Exam Objectives Reference

The CX-310-200 Sun Certified System Administrator for Solaris 10 (SCSA) exam is the first of two exams required for obtaining the SCSA certification and is a tangible first step in achieving your certification. Candidates can use this book to prepare for the SCSA Part I exam. The CX-310-200 exam tests a candidate's knowledge and skills required to successfully install and manage a Solaris 10 system. The exam includes topics on installation, file systems, boot procedures, user administration, managing printers, system processes, and backups.

Exam Topics

The following topics are general guidelines for the content likely to be included on the Sun Certified System Administrator for Solaris 10 Part I exam. The exam objectives could change at any time, so it is recommended that you visit the http://www.UnixEd.com website for any updates. Other related topics might also appear on any specific delivery of the exam. In order to better reflect the contents of the exam and for clarity purposes, the guidelines that follow might change at any time without notice.

Install Software

- Explain the Solaris 10 OS installation and upgrade options for CD / DVD, including how to provide Minimal Installations for SPARC, x64, and x86-based systems.
- Perform an OS installation from CD / DVD for SPARC, x64, and x86-based systems.

Manage File Systems

- Explain the Solaris 10 OS directory hierarchy, including root subdirectories, file components, and file types, and create and remove hard and symbolic links.
- Explain disk architecture including the UFS file system capabilities and naming conventions for devices for SPARC, x64, and x86-based systems.

- Use the `prtconf` and `format` commands to list devices, explain critical issues of the /etc/path_to_inst file and reconfigure devices by performing a reconfiguration boot or using the `devfsadm` command for SPARC, x64, and x86-based systems.
- Given a scenario, partition a disk correctly using the appropriate files, commands, and options, and manage disk labels using SMI and EFI labels as they relate to disk sets.
- Explain the Solaris 10 OS file system, including disk-based, distributed, devfs, and memory file systems related to SMF, and create a new UFS file system using options for <1Tbyte and > 1Tbyte file systems.
- Given a scenario, check and resolve Solaris 10 OS file system inconsistencies using `fsck`, and monitor file system usage using the command line (`df`, `du`, and `quot` commands).
- Perform mounts and unmounts on a Solaris 10 OS file system, and use volume management to access mounted diskettes and CD-ROMs, restrict access, troubleshoot volume management problems, and explain access methods without volume management.
- Perform Solaris 10 OS package administration using command-line interface commands and manage software patches for the Solaris OS, including preparing for patch administration, and installing and removing patches using the `patchadd` and `patchrm` commands.

Perform System Boot and Shutdown Procedures for SPARC, x64, and x86-based systems

- Given a scenario, explain boot PROM fundamentals, including OpenBoot Architecture Standard, boot PROM, NVRAM, POST, Abort Sequence, and displaying POST to serial port for SPARC.
- Given a scenario, explain the BIOS settings for booting, abort sequence, and displaying POST, including BIOS configuration for x64 and x86-based system.
- Execute basic boot PROM commands for a SPARC system.
- Perform system boot and shutdown procedures, including identifying the system's boot device, creating and removing custom device aliases, viewing and changing NVRAM parameters, and interrupting an unresponsive system.
- Explain the Service Management Facility and the phases of the boot process.
- Use SMF or legacy commands and scripts to control both the boot and shutdown procedures.

- Describe the purpose , functions and features of the Grand Unified Bootloader (GRUB), including how to modify x86 system boot behavior, manage GRUB boot archives, boot a system in the GRUB-based boot environment and interrupt an unresponsive system.

Perform User and Security Administration

- Explain and perform Solaris 10 OS user administration, and manage user accounts and initialization files.
- Monitor system access by using appropriate commands.
- Perform system security by switching users on a system, and by becoming root and monitoring `su` attempts.
- Control system security through restricting ftp access and using `/etc/hosts.equiv` and `$HOME/ .rhosts` files, and SSH fundamentals.
- Restrict access to data in files through the use of group membership, ownership, and special file permissions.

Manage Network Printers and System Processes.

- Configure and administer Solaris 10 OS print services, including client and server configuration, starting and stopping the LP print service, specifying a destination printer, and using the LP print service.
- Control system processes by viewing the processes, clearing frozen processes, and scheduling automatic one-time and recurring execution of commands using the command line.

Perform System Backups and Restores.

- Given a scenario, develop a strategy for scheduled backups, and backup an unmounted file system using the appropriate commands.
- Perform Solaris 10 OS file system restores using the appropriate commands, including restoring a regular file system, the `/usr` file system, the `/(root)` file system, and performing interactive and incremental restores for SPARC, x64, and x86 based systems.
- Backup a mounted file system by creating a UFS snapshot and performing a backup of the snapshot file.
- Restore data from a UFS snapshot and delete the UFS snapshot.

Solaris 10

System Administration (Exam CX-310-200), Part I

Bill Calkins

Solaris 10 System Administration Exam Prep (Exam CX-310-200), Part I

ISBN-13: 978-0-7897-3790-8

ISBN-10: 0-7897-3790-6

Library of Congress Cataloging-in-Publication Data:

Calkins, Bill.

Solaris 10 system administration exam prep (Exam CX-310-200) / Bill Calkins.

p. cm.

ISBN 978-0-7897-3790-8 (pbk. w/cd)

1. Electronic data processing personnel--Certification. 2. Operating systems (Computers)--Examinations--Study guides. 3. Solaris (Computer file) I. Title.

QA76.3.C34346 2008

005.4'32--dc22

2008031592

Printed in the United States on America

First Printing: September 2008

ASSOCIATE PUBLISHER
David Dusthimer

ACQUISITIONS EDITOR
Betsy Brown

SENIOR DEVELOPMENT EDITOR
Christopher Cleveland

TECHNICAL EDITOR
John Philcox

MANAGING EDITOR
Patrick Kanouse

PROJECT EDITOR
Mandie Frank

COPY EDITOR
Gayle Johnson

INDEXER
Ken Johnson

PROOFREADER
Matt Purcell

PUBLISHING COORDINATOR
Vanessa Evans

MULTIMEDIA DEVELOPER
Dan Scherf

DESIGNER
Gary Adair

PAGE LAYOUT
Mark Shriar

Bulk Sales

Que Certification offers excellent discounts on this book when ordered in quantity for bulk purchases or special sales. For more information, please contact

U.S. Corporate and Government Sales
1-800-382-3419
corpsales@pearsontechgroup.com

For sales outside the United States, please contact

International Sales
international@pearsoned.com

Contents at a Glance

Table of Contents

About the Author

Bill Calkins is a Sun Certified System Administrator for the Solaris operating environment. He is owner and president of Pyramid Consulting Inc., a computer training and consulting firm located near Grand Rapids, Michigan, specializing in the implementation and administration of Open Systems. He has more than 20 years of experience in Unix system administration, consulting, and training at more than 150 different companies. Bill has authored several Unix textbooks, which are currently best sellers and are used by universities and training organizations worldwide:

- *Solaris 2.6 Administrator Certification Training Guide Part I* (New Riders Publishing, ISBN: 157870085X)
- *Solaris 2.6 Administrator Certification Training Guide Part II* (New Riders Publishing, ISBN: 1578700868)
- *Solaris 7 Administrator Certification Training Guide: Parts I and II* (New Riders Publishing, ISBN: 1578702496)
- *Solaris 8 Training Guide (CX-310-011 and CX-310-012): System Administrator* (New Riders Publishing, ISBN: 1578702593)
- *Inside Solaris 9* (New Riders Publishing, ISBN: 0735711011)
- Solaris 9 Training Guide (CX-310-014 and CX-310-015): System Administrator (New Riders Publishing, ISBN: 0789729229)
- *Solaris 10 System Administration – First Edition* (Que, ISBN: 0789734613)

Bill has worked with Sun Press and Prentice Hall as a technical editor and a major contributor to many of their Solaris titles.

Bill's professional interests include consulting, writing, teaching, traveling, and developing Web-based training materials.

Bill works as a consultant with the certification group at Sun Microsystems and assists with the development of the Solaris 10 SCSA, SCNA, and SCSECA certification exams. Bill also consults with Sun Microsystems Professional Services and assists in the development of Solaris training and testing materials for the education division at Sun Microsystems.

Bill works as an instructor in government, corporate and university settings, and has helped thousands of administrators get their certification. Recently he was recognized by the United States Central Command (CENTCOM) as the "technical trainer of choice for the joint war fighting community."

His experience covers all varieties of Unix, including Solaris, HP-UX, AIX, IRIX, and Linux. When he's not working in the field, he writes Unix books and conducts training and educational seminars on various system administration topics. He draws on his many years of experience in system administration and training to provide a unique approach to Unix training.

Acknowledgments

I'd like to thank John Philcox of Mobile Ventures Limited, who once again has helped me get this book together. As always, John, you've done a great job. You've been a great asset and have become a good friend to have along on all of my books and projects. I want to thank all the editors who have contributed to this book; I value your input greatly. With each book, our tech editors get more refined, and their work is a huge contribution to the quality of this book. It's been a great team effort, and the book would not be as complete without your help. A special thanks goes out to Scott Howard and Edgar Danielyan.

A big thanks to Sun Microsystems for letting me participate in the Solaris 10 beta program and the input that they have provided for this book. A special thanks to Yvonne Prefontaine at Sun for her contributions and the information that she provided in the intro of this book.

Thank you, the reader, for buying my books and providing comments to improve the content with each new release. This book would not be what it is if it were not for your valuable input over the years. May the material in this book help you better your skills, enhance your career, and achieve your goal to become certified. Best of luck!

A lot of people behind the scenes make a book like this happen. After several books, I still don't have a clue how it all works, but it's a great team effort. A big thanks to everyone who edits the text, sets the type, prints the pages, and ships the book. My efforts would be lost in a closet somewhere if it weren't for your hard work.

We Want to Hear from You!

As the reader of this book, *you* are our most important critic and commentator. We value your opinion and want to know what we're doing right, what we could do better, what areas you'd like to see us publish in, and any other words of wisdom you're willing to pass our way.

As an associate publisher for Que Publishing, I welcome your comments. You can email or write me directly to let me know what you did or didn't like about this book—as well as what we can do to make our books better.

Please note that I cannot help you with technical problems related to the topic of this book. We do have a User Services group, however, where I will forward specific technical questions related to the book.

When you write, please be sure to include this book's title and author as well as your name, email address, and phone number. I will carefully review your comments and share them with the author and editors who worked on the book.

Email: feedback@quepublishing.com

Mail: Dave Dusthimer
Associate Publisher
Que Publishing
800 East 96th Street
Indianapolis, IN 46240 USA

Reader Services

Visit our website and register this book at www.quepublishing.com/register for convenient access to any updates, downloads, or errata that might be available for this book.

Introduction

Bill Calkins has been training Solaris system administrators for more than 15 years. This book contains the training material he uses in his basic and advanced Solaris administration courses. Over the years, this material has helped thousands of Solaris administrators become certified. This is our first edition of the *Solaris 10 System Administration Exam Prep*. It began with the *Training Guide* for Solaris 2.6, 7, 8, and 9 and is now the *Exam Prep* for Solaris 10. Instructors from universities and training organizations around the world have used this book as courseware in their Solaris administration courses. In addition, administrators from around the world have used this book as a self-study guide when instruction from a Sun training center is either unavailable or not within their budget. Many people have written with their success stories, suggestions, and comments. Their suggestions are what keep making this guide more valuable.

The SCSA Solaris 10 OS CX-310-200 and CX-310-202 *Exam Prep* books provide training materials for anyone who is interested in becoming a Sun Certified System Administrator for Solaris 10. When used as a study guide, these two books will save you a great deal of time and effort searching for information you will need to know when taking the exam. Each book covers the exam objectives in enough detail for the inexperienced administrator to learn the objectives and apply the knowledge to real-life scenarios. Experienced readers will find the material in these books to be complete and concise, making it a valuable study guide for the Sun Certified System Administrator (SCSA) exams.

This book is not a cheat sheet or cram session for the exam; it is a training manual. In other words, it does not merely give answers to the questions you will be asked on the exam. We have made certain that this book addresses the exam objectives in detail, from start to finish. If you are unsure about the objectives on the exams, this book teaches you what you need to know. After reading each chapter, assess your knowledge of the material covered using the review questions at the end of the chapter. When you have completed reading a section, use the practice exam at the end of the book and the ExamGear test engine on the CD-ROM to assess your knowledge of the objectives covered on each exam. This CD-ROM contains sample questions similar to what you are likely to see on the real exam. More sample questions are available at http://www.UnixEd.com, so be sure to visit this site to find additional training and study materials.

How This Book Helps You

This book teaches you how to administer the Solaris 10 operating system. It offers you a self-guided training course for all the areas covered on the CX-310-200 certification exam by showing you how to install, configure, and administer the Solaris 10 operating environment. You will learn the specific skills that are required to administer a system and to pass the first part of the Sun Certified System Administrator exam for Solaris 10 (CX-210-200). Experienced administrators who are upgrading an existing Solaris certification will find in-depth coverage of the new topics that they will need to learn for the CX-310-203 upgrade exam in both the SCSA Solaris 10 OS CX-310-200 and CX-310-202 *Exam Prep* books.

Throughout the book, we provide helpful tips and real-world examples that we have encountered as system administrators. In addition, we provide useful real-world exercises to help you practice the material you have learned. The following list describes this book's setup:

- **Organization**: This book is organized according to the individual exam objectives. Every objective you need to know for installing, configuring, and administering a Solaris 10 system is in this book. We have attempted to present the objectives in an order that is as close as possible to that listed by Sun. However, we have not hesitated to reorganize them as needed to make the material as easy as possible for you to learn. We have also attempted to make the information accessible in the following ways:
  - This Introduction includes the full list of exam topics and objectives.
  - Read the "Study and Exam Prep Tips" element early on to help you develop study strategies. This element provides valuable exam-day tips and information on exam/question formats.
  - Each chapter begins with a list of the objectives to be covered, exactly as they are defined by Sun. Throughout each section, material that is directly related to the exam objectives is identified.
  - Each chapter also begins with an outline that provides you with an overview of the material and the page numbers where particular topics can be found.
- **Instructional features**: This book is designed to provide you with multiple ways to learn and reinforce the exam material. The following are some of the helpful methods:
  - **Objective explanations**: As mentioned, each chapter begins with a list of the objectives covered in the chapter. In addition, immediately following each objective is an explanation in a context that defines it more meaningfully.
  - **Study Strategies**: The beginning of each chapter also includes strategies for studying and retaining the material in the chapter, particularly as it is addressed on the exam.

- **Exam Alerts**: Throughout each chapter you'll find exam tips that help you prepare for exam day. These tips were written by those who have already taken the Solaris 10 certification exams.
- **Notes**: Notes contain various types of useful information, such as tips on technology or administrative practices, historical background on terms and technologies, or side commentary on industry issues.
- **Cautions**: When you use sophisticated information technology, mistakes or even catastrophes are always possible because of improper application of the technology. Cautions alert you to such potential problems.
- **Step by Steps**: These are hands-on lab excercises that walk you through a particular task or function relevant to the exam objectives.
- **Key Terms**: A list of key terms appears near the end of each chapter.
- **Exercises**: Found at the end of the chapters in the "Summary" section, the exercises are performance-based opportunities for you to learn and assess your knowledge.
- **Suggested Readings and Resources**: At the end of each chapter is a list of additional resources that you can use if you are interested in going beyond the objectives and learning more about the topics presented in the chapter.

- **Extensive practice test options**: The book provides numerous opportunities for you to assess your knowledge and practice for the exam. The practice options include the following:
    - **Exam Questions**: These questions appear in the "Summary" section at the end of each chapter. They allow you to quickly assess your comprehension of what you just read. Answers to the questions are provided in the section "Answers to Exam Questions."
    - **Practice Exam**: A practice exam is included in Part II of this book, "Final Review," (as discussed in a moment).
    - **ExamGear**: The ExamGear software included on the CD-ROM provides further practice questions.

NOTE

ExamGear software For a complete description of the ExamGear test engine, see Appendix A, "What's on the CD-ROM."

- **Final Review**: This part of the book gives you two valuable tools for preparing for the exam:
    - **Fast Facts**: This condensed version of the information contained in the book will prove extremely useful for last-minute review.
    - **Practice Exam**: A full practice exam is included, with questions written in styles similar to those used on the actual exam. Use the practice exam to assess your readiness for the real exam.
- **Appendix and glossary**: This book also contains a glossary and a description of what is on the CD-ROM (Appendix A).

These and all the other book features will enable you to thoroughly prepare for the exam.

Conventions Used in This Book

- **Commands**: In the text, steps, and examples, the commands you type are displayed in a special `monospace` font.
- **Arguments and options**: In command syntax, command options and arguments are enclosed in < >. (The italicized words within the < > symbols stand for what you actually type. You don't type the < >.)

  ```
  lp -d<printer name> <filename> <return>
  ```

- **Using the mouse**: When using menus and windows, you select items using the mouse. Here is the default mapping for a three-button mouse:

  Left button: Select

  Middle button: Transfer/adjust

  Right button: Menu

  The Select button is used to select objects and activate controls. The middle mouse button is configured for either Transfer or Adjust. By default, it is set up for Transfer, which means that it is used to drag or drop list or text items. You use the left mouse button to highlight text, and then you use the middle button to move the text to another window or to reissue a command. The middle button can also be used to move around windows on the screen. The right mouse button, the Menu button, is used to display and choose options from pop-up menus.

- **Menu options**: The names of menus and the options that appear on them are separated by a comma. For example, "Select File, Open" means to pull down the File menu and choose the Open option.
- **Code-continuation character**: When a line of code is too long to fit on one line of a page, it is broken and continued to the next line. The continuation is preceded by a backslash.

Audience

This book is designed for anyone who has a basic understanding of UNIX and wants to learn more about Solaris system administration. Whether or not you plan to become certified, this book is the starting point to becoming a Solaris system administrator. It's the same training material that Bill uses in his Solaris 10 Intermediate System Administration course. This book covers the basics as well as intermediate system administration topics you need to know before you begin administering the Solaris operating system. Our goal was to present the material in an easy-to-follow format, with text that is easy to read and understand. The only prerequisite is that you have used UNIX, that you have attended a fundamentals of UNIX class for users, or that you have studied equivalent material so that you understand basic UNIX commands and syntax. Before you begin administering Solaris, it's important that you have actually used UNIX.

This book is also intended for experienced system administrators who want to become certified, update their current Solaris certification, or simply learn about the features of the Solaris 10 operating environment. To pass the certification exams, you need a solid understanding of the fundamentals of administering Solaris. This book will help you review the fundamentals required to pass the certification exams.

The Sun Certified System Administrator Exams

To become a Sun Certified System Administrator, you need to pass two exams: CX-310-200 (Part I) and CX-310-202 (Part II). This book covers the Part I exam, which is a prerequisite for Part II. You will not receive a certificate until you have passed both examinations. Also, if you are already certified in Solaris 2.6, 7, 8, or 9, you need to use materials found in volumes 1 and 2 of this series to take the upgrade exam, CX-310-203, to become certified on Solaris 10.

Beware of fakes. We have seen some websites that promote their own certification programs, so be sure to evaluate them carefully. Certification programs promoted by these sites are not the same as the Sun certification program, and you will not receive a certificate from Sun until you pass Sun's exams from a certified Sun testing center. Go to my website (http://www.UnixEd.com) for links to the real exams and information on Sun's certification program if you are in doubt. In addition, feel free to visit our online Solaris certification discussion forum at http://www.UnixEd.com, where you can ask me questions directly.

Exam CX-310-200

The following sections cover the Exam CX-310-200 objectives.

Manage File Systems

List the different types of file systems and file types in the Solaris operating environment. Understand how to add disk devices to a system and the device files associated with each disk on each Solaris platform (SPARC and x86/x64). Understand how to use the `format` and `fdisk` utilities. Understand how to create, mount, and repair file systems. Understand all the configuration files associated with managing file systems.

Install Software

Describe the methods used and the sequence of steps required to perform the Solaris 10 operating environment software installation on SPARC-, x64-, and x86-based systems. Identify the function of the package administration commands. Understand how to install, verify, and remove operating system patches.

Perform System Boot Procedures

Understand the entire boot process, with knowledge of the various configuration files and startup scripts on SPARC-, x64-, and x86-based systems. Understand how to use and execute boot PROM commands. Understand the role of the Solaris Management Facility (SMF) in the boot process, and become familiar with SMF-related commands. Understand the function of the files or directories accessed during the boot process. Understand the commands used to change the run level of a system to a specified state.

Perform User and Security Administration

Understand all aspects of administering users and groups. Understand how to set and verify file and directory permissions.

Manage Network Printers and System Processes

Describe the purpose, features, and functionality of the print management tools available in the Solaris operating environment. Understand the LP print service directory structure and the Solaris operating environment printing process. Understand the commands that display information for all active processes on the system. Understand the effect of sending a specified signal to a process. Understand the various methods used to terminate an active process.

Perform System Backups and Restores

Understand the functional capabilities of the various backup, archive, and restore utilities in Solaris 10. Identify the commands and steps required to back up and restore a file system. Given a specific scenario, be prepared to develop a strategy for scheduled backups and back up an unmounted file system using the appropriate commands.

Exam CX-310-203 (Solaris 10 Upgrade Exam)

If you're already certified on Solaris 2.6, 7, 8, or 9, you only need to take the CX-310-203 upgrade exam to update your certification. Here are the current objectives for that exam:

- Install Software
- Manage File Systems
- Perform System Boot and Shutdown Procedures for SPARC-, x64-, and x86-Based Systems
- Perform User and Security Administration
- Perform Advanced Installation Procedures

Summary

It's not uncommon for Sun to change the exam objectives or to shift them around after the exams have been published. I highly recommend that before you start this book, you visit my website at http://www.UnixEd.com to get the most up-to-date list of exam objectives, the errata for this book, up-to-date sample exam questions, and any other last-minute notes about these exams. We will provide all the information you need to pass the exam; all you need to do is devote the time. Learning the objectives is the first step; the next step is to practice. You need to have access to both SPARC- and x86/x64-based systems running Solaris 10 so that you can practice what you have learned. Unless you have a supernatural memory, it will be difficult to pass the exams without practice.

In the back of this book is the ExamGear software test CD that prepares you for the questions you might see on the exam. The CD-ROM-based test engine was designed by educational experts to help you learn as you test. It is a preview of the types of questions to expect on the exams, and it tests your knowledge on all the exam objectives. If you are weak in any area, the sample questions will help you identify that area so that you can go back to the appropriate chapter and study the topic. Each question on the CD-ROM has a flash card to help you in case you get stuck. This flash card contains brief, concise, textbook excerpts that explain why each answer is correct so that you can learn as you test.

Also, for an additional cost, you can purchase more questions for the ExamGear test engine from our website. You'll obtain hundreds of questions that will take you deep into each exam objective, providing a comprehensive skills assessment and helping you evaluate your readiness and retention of the materials.

Advice on Taking the Exam

More extensive tips are found in the "Study and Exam Prep Tips" element and throughout the book, but keep in mind the following advice as you study for the exam:

- **Read all the material**: This book includes information not reflected in the exam objectives to better prepare you for the exam and for real-world experiences. Read all the material to benefit from this.
- **Do the step-by-step lab exercises, and complete the exercises in each chapter**: This will help you gain experience and prepare for the scenario-type questions that you will encounter.
- **Use the questions to assess your knowledge**: Each chapter contains exam questions. Use these to asses your knowledge and determine where you need to review material.

- **Review the exam objectives**: Develop your own questions and examples for each topic listed. If you can develop and answer several questions for each topic, you should not find it difficult to pass the exam.
- **Relax and sleep before taking the exam**: Your time for taking the exam is limited. However, if you have prepared and you know Solaris network administration, you will find plenty of time to answer all the questions. Be sure to rest well the night before so that you can handle the stress that time limitations put on you as you take the exam.
- **Review all the material in the "Fast Facts" element the night before or the morning you take the exam.**
- **If you don't know the answer to a question, just skip it and don't waste much time**: You need to complete the exam in the time allotted. Don't be lazy during the exam; answer all the questions as quickly as possible. Any unfinished questions will be marked as incorrect.
- **Visit my website, http://www.UnixEd.com. It contains the following:**
  - Late-breaking changes that Sun might make to the exam or the objectives. You can expect Sun to change the exams frequently. Make sure you check my website before taking the exam.
  - A FAQs page with frequently asked questions and errata about this book or the exams.
  - Links to other informative websites.
  - Additional practice questions and sample exams for the ExamGear test engine. The ExamGear test engine has hundreds of questions that you can use to further assess your retention of the material presented in the book. The exams feature electronic flash cards that take the place of those sticky notes that you've used as bookmarks throughout the book. Don't attempt the real exam until you can pass every section of the practice exams with a 95% or better score.
  - An online forum where you can discuss certification-related issues with me and other system administrators, including some who have already taken the exam.
  - Additional study materials, training programs, and online seminars related to Solaris certification.
  - You can also email me directly from this website with questions or comments about this book. I always try to answer each one.

When you feel confident, take the real exams and become certified. Don't forget to drop me an email and let me know how you did (guru@UnixEd.com).

Study and Exam Prep Tips

These study and exam prep tips provide you with some general guidelines to help prepare for the Sun Certified Security Administrator exam. The information is organized into two sections. The first section addresses your pre-exam preparation activities and covers general study tips. The second section offers some tips and hints for the actual test-taking situation. Before tackling those areas, however, think a little bit about how you learn.

Learning as a Process

To better understand the nature of preparation for the exams, it is important to understand learning as a process. You probably are aware of how you best learn new material. You might find that outlining works best for you, or you might need to "see" things as a visual learner. Whatever your learning style, test preparation takes place over time. Obviously, you cannot start studying for this exam the night before you take it. It is important to understand that learning is a developmental process; as part of that process, you need to focus on what you know and what you have yet to learn.

Learning takes place when we match new information to old. You have some previous experience with computers, and now you are preparing for this certification exam. Using this book, software, and supplementary material will not just add incrementally to what you know. As you study, you will actually change the organization of your knowledge as you integrate this new information into your existing knowledge base. This will lead you to a more comprehensive understanding of the tasks and concepts outlined in the objectives and of computing in general. Again, this happens as a repetitive process rather than a singular event. Keep this model of learning in mind as you prepare for the exam, and you will make better decisions about what to study and how much more studying you need to do.

Study Tips

There are many ways to approach studying, just as there are many different types of material to study. The following tips, however, should work well for the type of material covered on the certification exam.

Study Strategies

Although individuals vary in the ways they learn, some basic principles apply to everyone. You should adopt some study strategies that take advantage of these principles. One of these principles is that learning can be broken into various depths. Recognition (of terms, for example) is a more surface level of learning in which you rely on a prompt of some sort to elicit recall. Comprehension or understanding (of the concepts behind the terms, for example) represents a deeper level of learning. The ability to analyze a concept and apply your understanding of it in a new way represents an even deeper level of learning.

Your learning strategy should help you understand the material at a level or two deeper than mere recognition. This will help you do well on the exam. You will know the material so thoroughly that you can easily handle the recognition-level types of questions used in multiple-choice testing. You also will be able to apply your knowledge to solve new problems.

Macro and Micro Study Strategies

One strategy that can lead to this deeper learning includes preparing an outline that covers all the objectives for the exam. You should delve a bit further into the material and include a level or two of detail beyond the exam's stated objectives. Then expand the outline by coming up with a statement of definition or summary for each point in the outline.

An outline provides two approaches to studying. First, you can study the outline by focusing on the organization of the material. Work your way through the points and subpoints of your outline with the goal of learning how they relate to one another. Be certain, for example, that you understand how each objective area is similar to and different from the others. Next, you can work through the outline by focusing on learning the details. Memorize and understand terms and their definitions, facts, rules and strategies, advantages and disadvantages, and so on. In this pass through the outline, attempt to learn details rather than the big picture (the organizational information that you worked on in the first pass through the outline).

Research has shown that attempting to assimilate both types of information at the same time seems to interfere with the overall learning process. To better perform on the exam, separate your studying into these two approaches.

Active Study Strategies

Develop and exercise an active study strategy. Write down and define objectives, terms, facts, and definitions. In human information-processing terms, writing forces you to engage in more active encoding of the information. Just reading over it would be more passive processing.

Next, determine whether you can apply the information you have learned by attempting to create examples and scenarios on your own. Think about how or where you could apply the concepts you are learning. Again, write down this information to process the facts and concepts in a more active fashion.

Commonsense Strategies

Finally, you also should follow commonsense practices when studying. Study when you are alert, reduce or eliminate distractions, take breaks when you become fatigued, and so on.

Pretesting Yourself

Pretesting enables you to assess how well you are learning. One of the most important aspects of learning is what has been called metalearning. Metalearning has to do with realizing when you know something well or when you need to study some more. In other words, you recognize how well or how poorly you have learned the material you are studying.

For most people, this can be difficult to assess objectively on their own. Practice tests are useful in that they reveal more objectively what you have learned and what you have not learned. You should use this information to guide review and further study. Developmental learning takes place as you cycle through studying, assessing how well you have learned, reviewing, and assessing again until you think you are ready to take the exam.

You might have noticed the practice exam included in this book. Use it as part of your learning process. The ExamGear software on the CD-ROM also provides a variety of ways to test yourself before you take the actual exam. By using the practice exam, you can take an entire timed, practice test that is quite similar to the actual Solaris exam. Set a goal for your pretesting. A reasonable goal would be to score consistently in the 95% range in all categories.

For a more detailed description of the exam simulation software, see Appendix A, "What's on the CD-ROM."

Exam Prep Tips

The Solaris certification exam reflects the knowledge domains established by Sun Microsystems for the Solaris OS administrators. The exam is based on a fixed set of exam questions. The individual questions are presented in random order during a test session. If you take the same exam more than once, you will see the same number of questions, but you won't necessarily see the same questions.

Solaris exams are similar in terms of content coverage, number of questions, and allotted time, but the questions differ. You might notice, however, that some of the same questions appear on, or rather are shared among, different final forms. When questions are shared among multiple final forms of an exam, the percentage of sharing generally is small.

You must complete the CX-310-200 exam before proceeding to the second exam, CX-310-202. You will not receive a certificate until you have successfully passed both exams.

Solaris exams also have a fixed time limit in which you must complete the exam.

Finally, the score you achieve on a fixed-form exam is based on the number of questions you answer correctly. The exam's passing score is the same for all final forms of a given fixed-form exam.

Table 1 shows the format for the exam.

Table 1 Time, Number of Questions, and Passing Score for the Exam

Exam	Time Limit in Minutes	Number of Questions	Passing Percentage
Sun Certified System Administrator for the Solaris 10 Operating System: Part 1	105	60	61%

Question types on the CX-310-200 exam are multiple-choice and drag-and-drop. Currently, the exam has no true-or-false or free-response-type questions.

Remember that you do not want to dwell on any one question for too long. Your 105 minutes of exam time can be consumed very quickly. Any unfinished questions will be marked as incorrect.

Correctly answered questions receive one point. Many of the multiple-choice questions are scenarios that have multiple correct answers. The question tells you how many answers to select. However, if you get one answer wrong, the entire question is marked wrong, and you do not receive a point.

When you finish the exam, you receive the results, with a report outlining your score for each section of the exam. You do not know which questions you answered correctly or incorrectly.

If you fail, purchase another voucher and retake the exam after a two-week waiting period. Every exam contains different questions.

If you feel that you were unfairly scored, you can request a review by sending an email to who2contact@sun.com.

Putting It All Together

Given all these different pieces of information, the task now is to assemble a set of tips that will help you successfully tackle the Solaris certification exam.

More Pre-Exam Prep Tips

Generic exam-preparation advice is always useful. Tips include the following:

- The certification exams are directed toward experienced Solaris system administrators—typically those who have six months to one year of experience. Although the Sun training courses help you prepare, some of the material found on the exam is not taught in the Sun training courses; however, everything on the exam is found in this book. To pass the exam, you need to retain everything that is presented in this book. To help you assess your skills, I've created the ExamGear test engine, which you will use to assess your retention of the materials. In addition, you can purchase hundreds of additional ExamGear test questions from http://www.UnixEd.com to assess your knowledge of the material. I don't recommend taking the Sun certification exams until you consistently pass these practice exams with a 95% or higher in *all* categories.

- Become familiar with general terminology, commands, and equipment. Hands-on experience is one of the keys to success. It is difficult, but not impossible, to pass the exam without that experience. Review the chapter-specific study tips at the beginning of each chapter for instructions on how best to prepare for the exam.

- Avoid using "brain dumps" available from various websites and newsgroups. Your exam may not match that particular user's exam, and you'll obtain a false sense of readiness. In addition, brain dumps do not prepare you for the scenario-type questions that you will see on the exam, and they may even be illegal. You need to know the objectives, and there is no shortcut for learning the material. Sun goes through a 13-step process to develop these exams and to prevent cheating. You cannot pass these exams without understanding the material. Besides, what good is your certification if you don't know the material? You'll never get through the job interview screening.

- Review the current exam-preparation guide on the Sun website. Visit my website, http://www.unixed.com, for late-breaking changes and up-to-date study tips from other administrators who have taken the exam. Use the forum to talk to others who have taken the exam.

- Memorize foundational technical detail, but remember that you need to be able to think your way through questions as well.

- Take any of the available practice tests that assess your knowledge against the stated exam objectives—not the practice exams that cheat and promise to show you actual exam questions and answers. Sun knows that these exams and brain dumps are available, and they change the questions too often for these types of practice exams to be useful. Too many users have written me to say that they thought they were prepared because they could pass the exam simulators, only to find that the questions and answers were different on the actual exam. I recommend the practice exams included in this book and the exams available using the ExamGear software on the CD-ROM. These are true skill assessment exams with flash cards to help you learn and retain while taking the exams. The test engine on the CD is designed to complement the material in this book and help you prepare for the real exam by helping you learn and assess your retention of the materials. If you know the material, you'll be able to handle any scenario-based question thrown at you. For more sample test questions, you can visit my website, http://www.unixed.com. I keep the questions up-to-date and relevant to the objectives. In addition, through our Solaris Certification online forum, you can share your experiences with other Solaris administrators who are preparing for the exam, just like you, and learn from those who have gone through the process. In addition, this website provides up-to-date links to the official Sun certification websites.

During the Exam Session

The following generic exam-taking advice that you have heard for years also applies when you're taking this exam:

- Take a deep breath and try to relax when you first sit down for your exam session. It is important to control the pressure you might (naturally) feel when taking exams.
- You will be given scratch paper. Take a moment to write down any factual information and technical details you've committed to short-term memory.
- Many questions are scenarios that require careful reading of all information and instruction screens. These displays have been put together to give you information relevant to the exam you are taking.
- Read the exam questions carefully. Reread each question to identify all relevant details. You may find that all the answers are correct, but you may be asked to choose the best answer for that particular scenario.
- Tackle the questions in the order they are presented. Skipping around will not build your confidence; the clock is always counting down.
- Do not rush, but also do not linger on difficult questions. The questions vary in their degree of difficulty. Don't let yourself be flustered by a particularly difficult or verbose question.
- Note the time allotted and the number of questions appearing on the exam you are taking. Make a rough calculation of how many minutes you can spend on each question, and use this to pace yourself.

- Take advantage of the fact that you can return to and review skipped or previously answered questions. Record the questions you cannot answer confidently, noting the relative difficulty of each question, on the scratch paper provided. After you have made it to the end of the exam, return to the more difficult questions.
- If session time remains after you have completed all the questions (and if you aren't too fatigued!), review your answers. Pay particular attention to questions that seem to have a lot of detail or that involve graphics.
- As for changing your answers, the general rule of thumb is *don't*! If you read the question carefully and completely the first time and felt like you knew the right answer, you probably did. Do not second-guess yourself. As you check your answers, if one clearly stands out as incorrectly marked, change it. If you are at all unsure, however, go with your first instinct.

If you have done your studying and follow the preceding suggestions, you should do well. Good luck!

PART I

Exam Preparation

CHAPTER ONE

Managing File Systems

Objectives

The following objectives for Exam CX-310-200 are covered in this chapter:

Explain disk architecture including the UFS file system capabilities and naming conventions for devices for SPARC, x64, and x86-based systems.

- Device drivers control every device connected to your system, and some devices use multiple device drivers. This chapter explains device drivers so that you can recognize and verify all devices connected to your system. In addition, the Solaris operating system accesses devices, such as disks and tape drives, through device and path names. The system administrator must be familiar with the various path names that point to each piece of hardware connected to the system.

Explain when and how to list devices, reconfigure devices, perform disk partitioning, and relabel a disk in a Solaris operating environment using the appropriate files, commands, options, menus, and/or tables.

- The system administrator is responsible for adding and configuring new hardware on the system. This chapter describes how new devices are configured into the Solaris operating environment. You'll need to describe disk architecture and understand naming conventions for disk devices as used in the Solaris operating environment on both SPARC-based and x86/x64-based Solaris systems.

- You'll need to know how to set up the disks and disk partitions when installing the Solaris operating environment. However, to properly set up a disk, you first need to understand the concepts behind disk storage and partitioning. You then need to determine how you want data stored on your system's disks.

Explain the Solaris 10 OS file system, including disk-based, distributed, devfs, and memory file systems related to SMF, and create a new UFS file system using options for <1Tbyte and >1Tbyte file systems.

- You'll need to understand all of the file systems that are available in the Solaris operating environment. In addition, you'll need to know when to use each type of file system.

Explain when and how to create a new UFS using the `newfs` command, check the file system using `fsck`, resolve file system inconsistencies, and monitor file system usage using associated commands.

- You'll need to be familiar with all of the commands used to create, check, and repair file systems. The system administrator needs to know how to use these tools and understand the effect that the various command options will have on performance and functionality.

Describe the purpose, features, and functions of root subdirectories, file components, file types, and hard links in the Solaris directory hierarchy.

Explain how to create and remove hard links in a Solaris directory.

- You'll need to know how to create, remove, and identify a hard link and understand why they are used in the Solaris operating environment. You'll need to be able to identify and describe all of the file types available in the Solaris operating environment. You'll need to understand the purpose of each subdirectory located in the root file system and the type of information that is stored in these subdirectories.

Explain the purpose and function of the vfstab file in mounting UFS file systems, and the function of the mnttab file system in tracking current mounts.

- You'll need to maintain the table of file system defaults as you configure file systems to mount automatically at bootup. You'll also need to understand the function of the mounted file system table (mnttab) and the entries made in this file.

Explain how to perform mounts and unmounts, and either access or restrict access to mounted diskettes and CD-ROMs.

- Each file system type supports options that control how the file system will function and perform. You'll need to understand all of these custom file system parameters. The system administrator needs to be familiar with mounting and unmounting file systems and all of the options associated with the process.

Outline

Study Strategies

The following study strategies will help you prepare for the exam:

- This chapter introduces many new terms that you must know well enough to match to a description if they were to appear on the exam. Know the terms I've provided in the "Key Terms" section at the end of this chapter.
- Understand what a device driver is and the various device driver names. They are rather difficult to remember, but keep going over them until you can describe them from memory. Many questions on the exam refer to the various types of device names.
- Practice all the commands and step by steps until you can describe and perform them from memory. The best way to memorize them is to practice them repeatedly on a Solaris system.
- As with every chapter of this book, you'll need a Solaris 10 system on which to practice. Practice every step-by-step example that is presented until you can perform the steps from memory. Also, as you practice creating file systems, you'll need some unused disk space with which to practice. I recommend an empty, secondary disk drive for this purpose.
- Familiarize yourself with the various types of file systems described in this chapter, but specifically, pay close attention to the UFS type and UFS parameters. Most questions on the exam revolve around the UFS. In addition, make sure you understand the Solaris Volume Manager. You don't need to know how to use it—just understand what it does and why you would use it.
- Make sure that you practice disk slicing. Understand how to create and delete disk slices and pay close attention to the limitations inherent with standard disk slices. Practice partitioning a disk using the `format` utility and SMC GUI tools until you have the process memorized.
- Finally, understand how to mount and unmount a file system as well as how to configure the /etc/vfstab file. Make sure that you understand all of the commands described in this chapter that are used to manage and display information about file systems, such as `df`, `fsck`, and `prtvtoc`.

Introduction

Before we can describe file systems, it's important that you understand how Solaris views the disk drives and various other hardware components on your system. In particular, you need to understand how these devices are configured and named before you can create a file system on them or install the Solaris operating environment.

Device management in the Solaris 10 environment includes adding and removing peripheral devices from a system, such as tape drives, disk drives, printers, and modems. Device management also involves adding a third-party device driver to support a device if the device driver is not available in Sun's distribution of the Solaris operating environment. System administrators need to know how to specify device names if using commands to manage disks, file systems, and other devices.

This chapter describes disk device management in detail. It also describes disk device naming conventions as well as adding, configuring, and displaying information about disk devices attached to your system.

Device Drivers

Objective:

Describe the basic architecture of a local disk and the naming conventions for disk devices as used in the Solaris operating environment.

Explain when and how to list and reconfigure devices.

A computer typically uses a wide range of peripheral and mass-storage devices such as a small computer system interface (SCSI) disk drive, a keyboard, a mouse, and some kind of magnetic backup medium. Other commonly used devices include CD-ROM drives, printers, and various Universal Serial Bus (USB) devices. Solaris communicates with peripheral devices through device files or drivers. A *device driver* is a low-level program that allows the kernel to communicate with a specific piece of hardware. The driver serves as the operating system's "interpreter" for that piece of hardware. Before Solaris can communicate with a device, the device must have a device driver.

When a system is started for the first time, the kernel creates a device hierarchy to represent all the devices connected to the system. This is the autoconfiguration process, which is described later in this chapter. If a driver is not loaded for a particular peripheral, that device is not functional. In Solaris, each disk device is described in three ways, using three distinct naming conventions:

- **Physical device name**—Represents the full device pathname in the device information hierarchy.

- **Instance name**—Represents the kernel's abbreviation name for every possible device on the system.
- **Logical device name**—Used by system administrators with most file system commands to refer to devices.

System administrators need to understand these device names when using commands to manage disks and file systems. We discuss these device names throughout this chapter.

EXAM ALERT

Memorize these device names. You'll encounter them in several questions and it's important that you understand when and where each name is used. Make sure you can identify a particular device driver name when it is presented as a filename.

Physical Device Name

Before the operating system is loaded, the system locates a particular device through the device tree, also called the full device pathname. Full device pathnames are described in Chapter 3, "Perform System Boot and Shutdown Procedures for SPARC, x64, and x86-Based Systems." After the kernel is loaded, however, a device is located by its physical device pathname. Physical device names represent the full device pathname for a device. Note that the two names have the same structure. For example, the full device pathname for a SCSI disk at target 0 on a SunFire V120 system is as follows:

```
/pci@1f,0/pci@1,1/ide@d/sd@0,0
```

On the x86/x64 platform, the primary IDE disk looks like this:

```
/pci@0,0/pci-ide@1f,1/ide@0/cmdk@0,0:a
```

Now let's look at the corresponding physical device name from the operating system level. Use the `dmesg` command, described later in this section, to obtain information about devices connected to your system. By typing `dmesg` at the command prompt, you'll receive the following information about the SunFire V120's SCSI disk 0:

```
May 13 13:40:50 sunfire scsi: [ID 193665 kern.info] sd15 at glm0: target 0 lun 0
May 13 13:40:50 sunfire genunix: [ID 936769 kern.info] sd15 is
/pci@1f,0/pci@1/scsi@8/sd@0,0
```

This same information is also available in the `/var/adm/messages` file.

The physical device pathnames for disks 3 and 4 are as follows:

```
Jul 25 14:06:47 smokey scsi: [ID 193665 kern.notice] sd19 at glm1: target 3 lun 0
Jul 25 14:06:47 smokey genunix: [ID 936769 kern.notice] sd19 is\
/pci@1f,0/pci@1/scsi@1,1/sd@3,0
```

```
Jul 25 14:06:48 smokey scsi: [ID 193665 kern.notice] sd20 at glm1: target 4 lun 0
Jul 25 14:06:48 smokey genunix: [ID 936769 kern.notice] sd20 is\
/pci@1f,0/pci@1/scsi@1,1/sd@4,0
```

As you can see, the physical device name and the full device name are the same. The difference is that the full device pathname is simply a path to a particular device. The physical device is the actual driver used by Solaris to access that device from the operating system.

Physical device files are found in the `/devices` directory. The content of the `/devices` directory is controlled by the devfs file system. The entries in the `/devices` directory dynamically represent the current state of accessible devices in the kernel and require no administration. New device entries are added when the devices are detected and added to the kernel. The physical device files for SCSI disks 3 and 4 would be

```
/devices/pci@1f,0/pci@1/scsi@1,1/sd@3,0:<#>
/devices/pci@1f,0/pci@1/scsi@1,1/sd@4,0:<#>
```

for the block device and

```
/devices/pci@1f,0/pci@1/scsi@1,1/sd@3,0:<#>,raw
/devices/pci@1f,0/pci@1/scsi@1,1/sd@4,0:<#>,raw
```

for the character (raw) device, where <#> is a letter representing the disk slice. Block and character devices are described later in this chapter in the section titled "Block and Raw Devices."

The system commands used to provide information about physical devices are described in Table 1.1.

TABLE 1.1 Device Information Commands

Command	Description
`prtconf`	Displays system configuration information, including the total amount of memory and the device configuration, as described by the system's hierarchy. This useful tool verifies whether a device has been seen by the system.
`sysdef`	Displays device configuration information, including system hardware, pseudo devices, loadable modules, and selected kernel parameters.
`dmesg`	Displays system diagnostic messages as well as a list of devices attached to the system since the most recent restart.
`format`	The `format` command displays both physical and logical device names for all available disks.

NOTE

prtconf Output The output produced by the `prtconf` command can vary depending on the version of the system's PROM.

Type the `prtconf` command:

```
# prtconf <cr>
```

The following output is displayed:

```
System Configuration:  Sun Microsystems  sun4u
Memory size: 1024 Megabytes
System Peripherals (Software Nodes):

SUNW,UltraAX-i2
    scsi_vhci, instance #0
    packages (driver not attached)
        terminal-emulator (driver not attached)
        deblocker (driver not attached)
        obp-tftp (driver not attached)
        disk-label (driver not attached)
        SUNW,builtin-drivers (driver not attached)
        dropins (driver not attached)
        kbd-translator (driver not attached)
        ufs-file-system (driver not attached)
    chosen (driver not attached)
    openprom (driver not attached)
        client-services (driver not attached)
    options, instance #0
    aliases (driver not attached)
    memory (driver not attached)
    virtual-memory (driver not attached)
    pci, instance #0
        pci, instance #0
            ebus (driver not attached)
                flashprom (driver not attached)
                eeprom (driver not attached)
```

*Output has been truncated.

Use the -v option to display detailed information about devices such as information about the attached SCSI disks:

```
dev_path=/pci@1f,0/pci@1/scsi@1,1/sd@2,0:a
            spectype=blk type=minor
            dev_link=/dev/dsk/c2t2d0s0
            dev_link=/dev/sd18a
dev_path=/pci@1f,0/pci@1/scsi@1,1/sd@2,0:a,raw
             spectype=chr type=minor
             dev_link=/dev/rdsk/c2t2d0s0
             dev_link=/dev/rsd18a
```

Next is an example of the output displayed by the `sysdef` command. Type the `sysdef` command:

```
# sysdef <cr>
```

The following output is displayed:

```
* Hostid
*
  831f857b
*
* sun4u Configuration
*
*
* Devices
*
scsi_vhci, instance #0
packages (driver not attached)
        terminal-emulator (driver not attached)
        deblocker (driver not attached)
        obp-tftp (driver not attached)
        disk-label (driver not attached)
        SUNW,builtin-drivers (driver not attached)
        dropins (driver not attached)
        kbd-translator (driver not attached)
        ufs-file-system (driver not attached)
chosen (driver not attached)
openprom (driver not attached)
        client-services (driver not attached)
options, instance #0
aliases (driver not attached)
memory (driver not attached)
virtual-memory (driver not attached)
pci, instance #0
        pci, instance #0
                ebus, instance #0
                        flashprom (driver not attached)
```

```
                    eeprom (driver not attached)
                    idprom (driver not attached)
                    SUNW,lomh (driver not attached)
            pmu, instance #0
```

*Output has been truncated.

```
* System Configuration
*
  swap files
swapfile             dev  swaplo blocks   free
/dev/dsk/c0t0d0s3   32,123     16 4096576 4096576
*
* Tunable Parameters
*
21241856        maximum memory allowed in buffer cache (bufhwm)
   16218        maximum number of processes (v.v_proc)
      99        maximum global priority in sys class (MAXCLSYSPRI)
   16213        maximum processes per user id (v.v_maxup)
      30        auto update time limit in seconds (NAUTOUP)
      25        page stealing low water mark (GPGSLO)
       1        fsflush run rate (FSFLUSHR)
      25        minimum resident memory for avoiding deadlock (MINARMEM)
      25        minimum swapable memory for avoiding deadlock (MINASMEM)
*
* Utsname Tunables
*
    5.10  release (REL)
 sunfire  node name (NODE)
   SunOS  system name (SYS)
Generic_127127-11  version (VER)
*
* Process Resource Limit Tunables (Current:Maximum)
*
0x0000000000000100:0x0000000000010000   file descriptors
*
* Streams Tunables
*
     9  maximum number of pushes allowed (NSTRPUSH)
 65536  maximum stream message size (STRMSGSZ)
  1024  max size of ctl part of message (STRCTLSZ)
*
* IPC Messages module is not loaded
*
*
* IPC Semaphores module is not loaded
*
*
* IPC Shared Memory module is not loaded
*
*
```

```
* Time Sharing Scheduler Tunables
*
60      maximum time sharing user priority (TSMAXUPRI)
SYS     system class name (SYS_NAME)
*
*
* IPC Shared Memory module is not loaded
*
*
* Time Sharing Scheduler Tunables
*
60      maximum time sharing user priority (TSMAXUPRI)
SYS     system class name (SYS_NAME) <$I~sysdef command>
```

*Output has been truncated.

Finally, here's an example of the device information for a SunFire system displayed using the dmesg command:

```
# dmesg <CR>
```

The following output is displayed:

```
Jan 24 09:19:36 sunfire halt: [ID 662345 auth.crit] halted by root
Jan 24 09:19:37 sunfire syslogd: going down on signal 15
Jan 24 09:19:37 sunfire rpcbind: [ID 564983 daemon.error] rpcbind terminating on
signal.
Jan 24 09:19:45 sunfire genunix: [ID 672855 kern.notice] syncing file systems...
Jan 24 09:19:45 sunfire genunix: [ID 904073 kern.notice]  done
Jan 24 14:29:31 sunfire genunix: [ID 540533 kern.notice] ^MSunOS Release 5.10 Version
Generic_120011-14 64-bit
Jan 24 14:29:31 sunfire genunix: [ID 943907 kern.notice] Copyright 1983-2007 Sun
Microsystems, Inc.  All rights reserved.
Jan 24 14:29:31 sunfire Use is subject to license terms.
Jan 24 14:29:31 sunfire genunix: [ID 678236 kern.info] Ethernet address =
0:3:ba:1f:85:7b
Jan 24 14:29:31 sunfire unix: [ID 673563 kern.info] NOTICE: Kernel Cage is ENABLED
Jan 24 14:29:31 sunfire unix: [ID 389951 kern.info] mem = 1048576K (0x40000000)
Jan 24 14:29:31 sunfire unix: [ID 930857 kern.info] avail mem = 1039745024
Jan 24 14:29:31 sunfire rootnex: [ID 466748 kern.info] root nexus = Sun Fire V120
(UltraSPARC-IIe 548MHz)
```

*Output has been truncated.

Use the output of the `prtconf` command to identify which disk, tape, and CD-ROM devices are connected to the system. As shown in the preceding `prtconf` and `sysdef` example, some devices display the `driver not attached` message next to the device instance. This message does not always mean that a driver is unavailable for this device. It means that no driver is currently attached to the device instance because there is no device at this node or the device is not in use. The operating system automatically loads drivers when the device is accessed, and it unloads them when it is not in use.

The system determines what devices are attached to it at startup. This is why it is important to have all peripherals powered on at startup, even if they are not currently being used. During startup, the kernel configures itself dynamically, loading needed modules into memory. Device drivers are loaded when devices, such as disk and tape devices, are accessed for the first time. This process is called autoconfiguration because all kernel modules are loaded automatically if needed. As described in Chapter 3, the system administrator can customize the way in which kernel modules are loaded by modifying the `/etc/system` file.

Device Autoconfiguration

Autoconfiguration offers many advantages over the manual configuration method used in earlier versions of Unix, in which device drivers were manually added to the kernel, the kernel was recompiled, and the system had to be restarted. Now, with autoconfiguration, the administrator simply connects the new device to the system and performs a reconfiguration startup. To perform a reconfiguration startup, follow the steps in Step by Step 1.1.

STEP BY STEP

1.1 Performing a Reconfiguration Startup

1. Create the `/reconfigure` file with the following command:

   ```
   # touch /reconfigure <cr>
   ```

   The `/reconfigure` file causes the Solaris software to check for the presence of any newly installed devices the next time you turn on or start up your system.

2. Shut down the system using the shutdown procedure described in Chapter 3.

   If you need to connect the device, turn off power to the system and all peripherals after Solaris has been properly shut down.

   After the new device is connected, restore power to the peripherals first and then to the system. Verify that the peripheral device has been added by attempting to access it.

NOTE

Automatic Removal of /reconfigure The file named `/reconfigure` automatically gets removed during the bootup process.

An optional method of performing a reconfiguration startup is to type `boot -r` at the OpenBoot prompt.

On an x86/x64 based system, perform a reconfiguration reboot by editing the `boot` command in the GRUB menu as described in Chapter 3.

NOTE

Specify a Reconfiguration Reboot As root, you can also issue the `reboot -- -r` command from the Unix shell. The `-- -r` passes the `-r` to the `boot` command.

During a reconfiguration restart, a device hierarchy is created in the `/devices` file system to represent the devices connected to the system. The kernel uses this to associate drivers with their appropriate devices.

Autoconfiguration offers the following benefits:

- Main memory is used more efficiently because modules are loaded as needed.
- There is no need to reconfigure the kernel if new devices are added to the system. When you add devices such as disks or tape drives other than USB and hot-pluggable devices, the system needs to be shut down before you connect the hardware so that no damage is done to the electrical components.
- Drivers can be loaded and tested without having to rebuild the kernel and restart the system.

NOTE

devfsadm Another option used to automatically configure devices on systems that must remain running 24×7, and one that does not require a reboot, is the `devfsadm` command.

Occasionally, you might install a new device for which Solaris does not have a supporting device driver. Always check with the manufacturer to make sure any device you plan to add to your system has a supported device driver. If a driver is not included with the standard Solaris release, the manufacturer should provide the software needed for the device to be properly installed, maintained, and administered.

Third-party device drivers are installed as software packages using the `pkgadd` command. At a minimum, this software includes a device driver and its associated configuration (.conf) file. The .conf file resides in the `/kernel/drv` directory. Table 1.2 describes the contents of the module subdirectories located in the `/kernel` directory.

TABLE 1.2 Kernel Module Subdirectories

Directory	Description
`drv/sparcv9`	Contains loadable device drivers and pseudo device drivers
`exec/sparcv9`	Contains modules used to run different types of executable files or shell scripts
`fs/sparcv9`	Contains file system modules such as ufs, nfs, procfs, and so on
`misc/sparcv9`	Contains miscellaneous system-related modules such as `swapgeneric` and `usb`
`sched/sparcv9`	Contains operating system schedulers
`strmod/sparcv9`	Contains System V STREAMS loadable modules (generalized connection between users and device drivers)
`sys/sparcv9`	Contains loadable system calls such as system semaphore and system accounting operations

USB Devices

Universal Serial Bus (USB) devices were developed to provide a method to attach peripheral devices such as keyboards, printers, cameras, and disk drives using a common connector and interface. Furthermore, USB devices are *hot-pluggable*, which means they can be connected or disconnected while the system is running. The operating system automatically detects when a USB device has been connected and automatically configures the operating environment to make it available.

The Solaris 10 operating environment supports USB devices on Sun Blade, Netra, Sunfire, and x86/x64-based system. In addition, a USB interface can be added to Sun systems that may not already have one.

When hot-plugging a USB device, the device is immediately displayed in the device hierarchy. For example, a full device pathname for a USB Zip drive connected to an Ultra system would appear as follows:

```
/pci@0,0/pci1462,5770@1d,7/storage@5/disk@0,0:a
```

A printer would look like this:

```
/pci@1f,4000/usb@5/hub@3/printer@1
```

Be careful when removing USB devices, however. If the device is being used when it is disconnected, you will get I/O errors and possible data errors. When this happens, you'll need to plug the device back in, stop the application that is using the device, and then unplug the device.

As stated in the "Volume Management" section later in this chapter, removable media such as floppy diskettes and CD-ROMs can be inserted and automatically mounted. When attaching a hot-pluggable device, it's best to restart `vold` after attaching the USB device as follows:

```
# svcadm restart volfs <cr>
```

Once `vold` identifies that the device has been connected, you'll see device names set up as follows:

```
zip1 -> /vol/dev/rdsk/c2t0d0/fat32        (USB Zip device)
zip0 -> /vol/dev/rdsk/c1t0d0/zip100       (USB Zip device)
jaz0 -> /vol/dev/rdsk/c3t0d0/jaz1gb       (USB Jaz device)
```

When disconnecting a USB device such as a Zip drive, unmount the device, stop `vold`, disconnect the device, and then restart `vold` as follows:

1. Stop any application that is using the device.
2. Unmount the USB device using the `volrmmount` command as follows:

   ```
   # volrmmount -e zip0 <cr>
   ```

   or the `eject` command as follows:

   ```
   # eject zip0 <CR>
   ```

   `zip0` is a nickname for the Zip device. The following nicknames are recognized:

   ```
   fd          /dev/rdiskette
   fd0         /dev/rdiskette
   fd1         /dev/rdiskette1
   ```

```
diskette        /dev/rdiskette
diskette0       /dev/rdiskette0
diskette1       /dev/rdiskette1
rdiskette       /dev/rdiskette
rdiskette0      /dev/rdiskette0
rdiskette1      /dev/rdiskette1
floppy          /dev/rdiskette
floppy0         /dev/rdiskette0
floppy1         /dev/rdiskette1
cdrom0          /vol/dev/rdsk/cXtYdZ/label
zip0            /vol/dev/rdsk/cXtYdZ/label
jaz0            /vol/dev/rdsk/cXtYdZ/label
rmdisk0         /vol/dev/rdsk/cXtYdZ/label
```

The `-e` option simulates the ejection of the media. For a more up-to-date listing of nicknames that might have been added since this writing, consult the `volrmmount` man page.

3. As root, stop `vold`:

```
# svcadm disable svc:/system/filesystem/volfs:default <cr>
```

4. Disconnect the USB device.

5. Start `vold`:

```
# svcadm enable svc:/system/filesystem/volfs:default <cr>
```

For more information on `vold` and USB devices, see the section titled "Volume Management" later in this chapter.

Instance Names

The instance name represents the kernel's abbreviated name for every possible device on the system. A few examples of instance names are:

- `sd0`: The instance name for a SCSI disk.
- `cmdk0`: The common disk driver used to represent SATA disks.
- `dad0`: the direct access device driver to represent IDE disks.
- `ata0`: Advanced technology attachment driver used to represent IDE disks.
- `hme0`: The instance name for a type of network interface

Instance names are mapped to a physical device name in the /etc/path_to_inst file. The following shows the contents of a path_to_inst file:

```
# more /etc/path_to_inst <cr>
#
#       Caution! This file contains critical kernel state
#
"/pseudo" 0 "pseudo"
"/scsi_vhci" 0 "scsi_vhci"
"/options" 0 "options"
"/pci@1f,0" 0 "pcipsy"
"/pci@1f,0/pci@1,1" 0 "simba"
"/pci@1f,0/pci@1,1/isa@7" 1 "ebus"
"/pci@1f,0/pci@1,1/isa@7/serial@0,3f8" 0 "su"
"/pci@1f,0/pci@1,1/isa@7/power@0,2000" 0 "power"
"/pci@1f,0/pci@1,1/isa@7/serial@0,2e8" 1 "su"
"/pci@1f,0/pci@1,1/usb@c,3" 0 "ohci"
"/pci@1f,0/pci@1,1/usb@5,3" 1 "ohci"
"/pci@1f,0/pci@1,1/ebus@c" 0 "ebus"
"/pci@1f,0/pci@1,1/pmu@3" 0 "pmubus"
"/pci@1f,0/pci@1,1/pmu@3/i2c@0,0" 0 "smbus"
"/pci@1f,0/pci@1,1/pmu@3/i2c@0,0/temperature@30" 0 "max1617"
"/pci@1f,0/pci@1,1/pmu@3/i2c@0,0/dimm@a8" 0 "seeprom"
"/pci@1f,0/pci@1,1/pmu@3/i2c@0,0/dimm@aa" 1 "seeprom"
"/pci@1f,0/pci@1,1/pmu@3/i2c@0,0/i2c-nvram@a0" 2 "seeprom"
"/pci@1f,0/pci@1,1/pmu@3/i2c@0,0/motherboard-fru@a2" 3 "seeprom"
"/pci@1f,0/pci@1,1/network@c,1" 0 "eri"
"/pci@1f,0/pci@1,1/ide@d" 0 "uata"
"/pci@1f,0/pci@1,1/ide@d/sd@0,0" 14 "sd"
"/pci@1f,0/pci@1,1/network@5,1" 1 "eri"
"/pci@1f,0/pci@1" 1 "simba"
"/pci@1f,0/pci@1/scsi@8" 0 "glm"
"/pci@1f,0/pci@1/scsi@8/sd@0,0" 15 "sd"
"/pci@1f,0/pci@1/scsi@8/sd@1,0" 16 "sd"
"/pci@1f,0/pci@1/scsi@8,1" 1 "glm"
"/pci@1f,0/pci@1/scsi@8,1/sd@6,0" 6 "sd"
"/iscsi" 0 "iscsi"
#
```

Although instance names can be displayed using the commands dmesg, sysdef, and prtconf, the only command that shows the mapping of the instance name to the physical device name is the dmesg command. For example, you can determine the mapping of an instance name to a physical device name by looking at the dmesg output, as shown in the following example from an Ultra system:

```
sd19 is /pci@1f,0/pci@1/scsi@1,1/sd@3,0
dad1 is /pci@1f,0/pci@1,1/ide@3/dad@0,0
```

In the first example, `sd19` is the instance name and `/pci@1f,0/pci@1/scsi@1,1/sd@3,0` is the physical device name. In the second example, `dad1` is the instance name and `/pci@1f,0/pci@1,1/ide@3/dad@0,0` is the physical device name. After the instance name has been assigned to a device, it remains mapped to that device. To keep instance numbers consistent across restarts, the system records them in the `/etc/path_to_inst` file. This file is only read at startup, and it is updated by the `devfsadmd` daemon described later in this section.

Devices already existing on a system are not rearranged when new devices are added, even if new devices are added to `pci` slots that are numerically lower than those occupied by existing devices. In other words, the `/etc/path_to_inst` file is appended to, not rewritten, when new devices are added.

It is generally not necessary for the system administrator to change the `path_to_inst` file because the system maintains it. The system administrator can, however, change the assignment of instance numbers by editing this file and doing a reconfiguration startup. However, any changes made in this file are lost if the `devfsadm` command is run before the system is restarted.

NOTE

Resolving Problems with `/etc/path_to_inst` If you can't start up from the startup disk because of a problem with the `/etc/path_to_inst` file, you should start up from the CD/DVD (`boot cdrom -s`) and remove the `/etc/path_to_inst` file from the startup disk. To do this, start up from the CD-ROM using `boot cdrom -s` at the OpenBoot prompt. Use the `rm` command to remove the file named `/a/etc/path_to_inst`. The `path_to_inst` file will automatically be created the next time the system boots.

You can add new devices to a system without requiring a reboot. It's all handled by the `devfsadmd` daemon that transparently builds the necessary configuration entries for those devices capable of notifying the kernel when the device is added (such as USB, FC-AL, disks, and so on). Before Solaris 7, you needed to run several `devfs` administration tools such as `drvconfig`, `disks`, `tapes`, `ports`, and `devlinks` to add in the new device and create the `/dev` and `/devices` entries necessary for the Solaris operating environment to access the new device. These tools are still available but only for compatibility purposes; `drvconfig` and the other link generators are symbolic links to the `devfsadm` utility. Furthermore, these older commands are not aware of hot-pluggable devices, nor are they flexible enough for devices with multiple instances. The `devfsadm` command should now be used in place of all these commands; however, `devfsadmd`, the `devfsadm` daemon, automatically detects device configuration changes, so there should be no need to run this command interactively unless the device is unable to notify the kernel that it has been added to the system.

An example of when to use the `devfsadm` command would be if the system had been started but the power to the CD-ROM or tape drive was not turned on. During startup, the system did not detect the device; therefore, its drivers were not installed. This can be verified by issuing the `sysdef` command and examining the output for sd6, the SCSI target ID normally used for the external CD-ROM:

```
sd, instance #6 (driver not attached)
```

To gain access to the CD-ROM, you could halt the system, turn on power to the CD-ROM, and start the system backup, or you could simply turn on power to the CD-ROM and issue the following command at the command prompt:

```
# devfsadm <cr>
```

When used without any options, `devfsadm` will attempt to load every driver in the system and attach each driver to its respective device instances. You can restrict `devfsadm` to only look at specific devices using the `-c` option as follows:

```
# devfsadm -c disk -c tape <cr>
```

This restricts the `devfsadm` command to devices of class *disk* and *tape*. As shown, the `-c` option can be used more than once to specify more than one device class.

Now, if you issue the `sysdef` command, you'll see the following output for the CD-ROM:

```
sd, instance #6
```

You can also use the `devfsadm` command to configure only the devices for a specific driver such as "st" by using the `-i` option as follows:

```
# devfsadm -i st <cr>
```

The `devfsadm` command will only configure the devices for the driver named "st."

Major and Minor Device Numbers

Each device has a major and minor device number assigned to it. These numbers identify the proper device location and device driver to the kernel. This number is used by the operating system to key into the proper device driver whenever a physical device file corresponding to one of the devices it manages is opened. The major device number maps to a device driver such as sd, st, or hme. The minor device number indicates the specific member within that class of devices. All devices managed by a given device driver contain a unique minor number. Some drivers of pseudo devices (software entities set up to look like devices) create new minor devices on demand. Together, the major and minor numbers uniquely define a device and its device driver.

Physical device files have a unique output when listed with the `ls -l` command, as shown in the following example:

```
# cd /devices/pci@1f,0/pci@1,1/ide@3 <cr>

# ls -l <cr>
```

The system responds with this:

```
total 4
drwxr-xr-x   2 root     sys         512 Mar 24 13:25 dad@0,0
brw-r-----   1 root     sys     136,  8 Aug  5 11:31 dad@0,0:a
crw-r-----   1 root     sys     136,  8 Aug  5 11:57 dad@0,0:a,raw
brw-r-----   1 root     sys     136,  9 Aug  5 11:32 dad@0,0:b
crw-r-----   1 root     sys     136,  9 Aug  5 11:57 dad@0,0:b,raw
brw-r-----   1 root     sys     136, 10 Aug  5 11:57 dad@0,0:c
crw-r-----   1 root     sys     136, 10 Aug  5 11:57 dad@0,0:c,raw
brw-r-----   1 root     sys     136, 11 Aug  5 11:55 dad@0,0:d
crw-r-----   1 root     sys     136, 11 Aug  5 11:57 dad@0,0:d,raw
brw-r-----   1 root     sys     136, 12 Aug  5 11:32 dad@0,0:e
crw-r-----   1 root     sys     136, 12 Aug  5 11:57 dad@0,0:e,raw
brw-r-----   1 root     sys     136, 13 Aug  5 11:32 dad@0,0:f
crw-r-----   1 root     sys     136, 13 Aug  5 11:57 dad@0,0:f,raw
brw-r-----   1 root     sys     136, 14 Aug  5 11:32 dad@0,0:g
crw-r-----   1 root     sys     136, 14 Aug  5 11:57 dad@0,0:g,raw
brw-r-----   1 root     sys     136, 15 Aug  5 11:32 dad@0,0:h
crw-r-----   1 root     sys     136, 15 Aug  5 11:57 dad@0,0:h,raw
```

This long listing includes columns showing major and minor numbers for each device. The `dad` driver manages all the devices listed in the previous example, which have a major number of 136. Minor numbers are listed after the comma.

During the process of building the /devices directory, major numbers are assigned based on the kernel module attached to the device. Each device is assigned a major device number by using the name-to-number mappings held in the `/etc/name_to_major` file. This file is maintained by the system and is undocumented. The following is a sample of the `/etc/name_to_major` file:

```
# more /etc/name_to_major <cr>
cn 0
rootnex 1
pseudo 2
ip 3
logindmux 4
icmp 5
fas 6
hme 7
p9000 8
p9100 9
sp 10
clone 11
sad 12
mm 13
iwscn 14
wc 15
conskbd 16
consms 17
ipdcm 18
dump 19
se 20
log 21
```

```
sy 22
ptm 23
pts 24
ptc 25
ptsl 26
bwtwo 27
audio 28
zs 29
cgthree 30
cgtwo 31
sd 32
st 33
...
...
envctrl 131
cvc 132
cvcredir 133
eide 134
hd 135
tadbat 136
ts102 137
simba 138
uata 139
dad 140
atapicd 141
```

To create the minor device entries, the `devfsadmd` daemon uses the information placed in the `dev_info` node by the device driver. Permissions and ownership information are kept in the `/etc/minor_perm` file.

Logical Device Name

The final stage of the autoconfiguration process involves the creation of the logical device name to reflect the new set of devices on the system. To see a list of logical device names for the disks connected to a SPARC system, execute a long listing on the `/dev/dsk` directory, as follows:

```
# ls -l /dev/dsk <cr>

total 96
lrwxrwxrwx    1 root      root           46 Mar 23 15:05 c0t0d0s0 -> \
../../devices/pci@1f,0/pci@1,1/ide@3/dad@0,0:a
lrwxrwxrwx    1 root      root           46 Mar 23 15:05 c0t0d0s1 -> \
../../devices/pci@1f,0/pci@1,1/ide@3/dad@0,0:b
lrwxrwxrwx    1 root      root           46 Mar 23 15:05 c0t0d0s2 -> \
../../devices/pci@1f,0/pci@1,1/ide@3/dad@0,0:c
lrwxrwxrwx    1 root      root           46 Mar 23 15:05 c0t0d0s3 -> \
../../devices/pci@1f,0/pci@1,1/ide@3/dad@0,0:d
lrwxrwxrwx    1 root      root           46 Mar 23 15:05 c0t0d0s4 -> \
../../devices/pci@1f,0/pci@1,1/ide@3/dad@0,0:e
lrwxrwxrwx    1 root      root           46 Mar 23 15:05 c0t0d0s5 -> \
../../devices/pci@1f,0/pci@1,1/ide@3/dad@0,0:f
```

```
lrwxrwxrwx   1 root     root          46 Mar 23 15:05 c0t0d0s6 -> \
../../devices/pci@1f,0/pci@1,1/ide@3/dad@0,0:g
lrwxrwxrwx   1 root     root          46 Mar 23 15:05 c0t0d0s7 -> \
../../devices/pci@1f,0/pci@1,1/ide@3/dad@0,0:h
```

*Output has been truncated.

On the second line of output from the `ls -l` command, notice that the logical device name **c0t0d0s0** is linked to the physical device name, as shown in the following:

```
../../devices/pci@1f,0/pci@1,1/ide@3/dad@0,0:a
```

On Sun SPARC systems, you'll see an eight string logical device name (c#t#d#s#) for each disk slice that contains the folowing:

Controller number (c#) — Identifies the host bus adapter (HBA), which controls communications between the system and disk unit. The controller number is assigned in sequential order, such as c0, c1, c2, and so on.

Target number (t#) — Target numbers, such as t0, t1, t2, and t3, correspond to a unique hardware address that is assigned to each disk, tape, or CD-ROM. Some external disk drives have an address switch located on the rear panel. Some internal disks have address pins that are jumpered to assign that disk's target number.

Disk number (d#) — The disk number is also known as the logical unit number (LUN). This number reflects the number of disks at the target location. The disk number is always set to 0 on embedded SCSI controllers.

Slice number (s#) — A slice number ranging from 0 to 7.

IDE and SATA disk drives do not use target controllers. Device names these types of disks represent the controller (c3), disk (d#), and slice(s#). Because IDE disks do not use target controllers, these disks use a t# value to represent the identity of the disks on its primary and secondary IDE busses. Target values on these systems are as follows:

- **t0**: Master device on the primary IDE bus.
- **t1**: Slave device on the primary IDE bus.
- **t2**: Master device on the secondary IDE bus.
- **t3**: Slave device on the secondary IDE bus.

The following is an example of IDE disks on a SunFire server:

```
# ls -l /dev/dsk <cr>
total 48
lrwxrwxrwx   1 root     root          45 Jan 23 18:11 c0t0d0s0 ->
../../devices/pci@1f,0/pci@1,1/ide@d/sd@0,0:a
lrwxrwxrwx   1 root     root          45 Jan 23 18:11 c0t0d0s1 ->
```

```
../../devices/pci@1f,0/pci@1,1/ide@d/sd@0,0:b
wxrwxrwx   1 root     root          44 Jan 23 18:11 c1t1d0s0 ->
../../devices/pci@1f,0/pci@1/scsi@8/sd@1,0:a
lrwxrwxrwx   1 root     root          44 Jan 23 18:11 c1t1d0s1 ->
../../devices/pci@1f,0/pci@1/scsi@8/sd@1,0:b
```

X86-based Solaris systems have a different disk naming convention, but before describing the logical device name for a disk on an x86-based system, it's worth pointing out a fundamental difference between disk slicing on a SPARC system and disk slicing on an x86-based system. Disk partitioning on the Solaris for the x86 platform has one more level than that of Solaris for SPARC. On Solaris for SPARC, slices and partitions are one and the same; on Solaris for x86, slices are "subpartitions" of a PC partition. This was done to allow Solaris to coexist with other PC operating systems, such as for dual boot configurations.

This difference in slicing brings some differences in the naming of disk devices on a Solaris x86-based PC. Slices are created in the first Solaris partition on a drive and, for SCSI disks, are named the same as with Solaris for SPARC (c#t#d0s#). However, because slices are within a PC partition, the PC partitions have their own device names. The entire drive is named c#t#d0p0, and the PC partitions (maximum of 4) are c#t#d0p1 through c#t#d0p4. To support the x86 environment, the `format` utility also has an added command called `fdisk` to deal with the PC partitions.

Solaris x86-based systems have 16 slices (numbered 0-15) versus 8 for SPARC. On the x86 PC, slice 8 is used to hold boot code and contains the GRUB `stage1` program in sector 0, the Solaris disk label, the VTOC in sectors 1 and 2 and GRUB `stage2` program beginning at sector 50. GRUB is described in Chapter 3. slice 8 also occupies the first cylinder (cylinder 0) of the Solaris `fdisk` partition.

On IDE and SATA disk drives, slice 9 is used for alternate sectors and contains blocks used to store bad block information. Higher slices are available for use, but not supported by `format` at this time and the `format` utility will only allow you to modify slices 0-7. The major differences between the logical device names used on SPARC-based systems versus x86-based systems are as follows:

- c is the controller number.
- t is the SCSI target number.
- s is the slice number ranging from 0-15.
- p represents the `fdisk` partition (not slice partition). This number ranges from p0 to p4. p0 represents the entire disk.
- d is the LUN number or IDE Drive Number.

If an IDE drive is used, *d* is used to determine MASTER or SLAVE and the *t* is not used for IDE drives. For example, two controllers are installed on an x86 PC:

- c0 is an IDE controller.
- c1 is a SCSI controller.

On an x86-based Solaris system, the following devices are listed in the `/dev/dsk` directory:

```
c0d0p0     c0d0s7      c1t0d0s4   c1t1d0s15  c1t2d0s12  c1t5d0s1   c1t6d0p3
c0d0p1     c0d0s8      c1t0d0s5   c1t1d0s2   c1t2d0s13  c1t5d0s10  c1t6d0p4
c0d0p2     c0d0s9      c1t0d0s6   c1t1d0s3   c1t2d0s14  c1t5d0s11  c1t6d0s0
c0d0p3     c1t0d0p0    c1t0d0s7   c1t1d0s4   c1t2d0s15  c1t5d0s12  c1t6d0s1
c0d0p4     c1t0d0p1    c1t0d0s8   c1t1d0s5   c1t2d0s2   c1t5d0s13  c1t6d0s10
c0d0s0     c1t0d0p2    c1t0d0s9   c1t1d0s6   c1t2d0s3   c1t5d0s14  c1t6d0s11
c0d0s1     c1t0d0p3    c1t1d0p0   c1t1d0s7   c1t2d0s4   c1t5d0s15  c1t6d0s12
c0d0s10    c1t0d0p4    c1t1d0p1   c1t1d0s8   c1t2d0s5   c1t5d0s2   c1t6d0s13
c0d0s11    c1t0d0s0    c1t1d0p2   c1t1d0s9   c1t2d0s6   c1t5d0s3   c1t6d0s14
c0d0s12    c1t0d0s1    c1t1d0p3   c1t2d0p0   c1t2d0s7   c1t5d0s4   c1t6d0s15
c0d0s13    c1t0d0s10   c1t1d0p4   c1t2d0p1   c1t2d0s8   c1t5d0s5   c1t6d0s2
c0d0s14    c1t0d0s11   c1t1d0s0   c1t2d0p2   c1t2d0s9   c1t5d0s6   c1t6d0s3
c0d0s15    c1t0d0s12   c1t1d0s1   c1t2d0p3   c1t5d0p0   c1t5d0s7   c1t6d0s4
c0d0s2     c1t0d0s13   c1t1d0s10  c1t2d0p4   c1t5d0p1   c1t5d0s8   c1t6d0s5
c0d0s3     c1t0d0s14   c1t1d0s11  c1t2d0s0   c1t5d0p2   c1t5d0s9   c1t6d0s
c0d0s4     c1t0d0s15   c1t1d0s12  c1t2d0s1   c1t5d0p3   c1t6d0p0   c1t6d0s7
c0d0s      c1t0d0s2    c1t1d0s13  c1t2d0s10  c1t5d0p4   c1t6d0p1   c1t6d0s8
c0d06      c1t0d0s3    c1t1d0s14  c1t2d0s11  c1t5d0s0   c1t6d0p2   c1t6d0s9
```

It's easy to see which devices are IDE disks because they do not have a "t" in the logical device name, while the SCSI disks with "c1" have a target number listed. This system has one IDE drive and five SCSI drives listed, targets 0, 1, 2, 5, and 6 (t6 is typically the CD-ROM).

NOTE

In this text and in the examples, unless otherwise noted, I will be using SPARC-based logical device names.

Examples of logical device names are the following:

- **c1t0d0s0**: A SCSI disk device name, that specifies controller 1, target 0, disk 0, and slice 0
- **c1d0p0**: An IDE or SATA disk name on an x86/864 system that specifies controller 1, disk 0, and fdisk partition 0
- **c1d0s0**: An IDE or SATA disk name that specifies controller 1, disk 0, and slice 0
- **c2t11d0p0**: A SCSI disk device name on an x86/864 system, that specifies controller 2, target 11, disk 0, and fdisk partition 0
- **c2t11d0s0**: A SCSI disk device name, that specifies controller 2, target 11, disk 0, and slice 0
- **c3t266000C0FFF7C140d31s2**: A Fibre-Channel attached LUN name that specifies controller 3, WWN 266000C0FFF7C140, LUN 31, and slice 2

On both SPARC-based and x86-based systems, the logical device name is the name that the system administrator uses to refer to a particular device when running various Solaris file system commands.

For example, if running the `mount` command, use the logical device name `/dev/dsk/c0t0d0s7` to mount the file system `/home`:

```
# mount /dev/dsk/c0t0d0s7 /home <cr>
```

Logical device files in the `/dev` directory are symbolically linked to physical device files in the `/devices` directory. Logical device names are used to access disk devices if you do any of the following:

- Add a new disk to the system.
- Move a disk from one system to another.
- Access (or mount) a file system residing on a local disk.
- Back up a local file system.
- Repair a file system.

Logical devices are organized in subdirectories under the `/dev` directory by their device types, as shown in Table 1.3.

TABLE 1.3 Device Directories

Directory	Description of Contents
`/dev/dsk`	Block interface to disk devices
`/dev/rdsk`	Raw or character interface to disk devices
`/dev/rmt`	Tape devices
`/dev/term`	Serial line devices
`/dev/cua`	Dial-out modems
`/dev/pts`	Pseudo terminals
`/dev/fbs`	Frame buffers
`/dev/sad`	STREAMS administrative driver
`/dev/md`	Metadevices managed by Solaris Volume Manager (SVM)
`/dev/vx`	Devices managed by Veritas Volume Manager

Block and Raw Devices

Disk drives have an entry under both the `/dev/dsk` and `/dev/rdsk` directories. The `/dsk` directory refers to the block or buffered device file, and the `/rdsk` directory refers to the character or raw device file. The "r" in `rdsk` stands for "raw." You may even hear these devices referred to as "cooked" and "uncooked" devices. If you are not familiar with these devices, refer to Chapter 2, "Installing the Solaris 10 Operating Environment," where block and character devices are described.

The /dev/dsk directory contains the disk entries for the block device nodes in /devices, as shown in the following command output:

```
# ls -l /dev/dsk <cr>
total 96
lrwxrwxrwx   1 root     root          46 Mar 23 15:05 c0t0d0s0 -> \
../../devices/pci@1f,0/pci@1,1/ide@3/dad@0,0:a
lrwxrwxrwx   1 root     root          46 Mar 23 15:05 c0t0d0s1 -> \
../../devices/pci@1f,0/pci@1,1/ide@3/dad@0,0:b
lrwxrwxrwx   1 root     root          46 Mar 23 15:05 c0t0d0s2 -> \
../../devices/pci@1f,0/pci@1,1/ide@3/dad@0,0:c
lrwxrwxrwx   1 root     root          46 Mar 23 15:05 c0t0d0s3 -> \
../../devices/pci@1f,0/pci@1,1/ide@3/dad@0,0:d
lrwxrwxrwx   1 root     root          46 Mar 23 15:05 c0t0d0s4 -> \
../../devices/pci@1f,0/pci@1,1/ide@3/dad@0,0:e
...
```

*Output has been truncated.

The /dev/rdsk directory contains the disk entries for the character device nodes in /devices, as shown in the following command:

```
# ls -l /dev/rdsk <cr>
total 96
lrwxrwxrwx   1 root     root          50 Mar 23 15:05 c0t0d0s0 -> \
../../devices/pci@1f,0/pci@1,1/ide@3/dad@0,0:a,raw
lrwxrwxrwx   1 root     root          50 Mar 23 15:05 c0t0d0s1 -> \
../../devices/pci@1f,0/pci@1,1/ide@3/dad@0,0:b,raw
lrwxrwxrwx   1 root     root          50 Mar 23 15:05 c0t0d0s2 -> \
../../devices/pci@1f,0/pci@1,1/ide@3/dad@0,0:c,raw
lrwxrwxrwx   1 root     root          50 Mar 23 15:05 c0t0d0s3 -> \
../../devices/pci@1f,0/pci@1,1/ide@3/dad@0,0:d,raw
lrwxrwxrwx   1 root     root          50 Mar 23 15:05 c0t0d0s4 -> \
../../devices/pci@1f,0/pci@1,1/ide@3/dad@0,0:e,raw
```

*Output has been truncated.

You should now have an understanding of how Solaris identifies disk drives connected to the system. The remainder of this chapter describes how to create file systems on these devices. It will also describe how to manage file systems and monitor disk space usage, some of the fundamental concepts you'll need for the first exam.

EXAM ALERT

Make sure you understand when to use a raw (character) device and when to use a block (buffered) device. You'll encounter several questions on the exam where you will need to select either the raw or block device for a particular command.

A File System Defined

A *file system* is a collection of files and directories stored on disk in a standard Unix file system (UFS) format. All disk-based computer systems have a file system. In Unix, file systems have two basic components: files and directories. A file is the actual information as it is stored on the disk, and a directory is a list of the filenames. In addition to keeping track of filenames, the file system must keep track of files' access dates, permissions, and ownership. Managing file systems is one of the system administrator's most important tasks. Administration of the file system involves the following:

- Ensuring that users have access to data. This means that systems are up and operational, file permissions are set up properly, and data is accessible.
- Protecting file systems against file corruption and hardware failures. This is accomplished by checking the file system regularly and maintaining proper system backups.
- Securing file systems against unauthorized access. Only authorized users should have access to files.
- Providing users with adequate space for their files.
- Keeping the file system clean. In other words, data in the file system must be relevant and not wasteful of disk space. Procedures are needed to make sure that users follow proper naming conventions and that data is stored in an organized manner.

You'll see the term *file system* used in several ways. Usually, *file system* describes a particular type of file system (disk-based, network based, or virtual). It might also describe the entire file tree from the root directory downward. In another context, the term *file system* might be used to describe the structure of a disk slice, described later in this chapter.

The Solaris system software uses the virtual file system (VFS) architecture, which provides a standard interface for different file system types. The VFS architecture lets the kernel handle basic operations, such as reading, writing, and listing files, without requiring the user or program to know about the underlying file system type. Furthermore, Solaris provides file system administrative commands that enable you to maintain file systems.

Defining a Disk's Geometry

Before creating a file system on a disk, you need to understand the basic geometry of a disk drive. Disks come in many shapes and sizes. The number of heads, tracks, and sectors and the disk capacity vary from one model to another. Basic disk terminology is described in Table 1.4.

TABLE 1.4 Disk Terminology

Disk Term	Description
Track	A concentric ring on a disk that passes under a single stationary disk head as the disk rotates.
Cylinder	The set of tracks with the same nominal distance from the axis about which the disk rotates.
Sector	Section of each disk platter. A sector holds 512 bytes.
Block	A data storage area on a disk. A disk block is 512 bytes.
Disk controller	A chip and its associated circuitry that control the disk drive.
Disk label	The first sector of a disk (block 0) that contains disk geometry and partition information. Also referred to as the Volume Table Of Contents (VTOC). To label a disk means to write slice information onto the disk. You usually label a disk after you change its slices using the `format` command.
Device driver	A kernel module that controls a hardware or virtual device.

A hard disk consists of several separate disk platters mounted on a common spindle. Data stored on each platter surface is written and read by disk heads. The circular path that a disk head traces over a spinning disk platter is called a *track*.

Each track is made up of a number of sectors laid end to end. A *sector* consists of a header, a trailer, and 512 bytes of data. The header and trailer contain error-checking information to help ensure the accuracy of the data. Taken together, the set of tracks traced across all the individual disk platter surfaces for a single position of the heads is called a *cylinder*.

Disk Controllers

Associated with every disk is a *controller*, an intelligent device responsible for organizing data on the disk. Some disk controllers are located on a separate circuit board, such as SCSI. Other controller types are integrated with the disk drive, such as Integrated Device Electronics (IDE) and Enhanced IDE (EIDE).

Defect List

Disks might contain areas where data cannot be written and retrieved reliably. These areas are called *defects*. The controller uses the error-checking information in each disk block's trailer to determine whether a defect is present in that block. When a block is found to be defective, the controller can be instructed to add it to a defect list and avoid using that block in the future. The last two cylinders of a disk are set aside for diagnostic use and for storing the disk defect list.

Disk Labels

A special area of every disk is set aside for storing information about the disk's controller, geometry, and slices. This information is called the disk's label or *volume table of contents (VTOC)*.

To label a disk means to write slice information onto the disk. You usually label a disk after defining its slices. If you fail to label a disk after creating slices, the slices will be unavailable because the operating system has no way of knowing about them.

Solaris supports two types of disk labels, the VTOC disk label and the EFI disk label. Solaris 10 (and later versions of Solaris 9) provides support for disks that are larger than 1 terabyte on systems that run a 64-bit Solaris kernel. The acronym EFI stands for Extensible Firmware Interface and this new label format is REQUIRED for all devices over 1TB in size.

The EFI label provides support for physical disks and virtual disk volumes. Solaris 10 also includes updated disk utilities for managing disks greater than 1 terabyte. The UFS file system is compatible with the EFI disk label, and you can create a UFS file system greater than 1 terabyte.

The traditional VTOC label is still available for disks less than 1 terabyte in size. If you are only using disks smaller than 1 terabyte on your systems, managing disks will be the same as in previous Solaris releases. In addition, you can use the `format -e` command to label a disk less than 1TB with an EFI label.

The advantages of the EFI disk label over the VTOC disk label are as follows:

- Provides support for disks greater than 1 terabyte in size.
- Provides usable slices 0–6, where slice 2 is just another slice.
- Partitions (or slices) cannot overlap with the primary or backup label, nor with any other partitions. The size of the EFI label is usually 34 sectors, so partitions start at sector 34. This feature means that no partition can start at sector zero (0).
- No cylinder, head, or sector information is stored in the EFI label. Sizes are reported in blocks.
- Information that was stored in the alternate cylinders area, the last two cylinders of the disk, is now stored in slice 8.
- If you use the `format` utility to change partition sizes, the unassigned partition tag is assigned to partitions with sizes equal to zero. By default, the format utility assigns the usr partition tag to any partition with a size greater than zero. You can use the partition change menu to reassign partition tags after the partitions are changed.
- Solaris ZFS (zettabyte file system) uses EFI labels by default.

The following lists restrictions of the EFI disk label:

- The SCSI driver, ssd or sd, currently supports only up to 2 terabytes. If you need greater disk capacity than 2 terabytes, use a disk and storage management product such as Solaris Volume Manager or ZFS to create a larger device to create a larger device.
- You cannot use the `fdisk` command on a disk with an EFI label that is greater than 1 terabyte in size.
- A disk with an EFI label is not recognized on systems running previous Solaris releases.
- The EFI disk label is not supported on IDE disks.
- As of this writing, you cannot boot from a disk with an EFI disk label.
- You cannot use the Solaris Management Console's Disk Manager tool to manage disks with EFI labels. Use the format utility to partition disks with EFI labels. Then, you can use the Solaris Management Console's Enhanced Storage Tool to manage volumes and disk sets with EFI-labeled disks.
- The EFI specification prohibits overlapping slices. The entire disk is represented by c#t#d#.
- The EFI disk label provides information about disk or partition sizes in sectors and blocks, but not in cylinders and heads.
- The following `format` options are either not supported or are not applicable on disks with EFI labels:
    - The `save` option is not supported because disks with EFI labels do not need an entry in the `format.dat` file.
    - The `backup` option is not applicable because the disk driver finds the primary label and writes it back to the disk.

Partition Tables

An important part of the disk label is the *partition table*, which identifies a disk's slices, the slice boundaries (in cylinders), and the total size of the slices. A disk's partition table can be displayed by using the `format` utility described in the "Disk Slices" section later in this chapter.

Solaris File System Types

Objective:

Describe the purpose, features, and functions of disk-based, networked, and pseudo file systems in a Solaris operating environment, and explain the differences among these file system types.

Solaris file systems can be put into three categories: disk-based, network-based, and virtual.

Disk-Based File Systems

Disk-based file systems reside on the system's local disk. As of this writing, the following are five types of disk-based file systems found in Solaris 10:

- **UFS (Unix File System)**—The Unix file system, which is based on the BSD FFS Fast file system (the traditional Unix file system). The UFS is the default disk-based file system used in Solaris.
- **HSFS (High Sierra File System)**—The High Sierra and ISO 9660 file system, which supports the Rock Ridge extensions. The HSFS file system is used on CD-ROMs and is a read-only file system.
- **PCFS (PC File System)**—The PC file system, which allows read/write access to data and programs on DOS-formatted disks written for DOS-based personal computers.
- **UDF (Universal Disk Format)**—The Universal Disk Format file system. UDF is the new industry-standard format for storing information on optical media technology called DVD (digital versatile disc).
- New to Solaris 10 is the ZFS file system. This file system features simplified administration, pool storage, self-healing data, snapshots, cloning, and scalability. ZFS is an objective on the CX-310-202 exam and is discussed in detail in the *Solaris 10 System Administration Exam Prep: Exam CX-310-202* book.

Network-Based File Systems

Network-based file systems are file systems accessed over the network. Typically, they reside on one system and are accessed by other systems across the network.

The network file system (NFS) or remote file systems are file systems made available from remote systems. NFS is the only available network-based file system bundled with the Solaris operating environment. NFS is discussed in detail in the *Solaris 10 System Administration Exam Prep: Exam CX-310-202* book.

Virtual File Systems

Virtual file systems, previously called pseudo file systems, are virtual or memory-based file systems that create duplicate paths to other disk-based file systems or provide access to special kernel information and facilities. Most virtual file systems do not use file system disk space, although a few exceptions exist. Cache file systems, for example, use a disk-based file system to contain the cache.

Some virtual file systems, such as the temporary file system, might use the swap space on a physical disk. The following is a list of some of the more common types of virtual file systems:

- **SWAPFS (Swap File System)**—A file system used by the kernel for swapping. Swap space is used as a virtual memory storage area when the system does not have enough physical memory to handle current processes.
- **PROCFS (Process File System)**—The Process File System resides in memory. It contains a list of active processes, by process number, in the `/proc` directory. Commands such as `ps` use information in the `/proc` directory. Debuggers and other development tools can also access the processes' address space by using file system calls.
- **LOFS (Loopback File System)**—The Loopback File System lets you create a new virtual file system, which can provide access to existing files using alternate pathnames. Once the virtual file system is created, other file systems can be mounted within it, without affecting the original file system.
- **CacheFS (Cache File System)**—The Cache File System lets you use disk drives on local workstations to store frequently used data from a remote file system or CD-ROM. The data stored on the local disk is the cache.
- **TMPFS (Temporary File System)**—The Temporary File System uses local memory for file system reads and writes. Because TMPFS uses physical memory and not the disk, access to files in a TMPFS is typically much faster than to files in a UFS. Files in the temporary file system are not permanent; they are deleted when the file system is unmounted and when the system is shut down or rebooted. TMPFS is the default file system type for the `/tmp` directory in the SunOS system software. You can copy or move files into or out of the `/tmp` directory just as you would in a UFS `/tmp`. When memory is insufficient to hold everything in the temporary file system, the TMPFS uses swap space as a temporary backing store, as long as adequate swap space is present.
- **MNTFS (Mounted File System Table)**—The Mounted File System Table maintains information about currently mounted file systems. MNTFS is described later in this chapter.
- **CTFS (Contract File System)**—The Contract File System is associated with the `/system/contract` directory and is the interface for creating, controlling, and observing contracts. The service management facility (SMF) uses process contracts (a type of contract) to track the processes which compose a service.
- **DEVFS (Device file System)**—The Device File Sysytem is used to manage the namespace of all devices on the system. This file system is associated with the `/devices` directory. The devfs file system is new in Solaris 10 and increases system boot performance

because only device entries that are needed to boot the system are attached. New device entries are added as the devices are accessed.

- **FDFS (File Descriptor File System)**—The File Descriptor File System provides explicit names for opening files by using file descriptors.
- **OBJFS (Object File System)**—The Object File System describes the state of all modules currently loaded by the kernel. This file system is used by debuggers to access information about kernel symbols without having to access the kernel directly.

Disk Slices

Objective:

Perform disk partitioning and relabel a disk in a Solaris operating environment using the appropriate files, commands, options, menus, and/or tables.

Disks are divided into regions called *disk slices* or *disk partitions*. A slice is composed of a single range of contiguous blocks. It is a physical subset of the disk (except for slice 2, which represents the entire disk). A Unix file system or the swap area is built within these disk slices. The boundaries of a disk slice are defined when a disk is partitioned using the Solaris `format` utility or the Solaris Management Console Disks Tool, and the slice information for a particular disk can be viewed by using the `prtvtoc` command. Each disk slice appears to the operating system (and to the system administrator) as though it were a separate disk drive.

Disk slicing differs between the SPARC and the x86 platforms. On the SPARC platform, the entire disk is devoted to the Solaris OS; the disk can be divided into 8 slices, numbered 0–7. On the x86 platform, the disk is divided into `fdisk` partitions using the `fdisk` command. The Solaris `fdisk` partition is divided into 10 slices, numbered 0–9.

NOTE

Slices Versus Partitions Solaris device names use the term *slice* (and the letter *s* in the device name) to refer to the slice number. Slices were called *partitions* in SunOS 4.*x*. This book attempts to use the term *slice* whenever possible; however, certain interfaces, such as the `format` and `prtvtoc` commands, refer to slices as partitions.

A *physical disk* consists of a stack of circular platters, as shown in Figure 1.1. Data is stored on these platters in a cylindrical pattern. Cylinders can be grouped and isolated from one another. A group of cylinders is referred to as a slice. A slice is defined with start and end points, defined from the center of the stack of platters, which is called the *spindle*.

Disk slices are defined by an offset and a size in cylinders. The offset is the distance from cylinder 0. To define a slice, the administrator provides a starting cylinder and an ending cylinder. A disk can have up to eight slices, named 0 to 7, but it is uncommon to use partition 2 as a file system. (See Chapter 2 for a discussion of disk-storage systems and sizing partitions.)

NOTE

Using Slice 2 As a Partition Sometimes a relational database uses an entire disk and requires one single raw partition. It's convenient in this circumstance to use slice 2, as it represents the entire disk, but is not recommended because you would be using cylinder 0. You should start your database partition on cylinder 1 so that you don't risk overwriting the disk's VTOC. UFS file systems are smart enough not to touch the VTOC, but some databases have proven to be not so friendly.

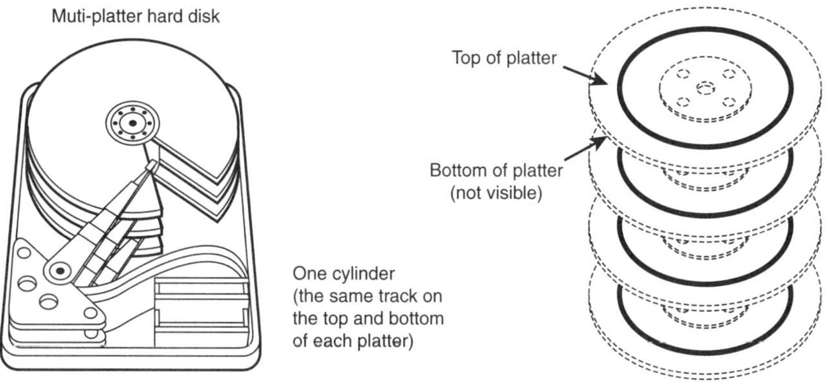

FIGURE 1.1 Disk platters and cylinders.

When setting up slices, remember these rules:

- Each disk slice holds only one file system.
- No file system can span multiple slices.
- After a file system is created, its size cannot be increased or decreased without repartitioning and destroying the partition directly before or after it.
- Slices cannot span multiple disks; however, multiple swap slices on separate disks are allowed.

When we discuss logical volumes later in this chapter, you'll learn how to get around some of these limitations in file systems.

Also follow these guidelines when planning the layout of file systems:

- Distribute the workload as evenly as possible among different I/O systems and disk drives. Distribute `/home` and swap directories evenly across disks. A single disk has limitations on how quickly data can be transferred. By spreading this load across more than one disk, you can improve performance exponentially. This concept is described in the *Solaris 10 System Administration Exam Prep: Exam CX-310-202* book, where I describe striping using the Solaris Volume Manager.

- Keep projects or groups within their own file system. This enables you to keep better track of data for backups, recovery, and security reasons. Some disks might have better performance than others. For multiple projects, you could create multiple file systems and distribute the I/O workload by putting high-volume projects on separate physical disks.
- Use the faster drives for file systems that need quick access and the slower drives for data that might not need to be retrieved as quickly. Some systems have drives that were installed as original hardware along with newer, better performing, drives that were added on some time later. Maybe you have a database dedicated to a high-volume project. This would be a perfect candidate to put on the newer, faster disk while a less accessed project could go on the slower disk drive.
- It is not important for most sites to be concerned about keeping similar types of user files in the same file system.
- Occasionally, you might have some users who consistently create small or large files. You might consider creating a separate file system with more inodes for users who consistently create small files. (See the section titled "The inode" later in this chapter for more information on inodes.)

We discuss disk slices again in Chapter 2, where we describe setting up disk storage and planning the layout of your disk slices.

Displaying Disk Configuration Information

As described earlier, disk configuration information is stored in the disk label. If you know the disk and slice number, you can display information for a disk by using the print volume table of contents (`prtvtoc`) command. You can specify the volume by specifying any slice defined on the disk (for example, `/dev/rdsk/c0t3d0s2` or `/dev/rdsk/c0t3d0s*`). Regardless of which slice you specify, all slices defined on the disk will be displayed. If you know the target number of the disk but do not know how it is divided into slices, you can show information for the entire disk by specifying either slice 2 or s*. Step by Step 1.2 shows how you can examine information stored on a disk's label by using the `prtvtoc` command.

STEP BY STEP

1.2 Examining a Disk's Label Using the `prtvtoc` Command

1. Become superuser.
2. Type **`prtvtoc /dev/rdsk/`*`cntndnsn`*** and press Enter.

   Information for the disk and slice you specify is displayed. In the following steps, information is displayed for all of disk 3:

1. Become superuser.
2. Type **`prtvtoc /dev/rdsk/c0t3d0s2`** and press Enter.

   The system responds with this:

```
* /dev/rdsk/c0t3d0s2 (volume "") partition map
*
* Dimensions:
*     512 bytes/sector
*      36 sectors/track
*       9 tracks/cylinder
*     324 sectors/cylinder
*    1272 cylinders
*    1254 accessible cylinders
*
* Flags:
*   1: unmountable
*  10: read-only
*
*                     First   Sector  Last
* Partition Tag Flags Sector  Count   Sector  Mount Directory
  2          5   01   0       406296  406295
  6          4   00   0       242352  242351
  7          0   00   242352  163944  406295  /files7
```

The `prtvtoc` command shows the number of cylinders and heads, as well as how the disk's slices are arranged.

The following is an example of running the `prtvtoc` command on a SCSI disk with an EFI label:

```
# prtvtoc /dev/rdsk/c2t1d0s1 <cr>
* /dev/rdsk/c2t1d0s1 partition map
*
* Dimensions:
*     512 bytes/sector
* 8385121 sectors
* 8385054 accessible sectors
*
```

```
* Flags:
*    1: unmountable
*   10: read-only
*
*                           First     Sector    Last
* Partition   Tag  Flags    Sector     Count    Sector  Mount Directory
       0       2    01          34     41006     41039
       1       2    00       41040   8327663   8368702   /mnt
       8      11    00     8368703     16384   8385086
```

Using the `format` Utility to Create Slices

Before you can create a file system on a disk, the disk must be formatted, and you must divide it into slices by using the Solaris `format` utility. Formatting involves two separate processes:

- Writing format information to the disk
- Completing a surface analysis, which compiles an up-to-date list of disk defects

When a disk is formatted, header and trailer information is superimposed on the disk. When the `format` utility runs a surface analysis, the controller scans the disk for defects. It should be noted that defects and formatting information reduce the total disk space available for data. This is why a new disk usually holds only 90–95% of its capacity after formatting. This percentage varies according to disk geometry and decreases as the disk ages and develops more defects.

The need to perform a surface analysis on a disk drive has dropped as more manufacturers ship their disk drives formatted and partitioned. You should not need to perform a surface analysis within the `format` utility when adding a disk drive to an existing system unless you think disk defects are causing problems. The primary reason that you would use `format` is if you want to view or change the partitioning scheme on a disk.

CAUTION

Always Back Up Your Data Formatting and creating slices is a destructive process, so make sure user data is backed up before you start.

The `format` utility searches your system for all attached disk drives and reports the following information about the disk drives it finds:

- Target location
- Disk geometry

- Whether the disk is formatted
- Whether the disk has mounted partitions

In addition, the `format` utility is used in disk repair operations to do the following:

- Retrieve disk labels
- Repair defective sectors
- Format and analyze disks
- Partition disks
- Label disks (write the disk name and configuration information to the disk for future retrieval)

The Solaris installation program partitions and labels disk drives as part of installing the Solaris release. However, you might need to use the `format` utility when doing the following:

- Displaying slice information
- Dividing a disk into slices
- Formatting a disk drive when you think disk defects are causing problems
- Repairing a disk drive

The main reason a system administrator uses the `format` utility is to divide a disk into disk slices.

EXAM ALERT

`format` Utility Pay close attention to each menu item in the format utility and understand what task each performs. Expect to see several questions pertaining to the format utility menus on Exam CX-310-200. Along with adding slices, make sure you know how to remove or resize slices. You may see a scenario where a production system is running out of swap and you need to go into the format utility and add another swap slice.

The process of creating slices is outlined in Step by Step 1.3.

NOTE

If you are using Solaris on an x86 or x64-based PC system, refer to the next Step by Step to create an FDISK partition before creating the slices.

STEP BY STEP

1.3 Formatting a Disk

1. Become superuser.
2. Type **`format`**.

   The system responds with this:

```
Searching for disks...done

AVAILABLE DISK SELECTIONS:
       0. c0t0d0 <SUN36G cyl 24620 alt 2 hd 27 sec 107>
          /pci@1f,0/pci@1/scsi@8/sd@0,0
       1. c0t1d0 <SUN36G cyl 24620 alt 2 hd 27 sec 107>
          /pci@1f,0/pci@1/scsi@8/sd@1,0
```

3. Specify the disk (enter its number).

   The system responds with the format main menu:

```
FORMAT MENU:
    disk - select a disk
    type - select (define) a disk type
    partition - select (define) a partition table
    current - describe the current disk
    format - format and analyze the disk
    repair - repair a defective sector
    label - write label to the disk
    analyze - surface analysis
    defect - defect list management
    backup - search for backup labels
    verify - read and display labels
    save - save new disk/partition definitions
    inquiry - show vendor, product and revision
    volname - set 8-character volume name
    !<cmd> - execute <cmd>, then return
    quit
```

   Table 1.5 describes the format main menu items.

TABLE 1.5 Format Main Menu Item Descriptions

Menu Item	Description
`disk`	Lists all the system's drives. Also lets you choose the disk you want to use in subsequent operations. This disk is referred to as the current disk.
`type`	Identifies the manufacturer and model of the current disk. Also displays a list of known drive types. Choose the Auto configure option for all SCSI-2 disk drives.
`partition`	Creates and modifies slices.
`current`	Describes the current disk (that is, device name, device type, number of cylinders, alternate cylinders, heads, sectors, and physical device name).
`format`	Formats the current disk by using one of these sources of information in this order: Information that is found in the `format.dat` file Information from the automatic configuration process Information that you type at the prompt if no format.dat entry exists This command does not apply to IDE disks. IDE disks are preformatted by the manufacturer.
`fdisk`	x86 platform only: Runs the fdisk program to create a Solaris fdisk partition.
`repair`	Used to repair a specific block on the current disk.
`label`	Writes a new label to the current disk. This is not the same as labeling the disk with `volname`.
`analyze`	Runs read, write, and compare tests.
`defect`	Retrieves and displays defect lists. This feature does not apply to IDE disks. IDE disks manage defects automatically.
`backup`	Searches for backup labels if the VTOC becomes corrupted or gets deleted.
`verify`	Displays information about the current disk such as device name, device type, number of cylinders, alternate cylinders, heads, sectors, and partition table.
`save`	Saves new disk and partition information.
`inquiry`	SCSI disks only—Displays the vendor, product name, and revision level of the current drive. This will also display the disk's current firmware.
`volname`	Labels the disk with a new eight-character volume name that you specify. This is not the same as writing the partition table to disk using `label`.
`quit`	Exits the format menu. Ctrl+D will also exit the format utility from the main menu or from any submenu.

4. Type **`partition`** at the format prompt. The partition menu is displayed.

NOTE

Using Shortcuts in the `format` Utility It is unnecessary to type the entire command. After you type the first two characters of a command, the `format` utility recognizes the entire command.

```
format> partition <cr>
PARTITION MENU:
    0 - change '0' partition
    1 - change '1' partition
    2 - change '2' partition
    3 - change '3' partition
    4 - change '4' partition
    5 - change '5' partition
    6 - change '6' partition
    7 - change '7' partition
    select - select a predefined table
    modify - modify a predefined partition table
    name - name the current table
    print - display the current table
    label - write partition map and label to the disk
    !<cmd> - execute <cmd>, then return
    quit
```

5. Type **print** to display the current partition map.

The system responds with this:

```
partition> print <cr>
Current partition table (original):
Total disk cylinders available: 24620 + 2 (reserved cylinders)

Part      Tag    Flag     Cylinders        Size            Blocks
  0       root    wm     1418 -  9924      11.72GB    (8507/0/0)   24576723
  1        var    wm     9925 - 13469       4.88GB    (3545/0/0)   10241505
  2     backup    wm        0 - 24619      33.92GB    (24620/0/0) 71127180
  3       swap    wu        0 -  1417       1.95GB    (1418/0/0)    4096602
  4 unassigned    wm    13470 - 14887       1.95GB    (1418/0/0)    4096602
  5 unassigned    wm    14888 - 16112       1.69GB    (1225/0/0)    3539025
  6 unassigned    wm    16113 - 16821    1000.15MB    (709/0/0)     2048301
  7       home    wm    16822 - 23910       9.77GB    (7089/0/0)   20480121
```

The columns displayed with the partition table are

- **Part**—The slice number (0–7).
- **Tag**—This is an optional value that indicates how the slice is being used. The value can be any of the following names that best fits the function of the file system you are creating:

  unassigned, boot, root, swap, usr, backup, stand, var, home, alternates, reserved

  You may also see tags labeled `public` or `private`, which represent Sun StorEdge Volume Manager tags:

- **Flag**—Values in this column can be
  - **wm**—The disk slice is writable and mountable.
  - **wu**—The disk slice is writable and unmountable (such as a swap slice).
  - **rm**—The disk slice is read-only and mountable.
  - **ru**—The disk slice is read-only and unmountable.
- **Cylinders**—The starting and ending cylinder number for the disk slice.
- **Size**—The slice size specified as
  - mb—megabytes
  - gb—gigabytes
  - b—blocks
  - c—cylinders
- **Blocks**—The total number of cylinders and the total number of sectors per slice.

> **NOTE**
>
> **Wasted Disk Space** Wasted disk space occurs during partitioning when one or more cylinders have not been allocated to a disk slice. This may happen intentionally or accidentally. If there are unallocated slices available, then wasted space can possibly be assigned to a slice later on.

You can use the `name` and `save` commands in the partition menu to name and save a newly created partition table to a file that can be referenced by name later, when you want to use this same partition scheme on another disk. When issuing the `name` command, you'll provide a unique name for this partition scheme and then issue the `save` command to save the information to the `./format.dat` file. Normally this file is located in the `/etc` directory, so provide the full pathname for `/etc/format.dat` to update the master file.

6. After you partition the disk, you must label it by typing **`label`** at the partition prompt:

```
partition> label <cr>
```

You are asked for confirmation on labeling the disk as follows:

```
Ready to label disk, continue?
```

Enter **Y** to continue.

> **NOTE**
>
> **Label Your Drive** To label a disk means to write slice information onto the disk. If you don't label the drive when exiting the `format` utility, your partition changes will not be retained. Get into the habit of labeling at the partition submenu, but you can also label at the `format` utility main menu as well—you get two chances to remember before exiting the utility.

7. After labeling the disk, type **quit** to exit the partition menu:

```
partition> quit <cr>
```

8. Type **quit** again to exit the `format` utility:

```
format> quit <cr>
```

It's important to point out a few undesirable things that can happen when defining disk partitions with the `format` utility if you're not careful. First, be careful not to waste disk space. Wasted disk space can occur when you decrease the size of one slice and do not adjust the starting cylinder number of the adjoining disk slice.

Second, don't overlap disk slices. Overlapping occurs when one or more cylinders are allocated to more than one disk slice. For example, increasing the size of one slice without decreasing the size of the adjoining slice will create overlapping partitions. The `format` utility will not warn you of wasted disk space or overlapping partitions.

As described earlier in this chapter, Solaris on the x86/x64 platform treats disk drives slightly differently than on the SPARC-based systems and the boot disk must have an SMI label. Disks on the x86/x64 platform maintain an `fdisk` partition table and a partition table for the Solaris `fdisk` partition.

These x86/x64-based systems use the `fdisk` partition table to identify parts of the disk reserved for different operating systems and to identify the partition that the system will boot from. This boot partition is referred to as the *active disk* partition. You can assign one `fdisk` partition on a disk to be used for Solaris.

On an x86 system, once a disk drive has been physically installed and verified as working, you'll use the `format` command to slice the disk, but first an `fdisk` partition must be created on the new drive. Use the `format` command as follows:

STEP BY STEP

1.4 Using the `format` Command

1. As root, type `format` to get into the `format` utility.

```
# format <cr>
```

The following menu appears:

```
AVAILABLE DISK SELECTIONS:
       0. c1t0d0 <FUJITSU-M1606S-512-6234 cyl 3455 alt 2 hd 6 sec 102>
          /pci@0,0/pci9004,8178@3/cmdk@0,0
       1. c1t1d0 <IBM-DFHSS1W!e-4141 cyl 4071 alt 2 hd 4 sec 135>
          /pci@0,0/pci9004,8178@3/cmdk@1,0
       2. c1t2d0 <DEFAULT cyl 2928 alt 2 hd 6 sec 120>
          /pci@0,0/pci9004,8178@3/cmdk@2,0
Specify disk (enter its number):
```

2. Enter the number corresponding to the new drive and the following menu will be displayed:

```
FORMAT MENU:
        disk       - select a disk
        type       - select (define) a disk type
        partition  - select (define) a partition table
        current    - describe the current disk
        format     - format and analyze the disk
        fdisk      - run the fdisk program
        repair     - repair a defective sector
        label      - write label to the disk
        analyze    - surface analysis
        defect     - defect list management
        backup     - search for backup labels
        verify     - read and display labels
        save       - save new disk/partition definitions
        inquiry    - show vendor, product and revision
        volname    - set 8-character volume name5
        quit
format>
```

3. Select the `fdisk` option and the following menu appears:

```
The recommended default partitioning for your disk is:
  a 100% "SOLARIS System" partition.

To select this, please type "y".  To partition your disk
differently, type "n" and the "fdisk" program will let you
select other partitions.
```

4. If you wish to use the entire drive for Solaris enter **y**. This will return to the format menu. If **n** is chosen, the fdisk menu will be displayed.

```
             Total disk size is 4073 cylinders
             Cylinder size is 540 (512 byte) blocks
                                                Cylinders
      Partition   Status    Type      Start   End   Length    %
      =========   ======    ========  =====   ===   ======   ===

THERE ARE NO PARTITIONS CURRENTLY DEFINED
SELECT ONE OF THE FOLLOWING:
     1.   Create a partition
     2.   Change Active (Boot from) partition
     3.   Delete a partition
     4.   Exit (Update disk configuration and exit)
     5.   Cancel (Exit without updating disk configuration)
Enter Selection:
```

5. Choose **1** to create a Solaris FDISK partition. This is not the same as a Solaris slice.

6. After creating the partition, choose **4** to exit and save. The format menu will return.

7. Choose **partition** and follow the Step by Step 1.3 procedure described earlier for formatting a disk, beginning at step number 4.

Disks on x86/x64-based Solaris systems can be divided into 10 slices labeled slice 0 through slice 9. Slices 0 through 7 are used for the same purposes as disk slices found on SPARC based Solaris systems. Slice 2 represents all of the space within the Solaris `fdisk` partition. As stated earlier, slices 8 and 9 are used for purposes specific to x86/x64 hardware. You cannot modify slices 8 and 9 using the `format` utility.

Here's an example of the partition table on an IDE or SATA disk on an x86/x64 system, as displayed by the `format` utility:

```
Part  Tag          Flag  Cylinders    Size         Blocks
(output omitted)
8     boot         wu    0 - 0        7.84MB       (1/0/0) 16065
9     alternates   wm    1 - 2        15.69MB      (2/0/0) 32130
```

In the previous example, notice that slice 9 is defined and tagged as the `alternates` slice.

The next example shows the partition table for a SCSI disk attached to an x86/x64-based system. Notice that partition 8 is assigned, but slice 9 is not used:

```
Part    Tag          Flag    Cylinders    Size      Blocks
(output omitted)
8       boot         wu      0 - 0        7.84MB    (1/0/0) 16065
9       unassigned   wm      0            0         (0/0/0) 0
```

One more item of note: On standard UFS file systems, don't change the size of disk slices that are currently in use. When a disk with existing slices is repartitioned and relabeled, any existing data will be lost. Before repartitioning a disk, first copy all the data to tape or to another disk.

The Free Hog Slice

When using the `format` utility to change the size of disk slices, a temporary slice is automatically designated that expands and shrinks to accommodate the slice resizing operations. This temporary slice is referred to as the *free hog*, and it represents the unused disk space on a disk drive. If a slice is decreased, the free hog expands. The free hog is then used to allocate space to slices that have been increased. It does not, however, prevent the overlapping of disk slices as described in the previous section.

The free hog slice exists only when you run the `format` utility. It is not saved as a permanent slice.

Using the `format` Utility to Modify Partitions

If you need to change the size of slices on a particular disk, you can either re-create the disk slices as outlined in the previous section or use the `modify` option of the `format` utility.

CAUTION

Copy Your Data to Avoid Loss You will lose all data when changing partition sizes. Make sure that you copy your data either to another disk or to tape before continuing.

The `modify` option allows root to create slices by specifying the size of each slice without having to keep track of starting cylinder boundaries. It also keeps track of any excess disk space in the temporary free hog slice. To modify a disk slice, follow the process outlined in Step by Step 1.5.

STEP BY STEP

1.5 Modifying a Disk Slice

1. Make a backup of your data. This process destroys the data on this disk slice.
2. As root, enter the partition menu of the `format` utility, as described in Step by Step 1.3.
3. After printing the existing partition scheme, type **`modify`** and press Enter.

NOTE

Mounted Partitions If you try to modify mounted partitions, you receive an error that states "Cannot modify disk partitions while it has mounted partitions."

When typing `modify`, you'll see the following output on a disk that does not have mounted partitions:

```
Select partitioning base:
        0. Current partition table (original)
        1. All Free Hog
Choose base (enter number) [0]?
```

4. Press Enter to select the default selection. The following is displayed:

```
Part      Tag    Flag     Cylinders         Size            Blocks
  0       root    wm      0                 0          (0/0/0)             0
  1       swap    wu      0                 0          (0/0/0)             0
  2     backup    wu      0 - 24619         33.92GB    (24620/0/0) 71127180
  3 unassigned    wm      0                 0          (0/0/0)             0
  4 unassigned    wm      0                 0          (0/0/0)             0
  5 unassigned    wm      0                 0          (0/0/0)             0
  6        usr    wm      0                 0          (0/0/0)             0
  7 unassigned    wm      0                 0          (0/0/0)             0


Do you wish to continue creating a new partition
table based on above table[yes]?
```

5. Press Enter to select the default selection. The following message is displayed:

```
Free Hog partition[6]?
```

6. Press Enter to select the default selection. If all the disk space is in use, the following message is displayed:

```
Warning: No space available from Free Hog partition.
Continue[no]?
```

7. Type **yes**. You'll be prompted to type the new size for each partition:

```
Enter size of partition '0' [0b, 0c, 0.00mb, 0.00gb]: 1gb
Enter size of partition '1' [0b, 0c, 0.00mb, 0.00gb]: 500mb
Enter size of partition '3' [0b, 0c, 0.00mb, 0.00gb]:
Enter size of partition '4' [0b, 0c, 0.00mb, 0.00gb]:
Enter size of partition '5' [0b, 0c, 0.00mb, 0.00gb]:
Enter size of partition '7' [0b, 0c, 0.00mb, 0.00gb]:
```

NOTE

Temporary Free Hog Slice 6 is not displayed because that is the temporary free hog.

When you are finished resizing the last partition, the following is displayed, showing you the revised partition map:

```
Part      Tag    Flag     Cylinders         Size            Blocks
  0       root    wm       0 -   725        1.00GB    (726/0/0)      2097414
  1       swap    wu     726 -  1080      500.78MB    (355/0/0)      1025595
  2     backup    wu       0 - 24619       33.92GB    (24620/0/0) 71127180
  3 unassigned    wm       0                0         (0/0/0)            0
  4 unassigned    wm       0                0         (0/0/0)            0
  5 unassigned    wm       0                0         (0/0/0)            0
  6        usr    wm    1081 - 24619       32.43GB    (23539/0/0) 68004171
  7 unassigned    wm       0                0         (0/0/0)            0
Okay to make this the current partition table[yes]?
```

NOTE

The Free Hog Slice 6, the free hog, represents the unused disk space. You might want to allocate this space to another partition so that it does not go unused, or you can save it and allocate it another time to an unused partition.

8. Press Enter to confirm your modified partition map. You'll see the following message displayed:

```
Enter table name (remember quotes):
```

9. Name the modified partition table and press Enter:

```
Enter table name (remember quotes): disk2
```

10. After you enter the name, the following message is displayed:

```
Ready to label disk, continue?
```

11. Type **yes** and press Enter to continue.

12. Type **quit** (or **q**) and press Enter to exit the partition menu. The main menu is displayed.

13. Type **quit** and press Enter to exit the `format` utility.

Using the Solaris Management Console Disks Tool

You can also partition a disk and view a disk's partition information by using the graphical interface provided by the Solaris Management Console (SMC) Disks Tool. To view partition information, follow the procedure outlined in Step by Step 1.6.

STEP BY STEP

1.6 Viewing a Disk's Partition Information Using Disks Tool

1. As root, start up the SMC by typing

   ```
   smc &
   ```

2. In the left navigation window, select the This Computer icon, then click on the Storage icon as shown in Figure 1.2.

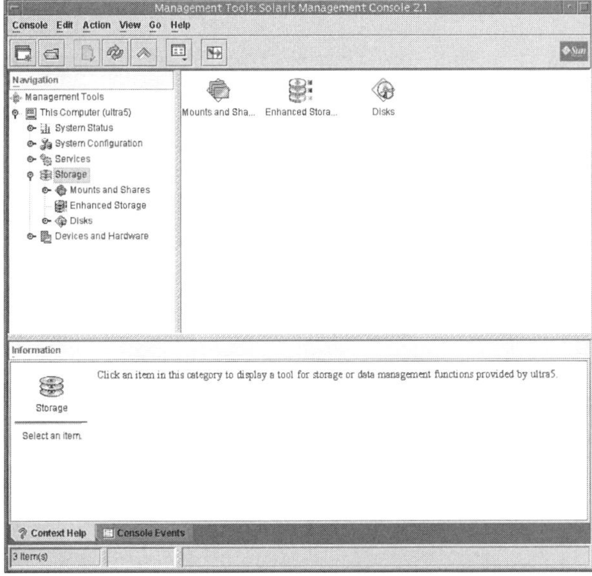

FIGURE 1.2 The SMC Storage icon.

3. From the SMC Main window, select the Disks icon as shown in Figure 1.3.

   The disk drives connected to your system will be displayed in the main window as shown in Figure 1.4.

4. Select the disk that you wish to view and the partition information for that disk will be displayed as shown in Figure 1.5.

You can use the SMC Disks Tool to perform the following tasks:

- Display information about a specific disk.
- Create Solaris disk partitions.
- List partitions.
- Copy the layout of one disk to another disk of the same type.
- Change the disk's label.

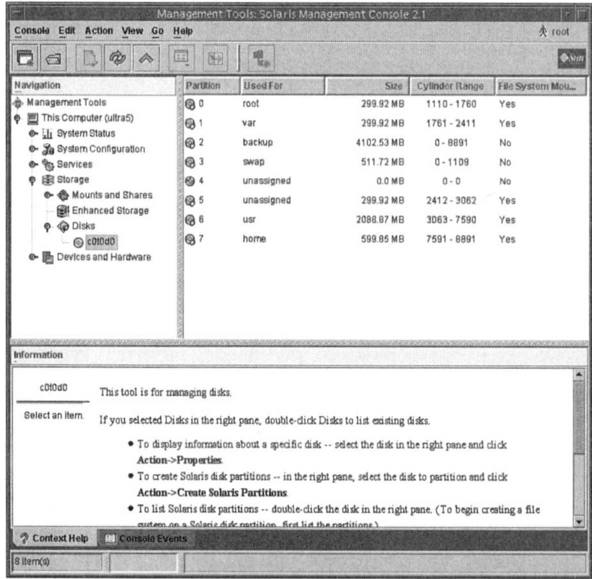

FIGURE 1.3 The SMC Disks icon.

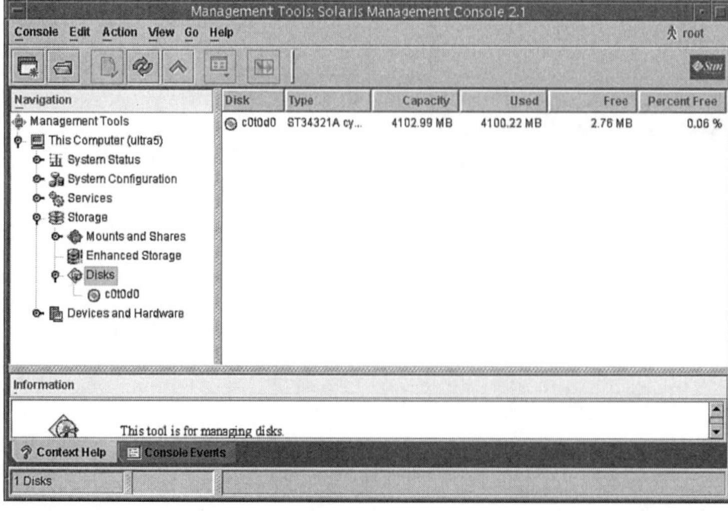

FIGURE 1.4 The SMC Disks tool.

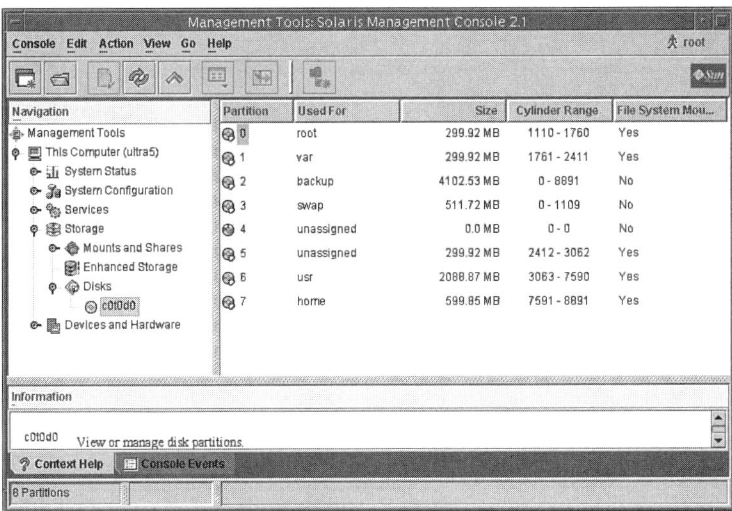

FIGURE 1.5 Selecting a disk.

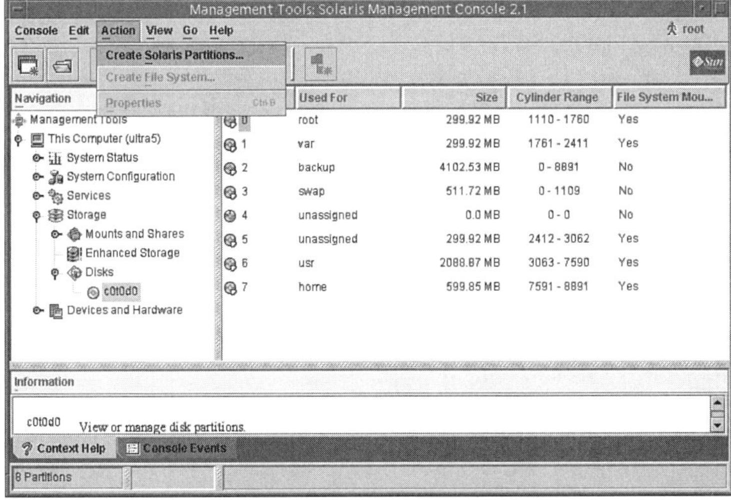

FIGURE 1.6 Partition a disk using Disks Tool.

To partition a disk using the SMC Disks Tool, follow the steps outlined in Step by Step 1.6. After selecting the disk that you want to partition, select the Create Solaris Partitions option from the pull-down Action menu as shown in Figure 1.6.

A Warning message will appear as shown in Figure 1.7.

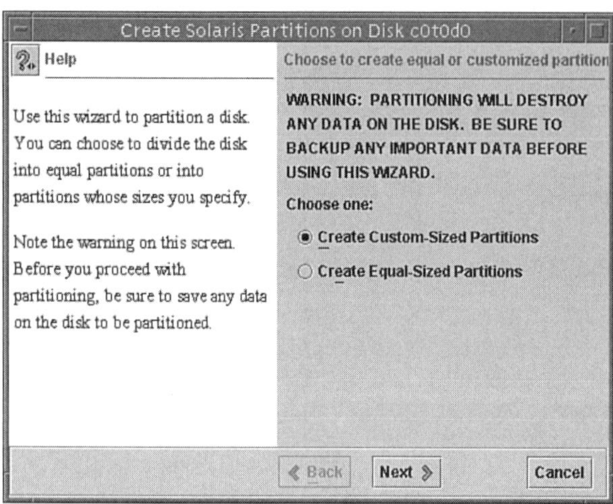

FIGURE 1.7 SMC warning message.

Click on the Next button and follow the prompts in each window to partition your disk. To partition a disk using the Disks Tool, follow the procedure outlined in Step by Step 1.7.

STEP BY STEP

1.7 Partitioning the Disk Using the SMC Disks Tool

1. In the window shown in Figure 1.7, specify whether you want to create custom-sized partitions or equal-sized partitions, then click the Next button. For this example, we are going to create custom-sized partitions. The window shown in Figure 1.8 will be displayed prompting you to specify the number of partitions to create.

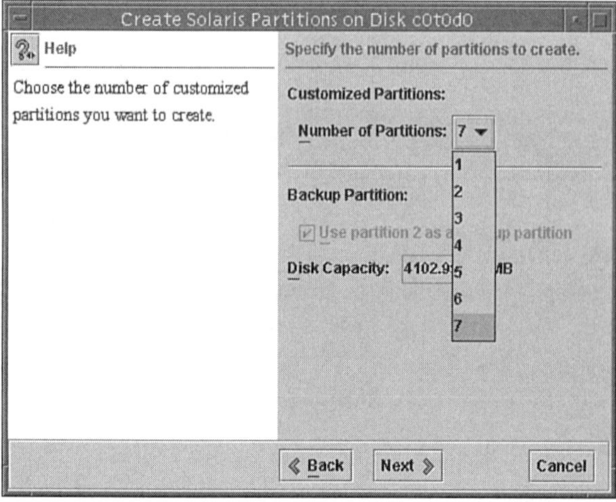

FIGURE 1.8 Specify number of partitions.

2. For this example, I selected 7 partitions and clicked on the Next button to continue. The next window prompts you to specify the size and use of the partition, as shown in Figure 1.9.

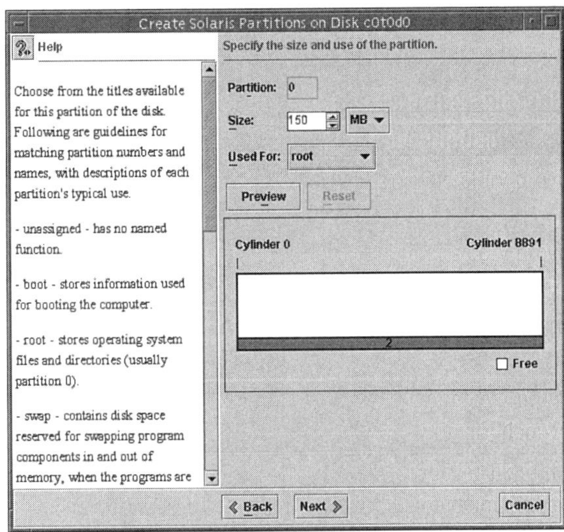

FIGURE 1.9 Specify the size and use of the partitions.

3. Next to the Size field, I selected MB and entered `150` into the Size field. Options for specifying size are MB (megabytes) or % (percentage of total disk).

   For the Used For field, I selected `root` because this is going to be the root partition. Options are `unassigned`, `boot`, `root`, `swap`, `usr`, `stand`, `var`, or `home`. Select the option that matches the function of the file system that you are creating. These options are described in the "Using the `format` Utility to Create Slices" section of this chapter.

   When you've made all of your selections, you can click on the Preview button to see a graphical layout of the disk. Click on the Next button when you are finished making all of your selections and you'll be asked to specify the size and use of the next partition. Continue sizing each partition. For this example, I left the remaining slices at 0 MB.

4. When you are finished sizing all of your partitions, you'll see a window summarizing all of your selections. Click Next and you'll see a warning window displayed as shown in Figure 1.10.

5. If you are satisfied with the partitions, click Finish. The new partitioning information is written and the `newfs` utility builds the partitions and creates each new file system.

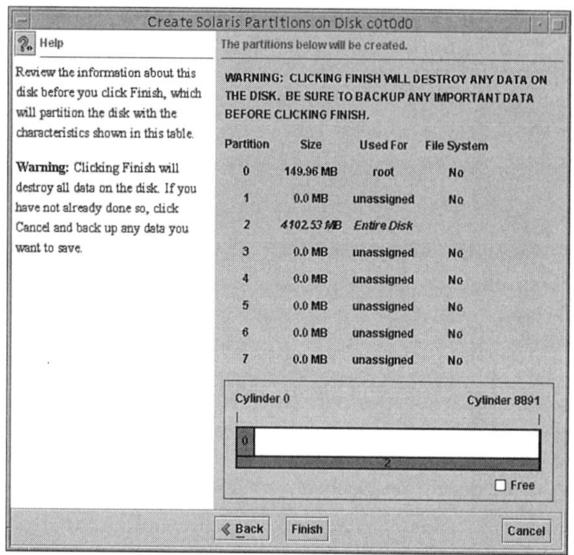

FIGURE 1.10 SMC warning window.

Recovering Disk Partition Information

It's always a good idea to save a disk's VTOC to a file using the `prtvtoc` command described earlier. This information can then be used later to restore the disk label if your current VTOC becomes corrupted or accidentally changed, or if you need to replace the disk drive.

NOTE

The disk label (VTOC) is stored in block 0 of each disk. The UFS file systems are smart enough not to touch the disk label, but be careful of any third party applications that create raw data slices. Ensure that these applications do not start at block 0; otherwise the disk label will be overwritten and the data on the disk will become inaccessible. I've seen some administrators start their raw slice at cylinder 2 or 3 just to ensure the disk label does not accidentally get overwritten.

By saving the output from the `prtvtoc` command into a file on another disk, you can reference it when running the `fmthard` command. The `fmthard` command updates the VTOC on hard disks. To recover a VTOC using `fmthard`, follow Step by Step 1.8.

STEP BY STEP

1.8 Recovering a VTOC

1. Run the `format` utility on the disk and label it with the default partition table.
2. Use the `fmthard` command to write the backup VTOC information back to the disk drive. The following example uses the `fmthard` command to recover a corrupt label on a disk named

/dev/rdsk/c0t3d0s2. The backup VTOC information is in a file named c0t3d0 in the /vtoc directory:

```
fmthard -s /vtoc/c0t3d0 /dev/rdsk/c0t3d0s2
```

Another use for the `fmthard` command is partitioning several disks with the same partitioning scheme. Get the VTOC information from the disk you want to copy (`c0t0d0`), and write the information to the new disk (`c1t0d0`) as follows:

```
prtvtoc /dev/rdsk/c0t0d0s2 | fmthard -s - /dev/rdsk/c1t0d0s2
```

Logical Volumes

On a large server with many disk drives, standard methods of disk slicing are inadequate and inefficient. File systems cannot span multiple disks, and the size of the file system is limited to the size of the disk. Another problem with standard file systems is that they cannot be increased in size without destroying data on the file system.

Sun has addressed these issues with three software packages: the Solaris Volume Manager (SVM), called Solstice DiskSuite in previous Solaris releases, ZFS, and the Veritas Volume Manager (VxVM). All packages allow file systems to span multiple disks and provide for improved I/O and reliability compared to the standard Solaris file system. We refer to these types of file systems as *logical volumes (LVMs)*.

SVM and ZFS are now part of Solaris 10 OE. The Veritas Volume Manager is purchased separately and is not part of the standard Solaris operating system distribution. SVM and ZFS are lower cost solutions and typically, SVM is used on Sun's multipacks and for mirroring the OS drives, whereas ZFS and the Veritas Volume Manager package are used on the larger SPARC storage arrays. LVMs, the SVM, and the Veritas Volume Manager are described in the *Solaris 10 System Administration Exam Prep: Exam CX-310-202* book.

Parts of a UFS

TIP

File Systems Although this section doesn't apply to any specific exam objective, the information is provided to help you better understand file systems in general.

UFS is the default disk-based file system used by the Solaris operating environment. It provides the following features:

- **State flags**—These show the state of the file system as clean, stable, active, or unknown. These flags eliminate unnecessary file system checks. If the file system is clean or stable, `fsck` (file system check) is not run when the system boots.

- **Extended fundamental types (EFT)**—These include a 32-bit user ID (UID), a group ID (GID), and device numbers.
- **Large file systems**—A UFS can be as large as 1 terabyte (TB) and can have regular files up to 2 gigabytes (GB). By default, the Solaris system software does not provide striping, which is required to make a logical slice large enough for a 1TB file system. However, the Solaris Volume Manager described in *Solaris 10 System Administration Exam Prep: Exam CX-310-202* book.
- **By default, a UFS can have regular files larger than 2GB**—You must explicitly use the `nolargefiles` mount option to enforce a 2GB maximum file size limit.
- **Logging**—UFS logging is the process of writing file system updates to a log before applying the updates to a UFS file system.
- **Multiterabyte file systems**—A multiterabyte file system enables creation of a UFS file system with up to approximately 16 terabytes of usable space, minus approximately one percent overhead. The system must be booted under a 64-bit kernel to support a multiterabyte file system. Systems booted under a 32-bit kernel are limited to a 1 TB file system.

During the installation of the Solaris software, several UFS file systems are created on the system disk. These are Sun's default file systems. Their contents are described in Table 1.6.

TABLE 1.6 Solaris Default File Systems

Slice	File System	Description
0	root	Root (/) is the top of the hierarchical file tree. It holds files and directories that make up the operating system. The root directory contains the directories and files critical for system operation, such as the kernel, the device drivers, and the programs used to boot the system. It also contains the mount point directories, in which local and remote file systems can be attached to the file tree. The root (/) file system is always in slice 0.
1	swap	Provides virtual memory or swap space. Swap space is used when you're running programs too large to fit in the computer's memory. The Solaris operating environment then "swaps" programs from memory to the disk and back, as needed. Although it is not technically required, it is common for the swap slice to be located in slice 1 unless /var is set up as a file system. If /var is set up, the interactive installation places /var on slice 1, and it places swap on slice 3. The /var file system is for files and directories likely to change or grow over the life of the local system. These include system logs, `vi` and `ex` backup files, printer and email spool files, backups of OS patches, and UUCP files. On a server, it's a good idea to have these files in a separate file system so that they cannot fill up the root slice.

TABLE 1.6 *Continued*

Slice	File System	Description
2	Entire Disk	Refers to the entire disk and is defined automatically by Sun's `format` utility and the Solaris installation programs. The size of this slice should not be changed.
3	/var	This slice is unassigned by default. In Solaris 10, if you let the Sun installation program auto layout the slices, it will place the /var directory under slice 0 with the root file system. However, if during the installation, /var is selected to have its own slice, the installation program will place /var onto slice 1 and will move swap to slice 3.
4		By default, slice 4 is unassigned and available for use.
5	/opt	This slice is unassigned by default. In Solaris 10, the /opt directory is put under slice 0 by default with the root file system. However, if during the installation, /opt is selected to have its own slice, the installation program will place /opt onto slice 5. /opt holds additional Sun software packages and optional third-party software that have been added to a system. If a slice is not allocated for this file system during installation, the /opt directory is put in slice 0, the root (/) file system.
6	/usr	This slice is unassigned by default. In Solaris 10, the /usr directory is put under slice 0 by default with the root file system. However, if during the installation, /usr is selected to have its own slice, the installation program will place /usr onto slice 6. /usr contains operating system commands—also known as executables—designed to be run by users. /usr also holds documentation, system programs (init and syslogd, for example), library routines, and system files and directories that can be shared with other users. Files that can be used on all types of systems (such as man pages) are in /usr/share. If /usr is placed on slice 0, slice 6 becomes an unallocated slice.
7	/export/home	Holds files created by users. On a standard system, /home is a mount point that points to /export/home and is managed by AutoFS.

Slice Numbers and Their Location on Disk

Although root may be located on slice 0, it doesn't necessarily mean that it is located first on the disk. For example, note the following partition scheme:

```
Part      Tag    Flag     Cylinders         Size            Blocks
  0      root     wm     258 -   759     1000.08MB    (502/0/0)      2048160
  1       var     wm     760 -  2265        2.93GB    (1506/0/0)     6144480
  2    backup     wm       0 - 39417       76.69GB    (39418/0/0) 160825440
  3      swap     wu       0 -   257      513.98MB    (258/0/0)      1052640
  4 unassigned    wm       0                 0        (0/0/0)              0
```

(continues)

(continued)

```
5 unassigned    wm     2266 -  2767      1000.08MB     (502/0/0)       2048160
6        usr    wm     2768 -  6783         7.81GB     (4016/0/0)     16385280
7       home    wm     6784 -  9293         4.88GB     (2510/0/0)     10240800
```

Notice how slice 3 starts at cylinder 0 and ends at cylinder 257. This puts slice 3 first on the disk. `root` is located on slice 0, which starts after slice 3 at cylinder 258. When using the interactive installation program to install the operating system, the swap partition is placed at the start of the disk beginning at cylinder 0 and the root partition is placed after the swap partition. A marginal performance increase is achieved by putting swap at the starting cylinder because of the faster rotation speeds on the outside perimeter of the disk. The interactive installation program is described in Chapter 2, "Installing the Solaris 10 Operating Environment."

You need to create (or re-create) a UFS only when you do the following:

- Add or replace disks.
- Change the slices of an existing disk.
- Do a full restore on a file system.
- Change the parameters of a file system, such as block size or free space.

The Root (/) File System

Objective:

Describe the purpose, features, and functions of root subdirectories, file components, file types, and hard links in the Solaris directory hierarchy.

Solaris comes with many file systems already created. These file systems were described earlier in this chapter. One of the most important file systems is the root file system. This file system is important because it is the first file system that is mounted when the system begins to boot. It is the file system that contains the kernel and all of the bootup scripts and programs. Without this file system, the system will not boot.

Furthermore, the root file system is at the top of the hierarchy of all file systems and contains all of the directory mount points for the other file systems. Taking a closer look at the contents of the root file system, we see that it contains many important directories, which are described in Table 1.7.

TABLE 1.7 Root Directories

Directory	Description of Contents
/	Root of the overall file system name space.
/bin	This is a symbolic link to the /usr/bin directory. See the section later in this chapter titled "Soft (Symbolic) Links."
/dev	Primary location for logical device names. Logical device names are described earlier in this chapter. Subdirectories within this directory are /dev/cfg—Symbolic links to physical ap_ids /dev/cua—Dial out devices for UUCP /dev/dsk—Block (buffered) disk devices /dev/fbs—Frame buffer device files /dev/fd—File descriptors /dev/md—Solaris Volume Manager metadisk devices /dev/pts—Pseudo terminal devices /dev/rdsk—Raw (character) disk devices /dev/rmt—Raw magnetic tape devices /dev/sad—Entry points for the STREAMS Administrative driver /dev/sound—Audio device and audio device control files /dev/swap—Default swap device /dev/term—Serial devices Logical device links in /dev point to device files in the /devices directory.
/devices	The devfs file system manages the /devices directory, which is the name space of all devices on the system. This directory represents the physical devices that consists of actual bus and device addresses.
/etc	Platform-dependent administrative and configuration files and databases that are not shared among systems. Most configuration files in this directory define the machine's identity. A few subdirectories within the /etc directory that you need to be aware of are /etc/acct—Accounting system configuration information. /etc/cron.d—Configuration information for cron(1M). /etc/default—Default information for various programs. /etc/dfs—Configuration information for shared file systems. /etc/dhcp—Dynamic Host Configuration Protocol (DHCP) configuration files. /etc/inet—Configuration files for Internet services. /etc/init.d—Contains legacy RC scripts for transitioning between run levels. This directory has been significantly reduced from previous versions of Solaris with the introduction of SMF, which is described in Chapter 3, "Perform System Boot and Shutdown Procedures." /etc/lib—Shared libraries needed during booting. /etc/lp—Configuration information for the printer subsystem. /etc/mail—Mail subsystem configuration. /etc/nfs—NFS server logging configuration file. /etc/opt—Configuration information for optional packages. /etc/rc<#>.d—Contains legacy RC scripts for transitioning between run levels. These are mainly hard links to the /etc/init.d directory and are described in Chapter 3. /etc/saf—Service Access Facility files. /etc/security—Basic Security Module (BSM) configuration files.

(continues)

TABLE 1.7 *Continued*

Directory	Description of Contents
	`/etc/skel`—Default profile scripts for new user accounts. This directory is discussed in Chapter 4, "User and Security Administration." `/etc/uucp`—UUCP configuration information.
`/export`	This directory contains commonly shared file systems such as user home directories.
`/home`	This is the system default directory (mount point) for user home directories. When you are running AutoFS, you cannot create new entries in this directory.
`/kernel`	This directory contains platform-independent loadable kernel modules required as part of the boot process. `/kernel` includes the generic part of the core kernel that is platform independent, named `/kernel/genunix`.
`/lib`	Shared executable files and Service Management Facility (SMF) executables.
`/mnt`	Default temporary mount point for file systems. Use this empty directory to temporarily mount any file system.
`/opt`	This is a default directory for add-on and third party application packages.
`/platform`	This directory contains platform-specific objects that need to reside on the root file system. It contains a series of directories, one per supported platform.
`/sbin`	The single-user `bin` directory contains essential commands used in the booting process. These commands are available when `/usr/bin` is not mounted. It contains many system administration commands and utilities.
`/usr`	The mount point for the `/usr` file system. The name "usr" is an acronym for Unix System Resources. Important subdirectories in `/usr` are `/usr/bin`—Most standard system commands are located here. `/usr/ccs`—C-compilation programs and libraries. `/usr/demo`—Demonstration programs. `/usr/dt`—CDE programs and files. `/usr/include`—Header files for C programs and other executables. `/usr/java`—Java programs and libraries. `/usr/lib`—Program libraries and databases. `/usr/openwin`—OpenWindows programs and files. `/usr/opt`—Configuration information for optional packages. `/usr/pub`—Files for online manual pages and character processing. `/usr/sadm`—System administration files and directories. `/usr/spool`—A symbolic link to `/var/spool`. `/usr/share`—A location for sharable files. Bundled Solaris software gets loaded here. `/usr/snadm`—Files related to system and network administration.

(continues)

TABLE 1.7 *Continued*

Directory	Description of Contents
	`/usr/tmp`—Symbolic link to `/var/tmp`. `/usr/ucb`—Berkeley compatibility package binaries.
`/var`	Directory for varying files such as logs, status files, mail, print files, and so on.

In addition, Solaris 10 introduces additional in-memory system directories and subdirectories that are described in Table 1.8. These in-memory directories are maintained by the kernel and system services. With the exception of `/tmp`, do not attempt to manually create, alter, or remove files from these directories.

TABLE 1.8 In-Memory System Directories

Directory	Description
`/dev/fd`	A directory containing special files relating to current file descriptors in use by the system.
`/devices`	The primary directory for physical device names.
`/etc/mnttab`	A memory-based file, in its own file system, which contains details of currently mounted file systems.
`/etc/svc/volatile`	A directory that contains log files and reference files relating to the current state of system services.
`/proc`	This directory stores current process-related information. Every process has its own subdirectory in `/proc`.
`/system/contract`	A file system used for creating, controlling, and observing contracts, which are relationships between processes and system resources. These process contracts are used by the Service Management Facility (SMF) to track the processes that compose a service. See Chapter 3 for a description of the SMF.
`/system/object`	This directory, used primarily for DTrace activity, describes the state of all modules currently loaded by the kernel.
`/tmp`	A memory-resident directory for temporary files. Be careful storing files in `/tmp`; this directory is cleared during the boot sequence.
`/var/run`	This directory contains lock files, special files, and reference files for a variety of system processes and services.

As you browse the directories in the root file system, you'll notice many file types. The file type can usually be identified by looking at the first character of the first column of information displayed when issuing the `ls -l` command.

A typical listing may look like this when listing the contents of the `/etc` directory:

```
ls -l /etc
total 583
lrwxrwxrwx   1 root     root          14 Aug  9 19:18 TIMEZONE -> ./default/init
drwxr-xr-x   6 root     other        512 Aug  9 20:51 X11
drwxr-xr-x   2 adm      adm          512 Aug 10 09:24 acct
lrwxrwxrwx   1 root     root          14 Aug  9 19:31 aliases -> ./mail/aliases
drwxr-xr-x   7 root     bin          512 Aug 10 09:34 apache
drwxr-xr-x   2 root     bin          512 Aug 10 09:26 apache2
drwxr-xr-x   2 root     other        512 Aug  9 20:29 apoc
-rw-r--r--   1 root     bin          226 Sep 13 14:17 auto_home
-rw-r--r--   1 root     bin          248 Aug  9 19:29 auto_master
lrwxrwxrwx   1 root     root          16 Aug  9 19:18 autopush -> ../sbin/autopush
drwxr-xr-x   2 root     other        512 Aug  9 20:19 bonobo-activation
drwxr-xr-x   2 root     sys          512 Aug  9 19:18 certs
lrwxrwxrwx   1 root     root          18 Aug  9 19:18 cfgadm -> ../usr/sbin/cfgadm
lrwxrwxrwx   1 root     root          18 Aug  9 20:18 chroot -> ../usr/sbin/chroot
    <output has been truncated>
```

The information displayed in the long listing is in the form of columns and is as follows (reading from left to right):

- **Column 1**—Ten characters that describe the mode of the file. The first character displays the file type where

d	The entry is a directory.
D	The entry is a door.
l	The entry is a symbolic link.
b	The entry is a block special file.
c	The entry is a character special file.
p	The entry is a FIFO (or "named pipe") special file.
s	The entry is an AF_UNIX address family socket.
-	The entry is an ordinary file.

The next nine characters in column one describe the file's permission mode, which is described in detail in Chapter 4, "User and Security Administration".

- **Column 2**—Displays the number of links to the file
- **Column 3**—Displays the file's owner
- **Column 4**—Displays the file's group
- **Column 5**—Displays the file size in bytes
- **Column 6**—Date/Time of the file's last modification

- **Column 7**—File name

The -> after a file name denotes a symbolic link, as follows:

```
lrwxrwxrwx   1 root    root    14 Feb 26  2005 TIMEZONE -> ./default/init
drwxr-xr-x   2 adm     adm    512 Feb 27  2005 acct
lrwxrwxrwx   1 root    root    14 Feb 26  2005 aliases -> ./mail/aliases
lrwxrwxrwx   1 root    root    16 Feb 26  2005 autopush -> ../sbin/autopush
lrwxrwxrwx   1 root    root    18 Feb 26  2005 cfgadm -> ../usr/sbin/cfgadm
lrwxrwxrwx   1 root    root    18 Feb 26  2005 chroot -> ../usr/sbin/chroot
lrwxrwxrwx   1 root    root    16 Feb 26  2005 clri -> ../usr/sbin/clri
```

A link is a pointer to another file or directory. Links provide a mechanism for multiple file names to reference the same data on disk. In Solaris, there are two types of links:

- Soft (symbolic) links
- Hard links

Both of these are discussed in the following sections.

Soft (Symbolic) Links

Sometimes symbolic links are used for shortcuts; other times we use them to link to a filename from each user's home directory to a centralized location or file. For example, perhaps we want to have a common directory named `documents` where every user stores their documents. This directory exists as `/export/data/documents`. In each user's directory, we create a link named documents that points to `/export/data/documents`. As a user, whenever I store something in the directory named `$HOME/documents`, the file actually gets directed to `/export/data/documents`. We can identify links when we perform a long listing on a directory as follows:

Notice the use of the `-i` option used with the **ls** command and the results displayed. This option is used to display the inode number (in the left column of the output) that has been assigned to each file and directory.

NOTE

I'll describe why this inode number is relevant to links later in this section when I describe hard links.

```
ls -li $HOME
```

The system displays the following:

```
75264 drwxr--r--    2 bcalkins staff  512 Jun  6 20:36 dir1
78848 drwxrwxr-x    2 bcalkins staff  512 Jun  6 20:38 dir2
82432 drw-r--r--    2 bcalkins staff  512 Jun  6 20:39 dir3
3593 lrwxrwxrwx     1 bcalkins staff  22 Jun 17 17:09 documents\
 -> /export/data/documents
```

Output has been truncated.

Notice the file that has an *l* as the first character of column 2. This is a soft or *symbolic* link. The sixth field shows a file size of 22 bytes and the last field shows which file or directory this link is pointing to. Each file has a unique inode number identified in column 1; the importance of this column is discussed later in this chapter.

When storing a file in $HOME/documents, the system is redirecting it to be stored in `/export/data`. Now when changing to the `/export/data` directory and issuing the `ls -li` command:

```
cd /export/data
ls -li
```

The system displays the following:

```
125461    drwxr-xr-x   2 root     other    512 Jun 17 17:09 documents
```

Notice the file that has a *d* as the first character of column 2. This is the directory that the `$HOME/documents` link points to. The first column shows the inode number, and the sixth column shows the file size as 512 bytes.

Symbolic links can point to files anywhere on the network. The file or directory could exist in another file system, on another disk, or on another system on the network.

The syntax for creating a symbolic link is as follows:

```
ln -s source-file link-name
```

For example, you might have a file named `file1` that has the following contents:

```
This is the contents of file1
```

To create a symbolic link named `link1`, which will be linked to the existing file named `file1`, you issue the following command:

```
ln -s file1 link1
```

Now when you list the contents of the directory you see two files:

```
3588 -rw-r--r--   1 bcalkins staff          30 Jun 17 17:51 file1
3594 lrwxrwxrwx   1 bcalkins staff           5 Jun 17 18:09 link1 -> file1
```

See the link named `link1` pointing to `file1`? If you display the contents of `link1`, it shows the following:

```
This is the contents of file1
```

If you remove `file1`, the source file, `link1` will still exist, but it points to a file that does not exist. Type the following:

```
cat link1
```

The `cat` command can't print out the contents of the file, so you get this message:

```
cat: Cannot open link1
```

When you re-create `file1`, `link1` will contain data again.

Hard Links

Objective:

Explain how to create and remove hard links in a Solaris directory.

A hard link is more difficult to determine, because they are not so obvious when viewed with the `ls -li` command. For example, when you go to the `/etc/rc2.d` directory and type

```
ls -li
```

the system displays the following:

```
total 102
<output has been truncated>
      2123 -rwxr--r--   5 root     sys         1718 Jan 21  2005 S47pppd
      2102 -rwxr--r--   2 root     sys          327 Jan 21  2005 S70uucp
      1368 -rwxr-xr-x   2 root     other       1558 Jan  9  2005 S72autoinstall
       241 -rwxr--r--   2 root     sys         1262 Jan 21  2005 S73cachefs.daemon
      1315 -rwxr--r--   2 root     sys         1028 Jan 21  2005 S81dodatadm.udaplt
       237 -rwxr--r--   2 root     sys          256 Jan 21  2005 S89PRESERVE
      2103 lrwxrwxrwx   1 root     root           31 Aug 10 09:49 S89bdconfig ->\
 ../init.d/buttons_n_dials-setup
      1898 -rwxr--r--   5 root     sys         3506 Jan 10  2005 S90wbem
      2100 -rwxr--r--   5 root     sys         1250 Jan 10  2005 S90webconsole
```

Output has been truncated.

The first character in the second column of information displays the file type as a regular file (-). The third column, link count, shows a number greater than 1. It displays the number of links used by this inode number. These are hard links, but they are not identified as links and the display does not show which file they are linked to.

Think of a hard link as a file that has many names. In other words, they all share the same inode number. As described in the section titled "The inode" later in this chapter, a file system identifies a file not by its name, but by its inode number. Looking at the file named `S90wbem` in the previous listing, we see an inode number of 1898. List all file names in this file system that share this inode number as follows:

```
find / -mount -inum 1898 -ls
```

The system displays the following list of files:

```
1898  4 -rwxr--r--   5 root   sys    3506 Jan 10  2005 /etc/init.d/init.wbem
1898  4 -rwxr--r--   5 root   sys    3506 Jan 10  2005 /etc/rc0.d/K36wbem
1898  4 -rwxr--r--   5 root   sys    3506 Jan 10  2005 /etc/rc1.d/K36wbem
1898  4 -rwxr--r--   5 root   sys    3506 Jan 10  2005 /etc/rc2.d/S90wbem
1898  4 -rwxr--r--   5 root   sys    3506 Jan 10  2005 /etc/rcS.d/K36wbem
```

All five of these files have the same inode number; therefore, they are the same file. You can delete any one of the filenames, and the data will still exist.

In this example, the file is named `file1` in `$HOME`:

```
3588 -rw-r--r--   3 bcalkins staff        30 Jun 17 17:51 file1
```

The contents of this file are displayed with the `cat` command:

```
This is the contents of file1
```

The syntax for creating a hard link is as follows:

```
ln source-file link-name
```

To create a hard link named `link1`, which will be linked to the existing file named `file1`, issue the following command:

```
ln file1 link1
```

Now when I list the contents of the directory, I see two files:

```
3588 -rw-r--r--   2 bcalkins staff        30 Jun 17 17:51 file1
3588 -rw-r--r--   2 bcalkins staff        30 Jun 17 17:51 link1
```

Both files share the same inode number, the number of links is two, and the file size is 30 bytes. If I display the contents of `link1`, it shows the following:

```
This is the contents of file1
```

If I remove `file1`, the source file, `link1` still exists and still contains the data. The data will not be deleted until I destroy the last file that shares this inode number.

A hard link cannot span file systems; it can only point to another file located within its file system. The reason is that hard links all share an inode number. Each file system has its own set of inode numbers; therefore, a file with inode number 3588 in the `/export/home` file system may not even exist in the `/var` file system.

An advantage of a symbolic link over a hard link is that you can create a symbolic link to a file that does not yet exist. You cannot create a hard link unless the source file already exists. Here's what happens when you create a symbolic link to a file that does not exist:

```
ln -s  nonexistentfile link5
```

When you list the file:

```
ls -l link5
```

The system responds with

```
lrwxrwxrwx   1 bcalkins staff   14 Jun 17 18:24 link5 -> nonexistentfile
```

Now, here's what happens when you create a hard link to a file that does not exist:

```
ln noexistentfile link6
```

The system responds with

```
ln: cannot access noexistentfile
```

Removing a Link

Remove a link using the `rm` command as follows:

```
rm <linkname>
```

For example, to remove the link named `link1`, type

```
rm link1
```

> **NOTE**
>
> **Removing Files and Links** When you remove a file, it's always a good idea to remove the symbolic links that pointed to that file, unless you plan to use them again if the file gets re-created.

Another advantage of symbolic links over hard links is that a symbolic link can link directories or files, whereas a hard link can link only files.

Components of the UFS

When you create a UFS, the disk slice is divided into cylinder groups. The slice is then divided into blocks to control and organize the structure of the files within the cylinder group. Each block performs a specific function in the file system. A UFS has the following four types of blocks:

- **Boot block**—Stores information used when booting the system
- **Superblock**—Stores much of the information about the file system
- **Cylinder Group**—File systems are divided into cylinder groups to improve disk access.
- **Inode**—Stores all information about a file except its name
- **Storage or data block**—Stores data for each file

The Boot Block

The boot block stores the code used in booting the system. Without a boot block, the system does not boot. Each file system has 15 sectors of space (sectors 1–15) allocated at the beginning for a boot block; however, if a file system is not to be used for booting, the boot block is left blank. The boot block appears only in the first cylinder group (cylinder group 0) and is the first 8KB in a slice.

The Superblock

The superblock resides in the 16 sectors (sectors 16–31) following the boot block and stores much of the information about the file system. Following are a few of the more important items contained in a superblock:

- Size and status of the file system
- Label (file system name and volume name)
- Size of the file system's logical block
- Date and time of the last update
- Cylinder group size
- Number of data blocks in a cylinder group
- Summary data block
- File system state (clean, stable, or active)
- Pathname of the last mount point

Without a superblock, the file system becomes unreadable. Because it contains critical data, the superblock is replicated in each cylinder group and multiple superblocks are made when the file system is created.

A copy of the superblock for each file system is kept up-to-date in memory. If the system gets halted before a disk copy of the superblock gets updated, the most recent changes are lost and the file system becomes inconsistent. The `sync` command saves every superblock in memory to the disk. The file system check program `fsck` can fix problems that occur when the `sync` command hasn't been used before a shutdown.

A summary information block is kept with the superblock. It is not replicated but is grouped with the first superblock, usually in cylinder group 0. The summary block records changes that take place as the file system is used, listing the number of inodes, directories, fragments, and storage blocks within the file system.

Cylinder Groups

Each file system is divided into cylinder groups with a minimum default size of 16 cylinders per group. Cylinder groups improve disk access. The file system constantly optimizes disk performance by attempting to place a file's data into a single cylinder group, which reduces the distance a head has to travel to access the file's data.

The inode

An inode contains all the information about a file except its name, which is kept in a directory. A filename is associated with an inode, and the inode provides access to data blocks. An inode is 128 bytes. The inode information is kept in the cylinder information block and contains the following:

- The type of the file (regular, directory, block special, character special, link, and so on)
- The mode of the file (the set of read/write/execute permissions)
- The number of hard links to the file
- The user ID of the file's owner
- The group ID to which the file belongs
- The number of bytes in the file
- An array of 15 disk-block addresses
- The date and time the file was last accessed
- The date and time the file was last modified
- The date and time the file was created

inodes are numbered and each file system maintains its own list of inodes. inodes are created for each file system when the file system is created. The maximum number of files per UFS is determined by the number of inodes allocated for a file system. The number of inodes depends on the amount of disk space that is allocated for each inode and the total size of the file system. Table 1.9 displays the default number of inodes created by the `newfs` command based on the size of the file system.

TABLE 1.9 Default Number of inodes

Disk Size	Density
Less than 1GB	2048
Less than 2GB	4096
Less than 3GB	6144
3GB to 1 Tbyte	8192
Greater than 1 Tbyte or file systems created with the `-T` option	1048576

You can change the default allocation by using the `-i` option of the `newfs` command. Also, the number of inodes will increase if a file system is expanded with the `growfs` command. The `newfs` command is described later in this chapter and `growfs` is described in the *Solaris 10 System Administration Exam Prep: Exam CX-310-202* book.

The Storage Block

Storage blocks, also called data blocks, occupy the rest of the space allocated to the file system. The size of these storage blocks is determined at the time a file system is created. Storage blocks are allocated, by default, in two sizes: an 8KB logical block size and a 1KB fragmentation size.

For a regular file, the storage blocks contain the contents of the file. For a directory, the storage blocks contain entries that give the inode number and the filename of the files in the directory.

Free Blocks

Blocks not currently being used as inodes, indirect address blocks, or storage blocks are marked as free in the cylinder group map. This map also keeps track of fragments to prevent fragmentation from degrading disk performance.

Creating a UFS

Objective:

Explain when and how to create a new UFS using the `newfs` command, check the file system using `fsck`, resolve file system inconsistencies, and monitor file system usage using associated commands.

Use the `newfs` command to create UFS file systems. `newfs` is a convenient front end to the `mkfs` command, the program that creates the new file system on a disk slice.

On Solaris 10 systems, information used to set some of the parameter defaults, such as number of tracks per cylinder and number of sectors per track, is read from the disk label. `newfs` determines the file system parameters to use, based on the options you specify and information provided in the disk label. Parameters are then passed to the `mkfs` (make file system) command, which builds the file system. Although you can use the `mkfs` command directly, it's more difficult to use and you must supply many of the parameters manually. (The use of the `newfs` command is discussed more in the next section.)

You must format the disk and divide it into slices before you can create a file system on it. `newfs` makes existing data on the disk slice inaccessible and creates the skeleton of a directory structure, including a directory named `lost+found`. After you run `newfs`, the slice is ready to be mounted as a file system.

CAUTION

Cleaning Sensitive Data from a Disk Removing a file system using the `newfs` or `rm` commands, or simply formatting the disk, is not sufficient to completely remove data bits from the disk. In order to wipe a hard disk clean of sensitive information, so that the data is beyond the recovery limits of any data recovery software or utility, use the `analyze` option within the `format` utility's main menu. When the `analyze` menu appears, select the `purge` option. Purging data from the disk complies with Department of Defense (DoD) wipe disk standards for completely removing data bits from a disk. This procedure destroys all the file systems on the disk.

To create a UFS on a formatted disk that has already been divided into slices, you need to know the raw device filename of the slice that will contain the file system (see Step by Step 1.9). If you are re-creating or modifying an existing UFS, back up and unmount the file system before performing these steps.

STEP BY STEP

1.9 Creating a UFS

1. Become superuser.
2. Type `newfs /dev/rdsk/`*<device-name>* and press Enter. You are asked if you want to proceed. The `newfs` command requires the use of the raw device name, not the block device name. If the block device name is used, it will be converted to a raw device name. For more information on raw (character) and block (buffered) devices, refer to the "Block and Raw Devices" section that appeared earlier in this chapter.

CAUTION

Prevent Yourself from Erasing the Wrong Slice Be sure you have specified the correct device name for the slice before performing the next step. The `newfs` command is destructive and you will erase the contents of the slice when the new file system is created. Be careful not to erase the wrong slice.

3. Type **y** to confirm.

The following example creates a file system on `/dev/rdsk/c2t1d0s1`:

1. Become superuser by typing **su**, and enter the root password.
2. Type **`newfs /dev/rdsk/c2t1d0s1`**.

   The system responds with this:

```
newfs: construct a new file system /dev/rdsk/c2t1d0s1: (y/n)? y
/dev/rdsk/c2t1d0s1:     8337600 sectors in 3860 cylinders of 16 tracks, 135
sectors
        4071.1MB in 84 cyl groups (46 c/g, 48.52MB/g, 6080 i/g)
super-block backups (for fsck -F ufs -o b=#) at:
 32, 99536, 199040, 298544, 398048, 497552, 597056, 696560, 796064, 895568,
 7354112, 7453616, 7553120, 7652624, 7752128, 7851632, 7948832, 8048336,
 8147840, 8247344,
```

The `newfs` command uses conservative and safe default values to create the file system. We describe how to modify these values later in this chapter. Here are the default parameters used by the `newfs` command:

- The file system block size is 8192.
- The file system fragment size (the smallest allocable unit of disk space) is 1024 bytes.
- The percentage of free space is now calculated as follows: (64MB/partition size) × 100, rounded down to the nearest integer and limited to between 1% and 10%, inclusive.
- The number of inodes allocated to a file system (see Table 1.9, titled "Default Number of inodes").

Understanding Custom File System Parameters

Before you choose to alter the default file system parameters assigned by the `newfs` command, you need to understand them. This section describes each of these parameters:

- Logical block size
- Fragment size
- Minimum free space
- Rotational delay (gap)
- Optimization type
- Number of inodes and bytes per inode

Logical Block Size

The *logical block size* is the size of the blocks that the Unix kernel uses to read or write files. The logical block size is usually different from the physical block size (usually 512 bytes), which is the size of the smallest block that the disk controller can read or write.

You can specify the logical block size of the file system. After the file system is created, you cannot change this parameter without rebuilding the file system. You can have file systems with different logical block sizes on the same disk.

By default, the logical block size is 8192 bytes (8KB) for UFS file systems. The UFS supports block sizes of 4096 or 8192 bytes (4KB or 8KB, with 8KB being the recommended logical block size).

To choose the best logical block size for your system, consider both the performance desired and the available space. For most UFS systems, an 8KB file system provides the best performance, offering a good balance between disk performance and use of space in primary memory and on disk.

NOTE

sun4u Only The sun4u architecture does not support the 4KB block size.

As a general rule, a larger logical block size increases efficiency for file systems in which most of the files are large. Use a smaller logical block size for file systems in which most of the files are small. You can use the `quot -c` file system command on a file system to display a complete report on the distribution of files by block size.

Fragment Size

As files are created or expanded, they are allocated disk space in either full logical blocks or portions of logical blocks called fragments. When disk space is needed to hold data for a file, full blocks are allocated first, and then one or more fragments of a block are allocated for the remainder. For small files, allocation begins with fragments.

The capability to allocate fragments of blocks to files rather than whole blocks saves space by reducing the fragmentation of disk space that results from unused holes in blocks.

You define the fragment size when you create a UFS. The default fragment size is 1KB. Each block can be divided into one, two, four, or eight fragments, resulting in fragment sizes from 512 bytes (for 4KB file systems) to 8192 bytes (for 8KB file systems only). The lower boundary is actually tied to the disk sector size, typically 512 bytes.

NOTE

Fragment Size for Large Files The upper boundary might equal the full block size, in which case the fragment is not a fragment at all. This configuration might be optimal for file systems with large files when you are more concerned with speed than with space.

When choosing a fragment size, look at the trade-off between time and space: A small fragment size saves space but requires more time to allocate. As a general rule, a larger fragment size increases efficiency for file systems in which most of the files are large. Use a smaller fragment size for file systems in which most of the files are small.

Minimum Free Space

The minimum free space is the percentage of the total disk space held in reserve when you create the file system. Before Solaris 7, the default reserve was always 10%. Since Solaris 7, the minimum free space is automatically determined. This new method of calculating free space results in less wasted disk space on large file systems.

Free space is important because file access becomes less efficient as a file system gets full. As long as the amount of free space is adequate, UFS file systems operate efficiently. When a file system becomes full, using up the available user space, only `root` can access the reserved free space.

Commands such as `df` report the percentage of space available to users

```
# df -k <cr>
Filesystem             kbytes     used    avail capacity  Mounted on
/dev/dsk/c0t0d0s0     12101980 3790346 8190615     32%     /
/devices                     0       0       0      0%    /devices
ctfs                         0       0       0      0%    /system/contract
proc                         0       0       0      0%    /proc
mnttab                       0       0       0      0%    /etc/mnttab
swap                   2781200    1272 2779928      1%    /etc/svc/volatile
objfs                        0       0       0      0%    /system/object
fd                           0       0       0      0%    /dev/fd
/dev/dsk/c0t0d0s1      5042614   63225 4928963      2%    /var
swap                   2779928       0 2779928      0%    /tmp
swap                   2779968      40 2779928      1%    /var/run
/dev/dsk/c0t0d0s7     10084544   10017 9973682      1%     /export/home
```

Notice that the sum of the values reported in the "`used`" and "`avail`" columns do not add up to the value reported in the "`size`" column. That's because the sum does not include the percentage of disk space allocated as minimum free space. Only the root user can use all of the space specified in the "size" column of the `df` output, while users can only use the amount specified in the "`avail`" column.

If you impose quotas on users, the amount of space available to the users does not include the free space reserve. You can change the value of the minimum free space for an existing file system by using the `tunefs` command.

Optimization Type

The optimization type is either space or time. When you select space optimization, disk blocks are allocated to minimize fragmentation and optimize disk use.

When you select time optimization, disk blocks are allocated as quickly as possible, with less emphasis on their placement. With enough free space, the disk blocks can be allocated effectively with minimal fragmentation. Time is the default.

You can change the value of the optimization type parameter for an existing file system by using the `tunefs` command.

Number of inodes and Bytes per inode

The number of inodes determines the number of files you can have in the file system because each file has one inode. The number of bytes per inode determines the total number of inodes created when the file system is made: the total size of the file system divided by the number of bytes per inode.

A file system with many symbolic links will have a lower average file size and the file system will require more inodes than a file system with a few very large files. If your file system will have many small files, you can use the `-i` option with `newfs` to specify the number of bytes per inode, which will determine the number of inodes in the file system. For a file system with very large files, give this parameter a lower value.

NOTE

Number of inodes Having too many inodes is much better than running out of them. If you have too few inodes, you could reach the maximum number of files on a disk slice that is practically empty.

The `mkfs` Command

EXAM ALERT

Expect to see several questions on creating, fixing, and managing file systems. All questions related to creating file systems will use `newfs`. It's important to understand the file system options described in this `mkfs` section, but don't be too concerned about understanding the `mkfs` method of creating file systems. Most system administrators use `newfs` and that is what you will be tested on.

Although it's highly recommended that the `newfs` command be used to create file systems, it's also important to see what is happening "behind the scenes" with the `mkfs` utility. The syntax for `mkfs` is as follows:

```
/usr/sbin/mkfs <options> <character device name>
```

The `mkfs` options are described in Table 1.10.

TABLE 1.10 The `mkfs` Command

Option	Description
`-F`	Used to specify the file system type. If this option is omitted, the `/etc/vfstab` and `/etc/default/fs` files are checked to determine a file system type.
`-m`	Shows the command line that was used to create the specified file system. No changes are made to the file system.
`-V`	Verbose. Shows the command line, but does not execute anything.
`-o <specific options>`	A list of options specific to the type of file system. The list must have the following format: `-o` followed by a space, followed by a series of `keyword [=value]` pairs, separated by commas, with no intervening spaces. `apc=`*<n>*—Reserved space for bad block replacement on SCSI devices. The default is `0`. N—Prints the file system parameters without actually creating the file system. `nsect=`*<n>*—The number of sectors per track on the disk. The default is 32. `ntrack=`*<n>*—The number of tracks per cylinder on the disk. The default is 16. This option is not applicable for disks with EFI labels. `bsize=`*<n>*—Logical block size, either `4096` (4KB) or `8192` (8KB). The default is `8192`. The sun4u architecture does not support the `4096` block size. `fragsize=`*<bytes>*—The smallest amount of disk space, in bytes, to allocate to a file. The value must be a power of 2 with a minimum value of `512` and a maximum of the logical block size. Thus, if the logical block size is `4096`, legal values are `512`, `1024`, `2048`, and `4096`. If the logical block size is `8192`, `8192` is also a legal value. The default is `1024`. `cgsize=`*<cyls>*—The number of cylinders per cylinder group. The default is `16`.

(continues)

TABLE 1.10 *Continued*

Option	Description
	free=<*n*>—The minimum percentage of free space to maintain in the file system. This space is off-limits to normal users. After the file system is filled to this threshold, only the superuser can continue writing to the file system. This parameter can be subsequently changed using the tunefs command. The default is ([64 Mbytes/partion size] x 100), rounded down to the nearest integer and limited between 1% and 10%, inclusively.
	rps=<*rps*>—The rotational speed of the disk, specified in revolutions per second. The default is 60.
	nbpi=<*value*>—The value specified is the number of bytes per inode, which specifies the density of inodes in the file system. The number is divided into the total size of the file system to determine the fixed number of inodes to create. It should reflect the expected average size of files in the file system. If fewer inodes are desired, a larger number should be used. To create more inodes, a smaller number should be given. The default is 2048. The number of inodes can be increased later if the file system is expanded with the growfs command.
	opt=<*value*>—Space or time optimization preference. The value can be s or t. Specify s to optimize for disk space. Specify t to optimize for speed (time). The default is t. Generally, you should optimize for time unless the file system is more than 90% full.
	nrpos=<*n*>—The number of different rotational positions into which to divide a cylinder group. The default is 8. This option is not applicable for disks with EFI labels.
	maxcontig=<*blocks*>—The maximum number of blocks belonging to one file that are allocated contiguously before inserting a rotational delay.

mkfs constructs a file system on the character (or raw) device found in the /dev/rdsk directory. Again, it is highly recommended that you do not run the mkfs command directly, but instead use the friendlier newfs command, which automatically determines all the necessary parameters required by mkfs to construct the file system. In the following example, the -v option to the newfs command outputs all the parameters passed to the mkfs utility. Type the following:

```
newfs -v /dev/rdsk/c2t4d0s1
```

The system outputs the following information and creates a new file system on /dev/rdsk/c2t4d0s1:

```
newfs: construct a new file system /dev/rdsk/c2t4d0s1: (y/n)? y
```

The following output appears on the screen:

```
mkfs -F ufs /dev/rdsk/c2t4d0s1 8359200 135 16 8192 1024 96 1 120 8192 t 0 -1 8 128 n
/dev/rdsk/c2t4d0s1:     8359200 sectors in 3870 cylinders of 16 tracks, 135 sectors
        4081.6MB in 85 cyl groups (46 c/g, 48.52MB/g, 6080 i/g)
super-block backups (for fsck -F ufs -o b=#) at:
 32, 99536, 199040, 298544, 398048, 497552, 597056, 696560, 796064, 895568,
 7453616, 7553120, 7652624, 7752128, 7851632, 7948832, 8048336, 8147840,
 8247344, 8346848,
```

You'll see in the output that all the `mkfs` parameters used to create the file system are displayed. The second line of output describes the disk. The third line describes the UFS file system being created. The remaining lines of output list the beginning sector locations of the backup superblocks.

The `newfs` command also creates a `lost+found` directory for the UFS file system. This directory is used by the `fsck` command and described later in this chapter.

The `fstyp` Command

A good command to use to view file system parameters is the `fstyp` command. Use the `-v` option to obtain a full listing of a file system's parameters:

```
fstyp -v /dev/rdsk/c0t0d0s7
```

The system responds with this:

```
ufs
magic    11954    format  dynamic time    Tue May 13 13:41:35 2008
sblkno   16       cblkno  24      iblkno  32      dblkno  760
sbsize   2048     cgsize  8192    cgoffset 64     cgmask  0xffffffc0
ncg      209      size    10240060        blocks  10084544
bsize    8192     shift   13      mask    0xffffe000
fsize    1024     shift   10      mask    0xfffffc00
frag     8        shift   3       fsbtodb 1
minfree  1%       maxbpg  2048    optim   time
maxcontig 128     rotdelay 0ms    rps     167
csaddr   760      cssize  4096    shift   9       mask    0xfffffe00
ntrak    48       nsect   128     spc     6144    ncyl    3334
cpg      16       bpg     6144    fpg     49152   ipg     5824
```

```
nindir  2048    inopb   64      nspf    2
nbfree  1259314 ndir    2       nifree  1217212 nffree  15
cgrotor 0       fmod    0       ronly   0       logbno  1568
version 2
fs_reclaim is not set
file system state is valid, fsclean is -3
blocks available in each rotational position
cylinder number 0:
```

*Output has been truncated.

NOTE

Copy the mkfs Options It's always a good idea to print the `mkfs` options used on a file system along with information provided by the `prtvtoc` command. Put the printout in your system log so that if you ever need to rebuild a file system because of a hard drive failure, you can re-create it exactly as it was before.

File System Operations

This section describes the Solaris utilities used for creating, checking, repairing, and mounting file systems. Use these utilities to make file systems available to the user and to ensure their reliability.

Synchronizing a File System

The UFS file system relies on an internal set of tables to keep track of inodes as well as used and available blocks. When a user performs an operation that requires data to be written to the disk, the data to be written is first copied into a buffer in the kernel. Normally, the disk update is not handled until long after the write operation has returned. At any given time, the file system, as it resides on the disk, might lag behind the state of the file system represented by the buffers located in physical memory (RAM). The internal tables finally get updated when the buffer is required for another use or when the kernel automatically runs the `fsflush` daemon (at 30-second intervals).

If the system is halted without writing out the memory-resident information, the file system on the disk will be in an inconsistent state. If the internal tables are not properly synchronized with data on the disk, inconsistencies result, data may be lost, and file systems will need repairing. File systems can be damaged or become inconsistent because of abrupt termination of the operating system in these ways:

- Experiencing power failure
- Accidentally unplugging the system
- Turning off the system without the proper shutdown procedure
- Performing a Stop+A (L1+A)
- Encountering a software error in the kernel
- Encountering a hardware failure that halts the system unexpectedly

To prevent unclean halts, the current state of the file system must be written to disk (that is, synchronized) before you halt the CPU or take a disk offline.

Repairing File Systems

EXAM ALERT

Understand all aspects of repairing a file system. Know everything from unmounting a faulty file system, checking a file system, creating a new file system, and restoring data to that file system.

During normal operation, files are created, modified, and removed. Each time a file is modified, the operating system performs a series of file system updates. When a system is booted, a file system consistency check is automatically performed. Most of the time, this file system check repairs any problems it encounters. File systems are checked with the `fsck` (file system check) command.

CAUTION

Never run the **fsck** command on a mounted file system. This could leave the file system in an unstable state and could result in the loss of data. Because the / (root), `/usr`, and `/var` file systems cannot be unmounted, these file systems should only have `fsck` run on them while in single-user mode.

Reboot the system immediately after running the `fsck` on these mounted file systems.

The Solaris `fsck` command uses a state flag, which is stored in the superblock, to record the condition of the file system. Following are the possible state values:

- `FSCLEAN`—If the file system was unmounted properly, the state flag is set to `FSCLEAN`. Any file system with an `FSCLEAN` state flag is not checked when the system is booted.
- `FSSTABLE`—On a mounted file system, this state indicates that the file system has not changed since the last `sync` or `fsflush`. File systems marked as `FSSTABLE` can skip `fsck` before mounting.
- `FSACTIVE`—The state flag gets set to `FSACTIVE` when a file system is mounted and modified. The `FSACTIVE` flag goes into effect before any modifications are written to disk, however. The exception is when a file system is mounted with UFS logging and the flag is set to `FSLOG`, as described later. When a file system is unmounted properly, the state flag is then set to `FSCLEAN`. A file system with the `FSACTIVE` flag must be checked by `fsck` because it might be inconsistent. The system does not mount a file system for read/write unless its state is `FSCLEAN`, `FSLOG`, or `FSSTABLE`.
- `FSBAD`—If the root file system is mounted when its state is not `FSCLEAN` or `FSSTABLE`, the state flag is set to `FSBAD`. A root file system flagged as `FSBAD` as part of the boot process is mounted as read-only. You can run `fsck` on the raw root device and then remount the root file system as read/write.
- `FSLOG`—If the file system was mounted with UFS logging, the state flag is set to `FSLOG`. Any file system with an `FSLOG` state flag is not checked when the system is booted. See the section titled "Mounting a File System with UFS Logging Enabled," where I describe mounting a file system from the command line later in this chapter.

`fsck` is a multipass file system check program that performs successive passes over each file system, checking blocks and sizes, pathnames, connectivity, reference counts, and the map of free blocks (possibly rebuilding it). `fsck` also performs cleanup. The phases (passes) performed by the UFS version of `fsck` are described in Table 1.11.

TABLE 1.11 `fsck` Phases

`fsck` Phase	Task Performed
Phase 1	Checks blocks and sizes
Phase 2	Checks pathnames
Phase 3	Checks connectivity
Phase 4	Checks reference counts
Phase 5	Checks cylinder groups

Normally, `fsck` is run noninteractively at bootup to preen the file systems after an abrupt system halt in which the latest file system changes were not written to disk. Preening automatically fixes any basic file system inconsistencies but does not try to repair more serious errors. While preening a file system, `fsck` fixes the inconsistencies it expects from such an abrupt halt. For more serious conditions, the command reports the error and terminates. It then tells the operator to run `fsck` manually.

Determining Whether a File System Needs Checking

File systems must be checked periodically for inconsistencies to avoid unexpected loss of data. As stated earlier, checking the state of a file system is automatically done at bootup; however, it is not necessary to reboot a system to check whether the file systems are stable as described in Step by Step 1.10.

STEP BY STEP

1.10 Determining the Current State of the File System

1. Become a superuser.
2. Type **`fsck -m /dev/rdsk/`*`cntndnsn`*** and press Enter. The state flag in the superblock of the file system you specify is checked to see whether the file system is clean or requires checking. If you omit the device argument, all the UFS file systems listed in `/etc/vfstab` with an `fsck` pass value of greater than `0` are checked.

In the following example, the first file system needs checking, but the second file system does not:

```
# fsck -m /dev/rdsk/c0t0d0s6 <cr>

** /dev/rdsk/c0t0d0s6
ufs fsck: sanity check: /dev/rdsk/c0t0d0s6 needs checking
fsck -m /dev/rdsk/c0t0d0s7
** /dev/rdsk/c0t0d0s7
ufs fsck: sanity check: /dev/rdsk/c0t0d0s7 okay
```

Running `fsck` Manually

You might need to manually check file systems when they cannot be mounted or when you've determined that the state of a file system is unclean. Good indications that a file system might need to be checked are error messages displayed in the console window or system crashes that occur for no apparent reason.

When you run `fsck` manually, it reports each inconsistency found and fixes innocuous errors. For more serious errors, the command reports the inconsistency and prompts you to choose a response. Sometimes corrective actions performed by `fsck` result in some loss of data. The amount and severity of data loss can be determined from the `fsck` diagnostic output. The procedure outlined in Step by Step 1.11 describes how to check a file system by running the `fsck` command manually.

STEP BY STEP

1.11 Manually Checking File Systems

1. Log in as root and unmount the file system.
2. After the file system is unmounted, type **`fsck /dev/rdsk/`*`<device>`*** and press Enter.

   If you do not specify a device, all file systems in the `/etc/vfstab` file with entries greater than `0` in the `fsck pass` field are checked, including root (/). As stated earlier, you must be in single-user mode to run fsck on root. You can also specify the mount point directory as an argument to `fsck`, and as long as the mount point has an entry in the `/etc/vfstab` file, `fsck` will be able to resolve the path to the raw device. The `fsck` command requires the raw device filename.
3. Any inconsistency messages are displayed. The only way to successfully change the file system and correct the problem is to answer `yes` to these messages.

> **NOTE**
>
> **Supply an Automatic Yes Response to fsck** The `fsck` command has a `-y` option that automatically answers `yes` to every question. But be careful: If `fsck` asks to delete a file, it will answer `yes` and you will have no control over it. If it doesn't delete the file, however, the file system remains unclean and cannot be mounted.

4. If you corrected any errors, type **`fsck /dev/rdsk/`*`<device>`*** and press Enter. `fsck` might not be capable of fixing all errors in one execution. If you see the message `FILE SYSTEM STATE NOT SET TO OKAY`, run the command again and continue to run `fsck` until it runs clean with no errors.
5. Rename and move any files put in `lost+found`. Individual files put in the `lost+found` directory by `fsck` are renamed with their inode numbers, so figuring out what they were named originally can be difficult. If possible, rename the files and move them where they belong. You might be able to use the `grep` command to match phrases with individual files and use the `file` command to identify file types, ownership, and so on. When entire directories are dumped into `lost+found`, it is easier to figure out where they belong and move them back.

> **NOTE**
>
> **Locating the Alternate Superblock** Occasionally the file system's superblock can become corrupted and `fsck` will ask you for the location of an alternate superblock. This information can be obtained by typing
>
> ```
> newfs -Nv <raw device name>
> ```

If you know the location of the backup superblock, you can tell `fsck` to rebuild the primary superblock when you run the fsck command. For example, if the backup superblock is located at block number 57632, enter the following command:

```
#   fsck -o b=57632 /dev/rdsk/c0t0d0s7 <cr>
```

The `labelit` Command

After you create the file system with `newfs`, you can use the `labelit` utility to write or display labels on unmounted disk file systems. The syntax for `labelit` is as follows:

```
labelit <-F <fstype>> <-V> <special> < fsname volume >
```

Labeling a file system is optional. It's required only if you're using a program such as `volcopy`, which will be covered soon. The `labelit` command is described in Table 1.12.

TABLE 1.12 The `labelit` Command

Parameter	Description
<special>	This name should be the physical disk slice (for example, `/dev/dsk/c0t0d0s6`).
<fsname>	This represents the mount point (for example, root [/], /home, and so on) of the file system.
<volume>	This can be used to represent the physical volume name.
-F *<fstype>*	This specifies the file system type on which to operate. The file system type should either be specified here or be determinable from the `/etc/vfstab` entry. If no matching entry is found, the default file system type specified in `/etc/default/fs` is used.
-V	This prints the command line but does not perform an action.

NOTE

View Current Labels If `fsname` and `volume` are not specified, `labelit` prints the current values of these labels. Both `fsname` and `volume` are limited to six or fewer characters.

The following is an example of how to label a disk partition using the `labelit` command. Type the following:

```
# labelit -F ufs /dev/rdsk/c0t0d0s6 disk1 vol1 <cr>
```

The system responds with this:

```
fsname:  disk1
volume:  vol1
```

The volcopy Command

The administrator (root) can use the volcopy command to make a copy of a labeled file system. This command works with UFS file systems, but the file system must be labeled with the labelit utility before the volcopy command is issued. To determine whether a file system is a UFS, issue this command:

```
# fstyp  /dev/rdsk/c0t0d0s6 <cr>
```

The system responds with this:

```
ufs
```

The volcopy command can be used to copy a file system from one disk to another.

The syntax for volcopy is as follows:

```
volcopy <options> <fsname> <srcdevice> <volname1> <destdevice> <volname2>
```

volcopy is described in Table 1.13.

TABLE 1.13 The volcopy Command

Option	Description
-F <***fstype***>	This specifies the file system type on which to operate. This should either be specified here or be determinable from the /etc/vfstab entry. If no matching entry is found, the default file system type specified in /etc/default/fs is used.
-V	This prints the command line but does not perform an action.
-a	This requires the operator to respond yes or no. If the -a option is not specified, volcopy pauses 10 seconds before the copy is made.
-o <***options***>	This is a list of options specific to the type of file system. The list must have the following format: -o followed by a space, followed by a series of keyword [=value] pairs, separated by commas, with no intervening spaces.
<***fsname***>	This represents the mount point (for example, /, /u1, and so on) of the file system being copied.
<***srcdevice***> / <***destdevice***>	This is the disk partition specified using the raw device (for example, /dev/rdsk/clt0d0s7, /dev/rdsk/clt0d1s7, and so on).
<***srcdevice***> / <***volname1***>	This is the device and physical volume from which the copy of the file system is being extracted.
<***destdevice***> / <***volname2***>	This is the target device and physical volume.

NOTE

fsname and volname Limits fsname and volname are limited to six or fewer characters and are recorded in the superblock. volname can be a dash (-) to use the existing volume name.

The following example copies the contents of /home1 (/dev/rdsk/c0t0d0s6) to /home2 (/dev/rdsk/c0t1d0s6):

```
volcopy -F ufs home1 /dev/rdsk/c0t0d0s6 home2 /dev/rdsk/c0t1d0s6 vol2
```

Other commands can also be used to copy file systems—ufsdump, cpio, tar, and dd, to name a few. These commands are discussed in Chapter 7, "Performing System Backups and Restorations."

Tuning File Systems

A situation might arise in which you want to change some of the parameters that were set when you originally created the file system. Perhaps you want to change the minfree value to free some additional disk space on a large disk drive. Using the tunefs command, you can modify the following file system parameters:

- maxcontig
- rotdelay
- maxbpg
- minfree
- optimization

See Table 1.14 for a description of these options.

CAUTION

tunefs can destroy a file system in seconds. Always back up the entire file system before using tunefs.

The syntax for tunefs is as follows:

```
tunefs [ -a <maxcontig> ] [ -d <rotdelay> ] [ -e <maxbpg> ]
[ -m <minfree> ] [ -o [ <value> ] <special>/<file system>
```

The tunefs command is described in Table 1.14.

TABLE 1.14 The `tunefs` Command

Option	Description
-a <*maxcontig*>	Specifies the maximum number of contiguous blocks that are laid out before forcing a rotational delay.
-e <*maxbpg*>	Sets the maximum number of blocks that any single file can allocate from a cylinder group before it is forced to begin allocating blocks from another cylinder group. Typically, this value is set to approximately one quarter of the total blocks in a cylinder group. The intent is to prevent any single file from using up all the blocks in a single cylinder group. The effect of this limit is to cause big files to do long seeks more frequently than if they were allowed to allocate all the blocks in a cylinder group before seeking elsewhere. For file systems with exclusively large files, this parameter should be set higher.
-m <*minfree*>	Specifies the minimum free space threshold, or the percentage of space held back from normal users. This value can be set to 0. However, up to a factor of three in throughput will be lost over the performance obtained at a 10% threshold. If the value is raised above the current usage level, users will be unable to allocate files until enough files have been deleted to get under the higher threshold is determined automatically.
-o <*value*>	Changes the optimization strategy for the file system. The value is either `space` or `time`. Use `space` to conserve space; use `time` to organize file layout and minimize access time. Generally, optimize a file system for time unless it is more than 90% full.
<*special*>/<*file system*>	Enters either the special device name (such as `/dev/rdsk/c0t0d0s6`) or the file system name (such as `/home`).

The file system does not need to be unmounted before using `tunefs`.

To change the minimum free space (`minfree`) on a file system from 10% to 5%, type the following:

```
# tunefs -m5 /dev/rdsk/c0t0d0s6 <cr>
minimum percentage of free space changes from 10% to 5%
```

Notice that the manual page of `tunefs` recommends that `minfree` be set at 10%; if you set the value under that, you lose performance. This means that 10% of the disk is unusable. This might not have been too bad in the days when disks were a couple hundred megabytes in size, but on a 9GB disk, you're losing 900MB of disk space. The mention of loss of performance in the manual page is misleading. With such large disk drives, you can afford to have `minfree` as low as 1%. This has been found to be a practical and affordable limit. In addition, performance does not become an issue because locating free blocks even within a 90MB area is efficient.

A rule of thumb is to use the default 10% minfree value for file systems up to 1GB and then adjust the minfree value so that your minfree area is no larger than 100MB. As for performance, applications do not complain about the lower minfree value. The one exception is the root (/) file system, in which the system administrator can use his judgment to allow more free space just to be conservative, in case root (/) ever becomes 100% full.

NOTE

Viewing the minfree Value On large file systems, the minfree is automatically determined so that disk space is not wasted. Use the mkfs -m command described next if you want to see the actual minfree value that newfs used.

Later, if you want to see what parameters were used when creating a file system, issue the mkfs command:

```
# mkfs -m /dev/rdsk/c2t1d0s1 <cr>
```

The system responds with this:

```
mkfs -F ufs -o nsect=135,ntrack=16,bsize=8192,fragsize=1024,cgsize=46,free=1,\
rps=120,nbpi=8179,opt=t,apc=0,gap=0,nrpos=8,maxcontig=128,mtb=n\
 /dev/rdsk/c2t1d0s1 8337600
```

Mounting File Systems

Objective:

Explain how to perform mounts and unmounts.

File systems can be mounted from the command line by using the mount command. The commands in Table 1.15 are used from the command line to mount and unmount file systems.

TABLE 1.15 File System Commands

Command	Description
mount	Mounts specified file systems and remote resources
mountall	Mounts all file systems specified in a file system table (vfstab)
umount	Unmounts specified file systems and remote resources
umountall	Unmounts all file systems specified in a file system table

> **NOTE**
>
> **/sbin/mountall** is actually a shell script that first checks the state of each file system specified in the /etc/vfstab file before issuing the `mount -a` command. If the file system flag indicates that the file system is not mountable, `mountall` will prompt for the root password on the console and try to fix the file system with `fsck` before running the `mount -a` command.

After you create a file system, you need to make it available. You make file systems available by mounting them. Using the `mount` command, you attach a file system to the system directory tree at the specified mount point, and it becomes available to the system. The root file system is mounted at boot time and cannot be unmounted. Any other file system can be mounted or unmounted from the root file system with few exceptions.

The syntax for `mount` is as follows:

```
mount -F <fstype> <options> [ -o <specific_options> ] <-O > device_to_mount mountpoint
```

Table 1.16 describes options to the `mount` command.

TABLE 1.16 The mount Command Options

Option	Description
`-F <fstype>`	Used to specify the file system type *<fstype>* on which to operate. If ***fstype*** is not specified, it must be determined from the `/etc/vfstab` file or by consulting `/etc/default/fs` or `/etc/dfs/fstypes`.
`-g`	Globally mount the file system. On a clustered system, this globally mounts the file system on all nodes of the cluster.
`-m`	Mounts the file system without making an entry in `/etc/mnttab`.
`-r`	Mounts the file system as read-only.
`-O`	Overlay mount. Allows the file system to be mounted over an existing mount point, making the underlying file system inaccessible. If a mount is attempted on a preexisting mount point without setting this flag, the mount fails, producing the error `device busy`.
`-p`	Prints the list of mounted file systems in the `/etc/vfstab` format. This must be the only option specified.
`-v`	Prints the list of mounted file systems in `verbose` format. This must be the only option specified.
`-V`	Echoes the complete command line but does not execute the command. `umount` generates a command line by using the options and arguments provided by the user and adding to them information derived from `/etc/mnttab`. This option should be used to verify and validate the command line.

(continues)

TABLE 1.16 *Continued*

Option	Description
`-o`	Specifies `fstype`-specific options. These are generic options that can be specified with the `-o` option. If you specify multiple options, separate them with commas (no spaces)—for example, `-o ro,nosuid`. Additionally, file system specific options are described later in this chapter and in their respective man pages (such as `man mount_ufs` and `man mount_nfs`). `devices` | `nodevices`—Allow or disallow the opening of device-special files. The default is devices. `exec` | `noexec`—Allow or disallow executing programs in the file system. `rw`|`ro`—Specifies read/write or read-only. The default is read/write. `nbmand` | `nonbmand`—Allow or disallow non-blocking mandatory locking semantics on this file system. Non-blocking mandatory locking is disallowed by default. `nosuid`—Disallows setuid execution and prevents devices on the file system from being opened. The default is to enable setuid execution and to allow devices to be opened. `remount`—With `rw`, remounts a file system with read/write access. `m`—Mounts the file system without making an entry in `/etc/mnttab`. `largefiles`—Specifies that a file system might contain one or more files larger than 2GB. It is not required that a file system mounted with this option contain files larger than 2GB, but this option allows such files within the file system. `largefiles` is the default. `nolargefiles`—Provides total compatibility with previous file system behavior, enforcing the 2GB maximum file size limit.

NOTE

Determining a File System's Type Because the `mount` commands need the file system type to function properly, the file system type must be explicitly specified with the `-F` option or determined by searching the following files:

`/etc/vfstab`—Search the FS type field for the file system type.

`/etc/default/fs`—Search for a local file system type.

`/etc/dfs/fstypes`—Search for a remote file system type.

If the file system type is not found in any of these locations, the system will report an error.

EXAM ALERT

Be very familiar with the mount options for a UFS file system along with the defaults used when an option is not specified. The exam has several questions related to creating and repairing file systems. You need to know all aspects of mounting and unmounting a file system on a production (active) system.

The following examples illustrate the options described in Table 1.16.

A file system has been created on disk `c0t0d0` on slice `s0`. The directory to be mounted on this disk slice is `/home2`. To mount the file system, first create the directory called `/home2` and then type the following:

```
# mount /dev/dsk/c0t0d0s0 /home2 <cr>
```

If the file system has been mounted, you return to a command prompt. No other message is displayed.

When the UFS file system is mounted with no options, a default set of file system specific options are used—they are explained in Table 1.17. Options specific to the UFS file system are also described in the `mount_ufs` man pages.

TABLE 1.17 Mount Default Options for a UFS File System

Option	Description
`read/write`	Indicates that file system can be read and written to.
`setuid`	Permits the execution of setuid programs in the file system.
`devices`	Allow the opening of device-special files.
`intr`	Allows keyboard interrupts to kill a process that is waiting for an operation on a locked file system.
`logging`	Indicates that logging is enabled for the UFS file system. This is the default for the Solaris 10 OS.
`largefiles`	Allows for the creation of files larger than 2 Gbytes. A file system mounted with this option can contain files larger than 2 Gbytes.
`xattr`	Supports extended attributes not found in standard Unix file systems.
`onerror=panic`	Specifies the action that the UFS file system should take to recover from an internal inconsistency on a file system. An action can be specified as: panic—Causes a forced system shutdown. This is the default. lock—Applies a file system lock to the file system. umount—Forcibly unmounts the file system.

In the next example, the `-v` option is used with the `mount` command to display a list of all mounted file systems:

```
# mount -v <cr>
```

The system responds with this:

```
/dev/dsk/c0t0d0s0 on / type ufs \
read/write/setuid/devices/intr/largefiles/logging/xattr/onerror=panic/dev=2200008 \
on Fri Aug  5 11:32:05 2005
/devices on /devices type devfs read/write/setuid/devices/dev=4380000 \
 on Fri Aug  5 11:31:47 2005 ctfs on /system/contract type ctfs \
```

```
read/write/setuid/devices/dev=43c0001 on Fri Aug  5 11:31:47 2005
proc on /proc type proc read/write/setuid/devices/dev=4400000 on\
 Fri Aug  5 11:31:47 2005
mnttab on /etc/mnttab type mntfs read/write/setuid/devices/dev=4440001 \
on Fri Aug  5 11:31:47 2005

swap on /etc/svc/volatile type tmpfs read/write/setuid/devices/xattr/dev=4480001 \
on Fri Aug  5 11:31:47 2005

objfs on /system/object type objfs read/write/setuid/devices/dev=44c0001 on \
Fri Aug  5 11:31:47 2005

/dev/dsk/c0t0d0s6 on /usr type ufs \
read/write/setuid/devices/intr/largefiles/logging/xattr/onerror=panic/dev=220000e \
on Fri Aug  5 11:32:06 2005
fd on /dev/fd type fd read/write/setuid/devices/dev=4640001 \
on Fri Aug  5 11:32:06 2005
/dev/dsk/c0t0d0s1 on /var type ufs \
read/write/setuid/devices/intr/largefiles/logging/xattr/onerror=panic/dev=2200009 \
on Fri Aug  5 11:32:09 2005
swap on /tmp type tmpfs read/write/setuid/devices/xattr/dev=4480002 \
on Fri Aug  5 11:32:09 2005
swap on /var/run type tmpfs read/write/setuid/devices/xattr/dev=4480003 \
on Fri Aug  5 11:32:09 2005
/dev/dsk/c0t0d0s4 on /data type ufs \
read/write/setuid/devices/intr/largefiles/logging/xattr/onerror=panic/dev=220000c \
on Fri Aug  5 11:32:16 2005
/dev/dsk/c0t0d0s5 on /opt type ufs \
read/write/setuid/devices/intr/largefiles/logging/xattr/onerror=panic/dev=220000d \
on Fri Aug  5 11:32:16 2005
/dev/dsk/c0t0d0s7 on /export/home type ufs \
read/write/setuid/devices/intr/largefiles/logging/xattr/onerror=panic/dev=220000f \
on Fri Aug  5 11:32:16 2005
```

The following example mounts a file system as read-only:

```
# mount -o ro /dev/dsk/c0t0d0s0 /home2 <cr>
```

The next example uses the `mount` command to mount a directory to a file system as read/writeable, disallow setuid execution, and allow the creation of large files:

```
# mount -o rw,nosuid,largefiles /dev/dsk/c0t0d0s0 /home2 <cr>
```

Type `mount` with no options to verify that the file system has been mounted and to review the mount options that were used:

```
# mount <cr>
```

The system responds with information about all mounted file systems, including `/home2`:

```
/home2 on /dev/dsk/c0t0d0s0 read/write/nosuid/largefiles on\
 Tue Jul 16 06:56:33 2005
```

NOTE

Using SMC to View Current Mounts You can also use the SMC Mounts Tool to view information about mounted file systems. The information provided is similar to the information displayed when you issue the `mount` command with no options. To access the Mounts Tool, follow the Step by Step procedure for using the SMC Usage Tool described in the section titled "Displaying a File System's Disk Space Usage."

Mounting a File System with Large Files

On a Solaris system, a large file is a regular file whose size is greater than or equal to 2GB. A small file is a regular file whose size is less than 2GB. Some utilities can handle large files, and others cannot. A utility is called *large file–aware* if it can process large files in the same manner that it does small files. A large file–aware utility can handle large files as input and can generate large files as output. The `newfs`, `mkfs`, `mount`, `umount`, `tunefs`, `labelit`, and `quota` utilities are all large file–aware for UFS file systems.

NOTE

Due to file system overhead, the largest file size that can be created on a multiterabyte file system is approximately 1 Tbyte. The data capacity of a 1 Tbyte file system is approximately 1 Tbyte minus 0.5% overhead and the recommended 1% free space.

On the other hand, a utility is called *large file–safe* if it causes no data loss or corruption when it encounters a large file. A utility that is large file–safe cannot properly process a large file, so it returns an appropriate error. Some examples of utilities that are not large file–aware but are large file–safe include the `vi` editor and the `mailx` and `lp` commands. A full list of commands that are large file–aware and large file–safe can be found in the online manual pages.

The `largefiles` mount option lets users mount a file system containing files larger than 2GB. The `largefiles` mount option is the default state for the Solaris 10 environment. The `largefiles` option means that a file system mounted with this option might contain one or more files larger than 2GB.

You must explicitly use the `nolargefiles` mount option to disable this behavior. The `nolargefiles` option provides total compatibility with previous file system behavior, enforcing the 2GB maximum file size limit.

NOTE

Mounting Largefile File Systems After you mount a file system with the default `largefiles` option and large files have been created, you cannot remount the file system with the `nolargefiles` option until you remove any large files and run `fsck` to reset the state to `nolargefiles`.

Mounting a File System with UFS Logging Enabled

The UFS logging feature eliminates file system inconsistency, which can significantly reduce the time of system reboots. UFS logging is the default in Solaris 10 and does not need to be specified when mounting a file system. Use the `nologging` option in the `/etc/vfstab` file or as an option to the `mount` command to disable UFS logging on a file system.

UFS logging is the process of storing file system operations to a log before the transactions are applied to the file system. Because the file system can never become inconsistent, `fsck` can usually be bypassed, which reduces the time to reboot a system if it crashes or after an unclean halt.

The UFS log is allocated from free blocks on the file system. It is sized at approximately 1MB per 1GB of file system, up to a maximum of 64MB. The default is logging for all UFS file systems.

NOTE

fsck on Logged File Systems Is it ever necessary to run `fsck` on a file system that has UFS logging enabled? The answer is yes. It is usually unnecessary to run `fsck` on a file system that has UFS logging enabled. The one exception to this is when the log is bad. An example of this is when a media failure causes the log to become unusable. In this case, logging puts the file system in an error state, and you cannot mount it and use it until `fsck` is run. The safest option is to always run `fsck`. It will quit immediately if logging is there and the file system is not in an error state.

Unmounting a File System

Unmounting a file system removes it from the file system mount point and deletes the entry from `/etc/mnttab`. Some file system administration tasks, such as `labelit` and `fsck`, cannot be performed on mounted file systems. You should unmount a file system if any of the following three conditions exist:

- The file system is no longer needed or has been replaced by a file system that contains software that is more current.
- When you check and repair it by using the `fsck` command.
- When you are about to do a complete backup of it.

To unmount a file system, use the `umount` command:

```
umount <mount-point>
```

<mount-point> is the name of the file system you want to unmount. This can be either the directory name in which the file system is mounted or the device name path of the file system. For example, to unmount the `/home2` file system, type the following:

```
umount /home2
```

Alternatively, you can specify the device name path for the file system:

```
umount /dev/dsk/c0t0d0s0
```

NOTE

Shutting Down the System File systems are automatically unmounted as part of the system shutdown procedure.

The `fuser` Command

Before you can unmount a file system, you must be logged in as the administrator (root) and the file system must not be busy. A file system is considered busy if a user is in a directory in the file system or if a program has a file open in that file system. You can make a file system available for unmounting by changing to a directory in a different file system or by logging out of the system. If something is causing the file system to be busy, you can use the `fuser` command, described in Table 1.18, to list all the processes that are accessing the file system and to stop them if necessary.

NOTE

Informing Users Always notify users before unmounting a file system.

The syntax for `fuser` is as follows:

```
/usr/sbin/fuser [options] <file>¦<file system>
```

Replace *<file>* with the filename you are checking, or replace *<file system>* with the name of the file system you are checking.

TABLE 1.18 The `fuser` Command Options

Option	Description
`-c`	Reports on files that are mount points for file systems and on any files within that mounted file system.
`-f`	Prints a report for the named file but not for files within a mounted file system.
`-k`	Sends the `SIGKILL` signal to each process.
`-u`	Displays the user login name in parentheses following the process ID.

The following example uses the `fuser` command to find out why `/home2` is busy:

```
# fuser -cu /home2 <cr>
```

The system displays each process and user login name that is using this file system:

```
/home2:     8448c(root)    8396c(root)
```

The following command stops all processes that are using the `/home2` file system by sending a `SIGKILL` to each one. Don't use it without first warning the users:

```
# fuser -c -k /home2 <cr>
```

Using the `fuser` command as described is the preferred method for determining who is using a file system before unmounting it. Added in Solaris 8 was another, less desirable method for unmounting a file system, using the `umount` command with the `-f` option, as follows:

```
# umount -f /home2 <cr>
```

The `-f` option forcibly unmounts a file system. Using this option can cause data loss for open files and programs that access files after the file system has been unmounted; it returns an error (EIO). The `-f` option should be used only as a last resort.

You can also use the `fuser` command to check on any device such as the system console. By typing:

```
# fuser /dev/console <cr>
```

The system displays the processes associated with that device as follows:

```
/dev/console:      459o     221o
```

/etc/mnttab

When a file system is mounted, an entry is maintained in the mounted file system table called `/etc/mnttab`. The file `/etc/mnttab` is really a file system that provides read-only access to the table of mounted file systems for the current host. The `mount` command adds entries to this table, and `umount` removes entries from this table. The kernel maintains the list in order of mount time. For example, the first mounted file system is first in the list, and the most recently mounted file system is last. When mounted on a mount point, the file system appears as a regular file containing the current `mnttab` information. Each entry in this table is a line of fields separated by spaces in this form:

```
<special> <mount_point> <fstype>  <options>  <time>
```

Table 1.19 describes each field.

TABLE 1.19 /etc/mnttab Fields

Field	Description
<*special*>	The resource to be mounted (that is, /dev/dsk/c0t0d0s0)
<*mount_point*>	The pathname of the directory on which the file system is mounted
<*fstype*>	The file system type
<*options*>	The list of mount options used to mount the file system
<*time*>	The time at which the file system was mounted

Following is a sample /etc/mnttab file:

```
# more /etc/mnttab <cr>
/dev/dsk/c0t0d0s0       /       ufs     \
rw,intr,largefiles,logging,xattr,onerror=panic,dev=2200008      1127941982
/devices        /devices        devfs   dev=4380000     1127941959
ctfs    /system/contract        ctfs    dev=43c0001     1127941959
proc    /proc   proc    dev=4400000     1127941959
mnttab  /etc/mnttab     mntfs   dev=4440001     1127941959
swap    /etc/svc/volatile       tmpfs   xattr,dev=4480001       1127941959
objfs   /system/object  objfs   dev=44c0001     1127941959
/dev/dsk/c0t0d0s6       /usr    ufs     \
rw,intr,largefiles,logging,xattr,onerror=panic,dev=220000e      1127941982
fd      /dev/fd fd      rw,dev=4640001  1127941982
/dev/dsk/c0t0d0s1       /var    ufs     \
rw,intr,largefiles,logging,xattr,onerror=panic,dev=2200009      1127941983
swap    /tmp    tmpfs   xattr,dev=4480002       1127941983
swap    /var/run        tmpfs   xattr,dev=4480003       1127941983
/dev/dsk/c0t0d0s5       /opt    ufs     \
rw,intr,largefiles,logging,xattr,onerror=panic,dev=220000d      1127941991
/dev/dsk/c0t0d0s7       /export/home    ufs     \
rw,intr,largefiles,logging,xattr,onerror=panic,dev=220000f      1127941991
-hosts  /net    autofs  nosuid,indirect,ignore,nobrowse,dev=4700001     1127942006
auto_home       /home   autofs  indirect,ignore,nobrowse,dev=4700002    1127942006
smokey:vold(pid487)     /vol    nfs     ignore,noquota,dev=46c0001      1127942024
/vol/dev/dsk/c0t2d0/s10_software_companion      /cdrom/s10_software_companion   hsfs\
ro,nosuid,noglobal,maplcase,rr,traildot,dev=16c0001     1127942029
/dev/dsk/c2t1d0s1       /mnt    ufs     rw,intr,largefiles,logging,xattr,\
onerror=panic,dev=800089        1128021589
```

Before Solaris 8, the /etc/mnttab file was a text file. The downside of being a text file was that it could get out of sync with the actual state of mounted file systems, or it could be manually edited. Now this file is a mntfs file system that provides read-only information directly from the kernel about mounted file systems for the local hosts.

You can display the contents of the mount table by using the `cat` or `more` commands, but you cannot edit them.

You can also view a mounted file system by typing `/sbin/mount` from the command line as shown earlier in this section.

Creating an Entry in the /etc/vfstab File to Mount File Systems

Objective:

Explain the purpose and function of the vfstab file in mounting UFS file systems, and the function of the mnttab file system in tracking current mounts.

The `/etc/vfstab` (virtual file system table) file contains a list of file systems, with the exception of the `/etc/mnttab` and `/var/run`, to be automatically mounted when the system is booted to the multiuser state. The system administrator places entries in the file, specifying what file systems are to be mounted at bootup. The following is an example of the `/etc/vfstab` file:

```
# cat /etc/vfstab <cr>
#device         device          mount           FS      fsck    mount   mount
#to mount       to fsck         point           type    pass    at boot options
#
fd      -       /dev/fd fd      -       no      -
/proc   -       /proc   proc    -       no      -
/dev/dsk/c0t0d0s3       -       -       swap    -       no      -
/dev/dsk/c0t0d0s0       /dev/rdsk/c0t0d0s0      /       ufs     1       no      -
/dev/dsk/c0t0d0s6       /dev/rdsk/c0t0d0s6      /usr    ufs     1       no      -
/dev/dsk/c0t0d0s1       /dev/rdsk/c0t0d0s1      /var    ufs     1       no      -
/dev/dsk/c0t0d0s7       /dev/rdsk/c0t0d0s7      /export/home    ufs     2       yes     -
/dev/dsk/c0t0d0s5       /dev/rdsk/c0t0d0s5      /opt    ufs     2       yes     -
/devices        -       /devices        devfs   -       no      -
ctfs    -       /system/contract        ctfs    -       no      -
objfs   -       /system/object  objfs   -       no      -
swap    -       /tmp    tmpfs   -       yes     -
```

EXAM ALERT

You'll need to make entries in the vfstab file on the exam. Understand the syntax and know how to create a new line in this file for both a UFS file system and swap.

Each column of information follows this format:

- **device to mount**—The buffered device that corresponds to the file system being mounted.

- **device to `fsck`**—The raw (character) special device that corresponds to the file system being mounted. This determines the raw interface used by `fsck`. Use a dash (`-`) when there is no applicable device, such as for swap, `/proc`, `tmp`, or a network-based file system.
- **mount point**—The default mount point directory.
- **FS type**—The type of file system.
- **`fsck pass`**—The pass number used by `fsck` to decide whether to check a file. When the field contains a `0` or a non-numeric value, the file system is not checked. When the field contains a value of `1`, the `fsck` utility gets started for that entry and runs to completion. When the field contains a value greater than `1`, that device is added to the list of devices to have the `fsck` utility run. The `fsck` utility can run on up to eight devices in parallel. This field is ignored by the `mountall` command.
- **mount at boot**—Specifies whether the file system should be automatically mounted when the system is booted. These file systems get mounted when SMF starts up the `svc:/system/file` system service instances.

NOTE

vfstab Entries for root (/), /usr, and /var For root (`/`), `/usr`, and `/var` file systems (if they are separate file systems), the `mount at boot field` option is no. The kernel mounts these file systems as part of the boot sequence before the `mountall` command is run. The `mount` command explicitly mounts the file systems root (`/`), `/usr`, and `/var` when SMF starts up the `svc:/system/file` system service instances.

- **`mount` options**—A list of comma-separated options (with no spaces) used when mounting the file system. Use a dash (`-`) to use default `mount` options.

Type the `mount` command with the `-p` option to display a list of mounted file systems in `/etc/vfstab` format:

```
# mount -p <cr>
```

The system responds with this:

```
/dev/dsk/c0t0d0s0 - / ufs - no rw,intr,largefiles,logging,xattr,onerror=panic
/devices - /devices devfs - no
ctfs - /system/contract ctfs - no
proc - /proc proc - no
mnttab - /etc/mnttab mntfs - no
swap - /etc/svc/volatile tmpfs - no xattr
objfs - /system/object objfs - no
```

```
/dev/dsk/c0t0d0s6 - /usr ufs - no rw,intr,largefiles,logging,xattr,onerror=panic
fd - /dev/fd fd - no rw
/dev/dsk/c0t0d0s1 - /var ufs - no rw,intr,largefiles,logging,xattr,onerror=panic
swap - /tmp tmpfs - no xattr
swap - /var/run tmpfs - no xattr
/dev/dsk/c0t0d0s4 - /data ufs - no rw,intr,largefiles,logging,xattr,onerror=panic
/dev/dsk/c0t0d0s5 - /opt ufs - no rw,intr,largefiles,logging,xattr,onerror=panic
/dev/dsk/c0t0d0s7 - /export/home ufs - no rw,intr,largefiles,logging,xattr,\
onerror=panic
```

The `-p` option is useful for obtaining the correct settings if you're making an entry in the `/etc/vfstab` file.

NOTE

Be aware that the current version of `mount -p` does not print out the raw device or the `fsck` pass number, which also needs to be included in the `/etc/vfstab` file.

Volume Management

Objective:

Explain how to perform access or restrict access to mounted diskettes and CD-ROMs.

Volume management (not to be confused with Solaris Volume Manager [SVM] described in the *Solaris 10 System Administration Exam Prep: Exam CX-310-202* book) with the `vold` daemon is the mechanism that manages removable media, such as the CD-ROM and floppy disk drives.

Mounting and unmounting a file system requires root privileges. How do you let users insert, mount, and unmount CD-ROMs and USB flash disks without being the administrator (root)? After a file system has been mounted and you remove the medium, what happens to the mount? Usually when you disconnect a disk drive while it is mounted, the system begins displaying error messages. The same thing happens if you remove a flash disk or CD-ROM while it is mounted.

Volume manager, with its `vold` daemon, provides assistance to overcome these problems. The `vold` daemon simplifies the use of disks and CDs by automatically mounting them. Volume manager provides three major benefits:

- By automatically mounting removable disks and CDs, volume management simplifies their use.
- Volume manager enables the user to access removable disks and CDs without having to be logged in as root.
- Volume manager lets the administrator (root) give other systems on the network automatic access to any removable disks and CDs that the users insert into your system.

To begin, let's look at the two devices that the system administrator needs to manage: the floppy disk drive and the CD-ROM. Volume manager provides access to both devices through the `/vol/dev` directory. In addition, Volume Manager creates links to the removable disk, CD-ROM, and USB devices through various directories, as shown in Table 1.20.

TABLE 1.20 Volume Manager Directories and Links

Link	Description
`/vol/dev/diskette0`	The directory providing block device access for the medium in floppy drive 0
`/vol/dev/rdiskette0`	The directory providing character device access for the medium in floppy drive 0
`/vol/dev/aliases/floppy0`	The symbolic link to the character device for the medium in floppy drive 0
`/dev/rdiskette`	The directory providing character device access for the medium in the primary floppy drive, usually drive 0
`/vol/dev/aliases/cdrom0`	Symbolic link to the directory providing character device access for the medium in the primary CD-ROM or DVD-ROM drive
`/vol/dev/aliases/zip0`	Symbolic link to the directory providing character device access for the medium in the primary Zip drive
`/vol/dev/aliases/jaz0`	Symbolic link to the directory providing character device access for the medium in the primary Jaz drive
`/vol/dev/aliases/PCMCIA`	Symbolic link to the directory providing character device access for the medium in the primary PCMCIA drive
`/vol/dev/aliases/rmdisk0`	Symbolic link to the directory providing character device access for the primary generic removable media that is not a Zip, Jaz, CD-ROM, floppy, DVD-ROM, or PCMCIA memory card
`/vol/dev/dsk/`	Symbolic link to the directory providing access to the CD-ROM buffered, or block, device
`/vol/dev/rdsk/`	Symbolic link to the directory providing access to the CD-ROM character, or raw, device
`/cdrom/cdrom0`	The symbolic link to the buffered device for the medium in CD-ROM or DVD-ROM drive 0
`/floppy/floppy0`	The symbolic link to the buffered device for the medium in floppy drive 0
`/rmdisk/zip0`	The symbolic link to the first mounted Zip medium in the local Zip drive
`/rmdisk/jaz0`	The symbolic link to the first mounted Jaz medium in the local Jaz drive
`/pcmem/pcmem0`	The symbolic link to the first mounted PCMCIA drive

The vold daemon automatically creates the mount point and mounts file systems when removable media containing recognizable file systems are inserted into the devices. For example, when a CD is inserted, vold automatically creates a mount point in the /cdrom directory and mounts the CD-ROM file system onto this mount point. It then creates a symbolic link to /vol/dev/aliases/cdrom0 and /cdrom/cdrom0 as described in the previous table.

NOTE

Most CDs and DVDs are formatted to the ISO 9660 standard, which is portable. So, most CDs and DVDs can be mounted by volume management. However, CDs or DVDs with UFS file systems are not portable between architectures. So, they must be used on the architecture for which they were designed. For example, a CD or DVD with a UFS file system for a SPARC platform cannot be recognized by an x86 platform. Likewise, an x86 UFS CD cannot be mounted by volume management on a SPARC platform. The same limitation generally applies to diskettes. However, some architectures share the same bit structure, so occasionally a UFS format specific to one architecture will be recognized by another architecture. Still, the UFS file system structure was not designed to guarantee this compatibility.

With a removable disk, however, the file system is not automatically mounted until you issue the volcheck command. The volcheck command instructs vold to look at each device and determine whether new media has been inserted into the drive. On some removable disks such as floppy disks, vold cannot continually poll the disk drive like it does on a CD because of the hardware limitation in these removable drives. Continuously polling a removable disk for media causes a mechanical action in the disk drive and causes the drive to wear out prematurely.

All USB devices are hot-pluggable, which means that the device is added and removed without shutting down the OS or the power. USB storage devices will be mounted by vold without any user interaction. When you hot-plug a USB device, the device is immediately seen in the system's device hierarchy, as displayed in the prtconf command output. When you remove a USB device, the device is removed from the system's device hierarchy, unless the device is in use.

If the USB device is in use when it is removed, the device node remains, but the driver controlling this device stops all activity on the device. Any new I/O activity issued to this device is returned with an error. In this situation, the system prompts you to plug in the original device. If the device is no longer available, stop the applications. After a few seconds, the port becomes available again.

The rmformat command is used to format, label, partition, and perform various functions on removable media such as USB storage devices. For example, to use the rmformat command to format a Zip drive, type the following:

```
# rmformat -F quick /vol/dev/aliases/zip0 <cr>
```

The system displays the following information:

```
Formatting will erase all the data on disk.
Do you want to continue? (y/n) y
.....................................................................
```

The `-F` option is used with one of the following options:

- `quick` Starts a format without certification or format with limited certification of certain tracks on the media.
- `long` Starts a complete format. For some devices this might include the certification of the whole media by the drive itself.
- `force` Provided to start a long format without user confirmation before the format is started. For drives that have a password protection mechanism, it clears the password while formatting. This feature is useful when a password is no longer available. On those media which do not have such password protection, force starts a long format.

After formatting the device, you can use the `newfs` command to create a file system on the device as follows:

```
# /usr/sbin/newfs -v /vol/dev/aliases/zip0 <cr>
```

You can also use the `rmformat -l` command to list the removable media devices on the system. Using this command provides detailed information about the device, such as the name used by vold and both the logical and physical device names as follows:

```
# rmformat -l <cr>
```

The system displays the following information:

```
Looking for devices...
       1. Volmgt Node: /vol/dev/aliases/rmdisk1
          Logical Node: /dev/rdsk/c5t0d0s2
          Physical Node: /pci@1e,600000/usb@b/hub@2/storage@4/disk@0,0
          Connected Device: TEAC     FD-05PUB        1026
          Device Type: Floppy drive
```

The `vold` daemon is the workhorse behind Volume Manager. It is automatically started by the Service Management Facility. `vold` reads the `/etc/vold.conf` configuration file at startup. The `vold.conf` file contains the Volume Manager configuration information. This information includes the database to use, labels that are supported, devices to use, actions to take if certain media events occur, and the list of file systems that are unsafe to eject without unmounting. The `vold.conf` file looks like this:

```
# ident "@(#)vold.conf  1.26    00/07/17 SMI"
#
# Volume Daemon Configuration file
#

# Database to use (must be first)
db db_mem.so
```

```
# Labels supported
label cdrom label_cdrom.so cdrom
label dos label_dos.so floppy rmdisk
label sun label_sun.so floppy rmdisk

# Devices to use
use cdrom drive /dev/rdsk/c*s2 dev_cdrom.so cdrom%d
use floppy drive /dev/rdiskette[0-9] dev_floppy.so floppy%d
use rmdisk drive /dev/rdsk/c*s2 dev_rmdisk.so rmdisk%d

# Actions
eject dev/diskette[0-9]/* user=root /usr/sbin/rmmount
eject dev/dsk/* user=root /usr/sbin/rmmount
insert dev/diskette[0-9]/* user=root /usr/sbin/rmmount
insert dev/dsk/* user=root /usr/sbin/rmmount
notify rdsk/* group=tty user=root /usr/lib/vold/volmissing -p
remount dev/diskette[0-9]/* user=root /usr/sbin/rmmount
remount dev/dsk/* user=root /usr/sbin/rmmount

# List of file system types unsafe to eject
unsafe ufs hsfs pcfs udfs
```

Each section in the `vold.conf` file is labeled with its function. Of these sections, you can safely modify the devices to use, which are described in Table 1.21, and actions, which are described in Table 1.22.

The "Devices to Use" section of the file describes the devices for `vold` to manage. `vold` has the following syntax:

```
use <device> <type> <special> <shared_object> <symname> < options >
```

TABLE 1.21 `vold.conf` Devices to Use

Parameter Field	Description
<device>	The type of removable media device to be used. Valid values are `cdrom`, `floppy`, `pcmem`, and `rmdisk`.
<type>	The device's specific capabilities. The valid value is `drive`.
<special>	The device or devices to be used. The path usually begins with /dev.
<shared_object>	The name of the program that manages this device. `vold` expects to find this program in /usr/lib/vold.
<symname>	The symbolic name that refers to this device. The `symname` is placed in the device directory.
<options>	The user, group, and mode permissions for the medium inserted (optional).

The *<special>* and *<symname>* parameters are related. If *<special>* contains any shell wildcard characters (that is, has one or more asterisks or question marks in it), *<symname>* must have a `%d` at its end. In this case, the devices that are found to match the regular expression are sorted and then numbered. The first device has a `0` filled in for the `%d`, the second device found has a `1`, and so on.

If the special specification does not have shell wildcard characters, the `symname` parameter must explicitly specify a number at its end.

The "Actions" section of the file specifies which program should be called if a particular event (action) occurs. The syntax for the `Actions` field is as follows:

```
insert <regex> < options > <program> <program_args>
eject <regex> < options > <program> <program_args>
notify <regex> < options> <program> <program_args>
```

The different actions are listed in Table 1.22.

TABLE 1.22 `vold.conf` Actions

<table>
<tr><th>Parameter</th><th>Description</th></tr>
<tr><td><code>insert|eject|notify</code></td><td>The media action prompting the event.</td></tr>
<tr><td><regex></td><td>This Bourne shell regular expression is matched against each entry in the <code>/vol</code> file system that is being affected by this event.</td></tr>
<tr><td><options></td><td>Which user or group name this event is to run (optional).</td></tr>
<tr><td><program></td><td>The full pathname of an executable program to be run if <code>regex</code> is matched.</td></tr>
<tr><td><program_args></td><td>Arguments to the program.</td></tr>
</table>

In the default `vold.conf` file, you see the following entries under the "Devices to Use" and "Actions" sections:

```
# Devices to use
use cdrom drive /dev/rdsk/c*s2 dev_cdrom.so cdrom%d
use floppy drive /dev/rdiskette[0-9] dev_floppy.so floppy%d
use rmdisk drive /dev/rdsk/c*s2 dev_rmdisk.so rmdisk%d
# Actions

eject dev/diskette[0-9]/* user=root /usr/sbin/rmmount
eject dev/dsk/* user=root /usr/sbin/rmmount
insert dev/diskette[0-9]/* user=root /usr/sbin/rmmount
insert dev/dsk/* user=root /usr/sbin/rmmount
notify rdsk/* group=tty user=root /usr/lib/vold/volmissing -p
remount dev/diskette[0-9]/* user=root /usr/sbin/rmmount
remount dev/dsk/* user=root /usr/sbin/rmmount
```

When a CD is inserted into the CD-ROM named `/dev/dsk/c0t6d0`, the following happens:

1. `vold` detects that the CD has been inserted and runs the `/usr/sbin/rmmount` command. `rmmount` is the utility that automatically mounts a file system on a CD-ROM

and floppy. It determines the type of file system, if any, that is on the medium. If a file system is present, rmmount creates a mount point in the /cdrom directory and mounts the CD-ROM file system onto this mount point. It then creates a symbolic link to /vol/dev/aliases/cdrom0 and /cdrom/cdrom0 as described in the previous table.

If the medium is read-only (either a CD-ROM or a floppy with the write-protect tab set), the file system is mounted as read-only. If a file system is not identified, rmmount does not mount a file system.

2. After the mount is complete, the action associated with the media type is executed. The action allows other programs to be notified that a new medium is available. For example, the default action for mounting a CD-ROM or a floppy is to start the File Manager.

   These actions are described in the configuration file /etc/rmmount.conf. Following is an example of the default /etc/rmmount.conf file:

```
# ident "@(#)rmmount.conf       1.27    06/01/20 SMI"
#
# Removable Media Mounter configuration file.
#

# File system identification
ident hsfs ident_hsfs.so cdrom
ident ufs ident_ufs.so cdrom floppy rmdisk
ident pcfs ident_pcfs.so floppy rmdisk
ident udfs ident_udfs.so cdrom floppy rmdisk

# Actions
action cdrom action_filemgr.so
action floppy action_filemgr.so
action rmdisk action_filemgr.so

# Mount
mount * hsfs udfs ufs -o nosuid
```

3. If the user issues the eject command, vold sees the media event and executes the action associated with that event. In this case, it runs /usr/sbin/rmmount. rmmount unmounts mounted file systems and executes actions associated with the media type called out in the /etc/rmmount.conf file. If a file system is "busy" (that is, it contains the current working directory of a live process), the eject action fails.

The program should be called if media events happen, such as eject or insert. If the vold.conf configuration file is modified, vold must be told to reread the /etc/vold.conf file as follows:

```
# svcadm refresh svc:/system/filesystem/volfs:default <cr>
```

This will instruct vold to re-read the configuration file.

Several other commands help you administer Volume Manager on your system. They are described in Table 1.23.

TABLE 1.23 Volume Manager Commands

Command	Description
rmmount	Removable media mounter. Used by vold to automatically mount a /cdrom, /floppy, Jaz, or Zip drive if one of these media types is installed.
volcancel	Cancels a user's request to access a particular CD-ROM or floppy file system. This command, issued by the system administrator, is useful if the removable medium containing the file system is not currently in the drive.
volcheck	Checks the drive for installed media. By default, it checks the drive pointed to by /dev/diskette.
volmissing	Specified in vold.conf, and notifies the user if an attempt is made to access a removable media type that is no longer in the drive.
vold	The Volume Manager daemon, controlled by /etc/vold.conf.
volrmmount	Simulates an insertion so that rmmount will mount the media, or simulates an ejection so that rmmount will unmount the media.

To some, volume management might seem like more trouble than it's worth. To disable volume management, type:

```
# svcadm disable svc:/system/filesystem/volfs:default <cr>
```

If you want to have volume management on the CD but not the floppy disk, comment out the entries in the "Devices to Use" and "Actions" sections of the vold.conf file with a #, as follows:

```
# Devices to use
use cdrom drive /dev/rdsk/c*s2 dev_cdrom.so cdrom%d
#use floppy drive /dev/rdiskette[0-9] dev_floppy.so floppy%d
use rmdisk drive /dev/rdsk/c*s2 dev_rmdisk.so rmdisk%d

# Actions
#eject dev/diskette[0-9]/* user=root /usr/sbin/rmmount
eject dev/dsk/* user=root /usr/sbin/rmmount
#insert dev/diskette[0-9]/* user=root /usr/sbin/rmmount
insert dev/dsk/* user=root /usr/sbin/rmmount
notify rdsk/* group=tty user=root /usr/lib/vold/volmissing -p
remount dev/diskette[0-9]/* user=root /usr/sbin/rmmount
remount dev/dsk/* user=root /usr/sbin/rmmount
```

With the changes made to /etc/vold.conf, when the vold daemon starts up, it manages only the CD-ROM and not the floppy disk.

Using Volume Management

`vold` is picky. Knowing this is the key to keeping `vold` from crashing or not working for some reason. With other computers, such as Windows PCs, you can eject CD-ROMs with no problems. With Solaris, `vold` isn't that robust, so the system administrator needs to follow a few ground rules when using volume management:

- Always use `vold` commands for everything to do with CD-ROMs and floppy disks. Use the commands listed in Table 1.23 to accomplish your task.
- Never press the button to eject a CD when a CD is already in the machine. This could cause `vold` to stop working. Use the `eject cdrom` command instead.
- If you can't stop or start `vold` using the `svcadm restart svc:/system/filesystem/volfs: default` command, you need to restart the system to get `vold` working properly.

I have found that the most reliable way to use floppy disks is via the Removable Media Manager GUI in the Common Desktop Environment (CDE) or Java Desktop Environment (JDE). Problems seem to be minimized when using floppy disks if I go through the media manager GUI versus the command line. Step by Step 1.12 describes how to access the Removable Media Manager GUI.

STEP BY STEP

1.12 Accessing the Removable Media Manager GUI

1. Open the File Manager GUI from the CDE front panel located at the bottom of the screen, as shown in Figure 1.11.

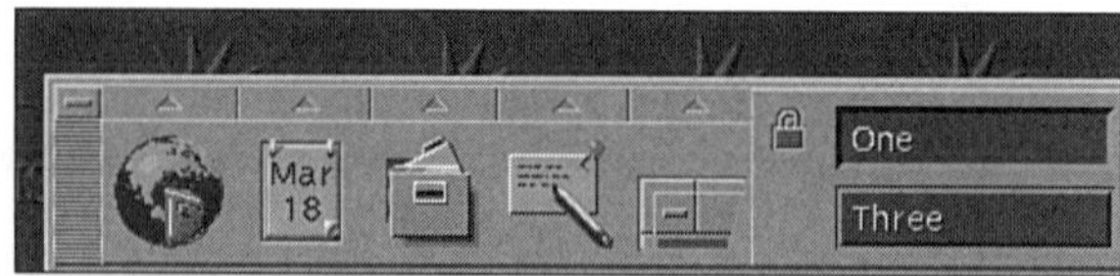

FIGURE 1.11 Front panel.

   The File Manager appears.

2. Click the File menu located in the menu bar, as shown in Figure 1.12.

   A pull-down menu will appear.

3. Select Removable Media Manager from the pull-down menu. The Removable Media Manager appears, as shown in Figure 1.13.

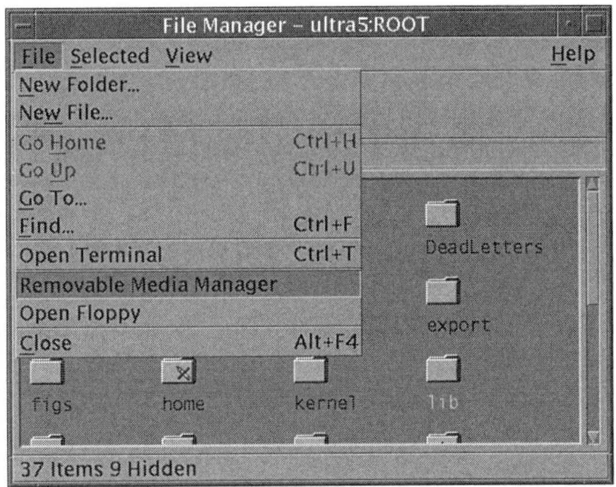

FIGURE 1.12 File Manager.

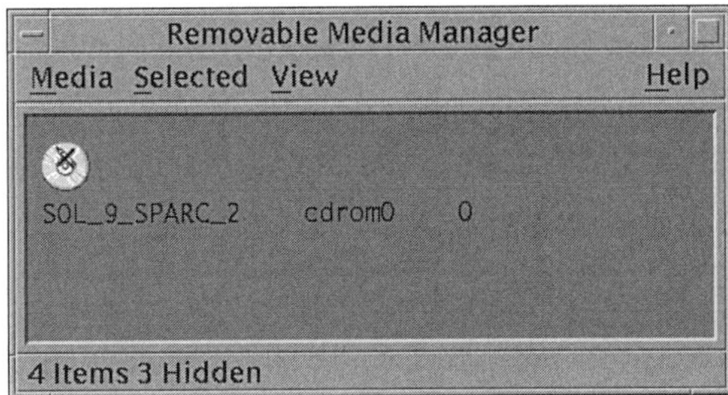

FIGURE 1.13 Removable Media Manager.

Troubleshooting Volume Manager

You might have problems with mounting a floppy or a CD-ROM. First, check to see if Volume Manager knows about the device. The best way to do this is to look in `/vol/dev/rdiskette0` and see if something is there. If not, the `volcheck` command has not been run or a hardware problem exists. If references to `/vol` lock up the system, it means that the daemon has died, and you need to restart the `vold` daemon as described earlier.

If `vold` is working properly, insert a formatted floppy disk and type `volcheck` followed by an `ls -l` as follows:

```
# volcheck <cr>
# ls -l /vol/dev/rdiskette0 <cr>
```

The system responds with this:

```
total 0
crw-rw-rw-   1 nobody   nobody    91,  7 Oct 13 14:56 unlabeled
```

NOTE

Unlabeled Volumes The volume is unlabeled; therefore, the file in `/vol/dev/rdiskette0` is called unlabeled.

Check to make sure that a link exists in `/floppy` to the character device in `/vol/dev/rdiskette0`. Type the following:

```
# ls -l /floppy <cr>
```

The system responds with this:

```
total 18
lrwxrwxrwx   1 root     nobody        11 Oct 13 14:56 floppy0 ->\
 ./noname
```

NOTE

Diskettes that are not named (that is, they have no "label") are assigned the default name of noname.

If a name is in `/vol/dev/rdiskette0`, as previously described, and nothing is mounted in `/floppy/`*<name_of_media>*, it's likely that data on the medium is an unrecognized file system. For example, perhaps it's a tar archive, a cpio backup, or a Macintosh file system. Don't use Volume Manager to get to these file types. Instead, access them through the block or character devices found in `/vol/dev/rdiskette0` or `/vol/dev/diskette0`, with user tools to interpret the data on them, such as `tar`, `dd`, or `cpio`.

If you're still having problems with Volume Manager, one way to gather debugging information is to run the `rmmount` command with the debug (`-D`) flag. To do this, edit `/etc/vold.conf` and change the lines that have `/usr/sbin/rmmount` to include the `-D` flag. For example:

```
insert /vol*/dev/diskette[0-9]/* user=root /usr/sbin/rmmount -D
```

This causes various debugging messages to appear on the console.

To see debugging messages from the Volume Manager daemon, run the daemon, `/usr/sbin/vold`, with the `-v -L10` flags. It logs data to `/var/adm/vold.log`. This file might contain information that could be useful in troubleshooting.

You might also want to mount a CD-ROM on a different mount point using volume management. By default, `vold` mounts the CD-ROM on the mount point `/cdrom/cdrom0`, but you can mount the CD-ROM on a different mount point by following the instructions in Step by Step 1.13.

STEP BY STEP

1.13 Mounting a CD-ROM on a Different Mount Point

1. If Volume Manager is running, bring up the File Manager and eject the CD-ROM by issuing the following command:

```
# eject cdrom <cr>
```

2. Stop the volume-management daemon by typing the following:

```
# svcadm disable svc:/system/filesystem/volfs:default <cr>
```

3. Create the directory called `/test`:

```
# mkdir /test <cr>
```

4. Insert the CD-ROM into the CD drive and issue this command:

```
# /usr/sbin/vold -d /test & <cr>
```

Now, instead of using the `/vol` directory, `vold` will use `/test` as the starting directory.

Displaying a File System's Disk Space Usage

Several options are available in Solaris for displaying disk usage. This chapter describes four commands:

- **df**—Displays information about currently mounted file systems and mount point, disk space allocation, usage, and availability.
- **SMC Usage Tool**—A GUI tool to display information about currently mounted file systems and mount point, disk space allocation, usage, and availability.
- **du**—Displays the disk usage of each file in each subdirectory. This command is described in the "Displaying Directory Size Information" section of this chapter.
- **quot**—Displays disk space used by each user. This command is described in the "Controlling User Disk Space Usage" section later in this chapter.

Use the `df` command and its options to see the capacity of each file system mounted on a system, the amount of space available, and the percentage of space already in use.

NOTE

Full File Systems File systems at or above 90% of capacity should be cleared of unnecessary files. You can do this by moving them to a disk, or you can remove them after obtaining the user's permission.

The following is an example of how to use the `df` command to display disk space information. The command syntax is as follows:

```
df -[F fstype] [options] <directory>
```

Table 1.24 explains the `df` command and its options.

TABLE 1.24 The df Command

Command	Description
`df`	With no options, lists all mounted file systems and their device names. It also lists the total number of 512-byte blocks used and the number of files.
<directory>	Is the directory whose file system you want to check. The device name, blocks used, and number of files are displayed.
`-F` *<fstype>*	Displays the unmounted file systems, their device names, the number of 512-byte blocks used, and the number of files on file systems of type `fstype`.
`-b`	Print the total number of kilobytes free.
`-h`	Scales disk space values to a more "human" readable format.
`-k`	Lists file systems, kilobytes used, free kilobytes, percent capacity used, and mount points.
`-t`	Displays total blocks as well as blocks used for all mounted file systems.

The following example illustrates how to display disk space information with the `df` command. Type the following:

```
# df -h <cr>
```

The system responds with this:

```
Filesystem             size   used  avail capacity  Mounted on
/dev/dsk/c0t0d0s0       12G   3.6G   7.8G    32%    /
/devices                 0K     0K     0K     0%    /devices
ctfs                     0K     0K     0K     0%    /system/contract
proc                     0K     0K     0K     0%    /proc
mnttab                   0K     0K     0K     0%    /etc/mnttab
swap                   2.7G   1.2M   2.7G     1%    /etc/svc/volatile
objfs                    0K     0K     0K     0%    /system/object
fd                       0K     0K     0K     0%    /dev/fd
/dev/dsk/c0t0d0s1      4.8G    62M   4.7G     2%    /var
swap                   2.7G     0K   2.7G     0%    /tmp
swap                   2.7G    40K   2.7G     1%    /var/run
/dev/dsk/c0t0d0s7      9.6G   9.8M   9.5G     1%    /export/home
```

The preceding example used the `-h` option to output the information in a more readable format.

Notice that the `-h` option scales the values to a more readable format.

In both examples, you'll see disk usage information displayed for each currently mounted file system.

You can also use the Solaris Management Console (SMC) Usage tool, which provides a graphical display of the available disk space for all mounted file systems. To use the Usage tool, follow the procedure outlined in Step by Step 1.14.

STEP BY STEP

1.14 Using the SMC Usage Tool

1. Launch the SMC by typing

   ```
   # smc& <cr>
   ```

2. In the left navigation window, select the This Computer icon from the left navigation pane, then select the Storage icon, and then click on the Mounts and Shares icon as shown in Figure 1.14.

   A window will open, prompting you to enter the root password. The Mounts and Shares tools will be displayed as shown in Figure 1.15.

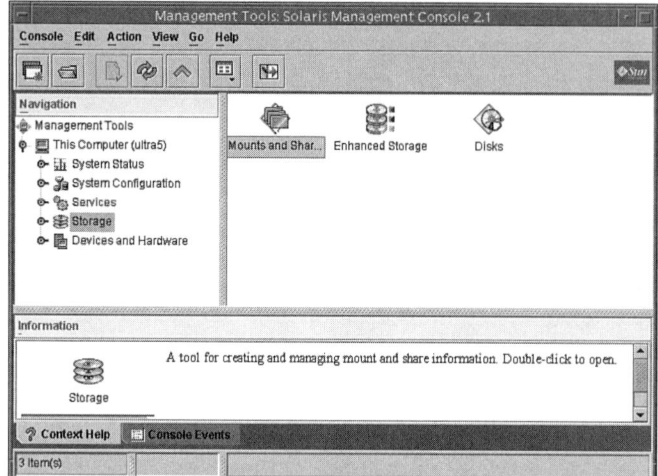

FIGURE 1.14 Selecting the Storage icon.

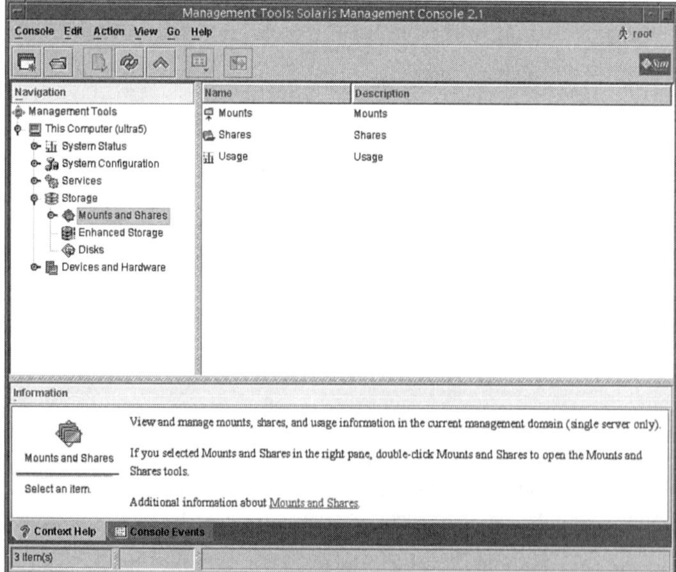

FIGURE 1.15 Mounts and Shares tools.

3. Select the Usage icon and the window shown in Figure 1.16 will be displayed.

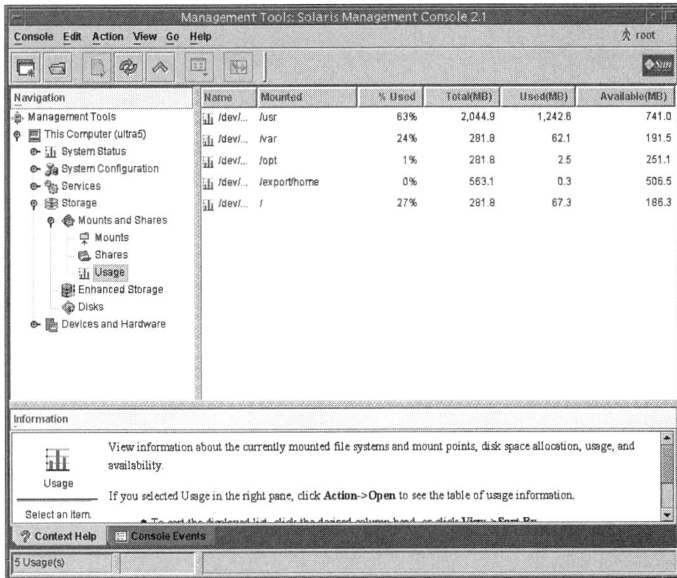

FIGURE 1.16 SMC Usage tool.

Displaying Directory Size Information

By using the `df` command, you display file system disk usage. You can use the `du` command to display the disk usage of a directory and all its subdirectories in 512-byte blocks. When used with the `-h` option, values are scaled to a more readable format.

The `du` command shows you the disk usage of each file in each subdirectory of a file system. To get a listing of the size of each subdirectory in a file system, type `cd` to the pathname associated with that file system and run the following pipeline:

```
du -s *| sort -r -n
```

This pipeline, which uses the reverse and numeric options of the `sort` command, pinpoints large directories. Use `ls -l` to examine the size (in bytes) and modification times of files within each directory. Old files or text files greater than 100KB often warrant storage offline.

The following example illustrates how to display the amount of disk space being consumed by the `/var/adm` directory using the `du` command. The largest files are displayed first, and the `-k` option displays the file size in 1024 bytes. Type the following:

```
# du -k /var/adm|sort -r -n <cr>
```

The system responds with this:

```
2230    /var/adm
1785    /var/adm/sa
4       /var/adm/acct
```

```
1       /var/adm/streams
1       /var/adm/sm.bin
1       /var/adm/passwd
1       /var/adm/log
1       /var/adm/exacct
1       /var/adm/acct/sum
1       /var/adm/acct/nite
1       /var/adm/acct/fiscal
```

In this example we use the `-h` option to output the information in a more readable format so that you can see the difference:

```
du -h /var/adm¦sort -r -n
```

The system responds with this:

```
   4K   /var/adm/acct
 2.3M   /var/adm
 1.8M   /var/adm/sa
   1K   /var/adm/streams
   1K   /var/adm/sm.bin
   1K   /var/adm/passwd
   1K   /var/adm/log
   1K   /var/adm/exacct
   1K   /var/adm/acct/sum
   1K   /var/adm/acct/nite
   1K   /var/adm/acct/fiscal
```

NOTE

The sort Command Notice that the files are not listed by file size. This is because the `-n` option to the `sort` command sorts data numerically, not by file size. The number 4 is a larger number, numerically, than the number 2. The `-n` option does not take into account that 4KB is smaller in size than 2.3MB.

Information on File Systems

The `df` command gives you capacity information on each mounted file system. The output of `df` and `fsck` is often misunderstood. This section goes into more detail about these two commands and describes their output so that you can better understand the information displayed. I begin with the `fsck` command. Remember, run `fsck` only on unmounted file systems, as shown in the following example. Type the following:

```
# umount /mnt <cr>
# fsck /dev/rdsk/c2t1d0s1 <cr>
```

The system responds with this:

```
** /dev/rdsk/c2t1d0s1
** Last Mounted on /mnt
** Phase 1 - Check Blocks and Sizes
** Phase 2 - Check Pathnames
** Phase 3 - Check Connectivity
** Phase 4 - Check Reference Counts
** Phase 5 - Check Cyl groups
2 files, 9 used, 4099509 free (13 frags, 512437 blocks, 0.0% fragmentation)
```

`fsck` first reports some things related to usage, as shown in Table 1.25.

TABLE 1.25 `fsck` Output

Field	Description
`files`	Number of files in the file system
`used`	Number of data blocks used
`free`	Number of data blocks free (fragments and whole blocks)

NOTE

Fragment Size A fragment is one data block in size, and a block consists of a number of data blocks, typically eight.

Then `fsck` reports more details of the free space, as shown in Table 1.26.

TABLE 1.26 `fsck` Output

Field	Description
`frags`	The number of free fragments (from fragmented blocks)
`blocks`	The number of free blocks (whole unfragmented blocks)
`% fragmentation`	Free fragments as a percentage of the whole disk size

Fragmentation does not refer to fragmentation in the sense of a file's disk blocks being inefficiently scattered across the whole file system, as you see in a Microsoft Windows file system.

In Solaris, a high percentage of fragmentation implies that much of the free space is tied up in fragments. In the previous example, fragmentation was 0%. High fragmentation affects creation of new files—especially those larger than a few data blocks. Typically, high fragmentation is caused by creating large numbers of small files.

Now let's review the output from the `df` command:

```
# mount /dev/dsk/c2t1d0s1 /mnt <cr>
# df -k /mnt <cr>
```

The system responds with this:

```
File system            kbytes    used   avail capacity  Mounted on
/dev/dsk/c2t1d0s1     4103598    4089 3894330      1%    /mnt
```

The `4103598` value in the output represents the total file system size in kilobytes. It includes the 5% `minfree` that you specified earlier with the `tunefs` command. The output is summarized in Table 1.27.

TABLE 1.27 Output from `df`

Field	Description
`4089KB used`	The amount of space used in the file system.
`3894330KB available`	Space available in the file system. This value is equal to the file system size minus the `minfree%` minus the space used (`4103598` – `5%` – `4089`). Because logging is enabled on this file system, a small amount of space is used for logging. The log size is 1MB per 1GB of space up to a max of 64MB.
`1% capacity`	Space used as a percentage, calculated as follows: kilobytes used/(kilobytes available – `minfree%`).

Controlling User Disk Space Usage

Quotas let system administrators control the size of UFS file systems by limiting the amount of disk space that individual users can acquire. Quotas are especially useful on file systems where user home directories reside. After the quotas are in place, they can be changed to adjust the amount of disk space or number of inodes that users can consume. Additionally, quotas can be added or removed as system needs change. Also, quota status can be monitored. Quota commands enable administrators to display information about quotas on a file system or search for users who have exceeded their quotas.

After you have set up and turned on disk and inode quotas, you can check for users who exceed their quotas. You can also check quota information for entire file systems by using the commands listed in Table 1.28.

TABLE 1.28 Commands to Check Quotas

Command	Description
`quota`	Displays the quotas and disk usage within a file system for individual users on which quotas have been activated
`repquota`	Displays the quotas and disk usage for all users on one or more file systems

You won't see quotas in use much today because the cost of disk space continues to fall. In most cases, the system administrator simply watches disk space to identify users who might be using more than their fair share. As you saw in this section, you can easily do this by using the `du` command. On a large system with many users, however, disk quotas can be an effective way to control disk space usage.

Another option for managing user space is the use of soft partitions described in the *Solaris 10 System Administration Exam Prep: Exam CX-310-202* book. With soft partitions, each user's home directory can be created within its own disk partition and would be limited to the space allocated to that partition.

The `quot` Command

Use the `quot` command to display how much disk space, in kilobytes, is being used by users. You do not need to implement disk quotas to use this command. The `quot` command can only be run by root. The syntax for the `quot` command is

```
quot -options <file system>
```

The `quot` command has two options:

`-a`	Reports on all mounted file systems
`-f`	Includes the number of files

To display disk space being used by all users on all mounted file systems, type the following:

```
# quot -af <cr>
```

The system responds with the following output:

```
/dev/rdsk/c0t0d0s0 (/):
68743    4370   root
  162      18   lp
   31      14   uucp
    1       1   adm
/dev/rdsk/c0t0d0s6 (/usr):
1270388 50748   root
 1254      19   lp
  766      15   uucp
   10       3   bin
    1       1   adm
/dev/rdsk/c0t0d0s1 (/var):
63327    5232   root
  208       9   adm
   22      27   lp
   16      17   uucp
    4       4   daemon
```

```
     4        8    nobody
     2        2    smmsp
     1        3    bill
     1        1    bin
/dev/rdsk/c0t0d0s5 (/opt):
  2608      253    root
     2        2    lp
/dev/rdsk/c0t0d0s7 (/export/home):
   212      131    root
    68       56    wcalkins
    58       39    bill
     5        5    sradmin
     4        4    jer
     4        4    jradmin
     2        2    tom
```

The columns of information displayed represent kilobytes used, number of files, and owner, respectively.

To display a count of the number of files and space owned by each user for a specific file system, enter

```
# quot -f /dev/dsk/c0t0d0s7 <cr>
```

The system responds with the following:

```
/dev/rdsk/c0t0d0s7:
   212      131    root
    68       56    wcalkins
    58       39    bill
     5        5    sradmin
     4        4    jer
     4        4    jradmin
     2        2    tom
```

Summary

This concludes the discussion of file systems. This chapter discussed the various device drivers and device names used in Solaris 10. You must understand the device naming conventions used on both the SPARC-based abd x86/x64-based Solaris systems. I described the Solaris commands and utilities used to obtain information about these devices and drivers. In addition to the devices that come standard with Solaris, this chapter also described Solaris Volume Manager and the added functionality it provides.

Device drivers are discussed in several chapters of this book because they are used in many aspects of the system administrator's job. Devices are referenced when we install and boot the operating system (see Chapter 2, "Installing the Solaris 10 Operating Environment," and Chapter 3), when creating and mounting file systems, when setting up printers (see Chapter 6, "Managing the LP Print Service"), and in general troubleshooting of system problems. It is very important that you have a good understanding of how device drivers are configured and named in the Solaris operating system.

This chapter also introduced you to the many options available for constructing file systems using the `mkfs` and `newfs` commands. Other Solaris utilities for managing, labeling, copying, and tuning file systems were also presented.

The process of creating a file system on a disk partition was described. Many file system creation parameters that affect performance were presented. This chapter also detailed all the parts of a file system so that, as you create file systems, you are familiar with terminology you'll encounter.

The `mount` and `umount` commands were described. In this chapter, I explained how to display mount options currently in use on a particular file system. In addition, the chapter showed you how to determine what process or user is using a file system before you unmount it.

In addition to showing how to manually mount file systems, this chapter described the Volume Manager for automatically mounting file systems on CD-ROM and disk. All the Volume Manager commands and associated configuration files were presented and explained.

Finally, the system administrator must monitor all file systems regularly. Commands and utilities used to monitor and manage file systems were described in detail.

Now that we've discussed devices, device and driver names, disk slices, and file systems, the next chapter will introduce the Solaris installation process.

Key Terms

- Block device
- Block size
- Buffered Devices
- Character device
- Cylinder
- Device autoconfiguration
- Device driver
- Device hierarchy

- Device tree
- Disk label
- Disk partition
- Disk quota
- Disk slice
- Disk-based file system
- fdisk
- File system
- File system `minfree` space
- File system type
- Fragment
- Free block
- Free hog slice
- Hard link
- Hot-pluggable
- inode
- Instance name
- Large files
- Large file–aware
- Large file–safe
- Logical device name
- Logical volume
- Major device number
- Minor device number
- Mounted file system table (`mnttab`)
- Network-based file system
- Partition table
- Physical device name
- Raw dence
- Reconfiguration startup
- Sector
- Service Management Facility (SMF)
- Storage block
- Superblock
- Swap
- Symbolic link
- UFS logging
- Virtual file system
- Volume manager
- Volume name

Exercises

1.1 Device Autoconfiguration

This exercise demonstrates three different methods that can be used to perform a reconfiguration boot so that the kernel recognizes new devices attached to the system.

Estimated time: 15 minutes

1. From the OpenBoot prompt, type the following:

```
# boot -r <cr>
```

The system performs a reconfiguration boot and a login prompt appears.

2. Log in as root and create an empty file named `/reconfigure` as follows:

```
# touch /reconfigure <cr>
```

Now reboot the system as follows:

```
# /usr/sbin/shutdown -y -g0 -i6 <cr>
```

The system performs a reconfiguration boot, and a login prompt appears.

3. Log in as root and issue the following command:

```
# reboot -- -r <cr>
```

The system performs a reconfiguration boot, and a login prompt appears.

1.2 Displaying Information About Devices

In this exercise, you'll use a few of the Solaris commands to display information about devices connected to your system.

Estimated time: 5 minutes

1. Use the `dmesg` command to determine the mapping of an instance name to a physical device name. Type the following:

```
# dmesg <cr>
```

In the output, identify the instance name assigned to each disk drive and peripheral attached to your system. On a system with IDE disks, you'll see entries similar to the following:

```
sd0 is /pci@1f,0/pci@1,1/ide@3/sd@2,0
```

On a system with SCSI disks, you'll see something like this:

```
sd17 is /pci@1f,0/pci@1/scsi@1,1/sd@1,0
```

2. Use the `prtconf` command to see which drivers are attached to the instance names identified in the previous step.

For example, you should see an entry something like this:

```
sd, instance #0
```

1.3 Adding a New Device

In this exercise, you'll use the `devfsadm` command to add in a new device without rebooting the system.

Estimated time: 15 minutes

1. Connect a tape drive, disk drive, or CD-ROM to the system and perform a reconfiguration reboot.

2. Log in and issue the `dmesg` command to verify that the device has been installed. You should see an entry something like this if you're adding an SCSI disk drive:

```
sd17 is /pci@1f,0/pci@1/scsi@1,1/sd@1,0
```

   Check to see that a driver is attached by issuing the `prtconf` command.

3. Halt the system, turn off the new device, and boot the system back up using the `boot` command. Do not do a reconfiguration reboot.
4. Issue the prtconf command. It should display (driver not attached) next to the instance device name for that device.
5. Turn the device back on and issue the `devfsadm` command.
6. Issue the `prtconf` command again. The message `(driver not attached)` next to the instance device name should be gone and the device is now available for use.

1.4 Displaying Disk Configuration Information

In this exercise, you determine the disk geometry and slice information of your disk drive.

Estimated time: 20 minutes

1. Log in as root.
2. Display and record your current disk configuration information using the `prtvtoc` command, as shown here:

```
prtvtoc <raw disk device name>
```

   How are the disk slices arranged? What disk geometry does it display?

3. Now, follow these steps to look at your disk information using the format utility:

   ❍ **A.** Type `format`. The Main menu appears, displaying your disk drives. You're going to select the disk numbered `0`, so note all of the information on that line.

   ❍ **B.** Type `0`. This will select the first disk listed. The Format menu will appear.

   ❍ **C.** Type `partition`. The Partition menu will appear.

   ❍ **D.** Type `print`. All of your disk partition information will be displayed.

   ❍ **E.** Press Ctrl+D. You'll exit the `format` utility.

1.5 Creating a File System

The following exercise requires that you have a spare disk drive connected to your system or a spare, unused slice on a disk. You will practice creating a disk slice and creating a file system.

Estimated time: 30 minutes

1. Practice creating a slice on your spare disk drive using the steps outlined in the earlier section titled "Using the `format` Utility to Create Slices."
2. Create a file system on the new or unused slice using the `newfs` command as follows:

```
# newfs <raw device name> <cr>
```

3. Create a directory in the root partition named `/test`, as shown here:

```
# mkdir /test <cr>
```

4. Mount the new file system to support large files using the following command:

```
# mount -o largefiles <block device name> /test <cr>
```

5. Unmount the file system, as shown here:

```
# umount /test <cr>
```

6. View the contents of the `/etc/vfstab` file on your system by typing `cat /etc/vfstab`.
7. Add the following line to the `/etc/vfstab` file for the file system you've just created so that it gets mounted automatically at boot time:

```
<block device name> <raw device> /test  ufs  2   yes  -
```

8. Reboot the system:

```
# /usr/sbin/shutdown -y -g0 -i6 <cr>
```

9. Verify that the file system was mounted automatically:

```
# mount <cr>
```

1.6 Tuning a File System

In this exercise, you'll modify some of the file system parameters that were specified when the file system was originally created with the **newfs** command.

Estimated time: 15 minutes

1. Log in as root.
2. List all of the parameters currently in use on the file system by typing the following:

```
# newfs -v <raw device name> <cr>
```

3. Open another window. Leave the information displayed in step 2 in the window for referencing later. In the new window, type the `tunefs` command to change the `minfree` value to 5% on the file system as follows:

```
# tunefs -m5 <raw device name> <cr>
```

4. View the new file system parameters, but this time you'll use the `mkfs` command as follows:

```
# mkfs -m <raw device name> <cr>
```

Compare the parameters displayed with the parameters that were displayed earlier in the other window.

5. Try the `fstyp` command for viewing the file system parameters as follows:

```
# fstyp -v <raw device name> <cr>
```

1.7 Using Volume Manager

In this exercise, you'll utilize Volume Manager to automatically mount a CD-ROM.

Estimated time: 10 minutes

1. Insert a CD-ROM into the CD-ROM player.
2. Type the `mount` command with no options to verify that the device was mounted. What is the mount point that was used?
3. Eject the CD-ROM as follows:

```
# eject cdrom <cr>
```

4. Type the following command to look for the Volume Manager process named `vold`:

```
# pgrep -l vold <cr> (or use svcs -p volfs)
```

5. Turn off the Volume Manager by typing the following:

```
# svcadm disable svc:/system/filesystem/volfs:default <cr>
```

6. Type the following command to look for the Volume Manager process named `vold`:

```
# pgrep -l vold <cr> (or use svcs -p volfs)
```

7. Insert the CD into the CD-ROM player. Did it mount the CD?
8. Restart the Volume Manager daemon by typing the following:

```
# svcadm enable svc:/system/filesystem/volfs:default <cr>
```

9. Type the `mount` command with no options to list all mounted file systems. Is the CD mounted now?

Exam Questions

1. Which of the following represents the kernel's abbreviated name for every possible device on the system?

   ❍ **A.** Instance name

   ❍ **B.** Logical device

   ❍ **C.** Physical device name

   ❍ **D.** Pseudo device name

2. Physical device files are found in which of the following?

   ❍ **A.** `/kernel/drv`

   ❍ **B.** `/dev`

   ❍ **C.** `/platform`

   ❍ **D.** `/devices`

3. Which of the following displays device configuration information, including system hardware, pseudo devices, loadable modules, and selected kernel parameters?

   ❍ **A.** `messages`

   ❍ **B.** `prtconf`

   ❍ **C.** `dmesg`

   ❍ **D.** `sysdef`

4. When you see the **driver not attached** message, it means which of the following?

   ❍ **A.** The device for this driver is not attached.

   ❍ **B.** A driver is unavailable for this device.

   ❍ **C.** No driver is currently attached to the device instance because there is no device at this node or the device is not in use.

   ❍ **D.** The kernel needs to be reconfigured to attach the device.

5. The .conf files reside in which directory?

   ❍ **A.** `/kernel/drv`

   ❍ **B.** `/dev`

   ❍ **C.** `/devices`

   ❍ **D.** `/platform`

6. Which of the following are mapped to a physical device name in the /etc/path_to_inst file?

❍ **A.** Logical devices

❍ **B.** Instance names

❍ **C.** Physical devices

❍ **D.** Pseudo devices

7. You can determine the mapping of an instance name to a physical device name by doing what? Choose all that apply.

❍ **A.** Looking at output from the `dmesg` command

❍ **B.** Viewing the `/var/adm/messages` file

❍ **C.** Looking at output from the `sysdef` command

❍ **D.** Looking at output from the `prtconf` command

8. The system relies on information found in which of the following files to find the root, usr, or swap device?

❍ **A.** `/etc/vfstab`

❍ **B.** `/etc/path_to_inst`

❍ **C.** `kernel`

❍ **D.** `/kernel/drv/`

❍ **E.** `/etc/driver`

9. Which of the following `shell` commands creates logical links to device nodes in the **/dev** and **/devices** directories?

❍ **A.** `boot -r`

❍ **B.** `drvconfig`

❍ **C.** `devfsadm`

❍ **D.** `devlinks`

10. Which of the following is the preferred command used to inform the system about newly installed device drivers?

❍ **A.** `devlinks`

❍ **B.** `drvconfig`

❍ **C.** `add_drv`

❍ **D.** `devfsadm`

11. Which of the following is the daemon responsible for handling both reconfiguration boot processing and updating `/dev` and `/devices` in response to dynamic reconfiguration event notifications from the kernel?

   ❍ **A.** `devfsadmd`

   ❍ **B.** `inetd`

   ❍ **C.** `devfsdadm`

   ❍ **D.** `svc.startd`

12. Your external CD-ROM was not turned on when the system was last booted with a reconfiguration reboot. To gain access to the CD-ROM, you could halt the system, turn on power to the CD-ROM, and start the system back up, or you could issue which of the following commands at the command prompt?

   ❍ **A.** `drvconfig cdrom`

   ❍ **B.** `add_drv cdrom`

   ❍ **C.** `devfsadm`

   ❍ **D.** `drvconfig -d`

13. Which of the following indicates the general device driver for devices such as disk, tape, or serial line?

   ❍ **A.** Minor device number

   ❍ **B.** Major device number

   ❍ **C.** Device tree

   ❍ **D.** Pseudo device

14. The minor device number:

   ❍ **A.** Indicates the general device driver for devices such as disk, tape, or serial line.

   ❍ **B.** Indicates the specific member within a driver.

   ❍ **C.** Uniquely defines a device and its device driver.

   ❍ **D.** Identifies the proper device location and device driver to the kernel.

15. Logical device files in the `/dev` directory are symbolically linked to which of the following in the `/devices` directory?

- ❍ **A.** Instance names
- ❍ **B.** Pseudo device files
- ❍ **C.** Full device path names
- ❍ **D.** Physical device files

16. Which of the following is a link from the `/dev` directory to the physical device name located in the `/devices` directory?

- ❍ **A.** Full device path name
- ❍ **B.** Pseudo device name
- ❍ **C.** Logical device name
- ❍ **D.** Instance name

17. `/dev/dsk/c0t0d0s7` is what type of device?

- ❍ **A.** Logical device name
- ❍ **B.** Pseudo device name
- ❍ **C.** Full device path name
- ❍ **D.** Instance name

18. Which of the following is the preferred command to create entries in the `/dev` directory for disk drives attached to the system?

- ❍ **A.** `devfsadm`
- ❍ **B.** `add_drv`
- ❍ **C.** `drvconfig`
- ❍ **D.** `boot -r`

19. Which directory contains the disk entries symbolically linked to the block device nodes in `/devices`?

- ❍ **A.** `/kernel/drv`
- ❍ **B.** `/dev/rdsk`
- ❍ **C.** `/vol/dev/aliases`
- ❍ **D.** `/dev/dsk`

20. Which of the following best describes a physical device name?

❍ **A.** It represents the full device pathname of a device.

❍ **B.** It is equivalent to the SCSI target ID of a device.

❍ **C.** It represents the actual name of a device, such as a disk, tape, and so on.

❍ **D.** It represents the kernel's abbreviated name for a device on the system.

21. In the standard device file naming convention "cXtYdZ," what does the "tY" portion of the filename identify?

❍ **A.** The controller card to which this device is attached

❍ **B.** The SCSI target address of the device

❍ **C.** The LUN of the device

❍ **D.** The function number as contained on the "Core I/O" board

22. Which of the following is a character device name?

❍ **A.** `/dev/dsk/c0t3d0s0`

❍ **B.** `/dev/rdsk/c0t3d0s0`

❍ **C.** `/dev/cua`

❍ **D.** `/devices/sbus@1,f8000000/esp@0,40000/sd@3,0:a`

23. What best describes an instance name?

❍ **A.** The kernel's abbreviated name for every possible device on the system

❍ **B.** A symbolic link to a physical device file

❍ **C.** The full device pathname of a device

❍ **D.** The SCSI address of a disk drive

24. Logical devices are organized in subdirectories under which directory?

❍ **A.** `/dev`

❍ **B.** `/devices`

❍ **C.** `/kernel`

❍ **D.** `/`

25. What best describes a logical device name?

- ❍ **A.** It is a symbolic link to a physical device file.
- ❍ **B.** It represents the kernel's abbreviated name for every possible device on the system.
- ❍ **C.** It represents the full device pathname of a device.
- ❍ **D.** It defines the SCSI address of a disk device.

26. What statement is *not* true about disk slices on standard Solaris?

- ❍ **A.** Each slice can hold only one file system.
- ❍ **B.** A file system cannot span multiple disk slices.
- ❍ **C.** A file system cannot be increased or decreased.
- ❍ **D.** Slices can span multiple disks.

27. Where is disk configuration information stored?

- ❍ **A.** On the disk label
- ❍ **B.** In several locations on the disk
- ❍ **C.** In the superblock
- ❍ **D.** In the partition table

28. Which of the following stores the procedures used to boot the system?

- ❍ **A.** Boot block
- ❍ **B.** Superblock
- ❍ **C.** inode
- ❍ **D.** Disk label

29. Which of the following commands will display partition information about a disk?

- ❍ **A.** `prtvtoc`
- ❍ **B.** `sysdef`
- ❍ **C.** `df -k`
- ❍ **D.** `sysinfo`

30. Which of the following is *not* a virtual file system?

❍ **A.** `/export/home`

❍ **B.** `Tmpfs`

❍ **C.** `Cachefs`

❍ **D.** `Procfs`

31. Which of the following tasks cannot be performed with the `format` utility?

❍ **A.** Repairing defective sectors

❍ **B.** Partitioning

❍ **C.** Retrieving corrupted disk labels

❍ **D.** Displaying disk usage

32. Which of the following does the superblock *not* contain?

❍ **A.** Size and status of the file system

❍ **B.** Cylinder group size

❍ **C.** Pathname of the last mount point

❍ **D.** Boot information

33. What information does the inode contain? Choose all that apply.

❍ **A.** The type of the file

❍ **B.** File directory information

❍ **C.** The number of bytes in the file

❍ **D.** Logical volume information

34. What is *not* true about logical block sizes?

❍ **A.** The logical block size is the size of the blocks the Unix kernel uses to read or write files.

❍ **B.** By default, the logical block size is 8192 bytes.

❍ **C.** A larger logical block size increases efficiency for file systems in which most of the files are large.

❍ **D.** A small logical block size increases efficiency for file systems in which most of the files are large.

35. What determines the number of inodes to be created in a new file system?

❍ **A.** The number of inodes depends on the amount of disk space that is allocated for each inode and the total size of the file system.

❍ **B.** 2048 inodes are created per 1GB of file system space.

❍ **C.** The number is dynamic and the kernel assigns inodes as required by the number of files in a file system.

❍ **D.** By default, one inode is allocated for each 2KB of data space.

36. In Solaris, which of the following is referred to as the smallest allocable unit of disk space?

❍ **A.** Fragment

❍ **B.** Data block

❍ **C.** Logical block

❍ **D.** Byte

37. What is another name for swap space and the total physical memory combined?

❍ **A.** Virtual memory

❍ **B.** Random Access Memory

❍ **C.** Partition C or Slice 2

❍ **D.** Static memory

38. When should a file system be checked with `fsck`? Choose all that apply.

❍ **A.** If the file system was unmounted improperly

❍ **B.** After a power outage

❍ **C.** Whenever a file system cannot be mounted

❍ **D.** When data has been accidentally deleted

39. What does `fsck` do when it preens a file system?

❍ **A.** Forces checking of the file system

❍ **B.** Checks and fixes the file system noninteractively

❍ **C.** Checks writeable file systems only

❍ **D.** Only checks to determine if a file system needs checking

40. Which of the following files contains a list of file systems to be automatically mounted at bootup?

❍ **A.** `/etc/fstab`

❍ **B.** `/etc/dfs/dfstab`

❍ **C.** `/etc/vfstab`

❍ **D.** `/etc/rc2.d/S74autofs`

41. The `mountall` command

❍ **A.** Mounts the CD-ROM and floppy automatically

❍ **B.** Mounts all file systems specified in the file system table

❍ **C.** Shares all files systems so that they can be mounted

❍ **D.** Mounts the tape in the tape drive

42. What command(s) is/are used to display disk space information?

❍ **A.** `du`

❍ **B.** `df`

❍ **C.** `quota`

❍ **D.** `repquota`

❍ **E.** All of the above

43. Which of the following mount options is used to mount file systems that have files larger than 2GB?

❍ **A.** `largefiles`

❍ **B.** `nolargefiles`

❍ **C.** `lf`

❍ **D.** `nlf`

44. What should you do to disable UFS logging on a file system?

❍ **A.** Use the `-o` nologging option with the `mount` command.

❍ **B.** Use the `-l` option with the `mount` command.

❍ **C.** You don't need to do anything; `nologging` is the default when mounting a file system.

❍ **D.** Use the logging feature in the `newfs` command when creating the file system.

45. Which of the following represents the correct format for an entry in the `/etc/vfstab` file?

❍ **A.** device to mount, device to fsck, mount point, FS type, fsck pass, mount at boot, mount options

❍ **B.** device to fsck, device to mount, mount point, FS type, fsck pass, mount at boot, mount point

❍ **C.** mount point, device to mount, device to fsck, mount point, FS type, fsck pass, mount at boot

❍ **D.** mount point, device to fsck, device to mount, mount point, FS type, fsck pass, mount at boot

46. Which of the following commands shows you the disk usage of each file in each subdirectory of a file system?

❍ **A.** `du`

❍ **B.** `df`

❍ **C.** `ls`

❍ **D.** `printenv`

47. Which of the following commands displays disk space occupied by mounted file systems?

❍ **A.** `df`

❍ **B.** `du`

❍ **C.** `ls`

❍ **D.** `printenv`

48. Which of the following causes high fragmentation?

❍ **A.** Creating large numbers of small files

❍ **B.** Creating large numbers of large files

❍ **C.** Not enough disk space

❍ **D.** A file's disk blocks being inefficiently scattered across the whole file system

49. Output from `df -k` does *not* contain which of the following fields?

❍ **A.** Total size in kilobytes

❍ **B.** Fragmentation

❍ **C.** Capacity

❍ **D.** Kilobytes available

50. Which of the following is the recommended way to create a file system?

❍ A. `mkfs`

❍ B. `format`

❍ C. `tunefs`

❍ D. `newfs`

51. Which of the following commands do you use to write or display labels on unmounted disk file systems?

❍ A. `format`

❍ B. `prtvtoc`

❍ C. `newfs`

❍ D. `labelit`

52. Which of the following commands do you issue to determine whether a file system is a UFS?

❍ A. `fstyp`

❍ B. `prtvtoc`

❍ C. `format`

❍ D. `newfs -v`

53. Which of the following commands is used to change the `minfree` value of a file system?

❍ A. `mkfs`

❍ B. `tunefs`

❍ C. `newfs`

❍ D. `format`

54. Which of the following commands do you use to view a full listing of file system parameters?

❍ A. `fstyp`

❍ B. `mkfs`

❍ C. `newfs`

❍ D. `prtvtoc`

55. A large file is a regular file whose size is greater than or equal to which of the following?

❍ **A.** 1TB

❍ **B.** 1GB

❍ **C.** 5GB

❍ **D.** 2GB

56. Which of the following commands is *not* large file–aware?

❍ **A.** `labelit`

❍ **B.** `vi`

❍ **C.** `mkfs`

❍ **D.** `mount`

57. Which of the following types of utility is able to handle large files as input and to generate large files as output?

❍ **A.** Large file–compatible

❍ **B.** Large file–safe

❍ **C.** Large file–aware

❍ **D.** Large file–capable

58. Which of the following options to the `mount` command provides total compatibility with previous file system behavior, enforcing the 2GB maximum file size limit?

❍ **A.** `-o compat`

❍ **B.** `largefiles`

❍ **C.** `-nolargefiles`

❍ **D.** `-o nolargefiles`

59. Which of the following options do you type the `mount` command with to display a list of mounted file systems in `/etc/vfstab` format?

❍ **A.** `-p`

❍ **B.** `-v`

❍ **C.** `-f`

❍ **D.** `-a`

60. Which of the following examples uses the `mount` command to map a directory to a file system as read/writeable, disallow `setuid` execution, and enable the creation of large files:

- ❍ **A.** `mount -o rw,nosuid,large /dev/dsk/c0t0d0s0 /home2`
- ❍ **B.** `mount -o rw,nosuid,largefiles /dev/dsk/c0t0d0s0 /home2`
- ❍ **C.** `mount -o rw,nosuid,largefiles /dev/rdsk/c0t0d0s0 /home2`
- ❍ **D.** `mount -o rw,suid,largefiles /dev/dsk/c0t0d0s0 /home2`

61. When a file system is mounted, where are entries maintained?

- ❍ **A.** `/etc/mnttab`
- ❍ **B.** `/etc/vfstab`
- ❍ **C.** `/etc/fstab`
- ❍ **D.** `/mnt`

62. Which of the following tasks can be performed on a mounted file system?

- ❍ **A.** `labelit`
- ❍ **B.** `fsck`
- ❍ **C.** `tunefs`
- ❍ **D.** `newfs`

63. If something is causing the file system to be busy, which of the following commands can you use to list all the processes accessing the file system?

- ❍ **A.** `fuser`
- ❍ **B.** `mount`
- ❍ **C.** `ps`
- ❍ **D.** `finger`

64. Which of the following commands stops all processes that are using the `/home2` file system?

- ❍ **A.** `fuser -c -k /home2`
- ❍ **B.** `fuser -k /home2`
- ❍ **C.** `kill -9 /home2`
- ❍ **D.** `umount /home2`

65. Which of the following is the mechanism that manages removable media, such as the CD-ROM and floppy disk drives?

- ❍ **A.** `autofs`
- ❍ **B.** NFS
- ❍ **C.** `vold`
- ❍ **D.** `init`

66. **`vold`** does all of the following except for what?

- ❍ **A.** Gives other systems on the network automatic access to any disks and CDs the users insert into your system
- ❍ **B.** Automatically mounts disks and CDs
- ❍ **C.** Enables the user to access disks and CDs without having to be logged in as root
- ❍ **D.** Automatically mounts a file system located on another system when that file system is accessed

67. Which of the following is the directory that provides character device access for the media in the primary floppy drive?

- ❍ **A.** `/vol/dev/diskette0`
- ❍ **B.** `/dev/rdiskette`
- ❍ **C.** `/vol/dev/aliases/floppy0`
- ❍ **D.** `/floppy/floppy0`

68. Which of the following contains the volume management configuration information used by `vold`?

- ❍ **A.** `/etc/init.d/volmgt`
- ❍ **B.** `/etc/vfstab`
- ❍ **C.** `/etc/vold.conf`
- ❍ **D.** `/etc/inittab`

69. Which of the following files can the system administrator modify to specify the program that should be called if media events happen, such as eject or insert?

- ❍ **A.** `/etc/vold.conf`
- ❍ **B.** `/etc/rmmount.conf`
- ❍ **C.** `/etc/inittab`
- ❍ **D.** `/etc/mnttab`

70. Which of the following actions notifies the user if an attempt is made to access a CD or disk that is no longer in the drive?

❍ A. `vold`

❍ B. `volcheck`

❍ C. `volmissing`

❍ D. `rmmount`

71. Which of the following commands is used to format a floppy disk and add a volume label?

❍ A. `format -d`

❍ B. `labelit`

❍ C. `format`

❍ D. `fdformat`

72. Which of the following should you issue to stop the volume management daemon?

❍ A. `svcadm stop svc:/system/filesystem/volfs:default`

❍ B. `/etc/init.d/volmgt stop`

❍ C. `ps -ef¦grep vold, then kill the process ID for vold`

❍ D. `svcadm disable volfs`

73. Which of the following commands displays capacity information on each mounted file system?

❍ A. `du`

❍ B. `format`

❍ C. `prtvtoc`

❍ D. `df`

74. Which of the following commands is used to instruct the system to mount the floppy automatically?

❍ A. `volcheck`

❍ B. `vold`

❍ C. `mount`

❍ D. `automount`

75. You can type `mount /opt` on the command line and not get an error message if which of the following conditions exits?

❍ **A.** `/opt` is listed in the `/etc/rmtab`.

❍ **B.** `/opt` is listed in the `/etc/mnttab`.

❍ **C.** `/opt` is listed in the `/etc/vfstab`.

❍ **D.** `/opt` is listed in the `/etc/dfs/dfstab`.

76. Volume Manager provides access to the CD-ROM and floppy devices through which of the following directories?

❍ **A.** `/vol/dev`

❍ **B.** `/dev/vol`

❍ **C.** `/dev`

❍ **D.** `/vold`

77. Which of the following is *not* true about volume management?

❍ **A.** Volume Manager is started via the `/etc/init.d/volmgt` script.

❍ **B.** Volume Manager automatically mounts CDs and floppy disks.

❍ **C.** Volume Manager reads the `/etc/vold.conf` configuration file at startup.

❍ **D.** Volume Manager automatically checks and performs an `fsck` on file systems at bootup.

❍ **E.** Volume Manager is started via the `svcadm enable volfs` command.

78. Which directory contains configuration files used to define a machine's identity?

❍ **A.** `/dev`

❍ **B.** `/usr`

❍ **C.** `/etc`

❍ **D.** `/opt`

❍ **E.** `/var`

79. Which type of link cannot span file systems?

❍ **A.** Symbolic link

❍ **B.** Hard link

❍ **C.** Hardware link

❍ **D.** Software link

80. Which type of link can point to a file that does not exist?

- ❍ **A.** Symbolic link
- ❍ **B.** Hard link
- ❍ **C.** Hardware link
- ❍ **D.** Software link

81. You can remove a link using which of the following commands?

- ❍ **A.** `rm`
- ❍ **B.** `rmdir`
- ❍ **C.** `rm -l`
- ❍ **D.** `rmlink`

82. Which task cannot be performed by the SMC Disks Tool?

- ❍ **A.** View partition information.
- ❍ **B.** Format a disk.
- ❍ **C.** Partition a disk.
- ❍ **D.** Copy one disk's partition scheme to another disk.

Answers to Review Questions

1. **A.** The instance name represents the kernel's abbreviation name for every possible device on the system. For more information, see the "Device Drivers" section.
2. **D.** Physical device files are found in the `/devices` directory. For more information, see the "Physical Device Name" section.
3. **D.** The `sysdef` command displays device configuration information, including system hardware, pseudo devices, loadable modules, and selected kernel parameters. For more information, see the "Physical Device Name" section.
4. **C.** When you see the `driver not attached` message, it means no driver is currently attached to the device instance because there is no device at this node or the device is not in use. For more information, see the "Physical Device Name" section.
5. **A.** The .conf files reside in the `/kernel/drv` directories. For more information, see the "Device Autoconfiguration" section.
6. **B.** Instance names are mapped to a physical device name in the /etc/path_to_inst file. For more

information, see the "Instance Names" section.

7. **A, B.** You can determine the mapping of an instance name to a physical device name by looking at the `dmesg` output and by viewing the `/var/adm/messages` file. For more information, see the "Instance Names" section.

8. **A, B.** The system relies on information found in both the `/etc/vfstab` file and the `/etc/path_to_inst` file to find the root, usr, and swap device. For more information, see the "Instance Names" section.

9. **C.** The `devfsadm` command a creates logical links to device nodes in /dev and `/devices` and loads the device policy. For more information, see the "Instance Names" section.

10. **D.** The `devfsadm` command is used to inform the system about newly installed device drivers. For more information, see the "Instance Names" section.

11. **A.** The `devfsadmd` daemon is the daemon responsible for handling both reconfiguration boot processing and updating `/dev` and /devices in response to dynamic reconfiguration event notifications from the kernel. For more information, see the "Instance Names" section.

12. **C.** An example of when to use the `devfsadm` command would be if the system has been started, but the power to the CD-ROM or tape drive was not turned on. During startup, the system did not detect the device; therefore, its drivers were not installed. The `devfsadm` command will perform these tasks. For more information, see the "Instance Names" section.

13. **B.** The major device number indicates the general device driver for devices such as disk, tape, or serial line. For more information, see the "Major and Minor Device Numbers" section.

14. **B.** The minor device number indicates the specific member within a driver. For more information, see the "Major and Minor Device Numbers" section.

15. **D.** The logical device name is a link from the `/dev` directory to the physical device name located in the `/devices` directory. For more information, see the "Logical Device Name" section.

16. **C.** The logical device name is a link from the `/dev` directory to the physical device name located in the `/devices` directory. For more information, see the "Logical Device Name" section.

17. **A.** The logical device name is a link from the `/dev` directory to the physical device name located in the `/devices` directory. The following is an example of a logical device name: `/dev/dsk/c0t0d0s7`. For more information, see the "Logical Device Name" section.

18. **A.** The `devfsadm` command can be used to create entries in the `/dev` directory for disk drives attached to the system. For more information, see the "Instance Names" section.

19. **D.** The `/dev/dsk` directory contains the disk entries for the block device nodes in `/devices`. For more information, see the "Block and Raw Devices" section.

20. **A.** A physical device name represents the full device pathname of the device. Physical device files are found in the `/devices` directory and have the following naming convention:

```
/devices/sbus@1,f8000000/esp@0,40000/sd@3,0:a
```

For more information, see the "Physical Device Name" section.

21. **B.** The fields of the logical device name cXtYdZ are as follows:

    - `cX`—Refers to the SCSI controller number
    - `tY`—Refers to the SCSI bus target number
    - `dZ`—Refers to the disk number (always 0, except on storage arrays)

    For more information, see the "Logical Device Name" section.

22. **B.** In the character device name `/dev/rdsk/c0t3d0s0`, the `/rdsk` directory refers to the character or raw device file. The *r* in *rdsk* stands for *raw*. For more information, see the "Block and Raw Devices" section.

23. **A.** The instance name represents the kernel's abbreviated name for every possible device on the system. For example, `sd0` and `sd1` represent the instance names of two SCSI disk devices. For more information, see the "Instance Names" section.

24. **A.** Logical device names are used with most Solaris file system commands to refer to devices. Logical device files in the `/dev` directory are symbolically linked to physical device files in the `/devices` directory. For more information, see the "Logical Device Name" section.

25. **A.** Logical device files in the `/dev` directory are symbolically linked to physical device files in the `/devices` directory. For more information, see the "Logical Device Name" section.

26. **D.** On a standard Solaris file system, a file system cannot span multiple disks or slices. It's only possible when using virtual file systems (that is, Solaris Volume Manager). For more information, see the "Disk Slices" section.

27. **A.** Disk configuration information is stored on the disk label. For more information, see the "Displaying Disk Configuration Information" section.

28. **A.** The boot block stores the procedures used in booting the system. Without a boot block, the system does not boot. For more information, see the "Components of the UFS" section.

29. **A.** The slice information for a particular disk can be viewed by using the `prtvtoc` command. For more information, see the "Disk Slices" section.

30. **A.** The following are virtual file systems: `swapfs`, `procfs`, `lofs`, `cachefs`, `tmpfs`, and `mntfs`. For more information, see the "Virtual File Systems" section.

31. **D.** The `format` utility is used to retrieve corrupted disk labels, repair defective sectors, format and analyze disks, partition disks, and label disks. For more information, see the "Using the `format` Utility to Create Slices" section.

32. **D.** Here are a few of the more important things contained in a superblock:

    - Size and status of the file system
    - Label (file system name and volume name)
    - Size of the file system's logical block
    - Date and time of the last update
    - Cylinder group size
    - Number of data blocks in a cylinder group
    - Summary data block
    - File system state (clean, stable, or active)
    - Pathname of the last mount point

    For more information, see the "The Superblock" section.

33. **A, C.** An inode contains all of the information about a file except its name, which is kept in a directory. The inode information is kept in the cylinder information block and contains the following:

    - The type of the file (regular, directory, block special, character special, link, and so on)
    - The mode of the file (the set of read/write/execute permissions)
    - The number of hard links to the file
    - The user id of the file's owner
    - The group id to which the file belongs
    - The number of bytes in the file
    - An array of 15 disk-block addresses
    - The date and time the file was last accessed
    - The date and time the file was last modified
    - The date and time the file was created

    For more information, see the "The inode" section.

34. **D.** As a general rule, a larger logical block size increases efficiency for file systems in which most of the files are large. Use a smaller logical block size for file systems in which most of the files are small. For more information, see the "Logical Block Size" section.

35. **A.** The number of inodes depends on the amount of disk space that is allocated for each inode and the total size of the file system. For more information, see the "inode" section.

36. **A.** The file system fragment size is the smallest allocable unit of disk space, which by default is 1024 bytes. For more information, see the "Information on File Systems" section.

37. **A.** Swap space plus the total amount of physical memory is also referred to as virtual memory. For more information, see the "Virtual File Systems" section.

38. **A, B, C.** `fsck` should be run after a power outage, when a file system is unmounted improperly, or whenever a file system cannot be mounted. For more information, see the "Repairing File Systems" section.

39. **B.** Normally, `fsck` is run noninteractively at bootup to preen the file systems after an abrupt system halt. Preening automatically fixes any basic file system inconsistencies and does not try to repair more serious errors. While preening a file system, `fsck` fixes the inconsistencies it expects from such an abrupt halt. For more serious conditions, the command reports the error and terminates. For more information, see the "Repairing File Systems" section.

40. **C.** The `/etc/vfstab` file contains a list of file systems to be automatically mounted when the system is booted to the multiuser state. For more information, see the "Creating an Entry in the `/etc/vfstab` File to Mount File Systems" section.

41. **B.** The `mountall` command mounts all file systems specified in the file system table (vfstab). For more information, see the "Mounting File Systems" section.

42. **E.** The following commands can be used to display disk space usage: `du`, `df`, `quota`, `repquota`. For more information, see the "Displaying a File System's Disk Space Usage" section.

43. **A.** The `largefiles` mount option lets users mount a file system containing files larger than 2GB. For more information, see the "Mounting File Systems" section.

44. **A.** Use the `-o nologging` option of the `mount` command to disable UFS logging on a file system. Logging is the default. For more information, see the "Mounting File Systems" section.

45. **A.** The correct format for the `/etc/vfstab` file is as follows:

    device to mount, device to fsck, mount point, FS type, fsck pass, mount at boot, mount options.

    For more information, see the "Creating an Entry in the `/etc/vfstab` File to Mount File Systems" section.

46. **A.** Use the `du` (directory usage) command to report the number of free disk blocks and files. For more information, see the "Displaying a File System's Disk Space Usage" section.

47. **A.** The `df` command with no options lists all mounted file systems and their device names. It also lists the total number of 512-byte blocks used and the number of files. For more information, see the "Displaying a File System's Disk Space Usage" section.

48. **A.** Typically, creating large numbers of small files causes high fragmentation. The solution is to either create a larger file system or to decrease the block size (finer granularity). For more information, see the "Displaying a File System's Disk Space Usage" section.

49. **B.** The `df -k` command does not display the percentage of fragmentation. For more information, see the "Displaying a File System's Disk Space Usage" section.

50. **D.** newfs is the friendly front end to the mkfs command. The newfs command automatically determines all the necessary parameters to pass to mkfs to construct new file systems. newfs was added in Solaris to make the creation of new file systems easier. It's highly recommended that the newfs command be used to create file systems. For more information, see the "Creating a UFS" section.

51. **D.** After you create the file system with newfs, you can use the labelit utility to write or display labels on unmounted disk file systems. For more information, see the "Creating a UFS" section.

52. **A.** Use the fstyp command to determine a file system type. For example, use it to check whether a file system is a UFS. For more information, see the "The fstyp Command" section.

53. **B.** Use the tunefs command to change the minfree value of a file system. For more information, see the "Tuning File Systems" section.

54. **A.** Use the fstyp command to view file system parameters. Use the -v option to obtain a full listing of a file system's parameters. For more information, see the "The fstyp Command" section.

55. **D.** A large file is a regular file whose size is greater than or equal to 2GB. For more information, see the "Mounting a File System with Large Files" section.

56. **B.** A utility is called large file–aware if it can process large files in the same manner that it does small files. A large file—aware utility can handle large files as input and can generate large files as output. The vi command is not large file–aware. For more information, see the "Mounting a File System with Large Files" section.

57. **C.** As stated in the previous question and answer, a utility is called large file–aware if it can process large files in the same manner that it does small files. A large file–aware utility can handle large files as input and can generate large files as output. For more information, see the "Mounting a File System with Large Files" section.

58. **D.** The -o nolargefiles option of the mount command provides total compatibility with previous file system behavior, enforcing the 2GB maximum file size limit. For more information, see the "Mounting a File System with Large Files" section.

59. **A.** Type the mount command with the -p option to display a list of mounted file systems in /etc/vfstab format. For more information, see the "Creating an Entry in the /etc/vfstab File to Mount File Systems" section.

60. **B.** The following command uses the mount command to map a directory to a file system as read/writeable, disallow setuid execution, and enable the creation of large files (more than 2GB in size):

    ```
    mount -o rw,nosuid,largefiles /dev/dsk/c0t0d0s0\
    /home2
    ```

    For more information, see the "Mounting a File System with Large Files" section.

61. **A.** When a file system is mounted, an entry is maintained in the mounted file system table called `/etc/mnttab`. This file is actually a read-only file system and contains information about devices that are currently mounted. For more information, see the "Mounting File Systems" section.

62. **C.** Do not use the following commands on a mounted file system: `fsck`, `newfs`, and `labelit`. `newfs` cannot be run on a mounted file system—it generates an error. For more information, see the "Unmounting a File System" section.

63. **A.** If something is causing the file system to be busy, you can use the `fuser` command to list all of the processes accessing the file system and to stop them if necessary. For more information, see the "The `fuser` Command" section.

64. **A.** The following command stops all processes that are using the `/home2` file system by sending a `SIGKILL` to each one: `fuser -c -k /home2`. For more information, see the "The `fuser` Command" section.

65. **C.** The `vold` daemon is the mechanism that manages removable media, such as the CD-ROM and floppy disk drives. For more information, see the "Volume Management" section.

66. **D.** `vold` does not automatically mount a file system located on another system when that file system is accessed. The facility responsible for that task is AutoFS. For more information, see the "Volume Management" section.

67. **B.** `/dev/rdiskette` and `/vol/dev/rdiskette0` are the directories providing character device access for the medium in the primary floppy drive, usually drive 0. For more information, see the "Volume Management" section.

68. **C.** `vold` reads the `/etc/vold.conf` configuration file at startup. The `vold.conf` file contains the Volume Manager configuration information used by `vold`. For more information, see the "Volume Management" section.

69. **A.** The "Actions" section of the `vold.conf` file specifies which program should be called if a particular event (action) occurs such as eject or insert. For more information, see the "Volume Management" section.

70. **C.** The `volmissing` action in the `vold.conf` file notifies the user if an attempt is made to access a CD or diskette that is no longer in the drive. For more information, see the "Volume Management" section.

71. **D.** Use the `fdformat` command to format a floppy disk, and then add a volume label. For more information, see the "Troubleshooting Volume Manager" section.

72. **B, D.** You can run the following run control script to stop the volume management daemon: `/etc/init.d/volmgt stop`. Or, stop the daemon using: `svcadm disable volfs`. For more information, see the "Troubleshooting Volume Manager" section.

73. **D.** The `df` command gives you capacity information on each mounted file system. For more information, see the "Displaying a File System's Disk Space Usage" section.

74. **A.** The `volcheck` command instructs `vold` to look at each device and determine if new media has been inserted into the drive. The system administrator issues this command to check the drive for installed media. By default, it checks the drive to which `/dev/diskette` points. For more information, see the "Volume Management" section.

75. **C.** You can type `mount /opt` on the command line and not get an error message if `/opt` is listed in the `/etc/vfstab` file. For more information, see the "Creating an Entry in the `/etc/vfstab` File to Mount File Systems" section.

76. **A.** Volume Manager provides access to the floppy disk and CD-ROM devices through the `/vol/dev` directory. For more information, see the "Volume Management" section.

77. **D.** Volume management does not automatically `fsck` file systems at bootup. It does, however, automatically mount CD-ROM and file systems when removable media containing recognizable file systems are inserted into the devices. For more information, see the "Volume Management" section.

78. **C.** The `/etc` directory contains configuration files that define a system's identity. For more information, see the "The Root (/) File System" section.

79. **B.** A hard link cannot span file systems, but a symbolic link can. For more information, see the "Hard Links" section.

80. **A.** An advantage of a symbolic link over a hard link is that you can create a symbolic link to a file that does not yet exist. For more information, see the "Soft (Symbolic) Links" section.

81. **A.** Remove a link using the `rm` command. For more information, see the "Soft (Symbolic) Links" section.

82. **B.** The SMC Disks Tool cannot be used to format a disk. For more information, see the "Using the Solaris Management Console Disks Tool" section.

Suggested Readings and Resources

- Calkins, Bill. *Inside Solaris 9*. New Riders Publishing, 2002.
- *Solaris 10 System Administration Guide: Devices and File Systems*, 2005, Sun Microsystems, Part number 817-5093-11. This manual is available online at `docs.sun.com`.

CHAPTER TWO

Installing the Solaris 10 Operating Environment

Objectives

The following test objectives for exam CX-310-200 are covered in this chapter:

This chapter describes how to install and manage the Solaris 10 operating system software on both the SPARC-based and x86/x64-based platforms.

Explain how to install the Solaris operating system from CD/DVD, including installation and upgrade options, hardware requirements, Solaris operating system software components (software packages, clusters, and groups) on SPARC-based and x86/x64-based systems.

- Many different methods can be used to install the Solaris 10 operating environment (OE). Which method you use depends on whether you are upgrading the operating system from a previous release, installing the operating system from scratch, or installing several systems that are configured exactly the same way. You also need to know if your system meets the minimum hardware requirements for the Solaris 10 OE.

  In addition to installing Solaris on Sun SPARC systems, you must also understand how to install the OS on x86- and x64-based systems.

Perform Solaris 10 OS package administration using command-line interface commands and manage software patches for the Solaris OS, including preparing for patch administration and installing and removing patches using the `patchadd` and `patchrm` commands.

- When installing the operating system, you need to understand how Sun packages their software into packages and groups. You need to understand how to install, list, verify, and remove individual software packages using the command-line interface commands described in this chapter.

  In addition, you need to understand how software updates are distributed via software patches. You need to understand how to obtain, install, list, and remove these patches using the various command-line interface utilities.

Outline

Study Strategies

The following strategies will help you prepare for the exam:

- Understand each of the methods used to install the operating system on both the SPARC and x86/x64 hardware platforms. Primarily, you need to know the difference between each method as well as where and when to use each one. Understand each step of the installation process on both the SPARC and x86/x64 platforms, including how to start the installation process from CD/DVD.
- Know all the hardware requirements for installing the Solaris 10 (version 08/07) operating environment on SPARC and x86/x64-based systems.
- Become familiar with all the tools used to manage software on a Solaris system. Understand which tool is best for a particular circumstance.
- Understand how to patch the operating system. Pay special attention to how to obtain patches, the various methods used to install and remove them, and how to verify patches on your system.
- Practice all the commands presented in this chapter until you can perform them and describe them from memory. In addition, practice installing the Solaris 10 OE and adding/removing software packages no less than three times or until you can perform all the tasks from memory.
- Finally, understand all the terminology and concepts described in this chapter as well as the terms outlined at the end of the chapter. Each term and concept is likely to appear on the exam.

Introduction

The Solaris installation process consists of three phases: system configuration, system installation, and post-installation tasks such as setting up printers, users, and networking. This chapter describes the various system configurations and the installation of the Solaris operating system on standalone SPARC-based and x86/x64-based systems.

After the software is installed, the system administrator is responsible for managing all software installed on a system. Installing and removing software is a routine task that is performed frequently. This chapter explains how to add and remove additional applications after the operating system has been installed.

Installing the Solaris 10 Software

When installing the operating system onto a machine, you'll be performing one of two types of installations: initial or upgrade.

You'll perform an initial installation either on a system that does not have an existing Solaris operating system already installed on it or when you want to completely wipe out the existing operating system and reinstall it.

An upgrade is performed on a system that is already running Solaris 7, Solaris 8, Solaris 9, or a previous release of Solaris 10. An upgrade will save as many modifications as possible from the previous version of Solaris that is currently running on your system.

CAUTION

Upgrading to a new software group You cannot upgrade your system to a software group that is not currently installed on the system. For example, you cannot upgrade to the Developer Solaris Software group if you previously installed the End User Solaris Software group. However, you can add to a system software that is not currently part of the installed software group.

Another option when upgrading your system is to take advantage of the Solaris live upgrade feature, which enables an upgrade to be installed while the operating system is running and can significantly reduce the downtime associated with an upgrade. The process involves creating a duplicate boot environment on an unused disk slice and upgrading the duplicate boot environment. When you're ready to switch and make the upgraded boot environment active, you simply activate it and reboot. The old boot environment remains available as a fallback to the original boot environment and allows you to quickly reactivate and reboot the old environment. This is useful if you need to back out of the upgrade and go back to the previous operating system release.

Regardless of whether you will perform an initial installation or an upgrade, you need to first determine whether your hardware meets the minimum requirements to support the Solaris 10 environment.

Requirements and Preparation for Installing the Solaris 10 Software

The first step in the installation is to determine whether your system type is supported under Solaris 10. Second, you need to decide which system configuration you want to install and whether you have enough disk space to support that configuration.

In preparation for installing Solaris 10 on a system, check whether your system type is supported. Also, make sure you have enough disk space for Solaris and all the packages you plan to install. (The section "Software Terminology" later in this chapter will help you estimate the amount of disk space required to hold the Solaris operating system.)

If your system is running a previous version of Solaris, you can determine your system type using the `uname -m` command. The system responds with the platform group and the platform name for your system. For example, to check for Sun platforms that support the Solaris 10 environment, use the command `uname -m`. On a SunFire, the system returns `sun4u` as the platform name and on an x86/x64-based system, the command returns `i86pc` as the platform name.

> **NOTE**
>
> **OpenBoot commands** To determine the system type on a system that is not currently running some version of Solaris, you need to use the OpenBoot commands described in the next chapter.

For a complete, up-to-date listing of all hardware that is compatible with the Solaris 10 OE, including all x86/x64-based systems, go to http://www.sun.com/bigadmin/hcl/. This site features a searchable database to quickly locate equipment in three categories: Sun Certified, Test Suite Certified, and Reported to Work. x86- and x64-based systems are available from many vendors, and the components can vary from system to system. Use this site to track down the specific components that are installed in your system to determine if it is compatible with Solaris 10. Overall, your x86/x64-based system needs to have a 120MHz or faster processor with hardware floating-point support required, a minimum of 512MB of RAM, and 6.8GB of disk space.

Check slice 2 by using the `format` command to determine whether your disk drive is large enough to hold Solaris. See Chapter 1, "Managing File Systems," for the correct use of this command. As described in Chapter 1, slice 2 represents the entire disk.

Minimum System Requirements

The computer must meet the following requirements before you can install Solaris 10 using the interactive installation method. The requirements for a SPARC system are different from those for the x86/x64 platform:

- A SPARC system must have a minimum of 256MB of physical memory for a CLI installation and 512MB for a graphical-based installation. Sun recommends 512MB and a minimum of 256MB.
- An x86/x64-based system must have a minimum of 384MB of physical memory for a CLI installation and 512MB for a graphical-based installation. 512MB is recommended.

CAUTION

Minimum memory requirements Although Sun provides minimum memory requirements, it is possible to install Solaris 10 on a system that has less RAM. Even with the minimum recommended RAM, the system runs sluggishly; more RAM typically is required to run your specific applications. It's important that you use Sun's RAM recommendations when you encounter this question on the exam. Also, pay close attention to the question, and understand the difference between "minimum" and "recommended."

- A SPARC system must have a 200MHz or faster processor, and an x86/x64-based system must have a 120MHz or faster processor.
- The media is distributed on CD-ROM and DVD only, so a bootable CD-ROM or DVD-ROM drive is required either locally or on the network. You can use all the Solaris installation methods to install the system from a networked CD-ROM or DVD-ROM. For the examples in this book, I will use the DVD.
- A minimum of 5GB of disk space is required for both SPARC- and x86-based platforms. See the next section for disk space requirements for the specific Solaris software you plan to install. Also, remember to add disk space to support your environment's swap space requirements.
- When upgrading the operating system, you must have an empty 512MB slice on the disk. The swap slice is preferred, but you can use any slice that will not be used in the upgrade, such as root (`/`), `/var`, and `/opt`.
- The system must be a SPARC-based or supported x86/x64-based system.

Software Terminology

The operating system is bundled in packages on the distribution media. Packages are arranged into software groups. The following sections describe the Solaris bundling scheme.

Software Packages

A *software package* is a collection of files and directories in a defined format. It describes a software application, such as manual pages and line printer support. The Solaris 10 entire distribution contains approximately 900 software packages that require 6.8GB of disk space.

A Solaris software package is the standard way to deliver bundled and unbundled software. Packages are administered by using the package administration commands, and they are generally identified by a SUNW*xxx* naming convention when supplied by Sun Microsystems. SUNW is Sun Microsystems's ticker symbol on the stock exchange, hence the SUNW prefix.

Software Groups

Software packages are grouped into *software groups*, which are logical collections of software packages. Sometimes these groups are referred to as clusters. For example, the online manual pages software group contains one package. Some software groups contain multiple packages, such as the CDE software cluster, which contains the CDE man pages, CDE desktop applications, CDE daemons, and so on.

For SPARC systems, software groups are grouped into seven configuration groups to make the software installation process easier. During the installation process, you will be asked to install one of the seven configuration groups. These seven configuration groups are minimal core metacluster, reduced networking support, core system support, end-user support, developer Solaris, entire Solaris software, and entire Solaris software plus OEM system support.

To view the names of cluster configurations on your system, look at the `/var/sadm/system/admin/.clustertoc` file using the following command:

```
# grep METACLUSTER /var/sadm/system/admin/.clustertoc <cr>
```

The following list describes each software group.

EXAM ALERT

Package name Be sure you know the package name for each software group. Most exam questions will refer to the software group by the package name (such as SUNWCmreq), not the description.

- **Minimal core metacluster (SUNWCmreq)**: The metacluster is hidden. It allows you to create a minimal core metacluster by deselecting packages from the core metacluster. Therefore, the disk requirements depend on which packages have been selected.
- **Reduced networking support (SUNWCrnet)**: Sun recommends 2GB to support the software, swap, and disk overhead required to support this software group. This group contains the minimum software that is required to boot and run a Solaris system with limited network service support. The Reduced Networking software group provides a multi-user text-based console and system administration utilities. This software group also enables the system to recognize network interfaces, but does not activate network services. A system installed with the Reduced Networking software group could, for example, be used as a thin-client host in a network.
- **Core system support (SUNWcreq)**: Sun recommends 2GB to support the software, swap, and disk overhead required to support this software group. This software group contains the minimum software required to boot and run Solaris on a system. It includes some networking software and the drivers required to run the OpenWindows (OW) environment, but it does not include the OpenWindows software.
- **End-user system support (SUNWcuser)**: Sun recommends 5.3GB to support the software, swap, and disk overhead required to support this software group. This group contains the core system support software plus end-user software, which includes OW compatibility and the Common Desktop Environment (CDE) software.
- **Developer system support (SUNWcprog)**: Sun recommends 6.6GB to support the software, swap, and disk overhead required to support this cluster. This software group contains the end-user software plus libraries, include files, man pages, and programming tools for developing software. Compilers and debuggers are purchased separately and are not included. However, you can use the open source GCC compiler supplied on the Solaris Companion CD.
- **Entire distribution (SUNWCall)**: Sun recommends 6.7GB to support the software, swap, and disk overhead required to support this software group. This software group contains the entire Solaris 10 release, which includes additional software needed for servers.
- **Entire distribution plus OEM system support (SUNWCXall)**: Sun recommends 6.8GB to support the software, swap, and disk overhead required to support this software group. This software group contains the entire Solaris 10 release software plus extended hardware support for non-Sun SPARC systems.

To determine which cluster configuration has been installed on your system, type

```
# cat /var/sadm/system/admin/CLUSTER <cr>
```

The system displays the following:

```
CLUSTER=SUNWCXall
```

NOTE

Recommended space requirements Swap space and necessary file system overhead is included in the disk space recommendations for each software group. A minimum of 512MB is required for swap space, but more space might be needed.

In addition, as new releases of Solaris 10 are made available, the size of these software groups might change. The requirements in this book are based on the 08/07 release of Solaris 10.

Solaris Media

The Solaris 10 operating system software is distributed on a DVD or CD-ROM set called "the installation media kit," and contains the following

- **Solaris 10 OS Software 1**: The only bootable CD. From this CD, you can access both the Solaris OS installation graphical user interface (GUI) and the CLI-based installation.
- **Solaris 10 OS Software 2**: This CD contains additional Solaris OS packages that the software prompts you to install if necessary.
- **Solaris 10 OS Software 3**: This CD contains additional Solaris OS packages that the software prompts you to install if necessary.
- **Solaris 10 OS Software 4**: This CD contains additional Solaris OS packages and ExtraValue software that the software prompts you to install if necessary.
- **Solaris 10 OS Languages CD**: This CD contains translated message files and other software in languages other than English.

The single DVD contains the contents of the entire CD set and is bootable.

If you've used previous versions of Solaris, the Supplemental CD and Installation CD are no longer supplied.

System Configuration to Be Installed

Before installing the operating system, you need to determine the system configuration to be installed. The configurations are defined by the way they access the root (/)file system and the swap area. The system configurations are as follows:

- Server
- Standalone

Each of these system configurations are discussed in the following sections.

Servers

A *server* is a system that provides services or file systems, such as home directories or mailboxes, to other systems on the network. An operating system server is a server that provides the Solaris software to other systems on the network.

There are file servers, startup servers, database servers, license servers, print servers, mail servers, web servers, installation servers, NFS servers, and even servers for particular applications. Each type of server has a different set of requirements based on the function it serves. For example, a database server will be disk- and memory-intensive, but it probably will not have many logged-in users. Therefore, when this system is configured, special thought needs to be put into setting up the file systems and fine tuning kernel parameters that relate to disk I/O and memory usage to optimize system performance.

A server system typically has the following file systems installed locally:

- The root (`/`) file system plus swap space
- The `/var` file system, which supports the print spooler, mail repository, and software spooler, and stores crash dumps, log files, and backups of software patches
- The `/export`, `/export/swap`, and `/export/home` file systems, which support client systems and provide home directories for users
- The `/opt` directory or file system for storing application software

Servers can also contain the following software to support other systems:

- Solaris CD-ROM or DVD image and boot software for networked systems to perform remote installations
- A JumpStart directory for networked systems to perform custom JumpStart installations

The server must meet a few minimum requirements before Solaris 10 can be installed:

- The Solaris 10 release supports all `sun4u`, `sun4us`, and `sun4v` platforms.
- To run a graphical user interface (GUI) installation, the system must have a minimum of 512MB of RAM. As a server, however, it is typical to have 1GB of RAM or more.
- The disk needs to be large enough to hold the Solaris operating system, swap space, and additional software. Plan on a minimum of 9GB of disk space, but realistically the server should have 18GB to 36GB or more, depending on the resources that this server will provide.

Clients

A *client* is a system that uses remote services from a server. Some clients have limited disk storage capacity or perhaps none at all, so they must rely on remote file systems from a server to function.

Other clients might use remote services (such as installation software) from a server, but they don't rely on a server to function. A standalone system, which has its own hard disk containing the root (`/`), `/usr`, and `/export/home` file systems and swap space, is a good example of this type of client.

Standalone Systems

On a standalone system, the operating system is loaded on a local disk, and the system is set to run independently of other systems. The operating system might be networked to other standalone systems. A networked standalone system can share information with other systems on the network, but it can function autonomously because it has its own hard disk with enough space to contain the root (`/`), `/var`, and `/export/home` file systems and swap space. The standalone system has local access to operating system software, executables, virtual memory space, and user-created files. Sometimes the standalone system accesses the server for data or accesses a CD-ROM, DVD-ROM, or tape drive from a server if one is not available locally.

Disk Storage

Before you begin to install a system, you need to think about how you want data stored on your system's disks. With one disk, the decision is easy. When multiple disks are installed, you must decide which disks to use for the operating system, the swap area, and the user data.

As described in Chapter 1, Solaris breaks disks into pieces called *partitions*, or *slices*. A Solaris disk can be divided into a maximum of seven slices.

Why would you want to divide the disk into multiple slices? Some administrators don't; they use the entire disk with one slice. By using one slice, all the space on the disk is available for anyone to use. When the system administrator creates a slice, the space in that slice is available only to the file system that is mounted on it. If another file system on the same disk runs out of space, it cannot borrow space from the other slice without repartitioning the disk. However, having multiple slices can provide some advantages. The following list describes some of the reasons why you might want to consider partitioning disks into multiple slices:

- Slices allow finer control over tasks such as creating backups. UNIX commands such as `ufsdump` work on entire file systems. For backups, you might want to separate data and swap space from the application software so that backups are completed faster with a `ufsdump`. For example, you might want to back up only data on a daily basis. On the other hand, you need to take the system down to single-user mode to back up `/`, so separating the data makes your backup finish much more quickly and results in less downtime.

- If one file system becomes corrupted, the others remain intact. If you need to perform a recovery operation, you can restore a smaller file system more quickly. Also, when data is separated from system software, you can modify file systems without shutting down the system or reloading operating system software.
- Slices allow you to control the amount of disk storage allocated to an activity or type of use. For example, `/var` can grow rapidly because it stores mail, log files, crash dumps and patch backups. To keep `/var` from filling up the root (`/`) file system, we typically create a slice specifically for the `/var` file system.
- If file systems are mounted remotely from other systems, you can share only the data that needs to be accessed, not the entire system disk.

The installation process gives you the option of creating slices. Start with the default partition scheme supplied with the installation program, which is to set up a file system for root (`/`) and swap. This scheme sets up the required slices and provides you with the sizes required, based on the software group you select to install. The following is a typical partitioning scheme for a system with a single disk drive:

- **root (`/`)**: Solaris creates the root (`/`) slice by default. The `auto_layout` function of the installation program determines how much space you need in root (`/`). Most of the files in these two slices are static. Information in these file systems does not increase in size unless you add software packages later. If you plan to add third-party software after the installation of Solaris, make sure you increase the root (`/`)slice to accommodate the additional files you plan to load. If the root (`/`) file system fills up, the system will not operate properly.
- **Swap**: This area on the disk doesn't have files in it. In UNIX, you're allowed to have more programs than will fit into memory. The pieces that aren't currently needed in memory are transferred into swap to free up physical memory for other active processes. Swapping into a dedicated slice is a good idea for two reasons: Swap slices are isolated so that they aren't put on tape with the daily backups, and a swap slice can be laid out on a disk in an area to optimize performance.
- **`/export/home`**: On a single-disk system, everything not in root (`/`), `/var`, or swap should go into a separate slice. `/export/home` is where you would put user-created files.
- **`/var` (optional)**: Solaris uses this area for system log files, print spoolers, crash dumps, patch backups and email. The name `/var` is short for variable; this file system contains system files that are not static but are variable in size. One day the print spooler direc-

tory might be empty; another day it might contain several large files. This separate file system is created to keep the root (`/`)file system from filling up with these files. If the `/var` file system does not exist, make sure you make root (`/`) larger.

- **`/opt` (optional)**: By default, the Solaris installation program loads optional software packages here. Also, third-party applications are usually loaded into `/opt`. If this file system does not exist, the installation program puts the optional software in the root file system. If the `/opt` file system does not exist, make sure you make root (`/`) larger.

File systems provide a way to segregate data, but when a file system runs out of space, you can't "borrow" from a file system that has some unused space. Therefore, the best plan is to create a minimal number of file systems with adequate space for expansion. This concept is discussed in Chapter 1, and the ability to make file systems larger is described in *Solaris 10 System Administration Exam Prep: Exam CX-310-202*.

Basic Considerations for Planning Partition (Slice) Sizes

Planning disk and partition space depends on many factors: the number of users, the application requirements, and the number and size of files and databases. The following are some basic considerations for determining your disk space requirements:

- Allocate additional disk space for each language selected (for example, Chinese, Japanese, and Korean).
- If you need printing or mail support, create a slice for a separate `/var` file system and allocate additional disk space. You need to estimate the number and size of email messages and print files to size this slice properly. In addition to this space, if you intend to use the crash dump feature `savecore`, allocate additional space in `/var` equal to twice the amount of physical memory.
- Allocate additional disk space on a server that will provide home file systems for users. Again, the number of users and the size of their files dictate the size of this file system. By default, home directories are usually located in the `/export` file system.
- Allocate additional disk space on an operating system server for JumpStart clients if this server will be used as a JumpStart installation server.
- Make sure you allocate enough swap space. The minimum size for the swap slice is 512MB. Factors that dictate the amount of swap space are the concurrent number of users and the application requirements. Consult with your application vendor for swap-space requirements. Vendors usually give you a formula to determine the amount of swap space you need for each application. In addition, the swap slice will be used for

core dumps and should contain enough space to hold a complete core dump—that is, exceed the size of the installed RAM.

NOTE

Sizing the swap area In the past, system administrators sized their swap based on the amount of RAM installed in their system. A simple rule of "set your minimum swap space at two times the amount of physical memory" was used. With newer systems now containing several gigabytes of RAM, this rule is no longer relevant.

- Determine the software packages you will install, and calculate the total amount of disk space required. When planning disk space, remember that the Solaris Interactive Installation program lets you add or remove individual software packages from the software group that you select.
- Create a minimum number of file systems. By default, the Solaris Interactive Installation program creates file systems for only root (`/`) and swap, although `/export` is also created when space is allocated for operating system services. Creating a minimum number of file systems helps with future upgrades and file system expansion because separate file systems are limited by their slice boundaries. Be generous with the size of your file systems, especially root (`/`) and `/usr`. Even when using logical volumes, these file systems cannot be increased without completely reloading the operating system.
- For each file system you create, allocate an additional 30% more disk space than you need to allow for future Solaris upgrades. This is because each new Solaris release needs approximately 10% more disk space than the previous release. By allocating an additional 30% more space for each file system, you allow for several Solaris upgrades before you need to repartition your system disk.
- Calculate additional disk space for copackaged or third-party software.
- If you will be using Solaris Volume Manager (SVM), you need to allocate an empty slice for the `metadb` replicas. Refer to *Solaris 10 System Administration Exam Prep: Exam CX-310-202* for more information on SVM.

Slice Arrangements on Multiple Disks

Although a single large disk can hold all slices and their corresponding file systems, two or more disks are often used to hold a system's slices and file systems.

> **NOTE**
>
> **Conventional file systems** Using conventional Solaris file systems, you cannot split a slice between two or more disks. Solaris Volume Manager and ZFS, which are described in *Solaris 10 System Administration Exam Prep: Exam CX-310-202*, allow us to overcome this limitation. For this chapter, however, I'll describe the use of conventional file systems.

For example, a single disk might hold the root (`/`) file system, a swap area, and the `/var` file system, and a second disk might be used for the `/export/home` file system and other file systems containing user data. In a multiple-disk arrangement, the disk containing the root (`/`) file system and swap space is referred to as the *system disk* or *boot disk*. Disks other than the system disk are called *secondary disks* or *nonsystem disks*.

Locating a system's file systems on multiple disks allows you to modify file systems and slices on the secondary disks without shutting down the system or reloading the operating system software. Also, using multiple disks allows you to distribute the workload as evenly as possible among different I/O systems and disk drives, such as distributing the `/home` and swap slices evenly across disks.

Having more than one disk increases input/output (I/O) volume. By distributing the I/O load across multiple disks, you can avoid I/O bottlenecks.

> **NOTE**
>
> **Improving system performance with multiple swap slices** A good way to improve system performance is to create more than one swap slice and assign each one to a separate disk drive. When the system needs to access swap, the disk I/O is spread evenly across the multiple disk drives.

Methods of Installing the Solaris 10 Software

Two methods are available for installing Solaris 10 on your system: `install-solaris` and Flash Archive installation.

- With `install-solaris`, the following installation procedures can be used:
    - Solaris installation Graphical User Interface (GUI)
    - Solaris installation Command-Line Interpreter (CLI)
    - Solaris Custom JumpStart software (JumpStart) installation
    - Solaris Upgrades

- With Flash Archive, the following installation procedures can be used:
  - Solaris Flash Archive installation
  - Solaris WAN boot installation

Each of these is discussed in the following sections.

Solaris Interactive Installation: Using the GUI

The default installation method uses a GUI if the host has sufficient memory and the display can display graphics. Otherwise, the installation aborts the GUI and uses the CLI.

The following minimum requirements determine if the system has sufficient RAM to run the GUI-based installation:

- **SPARC**: 128MB minimum physical memory for all installation types. 512MB minimum physical memory is required to run a GUI-based installation.
- **X86/x64**: 256MB minimum physical memory for all installation types. 512MB minimum physical memory is required to run a GUI-based installation.

Solaris Interactive Installation: Using the CLI

Hosts that do not have a graphical display or that have insufficient physical memory cannot run the GUI-based installation and use the CLI-based installation. On SPARC systems, you can also force a CLI-based installation by typing the following at the OpenBoot PROM:

```
# boot cdrom - nowin <cr>
```

On x86/x64-based systems, selecting the Solaris Interactive Text (Console session) option when booting to the CD or DVD causes the installation software to use the CLI on the system console. Choosing the Solaris Interactive Text (Desktop session) option causes the installation software to use the CLI in a terminal window within the Common Desktop Environment (CDE).

The Solaris Interactive Installation program, `install-solaris`, guides you step by step through installing the Solaris software. You'll be allowed to do a complete installation/reinstallation, perform an upgrade, or install a Solaris Flash archive. I like to refer to this installation as the conventional interactive installation. If you've installed previous versions of Solaris, this is the original interactive installation. With this installation, you need to know more about Solaris and other software products before installing them. The Interactive program does not allow you to install all the software (Solaris software and copackaged software) at once; it installs only the SunOS software. After you install the Solaris software, you must install the other copackaged software by using the copackaged installation programs.

> **NOTE**
>
> **`install-solaris` instead of `suninstall`** `install-solaris` is now the preferred command for starting and restarting the Solaris Installation program. You should use it instead of `suninstall`. `suninstall` is symbolically linked to `install-solaris`.

If your system does not have a directly attached CD-ROM or DVD-ROM drive, you can specify a drive that is attached to another system. The only requirement is that both systems must be attached to the same subnet.

JumpStart

JumpStart lets you install Solaris on a new system by inserting the DVD into the DVD drive and turning on power to the system. No interaction is required. The software components installed are specified by a default profile that is selected based on the model and disk size of the system.

All new SPARC-based systems have the JumpStart software (a preinstalled boot image) preinstalled on the boot disk. You can install the JumpStart software on existing systems by using the `re-preinstall` command.

Custom JumpStart

The Custom JumpStart method, formerly called autoinstall, allows you to automatically—and identically—install many systems with the same configuration without having to configure each of them individually. Custom JumpStart requires upfront setup of configuration files before the systems can be installed, but it's the most cost effective way to automatically install Solaris software for a large installation. Custom JumpStart provides the best solution for performing hands-off installation across the network.

> **NOTE**
>
> **JumpStart configuration on new systems** On a new system, the installation software is specified by a default profile based on the system's model and the size of its disks; you don't have a choice of the software to be installed. Make sure this JumpStart configuration is suited to your environment. The system loads the end-user distribution group and sets up minimal swap space. Slices and their sizes are set up by using default parameters that might not be suitable for the applications you plan to install.

When might you want to use JumpStart? For example, suppose you need to install the Solaris software on 50 systems. Of these 50 systems to be installed, 25 are in engineering as standalone systems with the entire distribution software group, and 25 are in the IT group with the developer distribution software group. JumpStart enables you to set up a configuration file for each department and install the operating system on all the systems. This process facilitates the installation by automating it, ensuring consistency between systems and saving you time and effort.

On a SPARC system, you initiate a custom JumpStart installation by typing the following command at the OpenBoot PROM:

```
# boot net - install <cr>
```

On an x86/x64-based system, you initiate a custom JumpStart installation by holding down the F12 key during the initial power-on sequence. This causes the system to initiate the Intel Preboot Execution Environment (PXE) installation process, which requires a server to respond to DHCP and other requests made by the x86/x64 system.

On both the SPARC- and x86/x64-based systems, no boot medium is required on the client system.

EXAM ALERT

JumpStart exam objective Custom JumpStart is an objective on the CX-310-202 exam and is described in detail in *Solaris 10 System Administration Exam Prep: Exam CX-310-202*. However, there are a couple of basic questions about Custom JumpStart on the CX-310-200 exam you need to know:

- Why would you use JumpStart over another type of installation, such as Web Start Flash or interactive?
- Which installation method is designed to allow hands-off installation across the network?
- How do you initiate a custom JumpStart installation?

Solaris Live Upgrade

Solaris Live Upgrade allows you to create a copy of the current operating environment and upgrade the copy while the system is running in the original environment. Solaris Live Upgrade utilizes Solaris Volume Manager (SVM) to create a mirror of the OS. When it is finished, you'll reboot to the upgraded version of the OS. If problems are encountered with the upgrade, you can boot back to the previous version, significantly reducing any downtime. For example, let's say that you are upgrading the OS using the Upgrade option in the interactive installation. If the power failed halfway through the upgrade and the system was powered off, your operating system would be incomplete and you would be unable to boot. Using Live Upgrade, because you're upgrading a copy of the OS, you simply boot to the original version of the OS and start over.

To perform a live upgrade, the SUNWlur and SUNWluu software packages must be installed. The packages are installed with the entire distribution software group in Solaris 10; however, the system you are upgrading is probably running an older version of the OS. Therefore, you need to install the Solaris 10 Live Upgrade packages on your current OS. The release of the Solaris Live Upgrade packages must match the release of the OS you are upgrading to. For example, if your current OS is the Solaris 8 release and you want to upgrade to the Solaris 10 release, you need to install the Solaris Live Upgrade packages from the Solaris 10 release. Solaris versions 7, 8, 9, or 10 can be upgraded to the most recent version of Solaris 10 using Live Upgrade.

CAUTION

Live upgrade Performing a live upgrade is beyond the scope of this chapter and is not covered in detail on the exam. For the exam, you'll need to describe a Solaris Live Upgrade and understand how it differs from the other installation methods, including a Solaris Interactive upgrade.

Solaris Flash Archives

The Solaris Flash Archive installation enables you to use a single reference installation (Flash Archive) of the Solaris OE on a system, which is called the *master system*. After installing the operating system onto the master system, you can add or delete software and modify system configuration information as necessary. You then create a flash archive from this master system and can use this archive to replicate that installation on a number of systems, which are called clone machines.

When you use any of the Solaris installation methods and you do not select to install a Solaris Flash archive, the installation method installs each Solaris package individually. The package-based installation method is time consuming because the installation method must extract each individual package from the installation media and then update the package map for each package. A Flash archive installs Solaris onto your system much faster because it is simply copying an image onto your drive and does not install the operating system package by package.

If you have many different Solaris configurations that you want to install on your systems, you need a Solaris Flash archive for each configuration. Solaris Flash archives are large files and require a significant amount of disk space. Also, after you create a Solaris Flash archive, you cannot change the archive. If you have many different installation configurations or if you want the flexibility to change your installation configuration, you might consider using the custom JumpStart installation method.

Custom JumpStart employs a command-line installation method that enables you to automatically install or upgrade several systems, based on profiles that you create. Custom Jumpstart can be configured to install Solaris from a Solaris Flash archive. The JumpStart configuration files define specific software installation requirements. You can also incorporate shell scripts to include preinstallation and postinstallation tasks. This is not a capability within the Solaris Flash archive.

If you have multiple systems to install, the custom JumpStart installation method might be the most efficient way for you to install your systems. However, if you plan to install only a few systems, the custom JumpStart installation method is less efficient. This is because the creation of a custom JumpStart environment and its associated configuration files is very time consuming.

WAN Boot

The WAN boot installation method enables you to boot and install software over a wide-area network (WAN) by using HTTP. Utilizing the WAN boot method of installation, you can install the Solaris OS on SPARC-based systems over a WAN. WAN boot can be used with security features to protect data confidentiality and installation image integrity.

The WAN boot installation method enables you to transmit an encrypted Solaris Flash archive over a WAN to a remote SPARC-based client. The WAN boot programs then install the client system by performing a custom JumpStart installation.

To perform a WAN boot installation:

- HTTPS must be enabled on the WAN boot server and install server.
- A hashing key and encryption key must exist on the WAN boot server and the client.
- You can use a WAN boot only on a SPARC-based system.

EXAM ALERT

WAN boot WAN boot is an advanced installation method and is covered in *Solaris 10 System Administration Exam Prep: Exam CX-310-202*, but you should know the preceding requirements for performing a WAN boot installation.

Upgrading the Operating System

An operating system upgrade merges the new version of the Solaris operating environment with the existing files on the system's disk. An upgrade saves as many modifications that you have made to the previous version of the Solaris operating environment as possible.

NOTE

Backups Make sure that you back up your entire system, and check the backup before performing an upgrade.

You can upgrade any system that is running the Solaris 7, 8, or 9 software. You can also update the Solaris 10 Update release if your system is running an older version of the Solaris 10 software. In this chapter, I will describe how to perform an initial installation but will not perform an upgrade. You'll see, however, in the later section "Using the Interactive Installation Process (`install-solaris`)" that after the system identification portion of the installation process is complete, `install-solaris` asks you if you want to perform an upgrade.

You cannot upgrade your system to a software group that is not installed on the system. For example, if you previously installed the end-user Solaris software group on your system, you cannot use the upgrade option to upgrade to the developer Solaris Software group. However, during the upgrade, you can add software to the system that is not part of the currently installed software group.

If you are already running the Solaris 10 operating environment and have installed individual patches, be aware of the following when upgrading to a Solaris 10 Update release:

- Any patches that were supplied as part of the Solaris 10 Update release are reapplied to your system. You cannot back out these patches.
- Any patches that were previously installed on your system and are not included in the Solaris 10 Update release are removed.

The Solaris Installation Precheckist

Before you begin installing the operating system, it's important to make sure you have everything you'll need. Adequate planning and preparation will save you time and trouble later. If the system is currently running a version of Solaris, make a full backup of all file systems before reloading the operating system. Even if the file systems are on separate disks than the operating system, make sure you have backups in place. As the saying goes, "Better safe than sorry." I recommend completing the installation worksheet in Table 2.1 so that all the information you'll need is handy during the installation.

Table 2.1 Installation Worksheet

Item or Option	Issue	Status
Network	Is the system connected to a network?	Yes/No
Hostname	The name for the system. Hostnames should be short, easy to spell, and lowercase, and they should have no more than 64 characters. If the system is on a network, the hostname should be unique.	
DHCP	Will the system use the Dynamic Host Configuration Protocol (DHCP) to configure its network interface?	Yes/No

Table 2.1 Installation Worksheet

Item or Option	Issue	Status
IP address	If not using DHCP, supply the static IP address for the system. This information must come from your site IP coordinator. `192.9.200.1` is one example of an IP address. IP addresses must be unique for every system on your network. For a large site or a site that has a presence on the Internet, you should apply for a unique IP address from the NIC to ensure that no other network node shares your address.	
Subnet	If not using DHCP, is the system part of a subnet? If using a subnet, make sure you also get the subnet mask used at your site. On an existing system, this information can be obtained from the `/etc/netmasks` file.	Yes/No
IPv6	You're be asked if support for IPv6, the next generation Internet protocol, should be installed.	Yes/No
Kerberos	Do you want to configure Kerberos security on this system? Kerberos provides selectable, strong, user- or server-level authentication based on symmetric key cryptography. Ask your in-house security personnel if Kerberos security is required. If yes, gather the following: Default realm: Administration server: First KDC: Additional KDCs:	Yes/No
Name service	NIS, NIS+, DNS, LDAP, or NONE. You need to specify which name service your system will be using (or NONE if you're not using one). On a running system, you can check which name service is being used by examining the `/etc/nsswitch.conf` file.	
Domain name	If the system uses a name service, supply the name of the domain in which the system resides. On a running system, this information can be obtained using the `/usr/bin/domainname` command.	
Default router	Do you want to specify a default IP router (gateway) or let the Solaris installation program find one? If you want to specify a default route, provide the following information. Router IP address:	
Time zone	You need to specify the geographic region and time zone in which this system will be operated. Geographic region: Offset from GMT: Time zone file:	
Power	Do you want to use power management? (Only available on management SPARC systems that support power management)	Yes/No

Table 2.1 Installation Worksheet

Item or Option	Issue	Status
Proxy server configuration	Do you have a direct connection to the Internet, or do you need to use a proxy server to gain access to the Internet? If you use a proxy server, provide the following: Host: Port:	
Locales	For which geographic regions do you want to install support?	
Software group	Which Solaris Software group do you want to install? (Reduced Networking Support, Entire Plus OEM, Entire, Developer, End User, or Core)	
Custom package selection	Do you want to add or remove software packages from the Solaris software group that you install?	
Select disks	On which disk(s) do you want to install the Solaris software? (for example, `c0t0d0`)	
Preserve data	Do you want to preserve data on any of the disk partitions? (Only available when using `install-solaris`)	Yes/No
Autolayout file systems	Do you want the installation program to automatically lay out file systems on your disks? If yes, which file systems should be used for autolayout? If no, you need to provide file system configuration information and you should have the layout of your disk slices prepared in advance.	Yes/No
Mount remote file systems	Does this system need to access software on another file system? If yes, provide the following information about the remote file system: Server: IP address: Remote file system: Local mount point: (Only available when using `install-solaris`)	Yes/No
Root password	During the installation, you are asked to assign a password to the root user account.	
Language	Determine the language to be used to install the Solaris 10 operating environment.	

You can use the `sysidcfg` file to preconfigure this information for a system. You must create a unique `sysidcfg` file for every system that requires different configuration information. You can use the same `sysidcfg` file to preconfigure parameters that are common between systems such as time zone, domain name, and so on. You need a system specific `sysidcfg` file to specify parameters that are unique to each system, such as IP address, hostname, and root password.

Next, verify that you have enough disk space for Solaris 10 and all the co-packaged and third-party software you plan to add. (Refer to the section "Software Groups" earlier in this chapter.) Normally, a server would have several gigabytes of disk space available for the operating system, so you'll be installing the full distribution software group. Also, you need to check with your software vendor regarding space requirements for any third-party software packages as well as swap space requirements.

Secure by Default

Traditionally, previous versions of Solaris always installed all the network services, and it was up to the system administrator to turn off unneeded services after the OS was installed. Until these services were disabled, the system was vulnerable.

New in Solaris 10 (version 11/06 and newer) is the Secure by Default (SBD) enhancement. SBD gives the system administrator the flexibility to disable numerous network services during the installation of the OS, thus limiting your risk of exposure over the network while still providing a useful system. The only network listening service left enabled under SBD is SSH (Secure Shell). When enabling SBD, some services are disabled, and others are limited to local connections only. Table 2.2 lists the services and how they are controlled with SBD.

Table 2.2 Controlled Services

Services Disabled by Secure by Default	
CDE subprocess control	telnetd
DMI	statd
SNMP	lockd
Solstice Enterprise Agent	NFS client
Seaport	NFS server
X font server	rquotad
Internet print protocol	NFS v4 callback daemon
SVM remote metaset	NFS id mapping
SVM remote mediator	ftpd
SVM remote multihost disk	fingerd
SVM communication	rlogind
rstatd	rshd
rusersd	Secure Shell
Services Limited to Local Connections by Secure by Default	
rpcbind	X server
syslogd	dtlogin
sendmail	ToolTalk
smcwebserver	dtcm
WBEM	BSD print

SBD can be enabled during the installation of the OS (as described in the next section), or it can be enabled anytime after the installation using the following command at the shell prompt:

```
# netservices limited <cr>
```

This command can be run only by the root user.

In addition, SBD can be disabled at any time. The network services are made available again using the following command:

```
# netservices open <cr>
```

The `netservices` command uses the Solaris service management facility, `smf`, to control services that accept requests over the network from remote clients.

Using the Interactive Installation Process (`install-solaris`) on a SPARC-Based System

After gathering the information for the installation worksheet, you are ready to begin the installation process. The following steps outline the process for installing Solaris 10 on a Sun SPARC system using the `install-solaris` interactive installation method. With the conventional interactive installation, Solaris is installed by using the Solaris install tool, `install-solaris`, a friendly and easy-to-use interface that has a dialog box for installing the operating system. The dialog box asks you several questions about the installation. This section provides an overview of the installation process using the conventional interactive installation program, `install-solaris`.

`install-solaris` brings up various menus and asks for your input. For this example, I'll use a character-based terminal and will use the Solaris CLI installation. Installation options are displayed in a menu-driven format. I'll use the spacebar to select options and the F2 key (or the equivalent Esc key sequence) to accept selected options. If you're using a bitmapped display, you see the same dialog box, but it is graphical, so you can click your selections. The `install-solaris` interface (GUI and CLI) allows you to go back to previous screens if you make a mistake. It doesn't actually do anything to your system until the installation program reaches the end and tells you it is about to start the loading process. During the installation, help is always available via the Help button.

I've broken the Solaris installation into two sections—SPARC and x86/x64. There are differences in how each platform begins the installation process. I'll begin with a SPARC-based installation.

CAUTION

Reinstalling the OS destroys data The following procedure reinstalls your operating system. That means it destroys all data on the target file systems. Optionally, you can select data file systems to be preserved (saved) during the installation, but I highly recommend a backup in case things go wrong.

If you're upgrading or installing Solaris on a running SPARC system, use the steps listed in Step by Step 2.1 to shut down and then perform the installation.

STEP BY STEP

NOTE

08/07 release of Solaris 10 This installation uses the 08/07 version of the Solaris 10 OS. As Sun releases new versions of Solaris 10, the specific installation steps could change.

2.1 Shutting Down and Installing SPARC-based Solaris on a Running System

1. Become root.
2. Issue the `shutdown` command. This command, described in Chapter 3, "Perform System Boot and Shutdown Procedures for SPARC-, x64-, and x86-Based Systems," brings the system to a single-user state by halting the window system and leaving you with a single root prompt on the console. It takes about a minute.
3. Issue the `halt` command. This command puts you into the PROM. You know you're in the PROM when you receive either an `ok` or > prompt.
4. Put the Solaris 10 CD-ROM 1 into the CD-ROM player and boot from the CD-ROM. Or, if your system has a DVD-ROM, place the Solaris 10 DVD into the drive and boot from the DVD. For this example, I'll install from DVD media.
5. At the `ok` prompt, type **`boot cdrom`**.

   This command starts the default GUI installation on a bitmapped console if your system has at least 512MB of RAM installed. If your system has less than 512MB of RAM, enter `boot cdrom - nowin` for the CLI (command-line interface) version of the installation program, which has no desktop windows. You can also type `boot cdrom - text` to specify the text installer. This option uses a text installer while still in a desktop windows setting.

   If the console does not support graphics, you're automatically put into the CLI version of the installation. I will use the CLI installation for this example.

NOTE

Clicking the Begin Installation button You can enter the installation program and complete all the selections, but no changes are made to the disk until you click the Begin Installation button at the end of the installation process.

The system starts from the DVD, the installation program is loaded into memory, and it begins configuring devices. Ignore any messages such as cables not connected or network interfaces that fail to respond. After a few minutes, you'll enter the system identification section of the installation. The installation program opens a dialog box, asking you various questions about your locale and language, as shown in Figure 2.1.

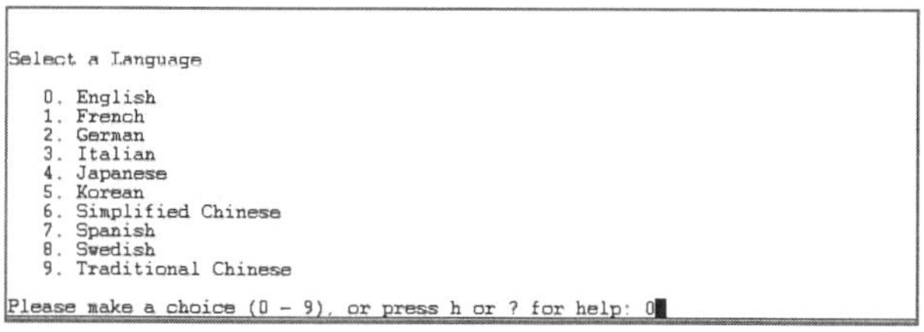

```
Select a Language

   0. English
   1. French
   2. German
   3. Italian
   4. Japanese
   5. Korean
   6. Simplified Chinese
   7. Spanish
   8. Swedish
   9. Traditional Chinese

Please make a choice (0 - 9), or press h or ? for help: 0
```

FIGURE 2.1 Select a language.

Select your language, and press Enter to continue.

6. Select a language by entering the corresponding number, and press Enter. In the example, I selected 0 for English. The system responded with the window shown in Figure 2.2, querying your terminal type.

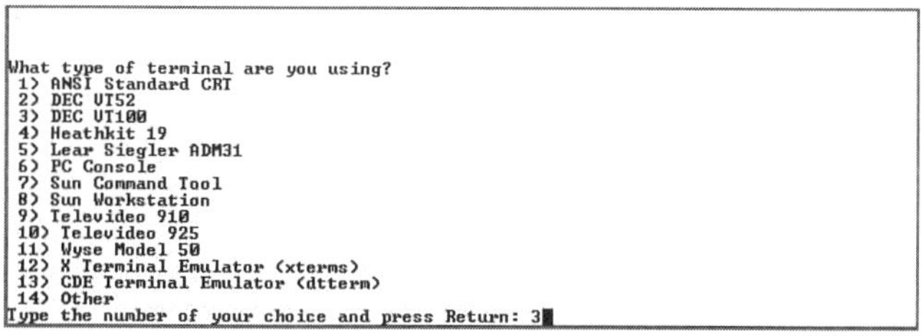

```
What type of terminal are you using?
 1) ANSI Standard CRT
 2) DEC VT52
 3) DEC VT100
 4) Heathkit 19
 5) Lear Siegler ADM31
 6) PC Console
 7) Sun Command Tool
 8) Sun Workstation
 9) Televideo 910
 10) Televideo 925
 11) Wyse Model 50
 12) X Terminal Emulator (xterms)
 13) CDE Terminal Emulator (dtterm)
 14) Other
Type the number of your choice and press Return: 3
```

FIGURE 2.2 Select a terminal type.

This menu appears only when you're using a character-based screen. You do not see this menu if you're using a bitmapped display.

7. For this example, I selected item **3** and pressed Enter. You see the window shown in Figure 2.3.

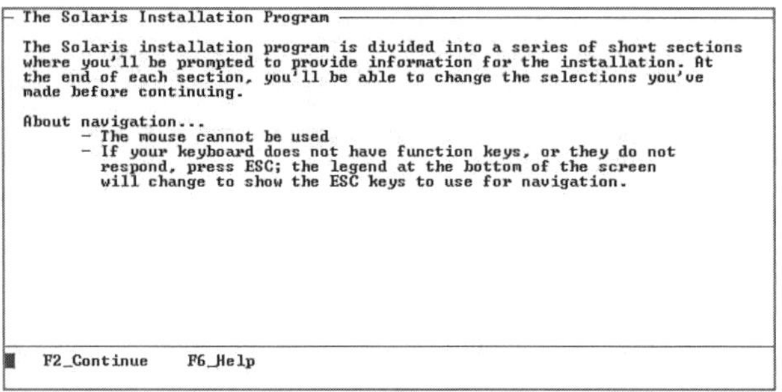

FIGURE 2.3 Welcome screen.

Again, this menu of options appears only when you use a character-based screen. On a bitmapped display, you do not see this menu.

8. I pressed the **F2** key to continue. You see the window shown in Figure 2.4.

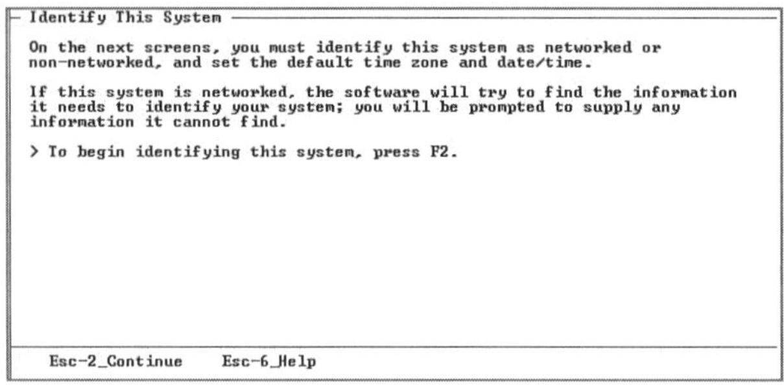

FIGURE 2.4 System identification.

The system tells you to Press F2 to continue. At the bottom of the window, I'm prompted to press **Esc+2** to continue. (Hold down the Esc key while pressing the 2 key.) This is because my keyboard/console does not support F2.

9. Press the **F2** key to continue. The window shown in Figure 2.5 appears.

Network Connectivity
Specify Yes if the system is connected to the network by one of the Solaris or vendor network/communication Ethernet cards that are supported on the Solaris CD. See your hardware documentation for the current list of supported cards.
Specify No if the system is connected to a network/communication card that is not supported on the Solaris CD, and follow the instructions listed under Help.
Networked
[X] Yes
[ ] No
Esc-2_Continue Esc-6_Help

FIGURE 2.5 Network connectivity.

If the system is connected to a Sun-supported network/communication card, select **`Yes`**. In rare circumstances, if the system is connected to a network card that is not supported on the Solaris CD-ROM, select `No` and complete the installation of Solaris software as follows:

a. Install the unbundled network/communication card.

b. As root, run the **`/usr/sbin/sys-unconfig`** program to return the system to its "as-manufactured" state. This command is entered with no options and simply unconfigures your system's hostname, network information, service domain name, time zone, IP address, subnet mask, and root password. When `sys-unconfig` is finished, it performs a system shutdown.

c. Attach the network adapter to the system.

d. At the `ok` prompt, type **`boot -r`**.

e. Provide network information as prompted on the screen, and the network will now be aware of the system.

f. After making your selection, press the **F2** key to continue. The window shown in Figure 2.6 appears.

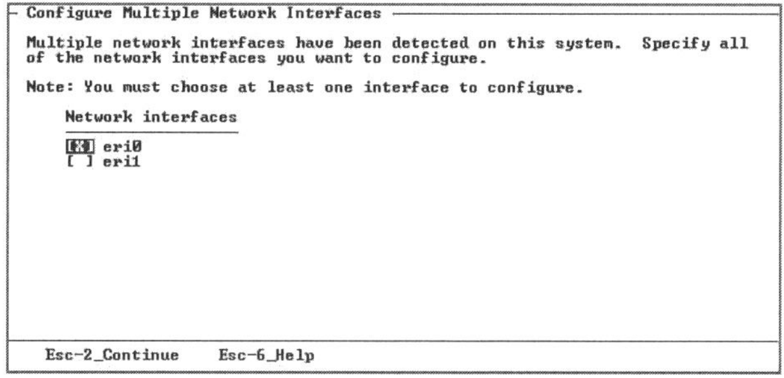

FIGURE 2.6 Select the primary network interface.

Specify the primary network interface for your system. This information is requested if the software detects multiple Ethernet cards or network adapter cards on your system. This screen is displayed if you're installing a gateway from a CD-ROM. On this system, I have the primary network adapter and one additional network adapter installed.

In most cases, the correct choice is to select the lowest-numbered interface. However, if you don't know, ask your system or network administrator for advice.

CAUTION

Specify the correct network interface If you specify the incorrect primary network interface, your system might not be able to find a name service.

In this example, I selected **eri0** as the interface and pressed **F2** to continue. The window shown in Figure 2.7 was displayed.

```
- DHCP for eri0 ---------------------------------------------------------

Specify whether or not this network interface should use DHCP to configure
itself.  Choose Yes if DHCP is to be used, or No if the network interface is
to be configured manually.

NOTE: DHCP support will not be enabled, if selected, until after the system
reboots.

     Use DHCP for eri0
     -------------------
     [ ] Yes
     [X] No

   Esc-2_Continue     Esc-6_Help
```

FIGURE 2.7 DHCP for the primary interface.

10. For this example, I selected **No** and pressed **F2** to continue. Most servers use static IP addresses, so I will specify a static IP address later in the installation. If you want the server to be assigned an IP address from the DHCP server, select `yes`. You see the window shown in Figure 2.8.

```
- Host Name for eri0 ----------------------------------------------------

Enter the host name which identifies this system on the network.  The name
must be unique within your domain; creating a duplicate host name will cause
problems on the network after you install Solaris.

A host name must have at least one character; it can contain letters,
digits, and minus signs (-).

  Host name for eri0 sunfire

   Esc-2_Continue     Esc-6_Help
```

FIGURE 2.8 Set the hostname.

11. Enter a unique hostname. In this example, I entered **sunfire** for the hostname and pressed **F2** to continue. The window shown in Figure 2.9 appears.

12. This menu appears if you did not select DHCP earlier in the process. Internet addresses are usually assigned by network or system administrators according to local and Internetwork policies. Because creating duplicate IP addresses can cause network problems, do not guess or make up a number; check with your system or network administrator for help. For this example, I set the IP address to **192.168.1.32** and pressed **F2** to continue. The window shown in Figure 2.10 appears.

```
- IP Address for eri0 -----------------------------------------------
  Enter the Internet Protocol (IP) address for this network interface.  It
  must be unique and follow your site's address conventions, or a
  system/network failure could result.

  IP addresses contain four sets of numbers separated by periods (for example
  129.200.9.1).

    IP address for eri0 192.168.1.32

  Esc-2_Continue    Esc-6_Help
```

FIGURE 2.9 Set the IP address.

```
- Subnet for eri0 ---------------------------------------------------
  On this screen you must specify whether this system is part of a subnet.  If
  you specify incorrectly, the system will have problems communicating on the
  network after you reboot.

  > To make a selection, use the arrow keys to highlight the option and
    press Return to mark it [X].

      System part of a subnet
      -----------------------
      [ ] Yes
      [X] No

  Esc-2_Continue    Esc-6_Help
```

FIGURE 2.10 Specify a subnet.

13. Specify whether your system is on a network that has subnets. If the network to which your system is connected is divided into subnets (usually using routers or gateways), answer Yes. If you do not know if your network has subnets, do not guess; check with your system administrator for help. For this example, my system was not part of a subnet, so I selected **No** and pressed **F2** to continue. The window shown in Figure 2.11 appears.

```
- Netmask for eri0 --------------------------------------------------
  On this screen you must specify the netmask of your subnet.  A default
  netmask is shown; do not accept the default unless you are sure it is
  correct for your subnet.  A netmask must contain four sets of numbers
  separated by periods (for example 255.255.255.0).

    Netmask for eri0 255.255.255.0

  Esc-2_Continue    Esc-6_Help
```

FIGURE 2.11 Set the netmask.

14. Specify whether this system will use IPv6, the next-generation Internet protocol. IPv6 is described in *Solaris 10 System Administration Exam Prep: Exam CX-310-202*. This system will not use IPv6, so I selected **No**, as shown in Figure 2.12, and pressed F2 to continue.

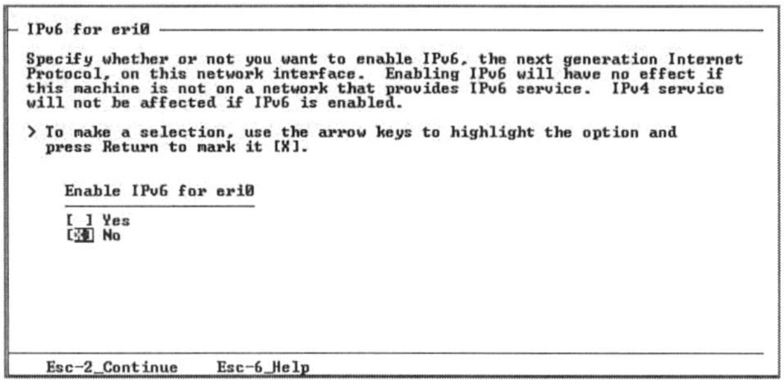

```
- IPv6 for eri0 ----------------------------------------------------------

Specify whether or not you want to enable IPv6, the next generation Internet
Protocol, on this network interface.  Enabling IPv6 will have no effect if
this machine is not on a network that provides IPv6 service.  IPv4 service
will not be affected if IPv6 is enabled.

> To make a selection, use the arrow keys to highlight the option and
  press Return to mark it [X].

    Enable IPv6 for eri0
    --------------------
    [ ] Yes
    [X] No

--------------------------------------------------------------------------
    Esc-2_Continue    Esc-6_Help
```

FIGURE 2.12 Enable IPv6.

15. From the window shown in Figure 2.13, specify whether a default route is needed and, if so, specify an IP address to the router (gateway) in the network. The router is used to forward all network traffic that is not addressed to the local subnet. If you know the address of your default router, select `Specify One`. If not, you can select `Find One`, and the system tries to locate the default router. In this example, I selected **`Find One`** and pressed **F2**. The summary window shown in Figure 2.14 appears.

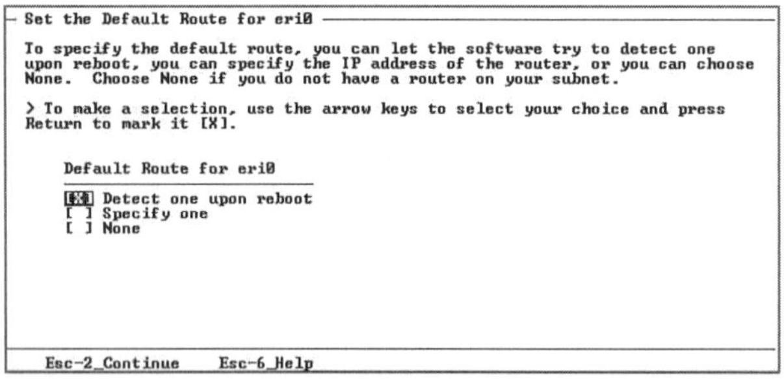

```
- Set the Default Route for eri0 -----------------------------------------

To specify the default route, you can let the software try to detect one
upon reboot, you can specify the IP address of the router, or you can choose
None.  Choose None if you do not have a router on your subnet.

> To make a selection, use the arrow keys to select your choice and press
Return to mark it [X].

    Default Route for eri0
    ----------------------
    [X] Detect one upon reboot
    [ ] Specify one
    [ ] None

--------------------------------------------------------------------------
    Esc-2_Continue    Esc-6_Help
```

FIGURE 2.13 Set the default route.

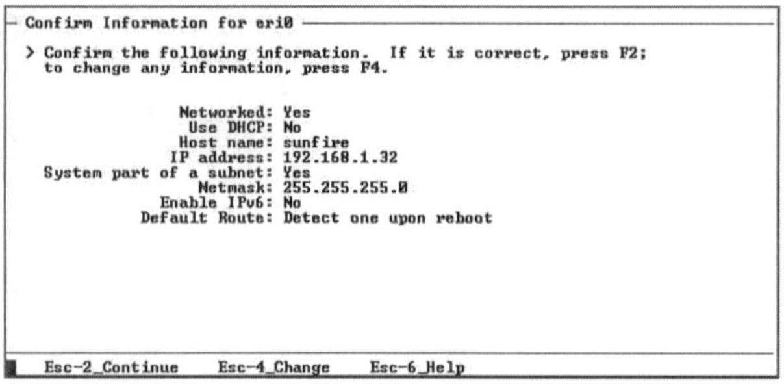

```
- Confirm Information for eri0 -------------------------------------------

> Confirm the following information.  If it is correct, press F2;
  to change any information, press F4.

                  Networked: Yes
                   Use DHCP: No
                  Host name: sunfire
                 IP address: 192.168.1.32
     System part of a subnet: Yes
                    Netmask: 255.255.255.0
                Enable IPv6: No
              Default Route: Detect one upon reboot

--------------------------------------------------------------------------
    Esc-2_Continue    Esc-4_Change    Esc-6_Help
```

FIGURE 2.14 System identification confirmation screen.

16. Confirm the settings by pressing **F2**. You see the window shown in Figure 2.15.

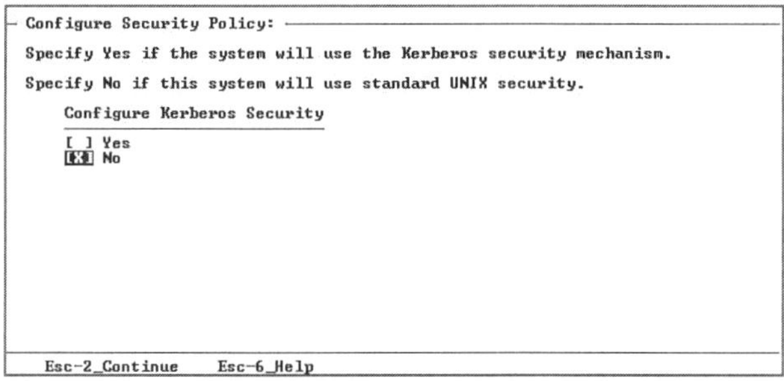

Configure Security Policy:
Specify Yes if the system will use the Kerberos security mechanism.
Specify No if this system will use standard UNIX security.
Configure Kerberos Security
[ ] Yes
[X] No
Esc-2_Continue Esc-6_Help

FIGURE 2.15 Configure the security policy.

This specifies the type of security policy being implemented on this system. If no special security policy is desired, select No. Normal UNIX security is implemented.

NOTE

Kerberos security Using Kerberos requires coordination with your network administrator. You need to know certain information, such as the fully qualified domain name of one or more KDCs. If you don't have or don't know this information, you can add it later to the `/etc/krb5/krb5.conf` file.

17. On this system, I will be using normal UNIX security, so I selected **No** and pressed **F2**. The confirmation window, shown in Figure 2.16, is displayed.

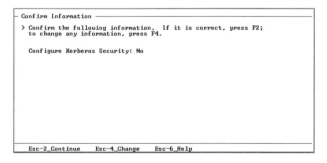

```
Confirm Information
> Confirm the following information.  If it is correct, press F2;
  to change any information, press F4.

  Configure Kerberos Security: No

Esc-2_Continue   Esc-4_Change   Esc-6_Help
```

FIGURE 2.16 Security confirmation screen.

18. If everything looks okay, press **F2** to continue. The window shown in Figure 2.17 appears.

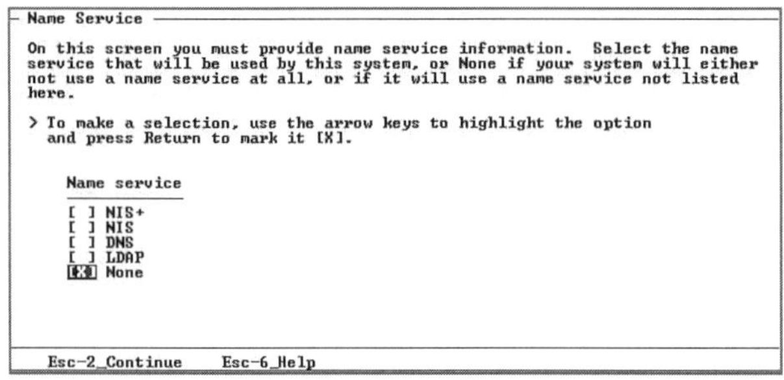
Name Service
On this screen you must provide name service information. Select the name service that will be used by this system, or None if your system will either not use a name service at all, or if it will use a name service not listed here.
> To make a selection, use the arrow keys to highlight the option and press Return to mark it [X].
Name service
[ ] NIS+
[ ] NIS
[ ] DNS
[ ] LDAP
[X] None
Esc-2_Continue Esc-6_Help

FIGURE 2.17 Select a name service.

Specify the name service you will be using. Name Services are described in *Solaris 10 System Administration Exam Prep: Exam CX-310-202*.

19. When you're asked to select a Name Service, the default is "NIS+." This system will not be using a name service, only local `/etc` files, so I selected **`None`** and pressed **F2** to continue. The confirmation window shown in Figure 2.18 appears.

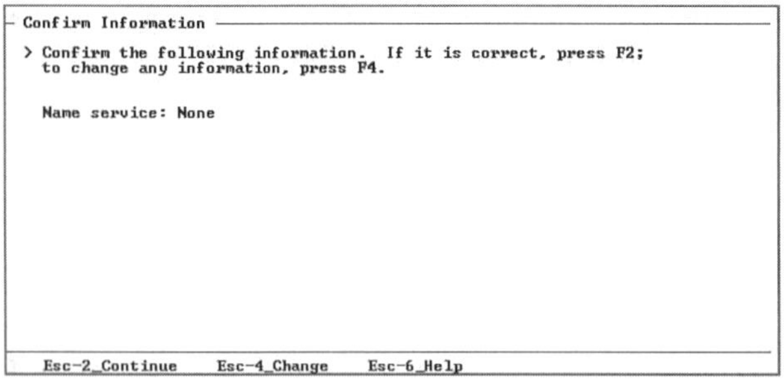

```
- Confirm Information --------------------------------------------------
 > Confirm the following information.  If it is correct, press F2;
   to change any information, press F4.

   Name service: None

   Esc-2_Continue    Esc-4_Change    Esc-6_Help
```

FIGURE 2.18 Confirm the name service.

20. The next window, shown in Figure 2.19, asks you to specify the NFSv4 domain name.

    As stated in the window, the derived domain name is sufficient for most configurations. I selected the option **`Use the NFSv4 domain derived by the system`** and pressed **F2** to continue. NFS is described in *Solaris 10 System Administration Exam Prep: Exam CX-310-202.* After you make your selection, a confirmation window appears, as shown in Figure 2.20.

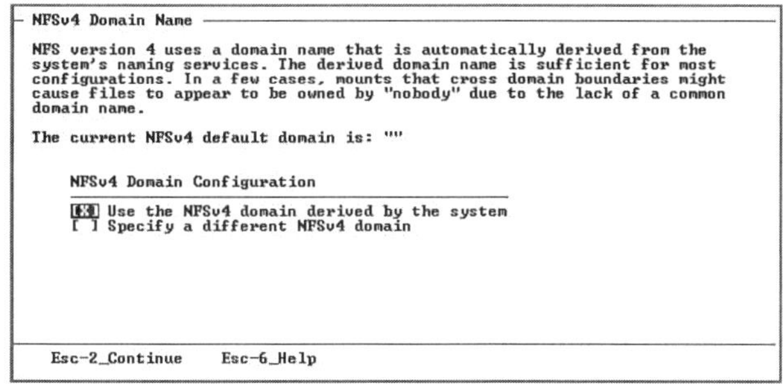

FIGURE 2.19 Specify the NFS domain name.

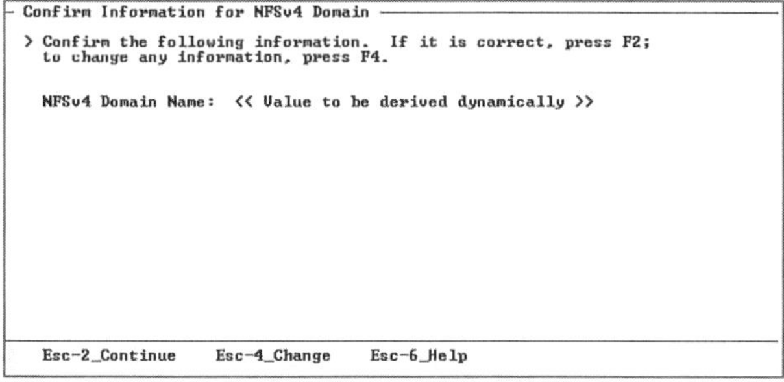

FIGURE 2.20 NFSv4 domain confirmation.

Press **F2** to continue.

21. If everything looks okay, press **F2** to continue.
22. The next window, shown in Figure 2.21, asks you to enter your time zone.

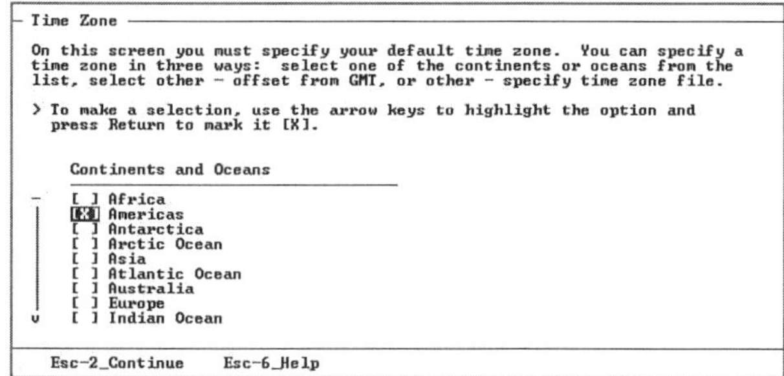

FIGURE 2.21 Specify the default time zone.

Select **`Americas`** and press **F2** to continue.

23. A subsequent menu appears, asking for specifics about that particular region, as shown in Figure 2.22.

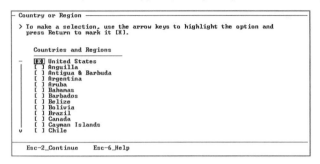

```
- Country or Region ----------------------------------------------------

  > To make a selection, use the arrow keys to highlight the option and
    press Return to mark it [X].

        Countries and Regions
        ----------------------------
  -     [X] United States
  |     [ ] Anguilla
  |     [ ] Antigua & Barbuda
  |     [ ] Argentina
  |     [ ] Aruba
  |     [ ] Bahamas
  |     [ ] Barbados
  |     [ ] Belize
  |     [ ] Bolivia
  |     [ ] Brazil
  |     [ ] Canada
  |     [ ] Cayman Islands
  v     [ ] Chile

    Esc-2_Continue    Esc-6_Help
```

FIGURE 2.22 Specify the country.

You see a confirmation window, as shown in Figure 2.23.

```
- Confirm Information --------------------------------------------------

  > Confirm the following information.  If it is correct, press F2;
    to change any information, press F4.

        Time zone: Eastern Time - Michigan - most locations
                   (US/Michigan)
    Date and time: 2008-01-23 15:50:00

    Esc-2_Continue    Esc-4_Change    Esc-6_Help
```

FIGURE 2.23 Confirm the time zone.

Review the information, and press **F2** to continue.

24. Continue to make your selection on subsequent menus to specify your time zone, and press **F2** to continue. The menu shown in Figure 2.24 appears, asking you to verify the date and time.

```
- Date and Time --------------------------------------------------------

  > Accept the default date and time or enter
    new values.

  Date and time: 2008-01-23 15:50

    Year   (4 digits) : 2008
    Month  (1-12)     : 01
    Day    (1-31)     : 23
    Hour   (0-23)     : 15
    Minute (0-59)     : 50

    Esc-2_Continue    Esc-6_Help
```

FIGURE 2.24 Set the date and time.

25. Modify the time as required, and press **F2** to continue. The confirmation screen shown in Figure 2.25 appears.

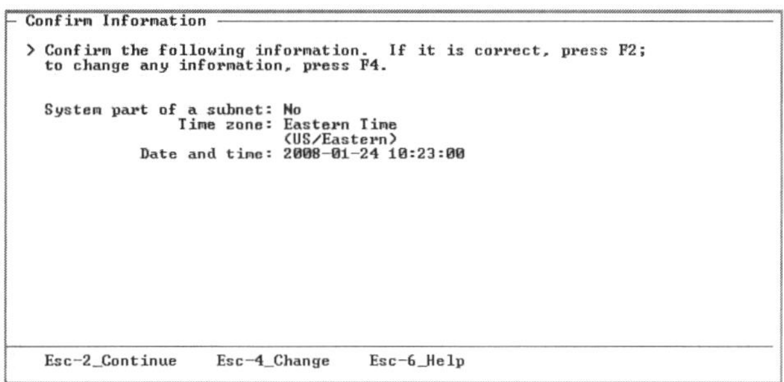

FIGURE 2.25 Confirm the time.

26. If everything is correct, press **F2** to continue. The menu shown in Figure 2.26 appears, asking you to set the root password.

```
Root Password

Please enter the root password for this system.

The root password may contain alphanumeric and special characters. For
security, the password will not be displayed on the screen as you type it.

> If you do not want a root password, leave both entries blank.

  Root password:
  Root password:

  Esc-2_Continue    Esc-6_Help
```

FIGURE 2.26 Set the root password.

27. Set the root password by entering it twice, and press **F2** to continue. The window shown in Figure 2.27 is displayed.

```
Identify This System

On the next screens, you must identify this system as networked or
non-networked, and set the default time zone and date/time.

If this system is networked, the software will try to find the information
it needs to identify your system; you will be prompted to supply any
information it cannot find.

> To begin identifying this system, press F2.

  F2_Continue    F6_Help
```

FIGURE 2.27 Begin to identify the system.

Press **F2** to continue.

28. You're asked if you want to enable remote services, as shown in Figure 2.28.

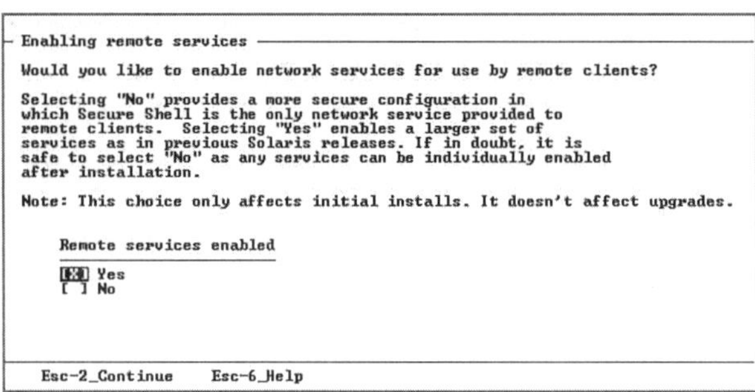

```
- Enabling remote services -------------------------------------------------
Would you like to enable network services for use by remote clients?

Selecting "No" provides a more secure configuration in
which Secure Shell is the only network service provided to
remote clients.  Selecting "Yes" enables a larger set of
services as in previous Solaris releases. If in doubt, it is
safe to select "No" as any services can be individually enabled
after installation.

Note: This choice only affects initial installs. It doesn't affect upgrades.

     Remote services enabled
     -----------------------
     [X] Yes
     [ ] No

-----------------------------------------------------------------------------
   Esc-2_Continue    Esc-6_Help
```

FIGURE 2.28 Enable remote services.

See the earlier section "Secure by Default." I answered `Yes` and pressed **F2** to continue.

29. The system identification portion of the installation is complete. Following the system identification portion of the installation, you see the dialog box shown in Figure 2.29.

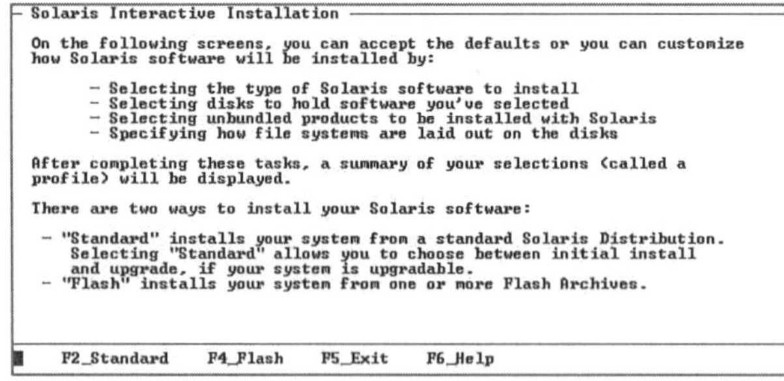

```
- Solaris Interactive Installation -----------------------------------------
On the following screens, you can accept the defaults or you can customize
how Solaris software will be installed by:

       - Selecting the type of Solaris software to install
       - Selecting disks to hold software you've selected
       - Selecting unbundled products to be installed with Solaris
       - Specifying how file systems are laid out on the disks

After completing these tasks, a summary of your selections (called a
profile) will be displayed.

There are two ways to install your Solaris software:

 - "Standard" installs your system from a standard Solaris Distribution.
   Selecting "Standard" allows you to choose between initial install
   and upgrade, if your system is upgradable.
 - "Flash" installs your system from one or more Flash Archives.

-----------------------------------------------------------------------------
    F2_Standard    F4_Flash    F5_Exit    F6_Help
```

FIGURE 2.29 Begin the interactive installation.

> **CAUTION**
>
> **The initial option destroys data** All data on the operating system slices will be lost. These slices include / (root), `/opt`, and `/var`.

30. The upgrade option is available if you are currently running Solaris 7, 8, or 9 and you want to upgrade to Solaris 10. As described earlier in this chapter, the upgrade option preserves all customizations you made in the previous version of Solaris. For this example, I pressed **F2** to select the Standard option, which is a complete reinstallation of the software, and the window shown in Figure 2.30 appeared.

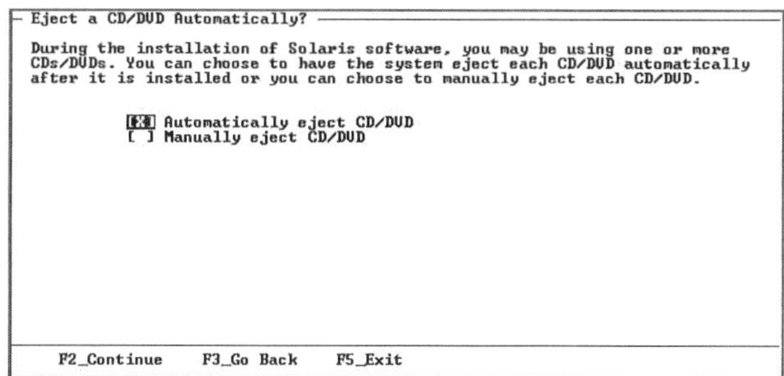

FIGURE 2.30 Eject the CD/DVD automatically.

31. I selected the option to have the CD/DVD automatically ejected when complete. After pressing **F2** to continue, you're asked about rebooting after the installation completes, as shown in Figure 2.31.

```
- Reboot After Installation? ----------------------------------------

After Solaris software is installed, the system must be rebooted. You can
choose to have the system automatically reboot, or you can choose to
manually reboot the system if you want to run scripts or do other
customizations before the reboot.  You can manually reboot a system by using
the reboot(1M) command.

          [X] Auto Reboot
          [ ] Manual Reboot

   F2_Continue    F3_Go Back    F5_Exit
```

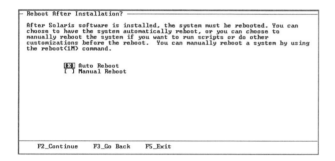

FIGURE 2.31 Reboot after the installation.

32. I selected Auto Reboot and pressed **F2** to continue. The Solaris Interactive Installation Window is displayed, as shown in Figure 2.32.

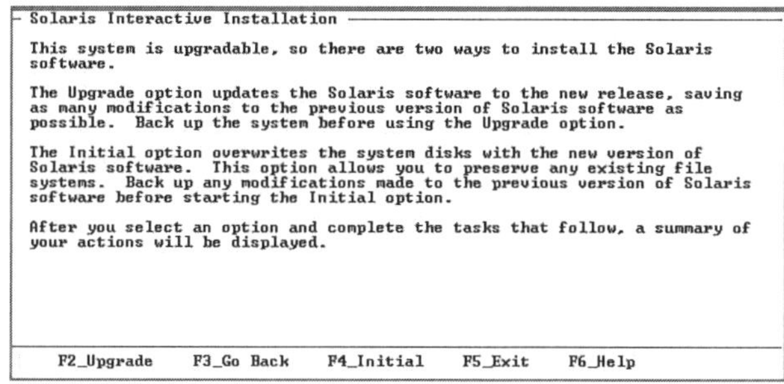

Solaris Interactive Installation
This system is upgradable, so there are two ways to install the Solaris software.
The Upgrade option updates the Solaris software to the new release, saving as many modifications to the previous version of Solaris software as possible. Back up the system before using the Upgrade option.
The Initial option overwrites the system disks with the new version of Solaris software. This option allows you to preserve any existing file systems. Back up any modifications made to the previous version of Solaris software before starting the Initial option.
After you select an option and complete the tasks that follow, a summary of your actions will be displayed.
F2_Upgrade F3_Go Back F4_Initial F5_Exit F6_Help

FIGURE 2.32 Select the method of installation.

Select whether you want to perform an Upgrade or an Initial Installation. I'll perform a complete reinstallation of the OS, so I pressed **F4** to continue with an Initial Installation.

33. You get a message that the system is initializing and loading the install media. The system hesitates for approximately 60 seconds as the media is being loaded from the CD/DVD. Then you see a license agreement, as shown in Figure 2.33.

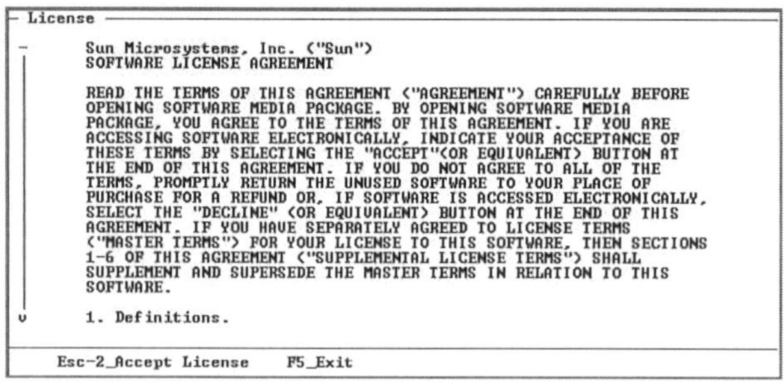

FIGURE 2.33 Review the license agreement.

34. Read the Licensing terms. If you agree to them, press **F2** to accept the agreement. The next menu that is displayed asks you to select the geographic regions for which support will be installed, as shown in Figure 2.34.

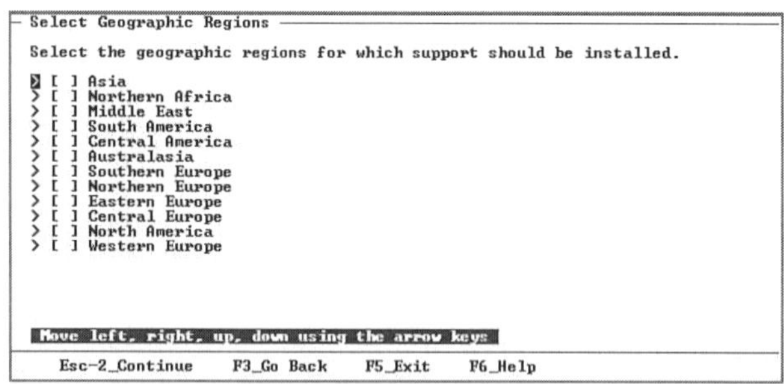

FIGURE 2.34 Select a geographic region.

35. A selection is optional. Select a region or leave it unselected, and press **F2**. I did not select a region; I pressed **F2**. The window shown in Figure 2.35 appeared.

36. Leaving the default selection of POSIX C as my locale, I pressed **F2** to continue. The screen shown in Figure 2.36 appeared.

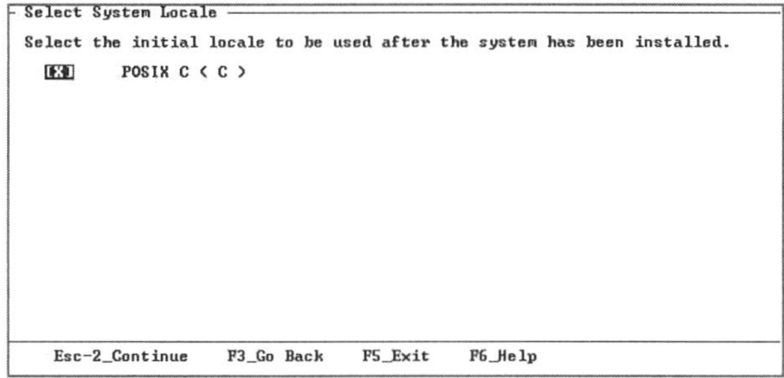

FIGURE 2.35 Select a system locale.

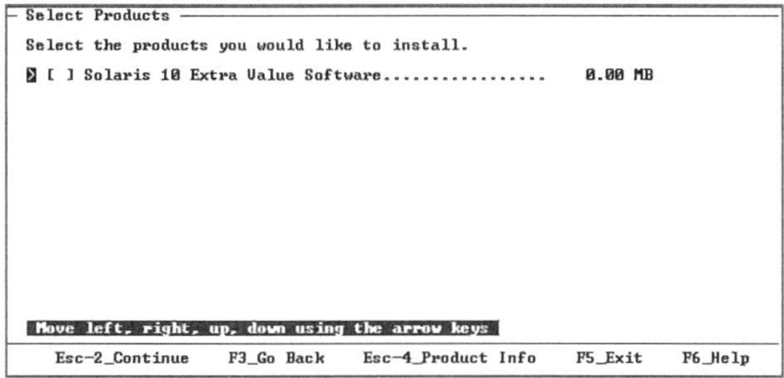

FIGURE 2.36 Extra value software selection.

Select to install the Extra Value software if you want to install the Solaris 10 Extra Value Software, which contains additional Solaris products and Early Access Software.

37. For the example, I did not select any additional software products to install. Select **F2** to continue. The next window asks if there are any applications from other sources to install, as shown in Figure 2.37.

```
Additional Products

To scan for additional products, select the location you wish to scan.
Products found at the selected location that are in a Web Start Ready
install form will be added to the Products list.

Web Start Ready product scan location:

   [X] None
   [ ] CD/DVD
   [ ] Network File System

Esc-2_Continue   F3_Go Back   F5_Exit
```

FIGURE 2.37 Install additional products.

38. For the example, I have no other application to install so I selected **none** and pressed **F2** to continue. The next window, shown in Figure 2.38, asks me to select the software group that I would like installed.

```
- Select Software ----------------------------------------------------------

  Select the Solaris software to install on the system.

  NOTE: After selecting a software group, you can add or remove software by
  customizing it. However, this requires understanding of software
  dependencies and how Solaris software is packaged.

      [ ]  Entire Distribution plus OEM support ....... 5851.00 MB
      [X]  Entire Distribution ........................ 5804.00 MB
      [ ]  Developer System Support ................... 5686.00 MB
      [ ]  End User System Support .................... 4715.00 MB
      [ ]  Core System Support ........................  861.00 MB
      [ ]  Reduced Networking Core System Support .....  801.00 MB

----------------------------------------------------------------------------
     Esc-2_Continue    F3_Go Back    F4_Customize    F5_Exit    F6_Help
```

FIGURE 2.38 Select a software cluster.

> **NOTE**
>
> **Default software group** The Entire Distribution software group is selected by default. After you select the software group you want to install, if you press F4, you see an interactive menu that allows you to select and deselect software packages within a particular software group.

39. Unless you don't have enough disk space, I recommend selecting the **Entire Distribution** so that the entire Solaris OE gets installed. After making your selection, press **F2** to continue. The Select Disks window appears, as shown in Figure 2.39.

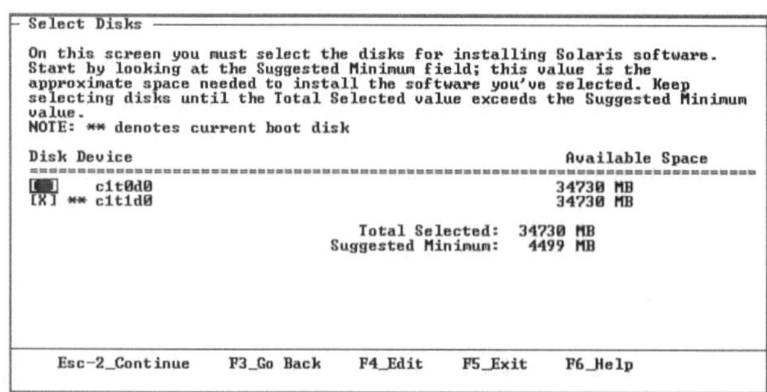

```
- Select Disks --------------------------------------------------------------

  On this screen you must select the disks for installing Solaris software.
  Start by looking at the Suggested Minimum field; this value is the
  approximate space needed to install the software you've selected. Keep
  selecting disks until the Total Selected value exceeds the Suggested Minimum
  value.
  NOTE: ** denotes current boot disk

  Disk Device                                          Available Space
  ===========================================================================
  [ ]     c1t0d0                                          34730 MB
  [X] **  c1t1d0                                          34730 MB

                                   Total Selected:  34730 MB
                                Suggested Minimum:   4499 MB

----------------------------------------------------------------------------
     Esc-2_Continue    F3_Go Back    F4_Edit    F5_Exit    F6_Help
```

FIGURE 2.39 Select the target installation (boot) disk.

40. Select the disk on which to install the operating system. This disk becomes your boot disk. Press **F2** after making your selection. The Preserve Data window appears, as shown in Figure 2.40.

41. If you want to preserve data on any of your partitions, press F4. I backed up my data before starting the installation, so I had no data to preserve. I was completely reinstalling the OS and building new disk slices, so I pressed **F2** to continue, and all the file systems were erased. This provides the most flexibility for laying out a new partition scheme on this disk. After you press **F2**, you see the window shown in Figure 2.41.

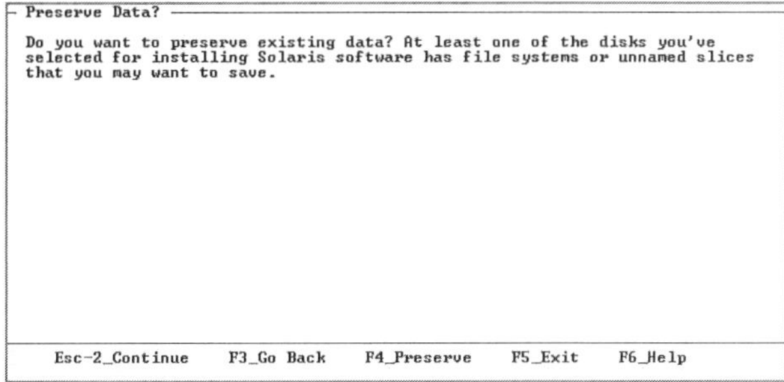

Preserve Data?
Do you want to preserve existing data? At least one of the disks you've selected for installing Solaris software has file systems or unnamed slices that you may want to save.
Esc-2_Continue
F3_Go Back
F4_Preserve
F5_Exit
F6_Help

FIGURE 2.40 Preserve data.

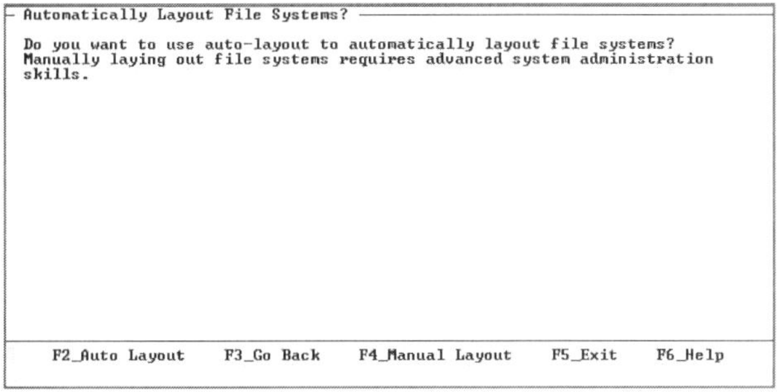

FIGURE 2.41 Automatically lay out file systems.

42. Press **F2**. The system automatically lays out the file systems. Sizes are determined by the software packages you selected. If you plan to add more software, you can modify the file system sizes in later steps. You see the dialog box shown in Figure 2.42.

```
- Automatically Layout File Systems

On this screen you must select all the file systems you want auto-layout to
create, or accept the default file systems shown.

NOTE: For small disks, it may be necessary for auto-layout to break up some
of the file systems you request into smaller file systems to fit the
available disk space. So, after auto-layout completes, you may find file
systems in the layout that you did not select from the list below.

          File Systems for Auto-layout
          ========================================
          [X] /
          [ ] /opt
          [ ] /usr
          [ ] /usr/openwin
          [ ] /var
          [X] swap

    Esc-2_Continue    F5_Cancel    F6_Help
```

FIGURE 2.42 Select file systems to be created.

43. Make your selection(s) and press **F2**.

NOTE

/usr, /var, and /opt I recommend adding /var as a separate file system. /var provides a dedicated slice for system log files, spooled software packages, patch information, and many other things that can take up a large amount of disk space. It's not recommended that you make /var part of the root file system. Some administrators also choose to create separate file systems for /usr and /opt to provide separate slices for additional software packages that you will add later. Again, it's not recommended that /var be part of the root file system.

For this example (see Figure 2.43), I selected **/var** as an additional file system and pressed **Esc+2**. You see the dialog box shown in Figure 2.44.

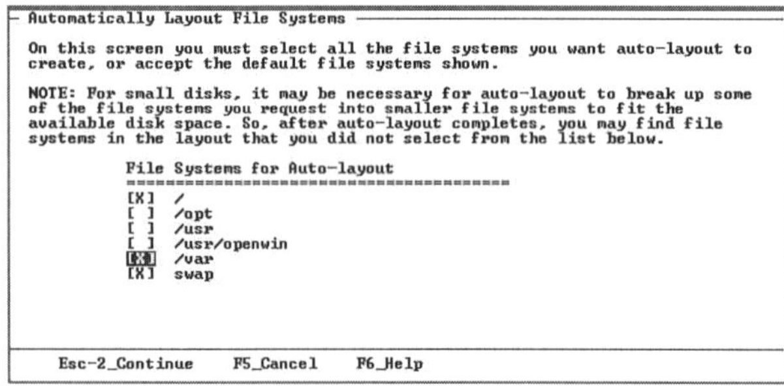

```
- Automatically Layout File Systems ----------------------------------

  On this screen you must select all the file systems you want auto-layout to
  create, or accept the default file systems shown.

  NOTE: For small disks, it may be necessary for auto-layout to break up some
  of the file systems you request into smaller file systems to fit the
  available disk space. So, after auto-layout completes, you may find file
  systems in the layout that you did not select from the list below.

            File Systems for Auto-layout
            ========================================
            [X] /
            [ ] /opt
            [ ] /usr
            [ ] /usr/openwin
            [X] /var
            [X] swap

      Esc-2_Continue    F5_Cancel    F6_Help
```

FIGURE 2.43 Add the /var file system.

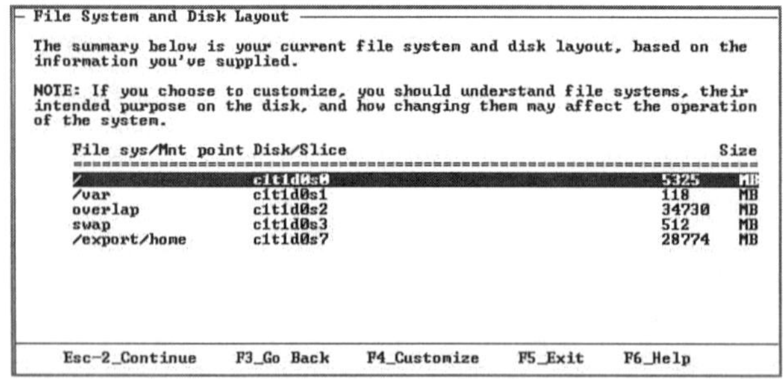

```
- File System and Disk Layout -----------------------------------------

  The summary below is your current file system and disk layout, based on the
  information you've supplied.

  NOTE: If you choose to customize, you should understand file systems, their
  intended purpose on the disk, and how changing them may affect the operation
  of the system.

      File sys/Mnt point Disk/Slice                                  Size
      ====================================================================
      /                  c1t1d0s0                                 5325  MB
      /var               c1t1d0s1                                 118   MB
      overlap            c1t1d0s2                                 34730 MB
      swap               c1t1d0s3                                 512   MB
      /export/home       c1t1d0s7                                 28774 MB

      Esc-2_Continue    F3_Go Back    F4_Customize    F5_Exit    F6_Help
```

FIGURE 2.44 File system summary screen.

44. At this point, you can further customize the slice sizes by pressing F4. You're then given a menu to select new sizes for each slice. I want to change a few slice sizes, so I press **F4**. The menu shown in Figure 2.45 appears.

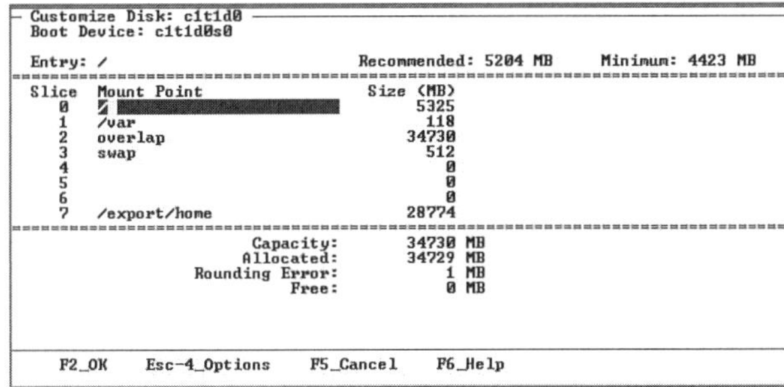

FIGURE 2.45 Customize file system sizes.

45. I begin by decreasing the size of `/export/home` to 5,000MB. Then I'll increase / to 10,000MB. I'll allocate 3,000MB to `/var` and 1,000MB to swap. Then I'll add another slice called `/data` and make it 6,000MB. I'll leave the rest of the disk unallocated so that I have space for later. When you're satisfied with how the slices are sized, press **F2** to continue. The dialog box shown in Figure 2.46 appears.

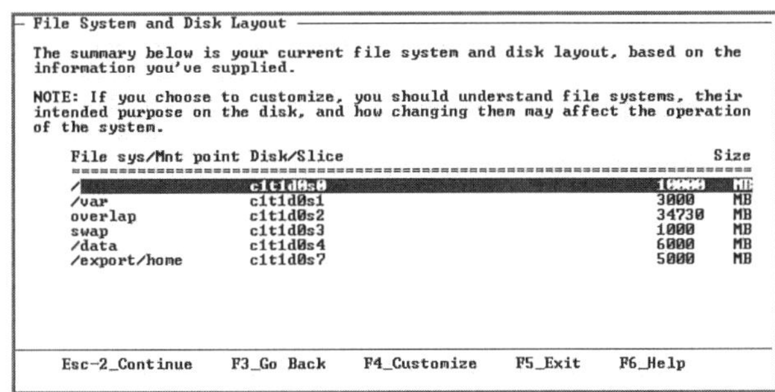

FIGURE 2.46 File system summary screen.

46. Double-check your selections, and press **F2** when you're ready to go to the next step. This is a good time to verify all your selections. Make sure swap is adequate for the type of server you are installing. It seems you can never have too much swap space or space on the / (root) or `/var` file systems. In other words, err on the side of being too large, not too small.

NOTE

Allow space for upgrades Sun recommends adding 30% to each file system that you create to enable you to upgrade to future Solaris versions. In the past, each new Solaris release has required approximately 10% more disk space than the previous release. By allowing 30% extra space, you can upgrade several times before you need to increase slice sizes.

Many servers today come with 72GB disk drives. I use the entire drive for the operating system. Most of my servers also run a third-party performance-monitoring package that can create huge log files in `/var`. Operating system patches can also use up a lot of space in `/var`. You'll find that you're constantly adding patches to a server because of the vast array of applications and hardware components you're supporting. I usually go crazy a little and allocate a few extra gigabytes to each file system.

Also, it's difficult to estimate your swap requirements on a server. These servers can run for months without a reboot and might be supporting several database applications or users. Again, allocate ample swap—no less than twice the amount of RAM. System performance will not be degraded if you allocate too much swap space. Too much swap space simply wastes disk space. Disk space is cheap, however, compared to the cost of running out of swap and crashing an application during peak production times. When you're satisfied with your selections, press **F2**. You see the dialog box shown in Figure 2.47.

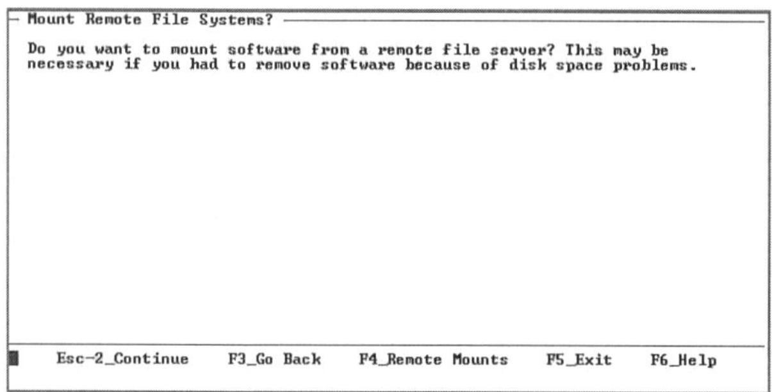

FIGURE 2.47 Mount remote file system.

47. Press **F2** to continue, unless you want to set up remote mounts.

NOTE

Setting up mount points I usually wait until after the initial software installation to set up these mounts. Many times, the system is not connected to a production network at this point, so the mount points are unavailable. It's also a personal preference to save this task for the post-installation phase, when I set up users, printers, and so on. I have a checklist of all the things I need to do after software installation, and setting up mount points is one of them.

Next you see the dialog box shown in Figure 2.48.

```
- Profile ----------------------------------------------------------------
The information shown below is your profile for installing Solaris software.
It reflects the choices you've made on previous screens.

=========================================================================

            Installation Option: Initial
                    Boot Device: c1t1d0
                Client Services: None
                  System Locale: C ( C )

                       Software: Solaris 10, Entire Distribution

      File System and Disk Layout: /                     c1t1d0s0 10000 MB
                                   /var                  c1t1d0s1 3000 MB
                                   swap                  c1t1d0s3 1000 MB
                                   /data                 c1t1d0s4 6000 MB
                                   /export/home          c1t1d0s7 5000 MB

-------------------------------------------------------------------------
    Esc-2_Begin Installation     F4_Change     F5_Exit     F6_Help
```

FIGURE 2.48 Interactive installation summary screen.

48. Verify the information, and press **F2** (Esc+2) if you agree.

> **CAUTION**
>
> **Pressing F2 versus pressing F5** When you press **F2** to begin the installation, all file systems, except any that were preserved, are destroyed. If you press F5 to cancel, the installation is aborted, all changes are undone, and the disk is unchanged.

> **NOTE**
>
> **Slice sizing** Slice sizes and disk space requirements were discussed earlier in this chapter. Review the sections "Software Groups" and "Disk Storage" if you are unsure of the slices and sizes that have been set up by the installation program.

If you did not allocate all the space on your disk, as I did, you see the message shown in Figure 2.49.

```
- Warning ----------------------------------------------------------------


      The following disk configuration condition(s) have been
      detected. Errors must be fixed to ensure a successful
      installation. Warnings can be ignored without causing the
      installation to fail.

      WARNING: Unused disk space (c1t1d0)


-------------------------------------------------------------------------
    F2_OK     F5_Cancel
```

FIGURE 2.49 Unused disk space warning.

Press **F2** to continue.

Next, you see the dialog box shown in Figure 2.50 as the software is being installed.

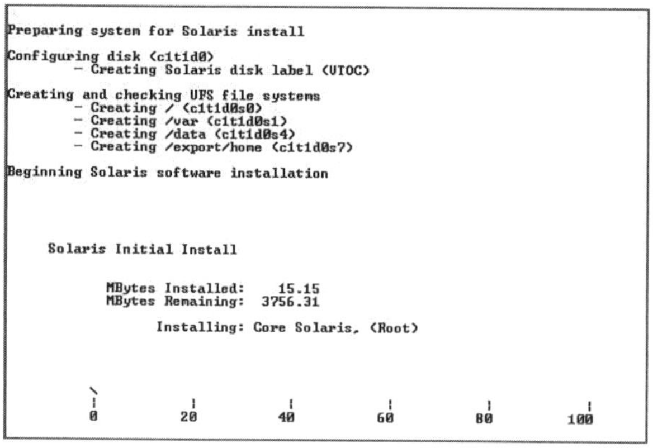

```
Preparing system for Solaris install

Configuring disk <c1t1d0>
        - Creating Solaris disk label (VTOC)

Creating and checking UFS file systems
        - Creating / (c1t1d0s0)
        - Creating /var (c1t1d0s1)
        - Creating /data (c1t1d0s4)
        - Creating /export/home (c1t1d0s7)

Beginning Solaris software installation



     Solaris Initial Install

            MBytes Installed:     15.15
            MBytes Remaining:   3756.31

                 Installing: Core Solaris, (Root)


            \
            |         |          |          |          |          |
            0         20         40         60         80         100
```

FIGURE 2.50 Installation progress screen.

A meter appears at the bottom of the screen, showing the progress of the installation. When it reaches 100%, the system reboots. After that, you see the following screen:

```
This system is configured with NFS version 4, which uses a domain
        name that is automatically derived from the system's name services.
        The derived domain name is sufficient for most configurations. In a
        few cases, mounts that cross different domains might cause files to
        be owned by "nobody" due to the lack of a common domain name.

        Do you need to override the system's default NFS version 4 domain
        name (yes/no) ? [no] :
```

Respond with `no` to continue. The system reboots and prompts you for the next media choice.

49. If you installed the OS using CDs, select the CD option, insert the Solaris 2 CD-ROM, and click OK to continue. As the installation continues, you'll continue to be prompted to load and unload the remaining CDs. After the system finishes loading all the CDs, it reboots, and the login screen is displayed.

NOTE

Power- saving feature Depending on the Energy Star version for your particular system, you may be prompted to enable your system's automatic power-saving feature. If your system uses Energy Star version 3 or later, you are not prompted for this information.

This completes the installation of the Solaris operating system.

You'll find various log files associated with the installation in the `/var/sadm` directory. For example, the `/var/sadm/install_data/install_log` contains all messages generated by the installation program.

If you're upgrading or installing Solaris on a running x86- or x64-based system, use the steps listed in Step by Step 2.2 to perform the installation.

STEP BY STEP

2.2 Installing x86- or x64 -based Solaris on a Running System

1. If you are installing Solaris on an x86- or x64-based system, you do not see the `ok` prompt as displayed on the SPARC-based system. Place the CD (or DVD) into the CD/DVD drive, and boot to the CD/DVD.

> **NOTE**
>
> **Configuring the BIOS** Your system's BIOS must be configured to boot from the CD-ROM or DVD. If necessary, get into the BIOS setup utility, as shown in Figure 2.51, and set the boot sequence, as shown in Figure 2.52.

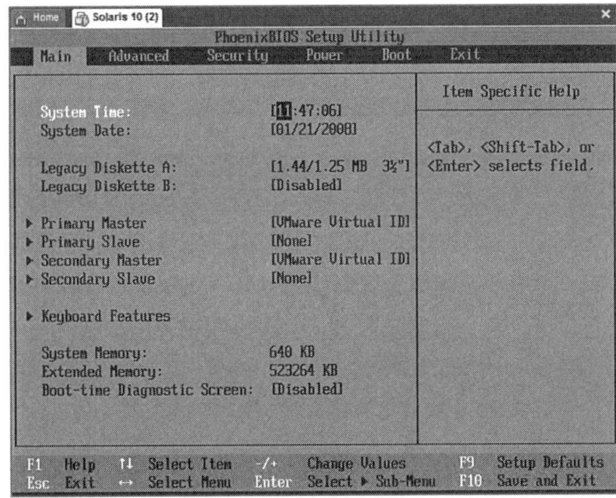

FIGURE 2.51 BIOS setup utility.

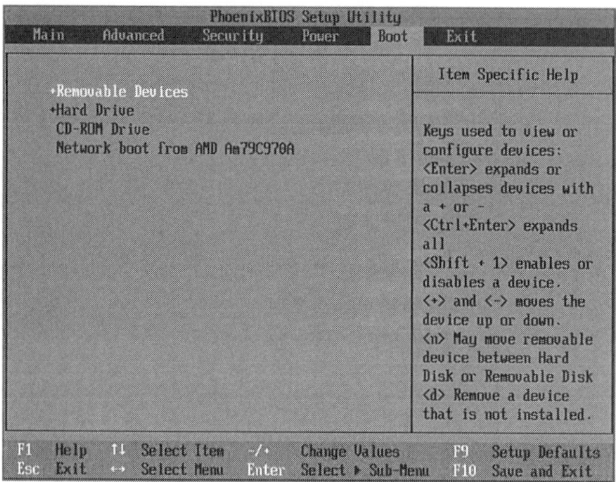

FIGURE 2.52 BIOS setup utility: boot sequence.

2. When the system boots to the Solaris CD/DVD, the GRUB menu appears, as shown in Figure 2.53.

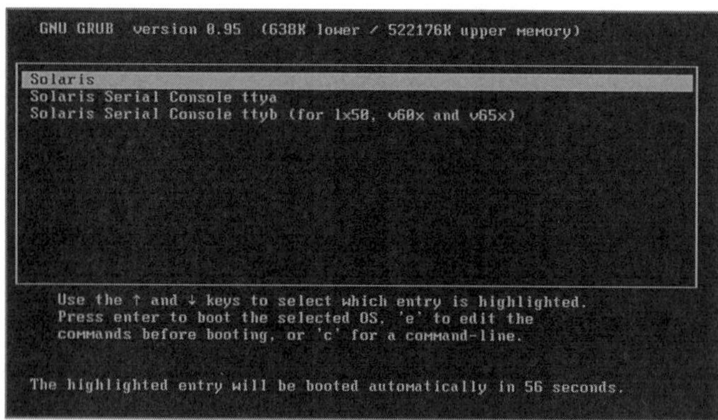

FIGURE 2.53 GRUB menu.

3. Three menu items appear in the GRUB menu. Select the first item—Solaris—and press Enter. The system continues booting from the CD/DVD and loads a memory-resident version of Solaris. The Configuring Devices window appears, as shown in Figure 2.54.

```
SunOS Release 5.10 Version Generic_120012-14 32-bit
Copyright 1983-2007 Sun Microsystems, Inc.  All rights reserved.
Use is subject to license terms.
NOTICE: MPO disabled because memory is interleaved

Configuring devices.
/

     1.     Solaris Interactive (default)
     2.     Custom JumpStart
     3.     Solaris Interactive Text (Desktop session)
     4.     Solaris Interactive Text (Console session)
     5.     Apply driver updates
     6.     Single user shell

Enter the number of your choice.
Automatically continuing in 29 seconds
```

FIGURE 2.54 Configuring devices.

4. Select item 1 and press Enter. The system begins to boot from the CD/DVD, as shown in Figure 2.55. The installation program attempts to configure all the devices.

```
Use is subject to license terms.
NOTICE: MPO disabled because memory is interleaved

Configuring devices.
/

     1.     Solaris Interactive (default)
     2.     Custom JumpStart
     3.     Solaris Interactive Text (Desktop session)
     4.     Solaris Interactive Text (Console session)
     5.     Apply driver updates
     6.     Single user shell

Enter the number of your choice.
Timed out, continuing.

Solaris Interactive

|
Using install cd in /dev/dsk/c1t0d0p0
Using RPC Bootparams for network configuration information.
Attempting to configure interface pcn0...
Skipped interface pcn0
Setting up Java. Please wait...
```

FIGURE 2.55 Booting from the CD/DVD.

NOTE

Adding third-party drivers The actual configuration of an x86/x64-based system will vary. Sometimes you may need to install a vendor-supplied driver for hardware such as a RAID controller or network interface. Item 5, Apply driver updates, allows you to temporarily stop the Solaris installation to add these third-party drivers.

As the program configures the devices, you're prompted to configure the keyboard layout, as shown in Figure 2.56. Previously, the USB keyboard assumed a self-identifying value of 1 during the installation. PS/2 keyboards are not self-identifying. You have to select the keyboard layout during the installation.

Select US-English, and press **F2** to continue.

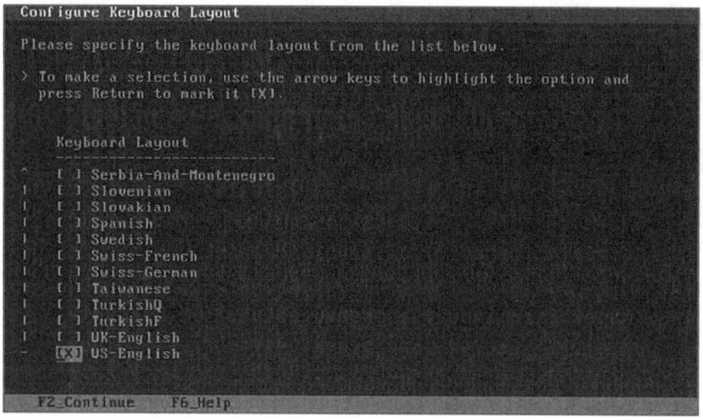

```
Configure Keyboard Layout

Please specify the keyboard layout from the list below.

> To make a selection, use the arrow keys to highlight the option and
  press Return to mark it [X].

    Keyboard Layout
    ---------------------------
^   [ ] Serbia-And-Montenegro
|   [ ] Slovenian
|   [ ] Slovakian
|   [ ] Spanish
|   [ ] Swedish
|   [ ] Swiss-French
|   [ ] Swiss-German
|   [ ] Taiwanese
|   [ ] TurkishQ
|   [ ] TurkishF
|   [ ] UK-English
-   [X] US-English

  F2_Continue    F6_Help
```

FIGURE 2.56 Configure the keyboard layout.

5. You're informed that the Solaris Interactive Installation is starting. You can select graphical mode or a console session, as shown in Figure 2.57.

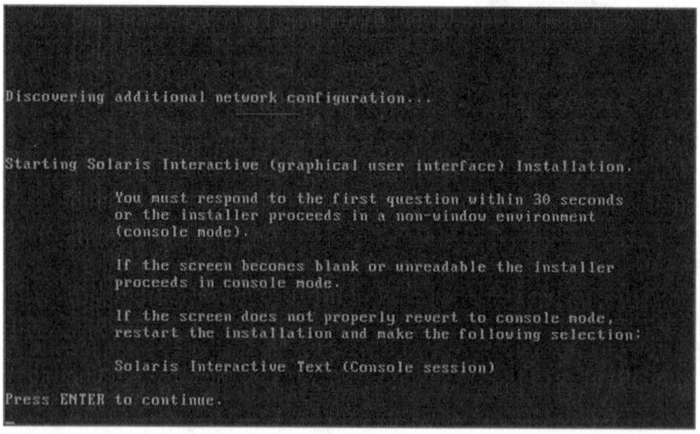

```
Discovering additional network configuration...

Starting Solaris Interactive (graphical user interface) Installation.

        You must respond to the first question within 30 seconds
        or the installer proceeds in a non-window environment
        (console mode).

        If the screen becomes blank or unreadable the installer
        proceeds in console mode.

        If the screen does not properly revert to console mode,
        restart the installation and make the following selection:

        Solaris Interactive Text (Console session)

Press ENTER to continue.
```

FIGURE 2.57 Start the installation.

Press Enter to continue. The system enters the Console mode of the installation program.

6. You're prompted to Select a Language, as shown in Figure 2.58.

   Enter `0` for English, and press Enter to continue.

7. The next two screens, Figures 2.59 and 2.60, provide information about navigating the installation program.

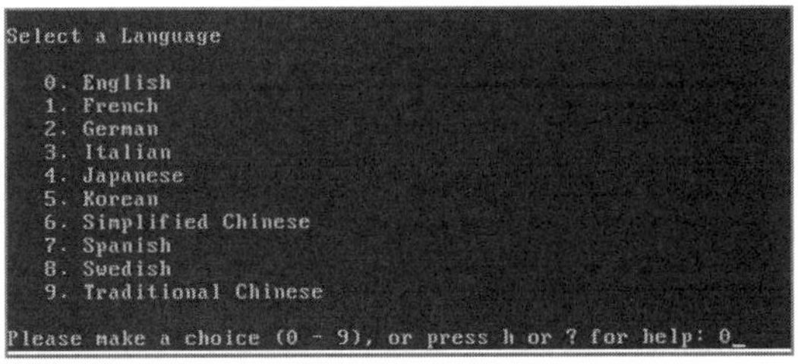

```
Select a Language

   0. English
   1. French
   2. German
   3. Italian
   4. Japanese
   5. Korean
   6. Simplified Chinese
   7. Spanish
   8. Swedish
   9. Traditional Chinese

Please make a choice (0 - 9), or press h or ? for help: 0_
```

FIGURE 2.58 Select a language.

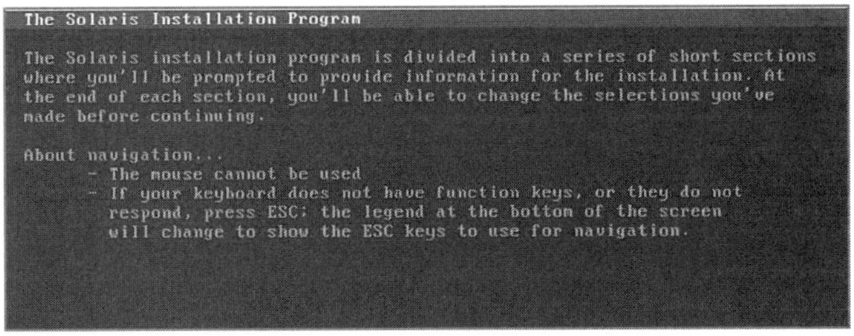

```
The Solaris Installation Program

The Solaris installation program is divided into a series of short sections
where you'll be prompted to provide information for the installation. At
the end of each section, you'll be able to change the selections you've
made before continuing.

About navigation...
      - The mouse cannot be used
      - If your keyboard does not have function keys, or they do not
        respond, press ESC; the legend at the bottom of the screen
        will change to show the ESC keys to use for navigation.
```

FIGURE 2.59 Solaris installation program.

```
Identify This System

On the next screens, you must identify this system as networked or
non-networked, and set the default time zone and date/time.

If this system is networked, the software will try to find the information
it needs to identify your system; you will be prompted to supply any
information it cannot find.

> To begin identifying this system, press F2.
```

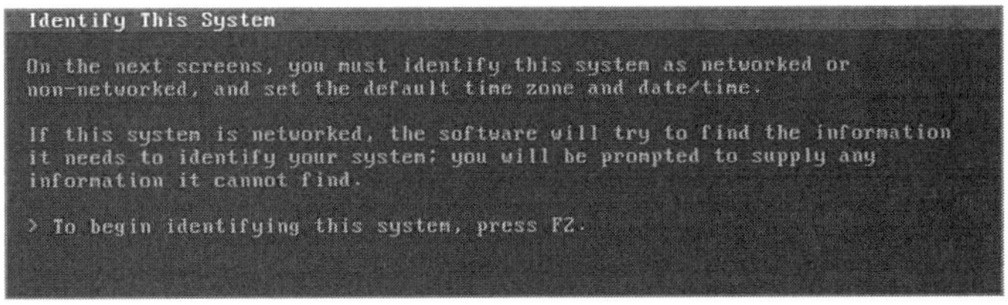

FIGURE 2.60 Identify this system.

Press **F2** to continue past each screen.

8. The Network Connectivity screen appears, as shown in Figure 2.61. Select Yes or No, and press **F2** to continue.

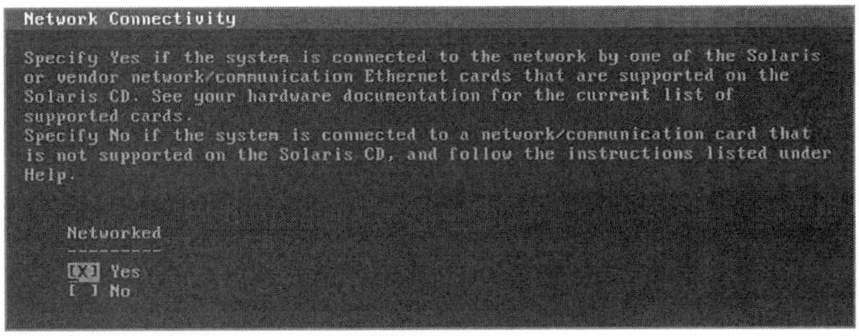

```
Network Connectivity

Specify Yes if the system is connected to the network by one of the Solaris
or vendor network/communication Ethernet cards that are supported on the
Solaris CD. See your hardware documentation for the current list of
supported cards.
Specify No if the system is connected to a network/communication card that
is not supported on the Solaris CD, and follow the instructions listed under
Help.

    Networked
    ---------
    [X] Yes
    [ ] No
```

FIGURE 2.61 Network connectivity.

9. If you chose to enable the network, you're prompted for additional network information. At this point, the installation on the x86/x64 platform is the same as what is displayed for the SPARC platform. Go back to the Step by Step 2.1 instructions for the SPARC platform, and begin at Step 10 to complete the installation dialog box.

Configuring Power Management

The `install-solaris` installation program prompts you to enable or disable the Power Management software after the installation is complete and the system reboots. If you are performing interactive installations, you cannot preconfigure the Power Management information and avoid the prompt. However, by using a custom JumpStart installation, you can preconfigure the Power Management information by using a finish script to create an `/autoshutdown` or `/noautoshutdown` file on the system. When the system reboots, the `/autoshutdown` file enables Power Management, and the `/noautoshutdown` file disables Power Management.

You can manually configure the power management configuration for your system by using the `pmconfig` command. A user has permission to change the Power Management configuration of his or her system using `pmconfig` only if the user is allowed to do so according to PMCHANGEPERM keyword of `/etc/default/power` file.

`pmconfig` first resets the Power Management state to its default and then reads the new Power Management configuration from `/etc/power.conf` and issues the commands to activate the new configuration. The `pmconfig` utility is run at system boot. This utility can also be run from the command line after manual changes have been made to the `/etc/power.conf` file. For editing changes made to the `/etc/power.conf` file to take effect, users must run `pmconfig`.

The following is what the /etc/power.conf file looks like on a system that has power management configured:

```
# more /etc/power.conf <cr>
# Copyright  1996 - 2001 by Sun Microsystems, Inc.
# All rights reserved.
#
#pragma ident   "@(#)power.conf 1.16    01/03/19 SMI"
#
# Power Management Configuration File
#
# This entry keeps removable media from being powered down unless the
# console framebuffer and monitor are powered down
# (See removable-media(9P))

device-dependency-property removable-media /dev/fb


autopm                  default
# Auto-Shutdown         Idle(min)       Start/Finish(hh:mm)     Behavior
autoshutdown            60              17:00 7:00              shutdown
autopm                  default
statefile               /export/home/.CPR
```

In this example, power management is configured to autoshutdown the system when it has been idle for 60 minutes anytime between 5 p.m. and 7 a.m. To disable autoshutdown, change the following lines in the `/etc/power.conf` file:

```
# Auto-Shutdown Idle(min)   Start/Finish(hh:mm)  Behavior
autoshutdown    60              17:00 7:00       noshutdown
```

Note that `shutdown` has been changed to `noshutdown` in the `/etc/power.conf` file.

The `dtpower` GUI also allows the configuration of `/etc/power.conf` file. For ease-of-use, it is recommended that you use `dtpower` GUI to configure the parameters in the `/etc/power.conf` file.

Tools for Managing Software

After installing the Solaris operating environment, you'll find it necessary to install additional software packages, or perhaps remove software from the system. In addition, you'll most likely need to install operating system patches on an on-going basis. Solaris provides the tools for adding and removing software from a system. These are described in Table 2.3.

Sun and its third-party vendors deliver software products in a form called a software package. As I described earlier, a package is a collection of files and directories in a defined format that conforms to the Application Binary Interface (ABI), a supplement to the System V Interface Definition. The Solaris operating environment provides a set of utilities that interpret the ABI format and provides the means to install or remove a package or to verify its installation.

Table 2.3 Tools for Managing Software

Command	Description
Managing Software from the Command Line	
`pkgadd`	Adds software packages to the system.
`pkgrm`	Removes software packages from the system.
`pkgchk`	Checks the accuracy of a software package installation.
`pkginfo`	Displays software package information.
`pkgask`	Stores answers in a response file so that they can be supplied automatically during an installation.
`pkgparam`	Displays package parameter values.
`pkgtrans`	Translates an installable package from one format to another.
Managing Software from the Graphical User Interface	
Solaris Product Registry	Manages all your Solaris software.
Web Start Installer	Installs or removes a software package with a GUI or text-based installer wizard.

Use the pkgadd or pkgrm commands directly from the command line to load or remove software packages. The pkgadd and pkgrm commands can be incorporated into scripts to automate the software installation process. Many third-party vendors use pkgadd in scripts as a means of installing their software.

The Solaris Product Registry is a front-end GUI for the software package commands. The Solaris Product Registry is a system for maintaining records of the software products installed on a Solaris system. The Product Registry includes a GUI tool to make managing your Solaris software easier. The Product Registry enables you to install, list, or uninstall Solaris software packages or clusters. The Solaris Product Registry is discussed in more detail later.

Also included on many CD-ROMs/DVDs that ship with Solaris is the installer utility. It invokes a Web Start install wizard sequence that leads the user through a sequence of installation windows. This installer utility is found in the top-level directory on many CD-ROMs/DVDs that ship with Solaris. When the installer is on a CD-ROM/DVD being accessed from a desktop file manager, double-click the installer to start the installation sequence. If the user is not currently the system's root user, the system requests the root user password.

Adding and Removing Software Packages

When you add a software package, the pkgadd command decompresses and copies files from the installation media, such as the CD-ROM/DVD, to a local system's disk. When you use packages, files are delivered in package format and are unusable as they are delivered. The pkgadd command interprets the software package's control files and then decompresses the product files and installs them on the system's local disk.

You should know the following before installing additional application software:

- Sun packages always begin with the prefix SUNW, as in SUNWvolr, SUNWadmap, and SUNWtcsh. Third-party packages usually begin with a prefix that corresponds to the company's stock symbol.
- You can use the pkginfo command or the Solaris Product Registry to view software already installed on a system.
- Clients might have software that resides partially on a server and partially on the client. If this is the case, adding software for the client requires adding packages to both the server and the client.
- You need to know where the software will be installed, and you need to make sure you have a file system with enough disk space to store the application software. If you know the name of the software package, you can use the pkgparam command to determine where the package will be loaded. For example, to find out information about the SUNWman package, type the following:

```
# pkgparam -d /cdrom/cdrom0/s0/Solaris_10/Product SUNWman SUNW_PKGTYPE <cr>
```

SUNW_PKGTYPE (and BASEDIR) is a special parameter that reports where a Solaris software package will be installed. If the package does not have the SUNW_PKGTYPE parameter set, the pkgparam command returns an empty string. For Sun packages, this usually means that the package is installed in /opt.

The system responds with the location where the application will be stored:

```
usr
```

NOTE

Obtaining pkgid Information It's not always clear what the pkgid is for a particular software package or application until it is actually installed. Sometimes the release documentation that comes with the package tells you the name of the pkgid. Other times you might need to call the vendor to get the pkgid information.

CAUTION

Use pkgrm to remove software When you remove a package, the pkgrm command deletes all the files associated with that package unless those files are also shared with other packages. If the files are shared with other packages, a system message warns you of that fact, and you are asked if you want to remove them anyway. Be sure you do not delete application software without using pkgrm. For example, some system administrators delete an application simply by removing the directory containing the application software. With this method, files belonging to the application that might reside in other directories are missed. With pkgrm, you'll be assured of removing all files associated with the application and not damaging installation of other packages.

Although the pkgadd and pkgrm commands do not log their output to a standard location, they do keep track of the product installed or removed. The pkgadd and pkgrm commands store information in a software product database about a package that has been installed or removed. By updating this database, the pkgadd and pkgrm commands keep a record of all software products installed on the system.

Using a Spool Directory

For convenience, you can copy frequently installed packages to a spool directory. If you copy packages to the default spool directory, /var/spool/pkg, you do not need to specify the source location of the package when using the pkgadd command. The pkgadd command, by default, looks in the /var/spool/pkg directory for any packages specified on the command line.

NOTE

Spooling packages versus installing them Copying packages to a spool directory is not the same as installing the packages on a system.

You can add a software package to a spool directory by following the steps described in Step by Step 2.3.

STEP BY STEP

2.3 Adding a Package to the Spool Directory

1. Log in as root.
2. Make sure the spool directory exists.
3. Add a software package to a spool directory using the pkgadd command, as follows:

```
# pkgadd -d <device-name> -s <spool directory> <pkgid> <cr>
```

   - -d *<device-name>* specifies the absolute path to the software package. *<device-name>* can be the path to a device, a directory, or a spool directory.
   - -s *<spool directory>* specifies the name of the spool directory where the software package will be spooled. You must specify *<spool directory>*, a directory where the software will be put.
   - *<pkgid>* is optional. It is the name of one or more packages, separated by spaces, to be added to the spool directory. If omitted, pkgadd copies all available packages.

4. Use the pkginfo command to verify that the package has been copied to the spool directory, as follows:

```
# pkginfo -d <spool directory> ¦ grep <pkgid> <cr>
```

   The pkginfo command returns a line of information about the package if it has been copied to the spool directory properly. If it returns an empty command line, the package has not been successfully copied to the spool directory.

The following is an example of how to copy a software package to the /var/spool/pkg directory:

```
# pkgadd -d /cdrom/sol_10_807_sparc_4/Solaris_10/Product -s /var/spool/pkg SUNNWman <cr>
```

The system responds with

```
Transferring <SUNWman> package instance
```

Now type the following to list the packages in the /var/spool/pkg directory:

```
# pkginfo -d /var/spool/pkg <cr>
```

The system responds with

```
system      SUNWman On-Line Manual Pages
```

Installing Software from the Command Line

Use the pkgadd command to install additional software packages from the command line. In the previous section, we used pkgadd to add software to a spool directory. To install this software on the system, type

```
# pkgadd <cr>
```

Any software that has been spooled to the /var/spool/pkg directory is listed. In this example, I spooled a package named SFWgawk. After you type the pkgadd command, the system responds with

```
The following packages are available:
  1  SFWgawk     gawk - pattern scanning and processing language
                 (sparc) 3.1.5,REV=2006.10.04.21.15

Select package(s) you wish to process (or 'all' to process
all packages). (default: all) [?,??,q]:
```

After pressing **Enter**, you may see a message like the following:

```
Using </opt> as the package base directory.
## Processing package information.
## Processing system information.
## Verifying package dependencies.
## Verifying disk space requirements.
## Checking for conflicts with packages already installed.
## Checking for setuid/setgid programs.

Installing gawk - pattern scanning and processing language as <SFWgawk>

## Installing part 1 of 1.
/opt/sfw/bin/gawk
/opt/sfw/bin/igawk
  <output has been truncated>
Installation of <SFWgawk> was successful.
```

Removing Software Using pkgrm

You can remove software packages from the command line using the pkgrm command. For example, to remove the software package named SUNWman, type

```
# pkgrm SUNWman <cr>
```

The system responds with

```
The following package is currently installed:
   SUNWman  On-Line Manual Pages
            (sparc) 43.0,REV=75.0

Do you want to remove this package? [y,n,?,q]
```

Type **y** and press **Enter**. You see a list of files being removed followed by a message similar to this one:

```
## Updating system information.
Removal of <SUNWman> was successful.
```

Solaris Product Registry

The Solaris Product Registry enables you to do the following:

- View a list of installed and registered software and some software attributes.
- Find and launch an installer.
- Install additional software products.
- Uninstall software.

The main difference between the Product Registry and the other tools is that the Product Registry is designed to be compatible with more of the newer installation wizards and Web Start 3.0.

To start up the Solaris Product Registry, type the following:

```
# /usr/bin/prodreg <cr>
```

The Product Registry window, shown in Figure 2.62, appears.

To view the contents of the system registry, double-click the magnifying glass next to Solaris System Software. The registry is expanded and the contents listed. Click any folder listed to get more information on that package. I clicked Entire Distribution and then Apache Web Server, and the information shown in Figure 2.63 was displayed.

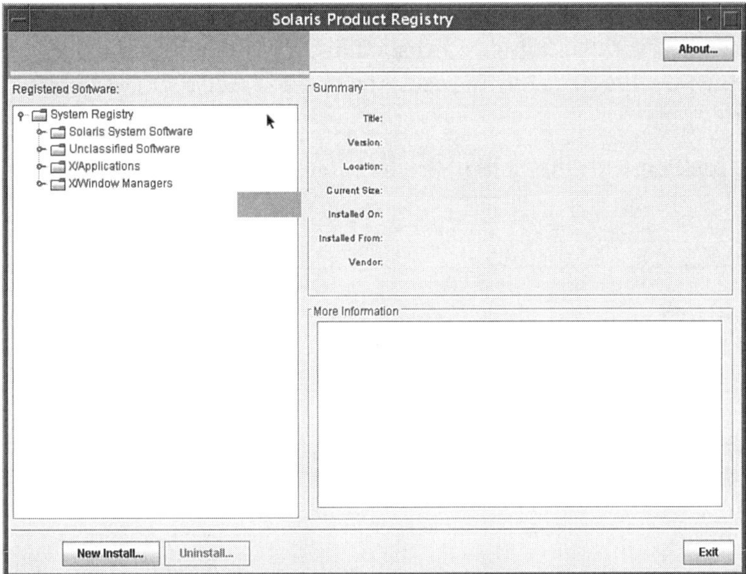

FIGURE 2.62 Product Registry window.

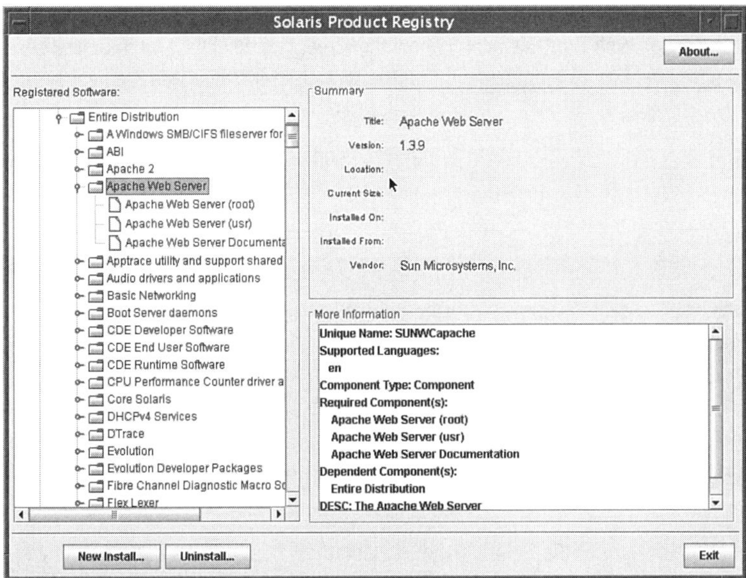

FIGURE 2.63 Apache Web Server information.

Along with listing information about all installed software products on your system, use the Solaris Product Registry to check the integrity of software products installed on the system.

Follow the steps outlined for listing installed software. After you see the package you want to check, click its name in the window titled Software Installed in Solaris Registry. If all or part of the product is missing, the message `Missing files in one or more components` appears after the Installed From attribute.

You can install a software package with the Solaris Product Registry by following the steps described in Step by Step 2.4.

STEP BY STEP

2.4 Installing Software Using the Solaris Product Registry

1. Log in as root.
2. Insert the CD-ROM/DVD that contains the software you want to add to the system. When you insert the CD-ROM/DVD, the Volume Manager automatically mounts the CD-ROM/DVD.
3. Start the Solaris Product Registry as outlined earlier in this section.
4. Click the New Install button at the bottom of the Solaris Product Registry window. The Product Registry displays the Select Installer dialog box, which initially points to the `/cdrom` directory.
5. When you find the installer you want, click its name in the Files box and then click OK.
6. The installer you selected launches Web Start installer. Follow the directions displayed by the installer you selected to install the software. For more information on the Web Start installer, see the next section.

You can also use the Product Registry to remove software by following the steps described in Step by Step 2.5.

STEP BY STEP

2.5 Uninstalling Software Using the Solaris Product Registry

To uninstall software, go into the Solaris Product Registry window and follow these steps:

1. Click the System Registry folder in the window titled Software Installed in Solaris Registry and click the software package you want to remove. Read the software attributes to make sure this is the software you want to uninstall.
2. Click the Uninstall button at the bottom of the Solaris Product Registry window. The software product you selected is uninstalled.

Web Start Installer

The Web Start installer enables you to add software to a system on which you have installed the Solaris operating environment. The Solaris Web Start program installs only those components in the software groups that you skipped when you initially installed the Solaris operating environment. You cannot change to another software group after installing or upgrading.

To add software to your system using the Web Start installer, follow Step by Step 2.6.

STEP BY STEP

2.6 Adding Software Using Web Start

1. Log in to the system as root.
2. Load the CD-ROM/DVD into the CD-ROM/DVD drive.

   This procedure assumes that the system is running volume management (`vold`). See Chapter 1 for more details.
3. Change directories to find the Solaris Web Start installer. It is a file named "installer" that's usually located in the top-level directory of the CD-ROM/DVD.
4. Execute the installer by typing `./installer` or by double-clicking the Installer icon in the File Manager or Solaris Product Registry window (as described in the preceding section). You can run the installer in a GUI interface or from the command line. To run the installer from the command line, execute the installer as follows:

   ```
   #./installer -nodisplay <cr>
   ```

   In the following example, I've installed the Solaris CD-ROM labeled "Solaris 10 Companion CD" into the CD-ROM drive. `vold` automatically mounts the CD-ROM.
5. After inserting the CD into the CD-ROM drive, type the following to begin the installation:

   ```
   # /cdrom/cdrom0/installer -nodisplay <cr>
   ```

   The following dialog begins:

   ```
   Select the type of installation you want for each product.

         No Install  Default Install  Custom Install  Product
         ----------  ---------------  --------------  -------
    0.   [ ]         [X]              [ ]             Application/Accessibility
    1.   [ ]         [X]              [ ]             Application/Editors
    2.   [ ]         [X]              [ ]             Application/Networking
    3.   [ ]         [X]              [ ]             Application/Publishing
    4.   [ ]         [X]              [ ]             Application/Utilities
    5.   [ ]         [X]              [ ]             Desktop/Environment
    6.   [ ]         [X]              [ ]             Development/Languages
   ```

```
 7.  [ ]        [X]             [ ]            Development/Libraries
 8.  [ ]        [X]             [ ]            Development/Tools
 9.  [ ]        [X]             [ ]            System/Daemons
10.  [ ]        [X]             [ ]            X/Applications
11.  [ ]        [X]             [ ]            X/Window Managers
12.                                            Done
  Enter the number next to the product you wish to change.  Select "Done" when
  finished [12]:
```

6. Deselect items 0 through 9 and press **Enter** to continue. The following messages are displayed on the screen:

```
Checking disk space.

The following items will be installed:

Product: X/Applications
Location: /opt
Size: 101.15 MB
-----------
stardic - Star Dictionary online translation tool, v1.3.1    3.14 MB
xterm - Terminal emulator for X Windows, v196    395.32 KB
sane -  Scanner Applications, v1.0.12    8.82 MB
rxvt - ouR eXtended Virtual Terminal, v2.7.10    177.44 KB
xcpustate - display CPU states and statistics, v2.5    40.05 KB
xmcd - Motif CD Audio Player, v3.2.1    5.66 MB
gimp - GNU Image Manipulation Program, v1.2.1    41.16 MB
vnc - Virtual Network Computing, v3.3.7    1.57 MB
xmms - X MultiMedia System, v1.2.10    6.04 MB
asclock - the AfterStep clock, v1.0    34.19 MB

Product: X/Window Managers
Location: /opt
Size: 14.34 MB
------------
afterstep - X11 window manager, v1.8.8    37.55 MB
WindowMaker - X11 Window Manager, v0.80.2    7.91 MB
fvwm - X11 virtual window manager, v2.4.3    3.08 MB


Ready to Install

1. Install Now
2. Start Over
3. Exit Installation

   What would you like to do [1]?
```

7. Press **Enter** to Install Now; a license agreement is displayed. Press `y` to accept the agreement and continue the install. The system shows you the progress of the installation. When it's complete, you see the following message:

```
Installing X/Window Managers
¦-1%--------25%----------50%----------75%--------100%¦


Installation details:

     Product              Result     More Info
  1. X/Applications       Installed  Available
  2. X/Window Managers    Installed  Available

  3. Done
```

8. Press **Enter** to complete the installation.

Listing and Verifying Installed Packages

At any time, you can use the Software Product Registry or issue the `pkginfo` command from the command line to obtain a complete listing of the software installed on a system. The Product Registry GUI displays information about installed software, as described in the previous section and as shown in Figure 2.64.

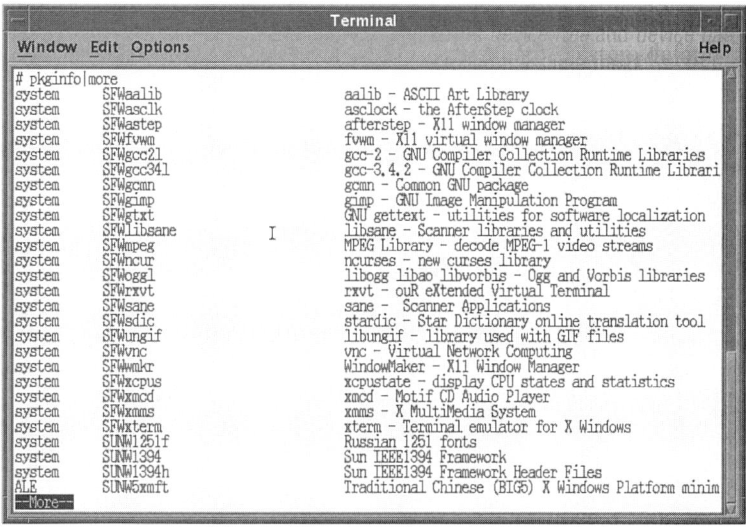

FIGURE 2.64 pkginfo output.

Figure 2.64 illustrates the `pkginfo` command used from the command line, piped to `more` to show the display of information one page at a time.

Table 2.4 lists some of the files and directories used with package administration.

Table 2.4 Software Package Files and Directories

File or Directory Name	Description
`/var/sadm/install/contents`	This file contains a complete record of all the software packages installed on the local system disk. It references every file and directory belonging to every software package and shows information about each software component, such as its default permission level and the package to which it belongs.
`/opt/`<*pkgname*>	The preferred location for the installation of unbundled packages.
`/etc/opt/`<*pkgname*>	The preferred location for log files of unbundled packages.

The `/var/sadm` directory is extremely important, especially when changes are made to the software installed on your system in any form. This directory is used to record the changes made to the system when installing or removing software and patches. Many Solaris change management utilities rely upon the information inside `/var/sadm` for an accurate picture of what actually resides on the system.

`/var/sadm/install/contents` is a file that can be used to determine which package an individual file belongs to. You can also use it to determine which files are associated with a certain software group. For example, you can find out what things are associated with the `format` command:

```
# grep /etc/format /var/sadm/install/contents <cr>
```

The system displays the following information:

```
/etc/format=../usr/sbin/format s none SUNWcsr
/etc/format.dat v none 0644 root sys 6986 55261 1106350052 SUNWcsr
```

`/var/sadm/pkg/`<*package name*> is the directory where all the information about your software packages is stored. It is critical to keep this directory intact and up to date by using the standard package installation commands described in this section.

Quite often, system administrators may be tempted to remove the files from `/var/sadm` when their `/var` file system begins to fill up.

CAUTION

Do not remove files from `/var/sadm` *Do not* remove files from `/var/sadm`. Removing files from this directory may not impact the system for quite some time, but as soon as a patch or package needs to be applied to or removed from the system, you will run into a variety of problems.

Software Patches

Another system administration task is managing system software patches. A *patch* is a fix to a reported software problem. Sun ships several software patches to customers so that problems can be resolved before the next release of software. The existing software is derived from a specified package format that conforms to the ABI.

A patch consists of several files and directories that replace files already installed on your system. Solaris patch types include the following:

- **Standard patches**: Patches that fix specific problems with the Solaris OS and other Sun hardware and software products.
- **Recommended and security patches**: Sun Customer Service designates operating system patches that are of universal interest or reflect security concerns to be "recommended" and "security" patches, respectively.
- **Firmware and PROM patches**: Hardware-related updates.
- **Patch clusters**: A group of standard, recommended, or security patches that have been bundled into a single archive for convenient downloading and installation.

Patches are identified by unique alphanumeric strings. The patch base code comes first, and then a hyphen, and then a number that represents the patch revision number. For example, patch 110453-01 is a Solaris patch to correct a known problem.

You might want to know more about patches that have previously been installed. Table 2.5 describes commands that provide useful information about patches already installed on a system.

Table 2.5 Helpful Commands for Patch Administration

Command	Function
`showrev -p`	Shows all patches applied to a system.
`pkgparam` *<pkgid>* `PATCHLIST`	Shows all patches applied to the package identified by *<pkgid>*.
`pkgparam` *<pkgid>* `PATCH INFO` *<patch-number>*	Shows the installation date and name of the host from which the patch was applied. *<pkgid>* is the name of the package (for example, SUNWadmap), and *<patch-number>* is the specific patch number.
`patchadd -R`	Shows all patches applied to a client, from the server's console. *<client_root_path>* `-p`
`patchadd -p`	Shows all patches applied to a system.
`patchrm` *<patchname>*	Removes a specified patch. *<patchname>* is the name of the patch to be removed.
`smpatch`	A new tool in Solaris 10 for managing patches.
`Patch Tool`	A Solaris Management Console Tool for managing patches.
`Sun Connection Services`	An automated patch management tool. This feature is New in the 08/07 release of Solaris 10.

NOTE

Sun Connection Service The Sun Connection Service method of obtaining patches is an objective on the CX-310-202 exam and is not covered on the CX-310-200 exam. Refer to *Solaris 10 System Administration Exam Prep: Exam CX-310-202.*

The tools described in Table 2.5 are tools you might already be accustomed to if you've managed patches using earlier versions of the Solaris operating environment. In Solaris 10, Patch Manager helps you manage patches by displaying information about installed patches. It also assists you in adding patches to one or more systems concurrently, removes patches, analyzes a system's patch requirements, and downloads patches from the SunSolve Online service.

I'll first describe how to manage patches using the conventional tools described in Table 2.5, and then I'll describe Patch Manager.

Obtaining a Patch

Sun customers can access security patches and other recommended patches via the World Wide Web. As of September 2006, you can no longer obtain patches via Sun's anonymous FTP server. You can download patches from the SunSolve website, which (as of this writing) is at http://sunsolve.sun.com. Look for the Patches and Updates link. Sun customers who have purchased a service contract can access an extended set of patches and a complete database of patch information. You can obtain individual patches or groups of patches called a *patch cluster*. Detailed information about how to install and remove a patch is provided in the README file included with each patch, which contains specific information about the patch.

As of this writing, you need a Sun Service Plan to download all patches, including restricted patches. Those without a contract can access only security patches and device drivers. In any case, you need a Sun Online Account to get patches from Sun's website. It is not required that you have a sun Service Plan to obtain an Online Account. You already have a Sun Online Account if you have an account on MySun, Sun Store, SunSolve, the Online Support Center, or the Sun Download Center.

Patches come in three different formats. Solaris 10 patches come in ZIP format, such as `104945-02.zip`. For Solaris 10 patches, use the `unzip` command to extract the patch files, as follows:

```
# /usr/bin/unzip 104945-02.zip <cr>
```

Signed patches are delivered as a jar file indicated by a `.jar` suffix in the name, such as `120292-01.jar`. To extract the jar file, type

```
# jar xvf 120292-01.jar <cr>
```

A signed patch is a patch that is signed with a valid digital signature. It provides greater security than an unsigned patch. The patch's digital signature can be verified before the patch is applied to your system. A valid digital signature ensures that the signed patch has not been modified since the signature was applied.

For more information about signed patches, see the "Managing Solaris Patches and Updates (Overview)" section of the *Solaris 10 System Administration Guide: Basic Administration*, found at http://docs.sun.com/app/docs/doc/817-1985/6mhm8o611.

NOTE

Compressed TAR files For Solaris 2.6 and earlier operating environments, patches might come in compressed TAR format, such as `104945-02.tar.Z`. Use the `zcat` command to decompress this type of patch file and the `tar` command to create the patch directories, as follows:

```
/usr/bin/zcat 104945-02.tar.Z ¦ tar xvf -
```

Other Solaris patches might come as GZIP compressed TAR files, such as `102945-02.tar.gz`. To extract a GZIP compressed TAR file, use the `gzcat` command to decompress and create the patch directories, as follows:

```
/usr/bin/gzcat 104945-02.tar.gz ¦ tar xvf -
```

The `patchadd` command is used to install directory-format patches to a Solaris 10 system. It is also used to list patches installed on a system. It must be run as root. The syntax is as follows:

```
patchadd [ -dpu ] [ -B backout_dir ] -R rootpath -M patchdir
```

The `patchadd` command is described in Table 2.6.

Table 2.6 `patchadd` **Command Options**

Command Option	Description
`-d`	Does not create a backup of the files to be patched. The patch cannot be removed when this option has been used to install the patch. By default, `patchadd` saves a copy of all files being updated so that the patch can be removed if necessary. Do not use the `-d` option unless you're positive the patch has been tested.
`-p`	Displays a list of the patches currently applied.
`-u`	Installs the patch unconditionally, with file validation turned off. The patch is installed even if some of the files to be patched have been modified since their original installation.
`-B <backout_dir>`	Saves backout data to a directory other than the package database. Specify `<backout_dir>` as an absolute pathname.

Table 2.6 `patchadd` **Command Options**

Command Option	Description
-M *<patch_dir>* tory *<patch_id>*	Specifies the patches to be installed. Specify patches to the -M option by direc- location and by patch number.
<patch_dir>	is the absolute pathname of the directory that contains the spooled patches. The *<patch_id>* is the patch number of a particular patch.
-M *<patch_dir>* *<patch_file list>*	Specifies the patches to be installed. Specify patches to the -M option by directory location and the name of a file containing a patch list. To use the directory location and a file containing a patch list, specify *<patch_dir>* as the absolute pathname of the directory containing the file with a list of patches to be installed. Specify *<patch_list>* as the name of the file containing the patches to be installed. See the example in the "Obtaining a Patch" section of this chapter.
-R *<client_root_path>*	Locates all patch files generated by `patchadd` under the directory *<client_root_path>*. *<client_root_path>* is the directory that contains the bootable root of a client from the server's perspective. Specify *<client_root_path>* as the absolute pathname to the beginning of the directory tree under which all patch files generated by `patchadd` are to be located. See the example in the "Obtaining a Patch" section of this chapter.

NOTE

patchadd options Additional options to the `patchadd` command can be found online in the Solaris system manual pages.

Installing a Patch

The following examples describe how to add patches to your system. A word of caution is in order before you install patches, however. It has been my personal experience—Murphy's Law, you might say—that things can go wrong. Because you're modifying the operating system with a patch, I highly recommend that you back up your file systems before loading patches. Although this can be a time-consuming and seemingly unnecessary task, I once encountered a power failure during a patch installation that completely corrupted my system. Another time, the patch installation script was defective, and the patch did not load properly. Without a backup, I would have had to reinstall the entire operating system.

The following example installs a patch to a standalone machine:

```
# patchadd /var/spool/patch/104945-02 <cr>
```

The following example installs multiple patches. The `patchlist` file specifies a file containing a list of patches to install:

```
# patchadd -M /var/spool/patch patchlist <cr>
```

Many times, a patch or patch cluster contains a script named `install_patch` or `install_cluster`. Simply executing this script installs the patch or patch cluster.

The following example displays the patches installed on a client system named client1:

```
# patchadd -R /export/root/client1 -p <cr>
```

When you're installing a patch, the `patchadd` command copies files from the patch directory to the local system's disk. More specifically, `patchadd` does the following:

- It determines the Solaris version number of the managing host and the target host.
- It updates the patch package's `pkginfo` file with information about patches made obsolete by the patch being installed, other patches required by this patch, and about patches incompatible with this patch.
- It moves outdated files and directories to the `/var` directory.
- It logs the patch installation to the `/var/sadm/patch/`<*patch-id*> directory.
- It updates the /var/sadm/pkg/<*pkg-name*>/pkginfo file.

The `patchadd` command will not install a patch under the following conditions:

- If the package is not fully installed on the host.
- If the patch architecture differs from the system architecture.
- If the patch version does not match the installed package version.
- If an installed patch already exists with the same base code and a higher version number.
- If the patch is incompatible with another, already-installed patch. (Each installed patch keeps this information in its `pkginfo` file.)
- If the patch being installed requires another patch that is not installed.

When a patch is installed, files that are replaced are moved into the `/var/sadm/pkg/`<*pkg-name*>`/save` directory. Files in this directory are used if you ever need to back out of a patch. These files are used to restore the system to the prepatch installation state. Backing out of a patch returns files and directories stored in the `/var` directory to their original locations and removes the versions installed by the patch. If you remove files in this directory, you cannot back out of a patch.

CAUTION

Don't remove patch files Do not remove patch files from the /var/sadm directory. These files may be needed to correct a problem in the future.

showrev -p gets its information from /var/sadm/pkg/<*pkgname*>/save as well, specifically from the pkginfo file in each pkg directory. This directory contains old information about the package as it existed prior to a patch install and contains backups of critical files for the package.

The file that you see in this directory will differ, depending on the package, but the save information for the patch IDs that have been installed should always exist and will look something like this:

```
# ls -l /var/sadm/pkg/SUNWcsu/save <cr>
total 8
drwxr-xr-x   2 root     other        512 Oct 10 15:25 112233-02
drwxr-xr-x   2 root     other        512 Oct 10 15:20 112963-01
drwxr-xr-x   2 root     other        512 Oct 10 15:27 112964-02
drwxr-xr-x   2 root     other        512 Oct 10 15:08 112998-02
```

Looking into each directory, we see a file named undo.Z, as follows:

```
# ls 112233-02 <cr>
undo.Z
```

If a file doesn't exist here, the patch was installed with the -d option. You did not save the backout information, and the patch cannot be backed out. This file is not always in .Z format. Sometimes it is just a regular uncompressed file.

A patch cluster contains a selected set of patches, conveniently wrapped for one-step installation. Typically, they are named "10_recommended." Clusters consist of operating system patches (including security fixes) deemed to be of universal interest. To install a patch cluster, follow these steps:

1. Uncompress or unzip the patch cluster and extract the tar file.
2. Change to the directory that contains the patch cluster, read the README file for any specific instructions, and run the install_cluster script.

Removing a Patch

Sometimes a patch does not work as planned and needs to be removed from the system. The utility used to remove, or back out of, a patch is the `patchrm` command, described in Table 2.7. Its syntax is as follows:

```
patchrm [ -f ] [ -B backout_dir ]
```

Table 2.7 `patchrm` **Command Options**

Command Options	Description
`-f`	Forces the patch removal regardless of whether the patch was superseded by another patch.
`-B` *<backout_dir>*	Removes a patch whose backout data has been saved to a directory other than the package database. This option is needed only if the original backout directory, supplied to the `patchadd` command at installation time, has been moved. Specify *backout_dir* as an absolute pathname.

The following example removes a patch from a standalone system:

```
# patchrm 104945-02 <cr>
```

The `patchrm` command removes a Solaris 10 patch package and restores previously saved files—restoring the file system to its state before a patch was applied—unless any of the following four conditions exist:

- The patch was installed with `patchadd -d`. (The `-d` option instructs `patchadd` not to save copies of files being updated or replaced.)
- The patch has been made obsolete by a later patch.
- The patch is required by another patch already installed on the system.
- The `patchrm` command calls `pkgadd` to restore packages saved from the initial patch installation.

Historical information about all installed patches that are able to be uninstalled using `patchrm` is stored in the `/var/sadm/patch` directory.

Patch Manager (`smpatch`)

Patch Manager is provided in Solaris 10 to assist you in managing patches on your system. Specifically, Patch Manager uses the `/usr/sbin/smpatch` utility to do the following:

- Analyze your system to determine if patches need to be installed.
- Download patches.
- Install patches.
- Remove patches.

The syntax for the `smpatch` utility is as follows:

```
smpatch subcommand <subcommand_option>
```

The `smpatch` command requires you to enter a *subcommand*, as described in Table 2.8.

Table 2.8 `smpatch` **Subcommands**

Subcommand	Description
`add`	Applies one or more patches to one or more systems. You must specify at least one patch to apply. By default, patches are applied to the local system. This subcommand attempts to apply only the patches you specify. If you specify a patch that depends on another that has not been applied, the `add` command fails to apply the patch you specified.
`analyze`	Analyzes a system to generate a list of the appropriate patches. After analyzing the system, use the `update` subcommand or the `download` and `add` subcommands to download and apply the patches to your systems. The smpatch analyze command depends on network services that are not available while the system is in single-user mode.
`download`	Downloads patches from the Sun patch server to a system. You can optionally specify which patches to download. You can also specify the name of a system and download the appropriate patches to that system.
`get`	Lists one or more of the `smpatch` configuration parameter values.
`order`	Sorts a list of patches into an order that can be used to apply patches.
`remove`	Removes a single patch from a single system.
`set`	Sets the values of one or more configuration parameters.
`unset`	Resets one or more configuration parameters to the default values.
`update`	Updates a single local or remote system by applying appropriate patches. This subcommand analyzes the system and then downloads the appropriate patches from the Sun patch server to your system. After the availability of the patches has been confirmed, the patches are applied based on the patch policy.

Each subcommand has specific options, which are described in Table 2.9.

Table 2.9 `smpatch` Subcommands and Options

Option	Description
Subcommand Options Supported by the `add` Command	
`-i` *patch_id1* `-i` *patch_id2*	Specifies the patch or patches that you want to install. You can list one or several patches to install, or you can specify the `-x` option to specify a file that contains the list of patches.
`-x mlist=`*patchlist_file*	Use this option instead of the `-i` option when you have many patches to install. With this option, you specify a file (*patchlist_file*) that contains the list of patches you want to install.
Subcommand Options for the `add` Subcommand	
`-d` *<patchdir>*	Specifies the directory where the patches are located. If you do not specify this option, the default patch spool directory (`/var/sadm/spool`) is assumed. The patch directory has the following syntax: *system_name*`:`*/directory_path*, where *system_name* is the name server containing the files and */directory_path* is a fully qualified, shared directory. You can specify just the */directory_path* if the directory is an NFS-mounted network directory or is located on the machine on which you want to install the patches.
`-h`	Displays information on how to use the command.
`-n` *system_name1 – system _name2 system_name2 ..*	Specifies the host or list of systems on n which you want to install the patches. You can specify the `–x mlist=`*system_name_file* operand instead of specifying this option.
`-x mlist=`*systemlist_file*	Specifies a file that contains the list of systems (machines) to which you want to install patches. You can specify the `-n` *system_name1* option instead of specifying this operand.
Options for the `analyze` Subcommand	
`-h`	Displays the command's usage statement.
`-n` *system_name*	Specifies the system you want to analyze.

Table 2.9 `smpatch` **Subcommands and Options**

Option	Description
The `download` **Subcommand Requires One of the Following Subcommand Options**	
`-I` *`patch_id1`* `-i` *`patch_id2`*	Specifies the patch or patches *`patch_id2`* `...` that you want to download. You can specify the `-x idlist=`*`patch_id_file`* operand instead of this option, or you can omit this argument in favor of the `-n` *`download_system`* option.
`-x idlist=`*`patchlist_file`*	Specifies the file containing the list of patches you want to download. You can specify this operand instead of specifying the `-i` *`patch_id1`* option.
Optional Subcommand Arguments for the `download` **Subcommand**	
`-n` *`download_system`*	Specifies the machine on which you want to download the recommended patches.
`-d` *`downloaddir`*	Specifies the directory where the patches are downloaded. This directory must have write permission and be accessible to the *`download_system`*. If you do not specify this option, the default patch spool directory (`/var/sadm/spool`) located on the download system is assumed.
The `remove` **Subcommand Requires the Following Options**	
`-i` *`patch_id`*	Specifies the patch you want to remove.
`-n systemname`	Specifies the system on which you want to remove the recommended patches. (Optional)

To use the `analyze` subcommand, the system needs to be connected to the Internet so that it can access the SunSolve site for patch information. To analyze a system, log in as root and type the following command:

```
# smpatch analyze <cr>
```

The system responds with a list of patches:

```
120199-01 SunOS 5.10: sysidtool Patch
119145-02 SunOS 5.10: usr/snadm/lib Patch
119252-02 SunOS 5.10: System Administration Applications Patch
119315-02 SunOS 5.10: Solaris Management Applications Patch
119313-02 SunOS 5.10: WBEM Patch
119250-02 SunOS 5.10: usr/sbin/install.d/pfinstall Patch
119534-02 SunOS 5.10: Flash Archive Patch
119254-02 SunOS 5.10: Install and Patch Utilities Patch
119783-01 SunOS 5.10 : bind patch
119065-01 SunOS 5.10: fc-cache patch
119812-01 X11 6.6.2: Freetype patch

. . . <output has been truncated > . . .
```

The following example analyzes the system named `zeus` and downloads the assessed patches from the SunSolve Online database to the default patch spool directory:

```
# /usr/sadm/bin/smpatch download <cr>
```

The system responds with the following:

```
120199-01 has been validated.
119145-02 has been validated.
119252-02 has been validated.
119315-02 has been validated.
119313-02 has been validated.
119250-02 has been validated.
119534-02 has been validated.
[Output has been truncated.]
```

The patches get downloaded to the `/var/sadm/spool` directory as jar files. Extract the files using `jar xvf` as described earlier in this chapter.

After extracting the jar file, install a patch from the download directory, by typing

```
# smpatch add -i 120469-01 <cr>
```

The system responds with:

```
add patch 120469-01
Patch 120469-01 has been successfully installed.
Validating patches...
Loading patches installed on the system...
Done!
Loading patches requested to install.
Done!
Checking patches that you specified for installation.
Done!
Approved patches will be installed in this order:
120469-01
```

I've generated a list of the patches I downloaded and want to install onto this system. To install the patches in this list, I type the following:

```
# smpatch add -x idlist=/var/sadm/spool/patchlist <cr>
```

The system responds with

```
add patch 120469-01
Validating patches...
Loading patches installed on the system...
Done!
Loading patches requested to install.
Done!
The following requested patches are already installed on the system
```

```
Requested to install patch 120469-01 is already installed on the system.
No patches to check dependency.
add patch 120292-01
Package SUNWmysqlS from patch 120292-01 is not installed on the system.
The original package SUNWmysqlS that 120292-01 is attempting to install to does \
not exist on this system.
wordlist too large
Patch 120292-01 failed to be copied to the pspool directory.
Validating patches...
Loading patches installed on the system...
Done!
Loading patches requested to install.
Done!
Checking patches that you specified for installation.
Done!
Approved patches will be installed in this order:
120292-01
add patch 120251-01
Patch 120251-01 has been successfully installed.
Validating patches...
Loading patches installed on the system...
Done!
Loading patches requested to install.
Done!
Checking patches that you specified for installation.
Done!
Approved patches will be installed in this order:
120251-01
add patch 120198-02
Patch 120198-02 has been successfully installed.
Validating patches...
Loading patches installed on the system...
Done!
Loading patches requested to install.
Done!
Checking patches that you specified for installation.
Done!
Approved patches will be installed in this order:
120198-02
```

Patch Tool

Patch Tool, a GUI-based tool for installing patches, is available in the Solaris Management Console (SMC), and mimics the `smpatch` command.

Access this Patch Tool by typing the following:

```
# smc <cr>
```

The Solaris Management Tool is displayed, as shown in Figure 2.65.

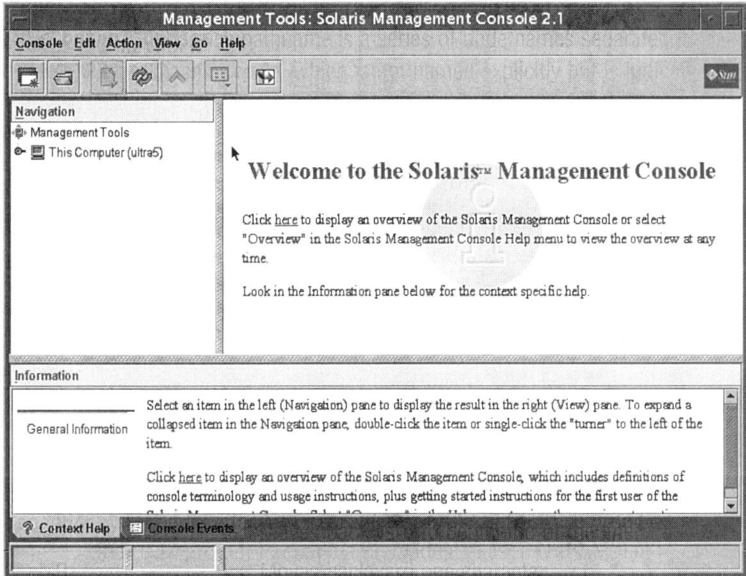

FIGURE 2.65 Solaris Management Tool.

In the left pane, click the This Computer icon. The icon expands as shown in Figure 2.66, displaying icons for various SMC tools.

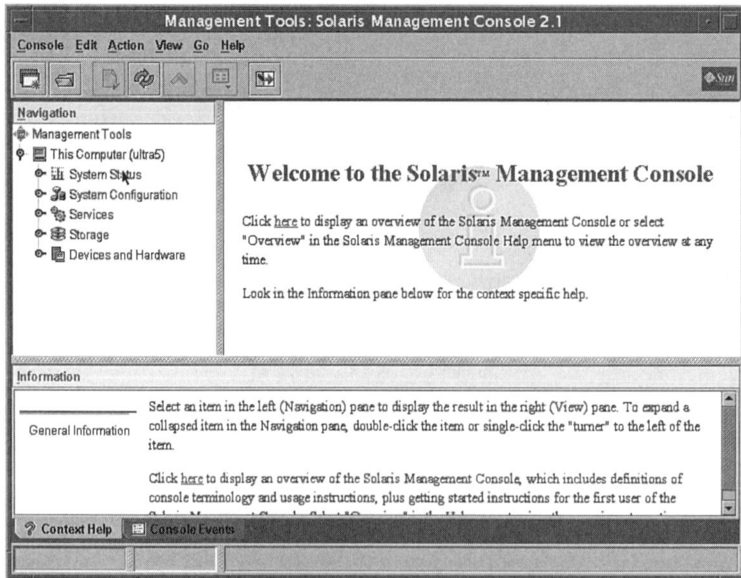

FIGURE 2.66 System Configuration tools.

Click on the System Configuration icon. The System Configuration icon expands and icons for the System Configuration tools are displayed, as shown in Figure 2.67.

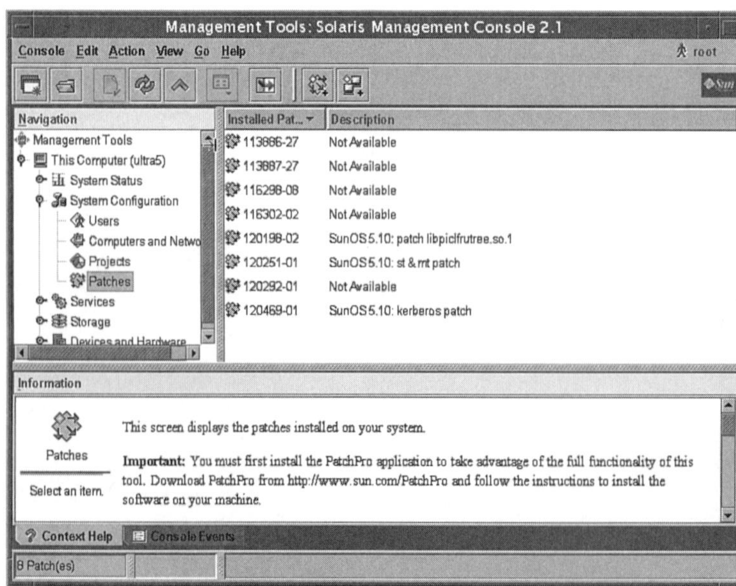

FIGURE 2.67 System Configuration icons.

Click the Patches icon, shown in Figure 2.67, enter the root password when prompted, and the main window on the Management Console displays information about any patches installed on the system. If the window is blank, no patches are installed.

When you click Action from the top toolbar, you have the option to add patches, analyze your system for patches, and download patches using the GUI as shown in Figure 2.68.

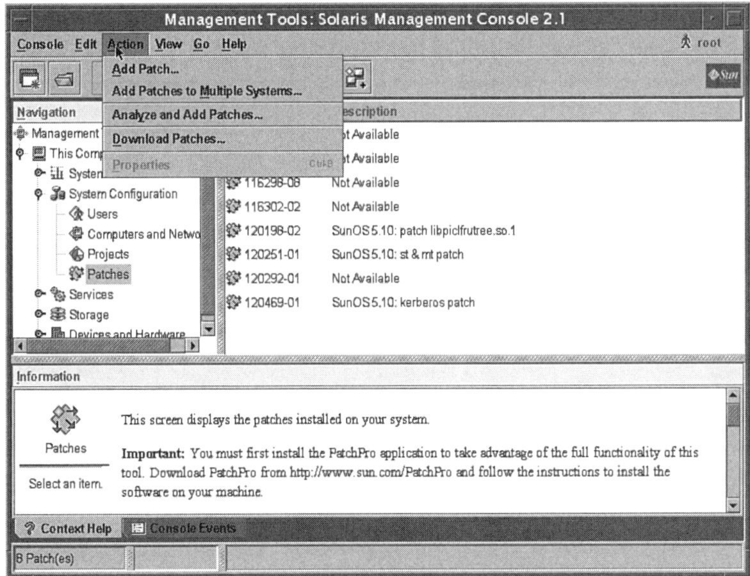

FIGURE 2.68 Patch actions.

General Guidelines

Some software packages do not conform to the ABI; therefore, they cannot be installed by using the Solaris Product Registry or the `pkgadd` command. For installation of products that do not conform to the ABI, follow the vendor's specific installation instructions. Here are a few additional guidelines to follow when installing new software on a system:

- Always be cautious with third-party or public-domain software. Make sure the software has been tested and is free of trojans and malicious code before installing it on a production system.
- Make sure the software package is supported under Solaris 10.
- Always read the vendor's release notes for special loading instructions. They might contain kernel parameters that need to be modified or suggest software patches that need to be applied.

- Do not install patches unless directed by Sun or one of your software providers. Some patches have not been tested thoroughly, especially when used in conjunction with other software patches. Adverse system performance could result.

NOTE

Recommended patch sets For each release of software, Sun usually has a prebundled set of patches called "Recommended and Security Patches." These patches have been thoroughly tested, and Sun recommends adding these patches to every system after the initial software installation is complete.

Adding and removing software packages is one of the simpler tasks you will encounter in system administration. As with all computer software, you should first load new software packages or patches on a nonproduction system for test purposes. Only after the software has been thoroughly tested should you install it on a production system.

Summary

This chapter described how to prepare for and install the Solaris operating environment on a SPARC-based and x86/x64-based system. You learned how to install the Solaris 10 operating environment onto a standalone system using the interactive installation program `installsolaris`. The interactive installation program provides a dialog box that allows the system administrator to select software packages and create file systems on the new server.

This chapter also described Software Package Administration, beginning with the methods Sun uses to package their bundled and unbundled operating system software. Then you learned about the tools and methods used to install, verify, and remove these software packages on a Solaris system.

The chapter also explained that occasionally, software deficiencies are discovered and need to be repaired. You learned how to obtain, install, and, if necessary, uninstall software patches.

Now that you understand how to install the Solaris operating environment, the next chapter will describe system startup and shutdown procedures.

Key Terms

- Platform group
- Platform name
- Installation media
- Disk slice
- Disk partition
- Software package
- Software group
- Configuration group
- Swap space
- Server
- Client
- JumpStart
- Standalone system
- Power management
- Hostname

- Initial installation
- IP address
- IPv6
- Solaris Interactive installation
- Upgrade (as it pertains to the Solaris Interactive method of installation)
- Solaris Live upgrade
- Web Start Installer
- WAN Boot
- Solaris Flash Archive
- Solaris product registry
- Software package
- Software patch
- Patch Manager
- Patch cluster
- Software spool directory
- Bundled software package
- Unbundled software package
- Compressed tar file
- Compressed jar file
- Patchlist file

Exercises

2.1 Preparing to Install the Solaris 10 Operating Environment

In this exercise, you will perform the steps necessary to prepare for a Solaris 10 operating system install on a networked standalone system.

Estimated time: 15 minutes

1. Identify your system type using the following command:

```
# uname -m <cr>
```

Is it a supported platform type and do you have the Solaris 10 Installation media kit for that platform?

2. Identify the peripherals connected to your system, and determine the device name for the CD-ROM/DVD and the disk drive that will be used as the boot device. Use the `prtconf`, `sysdef`, and `dmesg` commands to identify these devices.

   Make sure your system meets the minimum system requirements for Solaris 10. If it does not meet the minimum requirements, you cannot install Solaris 10. Check the amount of RAM as follows:

   ```
   # prtconf¦grep Memory <cr>
   ```

   Does the system have a CD-ROM?

   Check the amount of disk space using the `format` command and listing the size of slice 2, making sure that you select the correct device name for your boot disk.

NOTE

The `format` command Chapter 4, "User and Security Administration," describes the use of the `format` command.

3. Determine the software cluster that you want to install, and determine the amount of disk space it will require. Compare this value to the total size of your disk, which you determined in the preceding step. For example, if the size of disk slice 2 is 1.3GB, and I want to install the Entire Distribution cluster, I do not have enough disk space to complete the installation.
4. Plan your storage requirements as described in the "Disk Storage" section. Determine the file systems and slice sizes that you will want the installation program to create.
5. Obtain the following information that will be required by the Solaris 10 installation program:

   What is the system's hostname? Use the `hostname` command to determine the hostname on an existing system or ask your network administrator to assign a hostname.

   Does it have a static IP address or DHCP? Use the `ifconfig` command to determine the IP address on an existing system or ask your IP coordinator to assign an IP address. For more information on using the `ifconfig` command to determine a system's IP address, refer to *Solaris 10 System Administration Exam Prep: Exam CX-310-202*.

   Does IPv6, the next-generation Internet protocol, need to be enabled?

NOTE

Enabling the IPv6 services Enabling IPv6 has no effect if this machine is not on a network that provides IPv6 service. IPv4 service is unaffected if IPv6 is enabled.

Is a name service used, such as NIS, NIS+, DNS, or LDAP? Refer to *Solaris 10 System Administration Exam Prep: Exam CX-310-202*.

Should Kerberos security be configured? Ask your in-house security personnel if this is required.

What is the geographic region of your time zone (Eastern, Central, Alaska)?

During the installation, you are asked to assign a password to the root user account.

Determine the language to be used to install the Solaris 10 operating environment.

2.2 Installing Solaris 10 Using the Interactive Installation Program

For this exercise, you'll use the interactive installation program to install the Solaris 10 operating environment on your system.

Estimated time: 1 to 2 hours, depending on the speed of your system and CD-ROM

CAUTION

Destroyed data This exercise will destroy all the data on your hard drive.

1. Insert the Solaris 10 CD #1 or DVD into the CD-ROM/DVD drive.
2. If the system is currently running, either log in as root and shut down the system, or abort the operating system by pressing Stop+A.
3. Boot the operating system from the CD/DVD as follows:

```
# boot cdrom <cr>
```

4. The interactive installation program begins. Refer to the section titled "Using the Interactive Installation Process (`install-solaris`)," and follow the steps outlined in that section for installing the operating system.

2.3 Software Package Administration

This exercise takes you through the task of installing, verifying, and removing software on a Solaris system using the command line.

Estimated time: 20 minutes

1. List the software packages that are currently installed on your system:

   ```
   # pkginfo <cr>
   ```

2. Display a long-format listing of information for the SUNWman package installed on your system:

   ```
   # pkginfo -l SUNWman <cr>
   ```

   What is listed for the status, install date, number of files, and number of blocks used by this package?

3. Remove the SUNWman package from your system by using the following:

   ```
   # pkgrm SUNWman <cr>
   ```

   Verify that the software package has been removed by repeating step 1.

   Now you'll reinstall the software package. Log in as root and insert Solaris 10 CD #4 into the CD-ROM (or DVD into the DVD-Rom) drive. Use `pkgadd` to spool the SUNWman package into the default spool area as follows:

   ```
   # pkgadd -d /cdrom/sol_10_807_sparc_4/Solaris_10/Product-s /var/spool/pkg SUNWman <cr>
   ```

4. Use the following commands to verify the presence of SUNWman in the default spool area:

   ```
   # pkginfo -d /var/spool/pkg <cr>
   ```

5. Observe the messages displayed, and verify that the package is installed in `/var/spool/pkg`.

6. Reinstall the SUNWman package from the spool area as follows:

   ```
   # pkgadd <cr>
   ```

7. Select the SUNWman package when you are prompted; the package is reinstalled.

8. To remove the SUNWman package from the spool area, type the following:

   ```
   # pkgrm -s /var/spool/pkg <cr>
   ```

   Select the SUNWman package. It is removed from the spool directory.

9. You can now use the `pkgchk` command to check the completeness, pathname, file contents, and file attributes of the SUNWman package:

   ```
   # pkgchk SUNWman <cr>
   ```

Exam Questions

1. What is the minimum amount of RAM required to install Solaris 10 on a SPARC-based system?

   ❍ **A.** 256MB

   ❍ **B.** 512MB

   ❍ **C.** 96MB

   ❍ **D.** 128MB

2. What is the best command used to find out the name of your hardware's platform group and name?

   ❍ **A.** `uname -a`

   ❍ **B.** `sysdef`

   ❍ **C.** `arch`

   ❍ **D.** `uname -m`

3. What is a software group?

   ❍ **A.** A group of files and directories that describe a software application

   ❍ **B.** A logical collection of software packages

   ❍ **C.** Any software that can be installed on Solaris

   ❍ **D.** A collection of files that make up a software application

4. What is a software package?

   ❍ **A.** A group of files and directories that describe a software application

   ❍ **B.** A logical collection of software packages

   ❍ **C.** A collection of files that make up a software application

   ❍ **D.** A collection of files and directories

5. Which is *not* one of the six software groups in Solaris 10?

   ❍ **A.** Entire system support

   ❍ **B.** Reduced networking support

   ❍ **C.** Developer system support

   ❍ **D.** Entire distribution plus OEM system support

6. What are the default file systems created by the Solaris installation program?

❍ **A.** /, /opt, /usr, /var, and swap

❍ **B.** /, /usr, /var, and swap

❍ **C.** /, /usr, and swap

❍ **D.** / and swap

7. Which of the following is *not* a valid method of installing Solaris 10?

❍ **A.** Installing over a WAN using HTTP

❍ **B.** Interactive

❍ **C.** Installing from a remote CD-ROM on a system on the same subnet

❍ **D.** Web Start

8. Which of the following statements is *not* true of a software package?

❍ **A.** A software package is a group of files and directories that describe a software application, such as manual pages and line printer support.

❍ **B.** A software package is a standard way to deliver bundled and unbundled software.

❍ **C.** Software packages are grouped into software clusters.

❍ **D.** Software packages are administered using the `installf` command.

9. On a Sun system, what is the first step in installing a new operating system?

❍ **A.** Informing the users

❍ **B.** Repartitioning the hard drive

❍ **C.** Finding the source distribution media

❍ **D.** Performing a full backup

10. Which is *not* a valid software configuration group to choose during installation of the Solaris 10 operating environment?

❍ **A.** Core

❍ **B.** Client

❍ **C.** End user

❍ **D.** Developer

11. For which of the following is custom JumpStart used?

❍ **A.** To install the Solaris software on 50 identical systems

❍ **B.** To start a system that refuses to boot

❍ **C.** To set up AutoClient systems on a server

❍ **D.** To interactively guide you, step by step, in installing the Solaris software

12. Which of the following is a system that provides services to other systems in its networked environment?

❍ **A.** Server

❍ **B.** Client

❍ **C.** File server

❍ **D.** AutoClient server

13. Which of the following is a system that uses remote services from a server, has limited disk space, and requires a server to function?

❍ **A.** AutoClient server

❍ **B.** File server

❍ **C.** Client

❍ **D.** Standalone

14. Which type of installation preserves data and system configuration information?

❍ **A.** Initial

❍ **B.** Upgrade

❍ **C.** Preserve

❍ **D.** Interactive

15. What are the three phases of the installation process?

❍ **A.** System configuration, installation, and post installation

❍ **B.** Power on, boot from CD, execute the installation program

❍ **C.** Boot from CD, start installation program, post installation

❍ **D.** Boot from CD, system configuration, software installation

16. During installation, what default software group is selected to be installed?

- ❍ **A.** End-user distribution
- ❍ **B.** Core distribution
- ❍ **C.** Developer distribution
- ❍ **D.** Entire distribution

17. What is the kernel architecture of an ultra 5?

- ❍ **A.** `sun4m`
- ❍ **B.** `sun4c`
- ❍ **C.** `sun4u`
- ❍ **D.** `sun4`

18. What information is *not* required to install a server system?

- ❍ **A.** The server's Ethernet address
- ❍ **B.** The server's hostname
- ❍ **C.** The server's IP address
- ❍ **D.** The server's geographic region

19. Which of the following commands is used to show software package information?

- ❍ **A.** `pkgadd`
- ❍ **B.** `pkgchk`
- ❍ **C.** `pkgparam`
- ❍ **D.** `pkginfo`

20. Which of the following commands verifies the accuracy of a software package installation?

- ❍ **A.** `pkgadd`
- ❍ **B.** `pkgchk`
- ❍ **C.** `pkgask`
- ❍ **D.** `pkginfo`

21. Which of the following methods are used to remove software packages from a system?

- ❍ **A.** `pkgrm`
- ❍ **B.** `rm -r`
- ❍ **C.** AdminTool
- ❍ **D.** All of the above

22. What do software packages names usually start with?

- ❍ **A.** An abbreviation of the software package
- ❍ **B.** The company's stock symbol
- ❍ **C.** SUNW
- ❍ **D.** Anything the vendor chooses

23. Which of the following commands prepares a compressed tar patch file (with a `.Z` extension) for installation and saves approximately 25% on temporary disk space usage?

- ❍ **A.** `installpatch -u 104945-02.tar.Z`
- ❍ **B.** `installpatch -f 104945-02.tar.Z`
- ❍ **C.** `/usr/bin/zcat 104945-02.tar.Z ¦ tar xvf -`
- ❍ **D.** `unzip 104945-02.tar.Z ¦ tar xvf -`

24. Which of the following commands show all patches applied to a system? Choose all that apply.

- ❍ **A.** `patchadd -p`
- ❍ **B.** `pkginfo`
- ❍ **C.** `showrev -p`
- ❍ **D.** `smpatch`

25. Which of the following commands is used to remove a patch from a system?

- ❍ **A.** `uninstall`
- ❍ **B.** `pkgrm -s`
- ❍ **C.** `patchrm`
- ❍ **D.** `rm -r /var/sasdm/pkg/<pkgname>/save`

26. Sun distributes software patches in which of the following forms? Choose all that apply.

❍ **A.** Sun anonymous FTP site

❍ **B.** Email

❍ **C.** CD-ROM

❍ **D.** Sunsolve

❍ **E.** Sun Connection

27. The Solaris Product Registry enables you to do which of the following? Choose all that apply.

❍ **A.** View a list of installed software.

❍ **B.** Uninstall software.

❍ **C.** Launch the installer.

❍ **D.** Directly edit software packages with the registry editor.

28. When installing a patch using the `patchadd` command, which of the following options does not create a backup of the files to be patched?

❍ **A.** `-f`

❍ **B.** `-p`

❍ **C.** `-B`

❍ **D.** `-d`

29. Select all the conditions that prevent a patch from being installed.

❍ **A.** The patch being installed requires another patch that is not installed.

❍ **B.** The patch is incompatible with another, already installed patch.

❍ **C.** The patch was removed.

❍ **D.** The patch version is not the most up-to-date version.

❍ **E.** All of the above

30. Which method of installation creates a copy of the OS, upgrades the copy, and allows you to fall back to the original version of the OS if you encounter problems?

❍ **A.** Custom JumpStart

❍ **B.** Upgrade

❍ **C.** Live upgrade

❍ **D.** Solaris Flash Archive

31. Which of the following gives the system administrator the flexibility to disable numerous network services during the installation of the OS, thus limiting your risk of exposure over the network while still providing a useful system?

❍ **A.** Secure by Default

❍ **B.** `netservices limited`

❍ **C.** `netservices open`

❍ **D.** Comment selected services in the `inetd.conf` file

Answers to Exam Questions

1. **A.** The system on which you will install Solaris 10 must have a minimum of 256MB of RAM; however, 512MB of RAM is recommended. For more information, see the "Minimum System Requirements" section.

2. **D.** To determine your system type, use the `uname -m` command. The system responds with the platform group and platform name for your system. For more information, see the "Requirements and Preparation for Installing the Solaris 10 Software" section.

3. **B.** Software packages are grouped into software clusters, which are logical collections of software packages. For more information, see the "Software Terminology" section.

4. **A.** A software package is a collection of files and directories in a defined format. It is a group of files and directories that describe a software application. For more information, see the "Software Terminology" section.

5. **A.** The six software groups are reduced networking support, core system support, end-user support, developer system support, entire distribution, and entire distribution plus OEM system support. For more information, see the "Software Groups" section.

6. **D.** The default partition scheme setup with the interactive installation program is root (/) and swap. For more information, see the "Disk Storage" section.

7. **D.** Web Start is not a method of installing the OS. Web Start installers are used to install software packages, and Solaris Flash Archives are used when cloning systems. For more information on the methods of installation, see the "Methods of Installing the Solaris 10 Software" section.

8. **D.** The `installf` command is used to add a file to the software installation database, not to administer software packages. For more information, see the "Software Terminology" section.

9. **A, B, C, D.** All are correct. For more information, see the "The Solaris Installation Prechecklist" section.

10. **B.** The six configuration groups are reduced networking support, core system support, end-user support, developer system support, entire distribution, and entire distribution plus OEM system support. For more information, see the "Software Groups" section.

11. **A.** Custom JumpStart allows you to automatically and identically install many systems with the same configuration without having to configure each of them individually. For more information, see the "Custom JumpStart" section.

12. **A.** A server is a system that provides services or file systems, such as home directories or mail files, to other systems on the network. For more information, see the "Servers" section.

13. **C.** A client is a system that uses remote services from a server. Some clients have limited disk storage capacity, or perhaps none at all; these clients must rely on remote file systems from a server to function. For more information, see the "Servers" section.

14. **B.** The Upgrade option updates the Solaris software to the new release, preserving data, and saving as many modifications to the previous version of Solaris software as possible. For more information, see the "Upgrading the Operating System" section.

15. **A.** The three phases of the installation process are system configuration, installation, and post installation. For more information, see the "Introduction" section.

16. **D.** During the interactive installation, the entire distribution software group is selected by default. For more information, see the "Using the Interactive Installation Process (install-solaris)" section.

17. **C.** sun4u is the kernel architecture for all Sun UltraSPARC systems. For more information, see the "Requirements and Preparation for Installing the Solaris 10 Software" section.

18. **A.** The server's Ethernet address is not required to install a server system. During the installation, you are prompted to enter the IP address, hostname, and geographic region. For more information, see the "The Solaris Installation Prechecklist" section.

19. **D.** The `pkginfo` command displays software package information. For more information, see the "Tools for Managing Software" section.

20. **B.** The `pkgchk` command checks the accuracy of a software package installation. For more information, see the "Tools for Managing Software" section.

21. **A.** The `pkgrm` command removes software packages from the system. For more information, see the "Tools for Managing Software" section.

22. **B.** Software package names usually start with the company's stock symbol. For more information, see the "Adding and Removing Software Packages" section.

23. **C.** Patches might come in compressed tar format, such as `104945-02.tar.Z`. Use the `zcat` command to decompress this type of patch file. For more information, see the "Obtaining a Patch" section.

24. **A, C.** Use the `patchadd -p` command or the `showrev -p` command to show all patches that have been applied to a system. For more information, see the "Obtaining a Patch" section.

25. **C.** Use the `patchrm` command to remove a patch from a system. For more information, see the "Obtaining a Patch" section.

26. **D, E.** Today, Sun customers can access software updates (patches) through two main methods, SunSolve and Sun Connection. For more information, see the "Obtaining a Patch" section.

27. **A, B, C.** The Solaris Product Registry enables you to view all installed software, uninstall software, or launch the installer to install additional software. For more information, see the "Tools for Managing Software" section.

28. **D.** The `-d` option for the `patchadd` command does not create a backup of the files to be patched. For more information, see the "Obtaining a Patch" section.

29. **A, B.** The following conditions can prevent a patch from being installed:

    - The patch being installed requires another patch that is not installed.
    - The patch is incompatible with another, already installed patch.

    For more information, see the "Obtaining a Patch" section.

30. **C.** Live upgrade allows you to create a copy of the current operating environment and upgrade the copy while the system is running in the original environment. For more information, see the "Solaris Live Upgrade" section.

31. **A.** Secure by Default gives the system administrator the flexibility to disable numerous network services during the installation of the OS, thus limiting your risk of exposure over the network while still providing a useful system. SBD can also be disabled using the `netservices limited` command, but this command is used after the OS has been installed. For more information, see the "Secure by Default" section.

Suggested Readings and Resources

1. Websites

    - **http://docs.sun.com**: Solaris 10 Installation Guide by Sun Microsystems
    - **http://docs.sun.com**: Solaris 10 System Administration Guide: Basic Administration by Sun Microsystems

CHAPTER 3

Performing System Boot and Shutdown Procedures for SPARC, x64-, and x86-Based Systems

Objectives

The following objectives for the Solaris System Administrator Exam are covered in this chapter:

Given a scenario, explain boot PROM fundamentals, including OpenBoot Architecture Standard, boot PROM, NVRAM, POST, Abort Sequence, and displaying POST to serial port for SPARC.

Given a scenario, explain the BIOS settings for booting, abort sequence, and displaying POST, including BIOS configuration for x64- and x86-based systems.

Execute basic boot PROM commands for a SPARC system.

Perform system boot and shutdown procedures, including identifying the system's boot device, creating and removing custom device aliases, viewing and changing NVRAM parameters, and interrupting an unresponsive system.

Explain the Service Management Facility and the phases of the boot process.

Use Service Management Facility or legacy commands and scripts to control both the boot and shutdown procedures.

Describe the purpose, functions and features of the Grand Unified Bootloader (GRUB), including how to modify x86 system boot behavior, manage GRUB boot archives, boot a system in the GRUB-based boot environment and interrupt an unresponsive system.

- ► You need to understand the primary functions of the OpenBoot environment, which includes the programmable read-only memory (PROM). You need to have a complete understanding of how to use many of the OpenBoot commands and how to set and modify all the configuration parameters that control system bootup and hardware behavior.
- ► You must understand the entire boot process, from the proper power-on sequence to the steps you perform to bring the system into multi-user mode.

- You must be able to identify the devices connected to a system and recognize the various special files for each device.
- Occasionally, conventional shutdown methods might not work on an unresponsive system or on a system that has crashed. This chapter introduces when and how to use these alternative shutdown methods to bring the system down safely.
- You must understand how the Service Management Facility (SMF) controls which processes and services are started at various stages of the boot process. You need to understand how to use SMF or legacy commands and scripts to control both the boot and shutdown procedures.
- Understand the role GRUB has in the boot process on an x86/x64-based Solaris system. You need to be familiar with the boot process and related files that control the bootup process on the x86/x64-based platform.

Outline

Study Strategies

The following study strategies will help you prepare for the exam:

- When studying this chapter, you should practice on both Sun SPARC and x86/x64-based systems. Practice each step-by-step process that is outlined. In addition to practicing the processes, you should practice the various options described for booting each of the system types.
- You should display the hardware configuration of your Sun system by using the various OpenBoot commands presented in this chapter. You need to familiarize yourself with all the devices associated with your system. You should be able to identify each hardware component by its device pathname.
- You should display the hardware configuration of your x86/x64-based system by using the various commands presented in this chapter. You need to be familiar with all the devices associated with the x86/x64-based system. You should be able to identify each hardware component by its device pathname.
- You should practice creating both temporary and permanent device aliases. In addition, you should practice setting the various OpenBoot system parameters that are described in this chapter.
- You should practice booting the SPARC and x86/x64-based systems by using the various methods described. You need to understand how to boot into single-user and multi-user modes and how to specify an alternate kernel or system file during the boot process.
- During the boot process, you should watch the system messages and familiarize yourself with every stage of the boot process. You should watch the system messages that are displayed at bootup. You need to understand each message displayed during the boot process, from system power-on to bringing the system into multi-user mode.
- You need to thoroughly understand the Service Management Facility (SMF), service states, and milestones. You need to understand how the `svc.startd` daemon uses information from the service configuration repository to determine required milestones and how it processes the manifests located in the `/var/svc/manifest` directory. In addition, you must understand legacy run control scripts, run levels, and how they affect the system services.
- You should practice shutting down the system. You should make sure you understand the advantages and disadvantages of each method presented.

Introduction

System startup requires an understanding of the hardware and the operating system functions that are required to bring the system to a running state. This chapter discusses the operations that the system must perform from the time you power on the system until you receive a system login prompt. In addition, it covers the steps required to properly shut down a system. After reading this chapter, you'll understand how to boot both the Sun SPARC system and an x86/x64-based system. On both platforms, you'll understand which operations must take place to start up the kernel and UNIX system processes.

Booting a SPARC System

Bootstrapping is the process a computer follows to load and execute the bootable operating system. The term comes from the phrase "pulling yourself up by your bootstraps." The instructions for the bootstrap procedure are stored in the boot PROM.

The boot process goes through the following phases:

1. **Boot PROM phase:** After you turn on power to the system, the PROM displays system identification information and runs self-test diagnostics to verify the system's hardware and memory. It then loads the primary boot program, called `bootblk`, from its location on the boot device into memory.

2. **Boot programs phase:** The `bootblk` program finds and executes the secondary boot program (called `ufsboot`) from the UNIX file system (UFS) and loads it into memory. After the `ufsboot` program is loaded, the `ufsboot` program loads the two-part kernel.

3. **Kernel initialization phase:** The kernel initializes itself and begins loading modules, using `ufsboot` to read the files. When the kernel has loaded enough modules to mount the root file system, it unmaps the `ufsboot` program and continues, using its own resources.

4. **`init` phase:** The kernel creates a user process and starts the `/sbin/init` process. The `/sbin/init` process reads the `/etc/inittab` file for instructions on starting other processes, one of which is the `svc.startd` daemon (`/lib/svc/bin/svc.startd`).

5. **`svc.startd` phase:** The `svc.startd` daemon starts the system services and boots the system to the appropriate milestone. Specifically, `svc.startd` performs the following tasks:

   - Checks and mounts file systems.
   - Configures the network and devices.
   - Initiates various startup processes and performs system maintenance tasks.
   - In addition, `svc.startd` executes the legacy run control (RC) scripts for compatibility.

NOTE

Boot phases For the exam, you need to make sure you thoroughly understand each boot phase and the order in which each phase is run. The first two phases are described in this section, with the description of OpenBoot. The kernel, `init`, and `svc.startd` phases are described later in the chapter, in the sections "The Kernel" and "The Service Management Facility."

Powering on the System

Before you power on the system, you need to make sure everything is plugged in properly. Check the small computer system interface (SCSI) cables that connect any external devices to the system (such as disk drives and tape drives) to make sure they are properly connected. Check your network connection. Also make sure that the keyboard and monitor are connected properly. Loose cables can cause your system to fail during the startup process.

CAUTION

Connecting cables with the power turned off Always connect your cables before turning on the hardware; otherwise, you could damage your system.

The correct sequence for powering on your equipment is to first turn on any peripherals (that is, external disk drives or tape drives) and then turn on power to the system.

The Boot PROM and Program Phases

Objective:
Given a scenario, explain boot PROM fundamentals, including OpenBoot Architecture Standard, boot PROM, NVRAM, POST, Abort Sequence, and displaying POST to serial port for SPARC.

The bootstrap process begins after powerup, when the startup routines located in the hardware's PROM chip are executed. Sun calls this the *OpenBoot firmware*, and it is executed immediately after you turn on the system.

The primary task of the OpenBoot firmware is to test the hardware and to boot the operating system either from a mass storage device or from the network. OpenBoot contains a program called the *monitor* that controls the operation of the system before the kernel is available and before the operating system has been booted. When a system is turned on, the monitor runs a power-on self-test (POST) that checks such things as the hardware and memory on the system.

If no errors are found, the automatic boot process begins. OpenBoot contains a set of instructions that locate and start up the system's boot program and eventually start up the UNIX operating system.

NOTE

Automatic system recovery Sun server class systems can recognize failed components and disable the board that contains the failed component. If the server is configured with multiple central processing unit (CPU)/memory and input/output (I/O) boards, the system can boot in a degraded yet stable condition, even with failed components. See your server's *System Reference Manual* for details on automatic system recovery.

The boot program is stored in a predictable area (sectors 1 to 15) on the system hard drive, CD-ROM, or other bootable device and is referred to as the *bootblock* (`bootblk`). The bootblock is responsible for loading the secondary boot program (`ufsboot`) into memory, which is located in the UFS file system on the boot device. The path to `ufsboot` is recorded in the bootblock, which is installed by the Solaris `installboot` utility.

`ufsboot` locates and loads the two-part kernel. The *kernel* (which is covered in detail later in this chapter) is the part of the operating system that remains running at all times until the system is shut down. It is the core and the most important part of the operating system. The kernel consists of a two-piece static core called `genunix` and `unix`. `genunix` is the platform-independent generic kernel file, and `unix` is the platform-specific kernel file. When the system boots, `ufsboot` combines these two files into memory to form the running kernel.

The OpenBoot Environment

Objectives:
Execute basic boot PROM commands for a SPARC system.

Explain boot PROM fundamentals, including OpenBoot Architecture Standard, boot PROM, NVRAM, POST, Abort Sequence, and displaying POST to serial port on SPARC systems.

The hardware-level user interface that you see before the operating system starts is called the OpenBoot PROM (OBP). OpenBoot is based on an interactive command interpreter that gives you access to an extensive set of functions for hardware and software development, fault isolation, and debugging. The OBP firmware is stored in the system's PROM chip and on the system memory card. The card contains the values for the system's IDPROM (host ID, MAC address, date, and Cyclic Redundancy Check value).

Sun UltraSPARC systems use a programmable boot PROM that allows new boot program data to be loaded into the PROM by "flashing" the PROM with software. This type of PROM is called a flash PROM (FPROM).

The NVRAM chip stores user-definable system parameters, also referred to as NVRAM variables or EEPROM parameters. The parameters allow administrators to control variables such as the default boot device and boot command. The NVRAM also contains writeable areas for user-controlled diagnostics, macros, and device aliases. NVRAM is where the system identification information is stored, such as the host ID, Ethernet address, and time-of-day (TOD) clock. On older systems, a single lithium battery backup provides backup for the NVRAM and clock. Newer systems contain a non-removable Serial Electronically Erasable Programmable Read-Only Memory (SEEPROM) chip that does not require a battery. Other newer systems may contain a removable system configuration card to hold the system configuration information. Many software packages use the host ID for licensing purposes; therefore, it is important that the NVRAM chip (or memory card) can be removed and placed in any replacement system. Because NVRAM contains unique identification information for the machine, Sun sometimes refers to it as the identification programmable read-only memory (ID PROM).

OpenBoot is currently at version 5 but is available only on high-end Sun servers (Sun Fire and higher). Depending on the age of your system, you could have PROM version 3, 4, or 5 installed. The original boot PROM firmware, version 1, was introduced on the Sun SPARCstation 1. The first version of the OpenBoot PROM was version 2, and it first appeared on the SPARCstation 2 system. OpenBoot versions 3 and 4 are the versions that are currently available on the Ultra series systems and Enterprise servers. Versions 3, 4 and 5 of the OpenBoot architecture provide a significant increase in functionality over the boot PROMs in earlier Sun systems. One notable feature of the OpenBoot firmware is a programmable user interface based on the interactive programming language Forth. In Forth, sequences of user commands can be combined to form complete programs. This capability provides a powerful tool for debugging hardware and software. Another benefit of versions 3, 4, and 5 is the Flash update feature. You can update the version 3, 4, and 5 firmware without replacing the PROM chip, but you will not be tested on updating the firmware on the exam.

To determine the version of the OpenBoot PROM, type

```
/usr/sbin/prtdiag -v
```

or

```
prtconf -v
```

NOTE

No OpenBoot environment on the Intel platform The Intel environment has no OpenBoot PROM or NVRAM. On Intel systems, before the kernel is started, the system is controlled by the basic input/output system (BIOS), the firmware interface on a PC. Therefore, many features provided by OpenBoot are not available on Intel systems.

Entry-Level to High-End Systems

Every Sun workstation and server except the midrange, midframe, and high-end servers has only one system board and holds only one boot PROM and NVRAM chip.

Sun's midrange, midframe, and high-end servers, such as the Enterprise and Sun Fire, can be configured with multiple CPU/memory and I/O boards.

The following are some things you should be aware of on multiple-CPU systems:

- A multiple-CPU system has a clock board to oversee the backplane communications.
- The `host ID` and Ethernet address are on the clock board and are automatically downloaded to the NVRAM on all CPU boards when the POST is complete.
- PROM contents on each CPU are compared and verified via checksums.
- The CPU that is located in the lowermost card cage slot is the master CPU board.
- Each CPU runs its own individual POST.
- If these systems are configured with redundant CPU/memory and I/O boards, they can run in a degraded yet stable mode, even when some components have failed. Such systems are usually described as fault-tolerant or fault-resilient.

Accessing the OpenBoot Environment

You can get to the OpenBoot environment by using any of the following methods:

- Halting the operating system.
- Pressing the Stop and A keys simultaneously (Stop+A). On terminals that are connected to the serial port and do not have a Stop key, you press the Break key. This stops the operating system and transfers control to the OpenBoot monitor. In some cases, this method may lead to data loss or corruption and therefore should be used with caution.
- When the system is initially powered on. If your system is not configured to start up automatically, it stops at the user interface (the monitor prompt). If automatic startup is configured, you can make the system stop at the user interface by pressing Stop+A after the display console banner is displayed but before the system begins starting the operating system.
- When the system hardware detects an error from which it cannot recover. (This is known as a *watchdog*.)

System Console

Depending on the type of system you have, the console connection could vary. Some servers have a graphics card and keyboard connected to them, and the console goes through the graphics card. In most data centers, however, the console is connected to the serial port on the server. Most Sun Fire servers have a connection labeled Serial A/LOM, which is an RJ-45 connection, and the console is connected to this port. When the system is powered on, and if a keyboard is not detected, the console defaults to the serial port. Refer to the Server User's Guide to see how to connect a console to your particular server.

System Control Switch

On those servers with a power button and system control switch located on the system's front panel, the ability to turn the system on or off is controlled by the key position on the system control switch.

The four-position system control switch (key) located on the system's front panel controls the power-on modes of the system and prevents unauthorized users from powering off the system or reprogramming system firmware. Table 3.1 describes the function of each system control switch setting.

Table 3.1 Function of Each System Control Switch Setting

Position	Description
Normal	This key position allows the system Power button to power the system on or off. If the operating system is running, pressing and releasing the Power button initiates a graceful software system shutdown. Pressing and holding down the Power button for five seconds causes an immediate hardware power-off. This could cause disk corruption and loss of data and therefore should be used only as last resort.
Locked	Also referred to as the "secure" position, this key position disables the system Power button to prevent unauthorized users from powering the system on or off. It also disables the keyboard L1+A (Stop+A) command, terminal Break key command, and ~# tip window command, preventing users from suspending system operation to access the system ok prompt. The Locked setting, used for normal day-to-day operations, also prevents unauthorized programming of the system boot PROM.
Diagnostics	This key position forces the power-on self-test (POST) and OpenBoot Diagnostics software to run during system startup and system resets. The Power button functions the same as when the system control switch is in the Normal position.
Forced Off	This key position forces the system to power off immediately and to enter 5-volt standby mode. It also disables the system Power button. Use this setting when AC power is interrupted and you do not want the system to restart automatically when power is restored. With the system control switch in any other position, if the system were running prior to losing power, it restarts automatically after power is restored.
	The Forced Off setting also prevents a Remote System Control (RSC) session from restarting the system. However, the RSC card continues to operate using the system's 5-volt standby power.

NOTE

Alternative methods for stopping a system An alternative sequence that can be used to stop the system is Enter+~+Ctrl+B, which is equivalent to Stop+A. There must be an interval of more than 0.5 seconds between keypresses, and the entire string must be entered in less than 5 seconds. You can use this method only with serial devices acting as consoles and not for systems with keyboards of their own. To enable this alternative sequence, you must first modify the `/etc/default/kbd` file by removing the # from the entry:

```
#KEYBOARD_ABORT=alternate
```

To disable the abort key sequence, make the following entry to the `/etc/default/kbd` file:

```
KEYBOARD_ABORT=disable
```

Remember to uncomment the line by removing the #.

Then you save the changes and, as root, type

```
kbd -i
```

to put the changes into effect.

On a server with a physical keyswitch, the alternative Break does not work when the key is set to the Secure position.

If your console is connected to the serial port via a modem, you can send a break (Stop+A or L1+A) through the `tip` window by typing ~# (the tilde and then the pound sign).

CAUTION

Using Stop+A sparingly Forcing a system into the OpenBoot PROM by pressing Stop+A or Break abruptly breaks execution of the operating system. You should use these methods only as a last resort to restart the system. When you access the `ok` prompt from a running system, you are suspending the operating environment software and placing the system under firmware control. Any processes that were running under the operating environment software are also suspended, and the state of such software may not be recoverable.

The diagnostics and commands that you run from the `ok` prompt have the potential to affect the state of the system. Don't assume that you will be able to resume execution of the operating environment software from the point at which it was suspended. Although the `go` command resumes execution in most circumstances, as a rule, each time you drop the system to the `ok` prompt, you should expect to have to reboot it to get back to the normal operating state.

OpenBoot Firmware Tasks

The IEEE Standard 1275 defines the OpenBoot architecture and the primary tasks of the OpenBoot firmware are as follows:

- Test and initialize the system hardware.
- Determine the hardware configuration.

- Start the operating system from either a mass storage device or a network.
- Provide interactive debugging facilities for configuring, testing, and debugging.
- Allow modification and management of system startup configuration, such as NVRAM parameters.
- Servers such as the Sun Fire provide environmental monitoring and control capabilities at both the operating system level and the OpenBoot firmware level to monitor the state of the system power supplies, fans, and temperature sensors. If it detects any voltage, current, fan speed, or temperature irregularities, the monitor generates a warning message to the system console, and ultimately it initiates an automatic system shutdown sequence.

Specifically, the following tasks are necessary to initialize the operating system kernel:

1. OpenBoot displays system identification information and then runs self-test diagnostics to verify the system's hardware and memory. These checks are known as a POST—power-on self test.
2. OpenBoot then probes system bus devices, interprets their drivers, builds a device tree, and installs the console. After initializing the system, OpenBoot displays a banner on the console.
3. OpenBoot checks parameters stored in NVRAM to determine how to boot the operating system.
4. OpenBoot loads the primary startup program, `bootblk`, from the default startup device.
5. The `bootblk` program finds and executes the secondary startup program, `ufsboot`, and loads it into memory. The `ufsboot` program loads the operating system kernel.

The OpenBoot Architecture

Objective:
Explain boot PROM fundamentals, including OpenBoot Architecture Standard.

NOTE

The OpenBoot device tree In this section, pay close attention to the OpenBoot device tree. You're likely to see this topic on the exam.

The OpenBoot architecture provides an increase in functionality and portability compared to the proprietary systems of some other hardware vendors. Although this architecture was first implemented by Sun Microsystems as OpenBoot on SPARC (Scalable Processor Architecture) systems, its design is processor independent. The following are some notable features of OpenBoot firmware:

- **Plug-in device drivers:** A device driver can be loaded from a plug-in device such as a PCI card. The plug-in device driver can be used to boot the operating system from that device or to display text on the device before the operating system has activated its own software device drivers. This feature lets the input and output devices evolve without changing the system PROM.
- **The FCode interpreter:** Plug-in drivers are written in a machine-independent interpreted language called FCode. Each OpenBoot system PROM contains an FCode interpreter. This enables the same device and driver to be used on machines with different CPU instruction sets.
- **The device tree:** Devices called *nodes* are attached to a host computer through a hierarchy of interconnected buses on the device tree. A node representing the host computer's main physical address bus forms the tree's root node. Both the user and the operating system can determine the system's hardware configuration by viewing the device tree.

  Nodes with children usually represent buses and their associated controllers, if any. Each such node defines a physical address space that distinguishes the devices connected to the node from one another. Each child of that node is assigned a physical address in the parent's address space. The physical address generally represents a physical characteristic that is unique to the device (such as the bus address or the slot number where the device is installed). The use of physical addresses to identify devices prevents device addresses from changing when other devices are installed or removed.
- **The programmable user interface:** The OpenBoot user interface is based on the programming language Forth, which provides an interactive programming environment. It can be quickly expanded and adapted to special needs and different hardware systems. Forth is used not only by Sun but also utilized in the OpenFirmware boot ROMs provided by IBM, Apple, and Hewlett-Packard.

NOTE

Forth For more information on Forth, refer to American National Standards Institute (ANSI) Standard X3.215-1994 (see http://www.ansi.org).

The OpenBoot Interface

Objective:
Execute basic boot PROM commands for a SPARC system.

The OpenBoot firmware provides a command-line interface for the user at the system console called the *Forth Monitor*.

The Forth Monitor is an interactive command interpreter that gives you access to an extensive set of functions for hardware and software diagnosis. Sometimes you also see the Forth Monitor referred to as *new command mode*. These functions are available to anyone who has access to the system console.

The Forth Monitor prompt is `ok`. When you enter Forth Monitor mode, the following line displays:

```
Type help for more information
ok
```

Getting Help in OpenBoot

At any time, you can obtain help on the various Forth commands supported in OpenBoot by using the `help` command. The `help` commands from the `ok` prompt are listed in Table 3.2.

Table 3.2 OpenBoot `help` Commands

Command	Description
`help`	Displays instructions for using the help system and lists the available help categories.
`help` *<category>*	Shows help for all commands in the category. You use only the first word of the category description.
`help` *<command>*	Shows help for an individual command.

Because of the large number of commands, help is available only for commands that are used frequently.

The following example shows the `help` command with no arguments:

```
ok help <cr>
```

The system responds with the following:

```
ok help <cr>
Enter 'help command-name' or 'help category-name' for more help
```

```
(Use ONLY the first word of a category description)
Examples:  help select   -or-   help line
    Main categories are:
Breakpoints (debugging)
Repeated loops
Defining new commands
Numeric output
Radix (number base conversions)
Arithmetic
Memory access
Line editor
System and boot configuration parameters
Select I/O devices
Floppy eject
Power on reset
Diag (diagnostic routines)
Resume execution
File download and boot
nvramrc (making new commands permanent)
ok
```

If you want to see the help messages for all commands in the category `diag`, for example, you type the following:

```
ok help diag <cr>
```

The system responds with this:

```
test  <device-specifier>   Run selftest method for specified device
  Examples:
    test floppy       - test floppy disk drive
    test net          - test net
    test scsi         - test scsi
test-all        Execute test for all devices with selftest method
watch-clock     Show ticks of real-time clock
watch-net       Monitor network broadcast packets
watch-net-all   Monitor broadcast packets on all net interfaces
probe-scsi      Show attached SCSI devices
probe-scsi-all  Show attached SCSI devices for all host adapters
ok
```

```
ok help boot <cr>
```

The system responds with this:

```
ok help boot <cr>
boot <specifier>  ( — )    boot kernel ( default ) or other file
  Examples:
    boot                   - boot kernel from default device.
                             Factory default is to boot
                             from DISK if present, otherwise from NET.
    boot net               - boot kernel from network
    boot cdrom             - boot kernel from CD-ROM
    boot disk1:h           - boot from disk1 partition h
    boot tape              - boot default file from tape
    boot disk myunix -as   - boot myunix from disk with flags "-as"
dload <filename>  ( addr — )     debug load of file over network at address
  Examples:
     4000 dload /export/root/foo/test
     ?go        - if executable program, execute it
                  or if Forth program, compile it
```

PROM Device Tree (Full Device Pathnames)

Objective:
Identify the system's boot device on a SPARC system.

> **NOTE**
>
> **Device tree versus device pathname** The terms *device tree* and *device pathname* are often interchanged, and you'll see both used. They both mean the same thing.

OpenBoot deals directly with the hardware devices in the system. Each device has a unique name that represents both the type of device and the location of that device in the device tree. The OpenBoot firmware builds a device tree for all devices from information gathered at the POST. Sun uses the device tree to organize devices that are attached to the system. The device tree is loaded into memory, to be used by the kernel during boot to identify all configured devices. The paths built in the device tree by OpenBoot vary, depending on the type of system and its device configuration. The following example shows a full device pathname for an internal IDE cdrom on a peripheral component interconnect (PCI) bus system such as a Sun Fire server:

```
/pci@1f,0/pci@1,1/ide@d/cdrom
```

Typically, the OBP uses `disk` and `cdrom` for the boot disk and CD-ROM drive.

The following example shows the disk device on a Sun Fire server with a PCI-SCSI bus and a SCSI target address of 0:

```
/pci@1f,0/pci@1/scsi@8/disk@0,0
```

A *device tree* is a series of node names separated by slashes (/). The top of the device tree is the root device node. Following the root device node, and separated by a leading slash, is a list of bus devices and controllers. Each device pathname has this form:

```
driver-name@unit-address:device-arguments
```

The components of the device pathname are described in Table 3.3.

Table 3.3 Device Pathname Parameters

Parameter	Description
driver-name	This is the root device node, which is a human-readable string that consists of 1 to 31 letters, digits, and the following characters:
	, (comma)
	. (period)
	_ (underscore)
	+ (plus sign)
	- (minus sign)
	Uppercase and lowercase characters are distinct from one another. In some cases, the driver name includes the name of the device's manufacturer and the device's model name, separated by a comma. Typically, the manufacturer's uppercase, publicly listed stock symbol is used as the manufacturer's name (for example, `SUNW,hme0`). For built-in devices, the manufacturer's name is usually omitted (for example, `scsi` or `pci`).
	@ must precede the address parameter; it serves as a separator between the driver name and unit address.
unit-address	A text string that represents the physical address of the device in its parent's address space. The exact meaning of a particular address depends on the bus to which the device is attached. In this example,
	`/sbus@3,0/SUNW,fas@3,0/sd@0,0`
	`sbus@3,0` represents the I/O board in slot 1, located on the back of the system, and `SUNW,fas@3,0` is the onboard fast/wide SCSI controller of the same board.
	The following are common device driver names:
	`fas`: Fast/wide SCSI controller.
	`hme`: Fast (10/100Mbps) Ethernet.
	`isp`: Differential SCSI controllers and the SunSwift card.
	`ge`: Sun Gigabit Ethernet.
	`eri`: FastEthernet.
	`ce`: Gigaswift Ethernet.

Table 3.3 Device Pathname Parameters

Parameter	Description
	`qfe`: Quad FastEthernet.
	`dmfe`: Davicom FastEthernet.
	`glm`: UltraSCSI controllers.
	`scsi`: SCSI devices.
	`sf`: SCSI-compliant nexus driver that supports the Fibre Channel Protocol for SCSI on Private Fibre Channel Arbitrated Loops (FC-ALs).
	`soc`: Serial optical controller (SOC) device driver.
	`socal`: The Fibre Channel host bus adapter, which is an SBus card that implements two full-duplex Fibre Channel interfaces. Each Fibre Channel interface can connect to an FC-AL.
	`iprb`: An Intel network interface found on x86/x64-based systems. The network interface driver changes depending on which one of many possible third-party network interfaces you have installed on your x86/x64 platform. Others are `dnet` (Sohoware), `elxl` (3COM), `spwr` (SMC), and `nei` (Linksys).
	`sd@0,0` is the SCSI disk (`sd`) set to target `id 0`. (In this case, it is an internal disk because only internal disks should be controlled by the onboard SCSI controller of the I/O board in slot 1.)
`device-arguments`	A text string whose format depends on the particular device. *`device-arguments`* can be used to pass additional information to the device's software. In this example:
	`/pci@1f,0/pci@1,1/ide@3/atapicd@2,0:f`
	the argument for the disk device is `f`. The software driver for this device interprets its argument as a disk partition, so the device pathname refers to partition f on a CD-ROM.

You use the OpenBoot command `show-devs` to obtain information about the device tree and to display device pathnames. This command displays all the devices known to the system directly beneath a given device in the device hierarchy. `show-devs` used by itself shows the entire device tree. The syntax is as follows:

```
ok show-devs <cr>
```

The system outputs the entire device tree:

```
ok show-devs <cr>
/SUNW,UltraSPARC-IIe@0,0
/pci@1f,0
/virtual-memory
/memory@0,c0000000
/aliases
/options
```

```
/openprom
/chosen
/packages
/pci@1f,0/pci@1
/pci@1f,0/pci@1,1
/pci@1f,0/pci@1/scsi@8,1
/pci@1f,0/pci@1/scsi@8
/pci@1f,0/pci@1/scsi@8,1/tape
/pci@1f,0/pci@1/scsi@8,1/disk
/pci@1f,0/pci@1/scsi@8/tape
Output has been truncated
```

Commands that are used to examine the device tree are listed in Table 3.4.

Table 3.4 Commands for Browsing the Device Tree

Command	Description
`.properties`	Displays the names and values of the current node's properties.
`dev` *<device-path>*	Chooses the specified device node and makes it the current node.
`dev` *<node-name>*	Searches for a node with the specified name in the subtree below the current node and chooses the first such node found.
`dev ..`	Chooses the device node that is the parent of the current node.
`dev /`	Chooses the root machine node.
`cd /`	Same as `dev /`.
`device-end`	Leaves the device tree.
<device-path> `find-device`	Chooses the specified device node, similar to `dev`.
`ls`	Displays the names of the current node's children.
`pwd`	Displays the device pathname that names the current node.
`see` *<wordname>*	Decompiles the specified word.
`show-devs` *<device-path>*	Displays all the devices known to the system directly beneath a given device in the device hierarchy. `show-devs` used by itself shows the entire device tree.
`show-disks`	Displays only the disk devices currently connected to the system.
`show-nets`	Displays only the network interface devices currently connected to the system.
`words`	Displays the names of the current node's methods.
<device-path> `select-dev`	Selects the specified device and makes it the active node.

You can examine the device path from a UNIX shell prompt by typing the following:

```
prtconf -p
```

The system displays the following information:

```
# prtconf -p
System Configuration:  Sun Microsystems  sun4u
Memory size: 512 Megabytes
System Peripherals (PROM Nodes):

Node 'SUNW,UltraAX-i2'
    Node 'packages'
        Node 'terminal-emulator'
        Node 'deblocker'
        Node 'obp-tftp'
        Node 'disk-label'
        Node 'SUNW,builtin-drivers'
Output has been truncated -
```

OpenBoot Device Aliases

Objective:
Create and remove custom device aliases.

Device pathnames can be long and complex. Device aliases, like UNIX file system aliases, allow you to substitute a short name for a long name. An alias represents an entire device pathname, not a component of it. For example, the alias `disk0` might represent the following device pathname:

```
/pci@9,600000/SUNW,qlc@2/fp@0,0/disk@w2100000c50ebb5f7,0:a
```

OpenBoot provides the predefined device aliases listed in Table 3.5 for commonly used devices, so you rarely need to type a full device pathname. Be aware, however, that device aliases and pathnames can vary on each platform. The device aliases shown in Table 3.5 are from a Sun Fire server.

Table 3.5 Predefined Device Aliases

Alias	Device Pathname
disk	/pci@1f,0/pci@1/scsi@8/disk@0,0
disk3	/pci@1f,0/pci@1/scsi@8/disk@3,0
disk2	/pci@1f,0/pci@1/scsi@8/disk@2,0
disk1	/pci@1f,0/pci@1/scsi@8/disk@1,0
disk0	/pci@1f,0/pci@1/scsi@8/disk@0,0
cdrom	/pci@1f,0/pci@1,1/ide@d/cdrom@0,0:f
net	/pci@1f,0/pci@1,1/network@c,1

If you add disk drives or change the target of the startup drive, you might need to modify these device aliases. Table 3.6 describes the `devalias` commands, which are used to examine, create, and change OpenBoot aliases.

Table 3.6 `devalias` **Commands**

Command	Description
`devalias`	Displays all current device aliases.
`devalias_`*<alias>*	Displays the device pathname that corresponds to *alias*.
`devalias_`*<alias> <device-path>*	Defines an alias that represents device-path.

NOTE

Don't use existing `devalias` names If an alias with the same name already exists, you see two aliases defined: a `devalias` with the old value and a `devalias` with the new value. It gets confusing as to which `devalias` is the current `devalias`. Therefore, it is recommended that you do not reuse the name of an existing `devalias`, but choose a new name.

The following example creates a device alias named `bootdisk`, which represents SCSI disk with a target ID of 0 on a Sun Fire server:

```
bootdisk                  /pci@1f,0/pci@1/scsi@8/disk@0,0
```

To confirm the alias, you type `devalias`:

```
ok devalias <cr>
```

The system responds by printing all the aliases:

```
bootdisk                  /pci@1f,0/pci@1/scsi@8/disk@0,0
lom                       /pci@1f,0/pci@1,1/ebus@c/SUNW,lomh@14,200000
dload                     /pci@1f,0/pci@1,1/network@c,1:,
net2                      /pci@1f,0/pci@1,1/network@5,1
net                       /pci@1f,0/pci@1,1/network@c,1
disk                      /pci@1f,0/pci@1/scsi@8/disk@0,0
disk3                     /pci@1f,0/pci@1/scsi@8/disk@3,0
disk2                     /pci@1f,0/pci@1/scsi@8/disk@2,0
disk1                     /pci@1f,0/pci@1/scsi@8/disk@1,0
disk0                     /pci@1f,0/pci@1/scsi@8/disk@0,0
    Output has been truncated
```

NOTE

Viewing device aliases You can also view device aliases from a shell prompt by using the `prtconf -vp` command.

User-defined aliases are lost after a system reset or power cycle unless you create a permanent alias. If you want to create permanent aliases, you can either manually store the `devalias` command in a portion of NVRAM called `NVRAMRC` or you can use the `nvalias` and `nvunalias` commands. The following section describes how to configure permanent settings in the NVRAM on a Sun system.

OpenBoot NVRAM

Objective:
Viewing and changing NVRAM parameters.

System configuration variables are stored in system NVRAM. These OpenBoot variables determine the startup machine configuration and related communication characteristics. If you modify the values of the configuration variables, any changes you make remain in effect even after a power cycle. Configuration variables should be adjusted cautiously, however, because incorrect settings can prevent a system from booting.

EXAM ALERT

Device alias versus NVRAM parameter Understand the difference between a device alias and an NVRAM parameter, also called an NVRAM variable.

Table 3.7 describes OpenBoot's NVRAM configuration variables, their default values, and their functions.

Table 3.7 NVRAM Variables

Variable	Default	Description
`auto-boot?`	`true`	The system starts up automatically after power-on or reset if auto-boot? is true. If it is set to false, the system stops at the OpenBoot prompt (ok) after power-on or reset.
`boot-command`	`boot`	The command that is executed if auto-boot? is true.
`boot-device`	`disk` or `net`	The device from which to start up.
`boot-file`	Empty string	Arguments passed to the started program.
`diag-device`	`net`	The diagnostic startup source device.
`diag-file`	Empty string	Arguments passed to the startup program in diagnostic mode.

Table 3.7 NVRAM Variables

Variable	Default	Description
diag-level	*value*	Where value is either min or max (depending on the quantity of diagnostic information you want to see). max results in a longer boot time, so it's best to leave it at min.
diag-switch?	false	Whether to run in diagnostic mode. Set to true for POST diagnostics to run automatically when the server is powered on.
fcode-debug?	false	Whether name fields are included for plug-in device FCodes.
input-device	keyboard	A console input device (usually keyboard, ttya, or ttyb).
nvramrc	Empty	The contents of NVRAMRC.
oem-banner	Empty string	A custom original equipment manufacturer (OEM) banner (enabled with oem-banner? true).
oem-banner?	false	If true, use a custom OEM banner.
oem-logo	No default	A byte array custom OEM logo (enabled with oem-logo? true). Displayed in hexadecimal.
oem-logo?	false	If true, use a custom OEM logo; otherwise, use the Sun logo.
output-device	screen	A console output device (usually screen, ttya, or ttyb).
sbus-probe-list	0123	Which SBus slots to probe, and in what order.
screen-#columns	80	The number of onscreen columns (characters per line).
screen-#rows	34	The number of onscreen rows (lines).
security-#badlogins	No default	The number of incorrect security password attempts.
security-mode	none	The firmware security level (options: none, command, or full).
security-password	No default	The firmware security password (which is never displayed).
use-nvramrc?	false	If true, execute commands in NVRAMRC during system startup.

NOTE

OpenBoot versions Because older SPARC systems use older versions of OpenBoot, they might use different defaults or different configuration variables from those shown in Table 3.7. This text describes OpenBoot version 4.

You can view and change the NVRAM configuration variables by using the commands listed in Table 3.8.

Table 3.8 Commands for Viewing and Modifying Configuration Variables

Command	Description
`password`	Sets the security password.
`printenv`	Displays the current value and the default value for each variable. To show the current value of a named variable, you type the following: `printenv <parameter-name>`
`setenv <variable> <value>`	Sets `<variable>` to the given decimal or text `<value>`. Changes are permanent, but they often take effect only after a reset.
`set-default <variable>`	Resets the value of a specified `<variable>` to the factory default.
`set-defaults`	Resets *all* OpenBoot variable values to the factory defaults.

The following examples illustrate the use of the commands described in Table 3.8. All commands are entered at the `ok` OpenBoot prompt.

You use the `printenv` command at the OpenBoot prompt, with no argument, to display the current value and the default value for each variable:

```
ok printenv <cr>
```

The system responds with this:

```
Variable Name      Value              Default Value
tpe-link-test?     true               true
scsi-initiator-id   7                 7
keyboard-click?     false              false
keymap
ttyb-rts-dtr-off    false              false
ttyb-ignore-cd     true               true
ttya-rts-dtr-off    false              false
ttya-ignore-cd     true               true
ttyb-mode        9600,8,n,1,-         9600,8,n,1,-
ttya-mode        9600,8,n,1,-         9600,8,n,1,-
pcia-probe-list     1,2,3,4            1,2,3,4
pcib-probe-list     1,2,3              1,2,3
mfg-mode        off                off
diag-level       max                max
#power-cycles      89
system-board-serial#
system-board-date
```

```
fcode-debug?      false              false
output-device      screen              screen
input-device      keyboard             keyboard
load-base        16384              16384
boot-command      boot               boot
auto-boot?       false              true
watchdog-reboot?   false               false
diag-file
diag-device       net                net
boot-file
boot-device       disk:a disk net        disk net
local-mac-address?  false               false
Output has been truncated
```

> **NOTE**
>
> **The `printenv` command** Depending on the version of OpenBoot that you have on your system, the `printenv` command might show slightly different results. This example uses a system running OpenBoot version 4.17.

To set the `auto-boot?` variable to `false`, you type the following:

```
ok setenv auto-boot? false <cr>
```

The system responds with this:

```
auto-boot? =  false <cr>
```

You can verify the setting by typing the following:

```
ok printenv auto-boot? <cr>
```

The system responds with this:

```
auto-boot? =   false
```

To reset the variable to its default setting, you type the following:

```
ok set-default auto-boot? <cr>
```

The system does not respond with a message—only another OpenBoot prompt. You can verify the setting by typing the following:

```
ok printenv auto-boot? <cr>
```

The system responds with this:

```
auto-boot? =   true
```

To reset all variables to their default settings, you type the following:

```
ok set-defaults <cr>
```

The system responds with this:

```
Setting NVRAM parameters to default values.
```

It's possible to set device aliases and OpenBoot variables from the UNIX command line by issuing the `eeprom` command. You must be logged in as root to issue this command, and although anyone can view a parameter, only root can change the valuc of a parameter. For example, to set the `auto-boot?` variable to `true`, you type the following at the UNIX prompt (note the use of quotes to escape the ? from expansion by the shell):

```
# eeprom 'auto-boot?=true' <cr>
```

Any non-root user can view the OpenBoot configuration variables from a UNIX prompt by typing the following:

```
/usr/sbin/eeprom
```

For example, to change the OpenBoot parameter `security-password` from the command line, you must be logged in as root and issue the following command:

```
example# eeprom security-password=
Changing PROM password:
New password:
Retype new password:
```

CAUTION

Setting the OpenBoot security mode Setting the security mode and password can be dangerous: If you forget the password, the system is unable to boot. It is nearly impossible to break in without sending the CPU to Sun to have the PROM reset. OpenBoot security is discussed more in the section "OpenBoot Security," later in this chapter.

The security mode password you assign must have between zero and eight characters. Any characters after the eighth are ignored. You do not have to reset the system after you set a password; the security feature takes effect as soon as you type the command.

You can also use the `eeprom` command to add or modify device aliases from the command line as follows:

```
# eeprom "nvramrc=devalias bootdisk /pci@1f,0/pci@1/scsi@8/disk@0,0" <cr>
```

You can use the `nvramrc` configuration variable to store user-defined commands executed during startup. The preceding command creates an nvramrc script that contains a series of OBP commands that are executed during the boot sequence. If the `use-nvramrc?` configuration variable is `true`, the script is evaluated during the OpenBoot startup sequence, and the `bootdisk` alias gets created automatically at the next system reset.

With no parameters, the `eeprom` command displays all the OpenBoot configuration settings, similar to the OpenBoot `printenv` command.

Use the `prtconf` command with the `-vp` options to view OpenBoot parameters from the shell prompt:

```
prtconf -vp <cr>
```

The system responds with a great deal of output, but you see the following OpenBoot information embedded in the output:

```
. . . . <output truncated>
auto-boot-retry?:  'false'
        boot-command:  'boot'
        auto-boot?:  'false'
        watchdog-reboot?:  'false'
        diag-file:
        diag-device:  'net'
        boot-file:
        boot-device:  'bootdisk'
        local-mac-address?:  'false'

        bootdisk:  '/pci@1f,0/pci@1/scsi@8/disk@0,0'
        altboot:  '/pci@1f,0/pci@1/scsi@8/disk@0,0'
        lom:  '/pci@1f,0/pci@1,1/ebus@c/SUNW,lomh@14,200000'
        dload:  '/pci@1f,0/pci@1,1/network@c,1:,'
        net2:  '/pci@1f,0/pci@1,1/network@5,1'
        net:  '/pci@1f,0/pci@1,1/network@c,1'
        disk:  '/pci@1f,0/pci@1/scsi@8/disk@0,0'
        disk3:  '/pci@1f,0/pci@1/scsi@8/disk@3,0'
        disk2:  '/pci@1f,0/pci@1/scsi@8/disk@2,0'
        disk1:  '/pci@1f,0/pci@1/scsi@8/disk@1,0'
        disk0:  '/pci@1f,0/pci@1/scsi@8/disk@0,0'
. . . <output truncated>
```

NOTE

Resetting NVRAM variables On non-USB style keyboards, not USB keyboards, if you change an NVRAM setting on a SPARC system and the system no longer starts up, you can reset the NVRAM variables to their default settings by holding down Stop+N while the machine is powering up. When you issue the Stop+N key sequence, you hold down Stop+N immediately after turning on the power to the SPARC system; you then keep these keys pressed for a few seconds or until you see the banner (if the display is available).

On systems with USB keyboards, power on the system and wait for the front panel power button LED to blink. You hear an audible beep. Quickly press the front panel power button twice (similar to double clicking a mouse). The console displays a screen that says you have successfully reset the NVRAM contents to their default values. At this point, some NVRAM configuration parameters are reset to their defaults, and others are not. Only parameters that are more likely to cause problems, such as TTYA settings, are changed to the default. If you do nothing other than reset the machine at this point, the values are not permanently changed. Only settings that you change manually at this point become permanent. All other customized NVRAM settings are retained.

These are both good techniques for forcing a system's NVRAM variables to a known condition.

You can use the NVRAM commands listed in Table 3.9 to modify device aliases so that they remain permanent, even after a restart.

Table 3.9 NVRAM Commands

Command	Description
`nvalias` *<alias>* *<device-path>*	Stores the command `devalias` *<alias>* *<device-path>* in NVRAMRC. (The alias persists until the nvunalias or set-defaults command is executed.) This command turns on `use-nvramrc?`.
`nvunalias` *<alias>*	Deletes the corresponding alias from NVRAMRC.

For example, to permanently create a device alias named `bootdisk` that represents a SCSI disk with a target ID of 0 on a Sun Fire server, you type the following:

```
# nvalias bootdisk /pci@1f,0/pci@1/scsi@8/disk@0,0 <cr>
```

Because disk device pathnames can be long and complex, the `show-disks` command is provided to assist you in creating device aliases. Type the `show-disks` command, and you see a list of disk devices:

```
ok show-disks
a) /pci@1f,0/pci@1/scsi@8,1/disk
b) /pci@1f,0/pci@1/scsi@8/disk
c) /pci@1f,0/pci@1,1/ide@d/cdrom
d) /pci@1f,0/pci@1,1/ide@d/disk
e) /pci@1f,0/pci@1,1/ebus@c/SUNW,lomh@14,200000
q) NO SELECTION
Enter Selection, q to quit:
```

Type **b** to select a SCSI disk. The system responds with the following message:

```
/pci@1f,0/pci@1/scsi@8/disk has been selected.
Type ^Y ( Control-Y ) to insert it in the command line.
e.g. ok nvalias mydev ^Y
         for creating devalias mydev for
/pci@1f,0/pci@1/scsi@8/disk
ok
```

Now create a device alias named `bootdisk` and press Ctrl+Y:

```
ok nvalias bootdisk ^Y <cr>
```

The system pastes the selected device path:

```
ok nvalias bootdisk /pci@1f,0/pci@1/scsi@8/disk
```

Now all you need to do is add the target number and logical unit number (for example, `sd@0,0` or `disk@0,0`) to the end of the device name:

```
ok nvalias bootdisk /pci@1f,0/pci@1/scsi@8/disk@0,0
```

NOTE

Specifying the disk slice If the boot slice of the disk device that you want to boot to is not slice 0, you need to add the disk slice letter to the end of the device name:

```
ok nvalias bootdisk /pci@1f,0/pci@1/scsi@8/disk@0,0:b
```

In this example, I use the letter b, which corresponds to disk slice 1. This is one area where you'll find disk slices identified by an alpha character and not a number. The letter a corresponds to slice 0, b is slice 1, and so on. If no letter is specified, a for slice 0 is assumed. For example, `/pci@1f,0/pci@1/scsi@8/disk@0,0` is the same as specifying `/pci@1f,0/pci@1/scsi@8/disk@0,0:a` .

To remove an alias, type **nvunalias <aliasname>**. For example, to remove the `devalias` named `bootdisk`, type

```
ok nvunalias bootdisk <cr>
```

The alias named `bootdisk` will no longer be listed after the next OpenBoot reset.

The nvedit Line Editor

Optionally, you can use `nvedit` to create your device aliases. `nvedit` is an OpenBoot line editor that edits the NVRAMRC directly, has a set of editing commands, and operates in a temporary buffer. The following is a sample `nvedit` session:

```
ok setenv use-nvramrc? true <cr>
```

TIP

Learning `nvedit` This section is included for information purposes, to show an additional method for modifying the NVRAM. The `nvedit` line editor will not be covered on the certification exam.

The system responds with the following:

```
use-nvramrc? =   true
ok nvedit <cr>

 0: devalias bootdisk /pci@1f,0/pci@1,1/ide@3/disk@0,0
1: <Control-C> <cr>
ok nvstore <cr>
ok reset-all <cr>
  Resetting ......
ok boot bootdisk <cr>
```

The preceding example uses `nvedit` to create a permanent device alias named `bootdisk`. The example uses Ctrl+C to exit the editor and also uses the `nvstore` command to make the change permanent in the NVRAMRC. Then, issue the `reset-all` command to reset the system and boot the system from `bootdisk` by using the `boot bootdisk` command.

Table 3.10 lists some of the basic commands you can use while in the `nvedit` line editor.

Table 3.10 `nvedit` **Commands**

Command	Meaning
Ctrl+A	Moves backward to beginning of the line.
Ctrl+B	Moves backward one character.
Esc+B	Moves backward one word.
Ctrl+C	Exits the script editor, returning to the OpenBoot command interpreter. The temporary buffer is preserved but is not written back to the script. You use `nvstore` afterward to write it back.
Ctrl+D	Erases the next character.
Esc+D	Erases from the cursor to the end of the word, storing the erased characters in a save buffer.
Ctrl+E	Moves forward to the end of the line.
Ctrl+F	Moves forward one character.
Esc+F	Moves forward one word.
Ctrl+H	Erases the previous character.
Esc+H	Erases from the beginning of the word to just before the cursor, storing erased characters in a save buffer.

Table 3.10 `nvedit` Commands

Command	Meaning
Ctrl+K	Erases from the cursor position to the end of the line, storing the erased characters in a save buffer. If at the end of a line, it joins the next line to the current line (that is, deletes the new line).
Ctrl+L	Displays the entire contents of the editing buffer.
Ctrl+N	Moves to the next line of the script-editing buffer.
Ctrl+O	Inserts a new line at the cursor position and stays on the current line.
Ctrl+P	Moves to the previous line of the script-editing buffer.
Ctrl+Q	Quotes the next character (that is, allows you to insert control characters).
Ctrl+R	Retypes the line.
Ctrl+U	Erases the entire line, storing the erased characters in a save buffer.
Ctrl+W	Erases from the beginning of the word to just before the cursor, storing erased characters in a save buffer.
Ctrl+Y	Inserts the contents of the save buffer before the cursor.
Return (Enter)	Inserts a new line at the cursor position and advances to the next line.
Delete	Erases the previous character.
Backspace	Erases the previous character.

OpenBoot Security

Anyone who has access to a computer keyboard can access OpenBoot and modify parameters unless you set up the security variables. These variables are listed in Table 3.11.

Table 3.11 OpenBoot Security Variables

Variable	Description
`security-mode`	Restricts the set of operations that users are allowed to perform at the OpenBoot prompt.
`security-password`	Records the firmware security password. (It is never displayed.) You should not set this variable directly; you set it by using `password`.
`security-#badlogins`	Specifies the number of incorrect security password attempts.

CAUTION

Setting the OpenBoot security mode It is important to remember your security password and to set it before setting the security mode. If you later forget this password, you cannot use your system; you must call your vendor's customer support service to make your machine bootable again.

If you can get to a UNIX prompt as root, you can use the `eeprom` command to either change the security-mode parameter to none or reset the security password.

To set the security password, you type the `password` command at the `ok` prompt, as shown in the following:

```
ok password <cr>
New password (only first 8 chars are used): <enter password> <cr>
Retype new password: <enter password> <cr>
```

Earlier in this chapter you learned how to change the OpenBoot parameter `security-password` from the command line.

After you assign a password, you can set the security variables that best fit your environment.

You use `security-mode` to restrict the use of OpenBoot commands. When you assign one of the three values shown in Table 3.12, access to commands is protected by a password. The syntax for setting `security-mode` is as follows:

```
setenv security-mode <value>
```

Table 3.12 OpenBoot Security Values

Value	Description
`full`	Specifies that all OpenBoot commands except `go` require a password. This security mode is the most restrictive.
`command`	Specifies that all OpenBoot commands except `boot` and `go` require a password.
`none`	Specifies that no password is required. This is the default.

The following example sets the OpenBoot environment so that all commands except `boot` and `go` require a password:

```
setenv security-mode command <cr>
```

With `security-mode` set to `command`, a password is not required if you enter the `boot` command by itself or if you enter the `go` command. Any other command requires a password, including the `boot` command with an argument.

The following are examples of when a password might be required when `security-mode` is set to `command`:

Example	Description
`ok boot`	No password is required.
`ok go`	No password is required.
`ok reset-all`	You are prompted to enter a password.

Note that with `password`, the password is not echoed as it is typed.

If you enter an incorrect security password, there is a delay of about 10 seconds before the next startup prompt appears. The number of times that an incorrect security password can be typed is stored in the `security-#badlogins` variable, but you should not change this variable.

OpenBoot Diagnostics

You can run various hardware diagnostics in OpenBoot to troubleshoot hardware and network problems. The diagnostic commands are listed in Table 3.13.

Table 3.13 OpenBoot Diagnostic Commands

Command	Description
`.env`	On servers, this command is used to obtain status information about the system's power supplies, fans, and temperature sensors.
`probe-scsi`	Identifies devices attached to the internal SCSI bus.
`probe-scsi-all`	Identifies devices attached to any SCSI bus.
`probe-ide`	Identifies IDE devices attached to the PCI bus.
`probe-fcal-all`	Identifies devices on all Fibre Channel loops.
`reset-all`	Resets the entire system, similar to a power cycle.
`test` *<device-specifier>*	Executes the specified device's self-test method. For example, `test floppy` tests the floppy drive (if installed), and `test net` tests the network connection.
`test-all` *<device-specifier>*	Tests all devices that have built-in self-test methods below the specified device tree node. If *<device-specifier>* is absent, all devices beginning from the root node are tested.
`watch-clock`	Tests the clock function.
`watch-net`	Monitors the primary network connection.
`watch-net-all`	Monitors the primary network connection and any additional network interfaces.

The following examples use some of the diagnostic features of OpenBoot.

To identify peripheral devices currently connected to the system, such as disks, tape drives, or CD-ROMs, you use OpenBoot `probe` commands. To identify the various probe commands and their syntax, you use the OpenBoot `sifting` command:

```
ok sifting probe <cr>
```

The system responds with this:

```
(f006c444) probe-all
(f006bf14) probe-pci-slot
(f006baa4) probe-scsi-all
(f0060de8) probe-pci
. . . <output has been truncated>
```

The OpenBoot `sifting` command, also called a `sifting` dump, searches OpenBoot commands to find every command name that contains the specified string.

This first example uses the OpenBoot `probe` command, `probe-scsi`, to identify all the SCSI devices attached to a particular SCSI bus:

```
ok probe-scsi <cr>
```

This command is useful for identifying SCSI target IDs connected to the internal SCSI bus that are already in use or to make sure that all devices are connected and identified by the system. The system responds with this:

```
Target 0
  Unit 0   Disk     FUJITSU MAJ3364M SUN36G 0804
Target 1
  Unit 0   Disk     FUJITSU MAJ3364M SUN36G 0804
```

If the system has not been reset before the `probe-scsi` command is issued, the following message is displayed:

```
This command may hang the system if a Stop-A or halt command has been executed.  Please
type reset-all to reset the system before executing this command.
Do you wish to continue? (y/n) n
```

If you choose to continue, the system hangs and requires a power reset. Type `n` to abort the `probe-scsi` command. Before proceeding, it's best to have the `auto-boot?` value set to `false` so that the system does not try to boot after performing a reset. Next, type `reset-all` to reset the system. After the system resets, it's OK to use the `probe-scsi` command.

NOTE

OpenBoot probe commands The OpenBoot probe commands probe-scsi and probe-scsi-all are used to obtain a free open SCSI target ID number before adding a SCSI tape unit, a CD-ROM drive, a disk drive, or any other SCSI peripheral. Only devices that are powered on will be located, so you need to make sure everything is turned on. You can use this command after installing a SCSI device to ensure that it has been connected properly and that the system can see it. You can also use this command if you suspect a faulty cable or connection. If you have more than one SCSI bus, you use the probe-scsi-all command. If you have IDE devices, use the probe-ide command to look for them.

This example uses the probe-ide command to identify all IDE devices connected to the PCI bus:

```
ok probe-ide <cr>
 Device 0 ( Primary Master )
     ATA Model: ST34321A
 Device 1 ( Primary Slave )
     Not Present
 Device 2 ( Secondary Master )
     Removable ATAPI Model: CRD-8322B
 Device 3 ( Secondary Slave )
     Not Present
```

This example tests many of the system components, such as video, the network interface, and the floppy disk:

```
ok test all <cr>
```

To test the floppy disk drive to determine whether it is functioning properly, you put a formatted, high-density disk into the drive and type the following:

```
ok test floppy <cr>
```

The system responds with this:

```
Testing floppy disk system. A formatted disk should be in the drive.
Test succeeded.
```

You type **eject-floppy** to remove the disk.

Table 3.14 describes other OpenBoot commands you can use to gather information about the system.

Table 3.14 System Information Commands

Command	Description
`banner`	Displays the power-on banner
`show-sbus`	Displays a list of installed and probed SBus devices
`.enet-addr`	Displays the current Ethernet address
`.idprom`	Displays ID PROM contents, formatted
`.traps`	Displays a list of SPARC trap types
`.version`	Displays the version and date of the startup PROM
`.speed`	Displays CPU and bus speeds
`show-devs`	Displays all installed and probed devices

The following example uses the `banner` command to display the CPU type, the installed RAM, the Ethernet address, the host ID, and the version and date of the startup PROM:

```
ok banner <cr>
```

The system responds with this:

```
Sun Fire V120 (UltraSPARC-IIe 548MHz), No Keyboard
OpenBoot 4.0, 512 MB memory installed, Serial #51814587.
Ethernet address 0:3:ba:16:a0:bb, Host ID: 8316a0bb.
```

This example uses the `.version` command to display the OpenBoot version and the date of the startup PROM:

```
ok .version <cr>
```

The system responds with this:

```
Firmware CORE Release 1.0.17 created 2003/10/6 17:9
Release 4.0 Version 17 created 2003/10/06 17:10
cPOST version 1.0.17 created 2003/10/6
CORE 1.0.17 2003/10/06 17:09
```

NOTE

Checking the OpenBoot version from a shell prompt You can display the OpenBoot version from a shell prompt by typing this:

```
/usr/sbin/prtdiag -v
```

The system displays the following system diagnostic information and the OpenBoot version is displayed at the end of the output:

```
System Configuration:  Sun Microsystems  sun4u Sun Fire V120 (UltraSPARC-IIe
548MHz)
System clock frequency: 100 MHz
Memory size: 512 Megabytes

======================== CPUs ========================

                       Run   Ecache   CPU    CPU
Brd  CPU   Module   MHz     MB    Impl.   Mask
---  ---  -------  -----  ------  ------  ----
 0     0     0      548     0.5   13       3.3


======================== IO Cards ========================

     Bus#  Freq
Brd  Type  MHz   Slot  Name                              Model
---  ----  ----  ----  --------------------------------  ----------------------
 0   PCI-1  33    12   ebus
 0   PCI-1  33     3   pmu-pci10b9,7101
 0   PCI-1  33     3   lomp
 0   PCI-1  33     7   isa
 0   PCI-1  33    12   network-pci108e,1101              SUNW,pci-eri
 0   PCI-1  33    12   usb-pci108e,1103.1
 0   PCI-1  33    13   ide-pci10b9,5229
 0   PCI-1  33     5   network-pci108e,1101              SUNW,pci-eri
 0   PCI-1  33     5   usb-pci108e,1103.1
 0   PCI-2  33     8   scsi-glm                          Symbios,53C896
 0   PCI-2  33     8   scsi-glm                          Symbios,53C896


No failures found in System
===========================

======================== HW Revisions ========================

ASIC Revisions:
---------------
Cheerio: ebus Rev 1

System PROM revisions:
----------------------
  CORE 1.0.17 2003/10/06 17:09
```

This example shows how to use the `.enet-addr` command to display the Ethernet address:

```
ok .enet-addr <cr>
```

The system responds with this:

```
0:3:ba:16:a0:bb
```

To display the CPU information, type the following:

```
ok .speed <cr>
```

The system responds with this:

```
CPU  Speed    : 548.00 MHz
Primary PCI  : 66 Mhz
PCI  Bus A    : 33 MHz
PCI  Bus B    : 33 MHz
Memory Speed : 109.60 MHz    ( CPU:SDRAM = 5:1 )
```

To check network connectivity on all the network interfaces, type the following:

```
ok watch-net-all <cr>
```

The following is displayed, showing that only one interface has a functioning network cable connection:

```
/pci@1f,0/pci@1,1/network@5,1
Internal loopback test — succeeded.
Link is  — down
Looking for Ethernet Packets.
'.' is a Good Packet.  'X' is a Bad Packet.
Type any key to stop.

/pci@1f,0/pci@1,1/network@c,1
Internal loopback test — succeeded.
Link is  — up
Looking for Ethernet Packets.
'.' is a Good Packet.  'X' is a Bad Packet.
Type any key to stop.
```

Input and Output Control

The console is used as the primary means of communication between OpenBoot and the user. The console consists of an input device that is used to receive information supplied by the user and an output device that is used to send information to the user. Typically, the console is either the combination of a text/graphics display device and a keyboard, or an ASCII terminal connected to a serial port.

The configuration variables that are related to the control of the console are listed in Table 3.15.

Table 3.15 Console Configuration Variables

Variable	Description
input-device	Specifies the console input device (usually keyboard, ttya, or ttyb).
output-device	Specifies the console output device (usually screen, ttya, or ttyb).
screen-#columns	Specifies the number of onscreen columns. The default is 80 characters per line.
screen-#rows	Specifies the number of onscreen rows. The default is 34 lines.

You can use the variables in Table 3.15 to assign the console's power-on defaults. These values do not take effect until after the next power cycle or system reset.

If you select keyboard for input-device and the device is not plugged in, input is accepted from the ttya port as a fallback device. If the system is powered on and the keyboard is not detected, the system looks to ttya—the serial port—for the system console and uses that port for all input and output.

You can define the communication parameters on the serial port by setting the configuration variables for that port. These variables are shown in Table 3.16.

Table 3.16 Port Configuration Variables

Variable	Default Value
ttyb-rts-dtr-off	false
ttyb-ignore-cd	true
ttya-rts-dtr-off	false
ttya-ignore-cd	true
ttyb-mode	9600,8,n,1,-
ttya-mode	9600,8,n,1,-

The value for each field of the ttya-mode variable is formatted as follows:

<baud-rate>,<data-bits>,<parity>,<stop-bits>,<handshake>

The values for these fields are shown in Table 3.17.

Table 3.17 Fields for the `ttya-mode` Variable

Field	Values
<baud-rate>	110, 300, 1200, 4800, 9600, 19200
<data-bits>	5, 6, 7, 8
<parity>	n (none), e (even), o (odd), m (mark), s (space)
<stop-bits>	1, 1.5, 2
<handshake>	- (none), h (hardware: rts/cts), s (software: xon/xoff)

OpenBoot PROM Versions

Before you can run Solaris 10, your version of OpenBoot must meet the minimum firmware level for your system.

Sun SPARC systems must have PROM version 3.25.*xx* or later to use the Dynamic Host Configuration Protocol (DHCP) network boot, and must be aware of milestones that are used by the Service Management Facility in Solaris 10 and described later in this chapter. For examples in this book, I use OpenBoot version 4.17.

On Sun SPARC systems, you can install an updated version of the PROM's firmware to keep your PROM (and your version of OpenBoot) up-to-date. Updating your PROM is not covered on the exam, but if you would like more information on performing this procedure, visit http://sunsolve.sun.com and search the Sunsolve knowledgebase using the keywords `flash prom`. Each hardware platform has its own updates, so look for the firmware update that matches your particular hardware.

Booting a SPARC System

Objective:
Boot the system; access detailed information.

- Explain how to perform a system boot of SPARC-based systems.

Up to this point, this chapter describes the OpenBoot diagnostic utilities, variables, and parameters. At the OpenBoot PROM, the operating system is not yet running. In fact, the OpenBoot PROM works fine if the operating system is not even loaded. The primary function of the OpenBoot firmware is to start up the system. Starting up is the process of loading and executing a standalone program (for example, the operating system or the diagnostic monitor). In this discussion, the standalone program that is being started is the two-part operating system kernel. After the kernel is loaded, it starts the UNIX system, mounts the necessary file systems, and runs `/sbin/init`, which in turn starts the `svc.startd` daemon and SMF to bring the system to its default milestone. This process is described in the "The `init` Phase" section, later in this chapter.

Starting up can be initiated either automatically or with a command entered at the user interface. On most SPARC-based systems, the bootstrap process consists of the following basic phases:

1. The system hardware is powered on.
2. The system firmware (the PROM) executes a POST. (The form and scope of POSTs depend on the version of the firmware in the system.)
3. After the tests have been completed successfully, the firmware attempts to autoboot if the appropriate OpenBoot configuration variable (`auto-boot?`) has been set.

The OpenBoot startup process is shown here:

```
Sun Fire V120 (UltraSPARC-IIe 548MHz), No Keyboard
OpenBoot 4.0, 512 MB memory installed, Serial #51814587.
Ethernet address 0:3:ba:16:a0:bb, Host ID: 8316a0bb.



Executing last command: boot
Boot device: bootdisk  File and args:
SunOS Release 5.10 Version Generic_120011-14 64-bit
Copyright 1983-2007 Sun Microsystems, Inc.  All rights reserved.
Use is subject to license terms.
SUNW,eri0 : 100 Mbps full duplex link up
Hostname: sunfire1
/dev/rdsk/c2t0d0s7 is clean

sunfire1 console login:
```

The startup process is controlled by a number of configuration variables, as described in Table 3.18.

Table 3.18 Boot Configuration Variables

Variable	Description
`auto-boot?`	Controls whether the system automatically starts up after a system reset or when the power is turned on. The default for this variable is `true`. When the system is powered on, the system automatically starts up to the default run level.
`boot-command`	Specifies the command to be executed when `auto-boot?` is `true`. The default value of `boot-command` is `boot`, with no command-line arguments.
`diag-switch?`	Causes the system to run in diagnostic mode if the value is `true`. This variable is `false` by default.
`boot-device`	Contains the name of the default startup device used when OpenBoot is not in diagnostic mode.
`boot-file`	Contains the default startup arguments used when OpenBoot is not in diagnostic mode. The default is no arguments.
`diag-device`	Contains the name of the default diagnostic mode startup device. The default is `net`.
`diag-file`	Contains the default diagnostic mode startup arguments. The default is no arguments.

Typically, `auto-boot?` is set to `true`, `boot-command` is set to `boot`, and OpenBoot is not in diagnostic mode. Consequently, the system automatically loads and executes the program and arguments described by `boot-file` from the device described by `boot-device` when the system is first turned on or following a system reset.

The `boot` Command

The `boot` command has the following syntax:

```
boot <device specifier> [arguments] [options]
```

All arguments and options are optional.

The `boot` command and its options are described in Table 3.19.

Table 3.19 `boot` **Command Arguments and Options**

Argument	Description
<device specifier>	The full device name or `devalias` of the boot device. Typically this boot device is *<full device name>* For example, `pci@1f,0/pci@1/scsi@8/disk@3,0:a` indicates a SCSI disk (`sd`) at target 3, `lun0` on the SCSI bus, with the pci host adapter plugged in to slot 0. `cdrom`: Boot from a CD in the CD-ROM drive. `disk`: Boot from the hard drive. `net`: Boot from the network.
[*arguments*]	The name of the program to be booted (for example, stand/diag) and any program arguments. You can also specify the name of the standalone program to be started up (for example, `kernel/sparcv9/unix`). The default on a Sun SPARC system is to start up `kernel/sparcv9/unix` from the root partition.

The following options control the behavior of the `boot` command:

Option	Description
`-a`	The startup program interprets this flag to mean "Ask me," so it prompts for the name of the standalone program to load.
`-m verbose`	Displays more detailed messages during the boot process.
`-m milestone` *<level>*	Allows the operator to enter which milestone to enter upon bootup.
`-r`	Triggers device reconfiguration during startup.
`-s`	Boots to the single-user milestone.
`-v`	Boots in verbose mode. When this option is set, all system messages are displayed.
flags	The boot program passes all startup flags to [*argument*]. The startup flags are not interpreted by boot. (See the later section "The Kernel" for information on the options that are available with the default standalone program, `kernel/sparcv9/unix`.)

A noninteractive boot (`boot`) automatically boots the system by using default values for the boot path. You can initiate a noninteractive boot by typing the following command from the OpenBoot prompt:

```
ok boot
```

The system boots without requiring any additional interaction.

An interactive boot (`boot -a`) stops and asks for input during the boot process. The system provides a dialog box in which it displays the default boot values and gives you the option of changing them. You might want to boot interactively to make a temporary change to the system file or kernel. Booting interactively enables you to test your changes and recover easily if you have problems. To do this, follow the process in Step by Step 3.1.

TIP

The interactive boot process For the exam, you should make sure you understand what each step of an interactive boot process is asking for. For example, you should know the name of the default kernel, know what the default modules are and where they are located, understand what the `/etc/system` file is used for, and what is meant by the default root file system. Each of these is described in the section "The Kernel," later in this chapter.

STEP BY STEP

3.1 The Interactive Boot Process

1. At the `ok` prompt, type **`boot -a`** and press Enter. The boot program prompts you interactively.
2. Press Enter to use the default kernel as prompted, or type the name of the kernel to use for booting and then press Enter.
3. Press Enter to use the default modules directory path as prompted, or type the path for the modules directory and then press Enter.
4. Press Enter to use the default `/etc/system` file as prompted, or type the name of the system file and then press Enter.

NOTE

A missing *`/etc/system`* file If the `/etc/system` file is missing at bootup, you see this message:

```
Warning cannot open system file!
```

The system still boots, however, using all "default" kernel parameters. Because by default the lines in the `/etc/system` file are all commented by the asterisk (`*`) character, `/etc/system` is actually an "empty" file. The kernel doesn't use anything from this file until you edit this file and enter an uncommented line. You can specify `/dev/null` (an empty file) for the system filename, and the system still boots. In fact, if the `/etc/system` file gets corrupted and the system won't boot from the `/etc/system` file, you can specify a file named `/dev/null` to get the system to boot.

5. Press Enter to use the default root file system type as prompted (that is, `ufs` for local disk booting or `nfs` for diskless clients).
6. Press Enter to use the default physical name of the root device as prompted or type the device name.

The following output shows an example of an interactive boot session:

```
ok boot -a <cr>
Resetting ...


Sun Fire V120 (UltraSPARC-IIe 548MHz), No Keyboard
OpenBoot 4.0, 512 MB memory installed, Serial #51814587.
Ethernet address 0:3:ba:16:a0:bb, Host ID: 8316a0bb.



Executing last command: boot
Boot device: bootdisk  File and args:
SunOS Release 5.10 Version Generic_120011-14 64-bit
Copyright 1983-2007 Sun Microsystems, Inc.  All rights reserved.
Use is subject to license terms.
SUNW,eri0 : 100 Mbps full duplex link up
Hostname: sunfire1
/dev/rdsk/c2t0d0s7 is clean

sunfire1 console login:
```

To view more detailed information during the boot process, you use the `boot -v` or `boot -m verbose` options to the `boot` command:

```
ok boot -m verbose <cr>
```

The system outputs more detailed boot messages.

If you are not at the system console to watch the boot information, you can use the UNIX `dmesg` command to redisplay information that was displayed during the boot process, or you can view the information in the `/var/adm/messages` file. The `dmesg` command displays the contents of a fixed-size buffer. Therefore, if the system has been up for a long time, the initial boot messages may have been overwritten with other kernel log entries.

To view messages displayed during the boot process, you can use one of the following methods:

- At a UNIX prompt, type **`/usr/sbin/dmesg`** and press **Enter**.

NOTE

Viewing dmesg output Several pages of information are displayed when you use this method, so I recommend that you pipe the dmesg command to more:

```
/usr/sbin/dmesg¦more
```

- At a UNIX prompt, type **more /var/adm/messages** and press **Enter**.

Solaris 10 introduces the concept of services, described in the section "The Service Management Facility (SMF)." With SMF, there are additional tools for viewing system startup messages. Refer to that section for additional information.

When you specify an explicit device alias, such as disk3, with the boot command, the machine starts up from the specified startup device, using no startup arguments. Here's an example:

```
ok boot disk3 <cr>
```

In this case, the system boots from the disk drive defined by the device alias named disk3. It then loads kernel/sparcv9/unix as the default standalone startup program.

Various options affect the behavior of the boot command. You use the following syntax to specify any of the options listed in Table 3.19 with the boot command:

```
boot [options]
```

When you specify options with the boot command, the machine starts up from the default startup device. Here's an example:

```
ok boot -a <cr>
```

The -a option instructs the boot command to ask for the name of the standalone program to load. If you specify kernel/sparcv9/unix, which is the default, you are prompted to enter the directory that contains the kernel modules. (See the section "The Kernel," later in this chapter, for details on kernel modules.)

You can mix options and arguments with the boot command by using the following syntax:

```
boot [argument]<program filename> - <flags>
```

When you specify the boot command with an explicit startup device and option, the machine starts up from the specified device using the specified option. Here's an example:

```
ok boot disk3 -a <cr>
```

This gives the same prompts as the previous example, except that you are specifying the boot device and not using the default boot device. The system starts up the bootblock from the disk drive defined by the device alias named disk3.

During the startup process, OpenBoot performs the following tasks:

1. The firmware resets the machine if a client program has been executed since the last reset. The client program is normally an operating system or an operating system's loader program, but `boot` can also be used to load and execute other kinds of programs, such as diagnostics programs. For example, if you have just issued the `test net` command, when you next type `boot`, the system resets before starting up.
2. The boot program is loaded into memory, using a protocol that depends on the type of selected device. You can start up from disk, CD-ROM, or the network.
3. The loaded boot program is executed. The behavior of the boot program can be controlled by the `argument` string, if one is passed to the `boot` command on the command line.

The program that is loaded and executed by the startup process is a secondary boot program, the purpose of which is to load the standalone program. The second-level program is either `ufsboot`, when you're starting up from a disk, or `inetboot`, when you're starting up from the network.

Ifu're starting up from disk, the bootstrap process consists of two conceptually distinct phases: primary startup and secondary startup. The PROM assumes that the program for the primary startup (`bootblk`) is in the primary bootblock, which resides in sectors 1 through 15 of the startup device. The bootblock is created by using the `installboot` command. The software installation process typically installs the bootblock for you, so you don't need to issue this command unless you're recovering a corrupted bootblock.

On a SPARC system, to install a bootblock on disk `c0t0d0s0`, for example, you type the following:

```
installboot /usr/platform/'uname -i'/lib/fs/ufs/bootblk /dev/rdsk/c0t0d0s0
```

You cannot see the bootblock, because it resides outside the file system area. It resides in a protected area of the disk and will not be overwritten by a file system. The program in the bootblock area loads the secondary startup program, `ufsboot`.

When you're executing the `boot` command, if you specify a filename, that filename is the name of the standalone startup program to be loaded. If the pathname is relative (that is, it does not begin with a slash), `ufsboot` looks for the standalone program in a platform-dependent search path, which is `/platform/'uname-m'` and `/platform/'uname -i'`.

NOTE

Determining your system's platform name You can use the uname -i command to determine your system's platform name. For example, on a Sun Fire server, the path is /platform/SUNW,UltraAX-i2. You use the command uname -m to find a system's hardware classname; for a Sun Fire, the hardware classname is sun4u. ufsboot searches in both the /platform/'uname-m' and /platform/'uname -i' directories for the kernel files.

On the other hand, if the path to the filename is absolute, boot uses the specified path. The startup program then loads the standalone program and transfers control to it.

The following example shows how to specify the standalone startup program from the OpenBoot ok prompt:

```
ok boot disk5 kernel/sparcv9/unix -s <cr>
```

In this example, the PROM looks for the primary boot program (bootblk) on disk5 (/pci@1f,0/pci@1,1/ide@3/disk@5,0). The primary startup program then loads /platform/'uname -m'/ufsboot. ufsboot loads the appropriate two-part kernel. The core of the kernel is two pieces of static code called genunix and unix, where genunix is the platform-independent generic kernel file and unix is the platform-specific kernel file. When ufsboot loads these two files into memory, they are combined to form the running kernel. On systems running the 64-bit mode OS, the two-part kernel is located in the directory:

```
/platform/'uname -m'/kernel/sparcv9
```

Typical secondary startup programs, such as kernel/sparcv9/unix, accept arguments of the form *<filename>* -*<flags>*, where *filename* is the path to the standalone startup program and -*<flags>* is a list of options to be passed to the standalone program. The example starts up the operating system kernel, which is described in the later section "The Kernel." The -s flag instructs the kernel to start up in single-user mode.

Booting x86- and x64-Based Systems

EXAM ALERT

x86/x64 platform The CX-310-200 exam has several questions pertaining to Solaris on the x86/x64 platform—especially related to the boot process. Pay close attention to the topics in this section.

The procedure used to boot x64- and x86-based systems differs from that for SPARC-based systems. The x64/x86-based platform has boot subsystems used to boot and control the system before the kernel is loaded. In the previous section, I described how the OpenBoot environment controls the system startup after the power is turned on. On an x64/x86-based system, the system startup is controlled by the Basic Input/Output System (BIOS). After the system starts to boot, control is transferred from the BIOS to the Grand Unified Boot Loader (GRUB). GRUB then controls how the operating system is started.

Figure 3.1 illustrates the boot process on the x86/x64-based platform compared to the boot process on the SPARC platform.

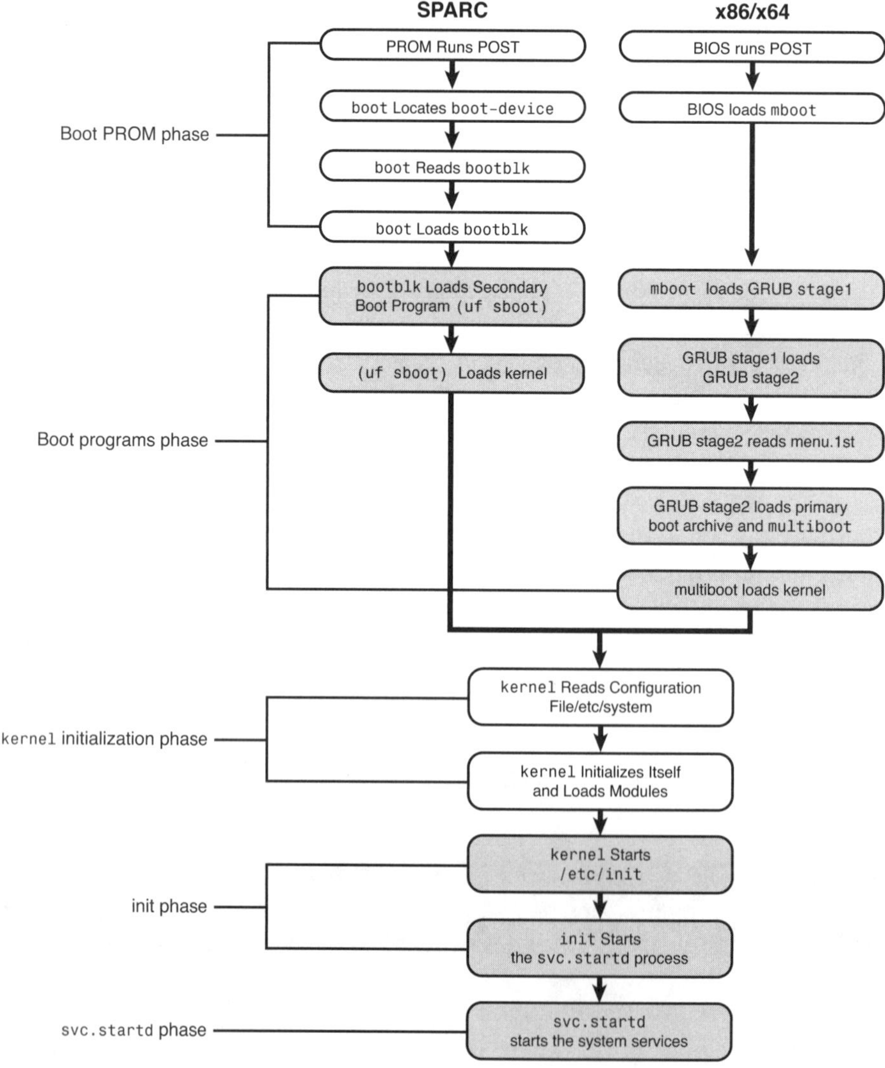

FIGURE 3.1 x86/x64 boot process

After the system is powered on, the BIOS ROM performs the following steps during the first part of the boot sequence:

1. The system firmware in the BIOS ROM executes a power-on self test (POST), runs BIOS extensions in peripheral board ROMs, and invokes software interrupt INT 19h, Bootstrap.

2. The INT 19h handler typically performs the standard PC-compatible boot, which consists of trying to read the first physical sector from the first diskette drive, or, if that fails, from the first hard disk. The processor then jumps to the first byte of the sector image in memory.

3. The first sector on a hard disk on an x86/x64 system contains the master boot block, which contains the master boot (mboot) program and the FDISK table, named for the PC program that maintains it.

   The master boot finds the active partition in the FDISK table, loads its first sector (GRUB stage1), and jumps to its first byte in memory.

4. If GRUB `stage1` is installed on the master boot block (see the `-m` option of `installgrub`) in the first sector of the Solaris FDISK partition. Then `stage2` is loaded directly from the Solaris FDISK partition regardless of the active partition. `stage2` is the core image of GRUB.

5. An x86 FDISK partition for the Solaris software begins with a one cylinder boot slice, which contains GRUB `stage1` in the first sector, the standard Solaris disk label and volume table of contents (VTOC) in the second and third sectors, and GRUB `stage2` in the fiftieth and subsequent sectors. The area from sector 4 to 49 might contain boot blocks for older versions of Solaris.

   When the FDISK partition for the Solaris software is the active partition, the master boot program (mboot) reads the partition boot program in the first sector of the active partition (GRUB `stage1`) into memory and jumps to it.

6. GRUB `stage1` in turn reads the GRUB `stage2` program into memory and jumps to it. The GRUB `stage2` program contains code that allows it to navigate the UFS structure on the root file system.

7. The GRUB `stage2` program locates the GRUB menu configuration file `/boot/grub/menu.lst` and displays the GRUB main menu.

8. When the GRUB menu displays, the user can choose to boot an operating system on a different partition, a different disk, or possibly from the network.

9. Either selected by the user or by default timeout, GRUB executes commands from `/boot/grub/menu.lst` to load a preconstructed boot archive containing a kernel program and data. The default primary boot archive for Solaris 10 is `/platform/i86pc/boot_archive`. The `boot_archive` is a ramdisk image containing Solaris kernel modules and data. GRUB places the `boot_archive` in memory without any interpretation.

10. GRUB then loads a program called multiboot, which implements the kernel side of the Multiboot Specification. The multiboot program is responsible for performing the following tasks:

    - Interpreting the contents of boot archive.
    - Autodetecting whether the system is 64-bit capable.
    - Selecting the best kernel mode for booting the system.
    - Assembling core kernel modules in memory.
    - Handing control of the system to the Solaris kernel.

11. The multiboot program assembles the core kernel modules from the boot archive and starts the operating system, links in the necessary modules from the boot archive and mounts the root file system on the real root device.

12. At this point, the kernel regains storage I/O, mounts additional file systems (see `vfstab`), and starts various operating system services as described in "The Service Management Facility" section later in this chapter.

NOTE

Archive information You cannot mix and match multiboot and boot archive information from different releases or OS instances.

As soon as the kernel gains control, it initializes CPU, memory, and I/O devices. It also mounts the root file system on the device as specified by the `bootpath` property with a file system type as specified by the property `fstype`. Boot properties can be set in `/boot/solaris/bootenv.rc` via the `eeprom` command or in the GRUB command line via the

GRUB edit menu or shell. If the properties are not specified, the root file system defaults to UFS on `/devices/ramdisk:a`, which is the case when booting the install miniroot from DVD. After the root device is mounted, the kernel initializes the `sched` and `init` commands. These commands start the Service Management Facility (SMF) services.

The BIOS

Objective:
Explain the BIOS settings for booting, including BIOS configuration, for x64 and x86-based systems.

Before the kernel is started, the x86/x64-based system is controlled by the read-only-memory (ROM) BIOS, the firmware interface on the x86/x64 platform.

Hardware adapters can also have an onboard BIOS that displays the physical characteristics of the device and can be used to access the device.

During the startup sequence, the PC BIOS checks for the presence of any adapter BIOS and if found, loads and executes each one. Each individual adapter's BIOS runs self-test diagnostics and displays device information.

When powered on, the system's BIOS initializes the CPU, memory, and platform hardware. When the BIOS completes its tasks, it loads the initial bootstrap software (bootloader) from the configured boot device and hands control to the bootloader (GRUB).

It might be necessary to modify the BIOS settings before installing the Solaris OS. For example, the system's BIOS must be configured to boot from the CD/DVD in order to install the Solaris OS from DVD. Entering the BIOS setup screen is performed by pressing a key early in the startup process. This keystroke may vary depending on the manufacturer. On some systems, you press the `F1` or `F2` key after powering on the system. On other systems, it may be the `Escape` key or the `Delete` key. Most times, the instructions to enter the BIOS setup are provided on the screen shortly after powering the system on. Figure 3.2 shows an example of the BIOS setup screen after pressing the `F2` key.

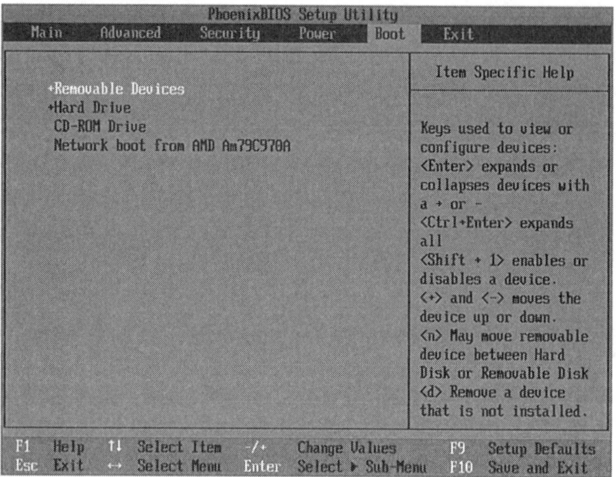

FIGURE 3.2 BIOS setup screen.

Notice that the boot sequence is set to first try booting from a removable device, and then a hard disk, followed by the CD-ROM drive, and finally the network. The boot sequence can be modified on this menu.

GRUB

Objectives:
Describe the purpose, functions and features of the Grand Unified Bootloader (GRUB), including how to modify x86 system boot behavior, manage GRUB boot archives, boot a system in the GRUB-based boot environment and interrupt an unresponsive system.

Identify the system's boot device on an x86/x64-based system.

Solaris 10 release 1/06 utilizes an open-source bootloader called the Grand Unified Boot Loader (GRUB):

- ▶ GRUB contains a boot menu where kernel and boot options can be configured.
- ▶ GRUB can be used to boot a multitude of operating systems, making it possible for the Solaris OS to coexist with other operating systems on the same disk.

After you power on the system and after the initialization phase is complete, the BIOS loads the GRUB, and the GRUB main menu is displayed, as shown in Figure 3.3. For the examples, I will use Solaris version 11/06.

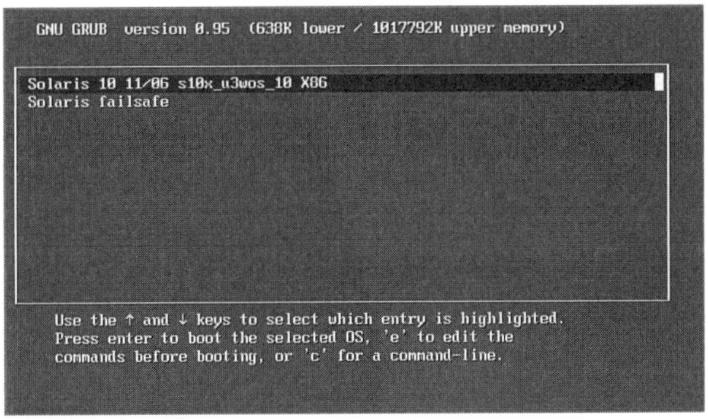

```
GNU GRUB  version 0.95  (638K lower / 1017792K upper memory)

Solaris 10 11/06 s10x_u3wos_10 X86
Solaris failsafe

   Use the ↑ and ↓ keys to select which entry is highlighted.
   Press enter to boot the selected OS, 'e' to edit the
   commands before booting, or 'c' for a command-line.
```

FIGURE 3.3 GRUB menu.

The two boot options shown are predefined in a configuration file named `/boot/grub/menu.lst`. If other operating systems are installed on this system, a boot entry for each operating system would appear in the GRUB main menu. If you install another operating system after the Solaris OS is installed, you would make an entry for the new operating system in the `/boot/grub/menu.lst file`. In the GRUB menu, you can

- Select a boot entry.
- Modify a boot entry using the GRUB edit option.
- Manually load an OS kernel from the command line.

The two boot options displayed in the main menu are the default boot options you see after installing the Solaris 10 OS. The first option boots the Solaris OS. You use this option to boot the system from disk into either single-user or multi-user mode. The second option is used to boot to the Solaris failsafe archive. This option is described later in this section, but it is used to boot the system when a damaged root file system is preventing the system from booting normally.

By default, the GRUB main menu appears, and booting continues after 10 seconds. To stop the autoboot process, use the arrow key to highlight a boot entry in the GRUB main menu. When you type `b`, the system begins booting.

NOTE

Keep the system bootable To ensure that the system remains bootable, the GRUB boot blocks, the GRUB menu, and the boot archive must be up to date. The GRUB boot blocks reside in the Solaris partition. If the boot blocks become corrupt, they should be reinstalled using the `installgrub` command:

```
installgrub -m /boot/grub/stage1 /boot/grub/stage2 /dev/rdsk/c0t2d0s3
```

where `/dev/rdsk/c0t2d0s3` is the boot disk. The `installboot` and `fmthard` commands are used on the Sun SPARC platform and cannot be used to write GRUB boot blocks.

Modifying the Boot Behavior

When the GRUB main menu appears, you can press `b` or `<cr>` to begin the boot process, or you can type `e` to display the GRUB edit menu. Press `e` when you want to temporarily modify the default boot behavior. In Figure 3.4, I used the arrow key to select the first entry and then typed `e` to edit that entry.

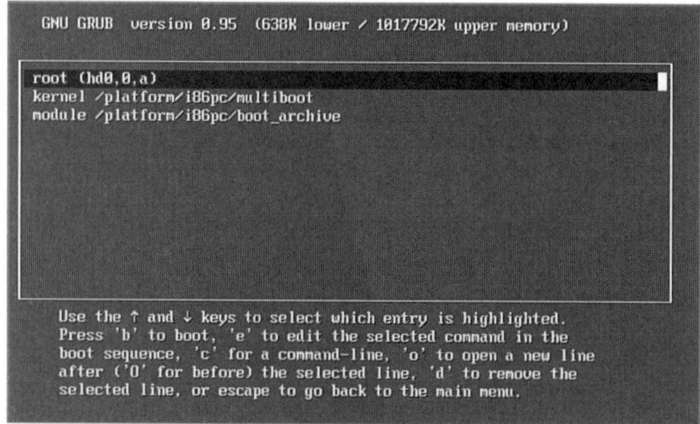
GNU GRUB version 0.95 (638K lower / 1017792K upper memory)
root (hd0,0,a)
kernel /platform/i86pc/multiboot
module /platform/i86pc/boot_archive
Use the ↑ and ↓ keys to select which entry is highlighted.
Press 'b' to boot, 'e' to edit the selected command in the
boot sequence, 'c' for a command-line, 'o' to open a new line
after ('O' for before) the selected line, 'd' to remove the
selected line, or escape to go back to the main menu.

FIGURE 3.4 GRUB edit menu.

The second line, `kernel /platform/i86pc/multiboot`, executes the `kernel` command, which determines the boot behavior of the Solaris OS. The multiboot program is responsible for assembling core kernel modules in memory by reading the boot archive (described later) and passing boot-related information (as specified in the Multiboot Specification) to the kernel. I can use the arrow key to highlight the kernel command and press `e` again to edit the `kernel` command, as shown in Figure 3.5.

```
[ Minimal BASH-like line editing is supported.  For the first word, TAB
  lists possible command completions.  Anywhere else TAB lists the possible
  completions of a device/filename.  ESC at any time exits. ]

grub edit> kernel /platform/i86pc/multiboot -s
```

FIGURE 3.5 GRUB command edit menu.

The `kernel` command supports several options and arguments that let you modify the boot behavior. The following are a few of the more common options:

- `kernel /platform/i86pc/multiboot` *`<kernel name>`*, where *`<kernel name>`* specifies the alternate kernel to boot from.
- `kernel /platform/i86pc/multiboot -a`, where `-a` performs an interactive boot and prompts for user configuration information during the boot process.
- Set the console property to ttya so that the system uses the serial port for the console:

  `kernel /platform/i86pc/multiboot -B console=ttya`
- `kernel /platform/i86pc/multiboot -s`, where `-s` boots the system into single-user mode.
- `kernel /platform/i86pc/multiboot -r`, where `-r` specifies a reconfiguration boot. The system probes all attached hardware devices and then assigns nodes in the file system to represent only those devices that are actually found.
- `kernel /platform/i86pc/multiboot -v`, where `-v` boots with verbose messages enabled.

I added the `-s` option to the `kernel` command to boot the system into single-user mode. When I press `Enter`, my changes are saved, and I return to the GRUB edit menu, as shown in Figure 3.6.

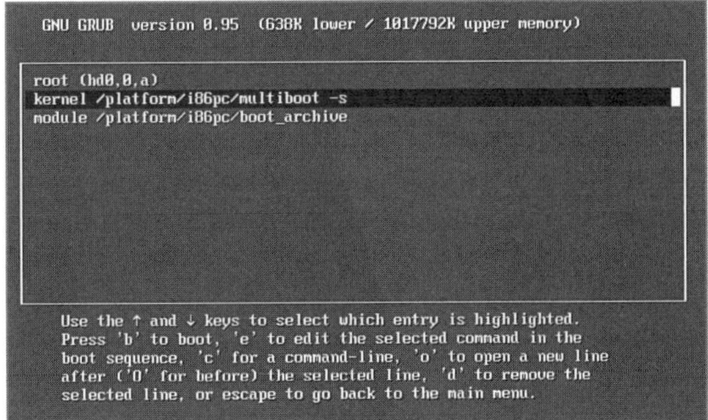
GNU GRUB version 0.95 (638K lower / 1017792K upper memory)
root (hd0,0,a)
kernel /platform/i86pc/multiboot -s
module /platform/i86pc/boot_archive
Use the ↑ and ↓ keys to select which entry is highlighted.
Press 'b' to boot, 'e' to edit the selected command in the
boot sequence, 'c' for a command-line, 'o' to open a new line
after ('O' for before) the selected line, 'd' to remove the
selected line, or escape to go back to the main menu.

FIGURE 3.6 Returning to the GRUB edit menu.

If I press the `Escape` key, I'm returned to the main menu, and the changes are not saved.

NOTE

GRUB menu changes Any modifications you make in the GRUB menu are temporary and persist only until the next time the system is booted.

Press **b** to boot using the new command string.

Another method for modifying the boot behavior is to use the `eeprom` command at the shell prompt. On the SPARC system, the `eeprom` command changes the OpenBoot NVRAM. On the x86/x64-based system, the `eeprom` command modifies boot variables stored in the `/boot/solaris/bootenv.rc` file. Changes made using the `eeprom` command persist over each system reboot. You can still temporarily override `eeprom` settings for a single boot cycle if you boot the system by specifying options and arguments to the `kernel` command in the GRUB edit menu.

The following is an example of entries in the `/boot/solaris/bootenv.rc` file:

```
setprop kbd-type 'US-English'
setprop ata-dma-enabled '1'
setprop atapi-cd-dma-enabled '0'
setprop console=text
setprop ttyb-ignore-cd 'true'
setprop ttya-rts-dtr-off 'false'
setprop ttya-ignore-cd 'true'
setprop ttyb-mode '9600,8,n,1,-'
setprop ttya-mode '9600,8,n,1,-'
setprop lba-access-ok '1'
setprop prealloc-chunk-size '0x2000'
setprop bootpath '/pci@0,0/pci-ide@1f,1/ide@0/cmdk@0,0:a'
setprop console 'text'
```

To change the `console` parameter in the `bootenv.rc` file, use the `eeprom` command to direct the console to run on ttya:

```
eeprom console=ttya <cr>
```

To identify the boot device on a x86/x64 system, type the following:

```
eeprom bootpath <cr>
```

The system displays the bootpath:

```
bootpath=/pci@0,0/pci-ide@1f,1/ide@0/cmdk@0,0:a
```

To remove a setting for a parameter, use double quotes to specify a null value. In the next example, the `boot-file` parameter is set to null:

```
eeprom boot-file="" <cr>
```

When the `boot-file` parameter is set to null, the x86/x64 system uses its default autodetect boot behavior.

GRUB Device Naming

To work with GRUB, you need to understand how GRUB names devices. The floppy disk is named as follows:

- `(fd0)`: First, second floppy diskette drive
- `(nd)`: Network interface

Hard disk device names start with `hd` followed by a number, where `0` maps to BIOS disk `0x80` (the first disk enumerated by the BIOS), `1` maps to `0x81`, and so on:

- `(hd0)`: First BIOS disk (also the BIOS boot disk 0x80)
- `(hd1)`: Second BIOS disk (BIOS disk 0x81)
- `(hd0,0), (hd0,1)`: First BIOS disk, first and second fdisk partition
- `(hd0,0,a)`: First BIOS disk, first fdisk partition, Solaris/BSD slice 0
- `(hd0,0,b)`: First BIOS disk, first fdisk partition, Solaris/BSD slice 1

All GRUB device names must be enclosed in parentheses.

The GRUB Menu

By default, the Solaris menu file resides in `/boot/grub/menu.lst`. The contents of this file dictate what is displayed in the GRUB menu when you boot the system. The GRUB menu file contains entries for all the OS instances that are installed on your system, as well as other important boot directives.

This file may be modified using a Solaris text editor. For example, I'll use the `vi` editor to modify the `menu.lst` file and change the console to the serial port by changing the following lines in the `menu.list` file from

```
#   serial —unit=0 —speed=9600
#   terminal serial
```

to

```
        serial —unit=0 —speed=9600
        terminal serial
```

When you uncomment these lines in the `menu.list` file, GRUB output is redirected to `ttya` (the serial port).

I can also turn off `autoboot` by changing the following line in the `menu.lst` file from

```
timeout=10
```

to

```
timeout=-1
```

Now, instead of the GRUB menu appearing for 10 seconds and automatically booting the system, the GRUB menu waits for user input.

The Boot Archive

The boot archive contains core kernel modules, including drivers and configuration files, that are needed to initialize the OS kernel. After the I/O subsystem is initialized, the kernel mounts the root (/) file system on the real root device. The Solaris OS updates the boot archive from files on the root (/) file system whenever necessary. This update typically occurs when a kernel patch is applied or when a driver package is added. To detect any file updates that were performed manually, the boot archive might also be updated during system shutdown.

If a system failure, power failure, or kernel panic occurs, immediately following a kernel file update, the boot archive and the root (/) file system might not be synchronized. Although the system might still boot with the old boot archive, you should boot the system in the failsafe archive to rebuild the boot archive. The boot archive is updated or rebuilt by using the `bootadm` command. Immediately after you perform a system upgrade or apply a patch, manually rebuild the boot archive by running the following command as superuser:

```
# bootadm update-archive <cr>
```

Two boot archives are maintained on the system:

- Failsafe boot archive
- Primary boot archive

A failsafe boot archive has the following characteristics:

- It is self-sufficient.
- It can boot on its own.
- It is created by default during installation of the OS.
- It requires no maintenance.

NOTE

Running `bootadm` with a cron job On mission-critical systems, where system availability is essential, you might choose to set up a cron job to run the `bootadm` command on a regular basis. If the boot archive does not need to be updated, this process uses very few resources and usually takes only 0.1 to 0.2 seconds to complete.

A primary boot archive shadows a root (/) file system. This boot archive contains all the kernel modules, `driver.conf` files, and a few configuration files. These files are located in the `/etc` directory. The kernel reads the files in the boot archive before the root (/) file system is mounted. After the root (/) file system is mounted, the kernel discards the boot archive from memory. Then, file I/O is performed against the root device.

Use the `bootadm` command to list the contents of the primary boot archive:

```
# bootadm list-archive <cr>
```

The system displays the list of files:

```
etc/rtc_config
etc/system
etc/name_to_major
etc/driver_aliases
etc/name_to_sysnum
etc/dacf.conf
etc/driver_classes
etc/path_to_inst
etc/mach
etc/devices/devid_cache
etc/devices/mdi_scsi_vhci_cache
etc/devices/mdi_ib_cache
kernel
platform/i86pc/biosint
platform/i86pc/kernel
boot/solaris.xpm
boot/solaris/bootenv.rc
boot/solaris/devicedb/master
boot/acpi/tables
```

The entire list of files contained in the boot archive can be found listed in the `/boot/solaris/filelist.ramdisk` file. When any of the files in the archive is updated, the boot archive must be rebuilt. You know when the boot archive is being updated, because you see the following message at shutdown:

```
updating /platform/i86pc/boot_archive...this may take a minute
```

Booting the Failsafe Archive for Recovery Purposes

Sometimes the boot archive can become corrupt—especially after a system crash or power failure. If the archive is corrupt, the system hangs when GRUB tries to boot Solaris. You also see a message about a corrupt RAM disk. To recover, you need to rebuild the boot archive, as described in this section.

You can rebuild the boot archive by selecting `failsafe archive` from the GRUB main menu. When booting to the failsafe archive, you are booting to the file `/boot/x86.miniroot-safe`, which is a bootable, standalone Solaris image. It's sort of like booting to the DVD, and it's on the disk for convenience. You could even copy this file to a USB memory stick as a recovery tool. The Solaris miniroot consists of the Solaris software that is required to install, repair, or upgrade systems.

During the failsafe boot procedure, the following messages appear:

```
Booting to milestone "milestone/single-user:default".
Configuring devices.
Searching for installed OS instances. . .

Solaris 10 11/06 s10x_u3wos_10 was found on /dev/dsk/c0d0s0.
Do you wish to have it mounted read-write on /a? [y,n,?]
```

Type **y** <cr>.

> **NOTE**
>
> **Metadevice mirror** If your system uses a metadevice mirror for the root partition, as described in the *Solaris 10 System Administration Exam Prep: Exam CX-310-202* book, you receive a message about the partitions being skipped because they are metadevices.

At this point, you boot the system from a mini-version of Solaris. The root (`/`) file system on the hard drive is mounted on `/a`.

Manually update the boot archive by issuing the following command:

```
# bootadm update-archive -R /a <cr>
```

The `-R /a` option specifies that the root file system, where the boot archive resides, is mounted on `/a`. When the boot archive is updated, reboot the system as follows:

```
# shutdown -i 6 <cr>
```

You should now have a working system.

Configuring the Video Display on the x86/x64 Platform

EXAM ALERT

The `kdmconfig` utility, Xorg, and Xsun You should know how to use the `kdmconfig` utility to configure the graphics device on an x86/x64-based system. You also should know how to configure both Xorg and Xsun.

Because of the wide array of video controllers available for x86/x64-based systems, sometimes getting the most from your video card can be tricky. For video support on x86/x64-based platforms, two Xservers are shipped with Solaris—Xsun and Xorg. The Xorg environment is the default server in Solaris 10.

To configure the Xorg server:

Create an `/etc/X11/xorg.conf` file with one of these commands:

```
/usr/X11/bin/Xorg -configure <cr>
```

or

```
/usr/X11/bin/xorgconfig <cr>
```

Xorg probes the hardware on the system and creates an Xorg configuration file called `xorg.conf.new` in the root directory. Edit the resultant `xorg.conf.new` file with any changes needed. (See the man pages or search the Web for an example for your graphics hardware and monitor.)

When you're ready to use the new configuration file, move the `xorg.conf.new` file to `/etc/X11/xorg.conf`.

Xorg uses the `xorg.conf` file as its configuration file for its initial setup. This configuration file is searched for in the following places (in the order listed) when the server is started:

```
/etc/X11/
/usr/X11/etc/X11/
/etc/X11/$XORGCONFIG
/usr/X11/etc/X11/$XORGCONFIG
/etc/X11/xorg.conf-4
/etc/X11/xorg.conf
/etc/xorg.conf
/usr/X11/etc/X11/xorg.conf.<hostname>
/usr/X11/etc/X11/xorg.conf-4
/usr/X11/etc/X11/xorg.conf
/usr/X11/lib/X11/xorg.conf.<hostname>
/usr/X11/lib/X11/xorg.conf-4
/usr/X11/lib/X11/xorg.conf
```

If you experience video problems or errors when starting the Xserver, review the log file named `/var/log/Xorg.0.log`. Information in that file is useful for debugging.

Some video cards are not supported by the Xorg X Window system server; however, support may be available with the Xsun server. To switch from the Xorg server to the Xsun server and configure the Xsun server to use a particular chipset, follow the steps described in Step by Step 3.2.

STEP BY STEP

3.2 Change Hardware Management from Xorg to Xsun

1. Run the program to configure the keyboard, display, and mouse:

   ```
   # kdmconfig <cr>
   ```

   The Introduction and X Server Selection screen, shown in Figure 3.7, is displayed.

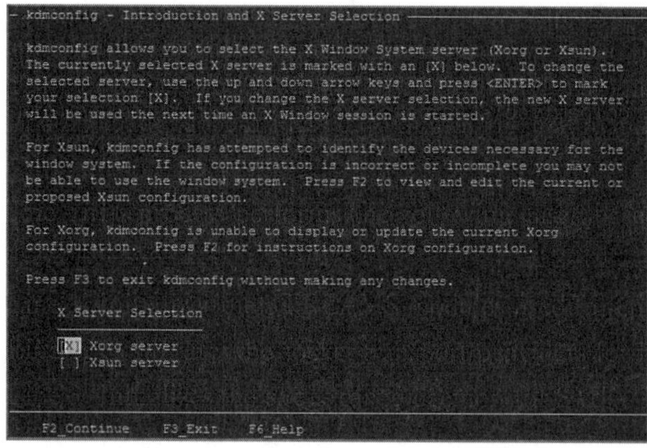

FIGURE 3.7 Selecting the X Window System server.

2. Select `Xsun server` and press **F2** to continue.

   The View and Edit Window System Configuration screen, shown in Figure 3.8, is displayed.

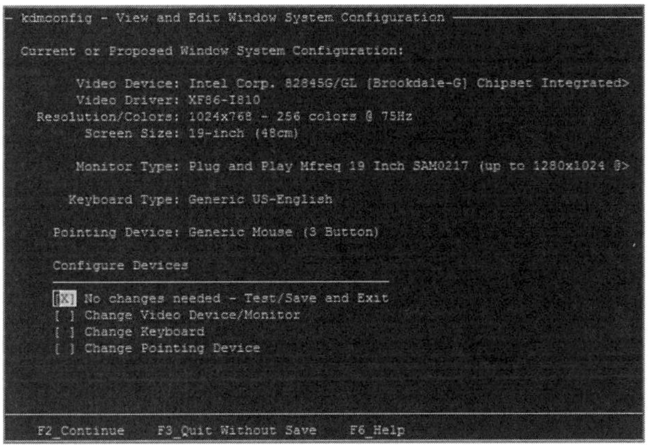

```
kdmconfig - View and Edit Window System Configuration

Current or Proposed Window System Configuration:

      Video Device: Intel Corp. 82845G/GL [Brookdale-G] Chipset Integrated>
      Video Driver: XF86-I810
 Resolution/Colors: 1024x768 - 256 colors @ 75Hz
       Screen Size: 19-inch (48cm)

      Monitor Type: Plug and Play Mfreq 19 Inch SAM0217 (up to 1280x1024 @>

     Keyboard Type: Generic US-English

   Pointing Device: Generic Mouse (3 Button)

   Configure Devices
   ________________________________________
   [X] No changes needed - Test/Save and Exit
   [ ] Change Video Device/Monitor
   [ ] Change Keyboard
   [ ] Change Pointing Device

 F2_Continue    F3_Quit Without Save    F6_Help
```

FIGURE 3.8 View and Edit Window System Configuration screen.

3. Select your video device. Use the `Change Video Device/Monitor` option to change the device if necessary.
4. Continue to select other `kdmconfig` options that may be necessary.
5. Press **F2** to save and exit.

The Kernel

After the `boot` command initiates the kernel, the kernel begins several phases of the startup process. The first task is for OpenBoot to load the two-part kernel. The secondary startup program, `ufsboot`, which was described in the section "The `boot` Command," loads the operating system kernel. The core of the kernel is two pieces of static code called `genunix` and `unix`. `genunix` is the platform-independent generic kernel file, and `unix` is the platform-specific kernel file. The platform-specific kernel used by `ufsboot` for systems running in 64-bit mode is named `/platform/'uname -m'/kernel/sparcv9/unix`. On x86/x64-based systems, Solaris runs in 32-bit or 64-bit mode. On SPARC systems, Solaris 10 runs only on 64-bit systems. However, early versions of Solaris gave you the option of running in 32-bit or 64-bit mode. On previous versions of Solaris for SPARC systems, the 32-bit platform-specific kernel was named `/platform/'uname -m'/kernel/unix`. Now, in Solaris 10, `/platform/'uname -m'/kernel/unix` is merely a link to the 64-bit kernel located in the `sparcv9` directory. When `ufsboot` loads `genunix` and `unix` into memory, they are combined to form the running kernel.

The kernel initializes itself and begins loading modules, using `ufsboot` to read the files. After the kernel has loaded enough modules to mount the root file system, it unmaps the `ufsboot` program and continues, using its own resources. The kernel creates a user process and starts the `/sbin/init` daemon, which starts other processes by reading the `/etc/inittab` file. (The `/sbin/init` process is described in the "The `init` Phase" section, later in this chapter.)

The kernel is dynamically configured in Solaris 10. It consists of a small static core and many dynamically loadable kernel modules. Many kernel modules are loaded automatically at boot time, but for efficiency, others—such as device drivers—are loaded from the disk as needed by the kernel.

A kernel module is a software component that is used to perform a specific task on the system. An example of a loadable kernel module is a device driver that is loaded when the device is accessed. Drivers, file systems, STREAMS modules, and other modules are loaded automatically as they are needed, either at startup or at runtime. This is referred to as *autoconfiguration*, and the kernel is referred to as a *dynamic kernel*. After these modules are no longer in use, they can be unloaded. Modules are kept in memory until that memory is needed. This makes more efficient use of memory and allows for simpler modification and tuning.

The `modinfo` command provides information about the modules that are currently loaded on a system. The modules that make up the kernel typically reside in the directories `/kernel` and `/usr/kernel`. Platform-dependent modules reside in the `/platform/'uname -m'/kernel` and `/platform/'uname -i'/kernel` directories.

When the kernel is loading, it reads the `/etc/system` file where system configuration information is stored. This file modifies the kernel's parameters and treatment of loadable modules. It specifically controls the following:

- The search path for default modules to be loaded at boot time as well as the search path for modules not to be loaded at boot time
- The root file system type and device
- The modules to be forcibly loaded at boot time rather than at first access
- The modules that are excluded from loading automatically at boot time
- The new values to override the default kernel parameter values

CAUTION

Modifying the `/etc/system` file A system administrator modifies the `/etc/system` file to modify the kernel's behavior. By default, the contents of the `/etc/system` file are completely commented out, and the kernel uses all default values. A default kernel is adequate for average system use, and you should not modify the `/etc/system` file unless you are certain of the results. A good practice is to always make a backup copy of any system file you modify, in case the original needs to be restored. Incorrect entries could prevent your system from booting. If a boot process fails because of an unusable `/etc/system` file, you should boot the system by using the interactive option `boot -a`. When you are asked to enter the name of the system file, you should enter the name of the backup system filename, or `/dev/null`, to use default parameters.

The `/etc/system` file contains commands that have this form:

```
set <parameter>=<value>
```

For example, the setting for the kernel parameter `nfs:nfs4_nra` is set in the `/etc/system` file with the following line:

```
set nfs:nfs_nra=4
```

This parameter controls the number of read-ahead operations that are queued by the NFS version 4 client.

Commands that affect loadable modules have this form:

```
set <module>:<variable>=<value>
```

NOTE

Editing the `/etc/system` file A command must be 80 or fewer characters in length, and a comment line must begin with an asterisk (`*`) and end with a hard return.

For the most part, the Solaris OE is self-adjusting to system load and demands minimal tuning. In some cases, however, tuning is necessary.

If you need to change a tunable parameter in the `/etc/system` file, you can use the `sysdef` command or the `mdb` command to verify the change. `sysdef` lists all hardware devices, system devices, loadable modules, and the values of selected kernel-tunable parameters. The following is the output that is produced from the `sysdef` command:

```
* Hostid
*
  831f857b
*
* sun4u Configuration
*
*
* Devices
*
scsi_vhci, instance #0
ib, instance #0 (driver not attached)
packages (driver not attached)
        terminal-emulator (driver not attached)
        deblocker (driver not attached)
        obp-tftp (driver not attached)
        disk-label (driver not attached)
```

```
Output has been truncated . . . . . . .
* System Configuration
*
  swap files
swapfile             dev  swaplo blocks   free
/dev/dsk/c0t0d0s3   32,123     16 4096576 4096576
*
* Tunable Parameters
*
21241856        maximum memory allowed in buffer cache (bufhwm)
   16218        maximum number of processes (v.v_proc)
      99        maximum global priority in sys class (MAXCLSYSPRI)
   16213        maximum processes per user id (v.v_maxup)
      30        auto update time limit in seconds (NAUTOUP)
      25        page stealing low water mark (GPGSLO)
       1        fsflush run rate (FSFLUSHR)
      25        minimum resident memory for avoiding deadlock (MINARMEM)
      25        minimum swapable memory for avoiding deadlock (MINASMEM)
*
* Utsname Tunables
*
    5.10  release (REL)
 sunfire  node name (NODE)
   SunOS  system name (SYS)
Generic_127127-11  version (VER)
*
* Process Resource Limit Tunables (Current:Maximum)
*
0x0000000000000100:0x0000000000010000   file descriptors
*
* Streams Tunables
*
      9  maximum number of pushes allowed (NSTRPUSH)
  65536  maximum stream message size (STRMSGSZ)
   1024  max size of ctl part of message (STRCTLSZ)
*
* IPC Messages module is not loaded
*
*
* IPC Semaphores module is not loaded
*
*
* IPC Shared Memory module is not loaded
*
*
* Time Sharing Scheduler Tunables
*
60      maximum time sharing user priority (TSMAXUPRI)
SYS     system class name (SYS_NAME)
```

The `mdb` command is used to view or modify a running kernel and must be used with extreme care. The use of `mdb` is beyond the scope of this book; however, more information can be obtained from The Solaris Modular Debugger Guide available at http://docs.sun.com.

> **NOTE**
>
> **Kernel tunable parameters in Solaris 10** You'll find in Solaris 10 that many tunable parameters that were previously set in `/etc/system` have been removed. For example, IPC facilities were previously controlled by kernel tunables, where you had to modify the `/etc/system` file and reboot the system to change the default values for these facilities. Because the IPC facilities are now controlled by resource controls, their configuration can be modified while the system is running. Many applications that previously required system tuning to function might now run without tuning because of increased defaults and the automatic allocation of resources.

Configuring the kernel and tunable parameters is a complex topic to describe in a few sections of a chapter. This introduction to the concept provides enough information for the average system administrator and describes the topics you need to know for the exam. If you are interested in learning more about the kernel and tunable parameters, refer to the additional sources of information described at the end of this chapter.

The `init` Phase

Objective:
Explain the Service Management Facility and the phases of the boot process.

The `init` phase has undergone major changes in Solaris 10. Even if you are experienced on previous versions of Solaris OE, this section introduces the `svc.startd` and `svc.configd` daemons and the Service Management Facility (SMF), which are new in Solaris 10 and will be covered extensively on the exam.

After control of the system is passed to the kernel, the system begins the last stage of the boot process—the `init` stage. In this phase of the boot process, the `init` daemon (`/sbin/init`) reads the `/etc/default/init` file to set any environment variables for the shell that `init` invokes. By default, the CMASK and TZ variables are set. These values get passed to any processes that `init` starts. Then, `init` reads the `/etc/inittab` file and executes any process entries that have `sysinit` in the action field so that any special initializations can take place before users log in.

After reading the `/etc/inittab` file, `init` starts the `svc.startd` daemon, which is responsible for starting and stopping other system services such as mounting file systems and configuring network devices. In addition, `svc.startd` starts the `svc.configd` daemon and also executes legacy run control (RC) scripts, which are described later in this section.

The `/sbin/init` command sets up the system based on the directions in `/etc/inittab`. Each entry in the `/etc/inittab` file has the following fields:

```
id:rstate:action:process
```

Table 3.20 describes each field.

Table 3.20 Fields in the `inittab` File

Field	Description
`id`	A unique identifier
`rstate`	The run level(s)
`action`	How the process is to be run
`process`	The name of the command to execute

Table 3.21 lists the valid action keywords:

Table 3.21 `inittab action` Field Values

Field	Description
sysinit	Executes the process before init tries to access the console via the console prompt. init waits for the completion of the process before it continues to read the inittab file.
powerfail	Indicates that the system has received a powerfail signal.

The following example shows a default `/etc/inittab` file:

```
ap::sysinit:/sbin/autopush -f /etc/iu.ap
sp::sysinit:/sbin/soconfig -f /etc/sock2path
smf::sysinit:/lib/svc/bin/svc.startd  >/dev/msglog 2<>/dev/msglog </dev/console
p3:s1234:powerfail:/usr/sbin/shutdown -y -i5 -g0 >/dev/msglog 2<>/dev/msglog
```

The `init` process performs the following tasks based on the entries found in the default `/etc/inittab` file:

Line 1: Initializes the STREAMS modules used for communication services.

Line 2. Configures the socket transport providers for network connections.

Line 3. Initializes the `svc.startd` daemon for SMF.

Line 4. Describes the action to take when the `init` daemon receives a power fail shutdown signal.

The Service Management Facility (SMF)

Objective:
Explain the Service Management Facility and the phases of the boot process.

- Use Service Management Facility or legacy commands and scripts to control both the boot and shutdown procedures.

In Solaris 10, the `svc.startd` daemon replaces the `init` process as the master process starter and restarter. In previous versions of Solaris, `init` would start all processes and bring the system to the appropriate "run level" or "init state." Now the SMF—or, more specifically, the `svc.startd` daemon—assumes the role of starting system services.

NOTE

SMF services A service can be described as an entity that provides a resource or list of capabilities to applications and other services. This entity can be running locally or remote, but at this phase of the boot process, the service is running locally. A service does not have to be a process; it can be the software state of a device or a mounted file system. Also, a system can have more than one instance of a service, such as with multiple network interfaces, multiple mounted file systems, or a set of other services.

Using the SMF to manage system services over the traditional UNIX startup scripts that, in the past, were run by the `init` process has the following advantages:

- The SMF automatically restarts failed services in the correct order, whether they failed as the result of administrator error or a software bug or were affected by an uncorrectable hardware error. The restart order is defined by dependency statements within the SMF.
- The system administrator can view and manage services as well as view the relationships between services and processes.
- The SMF allows the system administrator to back up, restore, and undo changes to services by taking automatic snapshots of service configurations.
- The SMF allows the system administrator to interrogate services and determine why a service may not be running.
- The SMF allows services to be enabled and disabled either temporarily or permanently.
- The SMF allows the system administrator to delegate tasks to nonroot users, giving these users the ability to modify, enable, disable, or restart system services.
- Large systems boot and shut down faster, because services are started and stopped in parallel according to dependencies setup in the SMF.

- The SMF allows customization of output sent to the boot console either to be as quiet as possible, which is the default, or to be verbose by using `boot -m verbose` from the OpenBoot prompt.
- The SMF provides compatibility with legacy RC scripts.

If you who have experience with previous versions of Solaris, you'll notice a few differences immediately:

- The boot process creates fewer messages. All the information that was provided by the boot messages in previous versions of Solaris is located in the `/var/svc/log` directory. You still have the option of booting the system with the `boot -v` option, which provides more verbose boot messages.
- Because the SMF can start services in parallel, the boot time is substantially quicker than in previous versions of Solaris.
- Because services are automatically restarted if possible, it may seem that a process refuses to die. Even a `kill -9` may initially kill the process, but the process could be immediately restarted by the SMF. The `svcadm` command should be used to disable any SMF service that should not be running.
- Many of the scripts in `/etc/init.d` and `/etc/rc*.d` have been removed, as well as entries in the `/etc/inittab` file so that the services can be administered using the SMF. You'll find a few RC scripts that still remain in the `/etc/init.d` directory, such as `sendmail`, `nfs.server`, and `dhcp`, but most of these legacy RC scripts simply execute the `svcadm` command to start the services through the SMF. Scripts and `inittab` entries that may still exist from legacy applications, or that are locally developed, continue to run. The legacy services are started after the SMF services so that service dependencies do not become a problem.

The `svc.startd` daemon obtains information about services from the *service configuration repository*. This daemon also can delegate responsibility for services to other delegated restarter daemons such as the `inetd` daemon. The `svc.startd` daemon uses information in the repository to start services for a given milestone by processing the manifests located in the `/var/svc/manifest` directory.

The *service instance* is the fundamental unit of administration in the SMF framework, and each SMF service has the potential to have multiple versions of it configured. A service instance is either enabled or disabled with the `svcadm` command described later in this chapter. An instance is a specific configuration of a service, and multiple instances of the same service can run in the same Solaris instance. For example, a web server is a service. A specific web server daemon that is configured to listen on port 80 is an instance. Another instance of the web server service could have different configuration requirements listening on port 8080. The service has system-wide configuration requirements, but each instance can override specific requirements as needed.

Services are represented in the SMF framework as *service instance objects*, which are children of service objects. These instance objects can inherit or override the configuration settings of the parent service object. Multiple instances of a single service are managed as child objects of the service object.

Services are not just the representation for standard long-running system services such as `httpd` or `nfsd`. Services also represent varied system entities that include third-party applications, such as Oracle software. In addition, a service can include less traditional entities such as the following:

- A physical network device
- A configured IP address
- Kernel configuration information

The services started by `svc.startd` are referred to as *milestones*. The milestone concept is much like the traditional run levels that were used in previous versions of Solaris. Milestones do not replace run levels. A milestone is a special type of service that represents a specific state of system readiness. A milestone is made up of several SMF services. For example, the services that constituted run levels S, 2, and 3 in the previous version of Solaris are also represented by the following milestone services:

`milestone/single-user` (equivalent to run level S)

`milestone/multi-user` (equivalent to run level 2)

`milestone/multi-user-server` (equivalent to run level 3)

Other milestones are available in the Solaris 10 OE:

`milestone/name-services`

`milestone/devices`

`milestone/network`

`milestone/sysconfig`

An SMF manifest is an XML (Extensible Markup Language) file that contains a complete set of properties that are associated with a service or a service instance. The properties are stored in files and subdirectories located in `/var/svc/manifest`. Manifests should not be edited directly to modify the properties of a service. The service configuration repository is the authoritative source of the service configuration information. It can only be manipulated or queried using SMF interfaces, which are command-line utilities described later in this section.

The repository database stores information about the state of each service instance along with information about the services and system. The repository is stored on disk in a database named `/etc/svc/repository.db`. It is managed by the `svc.configd` daemon. This daemon backs up the repository before any changes are applied from the SMF commands and utilities. You'll find copies of the database in the `/etc/svc` directory:

```
ls /etc/svc <cr>
```

The system displays the following:

```
repository-boot
repository-boot-20080313_103024
repository-boot-20080313_103702
repository-boot-20080314_124545
repository-boot-20080318_160859
repository-manifest_import
repository-manifest_import-20080212_173830
repository.db
repository.db_old_20080225_200233
volatile
```

The backup databases are named based on their type and the time they were taken. Those that contain the word `boot` are made before the first change after a system boot. Those that contain the phrase `manifest_import` are made after `svc:/system/manifest-import:default` finishes its processing.

A corrupt repository database keeps the system from booting. You can repair the corrupt database by booting the system to the single-user milestone and running the `/lib/svc/bin/restore_repository` command.

Each service instance is named with a Fault Management Resource Identifier or FMRI. The FMRI includes the service name and the instance name. For example, the FMRI for the ftp service is `svc:/network/ftp:default`, where the `svc` prefix indicates that the service is managed by the SMF. The category of the service is `network`. `ftp` identifies the service name, and `default` identifies the service instance.

You may see various forms of the FMRI that all refer to the same service instance:

```
svc://localhost/network/inetd:default
svc:/network/inetd:default
network/inetd:default
```

An FMRI for a legacy service has the following format:

```
lrc:/etc/rc3_d/S90samba
```

where the `lrc` (legacy run control) prefix indicates that the service is not managed by the SMF. The pathname `/etc/rc3_d` refers to the directory where the legacy script is located, and `S90samba` is the name of the run control script. See the section "Using the Run Control Scripts to Stop or Start Services" later in this chapter for information on run control scripts.

The service names include a general functional category that includes the following:

- Application
- Device
- Legacy
- Milestone
- Network
- Platform
- Site
- System

Service Dependencies

In earlier versions of Solaris, processes were started at bootup by their respective shell scripts, which ran in a predetermined sequence. Sometimes, one of these shell scripts failed for various reasons. Perhaps it was an error in the script, or one of the daemons did not start for various reasons. When a script failed, the other scripts were started regardless, and sometimes these scripts failed because a previous process failed to start. Tracking down the problem was difficult for the system administrator.

To remedy the problem with sequencing scripts, Sun uses the SMF to manage the starting and stopping of services. The SMF understands the dependencies that some services have on other services. If an SMF managed service fails or is terminated, all dependent processes are taken offline until the required process is restarted. The interdependency is started by means of a service contract. This contract is maintained by the kernel and describes the process interdependency, restarter process, and startup methods.

Most service instances have dependencies on other services or files. Those dependencies control when the service is started and automatically stopped. When the dependencies of an enabled service are not satisfied, the service is kept in the offline state. When the service instance dependencies are satisfied, the service is started or restarted by the `svc.startd` daemon. If the start is successful, the service is transitioned to the online state. There are four types of service instance dependencies:

- `require_all`: The dependency is satisfied when all cited services are running (online or degraded), or when all indicated files are present.
- `require_any`: The dependency is satisfied when one of the cited services is running (online or degraded), or when at least one of the indicated files is present.
- `optional_all`: The dependency is satisfied when all the cited services are running (online or degraded), disabled, in the maintenance state, or when cited services are not present. For files, this type is the same as `require_all`.
- `exclude_all`: The dependency is satisfied when all the cited services are disabled, in the maintenance state, or when cited services or files are not present.

Each service or service instance must define a set of methods that start, stop, and optionally refresh the service. These methods can be listed and modified for each service using the `svccfg` command described later in this chapter.

A service instance is satisfied and started when its criteria, for the type of dependency, are met. Dependencies are satisfied when cited services move to the online state. After it is running (online or degraded), if a service instance with a `require_all`, `require_any`, or `optional_all` dependency is stopped or refreshed, the SMF considers why the service was stopped and uses the `restart_on` attribute of the dependency to decide whether to stop the service. Table 3.22 defines the `restart_on` attributes.

Table 3.22 `restart_on` **Values**

Event	None	Error	Restart	Refresh
stop due to error	no	yes	yes	yes
non-error stop	no	no	yes	yes
refresh	no	no	no	yes

A service is considered to have stopped due to an error if the service has encountered a hardware error or a software error such as a core dump. For `exclude_all` dependencies, the service is stopped if the cited service is started and the `restart_on` attribute is not `none`.

You can use the `svcs` command, described later in this chapter, to view service instance dependencies and to troubleshoot failures. You'll also see how to use the `svccfg` command to modify service dependencies.

SMF Command-Line Administration Utilities

The SMF provides a set of command-line utilities used to administer and configure the SMF. Table 3.23 describes these utilities.

Table 3.23 SMF Command-Line Utilities

Command	Description
inetadm	Used to configure and view services controlled by the inetd daemon.
svcadm	Used to perform common service management tasks such as enabling, disabling, or restarting service instances.
svccfg	Used to display and manipulate the contents of the service configuration repository.
svcprop	Used to retrieve property values from the service configuration repository with output that is appropriate for use in shell scripts.
svcs	Used to obtain a detailed view of the service state of all service instances in the configuration repository.

Displaying Information About Services

Use the svcs command to display information about service instances. Some of the more common options to the svcs command are as follows:

- **-a**: Shows all services, even the disabled ones. Services are sorted by state and time.
- **-d**: Shows dependencies. Lists the services or service instances upon which the given service instances depend.
- **-D**: Shows dependents. Lists the service instances that depend on the given services or service instances.
- **-l**: Displays all available information.
- **-p**: Lists processes associated with a service.
- **-v**: Displays verbose output. When used with the -x option, this displays extra information for each explanation.
- **-x**: Describes service states.

To report the status of all enabled service instances and get a list of the various services that are running, use the svcs command with no options:

```
# svcs ¦ more <cr>
```

The svcs command obtains information about all service instances from the service configuration repository and displays the state, start time, and FMRI of each service instance:

```
STATE       STIME   FMRI
legacy_run    14:10:49 lrc:/etc/rc2_d/S10lu
legacy_run    14:10:49 lrc:/etc/rc2_d/S20sysetup
legacy_run    14:10:50 lrc:/etc/rc2_d/S40llc2
legacy_run    14:10:50 lrc:/etc/rc2_d/S42ncakmod
legacy_run    14:10:50 lrc:/etc/rc2_d/S47pppd
```

```
legacy_run   14:10:50 lrc:/etc/rc2_d/S70uucp
Output has been truncated . . . .

online       14:09:37 svc:/system/svc/restarter:default
online       14:09:48 svc:/network/pfil:default
online       14:09:48 svc:/network/loopback:default
online       14:09:48 svc:/milestone/name-services:default
online       14:09:50 svc:/system/filesystem/root:default
online       14:09:54 svc:/system/filesystem/usr:default
online       14:09:56 svc:/system/device/local:default
online       14:09:57 svc:/milestone/devices:default
online       14:09:57 svc:/network/physical:default
online       14:09:58 svc:/milestone/network:default
```

NOTE

Listing legacy services You'll notice that the list includes legacy scripts that were used to start up processes. Legacy services can be viewed, but they cannot be administered with the SMF.

The state of each service is one of the following:

- **degraded**: The service instance is enabled but is running at a limited capacity.
- **disabled**: The service instance is not enabled and is not running.
- **legacy_run**: The legacy service is not managed by the SMF, but the service can be observed. This state is only used by legacy services that are started with RC scripts.
- **maintenance**: The service instance has encountered an error that must be resolved by the administrator.
- **offline**: The service instance is enabled, but the service is not yet running or available to run.
- **online**: The service instance is enabled and has successfully started.
- **uninitialized**: This state is the initial state for all services before their configuration has been read.

Running the svcs command without options displays the status of all enabled services. Use the -a option to list all services, including disabled services:

```
# svcs -a <cr>
```

The result is a listing of all services:

```
. .. . <output has been truncated>
disabled     15:48:41 svc:/network/shell:kshell
disabled     15:48:41 svc:/network/talk:default
```

```
disabled     15:48:42 svc:/network/rpc/ocfserv:default
disabled     15:48:42 svc:/network/uucp:default
disabled     15:48:42 svc:/network/security/krb5_prop:default
disabled     15:48:42 svc:/network/apocd/udp:default
online      15:47:44 svc:/system/svc/restarter:default
online      15:47:47 svc:/network/pfil:default
online      15:47:48 svc:/network/loopback:default
online      15:47:50 svc:/system/filesystem/root:default
. .. . <output has been truncated>
```

To display information on selected services, you can supply the FMRI as an argument to the `svcs` command:

```
# svcs -l network <cr>
```

With the `-l` option, the system displays detailed information about the network service instance. The `network` FMRI specified in the previous example is a general functional category and is also called the network milestone. The information displayed by the previous command is as follows:

```
fmri       svc:/milestone/network:default
name       Network milestone
enabled     true
state      online
next_state  none
state_time  Wed Jul 27 14:09:58 2005
alt_logfile /etc/svc/volatile/milestone-network:default.log
restarter   svc:/system/svc/restarter:default
dependency  require_all/none svc:/network/loopback (online)
dependency  require_all/none svc:/network/physical (online)
```

Use the `-d` option to view which services are started at the `network:default` milestone:

```
# svcs -d milestone/network:default <cr>
```

The system displays the following:

```
STATE       STIME  FMRI
online       Jul_27  svc:/network/loopback:default
online       Jul_27  svc:/network/physical:default
```

Another milestone is the `multi-user` milestone, which is displayed as follows:

```
# svcs -d milestone/multi-user <cr>
```

The system displays all the services started at the `multi-user` milestone:

```
STATE       STIME  FMRI
online       Jul_27  svc:/milestone/name-services:default
online       Jul_27  svc:/milestone/single-user:default
```

```
online      Jul_27  svc:/system/filesystem/local:default
online      Jul_27  svc:/network/rpc/bind:default
online      Jul_27  svc:/milestone/sysconfig:default
online      Jul_27  svc:/network/inetd:default
online      Jul_27  svc:/system/utmp:default
online      Jul_27  svc:/network/nfs/client:default
online      Jul_27  svc:/system/system-log:default
online      Jul_27  svc:/network/smtp:sendmail
```

Many of these services have their own dependencies, services that must be started before they get started. We refer to these as subdependencies. For example, one of the services listed is the `svc:/network/inetd:default` service. You can see a listing of the subdependencies for this service by typing

```
# svcs -d network/inetd <cr>
```

The system displays the following dependencies:

```
STATE       STIME   FMRI
disabled     15:47:57 svc:/network/inetd-upgrade:default
online      15:47:48 svc:/network/loopback:default
online      15:48:01 svc:/milestone/network:default
online      15:48:30 svc:/milestone/name-services:default
online      15:48:33 svc:/system/filesystem/local:default
online      15:48:34 svc:/network/rpc/bind:default
online      15:48:36 svc:/milestone/sysconfig:default
```

The `-d` option, in the previous example, lists the services or service instances upon which the `multi-user` service instance depends. These are the services that must be running before the `multi-user` milestone is reached. The `-D` option shows which other services depend on the `milestone/multi-user` service:

```
# svcs -D milestone/multi-user <cr>
```

The system displays the following output, indicating that the `dhcp-server` and `multi-user-server` services are dependent on the `multi-user` service:

```
STATE       STIME   FMRI
online      Jul_27  svc:/network/dhcp-server:default
online      Jul_27  svc:/milestone/multi-user-server:default
```

To view processes associated with a service instance, use the `-p` option as follows:

```
# svcs -p svc:/network/inetd:default <cr>
```

The system displays processes associated with the `svc:/network/inetd:default` service. In this case, information about the `inetd` process is shown:

```
STATE       STIME   FMRI
online      Jul_27  svc:/network/inetd:default
        Jul_27     231 inetd
```

Viewing processes using `svcs -p` instead of the traditional `ps` command makes it easier to track all the processes associated with a particular service.

If a service fails for some reason and cannot be restarted, you can list the service using the `-x` option:

```
# svcs -x <cr>
```

The system displays the following:

```
svc:/application/print/server:default (LP print server)
 State: disabled since Thu Sep 22 18:55:14 2005
Reason: Disabled by an administrator.
   See: http://sun.com/msg/SMF-8000-05
   See: lpsched(1M)
Impact: 2 dependent services are not running. (Use -v for list.)
```

The example shows that the LP print service has not started and explains that the service has not been enabled.

Modifying the Service Configuration Repository

Use the `svccfg` command to manipulate data in the service configuration repository. The `svccfg` command interacts with the `svc.configd` daemon, which is started at system startup by the `svc.startd` daemon and is the repository daemon for the SMF. The repository can be manipulated from the command line or in interactive mode using the `svccfg` command. For example, to view and manipulate the properties for the `network/ftp` service, you could use the `svccfg` command in interactive mode, as shown in Step by Step 3.3.

> **CAUTION**
>
> **Using the `svccfg` command** Sun-delivered manifests should not be modified by customers. Customizations should occur in the repository using the `svccfg` command, as described in this Step by Step.

STEP BY STEP

3.3 Manipulating the Service Configuration Repository

In this Step by Step, I'll use the `svccfg` command to enable ftp logging by modifying the start property for the ftp service.

1. From the command line, type the following command to enter interactive mode:

   ```
   # svccfg <cr>
   ```

   The system displays the following prompt:

   ```
   svc:>
   ```

2. Type the `list` command to view all services:

   ```
   svc:> list <cr>
   ```

   The system displays all the services:

   ```
   system/boot-archive
   system/device/local
   milestone/devices
   Output has been truncated
   ```

3. Select the ftp service by typing the following:

   ```
   svc:> select network/ftp <cr>
   ```

   The prompt changes as follows:

   ```
   svc:/network/ftp>
   ```

4. Type the `listprop` command to list all the properties associated with the ftp service:

   ```
   svc:/network/ftp> listprop <cr>
   ```

   The following is displayed:

   ```
   general                         framework
   general/entity_stability        astring  Unstable
   general/restarter               fmri     svc:/network/inetd:default
   inetd                           framework
   inetd/endpoint_type             astring  stream
   inetd/isrpc                     boolean  false
   inetd/name                      astring  ftp
   inetd/proto                     astring  tcp6
   inetd/stability                 astring  Evolving
   inetd/wait                      boolean  false
   inetd_start                     method
   inetd_start/exec                astring  "/usr/sbin/in.ftpd -a"
   Output has been truncated -
   ```

   The output shows that the start method (the startup script) for the `ftp` service is `"/usr/sbin/in.ftpd -a"`.

5. I will add the -d option to the `in.ftpd` command to enable logging. I will modify the start method for the ftp service so that it starts up with the -a and -d options. Set the start method using the `setprop` command:

   ```
   svc:/network/ftp> setprop inetd_start/exec=astring: "/usr/sbin/in.ftpd -a -d" <cr>
   ```

6. Exit the session by typing end:

   ```
   svc:/network/ftp> end <cr>
   ```

An alternative is to change the start property for the ftp service using the default editor. Issue the following command at the shell prompt:

```
# svccfg -s ftp editprop <cr>
```

After setting the property, use the svcprop command to verify the change:

```
# svcprop -p inetd_start ftp <cr>
```

The system displays the following:

```
inetd_start/group astring root
inetd_start/limit_privileges astring :default
inetd_start/privileges astring :default
inetd_start/project astring :default
inetd_start/resource_pool astring :default
inetd_start/supp_groups astring :default
inetd_start/timeout_seconds count 0
inetd_start/type astring method
inetd_start/use_profile boolean false
inetd_start/user astring root
inetd_start/working_directory astring :default
inetd_start/exec astring /usr/sbin/in.ftpd\ -a\ -d
```

Now, the manifest needs to be reloaded as follows:

```
# svcadm refresh ftp <cr>
```

Starting and Stopping Services Using the SMF

To disable services in previous versions of Solaris, the system administrator had to search out and rename the relevant RC script(s) or comment out statements in a configuration file, such as modifying the inetd.conf file when disabling ftp.

The SMF makes it much easier to locate services and their dependencies. To start a particular service using the SMF, the service instance must be enabled using the svcadm enable command. By enabling a service, the status change is recorded in the service configuration repository. The enabled state persists across reboots as long as the service dependencies are met. The following example demonstrates how to use the svcadm command to enable the ftp server:

```
# svcadm enable network/ftp:default <cr>
```

To disable the ftp service, use the disable option as follows:

```
# svcadm disable network/ftp:default<cr>
```

To verify the status of the service, type

```
# svcs network/ftp <cr>
```

The system displays the following:

```
STATE       STIME    FMRI
disabled      16:07:08 svc:/network/ftp:default
```

The `svcadm` command allows the following subcommands:

- **`enable`**: Enables the service instances.
- **`disable`**: Disables the service instances.
- **`restart`**: Requests that the service instances be restarted.
- **`refresh`**: For each service instance specified, `refresh` requests that the assigned restarter update the service's running configuration snapshot with the values from the current configuration. Some of these values take effect immediately (for example, dependency changes). Other values do not take effect until the next service restart.
- **`clear`**: For each service instance specified, if the instance is in the maintenance state, signal to the assigned restarter that the service has been repaired. If the instance is in the degraded state, request that the assigned restarter take the service to the online state.

The `svcadm` command can also be used to change milestones. In Step by Step 3.4, I'll use the `svcadm` command to determine my current system state (milestone) and then change the system default milestone to single-user.

STEP BY STEP

3.4 Changing Milestones

1. I check to see at which milestone the system is currently running:

   ```
   # svcs | grep milestone <cr>
   ```

   The system responds with

   ```
   disabled     16:16:36 svc:/milestone/multi-user-server:default
   online      16:16:36 svc:/milestone/name-services:default
   online      16:16:43 svc:/milestone/devices:default
   online      16:16:45 svc:/milestone/network:default
   online      16:16:57 svc:/milestone/single-user:default
   online      16:17:03 svc:/milestone/sysconfig:default
   online      16:17:16 svc:/milestone/multi-user:default
   ```

   From the output, I see that `multi-user-server` is not running, but `multi-user` is running.

2. To start the transition to the single-user milestone, type

   ```
   # svcadm milestone single-user <cr>
   ```

The system responds with the following, prompting for the root password and finally entering single-user mode:

```
Root password for system maintenance (control-d to bypass): <enter root password>
single-user privilege assigned to /dev/console.
Entering System Maintenance Mode

Sep 22 17:22:09 su: 'su root' succeeded for root on /dev/console
Sun Microsystems Inc.  SunOS 5.10   Generic January 2005
#
```

3. Verify the current milestone with the following command:

```
# svcs -a ¦ grep milestone <cr>
```

The system responds with the following:

```
disabled     16:16:36 svc:/milestone/multi-user-server:default
disabled     17:21:37 svc:/milestone/multi-user:default
disabled     17:21:37 svc:/milestone/sysconfig:default
disabled     17:21:39 svc:/milestone/name-services:default
online      16:16:43 svc:/milestone/devices:default
online      16:16:45 svc:/milestone/network:default
online      16:16:57 svc:/milestone/single-user:default
```

The output indicates that the multi-user and multi-user-server milestones are disabled, and the single-user milestone is currently online.

Notice that when I check the run level:

```
# who -r <cr>
```

the system responds with the following:

```
   .        run-level 3  Mar 18 16:09     3      0  S
```

That's because, although changing milestones may disable or enable selected services, changing a milestone does not change the run level reported by the `who -r` command. Only the `init` process changes the current run level. The `svcadm milestone` command does not communicate directly with the init process.

4. Finally, I bring the system back up to the multi-user-server milestone:

```
# svcadm milestone milestone/multi-user-server:default <cr>
```

Issuing the `svcs` command again shows that the multi-user-server milestone is back online:

```
# svcs -a ¦grep milestone <cr>
online      16:16:43 svc:/milestone/devices:default
online      16:16:45 svc:/milestone/network:default
online      16:16:57 svc:/milestone/single-user:default
online      17:37:06 svc:/milestone/name-services:default
```

```
online      17:37:12 svc:/milestone/sysconfig:default
online      17:37:23 svc:/milestone/multi-user:default
online      17:37:31 svc:/milestone/multi-user-server:default
```

At bootup, `svc.startd` retrieves the information in the service configuration repository and starts services when their dependencies are met. The daemon is also responsible for restarting services that have failed and for shutting down services whose dependencies are no longer satisfied.

In the following example, users cannot telnet into the server, so I check on the telnet service using the `svcs -x` command:

```
# svcs -x telnet <cr>
```

The results show that the service is not running:

```
svc:/network/telnet:default (Telnet server)
 State: disabled since Wed Jun 04 12:09:01 2008
Reason: Temporarily disabled by an administrator.
   See: http://sun.com/msg/SMF-8000-1S
   See: in.telnetd(1M)
   See: telnetd(1M)
Impact: This service is not running.
```

I enable the service using the `svcadm` command:

```
# svcadm enable svc:/network/telnet:default <cr>
```

After enabling the service, check the status using the `svcs` command:

```
# svcs -x telnet <cr>
```

The system responds with the following:

```
svc:/network/telnet:default (Telnet server)
 State: online since Wed Jun 04 12:09:01 2008
   See: in.telnetd(1M)
   See: telnetd(1M)
Impact: None.
```

Also, if a service that has been running stops, try restarting the service using the `svcadm restart` command as follows:

```
# svcadm restart svc:/network/telnet:default <cr>
```

Starting Services During Boot

Under the SMF, the boot process is much quieter than previous versions of Solaris. This was done to reduce the amount of uninformative "chatter" that might obscure any real problems that might occur during boot.

Some new boot options have been added to control the verbosity of boot. One that you may find particularly useful is `-m verbose`, which prints a line of information when each service attempts to start up. This is similar to previous versions of Solaris where the boot messages were more verbose.

You can also boot the system using one of the milestones:

```
ok boot -m milestone=single-user <cr>
```

The system boots into single-user mode, where only the basic services are started, as shown when the `svcs` command is used to display services:

```
# svcs <cr>

STATE      STIME   FMRI
disabled    17:10:27 svc:/system/filesystem/local:default
disabled    17:10:27 svc:/system/identity:domain
disabled    17:10:27 svc:/system/sysidtool:net
disabled    17:10:28 svc:/system/cryptosvc:default
disabled    17:10:28 svc:/network/initial:default
disabled    17:10:28 svc:/network/rpc/bind:default
disabled    17:10:28 svc:/system/sysidtool:system
disabled    17:10:28 svc:/milestone/sysconfig:default
Output has been truncated . . . . .
```

This method of booting is slightly different than using the `boot -s` command. When the system is explicitly booted to a milestone, exiting the console administrative shell does not transition the system to multi-user mode, as `boot -s` does. To move to multi-user mode after `boot -m milestone=single-user`, use the following command:

```
# svcadm milestone milestone/multi-user-server:default <cr>
```

The milestones that can be specified at boot time are

- `none`
- `single-user`
- `multi-user`
- `multi-user-server`
- `all`

If you boot a system using one of the milestones and you do not include the -s option, the system stays in the milestone state that you booted it in. The system does not go into multi-user state automatically when you press Ctrl+D. You can, however, get into the multi-user state by using the following command, and all services will be restored:

```
# svcadm milestone all <cr>
```

To boot the system without any milestones, type

```
ok boot -m milestone=none <cr>
```

The `boot` command instructs the `svc.startd` daemon to temporarily disable all services except for the master restarter named `svc:/system/svc/restarter:default` and start `sulogin` on the console. The "none" milestone can be very useful in troubleshooting systems that have failures early in the boot process.

To bring the system back down to single-user mode from multi-user mode, type

```
# svcadm milestone milestone/single-user <cr>
```

The `-d` option can be used with the previous example to cause `svcadm` to make the given milestone the default boot milestone, which persists across reboots. This would be the equivalent of setting the default run level in the `/etc/inittab` file on previous versions of Solaris.

Other options that can be used with `svcadm` include

- **-r**: Enables each service instance and recursively enables its dependencies.
- **-s**: Enables each service instance and then waits for each service instance to enter the `online` or `degraded` state. `svcadm` returns early if it determines that the service cannot reach these states without administrator intervention.
- **-t**: Temporarily enables or disables each service instance. Temporary `enable` or `disable` only lasts until reboot.

NOTE

Changing run levels Run levels have not disappeared. You can still use the `init` command to change run levels. In fact, `init` is still the best command for changing the system state. `init` informs `svc.startd` that the run level is changing, and `svc.startd` restricts the system to the set of services for that corresponding milestone. The `svcadm` command does not change run levels, although it does change the set of services that are running. Using milestones to change the system state can be confusing and can lead to unexpected behavior. For example, running `svcadm milestone svc:/milestone/single-user:default` won't change the system's run level (as described by `who -r`). Running `init s` will. Also, continue to use `boot -s` if you want to; it works just fine.

So, if you're still confused about when to use milestones (`svcadm milestone`) and when to use run levels (the `init` command), most people still use run levels to transition between system states. In fact, Sun Microsystems recommends this method. Sun states that "using milestones to change the system state can be confusing and can lead to unexpected behavior." (Quote taken from Sun's System Administration Guide: Basic Administration)

A milestone is nothing more than a service that aggregates several other services and dependencies. It declares a specific state of readiness that other services can depend on. Other than occasionally using the `boot -m milestone=none` command to boot a system for recovery or troubleshooting purposes, most people typically use the `boot -s` command to bring the system into single-user mode and the `init` command to transition to the *desired* run level.

STEP BY STEP

3.5 Troubleshooting SMF Boot Problems

1. Boot the system as follows:

```
ok boot -m milestone=none <cr>
```

none starts the system with all services disabled, except the master restarter (`svc:/system/svc/restarter:default`). The system boots and asks you to enter the root password to enter system maintenance :

```
Root password for system maintenance (control-d to bypass):
```

2. After you log in, run `svcs`. You'll notice that all services are `disabled` or `uninitialized`. Next, step through the milestones as follows:

```
# svcadm milestone svc:/milestone/single-user:default <cr>
# svcadm milestone svc:/milestone/multi-user:default <cr>
# svcadm milestone svc:/milestone/multi-user-server:default <cr>
```

3. As you troubleshoot your system, follow these steps if a service fails to start:

a. Is the service in maintenance mode? Issue the following command to check the state:

```
# svcs -l <FMRI> <cr>
```

b. Check the log file. This file is specified in output from the `svcs -l` command as follows:

```
# svcs -l svc:/network/inetd:default <cr>
```

The system responds with the following:

```
fmri         svc:/network/inetd:default
name         inetd
enabled      true
state        online
next_state   none
```

```
state_time    Tue Mar 18 16:09:21 2008
logfile       /var/svc/log/network-inetd:default.log
restarter     svc:/system/svc/restarter:default
contract_id   46
dependency    require_any/error svc:/network/loopback (online)
dependency    require_all/error svc:/system/filesystem/local (online)
dependency    optional_all/error svc:/milestone/network (online)
dependency    optional_all/error svc:/network/rpc/bind (online)
dependency    optional_all/none svc:/network/inetd-upgrade (disabled)
dependency    require_all/none svc:/milestone/sysconfig (online)
  svc:/milestone/name-services (online)
```

c. Check the service dependencies with `svcs -d` *<FMRI>*. The output from `svcs -l` distinguishes between optional and mandatory dependencies.

d. Check the startup properties with `svcprop -p start` *<FMRI>*.

Secure By Default

New in Solaris 10 11/06 is the Secure By Default Network Profile, which allows the system administrator to restrict network services during the software installation process. Restricting network services during the installation process ensures that the system is secure before the system boots for the first time. Secure By Default helps the system administrator reduce the risk of exposure on the Internet or LAN. Secure By Default was covered in Chapter 2, "Installing the Solaris 10 Operating Environment."

When selecting this option during the installation process, I described how several network services are disabled, with the exception of `ssh`. With Secure By Default, Sun added the `netservices` command and two options: `open` and `limited`.

The `netservices open` command allows the system administrator to enable all the services that were disabled when the Secure By Default option was enabled during the installation process. In addition, if you did not select the Secure By Default option when installing the OS, or you simply want to make your system more secure, you can issue the `netservices limited` command at any time. It restricts the same network services that would have been restricted had the Secure By Default option been selected during the installation. Issue the following command from the shell prompt to enable Secure By Default:

```
# netservices limited <cr>
```

SMF Message Logging

In addition to the system logging methods described earlier in this chapter, each service has a log file in the `/var/svc/log` directory (or the `/etc/svc/volatile` directory, for services started before the single-user milestone) indicating when and how the system was started, whether it started successfully, and any messages it may have printed during its initialization. If a severe problem occurs during boot, you can log in on the console in maintenance mode, and you can use the `svcs` command to help diagnose the problem, even on problems that would have caused boot to hang. Finally, the new `boot -m` boot option allows the system administrator to configure the boot process to be more verbose, printing a simple message when each service starts.

Creating New Service Scripts

Objective:
Use Service Management Facility or legacy commands and scripts to control both the boot and shutdown procedures.

As you customize your system, you'll create custom scripts to start and stop processes or services on your system. The correct procedure for incorporating these scripts into the SMF is as follows:

- Determine the process for starting and stopping your service.
- Establish a name for the service and the category this service falls into.
- Determine whether your service runs multiple instances.
- Identify any dependency relationships between this service and any other services. Practically every service has a dependency so that the service does not startup too soon in the boot process.
- If a script is required to start and stop the process, create the script and place it in a local directory such as `/lib/svc/method`.
- Create a service manifest file for your service in the `/var/svc/manifest/site` directory. This XML file describes the service and any dependency relationships. Service manifests are incorporated into the repository either by using the `svccfg` command or at boot time. See the `service_bundle(4)` manual page for a description of the contents of the SMF manifests.
- Incorporate the script into the SMF using the `svccfg` utility.

Step by Step 3.6 describes the process of setting up and enabling an existing service instance.

STEP BY STEP

3.6 Enable the NFS Server Service

In the following example, I'll configure the SMF to share the NFS resources on an NFS server.

1. Log in as root or use a role that includes the Service Management rights profile.
2. The NFS server services are not running as displayed by the following `svcs` command:

   ```
   # svcs -a¦ grep -i nfs <cr>
   ```

   The system displays the following information about the NFS services:

   ```
   disabled     15:47:56 svc:/network/nfs/cbd:default
   disabled     15:47:59 svc:/network/nfs/server:default
   online       15:48:36 svc:/network/nfs/mapid:default
   online       15:48:36 svc:/network/nfs/status:default
   online       15:48:37 svc:/network/nfs/nlockmgr:default
   online       15:48:44 svc:/network/nfs/client:default
   online       15:54:26 svc:/network/nfs/rquota:default
   ```

   Notice that svc:/network/nfs/server:default is disabled.
3. Set up the required NFS configuration file on the server. To share a file system named `/data`, I need to configure the `/etc/dfs/dfstab` file as described in the *Solaris 10 System Administration Exam Prep: Exam CX-310-202* book. I add the following line to the NFS server configuration file:

   ```
   # share -F nfs -o rw /data <cr>
   ```

4. Enable the NFS service as follows:

   ```
   # svcadm enable svc:/network/nfs/server <cr>
   ```

5. Verify that the NFS server service is running by typing

   ```
   # svcs -a ¦ grep -i nfs <cr>
   ```

   The system displays the following information:

   ```
   disabled     15:47:56 svc:/network/nfs/cbd:default
   online       15:48:44 svc:/network/nfs/client:default
   online       11:22:26 svc:/network/nfs/status:default
   online       11:22:26 svc:/network/nfs/nlockmgr:default
   online       11:22:27 svc:/network/nfs/mapid:default
   online       11:22:28 svc:/network/nfs/server:default
   online       11:22:28 svc:/network/nfs/rquota:default
   ```

Step by Step 3.7 describes how to create a new service and incorporate it into the SMF. Taking the time to convert your existing RC scripts to the SMF allows them to take advantage of automated restart capabilities that could be caused by hardware failure, unexpected service failure, or administrative error. Participation in the service management facility also brings enhanced visibility with `svcs` (as well as future-planned GUI tools) and ease of management with `svcadm` and other Solaris management tools. The task requires the creation of a short XML file and making a few simple modifications to the service RC script.

STEP BY STEP

3.7 Converting an RC Script to the SMF

Before I start, I'll take an existing legacy RC script and place it under SMF control as a service. This script is named `/etc/init.d/legacy` and has the following entries:

```
#!/sbin/sh
case "$1" in
'start')
    /usr/local/legacyprog
    ;;

'stop')
    /usr/bin/pkill -x -u 0 legacyprog
    ;;

*)
    echo "Usage: $0 { start ¦ stop }"
    exit 1
    ;;

esac
exit 0
```

I'll move this script to /lib/svc/method/legacyservice.

The most complex part of this procedure is writing the SMF manifest in XML. Currently, these manifests need to be created with an editor, but in the future, expect a GUI-based tool to aid in the creation of the manifest file. The `service_bundle(4)` man page describes this XML-based file, but you need to be familiar with the XML programming language, and that is beyond the scope of this book. Here's a copy of my manifest for the service we will implement; I named it `/var/svc/manifest/site/legacyservice`, and I'll describe the contents of the file in this section:

```
<?xml version="1.0"?>
<!DOCTYPE service_bundle SYSTEM
"/usr/share/lib/xml/dtd/service_bundle.dtd.1">
<!—
ident "@(#)newservice.xml 1.2 04/09/13 SMI"
—>
<service_bundle type='manifest' name='OPTnew:legacyservice'>
```

```
<service
    name='site/legacyservice'
    type='service'
    version='1'>

<single_instance/>

<dependency
    name='usr'
    type='service'
    grouping='require_all'
    restart_on='none'>
    <service_fmri value='svc:/system/filesystem/local' />
</dependency>

<dependent
    name='newservice'
    grouping='require_all'
    restart_on='none'>
    <service_fmri value='svc:/milestone/multi-user' />
</dependent>

<exec_method
    type='method'
    name='start'
    exec='/lib/svc/method/legacyservice start'
    timeout_seconds='30' />

<exec_method
    type='method'
    name='stop'
    exec='/lib/svc/method/legacyservice stop'
    timeout_seconds='30' />

<property_group name='startd' type='framework'>
<propval name='duration' type='astring' value='transient'
/>
</property_group>

<instance name='default' enabled='true' />

<stability value='Unstable' />

<template>
    <common_name>
        <loctext xml:lang='C'>
        New service
        </loctext>
```

```
    </common_name>
  </template>
  </service>
  </service_bundle>
```

Now let's take a closer look at the XML-based manifest file and the steps I took to create it.

1. My file starts out with a standard header. After the header, I specify the name of the service, the type of service, the package providing the service, and the service name:

   ```
   <?xml version="1.0"?>
   <!DOCTYPE service_bundle SYSTEM
   "/usr/share/lib/xml/dtd/service_bundle.dtd.1">
   <!—
   ident "@(#)newservice.xml 1.2 04/09/13 SMI"
   —>

   <service_bundle type='manifest' name='OPTnew:legacyservice'>
   ```

2. I specify the service category, type, name, and version. These categories aren't used by the system, but help the administrator in identifying the general use of the service. These category types are

   application: Higher level applications, such as apache

   milestone: Collections of other services, such as name-services

   platform: Platform-specific services, such as Dynamic Reconfiguration daemons

   system: Solaris system services, such as coreadm

   device: Device-specific services

   network: Network/Internet services, such as protocols

   site: Site specific descriptions

   The service name describes what is being provided. It includes both any category identifier and the actual service name, separated by /. Service names should identify the service being provided. In this example, the entry I'll make to my manifest file is as follows:

   ```
   <service <cr>
       name='site/legacyservice' <cr>
       type='service' <cr>
       version='1'> <cr>
   ```

3. Identify whether your service will have multiple instances. The instance name describes any specific features about the instance. Most services deliver a "default" instance. Some (such as Oracle) may want to create instances based on administrative configuration choices. This service will have a single instance, so I'll make the following entry in the manifest:

   ```
   <single_instance /> <cr>
   ```

4. Define any dependencies for this service. I added the following entry to the manifest:

```
<dependency <cr>
    name='usr' <cr>
    type='service' <cr>
    grouping='require_all' <cr>
    restart_on='none'> <cr>
    <service_fmri value='svc:/system/filesystem/local' /> <cr>
</dependency> <cr>
```

   The first entry states that the *legacyservice* requires the *filesystem/local* service.

5. We now need to identify dependents. If I want to make sure that my service is associated with the multi-user milestone and that the multi-user milestone requires this service, I add the following entry to the manifest:

```
<dependent <cr>
     name='testservice' <cr>
     grouping='require_all' <cr>
     restart_on='none'> <cr>
      <service_fmri value='svc:/milestone/multi-user' /> <cr>
   <dependent> <cr>
```

   Because I can identify dependents, I can deliver a service that is a dependency of another service (milestone/multi-user) that I don't deliver. I can specify this in my *legacyservice* manifest without modifying the *milestone/multi-user* manifest, which I don't own. It's an easy way to have a service run before a Solaris default service.

   If all the dependent services have not been converted to SMF, you need to convert those too, because there is no way to specify a dependent on a legacy script.

   To avoid conflicts, it is recommended that you preface the dependent name with the name of your service. For example, if you're delivering a service (`legacyservice`) that must start before `syslog`, use the following entry:

```
<dependent <cr>
  name='legacyservice_syslog' <cr>
```

6. Specify how the service will be started and stopped. SMF interacts with your service primarily by its methods. The stop and start methods must be provided for services managed by `svc.startd`. They can directly invoke either a service binary or a script to achieve this. The refresh method is optional for svc.startd managed services. I'll use the following start and stop methods:

```
<exec_method <cr>
    type='method' <cr>
    name='start' <cr>
    exec='/lib/svc/method/legacyservice start' <cr>
    timeout_seconds='30' /> <cr>

<exec_method <cr>
    type='method' <cr>
```

```
name='stop' <cr>
exec='/lib/svc/method/legacyservice stop' <cr>
timeout_seconds='30' /> <cr>
```

Timeouts must be provided for all methods. The timeout should be defined to be the maximum amount of time in seconds that your method might take to run on a slow system or under heavy load. A method that exceeds its timeout is killed. If the method could potentially take an unbounded amount of time, such as a large file system `fsck`, an infinite timeout may be specified as 0.

7. Identify the service model. Will it be started by `inetd` or `svc.startd`? My service will be started by `svc.startd`. `svc.startd` provides three models of service:

   Transient services: These are often configuration services, which require no long-running processes to provide service. Common transient services take care of boot-time cleanup or load configuration properties into the kernel. Transient services are also sometimes used to overcome difficulties in conforming to the method requirements for contract or wait services. This is not recommended and should be considered a stopgap measure.

   Wait services: These services run for the lifetime of the child process, and are restarted when that process exits.

   Contract services: These are the standard system daemons. They require processes that run forever after they are started to provide service. Death of all processes in a contract service is considered a service error, which causes the service to restart.

   The default service model is *contract*, but it may be modified. For this example, I'll start the service with `svc.startd`. As a transient service, it will be started once and not restarted by adding the following lines to the manifest:

   ```
   <property_group name='startd' type='framework'> <cr>
   <propval name='duration' type='astring' value='transient' <cr>
   /> <cr>
   </property_group> <cr>
   ```

8. The next step is to create the instance name for the service by making the following entry:

   ```
   <instance name='default' enabled='true' /> <cr>
   ```

9. Finally, create template information to describe the service providing concise detail about the service. I'll assign a common name in the C locale. The common name should

   Be short (40 characters or less).

   Avoid capital letters (aside from trademarks like Solaris).

   Avoid punctuation.

   Avoid the word service (but do distinguish between client and server).

   I make the following entry in the manifest to describe my service as "New service":

```
<template> <cr>
    <common_name> <cr>
        <loctext xml:lang='C'> <cr>
        New service <cr>
        </loctext> <cr>
    </common_name> <cr>
</template> <cr>
```

10. When the manifest is complete, it is a good idea to verify the syntax using the `xmllint` program:

    ```
    # xmllint -valid /var/svc/manifest/site/legacyservice <cr>
    ```

    The `xmllint` program parses the XML file and identifies any errors in the code before you try to import it into the SMF. The `svccfg` program also can validate your file as follows, but the output is not as verbose as with the `xmllint` command:

    ```
    # svccfg validate /var/svc/manifest/site/legacyservice <cr>
    ```

11. After you've validated the syntax of your XML file, you need to import the new service into SMF by issuing the `svccfg` command:

    ```
    # svccfg import /var/svc/manifest/site/legacyservice <cr>
    ```

12. The service should now be visible using the `svcs` command:

    ```
    # svcs legacyservice <cr>
    STATE      STIME   FMRI
    -        svc:/site/legacyservice:default
    ```

13. You can also see on which services the `legacyservice` depends by using the `svcs -d` command:

    ```
    # svcs -d legacyservice <cr>
    STATE      STIME   FMRI
    online     Sep_20  svc:/system/filesystem/local:default
    ```

14. As a final step, enable the service using the `svcadm` command:

    ```
    # svcadm -v enable legacyservice <cr>
    svc:/site/legacyservice:default enabled.
    ```

    I used the -v option in this example because I wanted to see the message that says the service was enabled. Without the -v option, the result is silent.

15. At any time, I can view the properties of a service using the `svccfg` command:

    ```
    # svccfg -v -s legacyservice <cr>
    ```

    The system responds with the following prompt:

    ```
    svc:/site/legacyservice>
    ```

Use the listprop subcommand at the svccfg prompt to list the service properties:

```
svc:/site/legacyservice> listprop <cr>
usr               dependency
usr/entities         fmri   svc:/system/filesystem/local
usr/grouping         astring require_all
usr/restart_on        astring none
usr/type           astring service
general            framework
general/entity_stability astring Unstable
general/single_instance  boolean true
dependents          framework
dependents/newservice   astring svc:/milestone/multi-user
startd            framework
startd/duration        astring transient
start             method
start/exec          astring "/lib/svc/method/legacyservice start"
start/timeout_seconds   count  30
start/type          astring method
stop              method
stop/exec           astring "/lib/svc/method/legacyservice stop"
stop/timeout_seconds   count  30
stop/type           astring method
tm_common_name        template
tm_common_name/C      ustring "New service"
svc:/site/legacyservice>
```

Legacy Services

Objective:
Use Service Management Facility or legacy commands and scripts to control both the boot and shutdown procedures.

Solaris 10 still supports legacy RC scripts referred to as legacy services, but you will notice that the /etc/inittab file used by the init daemon has been significantly reduced. In addition, RC scripts that were located in the /etc/init.d directory and linked to the /etc/rc#.d directory have also been reduced substantially. For many of the scripts that remain, simply run the svcadm command to start the appropriate service.

SMF-managed services no longer use RC scripts or /etc/inittab entries for startup and shutdown, so the scripts corresponding to those services have been removed. In future releases of Solaris, the SMF will manage more services, and these directories will become less and less populated. RC scripts and /etc/inittab entries that manage third-party-provided or locally developed services will continue to be run at boot. These services may not run at exactly the same point in boot as they had before the advent of the SMF, but they are guaranteed to not run any earlier. Any services they had implicitly depended on will still be available.

For those readers who are experienced on Solaris versions prior to Solaris 10, you are accustomed to starting and stopping services via RC scripts. For instance, to stop and start the `sshd` daemon, you would type

```
# /etc/init.d/sshd stop <cr>
# /etc/init.d/sshd start <cr>
```

In the SMF, the correct procedure to start `sshd` is to type

```
# svcadm enable -t network/ssh:default <cr>
```

To temporarily stop `sshd`, you would type

```
# svcadm disable -t network/ssh:default <cr>
```

Or simply type

```
# svcadm restart network/ssh:default <cr>
```

to stop and restart the `sshd` daemon.

Prior to Solaris 10, to send a HUP signal to the `ssh` daemon, you would have typed

```
# kill -HUP 'cat /var/run/sshd.pid' <cr>
```

In Solaris 10, the correct procedure is to type

```
svcadm refresh network/ssh:default <cr>
```

Using the Run Control Scripts to Stop or Start Services

Although it is recommended that you use the SMF to start and stop services as described in the previous section "Creating New Service Scripts," functionality still exists to allow the use of run control scripts to start and stop system services at various run levels. Run control scripts were used in previous versions of Solaris to start and stop system services before the SMF was introduced.

A run level is a system state (run state), represented by a number or letter that identifies the services and resources that are currently available to users. The `who -r` command can still be used to identify a system's run state:

```
# who -r <cr>
```

The system responds with the following indicating that `run-level 3` is the current run state:

```
.    run-level 3 Aug 4 09:38   3   1 1
```

Since the introduction of the SMF in Solaris 10, some administrators refer to run states as if they are the same as milestones; however, that's not necessarily true. Run states can be compared to milestones, but they are not the same as milestones. As I described earlier in this chapter, run levels refer to specific run states that are achieved by running the `init` command. Milestones simply describe a specific state of system readiness. Sometimes, milestones are compared to run levels based on the processes and services that are started. Table 3.24 describes how the various legacy run states coincide with the Solaris 10 milestones.

Table 3.24 System Run States

Run State (Milestone)	Description
`0`	Stops system services and daemons. Terminates all running processes. Unmounts all file systems.
S, s (`single-user`)	Single-user (system administrator) state. Only root is allowed to log in at the console, and any logged-in users are logged out when you enter this run level. Only critical file systems are mounted and accessible. All services except the most basic operating system services are shut down in an orderly manner.
1	Single-user (system administrator) state. If the system is booted into this run level, all local file systems are mounted. All services except the most basic operating system services are shut down.
2 (`multi-user`)	Normal multi-user operation, without network file systems (NFSs) shared: directories; locks interfaces and starts processes; starts the `con` daemon; cleans up the `uucp tmp` files; starts the `lp` system; and starts the `sendmail` daemon and `syslog`.
3 (`multi-user-server`)	Normal multiuse operation of a file server, with NFSs shared. Completes all the tasks in run state 2 and starts the NFS daemons.
4	Alternative multi-user state (currently not used).
5	Power-down state. Shuts down the system so that it is safe to turn off power to the system. If possible, automatically turns off system power on systems that support this feature.
6	Reboot state.

To support legacy applications that still use run control scripts, these scripts have been carried over from Solaris 9. With run control scripts, each `init` state has a corresponding series of run control scripts—which are called RC scripts and are located in the `/sbin` directory—to control each run state. These RC scripts are as follows:

- `rc0`
- `rc1`
- `rc2`

- rc3
- rc5
- rc6
- rcS

NOTE

Run control scripts Solaris startup scripts can be identified by their rc prefix or suffix, which means *run control*.

You can still use the init command to transition between the various run states. The init daemon simply passes the required run state to the svc.startd daemon for execution.

The SMF executes the /sbin/rc<*n*> scripts, which in turn execute a series of other scripts that are located in the /etc/init.d directory. For each RC script in the /sbin directory, a corresponding directory named /etc/rc<*n*>.d contains scripts to perform various actions for that run state. For example, /etc/rc3.d contains files that are used to start and stop processes for run state 3.

NOTE

Legacy scripts Legacy scripts are run last—after the Solaris infrastructure services that are managed by the SMF are started.

The /etc/rc<*n*>.d scripts are always run in ASCII sort order shown by the ls command and have names of this form:

```
[K,S][#][filename]
```

A file that begins with K is referred to as a *stop script* and is run to terminate (kill) a system process. A file that begins with S is referred to as a *start script* and is run to start a system process. Each of these start and stop scripts is called by the appropriate /sbin/rc# script. For example, the /sbin/rc0 script runs the scripts located in the /etc/rc0.d directory. The /sbin/rc# script passes the argument start or stop to each script, based on their prefix and whether the name ends in .sh. There are no arguments passed to scripts that end in .sh.

All run control scripts are also located in the /etc/init.d directory, and all scripts must be /sbin/sh scripts. These files are hard linked to corresponding run control scripts in the /etc/rc<*n*>.d directories.

These run control scripts can also be run individually to start and stop services. For example, you can turn off NFS server functionality by typing `/etc/init.d/nfs.server stop` and pressing Enter. After you have changed the system configuration, you can restart the NFS services by typing `/etc/init.d/nfs.server start` and pressing Enter. If you notice, however, many of these RC scripts simply have `svcadm` commands embedded in them to perform the task of stopping and starting the service.

In addition to the `svcs -p` command, you can still use the `pgrep` command to verify whether a service has been stopped or started:

```
# pgrep -f <service> <cr>
```

The `pgrep` utility examines the active processes on the system and reports the process IDs of the processes. See Chapter 5, "Managing System Processes," for details on this command.

Adding Scripts to the Run Control Directories

If you add a script to the run control directories, you put the script in the `/etc/init.d` directory and create a hard link to the appropriate `rc<n>.d` directory. You need to assign appropriate numbers and names to the new scripts so that they will be run in the proper ASCII sequence, as described in the previous section.

To add a new run control script to a system, follow the process in Step by Step 3.8.

STEP BY STEP

3.8 Adding a Run Control Script

1. Become the superuser.
2. Add the script to the `/etc/init.d` directory:

```
# cp <filename> /etc/init.d <cr>
# cd /etc/init.d <cr>
# chmod 744 <filename> <cr>
# chown root:sys <filename> <cr>
```

3. Create hard links to the appropriate `rc<n>.d` directory:

```
# ln <filename> /etc/rc2.d/S<nnfilename> <cr>
# ln <filename> /etc/rc<n>.d/K<nnfilename> <cr>
```

4. Use the `ls` command to verify that the script has links in the specified directories:

```
# ls -li /etc/init.d/<filename> /etc/rc?.d/[SK]*<filename> <cr>
```

The following example creates an RC script named `program` that starts up at run level `2` and stops at run level `0`. Note the use of hard links versus soft links:

```
# cp program /etc/init.d <cr>
# cd /etc/init.d <cr>
# chmod 744 program <cr>
# chown root:sys program <cr>
# ln /etc/init.d/program /etc/rc2.d/S99program <cr>
# ln /etc/init.d/program /etc/rc0.d/K01program <cr>
```

You can verify the links by typing this:

```
# ls -li /etc/init.d/program /etc/rc?.d/[SK]*program
```

The system displays the following:

```
389928 -rwxr—r—   3 root   sys      69 Oct 26 23:31 /etc/init.d/program
389928 -rwxr—r—   3 root   sys      69 Oct 26 23:31 /etc/rc0.d/K01program
389928 -rwxr—r—   3 root   sys      69 Oct 26 23:31 /etc/rc2.d/S99progra
```

NOTE

Disabling a run control script If you do not want a particular script to run when the system is entering a corresponding `init` state, you can change the uppercase prefix (`S` or `K`) to some other character; I prefer to prefix the filename with an underscore or the word no. Only files beginning with uppercase prefixes of `S` or `K` are run. For example, you could change `S99mount` to `_S99mount` to disable the script.

System Shutdown

Objective:
Perform system shutdown procedures.

Solaris has been designed to run continuously—seven days a week, 24 hours a day. Occasionally, however, you need to shut down the system to carry out administrative tasks. Very seldom, an application might cause the system to go awry, and the operating system must be stopped to kill off runaway processes and then be restarted.

You can shut down the system in a number of ways, using various UNIX commands. With Solaris, taking down the operating system in an orderly fashion is important. When the system boots, several processes are started; they must be shut down before you power off the system. In addition, information that has been cached in memory and has not yet been written to disk will be lost if it is not flushed from memory and saved to disk. The process of shutting down Solaris involves shutting down processes, flushing data from memory to the disk, and unmounting file systems.

CAUTION

Improper shutdown can corrupt data Shutting down a system improperly can result in loss of data and the risk of corrupting the file systems.

NOTE

Protecting against power loss To avoid having your system shut down improperly during a power failure, you should use an uninterruptible power supply (UPS) that can shut down the system cleanly before the power is shut off. Be sure to follow the UPS manufacturer's recommendations for maintenance to eliminate the risk of the UPS becoming the cause of an improper shutdown.

Commands to Shut Down the System

When you're preparing to shut down a system, you need to determine which of the following commands is appropriate for the system and the task at hand:

`/usr/sbin/shutdown`

`/sbin/init`

`/usr/sbin/halt`

`/usr/sbin/reboot`

`/usr/sbin/poweroff`

Stop+A or L1+A

CAUTION

Aborting the operating system Using the Stop+A key sequence (or L1+A) abruptly breaks execution of the operating system and should be used only as a last resort to restart the system.

The first three commands—`/usr/sbin/shutdown`, `/sbin/init`, and `/usr/sbin/halt`—initiate shutdown procedures, kill all running processes, write data to disk, and shut down the system software to the appropriate run level. The `/usr/sbin/reboot` command does all these tasks as well, and it then boots the system back to the default milestone. The `/usr/sbin/poweroff` command is equivalent to `init` state `5`.

The `/usr/sbin/shutdown` Command

You use the `shutdown` command to shut down a system that has multiple users. The `shutdown` command sends a warning message to all users who are logged in, waits for 60 seconds (by default), and then shuts down the system to single-user state. The command option `-g` lets you choose a different default wait time. The `-i` option lets you define the `init` state to which the system will be shut down. The default is `S`.

The `shutdown` command performs a clean system shutdown, which means that all system processes and services are terminated normally, and file systems are synchronized. You need superuser privileges to use the `shutdown` command.

When the `shutdown` command is initiated, all logged-in users and all systems mounting resources receive a warning about the impending shutdown, and then they get a final message. For this reason, the `shutdown` command is recommended over the `init` command on a server with multiple users.

NOTE

Sending a shutdown message When using either `shutdown` or `init`, you might want to give users advance notice by sending an email message about any scheduled system shutdown.

The proper sequence of shutting down the system is described in Step by Step 3.9.

STEP BY STEP

3.9 Shutting Down a System

1. As superuser, type the following to find out if users are logged in to the system:

```
# who <cr>
```

2. A list of all logged-in users is displayed. You might want to send an email message or broadcast a message to let users know that the system is being shut down.
3. Shut down the system by using the `shutdown` command:

```
# shutdown -i<init-state> -g<grace-period> -y <cr>
```

Table 3.25 describes the options available for the `shutdown` command.

Table 3.25 Options for the `shutdown` Command

Option	Description
`-i`*`<init-state>`*	Brings the system to an `init` state that is different from the default, `S`. The choices are `0`, `S`, `1`, `2`, `5`, and `6`.
`-g`*`<grace-period>`*	Indicates a time (in seconds) before the system is shut down. The default is 60 seconds.
`-y`	Continues to shut down the system without intervention; otherwise, you are prompted to continue the shutdown process after 60 seconds. If you use the `shutdown -y` command, you are not prompted to continue; otherwise, you get the message `Do you want to continue? (y or n)`.

The `/sbin/init` Command

You use the `init` command to shut down a single-user system or to change its run level. The syntax is as follows:

```
init <run-level>
```

`<run-level>` is any run level described in Table 3.23. In addition, *`<run-level>`* can be `a`, `b`, or `c`, which tells the system to process only `/etc/inittab` entries that have the `a`, `b`, or `c` run level set. These are pseudo-states, which can be defined to run certain commands but that do not cause the current run level to change. *`<run-level>`* can also be the keyword `Q` or `q`, which tells the system to reexamine the `/etc/inittab` file.

You can use `init` to place the system in power-down state (`init` state `5`) or in single-user state (`init` state `1`). For example, to bring the system down to run level `1` from the current run level, you type the following:

```
# init 1 <cr>
```

The system responds with this:

```
svc.startd: Changing to state 1.
svc.startd: Killing user processes: done.
svc.startd: The system is ready for administration.
Requesting System Maintenance Mode
(See /lib/svc/share/README for more information.)

Root password for system maintenance (control-d to bypass):<enter root password>
single-user privilege assigned to /dev/console.
Entering System Maintenance Mode

Aug 4 09:18:13 su: 'su root' succeeded for root on /dev/console
Sun Microsystems Inc.  SunOS 5.10   Generic January 2005
```

NOTE

The `telinit` command The `/etc/telinit` command is the same as the `init` command. It is simply a link to the `/usr/sbin/init` command.

The /usr/sbin/halt Command

You use the `halt` command when the system must be stopped immediately and it is acceptable not to warn current users. The `halt` command shuts down the system without delay and does not warn other users on the system of the shutdown.

The /usr/sbin/reboot Command

You use the `reboot` command to shut down a single-user system and bring it into multi-user state. `reboot` does not warn other users on the system of the shutdown.

The Solaris `reboot`, `poweroff`, and `halt` commands stop the processor and synchronize the disks, but they perform unconditional shutdown of system processes. These commands are not recommended because they do not shut down any services and unmount any remaining file systems. They will, however, attempt to kill active processes with a SIGTERM, but the services will not be shut down cleanly. Stopping the services without doing a clean shutdown should be done only in an emergency or if most of the services are already stopped.

The speed of such a reboot is useful in certain circumstances, such as when you're rebooting from the single-user run state. Also, the capability to pass arguments to OpenBoot via the `reboot` command is useful. For example, this command reboots the system into run level `s` and reconfigures the device tables:

```
# reboot -- -rs
```

NOTE

The `/etc/nologin` file When a system will be unavailable for an extended time, you can create an `/etc/nologin` file to prevent users from logging in to it. When a user logs in to a system that has an `/etc/nologin` file, the message in the `/etc/nologin` file is displayed, and the user login is terminated. Superuser logins are unaffected by the `/etc/nologin` file.

The /usr/sbin/poweroff Command

The `poweroff` command is equivalent to the `init 5` command. As with the `reboot` and `halt` commands, the `poweroff` command synchronizes the disks and immediately shuts down the system, without properly shutting down services and unmounting all file systems. Users are not notified of the shutdown. If the hardware supports it, the `poweroff` command also turns off power.

NOTE

The `init` and `shutdown` Commands Using `init` and using `shutdown` are the most reliable ways to shut down a system, because these commands shut down services in a clean, orderly fashion and shut down the system with minimal data loss. The `halt`, `poweroff`, and `reboot` commands do not shut down services properly and are not the preferred method of shutting down the system.

Stopping the System for Recovery Purposes: SPARC

Objective:
Interrupting an unresponsive SPARC system.

Occasionally, a SPARC system might not respond to the `init` commands described earlier in this chapter. A system that doesn't respond to anything, including `reboot` or `halt`, is called a "crashed" or "hung" system. If you try to use the commands discussed in the previous sections but get no response, on non-USB style keyboards, you can press Stop+A or L1+A to get back to the boot PROM. (The specific Stop key sequence depends on your keyboard type.) On terminals connected to the serial port, you can press the Break key, as described in the section "Accessing the OpenBoot Environment," earlier in this chapter.

Some OpenBoot systems provide the capability of commanding OpenBoot by means of pressing a combination of keys on the system's keyboard, referred to as a *keyboard chord* or *key combination*. Table 3.26 describes these keyboard chords. When issuing any of these commands, you press the keys immediately after turning on the power to your system, and you hold down the keys for a few seconds until the keyboard light-emitting diodes (LEDs) flash. It should be noted, however, that these keyboard chords work only on non-USB keyboards and not USB-style keyboards.

Table 3.26 Keyboard Chords

Command	Description
Stop	Bypasses the POST. This command does not depend on the security mode. (Note that some systems bypass the POST as a default; in such cases, you use Stop+D to start the POST.)
Stop+A	Interrupts any program currently running and puts the system at the OpenBoot prompt, ready to accept OpenBoot PROM commands.
Stop+D	Enters diagnostic mode (sets the `diag-switch?` variable to `true`).
Stop+F	Enters Forth on the `ttya` port instead of probing. Uses `fexit` to continue with the initialization sequence. This chord is useful if hardware is broken.
Stop+N	Resets the contents of NVRAM to the default values.

NOTE

Disabling keyboard chords The commands listed in Table 3.26 are disabled if PROM security is on. Also, if your system has full security enabled, you cannot apply any of these commands unless you have the password to get to the `ok` prompt.

To change the default abort sequence on the keyboard, you need to edit the `/etc/default/kbd` file. In that file, you can enable and disable keyboard abort sequences, and change the keyboard abort sequence. After modifying this file, you issue the `kbd -i` command to update the keyboard defaults.

The process of breaking out of a hung system is described in Step by Step 3.10.

TIP

Interrupting a hung system Step by Step 3.10 describes an objective that is sure to be on the exam. Make sure that you understand each step and the order in which the steps are executed.

STEP BY STEP

3.10 Breaking Out of a Hung System

1. Use the abort key sequence for your system (Stop+A or L1+A). On a serial console, send a break signal.

   The monitor displays the `ok` PROM prompt.

2. Type the `sync` command to manually synchronize the file systems:

   ```
   ok sync <cr>
   ```

   The `sync` procedure synchronizes the file systems and is necessary to prevent corruption. During the `sync` process, the system panics, synchronizes the file systems, performs a crash dump by dumping the contents of kernel memory to disk, and finally performs a system reset to start the boot process.

3. After you receive the `login:` message, log in and type the following to verify that the system is booted to the specified run level:

   ```
   # who -r <cr>
   ```

4. The system responds with the following:

   ```
   run-level 3 Jun 9 09:19 3  0 S
   ```

Stopping the System for Recovery Purposes: x86/x64

Objective:
Explain the abort sequence on an x86/x64 system.

If your x86/x64-based system is unresponsive, follow these steps:

1. If the system is running, become superuser and type `init 0` to stop the system. After the `Press any key to reboot` prompt appears, press any key to reboot the system.
2. If the system is running, become superuser and type `init 6` to reboot the system.
3. If the system doesn't respond to any input from the mouse or keyboard, press the Reset key on the system tower, if it exists, to reboot the system. Or you can use the power switch to reboot the system.

Turning Off the Power to the Hardware

Only after shutting down the file systems should you turn off the power to the hardware. You turn off power to all devices after the system is shut down. If necessary, you should also unplug the power cables. When power can be restored, you use the process described in Step by Step 3.11 to turn on the system and devices.

STEP BY STEP

3.11 Turning on the Power

1. Plug in the power cables.
2. Turn on all peripheral devices, such as disk drives, tape drives, and printers.
3. Turn on the CPU and monitor.

Summary

This chapter has described the OpenBoot environment, the PROM, NVRAM, and the kernel. It described how to access OpenBoot and the various commands that are available to test and provide information about the hardware.

This chapter described the OpenBoot architecture, and it explained how OpenBoot controls many of the hardware devices. By using the programmable user interface available in OpenBoot, you can set several parameters that control system hardware and peripherals.

The device tree and OpenBoot device names were explained. This book mentions various device names used in Solaris. It's important that you understand each of them and how they differ between the SPARC and x86/x64-based platforms. Along with device names, this chapter explained how to set temporary and permanent device aliases.

The system startup phases were described, and you learned how Solaris processes and services are started, from bootup, to loading and initializing the two-part kernel, to continuing to the multi-user milestone. You can further control these services through the Service Management Facility (SMF). You need to understand the startup process and boot-related configuration files on both the SPARC and x86/x64-based platforms.

This chapter described how important it is to shut down the system properly, because the integrity of the data can be compromised if the proper shutdown steps are not performed. All the various commands used to shut down a system in an orderly manner were outlined.

Chapter 4, "User and Security Administration," describes how to protect your system and data from unauthorized access.

Key Terms

- Autoconfiguration
- Boot
- Bootblock
- Boot loader
- Bootstrapping
- Dependency
- Device alias
- Device tree
- Dynamic kernel

- Failsafe archive
- Full device name
- GRUB
- `init` state
- Interactive boot
- Kernel
- Loadable module
- miniroot
- Multi-user mode
- NVRAM
- OBP
- OpenBoot
- POST
- Primary boot archive
- PROM
- Reconfiguration boot
- Run control script
- Run level
- Service
- Service contract
- Service Instance Object
- Service Management Facility (SMF)
- Single-user mode
- Subdependencies
- `ufsboot`

Exercises

CAUTION

Don't do this on a production system! Because some of the steps involved in the following exercises could render a system unbootable if they're not performed properly, you should not perform these exercises on a production system.

3.1 Using OpenBoot Commands

Use a SPARC system for this exercise. In this exercise, you will halt the system and use the OpenBoot commands to set parameters and gather basic information about your system.

Estimated time: 30 minutes

1. Issue the OpenBoot command to display the banner:

```
ok banner <cr>
```

2. Reset the system:

```
ok reset-all <cr>
```

3. Set the `auto-boot?` parameter to false to prevent the system from booting automatically after a reset. From the OpenBoot ok prompt, type the following:

```
ok setenv auto-boot? false <cr>
```

   Verify that the parameter has been set:

```
ok printenv auto-boot? <cr>
```

4. Display the list of OpenBoot help topics:

```
ok help <cr>
```

5. Use the `banner` command to get the following information from your system:

   ROM revision
   Amount of installed memory
   System type
   System serial number
   Ethernet address
   Host ID

6. Display the following list of OBP parameters by using the `printenv` command:

```
output-device
input-device
auto-boot?
boot-device
```

7. Use the following commands to display the list of disk devices attached to your system:

```
ok probe-scsi <cr>
ok probe-scsi-all <cr>
ok probe-ide <cr>
```

Explain the main differences between these commands.

CAUTION

Preventing a system hang If any of these commands returns a message warning that your system will hang if you proceed, enter `n` to avoid running the command. Run `reset-all` before running `probe-` again, and then respond with `y` to this message.

8. List the target number and the device type of each SCSI device attached to your system by using the OpenBoot commands in step 7.

9. From the OpenBoot prompt, identify your default boot device:

```
ok printenv boot-device <cr>
```

10. Use the `show-disks` OpenBoot command to get a listing of the disk drives on your system:

```
ok show-disks <cr>
```

11. Create a permanent device alias named `bootdisk` that points to the IDE master disk:

```
ok nvalias bootdisk /pci@1f,0/pci@1,1/ide@3/disk@0,0 <cr>
```

You need to select a SCSI disk if your system does not have IDE disks attached to it. Make sure that the device alias points to a bootable disk.

12. Reset the system and verify that the device alias is set properly by typing the following:

```
ok reset-all <cr>
```

After the system resets, type the following:

```
ok devalias bootdisk <cr>
```

13. Set the system up so that it boots into single-user mode without any user intervention:

```
ok setenv boot-command 'boot -s' <cr>
```

14. I suggest changing the `auto-boot?` parameter back to `true` and resetting the system to validate that your `boot-command` parameter is set properly:

```
ok setenv auto-boot? true <cr>
ok reset-all <cr>
```

15. Boot the system, log on as root, and use the `eeprom` command to list all NVRAM parameters.

16. Use the `eeprom` command to list only the setting of the `boot-device` parameter:

```
# eeprom boot-device <cr>
```

17. Reset `boot-device` to its default parameter from the OpenBoot prompt:

```
ok set-default boot-device <cr>
```

18. From the OpenBoot prompt, remove the alias `bootdisk`:

```
ok nvunalias bootdisk <cr>
```

19. Reset the system and verify that `bootdisk` is no longer set:

```
ok reset-all <cr>
ok printenv <cr>
```

20. Set all the OpenBoot parameters back to their default values:

```
ok set-defaults <cr>
```

3.2 Booting the System

This exercise takes you through the steps of powering on and booting the system.

Estimated time: 5 minutes

1. Turn on power to all the peripheral devices, if any exist.

2. If the OpenBoot parameter `auto-boot?` is set to `false`, you should see the `ok` prompt shortly after you power on the system. If the system is set to `auto-boot`, you should see a message similar to the following:

```
SunOS Release 5.10 Version Generic 64-bit
Copyright 1983-2005 Sun Microsystems, Inc. All rights reserved.
Use is subject to license terms.
```

You should see the system begin the boot process. Interrupt the boot process by pressing Stop+A. The ok prompt appears.

3. At the ok prompt, type boot to boot the system.

3.3 Booting an Alternate Kernel

In this exercise, you'll practice booting from a backup copy of the /etc/system file. You should use this process if your /etc/system file ever becomes corrupt or unbootable.

Estimated time: 15 minutes

1. Log in as root.
2. Create a backup copy of the /etc/system file:

```
# cp /etc/system /etc/system.orig <cr>
```

3. Remove the /etc/system file:

```
# rm /etc/system <cr>
```

4. Halt the system:

```
# /usr/sbin/shutdown -y -g0 -i0 <cr>
```

5. At the ok prompt, boot the system by using the interactive option to supply the backup name of the /etc/system file. You do that by typing this:

```
ok boot -a <cr>
```

6. You are prompted to enter a filename for the kernel and a default directory for modules. Press Enter to answer each of these questions. When you are prompted with this message to use the default /etc/system file:

```
Name of system file [etc/system]:
```

enter the following:

```
/etc/system.orig <cr>
```

7. Later you'll be asked to enter the root file system type and the physical name of the root device. At that point, press Enter to answer both questions.
8. When the system is ready, log in as root, and put the original /etc/system file back in place:

```
# cp /etc/system.orig /etc/system <cr>
```

Exam Questions

1. The hardware-level user interface that you see before the operating system has been started is called what?

   ❍ **A.** OpenBoot

   ❍ **B.** EEPROM

   ❍ **C.** Firmware

   ❍ **D.** Boot PROM

2. Which of the following stores system identification information, such as the hostid?

   ❍ **A.** Firmware

   ❍ **B.** OpenBoot

   ❍ **C.** NVRAM

   ❍ **D.** Kernel

3. What tasks does OpenBoot perform? (Select the two best answers.)

   ❍ **A.** Executing POST

   ❍ **B.** Loading `bootblk`

   ❍ **C.** Executing `ufsboot`

   ❍ **D.** Loading the operating system kernel

4. Which of the following is *not* a task of the OpenBoot firmware?

   ❍ **A.** Testing and initializing the system hardware

   ❍ **B.** Loading the kernel

   ❍ **C.** Starting up the operating system from either a mass storage device or from a network

   ❍ **D.** Allowing modification and management of system startup configuration, such as NVRAM parameters

5. Which of the following is attached to a host computer through a hierarchy of interconnected buses on the device tree?

   ❍ **A.** SBus cards

   ❍ **B.** SCSI peripherals

   ❍ **C.** Plug-in device drivers

   ❍ **D.** Nodes

6. What is `/pci@1f,0/pci@1,1/ide@3/disk@0,0`?

- ❍ **A.** Full device pathname
- ❍ **B.** Physical device
- ❍ **C.** Logical device
- ❍ **D.** Instance

7. Which of the following is used to obtain information about devices and to display device pathnames in OpenBoot?

- ❍ **A.** `show-devs`
- ❍ **B.** `dmesg`
- ❍ **C.** `pwd`
- ❍ **D.** `sysdef`

8. Which of the following commands creates a temporary device alias named `bootdisk`?

- ❍ **A.** `setenv bootdisk /pci@1f,0/pci@1,1/ide@3/disk@0,0`
- ❍ **B.** `set bootdisk /pci@1f,0/pci@1,1/ide@3/disk@0,0`
- ❍ **C.** `nvalias bootdisk /pci@1f,0/pci@1,1/ide@3/disk@0,0`
- ❍ **D.** `devalias bootdisk /pci@1f,0/pci@1,1/ide@3/disk@0,0`

9. If you want to create permanent aliases in NVRAM (that show up after a reboot), which of the following commands should you use? (Choose two)

- ❍ **A.** `devalias`
- ❍ **B.** `nvalias`
- ❍ **C.** `setenv`
- ❍ **D.** `eeprom`

10. Which NVRAM variable specifies the device from which to start up?

- ❍ **A.** `boot-device`
- ❍ **B.** `boot-file`
- ❍ **C.** `output-device`
- ❍ **D.** `input-device`

11. If a system will not start due to a bad NVRAM variable, which of the following, performed before you see the OpenBoot prompt, resets the NVRAM variables to their default settings?

❍ **A.** `set-default` *<variable>*

❍ **B.** Stop+N

❍ **C.** `set-defaults`

❍ **D.** Ctrl+N

12. Which of the following can restrict the set of operations that users are allowed to perform at the OpenBoot prompt?

❍ **A.** `security-password`

❍ **B.** `security-mode`

❍ **C.** `set-secure`

❍ **D.** `set-security`

13. Which of the following is used in OpenBoot to test all devices that have built-in self-test methods below the specified device tree node?

❍ **A.** `diag`

❍ **B.** `probe-scsi`

❍ **C.** `test-all`

❍ **D.** `test`

14. Which option do you use with the OpenBoot `boot` command so that you are prompted for the name of the standalone program to load?

❍ **A.** `-v`

❍ **B.** `-f`

❍ **C.** `-s`

❍ **D.** `-a`

15. What resides in blocks 1 to 15 of the startup device?

❍ **A.** `bootblk`

❍ **B.** `superblock`

❍ **C.** `kernel`

❍ **D.** `ufsboot`

16. Which of the following loads the operating system kernel?

- ❍ **A.** `ufsboot`
- ❍ **B.** `openBoot`
- ❍ **C.** `bootblk`
- ❍ **D.** `init`

17. Which of the following commands lists all hardware devices, system devices, loadable modules, and the values of selected kernel tunable parameters?

- ❍ **A.** `more /var/adm/messages`
- ❍ **B.** `adb`
- ❍ **C.** `dmesg`
- ❍ **D.** `sysdef`

18. What key combination would you enter to interrupt a system that is not responding?

- ❍ **A.** Ctrl+B
- ❍ **B.** Ctrl+C
- ❍ **C.** Stop+A
- ❍ **D.** Ctrl+Alt+Delete
- ❍ **E.** Ctrl+Break

19. What is the function of the `auto-boot?` parameter that is set in the OpenBoot PROM?

- ❍ **A.** Boots automatically after power-on or reset
- ❍ **B.** Sets the default boot device
- ❍ **C.** Reboots after a watchdog reset
- ❍ **D.** Automatically performs a system reboot when a system core file has been generated

20. Which of the following commands is used to set the `auto-boot` parameter?

- ❍ **A.** `setenv auto-boot?=false`
- ❍ **B.** `set auto-boot=false`
- ❍ **C.** `eeprom auto-boot?=false`
- ❍ **D.** `nvset`

21. What do you type to display all OpenBoot parameter settings, such as `boot-device` and `ttya-mode`?

   ❍ **A.** `nvalias`

   ❍ **B.** `devalias`

   ❍ **C.** `printenv`

   ❍ **D.** `show all`

22. What do you type to check the target IDs on all the SCSI devices connected to all the SCSI controllers?

   ❍ **A.** `test-all`

   ❍ **B.** `probe-scsi`

   ❍ **C.** `probe-scsi-all`

   ❍ **D.** `test-scsi`

23. The kernel reads which of the following files when loading? (This is where system configuration information is stored.)

   ❍ **A.** `/etc/system`

   ❍ **B.** `kernel/sparcv9/unix`

   ❍ **C.** `/etc/inittab`

   ❍ **D.** `/kernel/unix`

24. Which sequence of events best describes the boot process on a Sun SPARC system?

   ❍ **A.** Boot PROM phase, boot program phase, kernel initialization phase, `init` phase, and `svc.startd` phase

   ❍ **B.** Boot program phase, boot PROM phase, kernel initialization phase, `svc.startd` phase, and `init` phase

   ❍ **C.** Boot program phase, boot PROM phase, `init` phase, kernel initialization phase, `svc.startd` phase

   ❍ **D.** Boot PROM phase, boot program phase, `svc.startd` phase, kernel initialization phase

25. What consists of a small static core and many dynamically loadable modules?

- ❍ **A.** The kernel
- ❍ **B.** `ufsboot`
- ❍ **C.** The shell
- ❍ **D.** The bootblock

26. After reading the `/etc/inittab` file, which daemon does the init process start?

- ❍ **A.** `sched`
- ❍ **B.** `/sbin/rc1`
- ❍ **C.** `ufsboot`
- ❍ **D.** `svc.startd`

27. How can you later view system messages displayed at bootup?

- ❍ **A.** By issuing the `dmesg` command
- ❍ **B.** By viewing the `/var/adm/messages` file
- ❍ **C.** By issuing the `sysdef` command
- ❍ **D.** By viewing logs in the `/var/svc/log directory`

28. To boot a system into a single-user state, which commands do you enter at the `ok` prompt? (Choose two.)

- ❍ **A.** `boot`
- ❍ **B.** `boot -s`
- ❍ **C.** `boot -a`
- ❍ **D.** `boot -m milestone=single-user`

29. Which command, typed at the `ok` prompt, stops and asks for boot information during the boot process?

- ❍ **A.** `boot -i`
- ❍ **B.** `boot -a`
- ❍ **C.** `boot -v`
- ❍ **D.** `boot -s`

30. Which of the following programs is responsible for executing `ufsboot`?

❍ **A.** `bootblk`

❍ **B.** `kernel`

❍ **C.** `init`

❍ **D.** `boot`

31. What command do you use to change run levels?

❍ **A.** `run`

❍ **B.** `init`

❍ **C.** `kill`

❍ **D.** `su`

32. This XML-based file contains a complete set of properties that are associated with an SMF service or a service instance. Where is this XML file stored?

❍ **A.** `/var/svc/method`

❍ **B.** `/lib/svc/method`

❍ **C.** `/var/svc/manifest`

❍ **D.** `/var/svc/profile`

33. Which command is used to transition your system into the single-user milestone from the multiuser milestone?

❍ **A.** `svcadm milestone single-user`

❍ **B.** `svcadm milestone/single-user`

❍ **C.** `init -s`

❍ **D.** `init single-user`

34. Which of the following is *not* the valid FMRI name of a service instance?

❍ **A.** `svc://localhost/network/inetd:default`

❍ **B.** `lrc:/etc/rc3_d/S90samba`

❍ **C.** `network/inetd:default`

❍ **D.** `svc:/inetd:default`

35. Which command is used to obtain a detailed view of the service state of all service instances in the configuration repository?

❍ **A.** `inetadm -a`

❍ **B.** `svcs -a`

❍ **C.** `svcadm -a`

❍ **D.** `svcprop -l`

36. Which of the following service states indicates that the service is configured to run, but is not yet running or available to run?

❍ **A.** Offline

❍ **B.** Maintenance

❍ **C.** Disabled

❍ **D.** Degraded

37. Which SMF command displays the services that must be running before the multi-user milestone is reached?

❍ **A.** `svcs -d milestone/multi-user`

❍ **B.** `svcs -D milestone/multi-user`

❍ **C.** `svcs -p milestone/multi-user`

❍ **D.** `svcs -l milestone/multi-user`

38. On an x86/x64-based system, which of the following is the bootloader?

❍ **A.** The BIOS

❍ **B.** GRUB

❍ **C.** The primary boot archive

❍ **D.** mboot

39. You need to modify the boot sequence on your x86/x64-based Solaris system. You want the system to try to boot from the DVD before it looks for a bootable partition on the internal disk drives. Where would you change this boot sequence?

❍ **A.** `menu.lst`

❍ **B.** Boot archive

❍ **C.** `bootenv.rc`

❍ **D.** System BIOS

40. How do you temporarily change your system configuration to boot your x86/x64-based Solaris system in single-user mode?

❍ **A.** Edit the `menu.lst` file

❍ **B.** Change the system BIOS

❍ **C.** Edit the `kernel` command in the GRUB menu at boot time

❍ **D.** Select "Solaris failsafe" from the GRUB main menu

41. On an x86/x64-based system, how do you configure the console to display on the serial port (ttya) and not the VGA monitor? (Choose two.)

❍ **A.** Use the `eeprom` command to direct the console to run on ttya:

```
eeprom console=ttya
```

❍ **B.** Set the console property to ttya so that the system uses the serial port for the console:

```
kernel /platform/i86pc/multiboot -B console=ttya
```

❍ **C.** Unplug the keyboard from the system. The console defaults to the serial port.

42. How do you permanently disable the autoboot feature on an x86/x64-based system?

❍ **A.** Add the line `timeout=false` to the `menu.lst` file

❍ **B.** `eeprom auto-boot?=false`

❍ **C.** Add the line `timeout=-1` to the `bootenv.rc` file

❍ **D.** Add the line `timeout=-1` to the `menu.lst` file

43. Where is the `bootpath` property stored on an x86/x64-based system?

❍ **A.** In the boot archive

❍ **B.** In the `bootenv.rc` file

❍ **C.** In the `menu.lst` file

❍ **D.** In the bootblock

Answers to Exam Questions

1. **A.** The hardware-level user interface that you see before the operating system starts is called the OpenBoot PROM (OBP). For more information, see the section "The OpenBoot Environment."

2. **C.** Nonvolatile RAM (NVRAM) is where the system identification information—such as the host ID, Ethernet address, and TOD clock—is stored. For more information, see the section "The OpenBoot Environment."

3. **A, B.** The two primary tasks of the OpenBoot firmware are to run the POST and to load the bootblock. For more information, see the section "The OpenBoot Environment."

4. **B.** OpenBoot runs POSTs to initialize the system hardware. It also loads the primary startup program, `bootblk`, from the default startup device. The `bootblk` program finds and executes the secondary startup program, `ufsboot`, and loads it into memory. From that point, the `ufsboot` program loads the operating system kernel. For more information, see the section "The OpenBoot Environment."

5. **D.** Devices called *nodes* are attached to a host computer through a hierarchy of interconnected buses on the device tree. A node that represents the host computer's main physical address bus forms the tree's root node. For more information, see the section "The OpenBoot Architecture."

6. **A.** A full device pathname is a series of node names separated by slashes (`/`). The root of the tree is the machine node, which is not named explicitly but is indicated by a leading slash. Each device pathname has this form:

   ```
   driver-name@unit-address:device-arguments
   ```

   For more information, see the section "PROM Device Tree (Full Device Pathnames)."

7. **A.** The OpenBoot command `show-devs` is used to obtain information about devices and to display device pathnames. For more information, see the section "PROM Device Tree (Full Device Pathnames)."

8. **D.** You use the `devalias` command to create a temporary device alias named `bootdisk`:

   ```
   devalias bootdisk /pci@1f,0/pci@1,1/ide@3/disk@0,0
   ```

   For more information, see the section "OpenBoot Device Aliases."

9. **B,D.** You use the `nvalias` command from the OpenBoot PROM or the `eeprom` command from the UNIX prompt to create a permanent alias in NVRAM that remains in effect even after a reboot. For more information, see the section "OpenBoot Device Aliases."

10. **A.** The NVRAM variable named `boot-device` contains the name of the default startup device. For more information, see the section "Booting a SPARC System."

11. **B.** To reset the NVRAM variables to their default settings, you hold down the Stop+N keys simultaneously while the machine is powering up. For more information, see the section "OpenBoot NVRAM."

12. **B.** The OpenBoot command `security-mode` restricts the set of operations that users are allowed to perform at the OpenBoot prompt. For more information, see the section "OpenBoot Security."

13. **C.** The OpenBoot command `test-all` tests all devices that have built-in self-test methods below the specified device tree node. For more information, see the section "OpenBoot Diagnostics."

14. **D.** You issue the OpenBoot `boot` command with the `-a` option to be prompted for the name of the standalone program to load. For more information, see the section "The `boot` Command."

15. **A.** The bootblock resides in blocks 1 to 15 of the startup device. For more information, see the section "The `boot` Command."

16. **A.** The secondary startup program, `ufsboot`, loads the two-part operating system kernel. For more information, see the section "Booting a SPARC System."

17. **D.** You use the `sysdef` command to list all hardware devices, system devices, and loadable modules, as well as the values of selected kernel tunable parameters. For more information, see the section "The Kernel."

18. **C.** You interrupt a system that is not responding by pressing Stop+A. For more information, see the section "Stopping the System for Recovery Purposes: SPARC."

19. **A.** `auto-boot?` controls whether the system automatically starts up after a system reset or when the power is turned on. The default for this variable is `true`. When the system is powered on, the system automatically starts up to the default run level. For more information, see the section "OpenBoot NVRAM."

20. **C.** `eeprom auto-boot?=false` is used to set the `auto-boot?` parameter from the UNIX shell. Option A is wrong because the = sign should not be used with the `setenv` command. Option B is wrong because there is not a `set` command at the OpenBoot prompt, and using `set` from the UNIX shell does not set an OpenBoot parameter. Option D is wrong because there is not an `nvset` command. For more information, see the section "OpenBoot NVRAM."

21. **C.** At the OpenBoot prompt, you use the `printenv` command to display all OpenBoot parameter settings. For more information, see the section "OpenBoot NVRAM."

22. **C.** You use the `probe-scsi-all` command to check the target IDs on all the SCSI devices that are connected to all the SCSI controllers. For more information, see the section "OpenBoot Diagnostics."

23. **A.** When the kernel is loading, it reads the `/etc/system` file, where system configuration information is stored. This file modifies the kernel's parameters and treatment of loadable modules. For more information, see the section "The Kernel."

24. **A.** The boot process goes through the following five phases: boot PROM phase, boot programs phase, kernel initialization phase, `init` phase, and `svc.startd` phase. For more information, see the section "Booting a SPARC System."

25. **A.** The kernel consists of a two-piece static core that is made up of `genunix` and `unix`. `genunix` is the platform-independent generic kernel file, and `unix` is the platform-specific kernel file. When the system boots, `ufsboot` combines these two files and many dynamically loadable modules into memory to form the running kernel. For more information, see the section "The Kernel."

26. **D.** The `init` process reads the `/etc/inittab` file and executes any process entries that have `sysinit` in the action field, so that any special initializations can take place before users log in. After reading the `/etc/inittab` file, `init` starts the `svc.startd` daemon, which is responsible for starting and stopping other system services such as mounting file systems and configuring network devices. In addition, `svc.startd` executes legacy run control (RC) scripts. For more information, see the section "The `init` Phase."

27. **D.** The boot process creates fewer messages. All the information that was provided by the boot messages in previous versions of Solaris is now located in the `/var/svc/log` directory. For more information, see the section "The Service Management Facility (SMF)."

28. **B, D.** You issue the `boot -s` command or the `boot -m milestone=single-user` at the OpenBoot `ok` prompt to boot the system into single-user mode. You can also boot to a specific milestone using the `boot -m` command. For more information, see the section "Booting a SPARC System."

29. **B.** The `boot -a` command performs an interactive boot. With this option, you are prompted to enter the name of the kernel, the default modules directory, the name of the system file, the root file system type, and the device name for the root device. For more information, see the section "Booting a SPARC System."

30. **A.** The `bootblk` program finds and executes the secondary boot program, called `ufsboot`, from the UFS and loads it into memory. For more information, see the section "Booting a SPARC System."

31. **B.** You use the `init` command to change run levels. For more information, see the sections "The `init` Phase" and "The Service Managmeent Facility."

32. **C.** An SMF manifest is an XML (Extensible Markup Language) file that contains a complete set of properties that are associated with a service or a service instance. The properties are stored in files and subdirectories located in `/var/svc/manifest`. For more information, see the section "The Service Management Facility (SMF)."

33. **A.** Use the `svcadm milestone single-user` command to switch into the single-user milestone. For more information, see the section "Starting Services During Boot."

34. **D.** A valid FMRI instance names has this form:

    ```
    svc://localhost/network/inetd:default
    svc:/network/inetd:default
    network/inetd:default
    ```

    `svc:/inetd:default` does not contain the service category name.

    `lrc:/etc/rc3_d/S90samba` is an FMRI for a legacy run control script not managed by the SMF.

    For more information, see the section "The Service Management Facility (SMF)."

35. **B.** Running the `svcs` command without options displays the status of all enabled services. Use the `-a` option to list all services, including disabled services. For more information, see the section "SMF Command-Line Administration Utilities."

36. **A.** The offline status indicates that a service instance is enabled (configured to run), but the service is not yet running or available to run. A disabled service is configured not to start. For more information, see the section "SMF Command-Line Administration Utilities."

37. **A.** The `-d` option for the `svcs` command lists the services or service instances upon which the multi-user service instance is dependent on. For more information, see the section "SMF Command-Line Administration Utilities."

38. **B.** Solaris 10 utilizes an open-source bootloader called GRUB (Grand Unified Boot Loader). For more information, see the section "GRUB."

39. **D.** If it becomes necessary to change the boot sequence, modify the BIOS settings before installing the Solaris OS. For example, the system's BIOS can be configured to boot from the CD/DVD in order to install the Solaris OS from DVD. Entering the BIOS setup screen is performed by pressing a key early in the startup process. For more information, see the section "Booting x86- and x64-Based Systems."

40. **C.** In the GRUB main menu, I can edit the kernel command as follows:

    ```
    kernel /platform/i86pc/multiboot -s
    ```

    to boot the system into single-user mode. The modification is temporary until the next time the system is booted. For more information, see the section "Modifying the Boot Behavior."

41. **A, B.** Use the `eeprom` command to direct the console to run on ttya as follows:

    ```
    eeprom console=ttya
    ```

    This is a permanent setting. Or, at bootup, edit the GRUB menu and set the console property to ttya so that the system uses the serial port for the console as follows: `kernel /platform/i86pc/multiboot -B console=ttya`. This temporarily changes the console to the ttya port until the next system boot. For more information, see the section "Modifying the Boot Behavior."

42. **D.** Turn off `autoboot` by changing the line in the `menu.lst` file from `timeout=10` to `timeout=-1`. For more information, see the section "The GRUB Menu."

43. **B.** The bootpath property is stored in the `/boot/solaris/bootenv.rc` file. For more information, see the section "Modifying the Boot Behavior."

Suggested Readings and Resources

For more information on the OpenBoot environment and the boot process, refer to *Inside Solaris 9*, by Bill Calkins (New Riders, 2002).

For more information on the Service Management Facility (SMF), refer to the "Managing Services" section of *Solaris 10 System Administration Guide: Basic Administration*, 2005, Sun Microsystems, Part Number Part No: 817-1985-11. This manual is available online at http://docs.sun.com.

For more information on the Solaris kernel and tuning its parameters, refer to the following publications:

- *The Solaris Tunable Parameters Reference Manual*, 2005, Sun Microsystems, Part number 817-0404-10. This manual is available online at http://docs.sun.com.
- *Solaris Performance and Tools: DTrace and MDB Techniques for Solaris 10 and OpenSolaris*, by Richard McDougall, Jim Mauro, and Brendan Gregg (Prentice Hall, 2006).
- *Solaris Internals: Solaris 10 and OpenSolaris Kernel Architecture*, Second Edition, by Jim Mauro and Richard McDougall (Prentice Hall, 2006).
- *Resource Management*, by Richard McDougall, Adrian Cockcroft, Evert Hoogendoorn, Enrique Vargas, Tom Bialaski, and Everet Hoogendoorn (Prentice Hall, 1999).

CHAPTER FOUR

User and Security Administration

Objectives

The following objectives for Exam CX-310-200 are covered in this chapter:

Explain and perform Solaris 10 OS user administration, and manage user accounts and initialization files.

- You need to know how to use the commands and utilities to set up user accounts, and you need to understand which files are configured and how the information is formatted in those files.

  When you set up user accounts, you can customize each user's session by using initialization files that are run each time the user logs in. This chapter describes how to administer each initialization file.

Monitor system access by using appropriate commands.

- You also need to control access to the operating system via user logins. Only users who have active logins should have access to the system. You need to control the level of access that each user will have. In addition to controlling system access, you need to monitor the system for unauthorized use.

Perform system security administration tasks by switching users on a system, and by becoming root and monitoring `su` attempts.

- Users sometimes obtain logins and passwords from other users. You need to monitor the system for any user that may be switching to a user account that they have not been authorized to use—this includes monitoring unauthorized use of the root account.

Control system security through restricting FTP access and using `/etc/hosts.equiv` and `$HOME/.rhosts` files and SSH fundamentals.

- You need to understand the vulnerabilities that are presented to your system by network services such as FTP, Telnet, and other forms of remote access. You need to restrict access to these facilities and ensure that unauthorized users do not gain access to your system over the network via an unsecured network service.

Restrict access to data in files through the use of group membership, ownership, and special file permissions.

- As a system administrator, you need to be able to assign access to directories and files by using the standard Solaris permissions scheme. Understanding this permission scheme and applying it to user and group IDs is necessary for controlling access to critical system data.

Outline

Study Strategies

The following study strategies will help you prepare for the exam:

- As you read this chapter, you should practice the step-by-step examples on a Solaris 10 system. You should practice the steps until you are able to perform them from memory.
- You should make sure you understand each of the attributes associated with a user account, such as the user ID (UID), primary group, default shell, and so on.
- You should practice using the command-line tools for adding, modifying, and removing user accounts, and you should pay attention to details. These commands will appear on the Sun exam, so you need to make sure you understand them thoroughly. You should continue practicing these commands until you can perform them from memory. You should modify the account attributes, such as the default shell, group, and UID value. You should modify variables in the initialization files for each user to see the results.
- You should pay special attention to the section "Controlling File Access." You need to understand everything discussed in that section because the exam tests heavily on those topics. You should know the commands described and understand permission values that are set on a file or directory.
- You should memorize all the configuration files described in this chapter. You won't need to understand how they are structured—just understand what they are used for and how they can be used to monitor and control security on a system.
- Various commands and files are described in the section "Auditing Users." You need to understand the commands and log files that are described in that section. Also, as you read through the "Controlling Network Security" section, you should pay special attention to the concept of trusted hosts and restrictions on superuser access and understand how to restrict these services
- You should study the terms at the end of the chapter. These terms might appear in questions on the exam, so you need to understand what they mean.

Introduction

Managing user accounts can be simple or complex, depending on the size of the network. Today, many Solaris servers are simply database servers or Web servers, and users do not log directly in to these systems. In addition, Solaris workstations may only require login accounts for one or two users. On the other hand, in a university setting, a server may hold hundreds of user login accounts. Managing these accounts is very complex because the accounts change every semester. The system administrator is not only responsible for managing user accounts but also for ensuring that system security is not compromised.

This chapter describes how to manage user accounts while maintaining a reasonable level of security on a system.

Administering User Accounts

Objective:

Explain and perform Solaris 10 OS user administration, and manage user accounts and initialization files.

Access to a system is allowed only through user login accounts that are set up by the system administrator. A user account includes information that a user needs to log in and use a system—a user login name, a password, the user's home directory, and login initialization files. Each of these items is described later in this chapter.

The following methods and tools are available in Solaris for adding new user accounts to a system:

- **User and Group Manager**—A graphical user interface (GUI) that is available in the Solaris Management Console.
- **The `/usr/sadm/bin/smuser` command**—A command that can be executed from the command line.
- **The `useradd` command**—A command that can be executed from the command line.

As with many Unix commands, the command-line method of adding user accounts can be difficult for inexperienced administrators. For this reason, Sun has added user account administration to the Solaris Management Console (SMC).

Managing User and Group Accounts with the SMC

The SMC is a GUI that is designed to ease several routine system administration tasks. When you use the SMC, you are presented with a menu-like interface that is much easier to use than the ASCII interface supplied at the command prompt. This chapter describes how to use the SMC and the command line to administer user accounts on a system.

Adding User Accounts with the SMC

To perform administrative tasks such as adding user accounts, SMC will prompt you for the root password or an authorized RBAC account before allowing permission to add, create, and modify user accounts. RBAC is a topic covered in *Solaris 10 System Administration Exam Prep: Exam CX-310-202* book.

NOTE

Editing User Accounts Files When you're adding or modifying user accounts, the SMC edits the files `/etc/passwd`, `/etc/shadow`, and `/etc/group`. These files are described later in this chapter. As root, you could edit these files directly, but that is not recommended. Errors in any of these files could cause adverse effects on the system.

The first step in setting up a new user account is to have the user provide the information you need in order to administer the account. You also need to set up proper permissions so that the user can share information with other members of his or her department. You need to know the user's full name, department, and any groups with which the user will be working. It's a good idea for the system administrator to sit down with the user and compile an information sheet (like the one shown in Table 4.1) so that you have all the information you need when you set up the account.

TABLE 4.1 User Information Data Sheet

Item
User name:
UID:
Primary group:
Secondary groups:
Comment:
Default shell:
Password status and aging:
Home directory server name:
Home directory path name:
Mail server:

(continues)

TABLE 4.1 *Continued*

Item
Department name:
Department administrator:
Manager:
Employee name:
Employee title:
Employee status:
Employee number:
Start date:
Desktop system name:

To use the SMC to add a new user login account, you should follow the procedure described in Step by Step 4.1.

EXAM ALERT

Using the SMC to Add a New User For the exam, you will not be asked to use the SMC to add a new user account, but you do need to know what tool within the SMC is used to add a user account. You also need to know what information the SMC asks for.

STEP BY STEP

4.1 Adding a New Login Account

1. Start the SMC by typing **smc** at the command prompt. The SMC Welcome window appears, as shown in Figure 4.1.
2. In the left pane of the Welcome window, click the This Computer icon. The icon expands, displaying five additional icons, as shown in Figure 4.2.
3. Click the System Configuration icon, and the system configuration icons appear in the main pane of the window, as shown in Figure 4.3. One of these icons is Users.

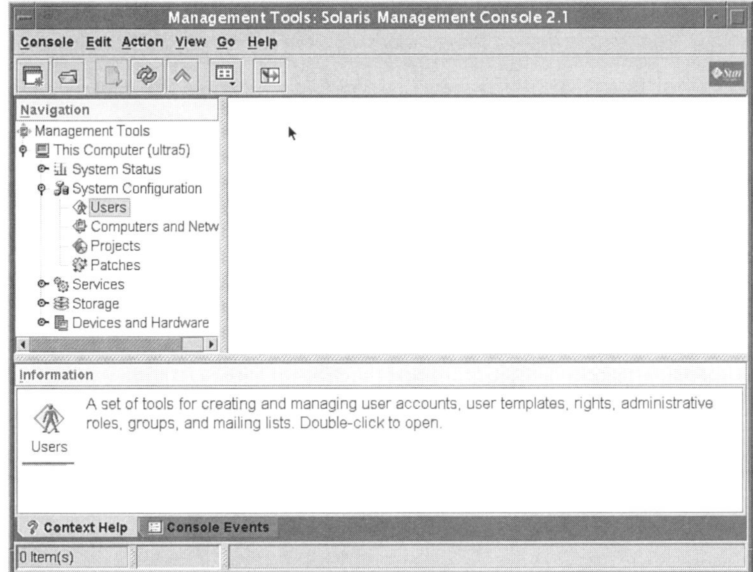

FIGURE 4.1 The SMC Welcome window.

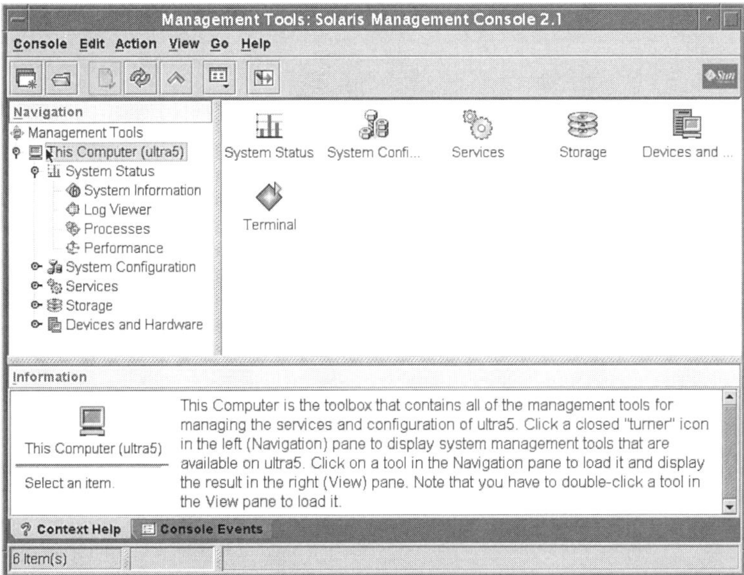

FIGURE 4.2 SMC tools.

4. Click the Users icon. You are prompted to enter a username and password. You can either enter the root password or enter your roll name and password if you have an RBAC account. After you enter the correct name and password, the User Accounts tool is loaded and displayed in the main pane of the window, as shown in Figure 4.4.

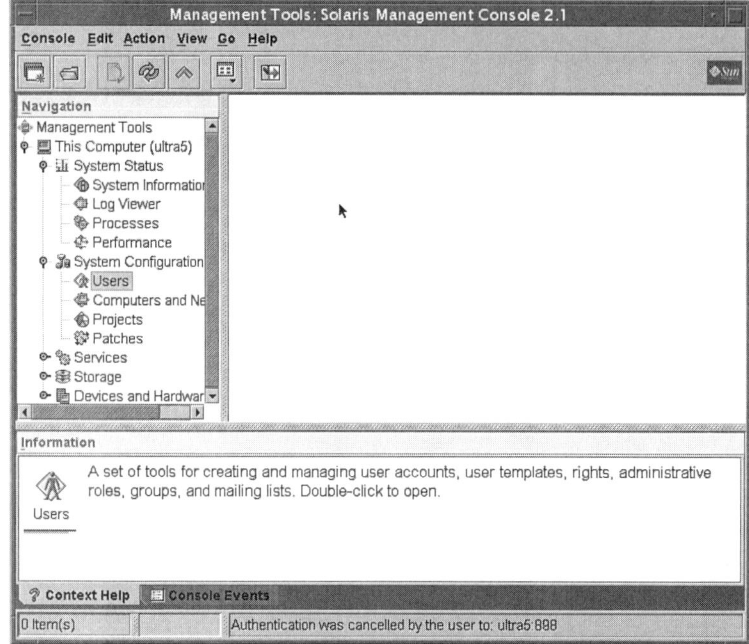

FIGURE 4.3 System configuration tools.

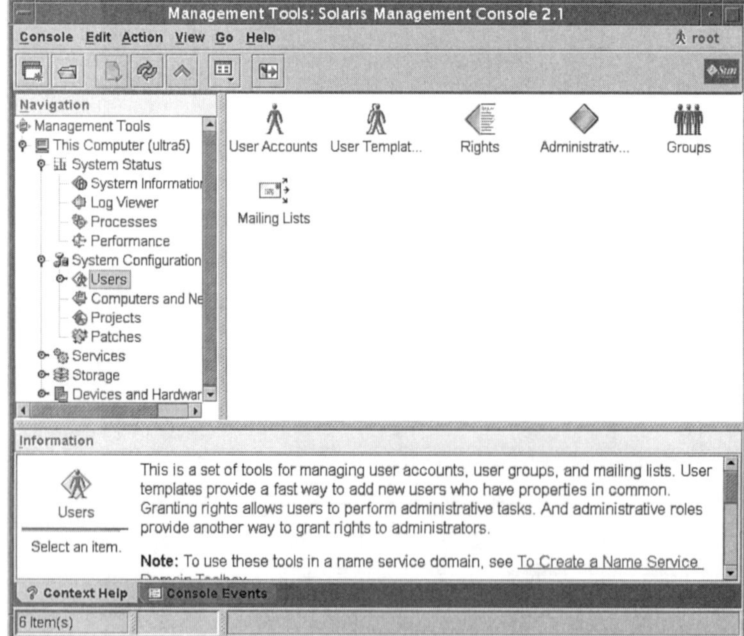

FIGURE 4.4 The Users Accounts tool.

5. Click the User Accounts icon. Current user accounts are displayed, then choose the Action menu and Add User, as shown in Figure 4.5.

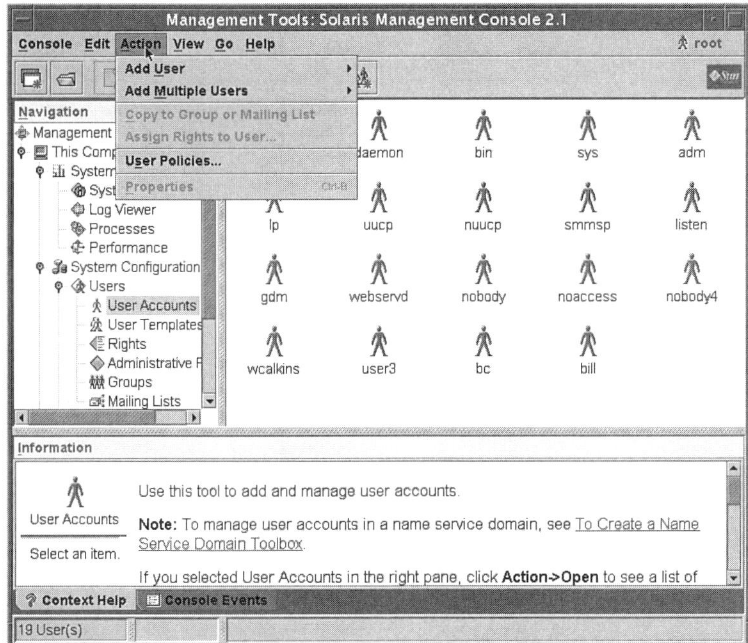

FIGURE 4.5 Displaying current user accounts.

6. From the top toolbar, select Action, Add User. Slide the mouse to the right, and you see two options for adding users, as shown in Figure 4.6. Select the With Wizard option.

   The Add User Wizard appears, as shown in Figure 4.7.

7. In the first wizard window that appears, all the fields are blank. Table 4.2 describes the information needed in this screen. If you aren't sure how to complete a field, read the Help screen in the left pane after you click on that field. After you enter the information in the first wizard window, click the Next button.

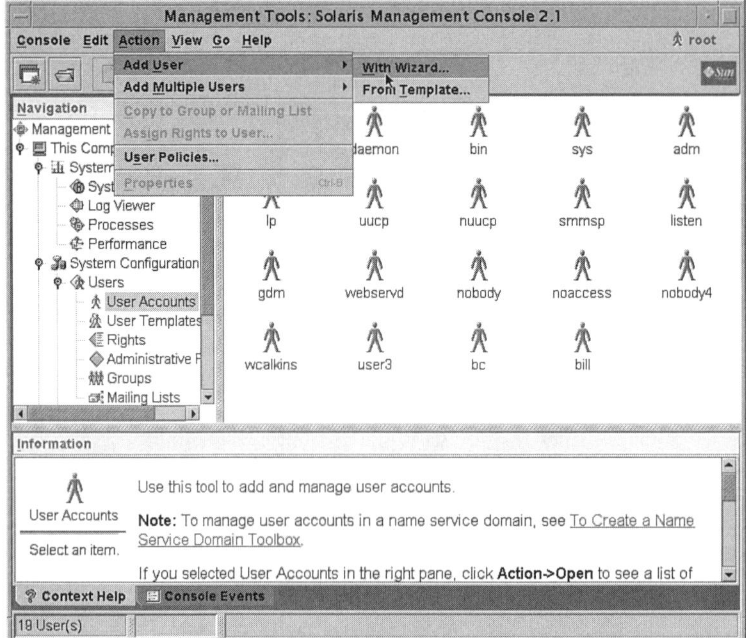

Figure 4.6 Adding a new user.

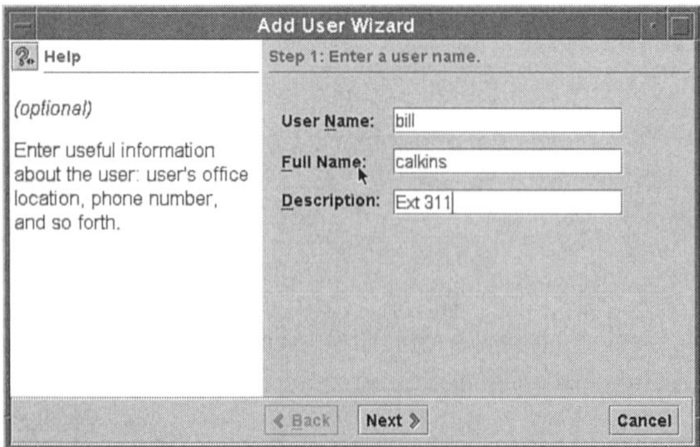

Figure 4.7 The Add User Wizard.

TABLE 4.2 Add User Fields

Field	Description
User Name	A unique login name that is entered at the Solaris login prompt. You should choose a name that is unique to the organization. The name can contain two to eight uppercase characters (A–Z), lowercase characters (a–z), or digits (0–9), but no underscores or spaces. The first character must be a letter, and at least one character must be a lowercase letter. The system allows you to use more than eight characters for the login name, but only the first eight characters are recognized.

TABLE 4.2 *Continued*

Field	Description
User ID	The unique UID. The SMC automatically assigns the next available UID; however, in a networked environment, you need to make sure this number is not duplicated by another user on another system. All UIDs must be consistent across the network. A UID is typically a number between 100 and 60,002, but it can be as high as 2,147,483,647. Note that Solaris releases prior to Solaris 9 use 32-bit data types to contain the UIDs, but UIDs in those versions are constrained to a maximum useful value of 60,000. Starting with the Solaris 2.5.1 release and compatible versions, the limit on UID values has been raised to the maximum value of a signed integer, or `2,147,483,647`. UIDs over `60,000` do not have full functionality and are incompatible with many Solaris features, so you should avoid using UIDs over `60,000`.
Primary Group	The primary group name for the group to which the user will belong. This is the group that the operating system will assign to files created by the user. `Group 10` (staff) is a predefined group that is sufficient for most users.
Full Name and Description	Optional comment fields. You can enter in these fields any comments, such as the full username, employee number, or phone number.
Password	The password status. You can select the following options: **User Account is Locked**—This is the default. If you choose this option, the user account is created and the account locked. **User Must Use This Password at First Login**—The account will have a password that you set in advance.
Home Directory	A field that points to an existing directory or specifies a new directory to create. This will be the location of the user's home directory and where the user's personal files will be stored. You should not include the username in this field. The username will automatically be added to the end of the path when the directory is created. Refer to the section "The Home Directory," later in this chapter.

8. Another window appears, asking you to enter a user ID (UID). Enter a UID and click Next.
9. In the third window of the wizard, you can either select to have the account locked or specify the password that the user will use the first time he or she logs in, as shown in Figure 4.8. Then click the Next button at the bottom of the window.

> **NOTE**
>
> **Changing a Password from the Command Line** A user can type the Unix command `passwd` at any time from the command prompt to change his or her password.

10. After you enter the user password information, a fourth window opens, asking you to select the primary group for that user. Select a group from the pull-down menu, as shown in Figure 4.9, and click the Next button.

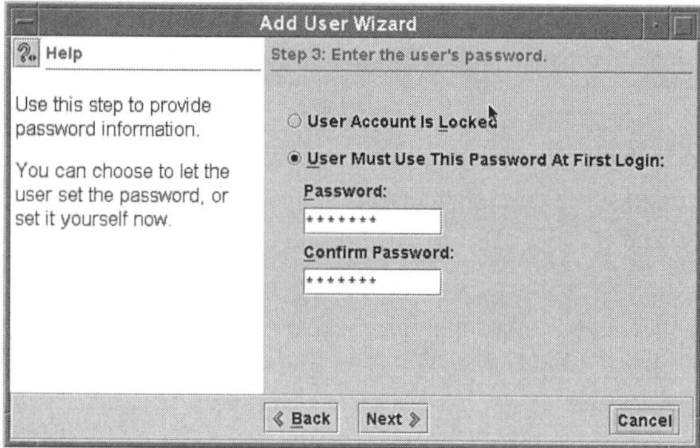

FIGURE 4.8 The Enter the User's Password window.

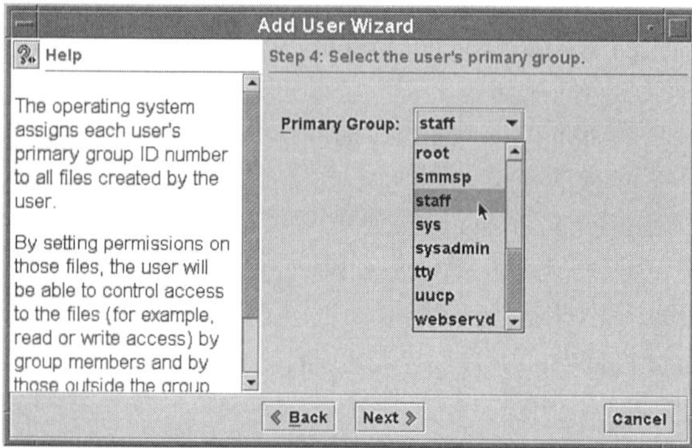

FIGURE 4.9 Selecting the user's primary group.

11. The fifth wizard window asks you to set the user's home directory, as shown in Figure 4.10. Fill in the information for the user's home directory and click the Next button.

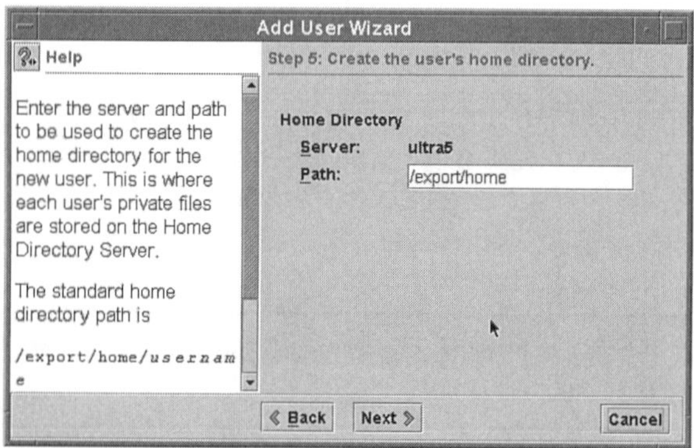

FIGURE 4.10 Selecting the user's home directory.

12. The sixth window displays the user's mail server and mailbox information, as shown in Figure 4.11. Click the Next button to continue.

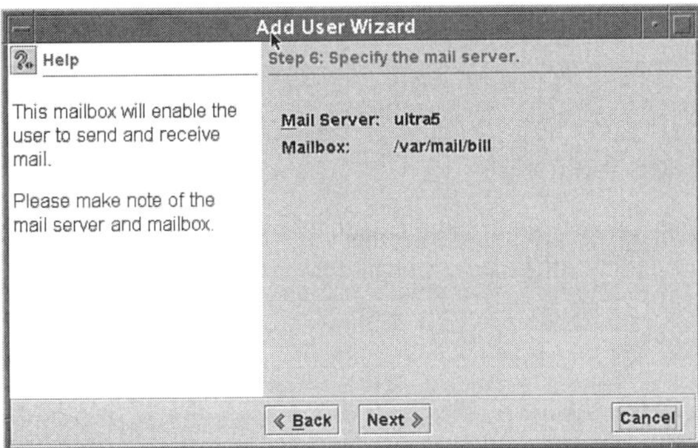

FIGURE 4.11 The user's mailbox and mail server information.

13. The next window displays a summary of the new user information, as shown in Figure 4.12. If the information is correct, click the Finish button, and you are returned to the main SMC window. Otherwise, click Back to go back and re-enter the information.

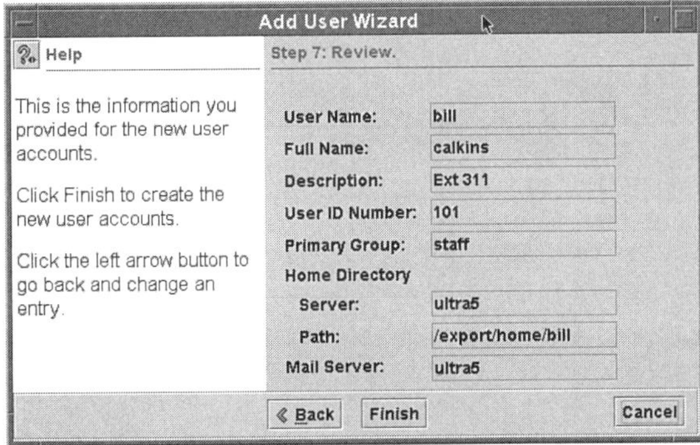

FIGURE 4.12 New user summary information.

When you use the Add User Wizard to create an account, the following defaults are assigned to the account:

- The default shell is the Bourne shell (`/bin/sh`).
- No secondary groups are set up.

To modify these settings, refer to the section "Modifying User Accounts with the SMC," later in this chapter.

Refer to the man pages for a description of this command.

Deleting User Accounts with the SMC

When a user account is no longer needed on a system, you need to delete it. Step by Step 4.2 describes how to perform this task.

STEP BY STEP

4.2 Using the SMC to Delete Existing User Accounts

1. Follow the steps in Step by Step 4.1 for adding a new login account through the SMC. When you get to the User Accounts tool (refer to Figure 4.5), right-click the user you want to delete. A pop-up menu appears, as shown in Figure 4.13.

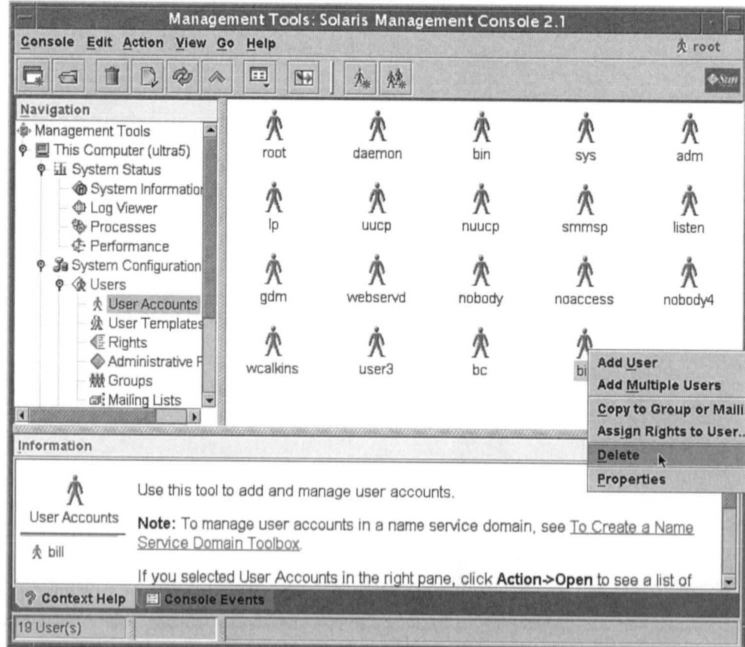

FIGURE 4.13 Deleting a user account.

2. Select Delete from the pop-up menu. A confirmation window appears, as shown in Figure 4.14.

   Select whether you want to delete the user's home directory and/or mailbox. Then click the Delete button at the bottom of the window to delete the account.

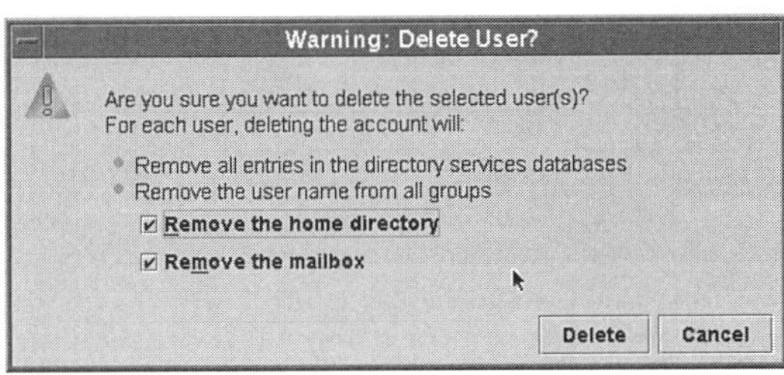

FIGURE 4.14 The Delete User confirmation window.

CAUTION

When selecting to remove the home directory, make sure that you are certain of the directory that will be removed. If you need data from this directory, do not remove it. Sometimes a user's home directory might point to an important directory such as "/" root. In this case, removing the home directory would remove important system files.

Modifying User Accounts with the SMC

If a login needs to be modified—to change a password or disable an account, for example—you can use the SMC to modify the user account settings, as described in Step by Step 4.3.

STEP BY STEP

4.3 Modifying User Accounts with the SMC

1. Follow the steps described in Step by Step 4.1 for adding a new login account through the SMC. When you get to the User Accounts tool (refer to Figure 4.5), double-click the user you want to modify. The window shown in Figure 4.15 appears.
2. Modify any of the following items in the User Properties window:
   - Change the username.
   - Change the full name.
   - Change the description of the account.
   - Change the login shell. By default the user is assigned to the Bourne shell (`/bin/sh`).
   - Change the account availability. This option allows you to specify a date on which the account is locked.
   - Lock an account to prevent logins using this user name.
   - Assign additional groups.

- Make the user a member of a project. Projects are described later in this chapter.
- Change the home directory.
- Share the home directory with other users or groups.
- Assign roles and grant rights to the account.
- Change the password or set password options, such as how often passwords should be changed, or expire passwords after a specified period of inactivity.

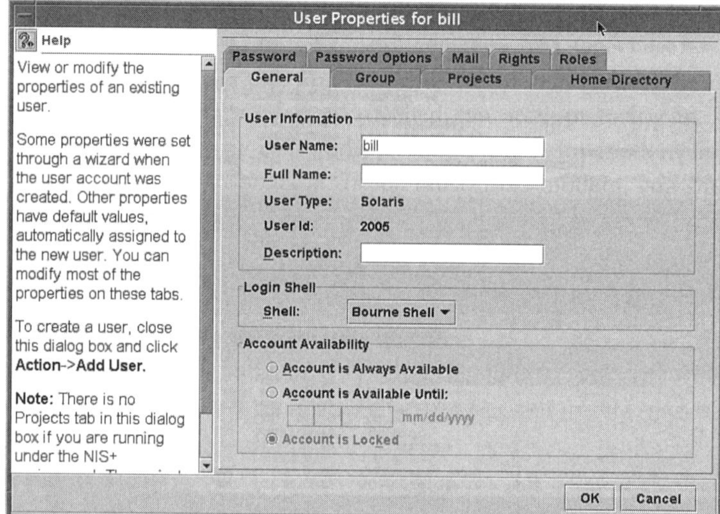

FIGURE 4.15 The User Properties window.

Adding Groups with the SMC

As a system administrator, you might need to add a group that does not already exist on the system. Perhaps a new group of users called `engrg` (from the Engineering Department) needs to be added. Step by Step 4.4 shows how to add this group to the system by using the SMC.

STEP BY STEP

4.4 Adding Groups with the SMC

1. Follow the steps described in Step by Step 4.1 for adding a new login account through the SMC. When you get to the Users tool (refer to Figure 4.4), double-click the Groups icon. The list of groups appears in the Groups tool, as shown in Figure 4.16.
2. From the top toolbar, select Action, Add Group, as shown in Figure 4.17.

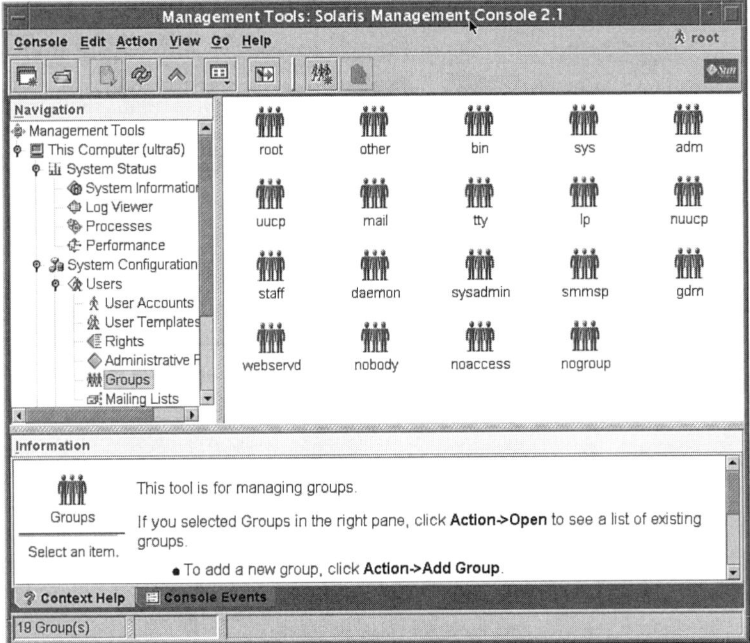

FIGURE 4.16 The Groups tool.

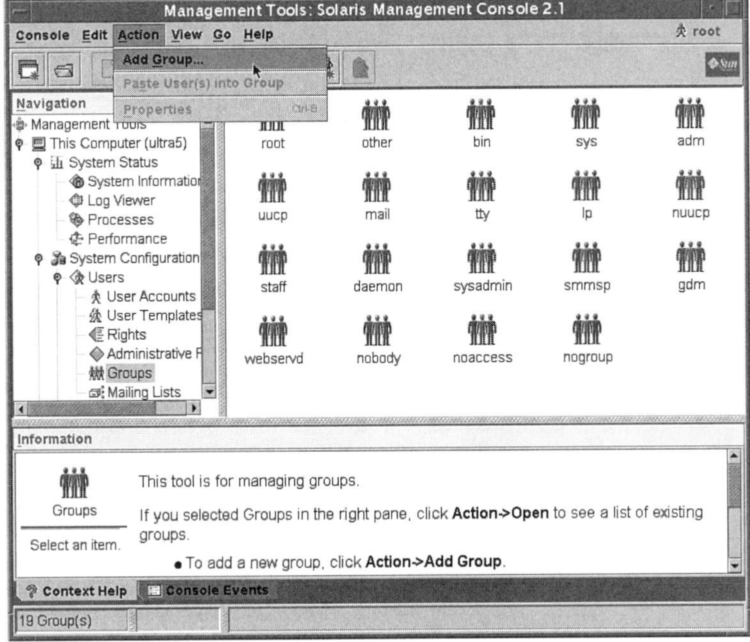

FIGURE 4.17 Adding a group.

The Add Group window appears, as shown in Figure 4.18.

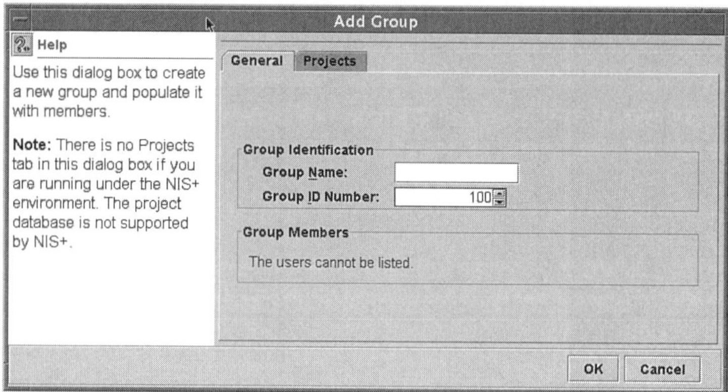

FIGURE 4.18 The Add Group window.

3. Enter the group name `engrg` and then enter the unique GID number `200`, then click on the OK button, as shown in Figure 4.19.

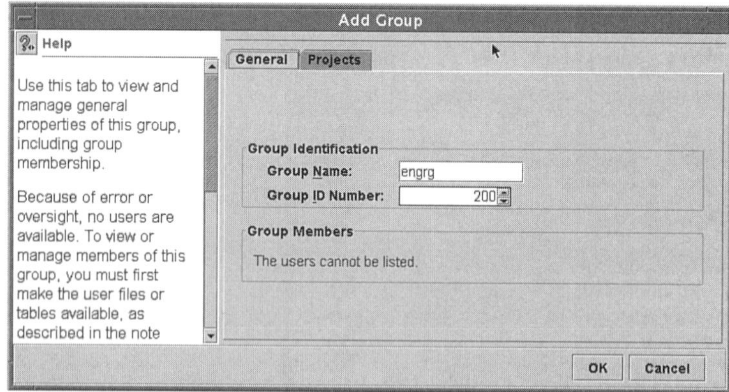

FIGURE 4.19 Adding the `engrg` group.

4. Click OK when you're finished, and you are returned to the main SMC window. The list of groups displayed in the Groups window is updated to include the new group. You can modify the group by double-clicking the icon that represents the group that you want to change.

The `/usr/sadm/bin/smgroup add` command is the command-line equivalent of the SMC tool for adding a new group. For example, to add a group named `development` with a GID of `300`, you enter this:

```
# /usr/sadm/bin/smgroup add -g 300 -n development <cr>
```

The system responds with this:

```
Authenticating as user: root
Type /? for help, pressing <enter> accepts the default denoted by [ ]
Please enter a string value for: password :: <Enter the Root Password>
Loading Tool: com.sun.admin.usermgr.cli.group.UserMgrGroupCli from ultra5
```

Refer to the man pages for a complete description of the `smgroup` command.

Managing User and Group Accounts from the Command Line

You can manage user accounts from the command line as well as through the SMC. Although using the command line is more complex than using the SMC GUI interface, the command line allows more options and provides a little more flexibility.

Solaris supplies the user administration commands described in Table 4.3 for setting up and managing user accounts.

TABLE 4.3 Account Administration Commands

Command	Description
`useradd`	Adds a new user account
`userdel`	Deletes a user account
`usermod`	Modifies a user account
`groupadd`	Adds a new group
`groupmod`	Modifies a group (for example, changes the GID or name)
`groupdel`	Deletes a group

NOTE

SMC Versus Conventional Administration Commands The SMC has its own command-line equivalents, such as `smuser` and `smgroup`. The difference between the SMC commands and the commands outlined in Table 4.3 is that the SMC can also update the name service. The commands in Table 4.3 only update the local files.

Adding User Accounts from the Command Line

You can add new user accounts on the local system by using the `useradd` command. This command adds an entry for the new user into the `/etc/passwd` and `/etc/shadow` files, which are described later in this chapter, in the section "Where User Account Information Is Stored."

Just like the SMC, the -k option to the useradd command copies all the user initialization files found in the /etc/skel directory into the new user's home directory. User initialization files are covered in the section "Setting Up Shell Initialization Files," later in this chapter.

The syntax for the useradd command is as follows:

```
useradd [-c comment] [-d dir] [-e expire]  [-f inactive]  [-g group] \
 [  -G group  [  , group...]] [ -m [-k skel_dir]] [-u uid  [-o]] \
 [-s shell]  [-A  authorization   [,authorization...]]
 [-P profile  [,profile...]] \
[-R role  [,role...]] [-p projname] [-K key=value] <loginname>
```

Table 4.4 describes these options.

TABLE 4.4 useradd Command Options

Option	Description
-A <authorization>	One or more comma-separated authorizations.
-b <base-dir>	The default base directory for the system if -d is not specified.
-u <uid>	Sets the unique UID for the user.
-o	Allows a UID to be duplicated. The default is not to let you choose a UID that is already in use.
-g <gid>	Specifies a predefined GID or name for the user that will be the user's primary group.
-G <gid>	Defines the new user's secondary group memberships. You can enter multiple groups, but they must be separated by commas. A user can belong to up to 15 additional groups. The number of groups can be increased to 32 by changing the kernel parameter ngroups_max.
-m	Creates a new home directory if one does not already exist.
-s <shell>	Defines the full pathname for the shell program to be used as the user's login shell. The default is /bin/sh if a shell is not specified.
-c <comment>	Specifies the user's full name, location, and phone number, in a comment.
-d <dir>	Specifies the home directory of the new user. It defaults to <base-dir>/<account-name>, where <base-dir> is the base directory for new login home directories and <account-name> is the new login name.
-D <dir>	Display the default values for group, basedir, skel-dir, and so on.
	When used with the -g, -b, -f, -e, -A, -P, -p, -R, or -K options, the -D option sets the default values for the specified fields.
-e <expiration>	Sets an expiration date on the user account. Specifies the date on which the user can no longer log in and access the account. After the specified date, the account is locked. Use the following format to specify the date: *mm/dd/yy*.

TABLE 4.4 *Continued*

Option	Description
-f *<inactive>*	Sets the number of inactive days allowed on a user account. If the account is not logged in to during the specified number of days, the account is locked.
-k *<skeldir>*	Specifies an alternate location for the user initialization template files. Files from this directory are copied into the user's home directory when the -m option is specified to create the home directory. The default location is /etc/skel.
-p *<project-name>*	Specifies the name of the project that the user is associated with.
-P *<profile>*	Specifies an execution profile for the account.
-R *<role>*	Specifies a role for the account.
<login-name>	Specifies the user login name to be assigned to this account.

Many additional options are available, although most of them are not used as often as the ones in Table 4.4. Additional options to the useradd command apply specifically to RBAC accounts and are described in the *Solaris 10 System Administration Exam Prep: Exam CX-310-202* book. You can also refer to the man pages to find a listing of all the options to the useradd command.

The useradd command can be used with just one argument and no options, as follows:

```
# useradd bcalkins <cr>
```

This creates the user account named bcalkins using all default options. To see all of the default values, type:

```
# useradd -D <cr>
```

The system responds with the following:

```
group=other,1  project=default,3  basedir=/home
skel=/etc/skel  shell=/bin/sh  inactive=0
expire=  auths=  profiles=  roles=  limitpriv=
defaultpriv=  lock_after_retries=
```

These defaults can be modified by using the -D option with the useradd command as follows:

```
# useradd -D home=/export/home <cr>
```

The defaults for the useradd command are stored in the /usr/sadm/defadduser file. This file is created the first time the useradd command is executed using the -D option. This file can then be edited manually or modified using one of the following options along with the –D option: -g, -b, -f, -e, -A, -P, -u, -R, or -K (see the useradd command described earlier or the useradd man pages for a description of these options).

For example, to change the default group, execute the following command:

```
# useradd -D -g staff <cr>
```

You can also temporarily override the default options by specifying them on the command line when executing the useradd command. The following example creates a new login account for Bill Calkins:

```
# useradd -u 3000 -g other -d /export/home/bcalkins -m -s /bin/sh \
 -c "Bill Calkins, ext. 2345" bcalkins <cr>
```

The login name is bcalkins, the UID is 3000, and the group is other. In this example, you instruct the system to create a home directory named /export/home/bcalkins. The default shell is /bin/sh, and the initialization files are to be copied from the /etc/skel directory.

NOTE

Assigning a UID If the -u option is not used to specify a UID, the UID defaults to the next available number above the highest number currently assigned. For example, if UIDs 100, 110, and 200 are already assigned to login names, the next UID that is automatically assigned is 201.

The /usr/sadm/bin/smuser add command is the command-line equivalent of the SMC tool for adding a new user. The advantage of using smuser over the useradd command is that smuser interacts with naming services, can use autohome functionality, and is well suited for remote management.

The smuser command has several subcommands and options. The syntax to add a user using smuser is

```
smuser add  [ auth args ] - [subcommand args]
```

A few of the more common arguments that can be used with the add subcommand are described in Table 4.5.

TABLE 4.5 add Subcommand Arguments

Argument	Description
-c *<comment>*	A short description of the login, typically the user's name and phone extension. This string can be up to 256 characters.
-d *<directory>*	Specifies the home directory of the new user. This string is limited to 1,024 characters.
-g *<group>*	Specifies the user's primary group membership.
-G *<group>*	Specifies the user's secondary group membership.
-n *<login>*	Specifies the user's login name.
-s *<shell>*	Specifies the user's login shell.
-u *<uid>*	Specifies the user ID of the user you want to add. If you do not specify this option, the system assigns the next available unique UID greater than 100.
-x autohome=Y¦N	Sets the home directory to automount if set to Y.

The following example adds a new user named "bcalkins" and a comment field of "Bill Calkins ext. 100":

```
# /usr/sadm/bin/smuser add -n bcalkins -c "Bill Calkins Ext 100" <cr>
Authenticating as user: root

Type /? for help, pressing <enter> accepts the default denoted by [ ]
Please enter a string value for: password :: <ENTER ROOT PASSWORD>
Loading Tool: com.sun.admin.usermgr.cli.user.UserMgrCli from Sunfirel
Login to Sunfirel as user root was successful.
Download of com.sun.admin.usermgr.cli.user.UserMgrCli from Sunfirel
was successful.
```

After you press Enter, the system asks for the root password to authenticate your credentials before adding the new login account. The next step would be to set a password for the account using the passwd command as follows:

```
# passwd bcalkins <cr>
passwd: Changing password for bcalkins
New Password: <ENTER PASSWORD>
Re-enter new Password: <RE_ENTER PASSWD>
passwd: password successfully changed for bcalkins
```

Options that can be used with the passwd command are described in Table 4.6.

TABLE 4.6 passwd Options

Option	Description
-s *<name>*	Shows password attributes for a particular user. When used with the -a option, attributes for all user accounts are displayed.
-d <name>	Deletes password for name and unlocks the account. The login name is not prompted for a password.
-e *<name>*	Changes the login shell, in the /etc/passwd file, for a user.
-f <name>	Forces the user to change passwords at the next login by expiring the password.
-h *<name>*	Changes the home directory, in the /etc/passwd file, for a user.
-l *<name>*	Lock a user's account. Use the -d or -u option to unlock the account.
-N *<name>*	Makes the password entry for *<name>* a value that cannot be used for login but does not lock the account.
-u <name>	Unlocks a locked account.

To force a user to change his or her password at the next login, type

```
# passwd -f bcalkins <cr>
passwd: password information changed for bcalkins
#
```

To change a user's home directory, type

```
# passwd -h bcalkins <cr>
```

The system responds with

```
Default values are printed inside of '[]'.
To accept the default, type <return>.
To have a blank entry, type the word 'none'.
```

Enter the new home directory when prompted:

```
Home Directory [/home/wcalkins]: /home/bcalkins <cr>
passwd: password information changed for bcalkins
```

Modifying User Accounts from the Command Line

You use the `usermod` command to modify existing user accounts from the command line. You can use `usermod` to modify most of the options that were used when the account was originally created.

The following is the syntax for the `usermod` command:

```
usermod [ -u uid [-o]] [-g group] [ -G group [ ,  group...]]
[  -d dir  [-m]]  [-s shell]  [-c comment]  [-l new_name] [-f inactive]
[-e expire]  [-A  authorization2   [,  authorization]]  [-P  profile
[,  profile]] [-R role  [, role]] [-K key=value] <loginname>
```

The options used with the `usermod` command are the same as those described for the `useradd` command, except for those listed in Table 4.7.

TABLE 4.7 `usermod` Command Options

Option	Description
`-l <new-login-name>`	Changes a user's login name on a specified account
`-m`	Moves the user's home directory to the new location specified with the `-d` option

Additional options to the `usermod` command apply specifically to RBAC accounts.

The following example changes the login name for user `bcalkins` to `wcalkins`:

```
# usermod -d /export/home/wcalkins -m -s /bin/ksh -l wcalkins bcalkins <cr>
```

This example also changes the home directory to `/export/home/wcalkins` and default shell to `/bin/ksh`.

NOTE

Modifying the Home Directory When you're changing the home directory, unless the `-d` and `-m` options are used, existing files still must be manually moved from the old home directory to the new home directory. In all cases, symbolic links, application-specific configuration files, and various other references to the old home directory must be manually updated.

To set a user's account expiration date, you enter this:

```
# usermod -e 10/15/2006 wcalkins <cr>
```

The account is now set to expire October 15, 2006. Notice the entry made to the `/etc/shadow` file:

```
wcalkins:1luzXWgmH3LeA:13005::::::
```

The syntax of the `/etc/shadow` file is described later in this chapter, in the section "Where User Account Information Is Stored."

The `/usr/sadm/bin/smuser modify` command is the command-line equivalent of the SMC tool for modifying an existing user account.

Deleting User Accounts from the Command Line

You use the `userdel` command to delete a user's login account from the system. You can specify options to save or remove the user's home directory. The syntax for the `userdel` command is as follows:

```
# userdel [-r] <login-name>
```

`-r` removes the user's home directory from the local file system. If this option is not specified, only the login is removed; the home directory remains intact.

> **CAUTION**
>
> Make sure you know where the user's home directory is located before removing it. Some users have / as their home directory, and removing their home directory would remove important system files.

The following example removes the login account for `bcalkins` but does not remove the home directory:

```
# userdel bcalkins <cr>
```

The `/usr/sadm/bin/smuser delete` command is the command-line equivalent of the SMC tool for deleting an existing user account.

Adding Group Accounts from the Command Line

You use the `groupadd` command to add new group accounts on the local system. This command adds an entry to the `/etc/group` file. The syntax for the `groupadd` command is as follows:

```
groupadd [-g <gid>] -o <group-name>
```

Table 4.8 describes the `groupadd` command options.

TABLE 4.8 groupadd Command Options

Option	Description
-g <*gid*>	Assigns the GID <*gid*> for the new group.
-o	Allows the GID to be duplicated. In other words, more than one group with *group-name* can share the same GID.

The following example adds to the system a new group named acct with a GID of 1000:

```
# groupadd -g 1000 acct <cr>
```

NOTE

Assigning a GID If the -g option is not used to specify a GID, the GID defaults to the next available number above the highest number currently assigned. For example, if group IDs 100, 110, and 200 are already assigned to group names, the next GID that is automatically assigned is 201.

The /usr/sadm/bin/smgroup add command is the command-line equivalent of the SMC tool for creating a new group.

Modifying Group Accounts from the Command Line

You use the groupmod command to modify the definitions of a specified group. The syntax for the groupmod command is as follows:

```
groupmod [-g <gid>] -o [-n <name>] <group-name>
```

Table 4.9 describes the groupmod command options.

TABLE 4.9 groupmod Command Options

Option	Description
-g <*gid*>	Assigns the new GID <*gid*> for the group.
-o	Allows the GID to be duplicated. In other words, more than one group with *group-name* can share the same GID.
-n <*name*>	Specifies a new name for the group.

The following example changes the engrg group GID from 200 to 2000:

```
# groupmod -g 2000 engrg <cr>
```

Any files that had the group ownership of "engrg" are now without a group name. A long listing would show a group ownership of 200 on these files, the previous GID for the engrg group. The group 200 no longer exists on the system, so only the GID is displayed in a long listing.

The /usr/sadm/bin/smgroup modify command is the command-line equivalent of the SMC tool for modifying an existing group.

Deleting Group Accounts from the Command Line

You use the `groupdel` command to delete a group account from the local system. The syntax for the `groupdel` command is as follows:

```
groupdel <group-name>
```

The following example deletes the group named `acct` from the local system:

```
# groupdel acct <cr>
```

The `/usr/sadm/bin/smgroup delete` command is the command-line equivalent of the SMC tool for deleting an existing group.

Setting Up Shell Initialization Files

Objective:

When you set up user accounts, you can customize each user's session by using initialization files that are referenced each time the user logs in. This chapter describes how to administer each initialization file.

As a system administrator, when you're setting up a user's home directory, you need to set up the shell initialization files for the user's login shell (also called *user initialization files*). A *shell initialization file* is a shell script that runs automatically each time the user logs in. The initialization file sets up the work environment and customizes the shell environment for the user. The primary job of the shell initialization file is to define the user's shell environment, such as the search path, environment variables, and windowing environment. Each Unix shell has its own shell initialization file (or files), located in the user's home directory, as described in the following sections.

C Shell Initialization Files

C shell initialization files run in a particular sequence after the user logs in to the system. For the C shell, initialization files are run in the following sequence:

1. Commands in `/etc/.login` are executed.
2. Commands from the `$HOME/.cshrc` file (located in the user's home directory) are executed. In addition, each time the user starts a new shell or opens a new window in CDE, commands from `$HOME/.cshrc` are run.
3. The shell executes commands from the `$HOME/.login` file (located in the user's home directory). Typically, the `$HOME/.login` file contains commands to specify the terminal type and environment.

4. When startup processing is complete, the C shell begins reading commands from the default input device, the terminal.

Although it is not part of the initialization of the shell, when the C shell terminates, it performs commands from the `$HOME/.logout` file (if that file exists in the user's home directory).

Bourne Shell Initialization Files

Bourne shell initialization files run in a particular sequence after the user logs in to the system. For the Bourne shell, initialization files are run in the following sequence:

1. Commands in `/etc/profile` are executed.
2. Commands from the `$HOME/.profile` file (located in the user's home directory) are executed. Typically, the `$HOME/.profile` file contains commands to specify the terminal type and environment.
3. When startup processing is complete, the Bourne shell begins reading commands from the default input device, the terminal.

Korn Shell Initialization Files

Korn shell initialization files run in a particular sequence after the user logs in to the system. For the Korn shell, initialization files are run in the following sequence:

1. Commands in `/etc/profile` are executed.
2. Commands from the `$HOME/.profile` file (located in the user's home directory) are executed. Typically, the `$HOME/.profile` file contains commands to specify the terminal type and environment.
3. If the `$HOME/.kshrc` file is present, commands located in this file are executed. In addition, this initialization file gets read (and the commands get executed) every time a new Korn shell is started after login. The `.kshrc` file name is defined by the `ENV` variable. This filename is user definable, but is typically named `.kshrc` or `.kshenv`.
4. When startup processing is complete, the Korn shell begins reading commands from the default input device, the terminal.

Additional Shells Included with Solaris 10

Solaris 10 also includes, as part of the operating environment, the `bash`, `zsh`, and `tcsh` shells. These shells, especially `bash` and `tcsh`, are gaining popularity with system administrators and contain extra options and functions. You can find further details about these shells and their additional functionality by consulting the man pages for them.

NOTE

The Effect of CDE on Shell Initialization Files Initialization files are executed in the order specified for each of the shells, except when you're logging in to the CDE, where the `$HOME/.dtprofile` file is also run. If the `DTSOURCEPROFILE` variable is not set to `TRUE` in the `.dtprofile` file, the `$HOME/.profile` file will not be run.

When you're using CDE, it may be necessary to add the following lines in the `$HOME/.profile` to get the `.kshrc` file to work properly in the Korn shell:

```
set -ha
ENV=$HOME/.kshrc
```

Without this entry, aliases and environment variables might not get passed to subshells (that is, additional shells spawned by the Korn shell). Therefore, when you open a new window in CDE, alias and environment variables are set in the initial shell but are not set in subsequent shells, even though they are listed in the `$HOME/.kshrc` file. The preceding entries fix this problem.

Default Initialization Files

When a user logs in to the system, the user's login shell is invoked. The shell program looks for its initialization files in the correct order for the shell. The shell program then executes the commands contained in each file and, when it is finished, displays the shell prompt on the user's screen.

Default user initialization files (such as `.cshrc`, `.profile`, and `.login`) are created automatically in the user's home directory when a new user account is added. You can predefine the contents of these files, or you can choose to use the system default files. The Solaris 10 system software provides default user initialization files for each shell in the `/etc/skel` directory on each system. These files are listed in Table 4.10.

TABLE 4.10 Default Initialization Files

Filename	Description
`local.cshrc`	The default `.cshrc` file for the C shell
`local.login`	The default `.login` file for the C shell
`local.profile`	The default `.profile` file for the Bourne and Korn shells

You can use these initialization files as a starting point and modify them to create a standard set of files that provides a work environment that is common to all users. You can also modify them to provide a working environment for different types of users.

Customizing User Initialization Files

When a user logs in to a system, the shell initialization files determine the work environment. The shell startup scripts can be modified to set environment variables and directory paths that are needed by a specific user. These startup scripts are located in the user's home directory.

When you are setting up user initialization files, it might be important to allow the users to customize their own initialization files. You can do this by having centrally located and globally distributed user initialization files called *site initialization files*. With these files, you can continually introduce new functionality to all the user work environments by editing one initialization file.

The *local initialization file*, located in the user's home directory, allows user-specific configuration. A local initialization file lets users further customize their own work environment.

Site initialization files are located in the `/etc` directory and can be edited only by root. They are designed to distribute sitewide changes to all user work environments. Individual user initialization files are located in each user's home directory and can be customized by the owner of the directory. When a user logs in, the site initialization file is run first, and then the initialization file located in the user's home directory is run.

NOTE

Sitewide Shell Initialization Files You should not use system initialization files located in the `/etc` directory (`/etc/profile`, `/etc/.login`) to manage an individual user's work environment. Files in that folder are site initialization files, which are considered to be global files and are meant to be generic and used to set work environments for all users. The system runs these startup files first and then runs each user's startup files, located in the home directories.

The most commonly customized aspects of shell startup scripts are environment variables. Table 4.11 describes the most common environment and shell variables, including some that you might want to customize in user initialization files.

TABLE 4.11 Shell and Environment Variables

Variable	Description
LOGNAME	Defines the user's login name. This variable is set by the login program and wouldn't normally be modified.
HOME	Defines the path to the user's home directory. The `cd` command uses this variable when an argument is not specified. This variable is set by the login program and wouldn't normally be modified.
SHELL	Defines the path to the default shell. This variable normally isn't modified manually by the user.

TABLE 4.11 *Continued*

Variable	Description
LPDEST	Sets the user's default printer.
PWD	Is set to the current working directory. This variable changes automatically each time the user changes directories. This variable isn't modified manually by the user.
PS1	Defines the shell prompts for the Bourne and Korn shells.
PATH (or path in the C shell)	Lists, in order, the directories that the shell searches to find the program to run when the user enters a command. If the directory is not in the search path, users must enter the complete pathname of a command. The default PATH variable is automatically defined in .profile (Bourne or Korn shell) or .cshrc (C shell) as part of the login process. The order of the search path is important. When identical commands exist in different locations, the first command found with that name is used. For example, suppose PATH is defined (in Bourne and Korn shell syntax) as PATH=/bin:/usr/bin:/usr/sbin:$HOME/bin and a file named sample resides in both /usr/bin and $HOME/bin. If the user enters the command sample without specifying its full pathname, the version found in /usr/bin is used.
prompt	Defines the shell prompt for the C shell.
TERM (or term in the C shell)	Defines the terminal. This variable should be reset in /etc/profile or /etc/.login. When the user invokes a program that uses advanced terminal properties such as an editor, the system looks for a file with the same name as the definition of this environment variable. The system searches the directory /usr/share/lib/terminfo to determine the terminal characteristics.
MAIL	Sets the path to the user's mailbox.
MANPATH	Sets the search path for system man pages.
umask	Sets the default user mask. Although umask is a command and not a variable, it is used to set the file-mode creation mask of the current shell execution environment, as described in the section "The Default User Mask," later in this chapter.

TIP

Modifying the Shell Prompt Some users find it helpful to make their login name, the hostname, and the current directory part of the prompt. Here's how you set it up in the Korn shell:

```
PS1="$(whoami)@$(hostname) [\$PWD] #"
```

The resulting prompt looks like this:

```
root@Sunfirel [/usr/bin] #
```

Step by Step 4.5 shows how to modify the shell environment by changing some of the variables in the shell startup file. It suggests some changes and shows the shell-specific syntax to use.

STEP BY STEP

4.5 Verifying and Changing a User's Environment

1. Log in as the user. This enables you to see the user's environment as the user would see it. You can use **su -** *<username>* to achieve this.
2. Set the user's default path to include the home directory as well as directories or mount points for the user's windowing environment and applications. To change the path setting, add or modify the line for PATH.

   For the Bourne or Korn shell, this is the syntax:

   ```
   $ PATH=/<dirname1>:/<dirname2>:/<dirname3>:.; export PATH
   ```

   For example, you could enter the following line in the user's `$HOME/.profile` file:

   ```
   $ PATH=$PATH:/usr/bin:/$HOME/bin:/net/glrr/files1/bin:.;export PATH
   ```

   For the C shell, notice that in the syntax, the colons are replaced with spaces:

   ```
   $ set path =(/<dirname1> /<dirname2> /<dirname3> .)
   ```

   For example, you could enter the following line in the user's `$HOME/.cshrc` file:

   ```
   $ set path=($path /usr/bin $HOME/bin /net/glrr/files1/bin .)
   ```

NOTE

Modifying the PATH Variable Prefixing $PATH (Korn shell) or `$path` (C shell) appends changes to the user's path settings that are already set by the site initialization file. When you set the PATH variable with this procedure, initial path settings are not overwritten and are not lost. Also note the dot (`.`) at the end of the list to denote the current working directory. The dot should always be at the end of the path for users and should not be used in the path for root, as discussed in the section "Setting the Correct Path," later in this chapter.

3. Make sure the environment variables are set to the correct directories for the user's windowing environments and third-party applications. To do so, enter `env`, and you see the following:

   ```
   $env <cr>
   HOME=/export/home
   HZ=100
   LOGNAME=bill
   MAIL=/var/mail/bill
   PATH=/usr/bin:
   SHELL=/bin/sh
   TERM=xterm
   TZ=US/Michigan
   ```

4. Add or change the settings of environment variables.

   For the Bourne or Korn shell, the syntax is as follows:

   ```
   VARIABLE=<value>;export VARIABLE
   ```

   The following example sets the user's default mail directory:

   ```
   MAIL=/var/mail/bcalkins;export MAIL
   ```

   For the C shell, the syntax is as follows:

   ```
   setenv VARIABLE <value>
   ```

   The following example sets the history to record the last 100 commands in C shell:

   ```
   $ set history = 100 <cr>
   ```

The Home Directory

The *home directory* is the portion of a file system that is allocated to a user for storing private files. The amount of space you allocate for home directories depends on the kinds of files the user creates and the type of work performed. An entire file system is usually allocated specifically for home directories, and the users all share this space. As the system administrator, you need to monitor user home directories so that one user does not use more than his or her fair share of space. You can use disk quotas to control the amount of disk space a user can occupy. (Disk quotas are discussed in Chapter 1, "Managing File Systems.") Or you can use soft partitions, which are described in the *Solaris 10 System Administration Exam Prep: Exam CX-310-202* book.

A home directory can be located either on the user's local system or on a remote file server. Although any directory name can be used for a home directory, it is customary that home directories are named using this convention: `/export/home/<username>`. When you put the home directory in `/export/home`, automounter can make it available across the network in case the user logs in from several different stations. For a large site, you should store home directories on a server.

Regardless of where their home directories are located, users usually access them through a mount point named `/home/<username>`. When AutoFS is used to mount home directories, you are not permitted to create any directories under the `/home` mount point on any system. The system recognizes the special status of `/home` when AutoFS is active. For more information about AutoFS and automounter, refer to the *Solaris 10 System Administration Exam Prep: Exam CX-310-202* book where these topics are covered in detail.

To access a home directory anywhere on the network, a user should always refer to it as `$HOME`, not as `/export/home/<username>`. The latter is machine specific, and its use should be discouraged. In addition, any symbolic links created in a user's home directory should use relative paths (for example, `../../../x/y/x`) so that the links will be valid no matter where the home directory is mounted. The location of user home directories might change. By not using machine-specific names, you maintain consistency and reduce system administration.

Projects

The concept of *projects* was introduced in Solaris 8. Projects are included in Solaris 10, and they allow much-improved tracking of resources and usage. The project concept is extremely useful when multiple projects use the same system and are charged for their usage of the system. With projects, it is now simple to identify and subsequently charge each project based on the resources used. In addition, a system administrator supporting multiple projects can perform duties associated with those projects so that his or her time is also booked to the project requesting the service. The system administrator would do this by using the `newtask` command. (See the `newtask` man page for further details about this command.)

You establish projects by using the configuration file `/etc/project`. The following example shows the standard `/etc/project` file:

```
system:0::::
user.root:1::::
noproject:2::::
default:3::::
group.staff:10::::
```

As you can see from this example, all members of the `staff` group (`GID 10`) belong to the project `group.staff`.

You can edit this file to create new projects and assign users and groups of users to the projects. Accounting software can produce reports on usage based on the projects specified in the `/etc/project` file.

For further information on projects, see the man page entry for projects as well as the entry for the `projects` command, which lists the projects a user or group belongs to.

Name Services

If you are managing user accounts for a large site, you might want to consider using a *name service* such as Network Information Service (NIS), Network Information Service Plus (NIS+), or Lightweight Directory Access Protocol (LDAP). A name service lets you store user account information in a centralized manner instead of storing it in every system's `/etc` file. When you use a name service for user accounts, users can move from system to system, using the same user account without having sitewide user account information duplicated in every system's `/etc` file. Using a name service also promotes centralized and consistent user account information. NIS, NIS+, and LDAP are discussed in *Solaris 10 System Administration Exam Prep: Exam CX-310-202* book.

System Security

Objective:

Restrict access to data in files through the use of group membership, ownership, and special file permissions.

In addition to setting up user accounts, keeping the system's information secure is one of a system administrator's primary tasks. System security involves protecting data against loss due to a disaster or system failure. In addition, the system administrator must protect systems from the threat of unauthorized access and protect data on the system from unauthorized users. Bad disasters often come from authorized personnel—even system administrators—destroying data unintentionally. Therefore, the system administrator is presented with two levels of security: protecting data from accidental loss and securing the system against intrusion or unauthorized access.

The first scenario—protecting data from accidental loss—is easy to achieve with a full system backup scheme that you run regularly. Regular backups provide protection in the event of a disaster. If a user accidentally destroys data, if the hardware malfunctions, or if a computer program simply corrupts data, you can restore files from the backup media. (Backup and recovery techniques are covered in Chapter 7, "Performing System Backups and Restorations.")

The second form of security—securing the system against intrusion or unauthorized access—is more complex. This book cannot cover every security hole or threat, but it does discuss Unix security fundamentals. Protection against intruders involves the following:

- **Controlling physical security**—You need to limit physical access to the computer equipment.
- **Controlling system access**—You need to limit user access via passwords and permissions.
- **Controlling file access**—You need to limit access to data by assigning file access permissions.
- **Auditing users**—You need to monitor user activities to detect a threat before damage occurs.
- **Controlling network security**—You need to protect against access through phone lines, serial lines, or the network.
- **Securing superuser access**—You need to reserve superuser access for system administrator use only.

The following sections describe these facets of security.

Controlling Physical Security

Physical security is simple: You need to lock the door. You should limit who has physical access to the computer equipment to prevent theft or vandalism. In addition, you should limit access to the system console. Anyone who has access to the console ultimately has access to the data. If the computer contains sensitive data, you need to keep it locked in a controlled environment with filtered power and adequate protection against fire, lightning, flood, and other disasters. You should restrict access to protect against tampering with the system and its backups. Anyone with access to the backup media could steal it and access the data. Furthermore, if a system is logged in and left unattended, anyone who can use that system can gain access to the operating system and the network. You need to make sure your users log out or lock their screens before walking away. In summary, you need to be aware of your users' computer surroundings, and you need to physically protect them from unauthorized access.

Controlling System Access

Controlling access to systems involves using passwords and appropriate file permissions. To control access, all logins must have passwords, and those passwords must be changed frequently. *Password aging* is a system parameter that you set to require users to change their passwords after a certain number of days. Password aging lets you force users to change their passwords periodically or prevent users from changing their passwords before a specified interval. You can set an expiration date for a user account to prevent an intruder from gaining undetected access to the system through an old and inactive account. For a high level of security, you should require users to change their passwords periodically (for example, every six weeks or every three months for lower levels of security). You should change system administration passwords (such as root and any other user who has administrative privileges through an RBAC account) monthly or whenever a person who knows the root password leaves the company or is reassigned. Each user should have his or her own account, and no user should disclose his or her password to anyone else.

Several files that control default system access are stored in the `/etc/default` directory. Table 4.12 describes a few of the files in the `/etc/default` directory.

TABLE 4.12 Files in the `/etc/default` Directory

Filename	Description
`/etc/default/passwd`	Controls the default policy on password aging.
`/etc/default/login`	Controls system login policies, including the policy on root access. The default is to limit root access to the console.
`/etc/default/su`	Specifies where attempts to use `su` to become root are logged and where those log files are located. This file also specifies whether attempts to use `su` to become root are displayed on a named device (such as a system console).

You can set default values in the /etc/default/passwd file to control user passwords. Table 4.13 lists the options that can be controlled through the /etc/default/passwd file.

TABLE 4.13 Flags in /etc/default/passwd

Flag	Description
MAXWEEKS	Specifies the maximum time period for which a password is valid. The MAXWEEKS value can be overridden by entries in the /etc/shadow file.
MINWEEKS	Specifies the minimum time period before the password can be changed. The MINWEEKS value can be overridden by entries in the /etc/shadow file.
PASSLENGTH	Specifies a minimum password length for all regular users. The value can be 6, 7, or 8.
WARNWEEKS	Specifies a time period after which the system warns of the password's expiration date. This entry does not exist in the file by default, but it can be added. The WARNWEEKS value can be overridden by entries in the /etc/shadow file.

Additional controls have been added to Solaris 10 that can be set in the /etc/default/passwd file and are as follows:

NAMECHECK=NO — Sets the password controls to verify that the user is not using the login name as a component of the password.

HISTORY=0 — HISTORY can have a value from 0–26. Setting a value higher than 0 forces the passwd program to log up to 26 changes to the user's password. The value entered specifies the number of changes to log preventing a user from reusing the same password for up to 26 changes. When the HISTORY value is set to zero (0), the password log for all users will be removed the next time a user changes his password. No password history will be checked if the flag is not present or has zero value.

DICTIONLIST= — Causes the passwd program to perform dictionary word lookups.

DICTIONDBDIR=/var/passwd — The location of the dictionary where the generated dictionary databases reside. This directory must be created manually.

Complexity of the password can be controlled using the following parameters:

MINDIFF=3 — The old and new passwords must differ by at least the MINDIFF value.

MINALPHA=2 — Password must contain at least this number of alpha characters.

MINUPPER=0 — Password must contain at least this number of uppercase characters.

`MINLOWER=0`	Password must contain at least this number of lowercase characters.
`MAXREPEATS=0`	The password must not contain more consecutively repeating characters than specified by the `MAXREPEATS` value.
`MINSPECIAL=0`	Password must contain at least this number of special characters.
`MINDIGIT=0`	Password must contain at least this number of digits.
`MINNONALPHA=1`	Describes the same character classes as `MINDIGIT` and `MINSPECIAL` combined; therefore you cannot specify both `MINNONALPHA` and `MINSPECIAL` (or `MINDIGIT`). You must choose which of the two options to use.
`WHITESPACE=YES`	Determines whether whitespace characters are allowed.

NOTE

Privileged users, such as root, are not forced to comply with password aging and password construction requirements. A privileged user can create a null password by entering a carriage return in response to the prompt for a new password. Therefore privileged users should be extra vigilant not to use bad (that is, easy to guess) passwords.

As a system administrator, your job is to ensure that all users have secure passwords. A system cracker can break weak passwords and put an entire system at risk. You should enforce the following guidelines on passwords:

- Passwords should contain a combination of six to eight letters, numbers, or special characters. Don't use fewer than six characters.
- Use a password with nonalphabetic characters, such as numerals or punctuation.
- Mix upper- and lowercase characters.
- The password must not contain any sequences of four or more letters (regardless of how you capitalize them) that can be found in a dictionary. Also, reversing the order of the letters doesn't do any good because a standard way of cracking a password is to try all the words in a dictionary, in all possible upper-/lowercase combinations, both forward and backward. Prefixing and/or appending a numeral or punctuation character to a dictionary word doesn't help either; on a modern computer, it doesn't take too long to try all those possible combinations, and programs exist (and are easy to get) to do exactly that.
- Use a password that is easy to remember, so you don't have to write it down. Never write down a password or email or give your password to anyone! You should be able to type it quickly, without having to look at the keyboard. This makes it harder for someone to steal your password by watching over your shoulder.

- Nonsense words made up of the first letter of every syllable in a phrase, such as `swotrb` for "Somewhere Over the Rainbow," work well for a password. Choose two short words and concatenate them together with a punctuation character between them (for example, `dog;rain`, `book+mug`, `kid?goat`).

> **NOTE**
>
> **Dictionaries and Password Cracking** Be aware that in addition to the standard American or English dictionaries, there are also crackers' dictionaries. These are collections of common computer terms and phrases, names, slang and jargon, easily typed key sequences (such as `asdfg` and `123456`), and commonly used phrases that one might be tempted to use for a password. These crackers' dictionaries are frequently updated and shared; programs to crack passwords are distributed with copies of these dictionaries.

The following are poor choices for passwords:

- Proper nouns, names, login names, and other passwords that a person might guess just by knowing something about the user.
- The user's name—forward, backward, or jumbled.
- Names of the user's family members or pets.
- Information that is easily obtained about you, such as the following:

  Car license plate numbers

  Telephone numbers

  Social Security numbers

  Employee numbers
- Names related to a hobby or an interest.
- Seasonal themes, such as Santa in December.
- Any word in the dictionary (English or foreign language).
- Simple keyboard patterns (such as `asdfgh`).
- Passwords the user has used previously.
- A password with fewer than six characters.
- A password of all digits, or all the same letter. This significantly decreases the search time for a cracker.

You might also want to lock a user's account after a specified number of failed logins. You can accomplish this by uncommenting the following line in the `/etc/security/policy.conf` file:

```
LOCK_AFTER_RETRIES=YES
```

If a user fails to enter the correct password after the number of RETRIES, as specified in the /etc/default/login file, the account is locked.

Where User Account Information Is Stored

When no network name service is used, user account and group information is stored in files located in the /etc directory. Even when you're using a name service, these local files still exist in the /etc directory, but most of the account information is stored in the name server's database.

Most user account information is stored in the /etc/passwd file; however, password encryption and password aging details are stored in the /etc/shadow file. Only root can view the /etc/shadow file. Group information is stored in the /etc/group file. Users are put together into groups based on their file access needs; for example, the acctng group might be users in the Accounting Department.

Each line in the /etc/passwd file contains several fields separated by colons (:), and each line is formatted as follows:

```
<username>:<password>:<uid>:<gid>:<comment>:<home-directory>:<login-shell>
```

Table 4.14 defines the fields in the /etc/passwd file.

TABLE 4.14 Fields in the /etc/passwd File

Field	Description
<username>	Contains the user or login name. A username should be unique and should consist of one to eight letters (A–Z, a–z) and numerals (0–9), but no underscores or spaces. The first character must be a letter, and at least one character must be a lowercase letter.
<password>	Contains an x, which is a placeholder for the encrypted password that is stored in the /etc/shadow file and that is used by the pwconv command, which is described later in this section.
<uid>	Contains a UID number that identifies the user to the system. UID numbers for regular users should range from 100 to 60,000, but they can be as high as 2,147,483,647. All UID numbers should be unique. UIDs lower than 100 are reserved. To minimize security risks, you should avoid reusing UIDs from deleted accounts.
<gid>	Contains a GID number that identifies the user's primary group. Each GID number must be a whole number between 0 and 60,000 (60,001 and 60,002 are assigned to nobody and noaccess, respectively). GIDs can go as high as 2,147,483,647, but GIDs higher than 60,002 might not be supported across other Unix platforms. GID numbers lower than 100 are reserved for system default group accounts.
<comment>	Usually contains the user's full name.
<home-directory>	Contains the user's home directory pathname.
<login-shell>	Contains the user's default login shell.

Each line in the /etc/shadow file contains several fields, separated by colons (:). The lines in the /etc/shadow file have the following syntax:

```
<username>:<password>:<lastchg>:<min>:<max>:<warn>:<inactive>:<expire>
```

Table 4.15 defines the fields in the /etc/shadow file.

TABLE 4.15 Fields in the /etc/shadow File

Field	Description
<username>	Specifies the user or login name.
<password>	Might ontain one of the following entries: a 13-character encrypted user password; the string *LK*, which indicates an inaccessible (locked) account; or the string NP, which indicates no valid password on the account and you cannot login directly to this account.
<lastchg>	Indicates the number of days between January 1, 1970, and the last password modification date.
<min>	Specifies the minimum number of days required between password changes.
<max>	Specifies the maximum number of days the password is valid before the user is prompted to specify a new password.
<inactive>	Specifies the number of days that a user account can be inactive before it is locked.
<expire>	Specifies the absolute date when the user account expires. Past this date, the user cannot log in to the system.

You should refrain from editing the /etc/passwd file directly, and you should never edit the /etc/shadow file directly. Any incorrect entry can prevent you from logging in to the system. These files are updated automatically, using one of the Solaris account administration commands or the SMC, as described earlier in this chapter.

If you must edit the /etc/passwd file manually, you should use the pwck command to check the file. The pwck command scans the password file and notes any inconsistencies. The checks include validation of the number of fields, login name, UID, GID, and whether the login directory and the program to use as shell exist.

Some experienced system administrators edit the /etc/passwd file directly for various reasons, but only after creating a backup copy of the original /etc/passwd file. For example, you might want to restore an /etc/passwd file from backup—perhaps because the original was corrupted or was incorrectly modified.

Use the /usr/ucb/vipw command to edit the /etc/passwd file. /usr/ucb/vipw edits the password file while setting the appropriate locks, and does any necessary processing after the password file is unlocked. If the password file is already being edited, you will be told to try again later. /usr/ucb/vipw also performs a number of consistency checks on the password entry for root and will not allow a password file with a "mangled" root entry to be installed. It also checks the /etc/shells file to verify that a valid login shell for root has been defined.

After modifying the /etc/passwd file, you run the pwconv command. This command updates the /etc/shadow file with information from the /etc/passwd file.

The pwconv command relies on the special value of x in the password field of the /etc/passwd file. The x indicates that the password for the user already exists in the /etc/shadow file. If the /etc/shadow file does not exist, pwconv re-creates everything in it from information found in the /etc/passwd file. If the /etc/shadow file does exist, the following is performed:

- Entries that are in the /etc/passwd file and not in the /etc/shadow file are added to the shadow file.
- Entries that are in the /etc/shadow file and not in the /etc/passwd file are removed from the shadow file.

Each line in the /etc/group file contains several fields, separated by colons (:). The lines in the /etc/group file have the following syntax:

<group-name>:*<group-password>*:*<gid>*:*<user-list>*

Table 4.16 defines the fields in the /etc/group file.

TABLE 4.16 Fields in the /etc/group File

Field	Description
<group-name>	Contains the name assigned to the group. For example, members of the Accounting Department group might be called acct. A group name can have a maximum of nine characters.
<group-password>	Usually contains an asterisk or is empty. See the information on the newgrp command in the section "Effective UIDs and GIDs," later in this chapter.
<gid>	Contains the group's GID number, which must be unique on the local system and should be unique across the entire organization. Each GID number must be a whole number between 0 and 60,002, but it can be as high as 2,147,483,647. However, GIDs above 60,002 might not be supported on some Unix platforms. Numbers lower than 100 are reserved for system default group accounts, so don't use them. User-defined groups can range from 100 to 60,000 (60,001 and 60,002 are reserved and assigned to nobody and noaccess, respectively).
<user-list>	Contains a list of groups and a comma-separated list of usernames that represent the user's secondary group memberships. Each user can belong to a maximum of 16 secondary groups.

NOTE

UID Values Earlier Solaris software releases use 32-bit data types to contain the GIDs, but GIDs are constrained to a maximum useful value of `60,000`. Starting with Solaris 2.5.1 and compatible versions, the limit on GID values has been raised to the maximum value of a signed integer, or `2,147,483,647`. GIDs greater than `60,000` do not have full functionality and are incompatible with many Solaris features, so you should avoid using them.

By default, all Solaris 10 systems have default groups already defined in the `/etc/group` file. Those entries are outlined in Table 4.17:

TABLE 4.17 Default Group File Entries

Entry	Description
`root::0:`	Super user group
`other::1:root`	Optional group
`bin::2:root,daemon`	Administrative group associated with running system binaries
`sys::3:root,bin,adm`	Administrative group associated with system logging or temporary directories
`adm::4:root,daemon`	Administrative group associated with system logging
`uucp::5:root`	Group associated with `uucp` functions
`mail::6:root`	Electronic mail group
`tty::7:root,adm`	Group associated with `tty` devices
`lp::8:root,adm`	Line printer group
`nuucp::9:root`	Group associated with `uucp` functions
`staff::10:`	General administrative group
`daemon::12:root`	Group associated with routine system tasks
`sysadmin::14:`	Administrative group associated with legacy Admintool and Solstice AdminSuite tools
`smmsp::25:`	Daemon for Sendmail message submission program
`gdm::50:`	Group reserved for the GNOME Display Manager daemon
`webservd::80:`	Group reserved for WebServer access
`nobody::60001:`	Group assigned for anonymous NFS access
`noaccess::60002:`	Group assigned to a user or a process that needs access to a system through some application but without actually logging in
`nogroup::65534:`	Group assigned to a user who is not a member of a known group

Other than the staff group, you should not use these groups for users. Also, some system processes and applications might rely on these groups, so you should not change the GIDs or remove these groups from the /etc/group file unless you are absolutely sure of the effect on the system.

If you edit the /etc/group file manually, you should use the grpck command to verify all entries in the group file. This verification includes a check of the number of fields, the group name, and the GID, as well as a check to ensure that all login names appear in the password file.

A user can display the list of groups that they belong to by typing the groups command as follows:

```
# groups <cr>
```

Their primary and secondary groups are listed as follows:

```
root other bin sys adm uucp mail tty lp nuucp daemon
```

A user can change their primary group using the newgrp command as follows:

```
# newgrp other <cr>
```

The root user has changed his or her primary group from root to other as displayed by the id command:

```
# id <cr>
uid=0(root) gid=1(other)
```

Restricted Shells

System administrators can use restricted versions of the Korn shell (rksh) and the Bourne shell (rsh) to limit the operations allowed for a particular user account. Restricted shells are especially useful for ensuring that time-sharing users and users' guests on a system have restricted permissions during login sessions. When an account is set up with a restricted shell, users cannot do the following:

- Change directories to a directory above their home directory
- Set the $PATH variable
- Specify path or command names that begin with /
- Redirect output

You can also provide users with shell procedures that have access to the full power of the standard shell but that impose a limited menu of commands.

NOTE

Don't Confuse `rsh` You should not confuse the restricted shell `/usr/lib/rsh` with the remote shell `/usr/bin/rsh`. When you specify a restricted shell, you should not include the following directories in the user's path—`/bin`, `/sbin`, or `/usr/bin`. Doing so allows the user to start another shell (a nonrestricted shell).

Controlling File Access

Objective:

Restrict access to data in files through the use of group membership, ownership, and special file permissions.

After you have established login restrictions, you need to control access to the data on the system. Some users only need to look at files; others need the ability to change or delete files. You might have data that you do not want anyone else to see. You control data access by assigning permission levels to a file or directory.

Three levels of access permission are assigned to a Unix file to control access by the owner, the group, and all others. You display permissions by using the `ls -la` command. The following example shows the use of the `ls -la` command to display permissions on files in the `/users` directory:

```
# ls -la   /users <cr>
```

The system responds with this:

```
drwxr-xr-x   2   bill   staff   512    Sep 23 07:02        .
drwxr-xr-x   3   root   other   512    Sep 23 07:02        ..
-rw-r--r--   1   bill   staff   124    Sep 23 07:02        .cshrc
-rw-r--r--   1   bill   staff   575    Sep 23 07:02        .login
```

The first column of information displays the type of file and its access permissions for the user, group, and others. The `r`, `w`, `x`, and `-` symbols are described in Table 4.18. The third column displays the owner of the file—usually the user who created the file. The owner of a file (and the superuser) can decide who has the right to read it, to write to it, and—if it is a command—to execute it. The fourth column displays the group to which this file belongs—normally the owner's primary group.

TABLE 4.18 File Access Permissions

Symbol	Permission	Means That Designated Users...
r	Read	Can open and read the contents of a file.
w	Write	Can write to the file (that is, modify its contents), add to it, or delete it.
x	Execute	Can execute the file (if it is a program or shell script).
-	Denied	Cannot read, write to, or execute the file.

When you list the permissions on a directory, all columns of information are the same as for a file, with one exception. The r, w, x, and - found in the first column are treated slightly different for a directory than for a file, as described in Table 4.19.

TABLE 4.19 Directory Access Permissions

Symbol	Permission	Means That Designated Users...
r	Read	Can list files in the directory.
w	Write	Can add files or links to or remove files or links from the directory.
x	Execute	Can open or execute files in the directory and can make the directory and the directories beneath it current.
-	Denied	Cannot read, write, or execute.

You use the commands listed in Table 4.20 to modify file access permissions and ownership, but you need to remember that only the owner of the file or root can assign or modify these values.

TABLE 4.20 File Access Commands

Command	Description
chmod	Changes access permissions on a file. You can use either symbolic mode (letters and symbols) or absolute mode (octal numbers) to change permissions on a file.
chown	Changes the ownership and optionally the group ownership of a file.
chgrp	Changes the group ownership of a file.

Use the chmod command to change the permissions on a file to rwxrwxrwx as follows:

```
# chmod rwxrwxrwx <filename> <cr>
```

Use the chown command to change the ownership on a file to bcalkins as follows:

```
# chown bcalkins <filename> <cr>
```

Use the chgrp command to change group ownership of a file to engrg as follows:

```
# chgrp engrg <filename> <cr>
```

The chown command can be used to change both the user and group ownership of a file as follows:

```
# chown bcalkins:engrg <filename> <cr>
```

Sometimes you don't have access to a file or directory if you use your current login and you want to switch from one login ID to another. As long as you know the login name and password, you can quickly switch to that login by using the su command, which is described in the following section.

Effective UIDs and GIDs

EXAM ALERT

Be very familiar with the concept of effective user IDs. Understand the difference between the commands who am i **and** whoami **especially as they report information on the effective user ID described later in this chapter.**

The su (switch user) command enables a user to become another user without logging off the system. To use the su command, you must supply the password for the user you are attempting to log in as. The root user can run su to any account without being prompted for passwords.

System administrators often use the su command. For example, as a safety precaution, rather than using the root account as a regular login, you might use a regular, nonroot login whenever you are not performing administration functions. When root access is required, you can quickly become the superuser by using the su command. When you are finished performing the task, you can exit the superuser account and continue working using your normal, nonroot account.

If the user enters the correct password, su creates a new shell process, as specified in the shell field of the /etc/passwd file for that particular user. In the following example, user1 runs the su command to become user2:

```
# su user2 <cr>
```

An option to the su command is -. This option specifies a complete login. The specified user's .profile file is run, and the environment is changed to what would be expected if the user actually logged in as the specified user.

Without the - option, the environment is passed along from the original login, with the exception of $PATH, which is controlled by PATH and SUPATH in the /etc/default/su file (which is described later in this chapter). When the administrator uses su to access the root account from an untrusted user's account, the - option should always be used. If it is not used, the administrator is logged in as root, using a PATH variable defined for a nonroot user. This could result in the administrator inadvertently running commands specified in the user's PATH variable.

A user can also switch his or her primary group by using the `newgrp` command. The `newgrp` command logs a user in to a new group by changing a user's real and effective GIDs. The user remains logged in, and the current directory is unchanged. The execution of `su` and `newgrp` always replaces the current shell with a new shell. The execution of `newgrp` always replaces the current shell with a new shell, even if the command terminates with an error (unknown group). Any variable that is not exported is reset to null or its default value. Exported variables retain their values.

With no operands and options, `newgrp` changes the user's real and effective GIDs back to the primary group specified in the user's password file entry.

A password is demanded if the group has a password (in the second field of the `/etc/group` file), the user is not listed in `/etc/group` as being a member of that group, and the group is not the user's primary group. The only way to create a password for a group is to use the `passwd` command and then cut and paste the password from `/etc/shadow` to `/etc/group`. Group passwords are antiquated and not often used.

The Default User Mask

When a user creates a file or directory, the *user mask* controls the default file permissions assigned to the file or directory. The `umask` command should set the user mask in the `/etc/default/login` file or a user initialization file, such as `/etc/profile` or `.cshrc`. You can display the current value of the user mask by typing **`umask`** and pressing Enter.

The user mask is set with a three-digit octal value, such as `022`. The first digit of this value sets permissions for the user, the second sets permissions for the group, and the third sets permissions for others. To set the user mask to `022`, you type the following:

```
# umask 022 <cr>
```

By default, the system sets the permissions on a file to `666`, granting read and write permission to the user, group, and others. The system sets the default permissions on a directory or executable file to `777`, or `rwxrwxrwx`. The value assigned by `umask` is subtracted from the default. To determine what `umask` value you want to set, you subtract the value of the permissions you want from `666` (for a file) or `777` (for a directory). The remainder is the value to use with the `umask` command. For example, suppose you want to change the default mode for files to `644` (`rw-r--r--`). The difference between `666` and `644` is `022`, so you would use this value as an argument to the `umask` command.

Setting the `umask` value has the effect of granting or denying permissions in the same way that `chmod` grants them. For example, the command `chmod 644` denies write permission to the group, while others, such as `umask 022`, deny write permission to the group and others.

The *sticky bit* is a permission bit that protects the files within a directory. If the directory has the sticky bit set, a file can be deleted only by the owner of the file, the owner of the directory, or root. This prevents a user from deleting other users' files from public directories. A `t` or `T` in the access permissions column of a directory listing indicates that the sticky bit has been set, as shown here:

```
drwxrwxrwt   5 root     sys          458 Oct 17 23:04 /tmp
```

You use the chmod command to set the sticky bit as follows:

```
# chmod +t  /export/home/bcalkins/public <cr>
```

Where the 't' option toggles the sticky bit on. Or, the sticky bit can be set by specifying the octal value as follows:

```
# chmod 1755 /export/home/bcalkins/public <cr>
```

If the sticky bit is set on a file or directory without the execution bit set for the others category (non-user-owner and non-group-owner), it is indicated with a capital T.

Access Control Lists (ACLs)

Objective:

Restrict access to data in files through the use of group membership, ownership, and special file permissions.

ACLs (pronounced *ackls*) can provide greater control over file permissions when the traditional Unix file protection in the Solaris operating system is not enough. The traditional Unix file protection provides read, write, and execute permissions for the three user classes: owner, group, and other. An ACL provides better file security by allowing you to define file permissions for the owner, owner's group, others, and specific users and groups, and allows you to set default permissions for each of these categories.

For example, assume you have a file you want everyone in a group to be able to read. To give everyone access, you would give "group" read permissions on that file. Now, assume you want only one person in the group to be able to write to that file. Standard Unix doesn't let you set that up; however, you can set up an ACL to give only one person in the group write permissions on the file. Think of ACL entries as an extension to regular Unix permissions.

ACL entries are the way to define an ACL on a file, and they are set through the ACL commands. ACL entries consist of the following fields, separated by colons:

```
entry_type:uid¦gid:perms
```

Table 4.21 defines ACL entries.

TABLE 4.21 ACL Entries

ACL Field	Description
entry_type	The type of ACL entry on which to set file permissions. For example, entry_type can be user (the owner of a file) or mask (the ACL mask).
uid	The username or identification number.
gid	The group name or identification number.
perms	The permissions set on entry_type. Permissions are indicated by the symbolic characters rwx or an octal number, as used with the chmod command.

Setting ACL Entries

Set ACL entries on a file or directory by using the setfacl command:

```
$ setfacl -s user::perms,group::perms,other:perms,mask:perms,\
acl_entry_list filename ... <cr>
```

TIP

Setting Versus Modifying an ACL The -s option sets a new ACL, but also replaces an entire existing ACL with the new ACL entries. You should read any exam questions on this topic very carefully, as it can be easily confused with the -m option to modify an existing ACL.

The ACL entries that can be specified with the setfacl command are described in Table 4.22.

TABLE 4.22 ACL Entries for Files and Directories

ACL Entry	Description
u[ser]::<perms>	File owner permissions.
g[roup]::<perms>	File group permissions.
o[ther]:<perms>	Permissions for users other than the file owner or members of the file group.
m[ask]:<perms>	The ACL mask. The mask entry indicates the maximum permissions allowed for users (other than the owner) and for groups. The mask is a quick way to change permissions on all the users and groups. For example, the mask:r-- mask entry indicates that users and groups cannot have more than read permissions, even though they might have write/execute permissions. The mask permission will override any specific user or group permissions.
u[ser]:<uid>:<perms>	Permissions for a specific user. For <uid>, you can specify either a username or a numeric UID.
g[roup]:<uid>:<perms>	Permissions for a specific group. For <gid>, you can specify either a group name or a numeric GID.
d[efault]:u[ser]::<perms>	Default file owner permissions.
d[efault]:g[roup]::<perms>	Default file group owner permissions.
d[efault]:o[ther]:<perms>	Default permissions for users other than the file owner or members of the file group.
d[efault]:m[ask]:<perms>	Default ACL mask.
d[efault]:u[ser]:<uid>:<perms>	Default permissions for a specific user. For <uid>, you can specify either a username or a numeric UID.
d[efault]:g[roup]:<gid>:<perms>`	Default permissions for a specific group. For <gid>, you can specify either a group name or a numeric GID.

EXAM ALERT

ACL Entries Make sure you understand the ACL entries and how they work. It is quite common to get a question on the exam that gives you the ACL for a number of users/groups, such as Bill, Emily, and the "Accounts" group, and then asks which permissions does "Bill" have? Additionally, make sure you take into account the ACL mask.

The following example sets the user permissions to read/write, sets the group permissions to read-only, and other permissions to none on the `txt1.doc` file. In addition, the user bill is given read/write permissions on the file, and the ACL mask permissions are set to read/write, which means that no user or group can have execute permissions.

```
$ setfacl -s user::rw-,group::r--,other:---,mask:rw-,user:bill:rw-txt1.doc <cr>
```

In addition to the ACL entries for files, you can set default ACL entries on a directory that apply to files created within the directory. For example, I'll use the `setfacl` command to add execute privileges on the `/export/home/bholzgen` directory for user `bcalkins`. This privilege on a directory allows the user `bcalkins` to change to that directory and do a long listing with the `ls -l` command to display the files in the directory. Before I set the ACL on this directory, let's look at the default permission that currently exists on this directory:

```
# ls -ld /export/home/bholzgen <cr>
drwxr-xr-x   2 bholzgen   staff    512 Jul 30 12:41 bholzgen
```

Now, issue the command to set the default ACL privileges:

```
# setfacl -s user::rwx,g::r--,o:---,d:user::rwx,d:group::r--,d:o:---\
,d:m:r-x,d:user:bcalkins:r-x /export/home/bholzgen <cr>
```

NOTE

Default ACL Entries When you set default ACL entries for specific users and groups on a directory for the first time, you must also set default ACL entries for the file owner, file group, others, and the ACL mask.

Use the `getfacl` command with the `-d` switch to display the default ACL entries for the `/export/home/bholzgen` directory as follows:

```
# getfacl -d /export/home/bholzgen <cr>
```

The system responds with the following:

```
# file: /export/home/bholzgen
# owner: bholzgen
# group: staff
```

```
default:user::rwx
default:user:bcalkins:rwx        #effective:rwx
default:group::r--               #effective:r--
default:mask:rwx
default:other:---
```

Now, the only people allowed to change to the `/export/home/bholzgen` directory are `bholzgen` and `bcalkins`. No other members, except root, will be able to access this directory—not even members of the same group.

Checking the New File Permissions

Check the new file permissions with the `ls -l` command. The plus sign (+) to the right of the mode field indicates that the file has an ACL:

```
$ ls -l <cr>
 total 210
 -rw-r-----+    1 mike  sysadmin   32100   Sep 11 13:11 txt1.doc
 -rw-r--r--     1 mike  sysadmin   1410    Sep 11 13:11 txt2.doc
 -rw-r--r--     1 mike  sysadmin   1700    Sep 11 13:11 labnotes
```

Verifying ACL Entries

To verify which ACL entries were set on the file, use the `getfacl` command:

```
$ getfacl txt1.doc <cr>
```

The system responds with this:

```
# file: txt1.doc
# owner: mike
# group: sysadmin
user::rw-
user:bill:rw-        #effective:rw-
group::r--           #effective:r--
mask:rw-
other:---
```

Copying a File's ACL to Another File

Copy a file's ACL to another file by redirecting the `getfacl` output as follows:

```
# getfacl <filename1> | setfacl  -f  -  <filename2>
```

The following example copies the ACL from `file1` to `file2`:

```
# getfacl file1 | setfacl -f - file2 <cr>
```

Issuing the getfacl command, you can verify that the change has been made:

```
# getfacl file* <cr>

# file: file1
# owner: root
# group: other
user::rw-
user:bcalkins:rw-          #effective:rw-
group::r--                 #effective:r--
mask:rw-
other:---

# file: file2
# owner: root
# group: other
user::rw-
user:bcalkins:rw-                   #effective:rw-
group::r--                 #effective:r--
mask:rw-
other:---
```

Modifying ACL Entries on a File

Modify ACL entries on a file by using the setfacl command:

```
setfacl -m <acl_entry_list> <filename1> [filename2 ...]
```

Table 4.23 describes the arguments for the setfacl command.

TABLE 4.23 setfacl Arguments

Argument	Description
-m	Modifies the existing ACL entry.
<acl_entry_list>	Specifies the list of one or more ACL entries to modify on the file or directory. You can also modify default ACL entries on a directory. (See Table 4.22 for the list of ACL entries.)
<filename>	Specifies the file or directory.

Deleting ACL Entries from a File

To delete an ACL entry from a file, use the setfacl -d *<acl_entry_list>* command. The following example illustrates how to remove an ACL entry for user bcalkins on file1 and file2:

```
# setfacl -d u:bcalkins file1 file2 <cr>
```

Use the getfacl command, described earlier, to verify that the entries have been deleted.

Setting the Correct Path

Setting your path variable (`$PATH`) correctly is important; if you do not set it correctly, you might accidentally run a program introduced by someone else that harms the data or your system. That kind of program, which creates a security hazard, is called a *Trojan horse*. For example, a substitute `su` program could be placed in a public directory where you, as system administrator, might run it. Such a script would look just like the regular `su` command. The script would remove itself after execution, and you would have trouble knowing that you actually ran a Trojan horse.

The path variable is automatically set at login time through the `/etc/default/login` file and the shell initialization files `.login`, `.profile`, and/or `.cshrc`. Setting up the user search path so that the current directory (`.`) comes last prevents you and your users from running a Trojan horse. The path variable for superuser should not include the current directory (`.`).

> **NOTE**
>
> **Checking Root's Path** Solaris provides a utility called the *Automated Security Enhancement Tool (ASET)* that examines the startup files to ensure that the path variable is set up correctly and does not contain a dot (`.`) entry for the current directory. ASET is discussed later in this chapter.

The `setuid` and `setgid` Programs

When the *set-user identification* (`setuid`) permission is set on an executable file, a process that runs the file is granted access based on the file's owner (usually root) rather than on the user who created the process. This enables a user to access files and directories that are normally available only to the owner. For example, the `setuid` permission on the `passwd` command makes it possible for a user to modify the `/etc/passwd` file to change passwords. When a user executes the `passwd` command, that user assumes the privileges of the root ID, which is UID `0`. The `setuid` permission can be identified by using the `ls -l` command. The `s` in the permissions field of the following example indicates the use of `setuid`, and the second `s` indicates the use of `setgid`:

```
# ls -l /usr/bin/passwd <cr>
  -r-sr-sr-x   1 root     sys     10332 May  3 08:23 /usr/bin/passwd
```

Many executable programs must be run by root (that is, by the superuser) in order to work properly. These executables run with the UID set to `0` (`setuid=0`). Anyone running these programs runs them with the root ID, which creates a potential security problem if the programs are not written with security in mind.

On the other hand, the use of `setuid` on an executable program presents a security risk. A determined user can usually find a way to maintain the permissions granted to him or her by the `setuid` process, even after the process has finished executing. For example, a particular command might grant root privileges through `setuid`. If a user could break out of this command, he or she could still have the root privileges granted by `setuid` on that file. An intruder who accesses a system will look for any files that have the `setuid` bit enabled.

Except for the executables shipped with Solaris that have `setuid` set to root, you should disallow the use of `setuid` programs—or at least restrict and keep them to a minimum. A good alternative to using `setuid` on programs is to use an RBAC account, as described in the *Solaris 10 System Administration Exam Prep: Exam CX-310-202* book.

NOTE

Locating `setuid` Programs To find files that have `setuid` permissions, you should become superuser. Then you can use the `find` command to find files that have `setuid` permissions set, as in this example:

```
# find / -user root -perm -4000 -ls
```

The following is displayed:

```
  369    21 -r-sr-xr-x   1 root     sys          21384 Jan 22  2005
/usr/bin/sparcv9/newtask
  376    21 -r-sr-xr-x   2 root     bin          20672 Jan 22  2005
/usr/bin/sparcv9/uptime
  376    21 -r-sr-xr-x   2 root     bin          20672 Jan 22  2005
/usr/bin/sparcv9/w
   <output has been truncated>
```

The *set-group identification* (`setgid`) permission is similar to `setuid`, except that with `setgid` the process's effective GID is changed to the group owner of the file, and a user is granted access based on permissions granted to that group. By using the `ls -l` command, you can see that the file `/usr/bin/mail` has `setgid` permissions:

```
# ls -l /usr/bin/mail <cr>
-r-x--s--x   1 bin   mail   61076 Nov  8 2001  /usr/bin/mail
```

The following example illustrates how to set the UID on an executable file named `myprog1`:

```
# chmod 4711  myprog1 <cr>
```

You can verify the change by entering this:

```
# ls -l myprog1 <cr>
```

The system responds with this:

```
-rws--x--x   1   root   other   25   Mar   6   11:52   myprog1
```

The following example illustrates how to set the GID on an executable file named `myprog1`:

```
# chmod 2751 myprog1 <cr>
```

You can verify the change by entering this:

```
# ls -l myprog1 <cr>
```

The system responds with this:

```
-rwxr-s--x   1   root   other   25   Mar   6   11:58   myprog1
```

A user can set the UID or GID permission for any file he or she owns.

Auditing Users

The following sections describe a few of the commands used to view information about users who have logged in to the system.

Monitoring Users and System Usage

As a system administrator, you need to monitor system resources and watch for unusual activity. Having a method to monitor the system is useful, especially when you suspect a breach in security. For example, you might want to monitor the login status of a particular user. In that case, you could use the `logins` command to monitor a particular user's activities, as described in Step by Step 4.6.

STEP BY STEP

4.6 Monitoring a User's Activity

1. Become superuser.
2. Display a user's login status by using the `logins` command:

   ```
   # logins -x -l <username>
   ```

   For example, to monitor login status for the user `calkins`, enter the following:

   ```
   # logins -x -l calkins <cr>
   ```

   The system displays the following information:

   ```
   calkins      200      staff          10   Bill S. Calkins
                         /export/home/calkins
                         /bin/sh
                         PS 060508 10 7 -1
   ```

   The following is the information displayed in the output of the `logins` command:

Field	Description
`calkins`	The login name
`200`	The UID
`staff`	The primary group
`10`	The GID
`Bill S. Calkins`	The comment field of the `/etc/passwd` file

`/export/home/calkins`	The user's home directory
`/bin/sh`	The user's default login shell
`PS 060508 10 7 -1`	The password aging information: the last date the password was changed, the number of days required between changes, the number of days allowed before a change is required, and the warning period

You should monitor user logins to ensure that their passwords are secure. A potential security problem is for users to use blank passwords (that is, users using carriage returns for passwords) or no password at all. When an account does not have a password, the password prompt will not be presented at login. Simply enter the user name, and you are in. You can periodically check user logins by using the method described in Step by Step 4.7.

STEP BY STEP

4.7 Checking for Users with No Passwords

1. Become superuser.
2. Display users who have no passwords by using the `logins` command:

   ```
   # logins -p <cr>
   ```

   The system responds with a list of users who do not have passwords.

Another good idea is to watch anyone who has tried to access the system but failed. You can save failed login attempts by creating the `/var/adm/loginlog` file with read and write permission for root only. After you create the `loginlog` file, all failed login activity is automatically written to this file after five failed attempts. This file does not exist by default; you, as the system administrator, must create it. To enable logging to this file as root, you can create the file as follows:

```
# touch /var/adm/loginlog <cr>
```

Then set the permission on the file to **600**:

```
# chmod 600 /var/adm/loginlog <cr>
```

The `loginlog` file contains one entry for each failed attempt. Each entry contains the user's login name, the `tty` device, and the time of the failed attempt. If a person makes fewer than five unsuccessful attempts, none of the attempts is logged.

The following is an example of an entry in which someone tried to log in as root but failed:

```
# more /var/adm/loginlog <cr>
root:/dev/pts/5:Wed Jun 4 11:36:40 2008
root:/dev/pts/5:Wed Jun 4 11:36:47 2008
root:/dev/pts/5:Wed Jun 4 11:36:54 2008
root:/dev/pts/5:Wed Jun 4  11:37:02 2008
```

The `loginlog` file might grow quickly. To use the information in this file and to prevent the file from getting too large, you must check it and clear its contents occasionally. If this file shows a lot of activity, someone might be attempting to break in to the computer system.

Checking Who Is Logged In

You use the Solaris `who` command to find out who is logged in to a system. To obtain the information it gives you, the `who` command examines the `/var/adm/utmpx` and `/var/adm/wtmpx` files. The `utmpx` file contains user access and accounting information for the `who` command (as well as for the `write` and `login` commands). The `wtmpx` file contains the history of user access and accounting information for the `utmpx` file.

Without arguments, the `who` command lists the login account name, terminal device, login date and time, and where the user logged in. Here is an example:

```
# who <cr>
root        pts/3        May 11 14:47     (10.64.178.2)
root        pts/1        May 10 15:42     (sparc1.PDESIGNINC.COM)
root        pts/2        May 10 15:53     (sparc1.PDESIGNINC.COM)
root        pts/4        May 11 14:48     (pluto)
```

Table 4.24 lists some of the most common options used with the `who` command.

TABLE 4.24 Common Options Used with the `who` Command

Options	Description
`-a`	Processes `/var/adm/utmpx` or the named file with `-b`, `-d`, `-l`, `-p`, `-r`, `-t`, `-T`, and `-u` options turned on.
`-b`	Indicates the time and date of the last reboot, as shown in the following example: `who -b`
`-m`	Outputs only information about the current terminal. Here's an example: `who -m`
`-n` <x>	Takes a numeric argument, <x>, which specifies the number of users to display per line. <x> must be at least 1. The `-n` option can be used only with the `-q` option.
`-q`	Displays only the names and the number of users currently logged on. When this option, which stands for *quick who*, is used, all other options are ignored. The following is an example of the `-q` and `-n` options being used together: `who -q -n2`

TABLE 4.24 Common Options Used with the who Command

Options	Description

	The system responds with this:
	`root      bcalkins`
	`sburge      czimmerman`
	`# users=4`

-r	Indicates the current run level of the `init` process. Here's an example of the output returned by who -r: `   .      run-level 3  Oct 18 09:02     3      0  S`
-s	Lists only the name, line, and time fields. This is the default when no options are specified.

The `rusers` command is similar to the who command, but it can be used to list users logged in on a remote host. To use `rusers`, the `rpc.rusers` daemon must be running. Check whether the `rpc.rusers` daemon is running by typing

```
# svcs rusers <cr>
```

For more information on the `svcs` command, refer to Chapter 3.

To list users logged into other systems on your network, use the `rusers` command as follows:

```
# rusers -l <cr>
Sending broadcast for rusersd protocol version 3...
root         smokey:pts/1              Aug 12 10:07      29 (192.168.1.87)
root         ultra5:pts/1              Aug 12 17:33      (billsgateway.wca)
Sending broadcast for rusersd protocol version 2...
#
```

The whoami Command

The command `whoami` displays the effective current username. It is a lot like the who command used with the `am` and `i` options. These two options to the who command limit the output to describing the invoking user, which is equivalent to the `-m` option. `am` and `i` must be separate arguments.

`whoami` is a carryover from Berkeley Software Distribution (BSD) Unix. This old BSD command is found under the `/usr/ucb` directory with other BSD commands. `/usr/ucb/whoami` displays the login name that corresponds to the current effective UID. If you have used `su` to temporarily change to another user, `/usr/ucb/whoami` reports the login name associated with that user ID. For example, suppose you are logged in as `root` and issue the following `su` command to become `wcalkins`:

```
# su - wcalkins <cr>
```

Now issue the `who am i` command:

```
# who am i <cr>
```

The system reports that you are logged in as `root`. The `who am i` command looks up the entry for your current tty in the `utmpx` file:

```
root    pts/7         Oct 18 19:08
```

Next, you can issue the `/usr/ucb/whoami` command:

```
# /usr/ucb/whoami <cr>
```

The system reports your current effective UID as follows:

```
wcalkins
```

The whodo Command

The `whodo` command produces formatted and dated output from information in the `/var/adm/utmpx`, `/tmp/ps_data`, and `/proc/pid` files. It displays each user logged in and the active processes owned by that user. The output of the `whodo` command shows the date, time, and machine name. For each user who is logged in, the system displays the device name, UID, and login time, followed by a list of active processes associated with the UID. The process list includes the device name, process ID, CPU minutes and seconds used, and process name. You issue the `whodo` command as follows:

```
# whodo <cr>
```

The system responds with this:

```
Thu May 11 15:16:56 EDT 2008
holl300s

pts/3         root       14:47
    pts/3           505     0:00 sh
    pts/3           536     0:00 whodo

pts/1         root       15:42
    pts/1           366     0:00 sh
    pts/1           514     0:00 rlogin
    pts/1           516     0:00 rlogin

pts/2         root       15:53
    pts/2           378     0:00 sh

pts/4         root       14:48
    pts/4           518     0:00 sh
```

You use the `-l` option with the `whodo` command to get a long listing:

```
# whodo -l <cr>
```

The system responds with this:

```
  1:11pm  up 4 day(s), 18 hr(s), 20 min(s)  3 user(s)
User    tty       login@  idle   JCPU  PCPU  what
root    console  Mon 9am  22:00              /usr/dt/bin/sdt_shell -c   u
root    pts/4    Mon 9am  22:00    4         -ksh
```

The fields displayed are the user's login name; the name of the `tty` the user is on; the time of day the user logged in; the idle time (which is the time since the user last typed anything in *`hours:minutes`*); the CPU time used by all processes and their children on that terminal (in *`minutes:seconds`*); the CPU time used by the currently active processes (in *`minutes:seconds`*); and the name and arguments of the current process.

The `last` Command

The Solaris `last` command looks in the `/var/adm/wtmpx` file for information about users who have logged in to the system. The `last` command displays the sessions of the specified users and terminals in reverse chronological order, displaying the most recent login first. For each user, `last` displays the time when the session began, the duration of the session, and the terminal where the session took place. The `last` command also indicates whether the session is still active or was terminated by a reboot.

For example, the command `last root console` lists all of root's sessions, as well as all sessions on the console terminal:

```
# last root console ¦more <cr>
```

The system responds with this:

```
root       pts/1         192.168.1.27      Thu Jun  5 15:28   still logged in
root       pts/1         192.168.1.27      Wed Jun  4 13:54 - 16:41  (02:47)
root       console                         Wed Jun  4 12:05 - 12:05  (00:00)
root       pts/1         192.168.1.27      Thu May 15 10:25 - 08:54 (3+22:28)
root       console                         Tue May 13 13:48 - down  (16+02:27)
root       console                         Tue May 13 13:12 - down   (00:28)

wtmp begins Fri May  9 14:15
```

Controlling Network Security

Objective:

Control system security through restricting FTP access and using `/etc/hosts.equiv` and `$HOME/.rhosts` files, and SSH fundamentals.

The most difficult system administration issue to address is network security. When you connect your computer to the rest of the world via a network such as the Internet, someone can find an opening and breach your security. The following sections describe a few fundamental recommendations for tightening up a system in a networked environment.

Securing Network Services

Solaris is a powerful operating system that executes many useful services such as FTP and HTTP services. However, some of the services aren't needed and can pose potential security risks, especially for a system that is connected to the Internet. The first place to start tightening up a system is by disabling unneeded network services.

In past releases of Solaris, these services were managed by `inetd`, which obtained its instructions from the `/etc/inetd.conf` file. In Solaris 10, you'll notice that this file is substantially smaller because inetd is now started by the SMF, which is described in Chapter 3. The `inetd` daemon is configured using the `inetadm` command, which is described in the *Solaris 10 System Administration Exam Prep: Exam CX-310-202* book.

By default, `inetd` is configured for 40 or more services, but you probably need only some of them. You can list all of the network services and view their state with the `inetadm` command as follows:

```
# inetadm <cr>
ENABLED   STATE          FMRI
enabled   online         svc:/network/rpc/gss:default
enabled   online         svc:/network/rpc/mdcomm:default
enabled   online         svc:/network/rpc/meta:default
enabled   online         svc:/network/rpc/metamed:default
enabled   online         svc:/network/rpc/metamh:default
disabled  disabled       svc:/network/rpc/rex:default
enabled   online         svc:/network/rpc/rstat:default
enabled   online         svc:/network/rpc/rusers:default
disabled  disabled       svc:/network/rpc/spray:default
disabled  disabled       svc:/network/rpc/wall:default
 <output is truncated> . . .
```

Chapter 2 described the Secure by Default option of hardening the system and disabling many unneeded network services during the installation of the operating system. Chapter 3 described the `netservices` command which is a convenient method of disabling and enabling all unneeded network services except `ssh`.

You can individually deactivate unnecessary services by disabling them. For example, to disallow Telnet connections to the system, you would disable it as follows:

```
# inetadm -d telnet <cr>
```

To disable FTP, type

```
# inetadm -d ftp <cr>
```

You can verify that the FTP service has been disabled by typing

```
# inetadm|grep ftp <cr>
```

The system responds with

```
disabled  disabled       svc:/network/ftp:default
```

You also can type

```
# svcs ftp <cr>
```

The system responds with

```
STATE          STIME    FMRI
disabled        9:02:23 svc:/network/ftp:default
```

You can disable `nfs`, `spray`, `rexec`, `finger`, and many other Internet services in a similar manner.

It is critical that you turn off all unneeded network services because many of the services that are run by `inetd`, such as `rexd`, pose serious security vulnerabilities. `rexd` is a daemon that is responsible for remote program execution. On a system that is connected to the rest of the world via the Internet, this could create a potential entry point for a hacker. You should absolutely disable TFTP unless it's required, as with a JumpStart server. TFTP is managed by SMF, under the service identifier `svc:/network/tftp/udp6:default`. Administrative actions on this service, such as enabling, disabling, or requesting restart, can be performed using `svcadm`. Responsibility for initiating and restarting this service is delegated to `inetd`. Use `inetadm` to make configuration changes and to view configuration information for this service. The service status can be queried using the `svcs` command.

You might also want to disable `finger` so that external users can't figure out the usernames of your internal users—which would make breaking in much easier. Whether you keep the other services much depends on the needs of your site. Disable `finger` as follows:

```
# inetadm -d finger <cr>
```

Other services that you may want to consider disabling are

- `svc:/network/nfs/client:default`
- `svc:/network/nfs/server:default`
- `svc:/system/filesystem/autofs:default`
- `svc:/network/smtp:sendmail`
- `svc:/network/rpc/rusers:default`
- `lrc:/etc/rc2_d/S99dtlogin`
- `lrc:/etc/rc3_d/S76snmpdx`

The `lrc` services are disabled through their respective run control scripts.

The /etc/default/login File

One way to protect your system from unauthorized access—regardless of whether it's on the Internet or not —is via the /etc/default/login file. You need to make sure the following line is not commented:

```
CONSOLE=/dev/console
```

With this entry, root is allowed to log in only from the secure system console and not via the network by using telnet or rlogin. However, this entry does not disallow a user from using the su command to switch to root after logging in as a regular user if he or she knows the root password.

Modems

Modems are always a potential point of entry for intruders. Anyone who discovers the phone number to which a modem is attached can attempt to log in. Low-cost computers can be turned into automatic calling devices that search for modem lines and then try endlessly to guess passwords and break in. If you must use a modem, you should use it for outgoing calls only. An outgoing modem will not answer the phone. If you allow calling in, you should implement a callback system. A callback system guarantees that only authorized phone numbers can connect to the system. Another option is to have two modems that establish a security key between them. This way, only modems with the security key can connect with the system modem and gain access to the computer.

Trusted Hosts

EXAM ALERT

Although many sites restrict the use of trusted hosts, be prepared to answer several questions on the exam pertaining to trusted hosts. Be familiar with the .rhosts and the /etc/hosts.equiv files and how they affect commands like rlogin.

Along with protecting passwords, you need to protect your system from a root user coming in from across the network. For example, say systemA is a trusted host from which a user can log in without being required to enter a password. A user who has root access on systemA could access the root login on systemB simply by logging in across the network, if systemA is set up as a trusted host on systemB. When systemB attempts to authenticate root from systemA, it relies on information in its local files—specifically, /etc/hosts.equiv and /.rhosts. Because of the many risks posed by rlogin and other r commands, you should not use them. Instead, you should use the Secure Shell (SSH) commands, which are described in the section "The Secure Shell (ssh)," later in this chapter.

The /etc/hosts.equiv File

The /etc/hosts.equiv file contains a list of trusted hosts for a remote system, one per line. An /etc/hosts.equiv file has the following structure:

```
system1
system2 user_a
```

If a user attempts to log in remotely by using `rlogin` from one of the hosts listed in this file, and if the remote system can access the user's password entry, the remote system enables the user to log in without a password.

When an entry for a host is made in `/etc/hosts.equiv` (for example, the sample entry for `system1` shown earlier), the host is trusted and so is any user at that machine. If the username is also mentioned, as in the second entry shown in the previous example, the host is trusted only if the specified user is attempting access. A single line of + in the `/etc/hosts.equiv` file indicates that any host is trusted.

NOTE

Don't Trust Everyone Using a + in the `hosts.equiv` or `.rhosts` file is very bad practice and could pose a serious security problem because it specifies that *all* systems are trusted. You should get into the habit of listing the trusted systems and not using the + sign. Better yet, you should use a more secure alternative to `rlogin`, such as the Secure Shell (`ssh`).

TIP

Security and the `/etc/hosts.equiv` File The `/etc/hosts.equiv` file presents a security risk. If you maintain an `/etc/hosts.equiv` file on your system, this file should include only trusted hosts in your network. The file should not include any host that belongs to a different network or any machines that are in public areas. Also, you should never put a system name into the `/etc/hosts.equiv` file without a username or several names after it.

The `.rhosts` File

The `.rhosts` file is the user equivalent of the `/etc/hosts.equiv` file. It contains a list of hosts and users. If a host/user combination is listed in this file, the specified user is granted permission to log in remotely from the specified host without having to supply a password. Note that an `.rhosts` file must reside at the top level of a user's home directory because `.rhosts` files located in subdirectories are not consulted. Users can create `.rhosts` files in their home directories; this is another way to allow trusted access between their own accounts on different systems without using the `/etc/hosts.equiv` file.

The `.rhosts` file presents a major security problem. Although the `/etc/hosts.equiv` file is under the system administrator's control and can be managed effectively, any user can create an `.rhosts` file that grants access to whomever the user chooses—without the system administrator's knowledge.

NOTE

Disabling `.rhosts` and `hosts.equiv` Files To disable `.rhosts` and `/etc/hosts.equiv` access altogether while still allowing the `rlogin` protocol, you comment the lines that reference `pam_rhosts_auth.so.1` from `/etc/pam.conf`. This forces `rlogin` to use a password during authentication and effectively disables `in.rshd` and `in.rexecd`.

The only secure way to manage `.rhosts` files is to completely disallow them.

Restricting FTP

EXAM ALERT

Although many sites restrict the use of FTP and favor SFTP (secure FTP) in its place, be prepared to answer questions regarding `ftp` and be familiar with the files related to restricting FTP access.

File Transfer Protocol (FTP) is a common tool for transferring files across a network. Although most sites leave FTP enabled, you need to limit who can use it. Solaris contains various configuration files in the `/etc/ftpd` directory to control access to the FTP server. One of these files is a file named `/etc/ftpd/ftpusers`, which is used to restrict access via FTP. The `/etc/ftpd/ftpusers` file contains a list of login names that are prohibited from running an FTP login on the system. The following is an example of a default `/etc/ftpd/ftpusers` file:

```
# more /etc/ftpd/ftpusers <cr>

# ident "@(#)ftpusers   1.5     04/02/20 SMI"
#
# List of users denied access to the FTP server, see ftpusers(4).
#
root
daemon
bin
sys
adm
lp
uucp
nuucp
smmsp
listen
gdm
webservd
nobody
noaccess
nobody4
```

Names in the `/etc/ftpd/ftpusers` file must match login names in the `/etc/passwd` file.

NOTE

Root Access to FTP The default in Solaris 10 is to not allow FTP logins by root. It is dangerous to allow root access via FTP because that would allow anyone who knows the root password to have access to the entire system.

The FTP server `in.ftpd` reads the `/etc/ftpd/ftpusers` file each time an FTP session is invoked. If the login name of the user trying to gain access matches a name in the `/etc/ftpd/ftpusers` file, access is denied.

The `/etc/ftpd/ftphosts` file is used to allow or deny access to accounts from specified hosts. The following example allows the user `ftpadmin` to connect via FTP from the explicitly listed addresses `208.164.186.1`, `208.164.186.2`, and `208.164.186.4`; and deny the specified `ftpadmin` user to connect from the site `208.164.186.5`:

```
# Example host access file
#
# Everything after a '#' is treated as comment,
# empty lines are ignored
allow ftpadmin 208.164.186.1 208.164.186.2 208.164.186.4
deny ftpadmin 208.164.186.5
```

The file `/etc/shells` contains a list of the shells on a system. Whereas the `/etc/ftpd/ftpusers` file contains a list of users not allowed to use FTP, the `/etc/shells` file enables FTP connections only to those users running shells that are defined in this file. If this file exists and an entry for a shell does not exist in this file, any user running the undefined shell is not allowed FTP connections to this system.

The `/etc/shells` file does not exist by default. If the file does not exist, the system default shells are used. The following are the system default shells:

```
/bin/bash        /bin/tcsh        /usr/bin/ksh
/bin/csh         /bin/zsh         /usr/bin/pfcsh
/bin/jsh         /sbin/jsh        /usr/bin/pfksh
/bin/ksh         /sbin/sh         /usr/bin/pfsh
/bin/pfcsh       /usr/bin/bash    /usr/bin/sh
/bin/pfksh       /usr/bin/csh     /usr/bin/tcsh
/bin/pfsh        /usr/bin/jsh     /usr/bin/zsh
/bin/sh
```

You can create the `/etc/shells` file by using the `vi` editor and listing each shell that you want to be recognized by the system. The following is an example `/etc/shells` file:

```
# more /etc/shells <cr>
        /sbin/sh
        /bin/sh
        /bin/ksh
```

NOTE

`/etc/shells` May Deny Access If you don't list all the default shells in the `/etc/shells` file, as done in the previous example, users using those shells are not allowed access.

Securing Superuser Access

The Unix superuser (root) is immune from restrictions placed on other users of the system. Any Unix account with a UID of `0` is the superuser. All Unix systems have a default superuser login named root. The user of this account can access any file and run any command. This login is valuable because any user who might have gotten himself or herself into trouble by removing access permissions, forgetting his or her password, or simply needing a file from an area to which he or she doesn't have access can be helped by root.

However, root access can be dangerous. Root can delete anything, including the operating system. The root login is both dangerous and necessary. System administrators must not give the root password to anyone and should use it themselves only when required. If it becomes necessary to grant superuser privileges to non-root users, you should utilize `roles`, as described in the *Solaris 10 System Administration Exam Prep: Exam CX-310-202* book.

Restricting Root Access

Root access needs to be safeguarded against unauthorized use. You should assume that any intruder is looking for root access. You can protect the superuser account on a system by restricting access to a specific device through the `/etc/default/login` file. For example, if superuser access is restricted to the console, the superuser can log in only at the console, which should be in a locked room. Anybody who remotely logs in to the system to perform an administrative function must first log in with his or her login and then use the `su` command to become superuser.

Step by Step 4.8 describes the procedure for restricting root from logging in to the system console from a remote system.

STEP BY STEP

4.8 Restricting Root Access

1. Become superuser.
2. Edit the `/etc/default/login` file and uncomment the following line:

   ```
   CONSOLE=/dev/console
   ```

In Step by Step 4.8, you set the variable `CONSOLE` to `/dev/console`. If the variable `CONSOLE` were set as follows with no value defined, root could not log in from anywhere, not even from the console:

```
CONSOLE=
```

With the `CONSOLE` value set to nothing, the only way to get into the system as root is to first log in as a regular user and then become root by issuing the `su` command. If the system console is not in a controlled environment, the option of not being able to log in to the console as root might be useful.

Monitoring Superuser Access

Solaris can be set up to log all attempts to become superuser. The logs that contain this information are useful when you're trying to track down unauthorized activity. Whenever someone issues the `su` command to switch from being a user to being root, this activity is logged in the file `/var/adm/sulog`. The `sulog` file lists all uses of the `su` command—not only those used to switch from being a user to being superuser. The entries in the `sulog` file show the date and time the command was entered, whether the command was successful, the port from which the command was issued, and the name of the user and the switched identity.

To monitor who is using the `su` command, the `sulog` logging utility must be turned on in the `/etc/default/su` file. By default, `su` logging is enabled. Step by Step 4.9 describes how to turn on logging of the `su` command if it has been disabled.

STEP BY STEP

4.9 Monitoring Superuser Access

1. Become superuser.
2. Edit the `/etc/default/su` file and uncomment the following line:

```
SULOG=/var/adm/sulog
```

Through the `/etc/default/su` file, you can also set up the system to display a message on the console each time an attempt is made to use the `su` command to gain superuser access from a remote system. This is a good way to immediately detect when someone is trying to gain superuser access to the system on which you are working. Step by Step 4.10 describes how to display root access attempts to the console.

STEP BY STEP

4.10 Monitoring Superuser Access Attempts

1. Become superuser.
2. Edit the `/etc/default/su` file and uncomment the following line:

```
CONSOLE=/dev/console
```

3. Use the `su` command to become root. Verify that a message is printed on the system console.

The Secure Shell (`ssh`)

The Secure Shell (`ssh`) enables users to securely access a remote system over an insecure network. You use the Secure Shell to do the following:

- Log in to a remote system (by using `ssh`).
- Copy files over the network between hosts (by using `scp` or `sftp`).

Before the Secure Shell was available, remote connections were—and still can be—handled via `rlogin`, `rsh`, and `rcp`. These commands create insecure connections and are prone to security risks.

With the Secure Shell, you establish secure communication between two hosts on an insecure network. The two hosts are referred to as the *client* (the host that requests the connection) and the *server* (the host being connected to). The Secure Shell daemon, `sshd`, starts up on each host at system boot, when the `svc:/network/ssh:default` service has been enabled by SMF. The `sshd` daemon listens for connections, and it handles the encrypted authentication exchange between the hosts. When authentication is complete, the user can execute commands and copy files remotely.

The `ssh` on the client side is controlled by the `/etc/ssh/ssh_config` file and by `ssh` command line options. The `ssh_config` file controls which types of authentication are permitted for accessing the server. Optionally, a user can also provide `ssh` settings in his or her own `$HOME/.ssh/config` file.

The `sshd` on the server side is controlled by the `/etc/ssh/sshd_config` file, which is controlled by the system administrator.

Normally, each user wanting to use SSH with authentication runs the `ssh-keygen` command once to create the authentication key in `$HOME/.ssh/identity`, `$HOME/.ssh/id_dsa`, or `$HOME/.ssh/id_rsa`. The client maintains the private key, and the server is provided with the public key that is needed to complete authentication. Public-key authentication is a stronger type of authentication than typical password authentication because the private key never travels over the network. To create a public/private key for public key authentication, follow Step by Step 4.11.

STEP BY STEP

4.11 Setting Up Public Key Authentication for Solaris Secure Shell

In the following step by step, you'll set up Public Key Authentication so that `bcalkins` can log in to a remote host using `ssh`. For this step by step, you'll need two systems. One will be the client, and the other will be the remote host.

1. Make sure both systems have a user account named `bcalkins`, a password assigned to the account, and an established home directory named `/export/home/bcalkins`.
2. Make sure each account has a `.ssh` directory in the `/export/home/bcalkins` home directory. If not, you can create the `.ssh` directory by running the `ssh-keygen` command described in step 7.
3. As root, enable host-based authentication on the client by adding the following line to the `/etc/ssh/ssh_config` file:

```
HostbasedAuthentication yes
```

4. On the remote host, enable host based authentication by adding the following line to the `/etc/ssh/sshd_config` file:

```
HostbasedAuthentication yes
```

5. Start up `sshd` on the remote host if it is not currently running by typing

```
# svcadm svc:/network/ssh:default <cr>
```

If the `ssh` service is already running, restart it.

6. On the remote host, ensure that the `sshd` daemon can access the list of trusted hosts by setting `IgnoreRhosts` to no in the `/etc/ssh/sshd_config` file as follows

```
IgnoreRhosts no
```

7. On the client, log in as `bcalkins` and create the client's public key. To generate the public key on the client, issue the following command:

```
# ssh-keygen -t rsa <cr>
```

Use the `-t` option to specify the type of algorithm; `rsa`, `dsa`, or `rsa1`. The system responds with

```
Generating public/private rsa key pair.
Enter file in which to save the key (//.ssh/id_rsa):
```

When you press **Enter**, the system responds with

```
Created directory '/export/home/bcalkins/.ssh'.
Enter passphrase(empty for no passphrase):
```

The `passphrase` is used for encrypting the private key. A good `passphrase` is 10–30 characters long, mixes alphabetic and numeric characters, and avoids simple English prose and English names. A carriage return entry means that no `passphrase` is used; this type of blank `passphrase` is strongly discouraged for user accounts. The `passphrase` is not displayed when you type it in, as shown here:

```
Enter same passphrase again:
```

Enter the `passphrase` again to confirm it. The system responds with

```
Your identification has been saved in /export/home/bcalkins/.ssh/id_rsa.
Your public key has been saved in /export/home/bcalkins/.ssh/id_rsa.pub.
```

```
The key fingerprint is:
c9:8e:d8:f9:69:6e:01:e7:c4:82:05:8a:8e:d3:03:56 root@ultra5
```

8. The key fingerprint is displayed as a colon-separated series of two-digit hexadecimal values. You should check to make sure the path to the key is correct. In this example, the path is `/export/home/bcalkins/.ssh/id_rsa.pub`. At this point, you have created a public/private key pair. Now, copy the public key and append the key to the `$HOME/.ssh/authorized_keys` file in your home directory on the remote host.

9. When the public key has been created on the client and copied to the remote host, you can start using the Secure Shell to log in to the remote system by typing this line, where *<hostname>* is the name of the remote host that you want to connect to:

   ```
   # ssh <hostname>
   ```

   The first time you run `ssh`:

   ```
   # ssh 192.168.0.252 <cr>
   ```

   you're prompted with questions regarding the authenticity of the remote host as follows:

   ```
   The authenticity of host '192.168.0.252' can't be established.
    RSA key fingerprint in md5 is: \
   78:28:11:cb:41:81:a2:73:50:5a:d4:49:bb:12:85:03
    Are you sure you want to continue connecting(yes/no)? yes
   ```

   This is a normal message for initial connections to the remote host. If you enter `yes`, the system responds with

   ```
   Warning: \
   Permanently added '192.168.0.252' (RSA) to the list of known hosts.
   Enter passphrase for key '/export/home/bcalkins/.ssh/id_rsa':
   ```

   After you enter your `passphrase`, the system will log you into the remote host.

   ```
   Last login: Wed Jun 4 20:43:57 2008 from Sunfire1
   Sun Microsystems Inc.   SunOS 5.10      Generic January 2005
   ```

To copy files by using the Secure Shell, you start the secure copy program by typing the `scp` command, using the following syntax:

```
scp <sourcefile> <username>@<hostname>:</destinationdir>
```

Table 4.25 describes the arguments to the `scp` command.

TABLE 4.25 scp Command Arguments

Argument	Description
<sourcefile>	The name of the local file that you want to copy
<username>	The username on the remote host to which you want to connect
<hostname>	The name of the remote system to which the file will be copied
<destinationdir>	The name of the directory on the remote host to which you will copy the file

You should type the secure `passphrase` when prompted. The system responds by displaying the following:

- The filename
- The percentage of the file transferred as it is being copied
- The quantity of data transferred as it is being transferred
- The estimated time of arrival when the entire file will be copied to the remote directory

This example copies the file named `file1` to the home directory of `bcalkins` on the remote host:

```
# scp file1 bcalkins@192.168.0.252:~ <cr>
```

The system responds with this:

```
Password:
```

If you enter the user login password, you are then logged in to the remote host:

```
file1  100%  |*************************************| 12540  0:00
```

For more information on using the Secure Shell, refer to the `ssh` and `sshd` man pages.

ASET

The Solaris 10 system software includes ASET (Automated Security Enhancement Tool), which helps you monitor and control system security by automatically performing tasks that you would otherwise do manually. ASET performs the following seven tasks, each of which makes specific checks and adjustments to system files and permissions to ensure system security:

- Verifies appropriate system file permissions
- Verifies system file contents

- Checks the consistency and integrity of /etc/passwd and /etc/group file entries
- Checks the contents of system configuration files
- Checks environment files (.profile, .login, and .cshrc)
- Verifies appropriate electrically erasable programmable read-only memory (EEPROM) settings
- Ensures that the system can be safely used as a network relay

The ASET security package provides automated administration tools that let you control and monitor a system's security. You specify a low, medium, or high security level at which ASET runs. At each higher level, ASET's file-control functions increase to reduce file access and tighten system security.

ASET tasks are disk intensive and can interfere with regular activities. To minimize their impact on system performance, you should schedule ASET to run when the system activity level is lowest—for example, once every 24 or 48 hours, at midnight.

The syntax for the aset command is as follows:

```
/usr/aset/aset -l <level> -d <pathname>
```

Table 4.26 describes the aset command options.

TABLE 4.26 aset Command Options

Option	Description
<level>	Specifies the level of security. Valid values are low, medium, and high: **low**—This level ensures that attributes of system files are set to standard release values. At this level, ASET performs several checks and reports potential security weaknesses. At this level, ASET takes no action and does not affect system services. **medium**—This level provides adequate security control for most environments. At this level, ASET modifies some of the settings of system files and parameters, restricting system access to reduce the risks from security attacks. ASET reports security weaknesses and any modifications that it makes to restrict access. At this level, ASET does not affect system services. **high**—This level renders a highly secure system. At this level, ASET adjusts many system files and parameter settings to minimum access permissions. Most system applications and commands continue to function normally, but at this level, security considerations take precedence over other system behavior.
<pathname>	Specifies the working directory for ASET. The default is /usr/aset.

The following example runs ASET at low security, using the default working directory /usr/aset:

```
# /usr/aset/aset -l low <cr>
======= ASET Execution Log =======
ASET running at security level low
Machine = Sunfirel; Current time = 0530_14:03
aset: Using /usr/aset as working directory
Executing task list ...
        firewall
        env
        sysconf
        usrgrp
        tune
        cklist
        eeprom
All tasks executed. Some background tasks may still be running.
Run /usr/aset/util/taskstat to check their status:
     /usr/aset/util/taskstat     [aset_dir]
where aset_dir is ASET's operating directory,currently=/usr/aset.
When the tasks complete, the reports can be found in:
     /usr/aset/reports/latest/*.rpt
You can view them by:
     more /usr/aset/reports/latest/*.rpt
#
```

Common-Sense Security Techniques

A system administrator can have the best system security measures in place, but without the users' cooperation, system security may be compromised. The system administrator must teach common-sense rules regarding system security, such as the following:

- Use proper passwords. Countless sites use weak passwords such as `admin` or `supervisor` for their root accounts.
- Don't give your password to anyone, no matter who the person says he or she is. One of the best system crackers of our time said that he would simply pose as a system support person, ask a user for a password, and get free reign with the system.
- Only give out a password to a known, trusted person. Users should know that no one would ever email or call asking for the password.
- If you walk away from a system, log out or lock the screen.
- Don't connect modems to the system without approval from the system administrator.

Summary

This chapter describes how to add, modify, and remove user accounts using both the SMC and the command line. The GUI of the SMC makes managing user accounts much easier than using the command-line method.

This chapter also describes the user shell initialization files. It describes how to use these files to customize the user work environment. In addition, this chapter describes many of the default shell environment variables that control the user shell environment.

This chapter also discusses fundamental concepts in system security. When you're considering security, you need to begin by securing the hardware in a safe location. Remember that anyone who has physical access to a computer can access the operating system and data, regardless of how secure you've made everything else.

Keep your data secure by controlling the user logins on the system. You should make sure that users have secure passwords and are not making their logins and passwords public. You should implement password aging and restricted shells where they make sense.

You should set up file and directory permissions to ensure that users have access to only the data that they are authorized to see. You should utilize secure `umask` values and, if necessary, ACLs. You should monitor all user activities by using the Solaris utilities described in this chapter. Finally, you should not set `setuid` and `setgid` permissions unless absolutely necessary.

If your system is on a network, you should implement the network security measures that are described in this chapter. You should turn off unneeded services, using the "deny first, then allow" rule. In other words, you should turn off as many services and applications as possible, and then you should selectively turn on those that are essential. You should utilize trusted systems carefully. Also, you should keep your operating system security patches up-to-date. As new threats are discovered, you should quickly fix them by installing security patches as they become available. Chapter 2, "Installing the Solaris 10 Operating Environment," describes the process of obtaining and loading system patches.

In this chapter you have learned about securing the superuser password. You need to keep it under tight control and make sure that it is never made available to anyone except those who are authorized. You should limit using the superuser login unless the task to be performed requires root privileges. The *Solaris 10 System Administration Exam Prep: Exam CX-310-202* book describes RBAC, which is a great alternative to giving out the root password to system operators and junior-level administrators.

Key Terms

- ACL
- ASET
- Default shell
- Effective GID
- File access permissions
- GID
- Group
- High ASET security
- Home directory
- Login shell
- Low ASET security
- Medium ASET security
- Network service
- Password aging
- Password encryption
- Primary group
- Restricted shell
- Secondary group
- Secure Shell
- Set-user identification permission
- Set-group identification permission
- Shell variable
- Sticky bit
- Trusted host
- UID
- User initialization file
- User mask

Exercises

4.1 Managing User Accounts

In this exercise, you use the SMC to add new users to your system, lock user accounts, and set up password aging.

Estimated time: 20 minutes

1. After the SMC GUI appears, use the SMC to add the following list of users:

Login	Password	UID	Pri GID	Secondary GID
`user3`	`trng`	1003	10	14
`user4`	`trng`	1004	10	14
`user5`	`trng`	1005	10	
`locked1`	(lock accnt)	1006	10	
`nopass1`	(no password)	1008	10	

2. Log out.
3. Try logging in as the user `locked1`.

4.2 User Initialization Files

In this exercise, you work with user initialization files.

Estimated time: 20 minutes

1. Use the `vi` editor to edit the `/etc/skel/local.profile` file by adding the following entries and setting the following variables:

```
EDITOR=/usr/bin/vi; export EDITOR
PATH=$PATH:/usr/lib/lp; export EDITOR
```

2. Use the SMC to create a new user called `user9` that uses the Korn shell. Log in as `user9` and verify that all the variables you set in `/etc/skel/local.profile` are set correctly in the user's environment by typing the following:

```
# env <cr>
```

3. Create a `.profile` file for `user9` that includes two aliases and sets the primary prompt to display the current working directory. Use the `vi` editor to add the following three lines to the `.profile` file that is located in `user9`'s home directory:

```
alias del='rm -i'
alias hi='echo hello'
PS1=\$PWD' $'
```

4. Log out and log back in as the same user to verify that the `.profile` file works. Do you have a new shell prompt?
5. Verify that your new aliases are defined by typing the following:

```
# alias <cr>
```

6. Log out and log back in again as root.
7. Use `useradd` to create a new user named `user10`, specify the Korn shell as the default shell, and assign the password `trng`:

```
# useradd -u 1010 -g 10 -d /export/home/user10 -m \
-s /bin/ksh -c "Solaris Student" user10 <cr>
# passwd user10 <cr>
 New Passwd:
 Re-enter new passwd:
```

8. Log out and log back in as `user10`. Record the list of initialization files in your home directory by issuing the `ls -la` command. Which of these files is the same as `/etc/skel/local.profile`?

9. Copy `/etc/skel/local.profile` to `.profile`.

10. Log out and log back in as `user10`. Verify that the variables set in the `.profile` file for `user9` are also set in `user10`'s login (`PATH` and `EDITOR`). Are they correct?

4.3 Monitoring Users

In this exercise, you use the various utilities to monitor users who are accessing your system.

Estimated time: 5 minutes

1. Log in as root.

2. Create a file called `loginlog` in the `/var/adm` directory and set the file permission to 600:

```
# cd /var/adm <cr>
# touch loginlog <cr>
# chmod 600 loginlog <cr>
```

3. Log out and log back in. Do not log in using the CDE; log in using the command line.

4. Enter `root` after the login prompt and supply an incorrect password. Do this five times. After the fifth attempt, log in as root using the correct password and examine the `/var/adm/loginlog` file:

```
# more /var/adm/loginlog <cr>
```

5. Use the `finger` command to display information about the user named `user9`:

```
# finger user9 <cr>
# finger -m user9 <cr>
```

6. User the `finger` command to display information about a user on another system:

```
# finger user9@<hostname> <cr>
# finger -m user9@<hostname> <cr>
```

7. Use the `last` command to display user and reboot activity.

8. Use the `logins` command to obtain information about the `user9` login account:

```
# logins -x -l user9 <cr>
```

4.4 File Access

In this exercise, you use Unix permissions to control file access by allowing/disallowing access to files and directories.

Estimated time: 20 minutes

1. Log in as `user9`.
2. Enter the `umask` command to determine your current `umask` value:

   ```
   # umask <cr>
   ```

   If the `umask` is not `002`, change it by entering the following:

   ```
   # umask 002 <cr>
   ```

3. Create a file called `file1` in your home directory:

   ```
   # cd $HOME <cr>
   # touch file1 <cr>
   ```

4. Enter `ls -l` to see the default permission that was assigned to the `file1` file.
5. Set your `umask` to `022`:

   ```
   # umask 022 <cr>
   ```

6. Create a file named `file2` and look at the default permission value:

   ```
   # touch file2 <cr>
   # ls -l <cr>
   ```

7. Create a new user called `newuser`:

   ```
   # useradd -u 3001 -g 10 -d /export/home/user20 -m \
   -s /bin/ksh -c "Temporary User" user20 <cr>
   ```

8. Set the password for `user20`:

   ```
   # passwd user20 <cr>
   ```

9. Log out and log back in as `user9`. You are placed in your home directory, `/export/home/user9`.
10. Create a new file named `file10` and list the permissions:

    ```
    # touch file10 <cr>
    # ls -l <cr>
    ```

11. Use `chmod` to set the UID permissions on `file10` and list the permissions:

    ```
    # chmod 4555 file10 <cr>
    # ls -l <cr>
    ```

12. Use `chmod` to set the UID and GID permissions on `file10`, and then display the permissions:

    ```
    # chmod 6555 file10 <cr>
    # ls -l <cr>
    ```

    What changes?

13. Use chmod to remove all execute permissions from file10, and then display the new permissions:

```
# chmod 6444 file10 <cr>
# ls -l <cr>
```

14. List the directory permissions on /tmp:

```
# ls -ld /tmp <cr>
```

Note that the sticky bit is set on /tmp.

15. As user9, change to the /tmp directory and create a file called file1:

```
# cd /tmp <cr>
# touch file1 <cr>
# ls -l <cr>
```

Note the permissions on the file. They should be 644 (rw-r---r--).

16. Become user20, and in the /tmp directory, remove the file named file1:

```
# su user20 <cr>
# cd /tmp <cr>
# rm file1 <cr>
```

What message do you receive?

17. Exit the current shell to return to being user9. Change to the user9 home directory and set the ACL on file10 so that user20 has read and write permissions on the file:

```
# exit <cr>
# cd $HOME <cr>
# setfacl -m user:user20:6 file10 <cr>
```

18. List the file permissions on file10 by issuing **ls -l**. Note the +, which indicates that an ACL is set on the file.

19. List the ACL entry on file10 as follows:

```
# getfacl file10 <cr>
```

20. Remove the ACL from file10 as follows:

```
# setfacl -d u:user20 file10 <cr>
```

4.5 Restricting Root Access

In this exercise, you make changes to the system to restrict root logins.

Estimated time: 10 minutes

1. Try to log in to your system as root from a remote system. If the `/etc/default/login` file has not been modified from its default settings, you should not be able to log in.
2. Log in to your system from the console as root.
3. Use `vi` to edit the file `/etc/default/login`, adding a pound sign (#) at the beginning of the following line:

```
#CONSOLE=/dev/console
```

4. Try to log in to your system as root from a remote system. Does it work?
5. Now try to open an FTP connection from a remote system:

```
# ftp <hostname> <cr>
```

6. When you are prompted with a login name, try to get in as root. If the `/etc/ftpd/ftpusers` file has not been modified from its default settings, you get a `Login Incorrect` message and are not able to log in.
7. Remove root from the `/etc/ftpd/ftpusers` files. Does the FTP session work now?
8. Disallow all FTP connections using the `inetadm` command as follows:

```
# inetadm -d ftp <cr>
```

9. Try to connect from a remote system via FTP.

Exam Questions

1. What is the maximum length of a username?

   ❍ **A.** Eight characters

   ❍ **B.** Six characters

   ❍ **C.** Seven characters

   ❍ **D.** Unlimited

2. UID `0` is typically which of the following?

   ❍ **A.** root

   ❍ **B.** A daemon

   ❍ **C.** `adm`

   ❍ **D.** `lpr`

3. How many groups can a user belong to?

   ❍ **A.** 1

   ❍ **B.** 32

   ❍ **C.** Unlimited

   ❍ **D.** 16

4. When you add a new user account via the Add User Wizard, which of the following options are not available for setting the password? (Select the three best answers.)

   ❍ **A.** The password is cleared until first login.

   ❍ **B.** The account is locked.

   ❍ **C.** No password is assigned.

   ❍ **D.** Have the system generate a password.

5. What is the best way to delete a login but retain the user's files?

   ❍ **A.** Delete the login but deselect the Delete Home Directory check box.

   ❍ **B.** Change the password on the login.

   ❍ **C.** Change the UID of the login.

   ❍ **D.** Delete the login, but don't delete files by using the `rm` command.

6. Which of the following is not a default user initialization file?

   ❍ **A.** `.cshrc`

   ❍ **B.** `.login`

   ❍ **C.** `.profile`

   ❍ **D.** `.exrc`

7. Which directory contains the Solaris default initialization files?

   ❍ **A.** `/etc/default`

   ❍ **B.** `/etc/skel`

   ❍ **C.** `/etc/dfs`

   ❍ **D.** `/home`

8. What is the proper syntax to set the default path in the Korn shell?

❍ **A.** PATH=</dirname1>:</*dirname2*>:</*dirname3*>:.; export PATH

❍ **B.** setenv path =(</*dirname1*> </*dirname2*> /*dirname3*> .)

❍ **C.** set path =(</*dirname1*> </*dirname2*> </*dirname3*> .)

❍ **D.** setenv PATH </*dirname1*>:</*dirname2*>:</*dirname3*>

9. What is the proper syntax to set the default path in the C shell?

❍ **A.** set path = (</*dirname1*> </*dirname2*> </*dirname3*> .)

❍ **B.** PATH=</dirname1:/*dirname2*>:</*dirname3*>:.; export PATH

❍ **C.** setenv path =(</*dirname1*> </*dirname2*> </*dirname3*> .)

❍ **D.** set path=</*dirname1*> </*dirname2*> </*dirname3*> .

10. Which of the following files contains encrypted password information?

❍ **A.** /etc/shadow

❍ **B.** /etc/passwd

❍ **C.** /etc/default/password

❍ **D.** /etc/password

11. What is the sitewide initialization file for the Korn shell called?

❍ **A.** /etc/profile

❍ **B.** $HOME/.profile

❍ **C.** /etc/.profile

❍ **D.** /etc/skel/local.profile

12. What is the sitewide initialization file for the C shell called?

❍ **A.** /etc/.login

❍ **B.** /etc/login

❍ **C.** $HOME/.login

❍ **D.** /etc/skel/local.login

13. What is the maximum UID number in Solaris 10?

❍ **A.** `2,147,483,647`

❍ **B.** `60,000`

❍ **C.** `120,000`

❍ **D.** Unlimited

14. What can you do if `CONSOLE=` is included in the `/etc/default/login` file?

❍ **A.** Log in as root from the network and console.

❍ **B.** Log in as a regular user and then use `su` to become root.

❍ **C.** Log in as root from the console but not from the network.

❍ **D.** Log in as root from the network but not from the console.

15. Which of the following are functions of the `/etc/group` file? (Select the two best answers.)

❍ **A.** Assigns users to secondary groups

❍ **B.** Assigns a name to a group ID number

❍ **C.** Provides a special group for `su` privileges

❍ **D.** Specifies which users can access network resources, such as printers

16. You are a system administrator and suspect that one of your users has repeatedly tried to use `su` to gain root privileges. Which of the following files would you look at to see if your suspicion is correct?

❍ **A.** `/usr/adm/syslog`

❍ **B.** `/usr/adm/lastlog`

❍ **C.** `/usr/adm/utmpx`

❍ **D.** `/var/adm/sulog`

17. What effect does the sticky bit have if it is set on the `/tmp` directory as `drwxrwxrwt 2 sys sys 512 May 26 11:02 /tmp`?

❍ **A.** It permits superuser access only.

❍ **B.** It prohibits all read-write permissions.

❍ **C.** It allows only the owner to remove and rename his or her files.

❍ **D.** It is a security risk because any user can delete another user's files.

18. Which of the following files controls the default policy on password aging?

❍ **A.** `/etc/default/login`

❍ **B.** `/etc/default/passwd`

❍ **C.** `/etc/shadow`

❍ **D.** `/etc/passwd`

19. Which of the following do not make secure passwords?

❍ **A.** Phrases

❍ **B.** Nonsense words

❍ **C.** Words with numbers or symbols

❍ **D.** Employee numbers

20. Which of the following makes a secure password?

❍ **A.** A combination of six or more letters

❍ **B.** Your name forward, backward, or jumbled

❍ **C.** Keyboard patterns (such as `asdfgh`)

❍ **D.** Any word in the dictionary

21. Password aging and encryption are stored in which of the following files?

❍ **A.** `/etc/passwd`

❍ **B.** `/etc/shadow`

❍ **C.** `/etc/default/passwd`

❍ **D.** `/etc/default/login`

22. On file permissions, what does the w in the example `-rwxr-xr-x` mean?

❍ **A.** Write privileges for the owner

❍ **B.** Write privileges for the owner and group

❍ **C.** Write privileges for everyone

❍ **D.** Write privileges for root only

23. What command is used to change read, write, and execute permissions on a file?

❍ **A.** `chgrp`

❍ **B.** `chown`

❍ **C.** `chmod`

❍ **D.** `passwd`

24. When a user creates a file or directory, which of the following controls the default file permissions assigned to the file or directory?

❍ **A.** `chmod`

❍ **B.** Permissions assigned

❍ **C.** `umask`

❍ **D.** `chown`

25. To what does a `umask` value of `022` set the default permissions on a directory?

❍ **A.** 644

❍ **B.** 755

❍ **C.** 022

❍ **D.** 533

26. To what does a `umask` value of `022` set the default permissions on a file?

❍ **A.** 644

❍ **B.** 755

❍ **C.** 022

❍ **D.** 533

27. What do the permissions `dr-xr--r--` on a directory mean?

❍ **A.** Only the owner and group member can list files in this directory.

❍ **B.** Only the owner can open files in this directory.

❍ **C.** Neither read, write, nor execute privileges have been assigned.

❍ **D.** Only the owner can remove files in this directory.

28. What is the difference between chmod and umask?

❍ **A.** A chmod value can be set by individual users, whereas umask operates on the system level.

❍ **B.** chmod uses the sticky bit, and umask doesn't.

❍ **C.** umask permissions are stored in a directory rather than in files.

❍ **D.** umask changes the default permissions for every file and directory created in the future, whereas chmod works on a specific directory or file that already exists.

29. What does a restricted shell not allow the user to do?

❍ **A.** Change directories.

❍ **B.** Redirect output.

❍ **C.** Remove files.

❍ **D.** Execute scripts.

30. To what can rsh refer?

❍ **A.** The default system shell or the remote shell command

❍ **B.** A combination of the Bourne and C shell or a restricted shell

❍ **C.** The variable used to limit the number of login attempts or a restricted shell

❍ **D.** A restricted shell or the remote shell command

31. Which of the following commands displays users who don't have passwords?

❍ **A.** Use more /etc/passwd

❍ **B.** logins -p

❍ **C.** passwd

❍ **D.** attributes

32. Which of the following files contains a list of trusted hosts for a remote system?

❍ **A.** /.rhosts

❍ **B.** /etc/hosts.equiv

❍ **C.** /etc/default/login

❍ **D.** /etc/hosts

33. Which of the following files gives a specified user permission to log in remotely from the specified host without having to supply a password?

❍ **A.** `.rhosts`

❍ **B.** `/etc/hosts.equiv`

❍ **C.** `/etc/default/login`

❍ **D.** `/etc/hosts`

34. You can protect the superuser account on a system by restricting access to a specific device through what file?

❍ **A.** `/etc/hosts.equiv`

❍ **B.** `/etc/default/login`

❍ **C.** `/etc/default/passwd`

❍ **D.** `/etc/default/su`

35. Which of the following files lists all uses of the `su` command?

❍ **A.** `/var/adm/wtmpx`

❍ **B.** `/var/adm/messages`

❍ **C.** `/var/adm/lastlog`

❍ **D.** `/var/adm/sulog`

36. Which of the following makes specific checks and adjustments to system files and permissions to ensure system security?

❍ **A.** `chmod`

❍ **B.** `aset`

❍ **C.** An ACL

❍ **D.** The proper entry in the `/etc/default/login` file

37. Shell scripts that run `setuid` or `setgid` can be sufficiently secure.

❍ **A.** True

❍ **B.** False

38. Which of the following commands is used to set ACL entries on a file?

❍ **A.** `setfacl`

❍ **B.** `chmod`

❍ **C.** `chown`

❍ **D.** `getfacl`

39. What does the plus sign (+) to the right of the permission mode field indicate (`-rw-r-----+`)?

❍ **A.** The file has an ACL.

❍ **B.** The sticky bit is set.

❍ **C.** `setuid` permission has been set on the file.

❍ **D.** It sets group ID on execution.

40. Which of the following commands is used to delete an ACL?

❍ **A.** `setfacl -d` *<acl-entry-list>*

❍ **B.** `delfacl`

❍ **C.** `chown -acl`

❍ **D.** `setfacl -m`

41. Which of the following commands displays each user logged in and the active processes owned by each user?

❍ **A.** `whodo`

❍ **B.** `who`

❍ **C.** `w`

❍ **D.** `who -u`

42. Which of the following commands displays the time and date of the last reboot?

❍ **A.** `who -b`

❍ **B.** `who -i`

❍ **C.** `uptime`

❍ **D.** `uname`

Answers to Exam Questions

1. **A.** A user login name can contain two to eight uppercase characters (A–Z) or lowercase characters (a–z) or digits (0–9), but no underscores or spaces. The first character must be a letter, and at least one character must be a lowercase letter. For more information, see the section "Adding User Accounts with the SMC."

2. **A.** The UID for the root login is always 0. For more information, see the section "Securing Superuser Access."

3. **D.** A user can belong to as many as 15 secondary groups. Added to the primary group, a user can belong to 16 total groups. For more information, see the section "Where User Account Information Is Stored."

4. **A, B, D.** The password is cleared until first login is no longer an option in Solaris 10. You cannot lock an account via the Add User Wizard in the SMC. The SMC cannot automatically generate a password for a user account. For more information, see the section "Adding User Accounts with the SMC."

5. **A.** When you delete a user account in the SMC, you deselect the Delete Home Directory check box to retain all the user's files. For more information, see the section "Deleting User Accounts with the SMC."

6. **D.** The following are default user initialization files that are put into a user's home directory when the user's account is created: .cshrc, .login, and .profile. For more information, see the section "Customizing User Initialization Files."

7. **B.** The /etc/skel directory contains the Solaris default initialization files. For more information, see the section "Customizing User Initialization Files."

8. **A.** To set the default path in the Korn shell, you issue the following command: PATH=</dirname1>:</dirname2>:</dirname3>:.; export PATH. For more information, see the section "Setting Up Shell Initialization Files."

9. **A.** To set the default path in the C shell, you issue the following command: set path = (</dirname1> </dirname2> </dirname3>.) For more information, see the section "Setting Up Shell Initialization Files."

10. **A.** The /etc/shadow file contains the encrypted password information for each user account. For more information, see the section "Where User Account Information Is Stored."

11. **A.** The sitewide initialization file for the Korn shell is /etc/profile. For more information, see the section "Setting Up Shell Initialization Files."

12. **A.** The sitewide initialization file for the C shell is /etc/.login. For more information, see the section "Setting Up Shell Initialization Files."

13. **A.** UID numbers for regular users should range from 100 to 60,000, but they can be as high as 2,147,483,647. For more information, see the section "Adding User Accounts with the SMC."

14. **B.** In the /etc/default/login file, with no value defined for the variable CONSOLE, root cannot log in from anywhere—not even the console. The only way to get in to the system as root is to first log in as a regular user and become root by issuing the su command. For more information, see the section "Restricting Root Access."

15. **A, B.** The /etc/group file assigns users to secondary groups and assigns a name to a group ID number. For more information, see the section "Where User Account Information Is Stored."

16. **D.** Whenever someone issues the su command to switch from a user and become root, this activity is logged in a file called /var/adm/sulog. The sulog file lists all uses of the su command, not only those used to switch from a user to superuser. The entries in this file show the date and time the command was entered, whether it was successful, the port from which the command was issued, and the name of the user and the switched identity. For more information, see the section "Monitoring Superuser Access."

17. **C.** If the sticky bit is set on the /tmp directory as rwxrwxrwx, only the owner can remove and rename his or her files. For more information, see the section "Sticky Bits."

18. **B.** The /etc/default/passwd file controls the default policy on password aging. For more information, see the section "Controlling System Access."

19. **D.** Employee numbers are not secure passwords. For more information, see the section "Controlling System Access."

20. **A.** You should ensure that passwords contain a combination of 6–8 letters, numbers, or special characters. For more information, see the section "Controlling System Access."

21. **B.** Password encryption and password aging details are stored in the /etc/shadow file. For more information, see the section "Where User Account Information Is Stored."

22. **A.** On files, the w in the first field of the permissions list designates write privileges for the owner. For more information, see the section "Controlling File Access."

23. **C.** The chmod command changes access permissions on a file. You can use either symbolic mode (letters and symbols) or absolute mode (octal numbers) to change permissions on a file. For more information, see the section "Controlling File Access."

24. **C.** When a user creates a file or directory, the umask value controls the default file permissions assigned to the file or directory. For more information, see the section "Controlling File Access."

25. **B.** A umask value of 022 sets the default permission on a directory to 755 (rwxr-xr-x). For more information, see the section "Controlling File Access."

26. **A.** A umask value of 022 sets the default permission on a file to 644 (rw-r--r--). For more information, see the section "Controlling File Access."

27. **B.** The permissions r-xr--r-- on a directory allow only the owner to open files in that directory. For more information, see the section "Controlling File Access."

28. **D.** `umask` changes the default permissions for every file and directory created in the future, whereas `chmod` works on a specific directory or file that already exists. For more information, see the section "Controlling File Access."

29. **B.** A restricted shell does not allow the user to change directories or redirect output. For more information, see the section "Restricted Shells."

30. **D.** `rsh` refers to either a restricted shell or the remote shell command. You should not confuse the restricted shell `/usr/lib/rsh` with the remote shell `/usr/bin/rsh`. When you specify a restricted shell, you should not include the following directories in the user's path—`/bin`, `/sbin`, or `/usr/bin`. If you do include the m in the user's path, you will allow the user to start another shell (a nonrestricted shell). For more information, see the section "Restricted Shells."

31. **B.** You use the `logins -p` command to display usernames that do not have passwords associated with them. For more information, see the section "Monitoring Users and System Usage."

32. **B.** The `/etc/hosts.equiv` file contains a list of trusted hosts for a remote system, one per line. For more information, see the section "Trusted Hosts."

33. **A.** The `.rhosts` file is the user equivalent of the `/etc/hosts.equiv` file. It contains a list of trusted hosts for a remote system, as well as a list of users. If a host/user combination is listed in this file, the specified user is granted permission to log in remotely from the specified host without having to supply a password. For more information, see the section "The `.rhosts` File."

34. **B.** You can protect the superuser account on a system by restricting access to a specific device through the `CONSOLE` variable located in the `/etc/default/login` file. For more information, see the section "Restricting Root Access."

35. **D.** The `sulog` file lists all uses of the `su` command, not only those that are used to switch a user to superuser. The entries in the `sulog` file show the date and time the command was entered, whether it was successful, the port from which the command was issued, and the name of the user and the switched identity. For more information, see the section "Monitoring Superuser Access."

36. **B.** The Solaris 10 system software includes ASET, which helps you monitor and control system security by automatically performing tasks you would otherwise do manually. ASET performs seven tasks, making specific checks and adjustments to system files and permissions to ensure system security. For more information, see the section "ASET."

37. **B.** Except for the executables that are shipped with the `setuid` bit set to root, you should disallow the use of `setuid` programs. For more information, see the section "The `setuid` and `setgid` Programs."

38. **A.** You use the `setfacl` command to set ACL entries on a file or directory. For more information, see the section "Setting ACL Entries."

39. **A.** The plus sign (+) to the right of the permission mode field (`-rw-r-----+`) indicates that the file has an ACL. For more information, see the section "Setting ACL Entries."

40. **A.** You use the `setfacl -d` command to delete an ACL on a file or directory. For more information, see the section "Setting ACL Entries."

41. **A.** Use the `whodo` command to display each user logged in and the active processes owned by that user. For more information, see the section "The `whodo` Command."

42. **A.** The `who -b` command displays the time and date of the last reboot. For more information, see the section "Checking Who Is Logged In."

Suggested Reading and Resources

For more information on this topic, refer to the *Solaris 10 System Administration Guide: Security Services* by Sun Microsystems, Part number 816-4557-10. This guide is available at `http://docs.sun.com`.

CHAPTER FIVE

Managing System Processes

Objectives

The following test objectives for Exam CX-310-200 are covered in this chapter:

Explain how to view system processes and clear frozen processes.

- Managing system processes is a common task for any system administrator. You should know how to use the commands that display information for all active processes on the system, and how to terminate an active or deadlocked process.

Explain how to schedule an automatic one-time execution of a command and the automatic recurring execution of a command.

- Many processes compete for execution time so scheduling jobs to run at off-peak hours can dramatically improve system performance. The system administrator needs to understand how to use the Solaris batch processor to schedule execution of commands.

Outline

Study Strategies

The following study strategies will help you prepare for the test:

- Understand each of the commands in this chapter enough so that you can match the command and option with a description. Practice them on a Solaris system so that you can become familiar with the output they produce.
- Know all the commands used to display information about a process. When viewing processes, understand each of the fields that are displayed in the output.
- Finally, understand how to schedule commands via the Solaris batch-processing facilities. Become familiar with all of the associated configuration files: what they do and how they are formatted.

EXAM ALERT

Managing System Processes As of this writing, the topic of managing system processes is covered lightly on the CX-310-200 exam. This could change in the future as Sun keeps updating and changing its exams. The best approach is to be prepared and learn the material thoroughly. After all, it's a topic every system administrator needs to know to effectively perform the job.

Introduction

This chapter covers Solaris processes—how to view processes, understand the effects signals have on processes, and how to manage processes.

Viewing a Process

Objective:

Explain how to view system processes.

Solaris is a multitasking environment in which a number of programs run at the same time. This means that many users can be active on the system at the same time, running many jobs (processes) simultaneously. Each Solaris program can start and stop multiple processes while it is running, but only one job is active per processor at any given time while the other jobs wait in a job queue. Because each process takes its turn running in very short time slices (much less than a second each), multitasking operating systems give the appearance that multiple processes are running at the same time. A parent process forks a child process, which, in turn, can fork other processes.

NOTE

Forks The term *fork* is used to describe a process started from another process. As with a fork in the road, one process turns into two. You'll also see the term *spawn* used—the two words are interchangeable for the purposes of this subject.

A program can be made up of many processes. A *process* is part of a program running in its own address space. A process under Solaris consists of an *address space* and a set of data structures in the *kernel* to keep track of that process. The address space is divided into various sections that include the instructions that the process may execute, memory allocated during the execution of the process, the *stack*, and memory-mapped files. The kernel must keep track of the following data for each process on the system:

- Address space
- Current status of the process
- Execution priority of the process
- Resource usage of the process
- Current signal mask
- Ownership of the process

A process is distinct from a job, command, or program that can be composed of many processes working together to perform a specific task. For example, a computer-aided design application is a single program. When this program starts, it spawns other processes as it runs. When a user logs in to the program, it spawns yet other processes. Each process has a process ID associated with it and is referred to as a *PID*. You can monitor processes that are currently executing by using one of the commands listed in Table 5.1.

TABLE 5.1 Commands to Display Processes

Command	Description
`mpstat`	Executed from the command line, `mpstat` reports processor statistics in tabular form. Each row of the table represents the activity of one processor.
`ps`	Executed from the command line to display information about active processes.
`pgrep`	Executed from the command line to find processes by a specific name or attribute.
`prstat`	Executed from the command line to display information about active processes on the system.
`ptree`	Prints the process trees containing the specified pids or users, with child processes indented from their respective parent processes.
`sdtprocess`	A GUI used to display and control processes on a system. This utility requires the X Window System (also known as X Windows).
`SMC process tool`	A GUI available in the Solaris Management Console used to monitor and manage processes on a system.
`pargs`	Executed from the command line to examine the arguments and environment variables of a process.
`svcs`	With the `-p` option, this Service Management Facility command will list processes associated with each service instance.
`time`	Time a simple command.

Before getting into the commands used to monitor processes, you first need to become familiar with process attributes. A process has certain attributes that directly affect execution. These are listed in Table 5.2.

TABLE 5.2 Process Attributes

Attribute	Description
`PID`	The process identification (a unique number that defines the process within the kernel)
`PPID`	The parent PID (the parent of the process)
`UID`	The user ID number of the user who owns the process
`EUID`	The effective user ID of the process
`GID`	The group ID of the user who owns the process
`EGID`	The effective group ID that owns the process
`Priority`	The priority at which the process runs

Use the ps command to view processes currently running on the system. Use the ps command when you're on a character-based terminal and don't have access to a graphical display. Adding the -l option to the ps command displays a variety of other information about the processes currently running, including the state of each process (listed under S). The codes used to show the various process states are listed in Table 5.3.

TABLE 5.3 Process States

Code	Process State	Description
O	Running	The process is running on a processor.
S	Sleeping	The process is waiting for an event to complete.
R	Runnable	The process is on the run queue.
Z	Zombie state	The process was terminated and the parent is not waiting.
T	Traced	The process was stopped by a signal because the parent is tracing it.
W	Waiting	The process is waiting for CPU usage to drop to the CPU-caps enforced limits

To see all the processes that are running on a system, type the following:

```
ps -el
```

The system responds with the following output:

```
# ps -el

F  S  UID   PID  PPID C PRI NI  ADDR SZ    WCHAN TTY  TIME CMD
19 T   0     0     0  0   0 SY   ?     0          ?   0:18 sched
 8 S   0     1     0  0  40 20   ?   150        ? ?   0:00 init
19 S   0     2     0  0   0 SY   ?     0        ? ?   0:00 pageout
19 S   0     3     0  0   0 SY   ?     0        ? ?   0:01 fsflush
 8 S   0   309     1  0  40 20   ?   217        ? ?   0:00 sac
 8 S   0   315     1  0  40 20   ?   331        ? ?   0:00 sshd
 8 S   0   143     1  0  40 20   ?   273        ? ?   0:00 rpcbind
 8 S   0    51     1  0  40 20   ?   268        ? ?   0:00 sysevent
 8 S   0    61     1  0  40 20   ?   343        ? ?   0:01 picld
 8 S   0   453   403  0  50 20   ?  1106        ? ?   0:00 dtfile
 8 S   0   189     1  0  40 20   ?   509        ? ?   0:00 automoun
 8 S   0   165     1  0  40 20   ?   292        ? ?   0:00 inetd
 8 S   0   200     1  0  40 20   ?   415        ? ?   0:00 syslogd
 8 S   0   180     1  0  40 20   ?   266        ? ?   0:00 lockd
 8 S   0   219     1  0  40 20   ?   391        ? ?   0:00 lpsched
 8 S   1   184     1  0  40 20   ?   306        ? ?   0:00 statd
 8 S   0   214     1  0  40 20   ?   365        ? ?   0:00 nscd
 8 S   0   204     1  0  40 20   ?   254        ? ?   0:00 cron
 8 S   0   232     1  0  40 20   ?   173        ? ?   0:00 powerd
 8 S   0   255   254  0  40 20   ?   215        ? ?   0:00 smcboot
 8 S   0   258     1  0  40 20   ?   356        ? ?   0:02 vold
```

The manual page for the ps command describes all the fields displayed with the ps command, as well as all the command options. Table 5.4 lists some important fields.

TABLE 5.4 Process Fields

Field	Description
F	Flags associated with the process.
S	The state of the process.
UID	The user ID of the process owner. For many processes, this is 0 because they run setuid.
PID	The process ID of each process. This value should be unique. Generally, PIDs are allocated lowest to highest, but they wrap at some point. This value is necessary for you to send a signal, such as the kill signal, to a process.
PPID	The parent process ID. This identifies the parent process that started the process. Using the PPID enables you to trace the sequence of process creation that took place.
PRI	The priority of the process. Without the -c option, higher numbers mean lower priority. With the -c option, higher numbers mean higher priority.
NI	The nice value, used in priority computation. This is not printed when the -c option is used. The process's nice number contributes to its scheduling priority. Making a process nicer means lowering its priority.
ADDR	The memory address of the process.
SZ	The SIZE field. This is the total number of pages in the process. Page sizes are 8192 bytes on sun4u systems, but vary on different hardware platforms. Issue the /usr/bin/pagesize command to display the page size on your system.
WCHAN	The address of an event for which the process is sleeping (if it's -, the process is running).
STIME	The starting time of the process (in hours, minutes, and seconds).
TTY	The terminal assigned to your process.
TIME	The cumulative CPU time used by the process in minutes and seconds.
CMD	The command that generated the process.

You often want to look at all processes. You can do this using the command ps -el. A number of options available with the ps command control what information gets printed. A few of them are listed in Table 5.5.

TABLE 5.5 ps Command Options

Option	Description
-A	Lists information for all processes. Identical to the -e option.
-a	Lists information about all the most frequently requested processes. Processes not associated with a terminal will not be listed.
-e	Lists information about every process on the system.

(continues)

TABLE 5.5 *Continued*

Option	Description
`-f`	Generates a full listing.
`-l`	Generates a long listing.
`-P`	Prints the number of the processor to which the process is bound, if any, under an additional column header `PSR`. This is a useful option on systems that have multiple processors.
`-u <username>`	Lists only process data for a particular user. In the listing, the numerical user ID is printed unless you give the `-f` option, which prints the login name.

For a complete list of options to the `ps` command, refer to the Solaris online manual pages.

NOTE

`sort` Command The `sort` command is useful when you're looking at system processes. Use the `sort` command as the pipe output to sort by size or PID. For example, to sort by the `SZ` field, use the command `ps -el | sort +9` (remember, `sort` starts numbering fields with 0).

pgrep

The `pgrep` command replaces the combination of the `ps`, `grep`, `egrep`, and `awk` commands that were used to manage processes in earlier releases of Solaris. The `pgrep` command examines the active processes on the system and reports the process IDs of the processes whose attributes match the criteria you specify on the command line. The command syntax for the `pgrep` command is shown here:

```
pgrep <options> <pattern>
```

`pgrep` options are described in Table 5.6.

TABLE 5.6 `pgrep` Options

Option	Description
`-d <delim>`	Specifies the output delimiter string to be printed between each matching process ID. If no `-d` option is specified, the default is a newline character.
`-f`	The regular expression pattern should be matched against the full process argument string. If no `-f` option is specified, the expression is matched only against the name of the executable file.
`-g <pgrplist>`	Matches only processes whose process group ID is in the given list.
`-G <gidlist>`	Matches only processes whose real group ID is in the given list. Each group ID may be specified as either a group name or a numerical group ID.

TABLE 5.6 *Continued*

Option	Description
`-l`	Long output format. Prints the process name along with the process ID of each matching process.
`-n`	Matches only the newest (most recently created) process that meets all other specified matching criteria.
`-P` *<ppidlist>*	Matches only processes whose parent process ID is in the given list.
`-s` *<sidlist>*	Matches only processes whose process session ID is in the given list.
`-t` *<termlist>*	Matches only processes that are associated with a terminal in the given list. Each terminal is specified as the suffix following `/dev/` of the terminal's device pathname in `/dev` (for example, `term/a` or `pts/0`).
`-u` *<euidlist>*	Matches only processes whose effective user ID is in the given list. Each user ID may be specified as either a login name or a numerical user ID.
`-U` *<uidlist>*	Matches only processes whose real user ID is in the given list. Each user ID may be specified as either a login name or a numerical user ID.
`-v`	Matches all processes except those that meet the specified matching criteria.
`-x`	Considers only processes whose argument string or executable filename exactly matches the specified pattern.
<pattern>	A pattern to match against either the executable filename or full process argument string.

For example, the following `pgrep` command finds all processes that have `"dt"` in the process argument string:

```
# pgrep -l -f "dt"
```

The system responds with this:

```
  500 /usr/dt/bin/dtlogin -daemon
16224 ./dtterm
  438 /usr/dt/bin/dtlogin -daemon
  448 /usr/openwin/bin/Xsun :0 -defdepth 24 -nobanner -auth /var/dt/A:0-p_aW2a
  520 dtgreet -display :0
```

To find the process ID for the `lpsched` process, issue this command:

```
# pgrep -l lpsched
```

The system responds with this:

```
6899 lpsched
```

prstat

Use the prstat command from the command line to monitor system processes. Again, like the ps command, it provides information on active processes. The difference is that you can specify whether you want information on specific processes, UIDs, CPU IDs, or processor sets. By default, prstat displays information about all processes sorted by CPU usage. Another nice feature with prstat is that the information remains on the screen and is updated periodically. The information displayed by the prstat command is described in Table 5.7.

TABLE 5.7 Column Headings for the prstat Command

Column Heading	Description
PID	The process identification (a unique number that defines the process within the kernel)
USERNAME	The login ID name of the owner of the process
SIZE	The total virtual memory size of the process in kilobytes (K), megabytes (M), or gigabytes (G)
RSS	The resident set size of the process in kilobytes, megabytes, or gigabytes
STATE	The state of the process:
	cpu<*n*>—Process is running on CPU.
	sleep—Process is waiting for an event to complete.
	run—Process is in the run queue.
	zombie—Process has terminated and parent is not waiting.
	stop—Process is stopped.
PRI	The priority of the process
NICE	The value used in priority computation
TIME	The cumulative execution time for the process
CPU	The percentage of recent CPU time used by the process
PROCESS	The name of the process
NLWP	The number of lightweight processes (LWPs) in the process

This section will introduce some new terminology, so Table 5.8 defines a few terms related to processing in general.

TABLE 5.8 Process Terminology

Term	Description
Multitasking	A technique used in an operating system for sharing a single processor among several independent jobs. Multitasking introduces overhead because the processor spends some time choosing the next job to run and saving and restoring tasks' state. However, it reduces the worst-case time from job submission to completion compared with a simple batch system, in which each job must finish before the next one starts. Multitasking also means that while one task is waiting for some external event, the CPU is free to do useful work on other tasks. A multitasking operating system should provide some degree of protection of one task from another to prevent tasks from interacting in unexpected ways, such as accidentally modifying the contents of each other's memory areas. The jobs in a multitasking system may belong to one or many users. This is distinct from parallel processing, in which one user runs several tasks on several processors. Time sharing is almost synonymous with multitasking, but it implies that there is more than one user.
Parallel processing	The simultaneous use of more than one CPU to solve a problem. The processors either may communicate to cooperate in solving a problem or may run completely independently, possibly under the control of another processor that distributes work to the others and collects results from them.
Multithreaded	Multithreaded is a process that has multiple flows (threads) of control. The traditional Unix process contained, and still contains, a single thread of control. Multithreading (MT) separates a process into many execution threads, each of which runs independently. For more information, see the Multithreaded Programming Guide at `http://docs.sun.com/` Part number 816-5137-10.
Lightweight process (LWP)	A single-threaded subprocess. LWPs are scheduled by the kernel to use available CPU resources based on their scheduling class and priority. LWPs include a kernel thread, which contains information that must be in memory all the time, and a LWP, which contains information that is swappable. A process can consist of multiple LWPs and multiple application threads. A lightweight process is somewhere between a thread and a full process.
Application thread	A series of instructions with a separate stack that can execute independently in a user's address space. The threads can be multiplexed on top of LWPs.
Address space	The range of addresses that a processor or process can access, or at which a device can be accessed. The term may refer to either a physical address or a virtual address. The size of a processor's address space depends on the width of the processor's address bus and address registers. Processes running in 32-bit mode have a 4 gigabyte address space (2^{32} bytes) and processes running in 64-bit mode have a 16 terabyte (2^{64} bytes) address space.
Shared memory	Usually refers to RAM, which can be accessed by more than one process in a multitasking operating system with memory protection.

The syntax for the `prstat` command is as follows:

```
prstat [options] <count> <interval>
```

Table 5.9 describes a few of the `prstat` command options and arguments.

TABLE 5.9 `prstat` Options and Arguments

Option	Description
`prstat` Options	
`-a`	Displays separate reports about processes and users at the same time.
`-c`	Continuously prints new reports beneath previous reports instead of overwriting them.
`-j` *<projlist>*	Reports only processes or LWPs whose project ID is in the given list. Each project ID can be specified as either a project name or a numerical project ID.
`-J`	Reports information about processes and projects.
`-k` *<tasklist>*	Reports only processes or LWPs whose task ID is in *tasklist*.
`-m`	Reports microstate process accounting information. In addition to all fields listed in `-v` mode, this mode also includes the percentage of time the process has spent processing system traps, text page faults, and data page faults, and waiting for user locks and waiting for CPU (latency time).
`-n` *<nproc>*	Restricts the number of output lines. The *<nproc>* argument specifies how many lines of process or LWP statistics are reported.
`-p` *<pidlist>*	Reports only processes that have a PID in the given list.
`-P` *<cpulist>*	Reports only processes or LWPs that have most recently executed on a CPU in the given list. The *<cpulist>* argument identifies each CPU by an integer as reported by `psrinfo`.
`-S` *<key>*	Sorts output lines by *<key>* in descending order. Values for *<key>* can be `cpu`—Sorts by process CPU usage. This is the default. `time`—Sorts by process execution time. `size`—Sorts by size of process image. `rss`—Sorts by resident set size. `pri`—Sorts by process priority.
`-s` *<key>*	Sorts output lines by *<key>* in ascending order. See the `-S` option for a list of valid *keys* to use.
`-t`	Reports total usage summary for each user.
`-u` *<uidlist>*	Reports only processes whose effective user ID is in the given list. The value for *<uidlist>* may be specified as either a login name or a numerical user ID.

TABLE 5.9 *Continued*

Option	Description
`-U <uidlist>`	Reports only processes whose real user ID is in the given list. The value for `<uidlist>` may be specified as either a login name or a numerical user ID.
`prstat` Arguments	
`<count>`	Specifies the number of times that the statistics are repeated. By default, `prstat` reports statistics until a termination signal is received.
`<interval>`	Specifies the sampling interval in seconds; the default interval is 5 seconds.

NOTE

psrinfo Command `psrinfo` displays one line for each configured processor, displaying whether it is online, non-interruptible, offline, or powered off, as well as when that status last changed.

The following example uses the `prstat` command to view the four most active root processes running. The `-n` option is used here to restrict the output to the top four processes. The next number, `5`, specifies the sampling interval in seconds, and the last number, `3`, runs the command three times:

```
# prstat -u root -n 4 5 3
```

The system displays the following output:

```
PID USERNAME  SIZE   RSS  STATE  PRI  NICE  TIME     CPU  PROCESS/NLWP
4375 root     4568K 4344K cpu0    59    0   0:00:00 0.4% prstat/1
4298 root     7088K 5144K sleep   59    0   0:00:02 0.2% dtterm/1
 304 root     2304K 1904K sleep   59    0   0:02:35 0.0% mibiisa/7
 427 root     1832K 1304K sleep   59    0   0:00:00 0.0% rpc.rstatd/1
Total: 53 processes, 111 lwps, load averages: 0.02, 0.01, 0.01
```

The output updates on your display five times every three seconds.

I described projects in Chapter 4, “User and Security Administration,” where user accounts can be assigned to project groups. These projects can also be used to label workloads and separate projects and a project’s related processes from one another.

The project provides a networkwide administrative identifier for related work. A project consists of tasks, which collect a group of processes into a manageable entity that represents a workload component.

You can use the prstat command with the -J option to monitor the CPU usage of projects and the -k option to monitor tasks across your system. Therefore, you can have prstat report on the processes related to a project rather than just list all system processes. In addition, the system administrator can set processing limits on the project, such as setting a limit on the total amount of physical memory, in bytes, that is available to processes in the project. For more information on projects and resource capping, read the man pages on the following commands: rcapd(1M), project(4), rcapstat(1), and rcapadm(1M).

mpstat

Use the mpstat command to report processor statistics on a multi-processor system. When executing the mpstat command, we'll usually want to see more than one result, so we specify the number of seconds between each mpstat as follows:

```
mpstat 30
```

The argument 30, specifies that I want to get a report every 30 seconds. The system displays the following information every 30 seconds:

```
CPU minf mjf xcal  intr ithr  csw icsw migr smtx  srw syscl  usr sys  wt idl
  0    6   0    0   114   14   25    0    6    3    0    48    1   2  25  72
  1    6   0    0    86   85   50    0    6    3    0    66    1   4  24  71
  2    7   0    0    42   42   31    0    6    3    0    54    1   3  24  72
  3    8   0    0     0    0   33    0    6    4    0    54    1   3  24  72
```

The results are from a system with four processors. Typically, a system administrator will use the mpstat command to check CPU utilization. In this example, I look at the idl column (percent idle time) and see that the server's CPUs are approx 28% used. For more information on the other columns of information, refer to the mpstat man pages.

ptree

The `ptree` command will display the process tree. The parent process is displayed with the respective child processes indented beneath it. Here is an example showing the processes that belong to the `inetd` process (PID 270):

```
# ptree 270<cr>
```

The system displays:

```
270   /usr/lib/inet/inetd start
  780   /usr/sbin/in.telnetd
    783   -sh
      1250  ptree 270
```

With no arguments, the `ptree` command will display every process along with the associated child processes.

time

The `time` command is used to display the time that the system has spent executing a command. It's a useful command for benchmarking performance. Use this command to time a command on a particular system configuration and compare to another system. In the following example, I'll check the system processing time for a script I wrote named "`longtime`":

```
# time ./longtime<cr>
```

The system displays:

```
real       14.7
user        9.9
sys         2.3
```

The `real` time is the total time that has elapsed between invoking the script and its termination. The `user` time is the time the processor spends executing your user code. Finally, the `system` time is the time the processor spends executing Operating System code on behalf of your process.

Process Manager

In the Desktop Environment (CDE & JAVA Desktop) you have access to the Process Manager GUI, `sdtprocess`, a graphical tool that provides a process manager window for monitoring and controlling system processes.

EXAM ALERT

The exam will most likely ask you about the command-line tools used to manage system processes, such as `kill`, `pkill`, `pargs`, and `pgrep`. You only need to understand that GUI tools can be used to manage processes and you should be prepared to identify these GUI tools.

The advantage of using the Process Manager is that you can view and control processes without knowing all the complex options associated with the `ps` and `kill` commands. For example, you can display processes that contain specific character strings, and you can sort the process list alphabetically or numerically. You can initiate a search using the `find` command, or you can terminate a process simply by highlighting it and clicking `kill`.

To open the Process Manager, you need to log into the Desktop windowing environment. You can start the GUI by executing the command `sdtprocess`, as follows:

```
# sdtprocess &
```

Or, you can click Find Process on the Tools subpanel, as shown in Figure 5.1.

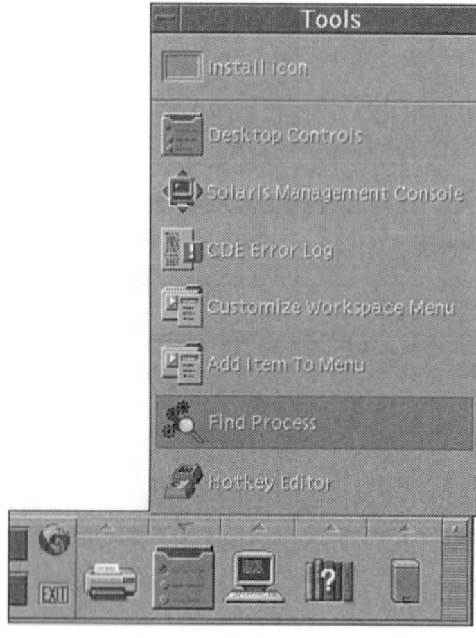

FIGURE 5.1 Front panel.

The Process Manager window opens, as shown in Figure 5.2.

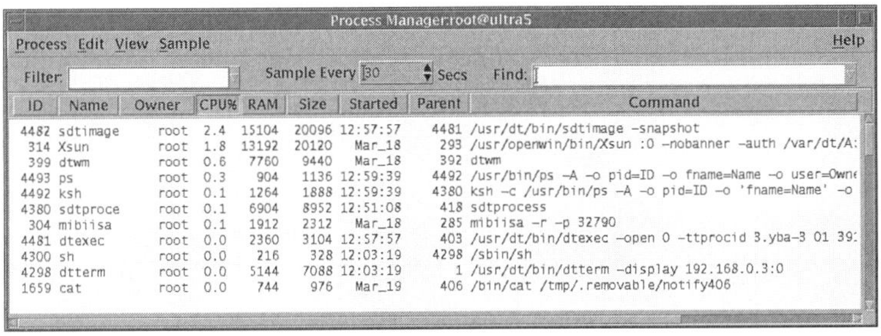

Figure 5.2 Process Manager window.

Each process attribute in the header of the Process Manager window provides detailed information about the process and is described in Table 5.10.

TABLE 5.10 Process Manager Window

Column Heading	Description
`ID`	Process ID
`Name`	Process name
`Owner`	Login ID name of the owner of the process
`CPU%`	Ratio of CPU time available in the same period, expressed as a percentage
`RAM`	Amount of RAM currently occupied by this process
`Swap`	Total swap size in virtual memory
`Started`	Actual start time (or date, if other than current)
`Parent`	Process ID of parent process, or PPID
`Command`	Actual Unix command (truncated) being executed

Click any of the column headings to sort the processes by that attribute. For example, click the `CPU` heading to sort all processes by their CPU usage. The list updates every 30 seconds, but you can enter a value in the `Sampling` field to update the list as frequently as you like. Finally, you can enter a text string that is common to the process entries of all the processes you want to display in the Find drop-down menu. In Figure 5.3, I entered "root" in the `Find` field to display all processes owned by root. I also changed the sampling rate to every 5 seconds and clicked the `CPU` heading to sort processes by their CPU usage.

Another nice feature of the Process Manager is the capability to display the ancestry of a process. When a Unix process initiates one or more processes, these are *child processes*, or children. Child and parent processes have the same user ID. To view a parent process and all the child processes that belong to it, highlight the process in the Process Manager window. Click Process from the toolbar at the top of the window and select Show Ancestry, as shown in Figure 5.4.

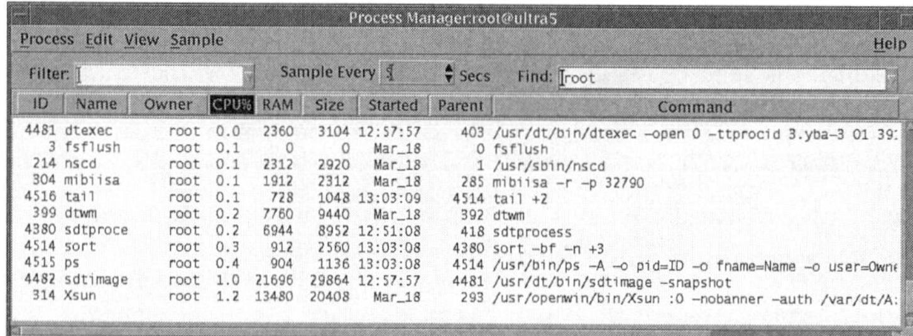

FIGURE 5.3 Sorted Process Manager window.

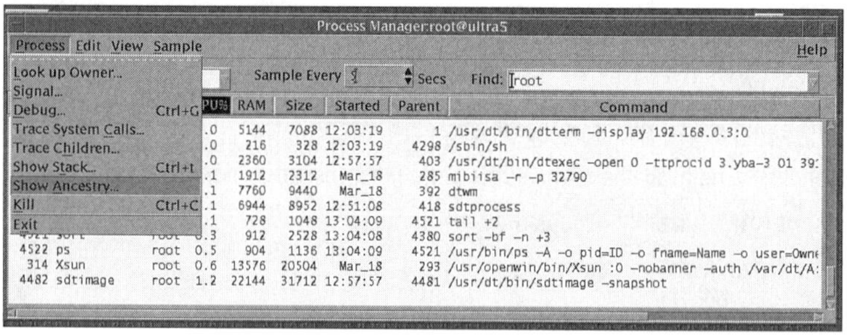

FIGURE 5.4 Selecting Show Ancestry.

The window shown in Figure 5.5 displays showing all the processes belonging to the parent.

The command-line equivalent to the Ancestry selection in the Process Manager is the `ptree` command. Use this command when you don't have a graphical display terminal. The `ptree` command displays the process ancestry trees containing the specified PIDs or users. The child processes are displayed indented from their respective parent processes. For example, here is the process tree for the `-sh` process, which has a PID of `293`:

```
# ptree 293
```

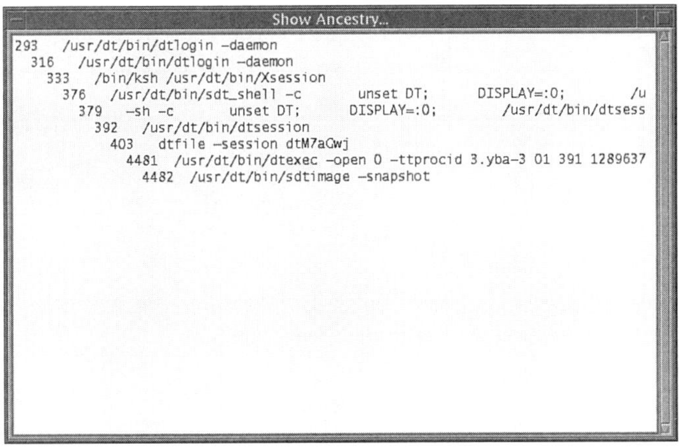

```
293   /usr/dt/bin/dtlogin -daemon
  316   /usr/dt/bin/dtlogin -daemon
    333   /bin/ksh /usr/dt/bin/Xsession
      376   /usr/dt/bin/sdt_shell -c        unset DT;       DISPLAY=:0;         /u
        379   -sh -c        unset DT;       DISPLAY=:0;         /usr/dt/bin/dtsess
          392   /usr/dt/bin/dtsession
            403   dtfile -session dtM7aGwj
              4481  /usr/dt/bin/dtexec -open 0 -ttprocid 3.yba-3 01 391 1289637
                4482  /usr/dt/bin/sdtimage -snapshot
```

Figure 5.5 Show Ancestry window.

The system responds with this:

```
293  /usr/dt/bin/dtlogin -daemon
  316   /usr/dt/bin/dtlogin -daemon
    333   /bin/ksh /usr/dt/bin/Xsession
      376   /usr/dt/bin/sdt_shell -c  unset DT;DISPLAY=:0;/usr/dt/bin/dt
        379  -sh -c unset DT; DISPLAY=:0; usr/dt/bin/dtsession_res - \
               merge
          392   /usr/dt/bin/dtsession
            402   /usr/dt/bin/dtterm -session dthIaGth -C -ls
              418   -sh
```

SMC Process Tool

The Solaris Management Console (SMC) includes a GUI called the Process Tool, which is used for viewing and managing processes, similar to the Desktop Process Manager tool described in the previous section. You can use the job scheduler tool to

- Suspend a process
- Resume a suspended process
- Kill a process
- Display information about a process

To open the Process Tool, follow Step by Step 5.1.

STEP BY STEP

5.1 Opening the Process Tool

1. Start up the Solaris Management Console in the background by typing

```
# smc &
```

2. The SMC Welcome window appears as shown in Figure 5.6.
3. In the SMC navigation pane, open the Process Tool by clicking on the This Computer icon, then click on the System Status icon, then click on the Processes icon as shown in Figure 5.7.
4. The Process Tool displays as shown in Figure 5.8

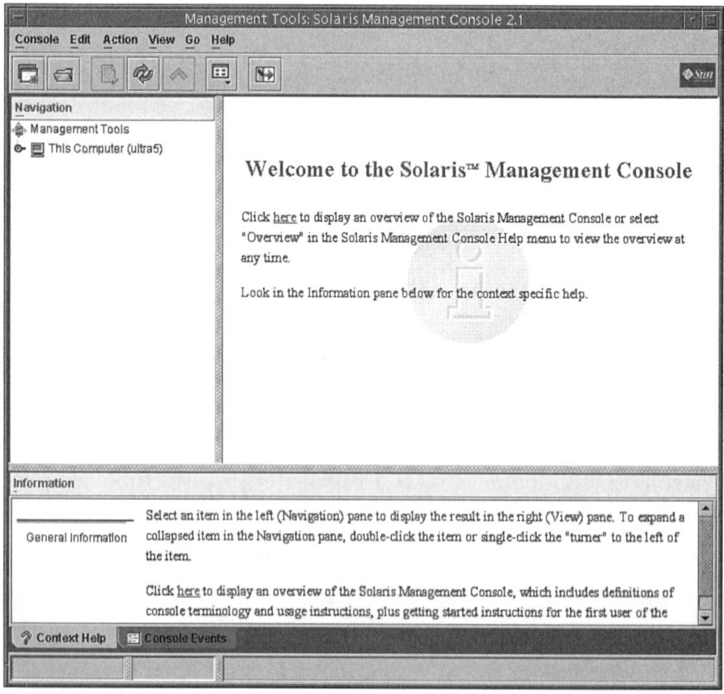

FIGURE 5.6 SMC Welcome Window.

The Process Tool works much the same way as the Process Manager tool described earlier.

pargs

The `pargs` command is used from the command line to examine the arguments and environment variables of a process (or number of processes). `pargs` can also be used to examine core files.

The syntax for the `pargs` command is as follows:

```
pargs [options] [pid ¦ core]
```

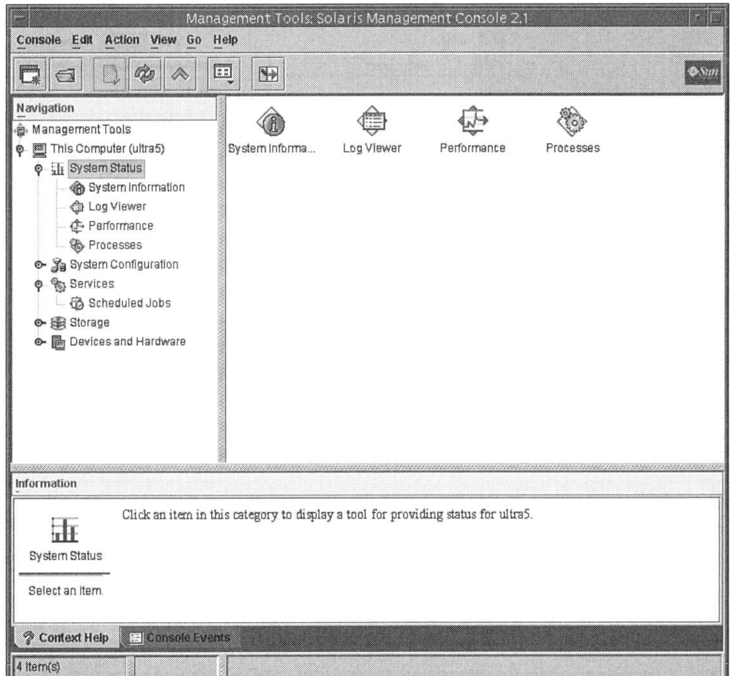

FIGURE 5.7 Opening the Job Scheduler.

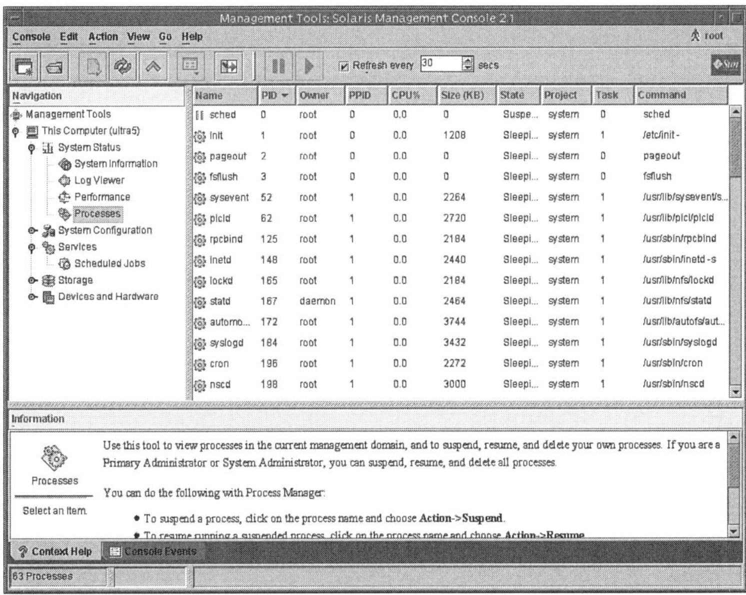

FIGURE 5.8 Process Tool.

Table 5.11 describes the pargs command options and arguments.

TABLE 5.11 pargs Options and Arguments

Option/Arguments	Description
-a	Prints the process arguments.
-c	Treats strings in the target process as though they were encoded in 7-bit ASCII.
-e	Prints process environment variables and values.
-F	Force. Grabs the target process even if another process has control.
-x	Prints process auxiliary vector.
<pid>	Process ID list. The PID list can be a single process ID or multiple PIDs separated by a space.
core	Processes a core file.

For example, to use the pargs command to view all of the environment variables associated with the telnetd process, I first need to find the PID of the telnetd process using pgrep as follows:

```
# pgrep telnetd
16173
```

Next, I issue the pargs command using the PID for the telnetd process as an argument:

```
# pargs -e 16173
```

The system responds with

```
16173:  /usr/sbin/in.telnetd
envp[0]: SMF_RESTARTER=svc:/network/inetd:default
envp[1]: SMF_FMRI=svc:/network/telnet:default
envp[2]: SMF_METHOD=inetd_start
envp[3]: PATH=/usr/sbin:/usr/bin
envp[4]: TZ=US/Michigan
```

SVCS

The Service Management Facility (SMF) was described in Chapter 3, “Perform System Boot and Shutdown Procedures for SPARC, x64, and x86-Based Systems,” so I won't be redundant by describing it again here. However, this is just a reminder that you can use the svcs command with the -p option to list all processes associated with each service instance.

Process Types

When sitting at a terminal and typing in commands, the user is typically executing *foreground processes*. Commands such as `vi` are foreground processes—they read input from the keyboard and display output to the terminal. Foreground processes maintain control of the terminal, and the user cannot do anything else in that terminal window until the execution of that command is complete.

Some processes are not interactive and don't need to run in the foreground. These are referred to as *background processes* or *jobs*. A background process gets detached from the terminal, freeing up the terminal while it is running. When a user decides to run a process in the background, you must arrange for the process to get its input from another source. In addition, you need to arrange for the process to output to a device other than the terminal, such as a file.

To run a process in the background, enter an `&` (ampersand) after the command:

```
# find . -name core -print &
```

After typing in this command, you're returned to a command prompt. The `find` command executes in the background. One problem, however, is the standard output is still on your terminal. In other words, as the `find` command executes, the results still are displayed on your screen, which can become quite annoying. It's best to redirect the output to a file, as follows:

```
# find . -name core -print  > /tmp/results &
```

After you put the `find` command in the background, the system displays two numbers associated with that process—the job number and the process ID number (PID) as follows:

```
    [1]    14919
```

You use this job number to control background processes.

NOTE

No Job Control in the `sh` shell The Bourne shell does not provide job control. Job control enables you to check and manage your background jobs. Thus, with the Bourne shell, you can submit jobs to the background, but you cannot manage them. Use `jsh` (job shell), which provides all the functionality of `sh` and enables job control. The Korn shell (`ksh`) and the C shell (`csh`) both allow for job control.

The shell maintains a table containing information about processes that are currently in the background. This is referred to as the *jobs table*. The jobs table is unique to the user, and each user has his own jobs table. Furthermore, the jobs table contains only entries for jobs that are running in your current shell. If you start a new shell, the jobs table for the new shell is empty. Each job in the table is assigned a number that is unique to that user only. In other words, two users can each have a job numbered 1. Don't confuse this job number with a process ID number; remember, process IDs are unique, and no two share the same number. Any jobs that the user has placed in the background are displayed here by typing in the `jobs` command, as follows:

```
# jobs
```

The system responds with this:

```
[3] +  Running   find / -name bill -print > /tmp/results3 &
[2] -  Running   find / -name junk -print > /tmp/results2 &
[1]    Running   find / -name core -print > /tmp/results1 &
```

The jobs table contains the following information:

- A numeric value for each job
- A + (plus) symbol to designate the current job that user commands will operate on
- A - (minus) symbol to designate the next job that the user commands will operate on
- The status of the job
- The name of the job

Each job in the job table has one of the following states:

- `Running`—An active job
- `Stopped`—A job that has been suspended
- `Terminated`—A job that has been killed
- `Done`—A completed job

When the job finishes, the following is displayed on your terminal:

```
[1] +  Done      find / -name core -print > /tmp/results &
```

Note the job number of `1` and the status of `Done`.

If you want to terminate a job, use the `kill` command followed by a `%` (percent sign) and then the job number, as follows:

```
# kill %1
```

CAUTION

Pay special attention to the use of the `%` (percent) symbol—it's absolutely required. Without it, you could kill the wrong process and potentially crash the system. Get familiar with the `kill` command in the next section of this chapter before you use it.

If you do not enter a number following the `%` sign, the command acts upon the current job entry listed in the jobs table. For this example, you are going to kill job number 1, as follows:

```
# kill %1
```

The following message is displayed indicating successful termination:

```
[1] + Terminated   find / -name core -print > /tmp/results &
```

You can also bring a job back into the foreground with the `fg` command. Typing `fg` with no arguments brings the current job (the job with the + sign next to it in the jobs table) into the foreground. You can also specify the job by typing `fg %<job number>`, as follows:

```
# fg %2
```

This brings job 2 back into the foreground on your terminal.

In a windowing environment such as Java Desktop System, placing jobs in the background is not an issue. Typically, you start a job in one window and open another window to continue working. Therefore, placing jobs into the background has all but disappeared unless you are working on a character-based terminal.

Using Signals

Objective:

Clearing frozen processes.

Solaris supports the concept of sending software *signals* to a process. These signals are ways for other processes to interact with a running process outside the context of the hardware. The `kill` command is used to send a signal to a process. System administrators most often use the signals `SIGHUP`, `SIGKILL`, `SIGSTOP`, and `SIGTERM`. The `SIGHUP` signal is used by some utilities as a way to notify the process to do something, such as re-read its configuration file. The `SIGHUP` signal is also sent to a process if the remote connection is lost or hangs up. The `SIGKILL` signal is used to abort a process, and the `SIGSTOP` signal is used to pause a process. The SIGTERM signal is the default signal sent to processes by commands such as `kill` and `pkill` when no signal is specified. Table 5.12 describes the most common signals an administrator is likely to use.

EXAM ALERT

Don't worry about remembering all of the signals listed; just be familiar with the more common signals, such as `SIGHUP`, `SIGKILL`, `SIGSTOP`, and `SIGTERM`.

TABLE 5.12 Signals Available Under Solaris

Signal	Number	Description
SIGHUP	1	Hangup. Usually means that the controlling terminal has been disconnected.
SIGINT	2	Interrupt. The user can generate this signal by pressing Ctrl+C or Delete.

(continues)

TABLE 5.12 *Continued*

Signal	Number	Description
SIGQUIT	3	Quits the process and produces a core dump.
SIGILL	4	Illegal instruction.
SIGTRAP	5	Trace or breakpoint trap.
SIGABRT	6	Abort.
SIGEMT	7	Emulation trap.
SIGFPE	8	Arithmetic exception. Informs a process of a floating-point error.
SIGKILL	9	Killed. Forces the process to terminate. This is a sure kill.
SIGBUS	10	Bus error.
SIGSEGV	11	Segmentation fault.
SIGSYS	12	Bad system call.
SIGPIPE	13	Broken pipe.
SIGALRM	14	Alarm clock.
SIGTERM	15	Terminated. A gentle kill that gives processes a chance to clean up.
SIGUSR1	16	User signal 1.
SIGUSR2	17	User signal 2.
SIGCHLD	18	Child status changed.
SIGPWR	19	Power fail or restart.
SIGWINCH	20	Window size change.
SIGURG	21	Urgent socket condition.
SIGPOLL	22	Pollable event.
SIGSTOP	23	Stopped (signal). Pauses a process.
SIGTSTP	24	Stopped (user).
SIGCONT	25	Continued.
SIGTTIN	26	Stopped (tty input).
SIGTTOU	27	Stopped (tty output).
SIGVTALRM	28	Virtual timer expired.
SIGPROF	29	Profiling timer expired.
SIGXCPU	30	CPU time limit exceeded.
SIGXFSZ	31	File size limit exceeded.
SIGWAITING	32	Concurrency signal reserved by threads library.
SIGLWP	33	Inter-LWP signal reserved by threads library.
SIGFREEZE	34	Checkpoint freeze.
SIGTHAW	35	Checkpoint thaw.
SIGCANCEL	36	Cancellation signal reserved by the threads library.

NOTE

Obtain a list of the signals by typing: `man signal.h`

In addition, you can write a *signal handler*, or *trap*, in a program to respond to a signal being sent. For example, many system programs, such as the name server daemon, respond to the `SIGHUP` signal by re-reading their configuration files. This signal can then be used to update the process while running, without having to terminate and restart the process. Signal handlers cannot be installed for `SIGSTOP` (23) or `SIGKILL` (9). Because the process cannot install a signal handler for signal 9, an otherwise well-behaved process may leave temporary files around or not be able to finish out critical operations that it is in the middle of. Thus, `kill -9` invites corruption of application data files and should only be used as a last resort.

Here's an example of how to trap a signal in a script:

```
# trap '/bin/rm tmp$$;exit 1' 1 2 3 15
```

As the name suggests, `trap` traps system interrupt until some command can be executed. The previous example traps the signals `1`, `2`, `3`, and `15`, and executes the `/bin/rm tmp$$` command before exiting the program. The example deletes all `tmp` files even if the program terminates abnormally.

The `kill` command sends a terminate signal (signal 15) to the process, and the process is terminated. Signal 15, which is the default when no options are used with the `kill` command, is a gentle kill that allows a process to perform cleanup work before terminating. Signal 9, on the other hand, is called a sure, unconditional kill because it cannot be caught or ignored by a process. If the process is still around after a `kill -9`, either it is hung up in the Unix kernel, waiting for an event such as disk I/O to complete, or you are not the owner of the process.

The `kill` command is routinely used to send signals to a process. You can kill any process you own, and the superuser can kill all processes in the system except those that have process IDs `0`, `1`, `2`, `3`, and `4`. The `kill` command is poorly named because not every signal sent by it is used to kill a process. This command gets its name from its most common use—terminating a process with the `kill -15` signal.

NOTE

Forking Problem A common problem occurs when a process continually starts up new copies of itself—this is referred to as *forking* or *spawning*. Users have a limit on the number of new processes they can fork. This limit is set in the kernel with the `MAXUP` (maximum number of user processes) value. Sometimes, through user error, a process keeps forking new copies of itself until the user hits the `MAXUP` limit. As a user reaches this limit, the system appears to be waiting. If you kill some of the user's processes, the system resumes creating new processes on behalf of the user. It can be a no-win situation. The best way to handle these runaway processes is to send the `STOP` signal to all of the runaway processes to suspend the processes and then send a `KILL` signal to terminate the processes. Because the processes were first suspended, they can't create new ones as you kill them off.

You can send a signal to a process you own with the `kill` command. Many signals are available, as listed in Table 5.12. To send a signal to a process, first use the `ps` command to find the process ID (PID) number. For example, type `ps -ef` to list all processes and find the PID of the process you want to terminate:

```
# ps -ef

UID     PID  PPID  C    STIME  TTY   TIME   CMD
root      0     0  0   Nov 27  ?     0:01   sched
root      1     0  0   Nov 27  ?     0:01   /etc/init -
root      2     0  0   Nov 27  ?     0:00   pageout
root      3     0  0   Nov 27  ?    12:52   fsflush
root    101     1  0   Nov 27  ?     0:00   /usr/sbin/in.routed -q
root    298     1  0   Nov 27  ?     0:00   /usr/lib/saf/sac -t 300
root    111     1  0   Nov 27  ?     0:02   /usr/sbin/rpcbind
root    164     1  0   Nov 27  ?     0:01   /usr/sbin/syslogd -n -z 12
root    160     1  0   Nov 27  ?     0:01   /usr/lib/autofs/automountd
.
.
.
root   5497   433  1 09:58:02  pts/4  0:00   script psef
```

To kill the process with a PID number of `5497`, type this:

```
# kill 5497
```

Another way to kill a process is to use the `pkill` command. `pkill` functions identically to `pgrep`, which was described earlier, except that instead of displaying information about each process, the process is terminated. A signal name or number may be specified as the first command-line option to `pkill`. The value for the signal can be any value described in Table 5.12. For example, to kill the process named `psef` with a `SIGKILL` signal, issue the following command:

```
# pkill -9 psef
```

> **NOTE**
>
> **Killing a Process** If no signal is specified, `SIGTERM (15)` is sent by default. This is the preferred signal to send when trying to kill a process. Only when a `SIGTERM` fails should you send a SIGKILL signal to a process. As stated earlier in this section, a process cannot install a signal handler for signal 9 and an otherwise well-behaved process might not shut down properly.

In addition, the Desktop Process Manager, which was described earlier, can be used to kill processes. In the Process Manager window, highlight the process that you want to terminate, click Process from the toolbar at the top of the window, and then select Kill from the pull-down menu, as shown in Figure 5.9.

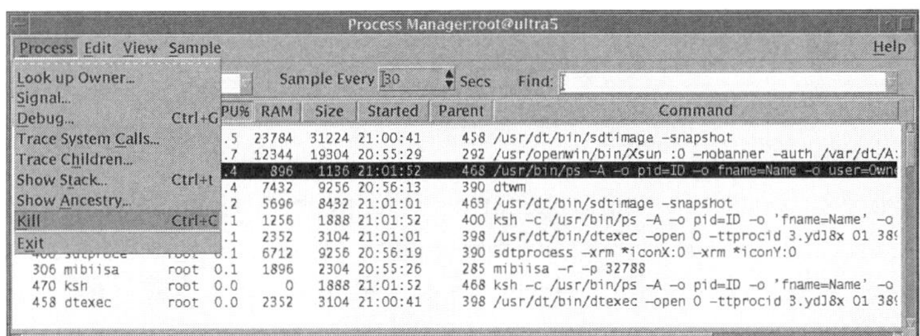

Figure 5.9 Killing processes.

The equivalent Unix command used by the Process Manager to terminate a process is shown here:

```
# kill -9 <PID>
```

`<PID>` is the process ID of the selected process.

The `preap` command forces the killing of a defunct process, known as a *zombie*. In previous Solaris releases, zombie processes that could not be killed off remained until the next system reboot. Defunct processes do not normally impact system operation; however, they do consume a small amount of system memory. See the `preap` manual page for further details of this command.

Scheduling Processes

Processes compete for execution time. *Scheduling*, one of the key elements in a time-sharing system, determines which of the processes executes next. Although hundreds of processes might be present on the system, only one actually uses a given CPU at any given time. Time sharing on a CPU involves suspending a process and then restarting it later. Because the suspension and resumption of active processes occurs many times each second, it appears to the user that the system is performing many tasks simultaneously.

Unix attempts to manage the priorities of processes by giving a higher priority to those that have used the least amount of CPU time. In addition, processes that are waiting on an event, such as a keyboard press, get higher priority than processes that are purely CPU-driven.

On any large system with a number of competing user groups, the task of managing resources falls to the system administrator. This task is both technical and political. As a system administrator, you must understand your company goals to manage this task successfully. When you understand the political implications of who should get priority, you are ready to manage the technical details. As root, you can change the priority of any process on the system by using the `nice` or `priocntl` commands. Before you do this, you must understand how priorities work.

Scheduling Priorities

All processes have assigned to them an execution priority—an integer value that is dynamically computed and updated on the basis of several different factors. Whenever the CPU is free, the scheduler selects the most favored process to resume executing. The process selected is the one with the lowest-priority number because lower numbers are defined as more favored than higher ones. Multiple processes at the same priority level are placed in the run queue for that priority level. Whenever the CPU is free, the scheduler starts the processes at the head of the lowest-numbered nonempty run queue. When the process at the top of a run queue stops executing, it goes to the end of the line and the next process moves up to the front. After a process begins to run, it continues to execute until it needs to wait for an I/O operation to complete, receives an interrupt signal, or exhausts the maximum execution time slice defined on that system. A typical time slice is 10 milliseconds.

A Unix process has two priority numbers associated with it. One of the priority numbers is its requested execution priority with respect to other processes. This value (its `nice` number) is set by the process's owner and by root; it appears in the `NI` column in a `ps -l` listing. The other priority assigned to a process is the execution priority. This priority is computed and updated dynamically by the operating system, taking into account such factors as the process's `nice` number, how much CPU time it has had recently, and other processes that are running and their priorities. The execution priority value appears in the `PRI` column on a `ps -l` listing.

Although the CPU is the most-watched resource on a system, it is not the only one. Memory use, disk use, I/O activity, and the number of processes all tie together in determining the computer's throughput. For example, suppose you have two groups, A and B. Both groups require large amounts of memory—more than is available when both are running simultaneously. Raising the priority of Group A over Group B might not help if Group B does not fully relinquish the memory it is using. Although the paging system does this over time, the process of swapping a process out to disk can be intensive and can greatly reduce performance. A better alternative might be to completely stop Group B with a signal and then continue it later, when Group A has finished.

Changing the Priority of a Time-Sharing Process with `nice`

The `nice` command is supported only for backward compatibility with previous Solaris releases. The `priocntl` command provides more flexibility in managing processes. The priority of a process is determined by the policies of its scheduling class and by its `nice` number. Each time-sharing process has a global priority that is calculated by adding the user-supplied priority, which can be influenced by the `nice` or `priocntl` commands, and the system-calculated priority.

The execution priority number of a process is assigned by the operating system and is determined by several factors, including its schedule class, how much CPU time it has used, and its `nice` number. Each time-sharing process starts with a default `nice` number, which it inherits from its parent process. The `nice` number is shown in the `NI` column of the `ps` report.

A user can lower the priority of a process by increasing its user-supplied priority number. Only the superuser can increase the priority of a process by lowering its `nice` value. This prevents users from increasing the priorities of their own processes, thereby monopolizing a greater share of the CPU.

Two versions of the `nice` command are available: the standard version, `/usr/bin/nice`, and a version that is integrated into the C shell as a C shell built-in. `/usr/bin/nice` numbers range from `0` to `+39` and the default value is 20, while the C-shell built-in version of `nice` has values that range from –20 to +20. The lower the number, the higher the priority and the faster the process runs.

Use the `/usr/bin/nice` command as described in Table 5.13 when submitting a program or command.

TABLE 5.13 Setting Priorities with `nice`

Command	Description
Lowering the Priority of a Process Using `/usr/bin/nice`	
`nice` <*process_name*>	Increases the `nice` number by 4 units (the default)
`nice -4` <*process_name*>	Increases the `nice` number by 4 units
`nice -10` <*process_name*>	Increases the `nice` number by 10 units
Increasing the Priority of a Process	
`nice -n -10` <*process_name*>	Raises the priority of the command by lowering the `nice` number

NOTE

Root may run commands with a priority higher than normal by using a negative increment, such as -10. A negative increment assigned by an unprivileged user is ignored.

As a system administrator, you can use the `renice` command to change the priority of a process after it has been submitted. The `renice` command has the following form:

```
renice priority -n <value> -p <pid>
```

Use the ps -elf command to find the PID of the process for which you want to change the priority. The process that you want to change in the following example is named largejob:

```
# ps -elf¦grep largejob
9 S   0   8200  4100  0  84  20  f0274e38  193        Jun 04 ?    0:00 largejob
```

Issue the following command to increase the priority of PID 8200:

```
renice -n -4 -p 8200
```

Issuing the ps -elf command again shows the process with a higher priority:

```
# ps -elf¦grep largejob
9 S   0  8200  4100  0  60  16   f0274e38  193      Jun 04  ?    0:00  largejob
```

Changing the Scheduling Priority of Processes with priocntl

The standard priority scheme has been improved since earlier versions of Solaris as part of its support for real-time processes. Real-time processes are designed to work in application areas in which a nearly immediate response to events is required. These processes are given nearly complete access to all system resources when they are running. Solaris uses time-sharing priority numbers ranging from -20 to 20. Solaris uses the priocntl command, intended as an improvement over the nice command, to modify process priorities. To use priocntl to change a priority on a process, type this:

```
priocntl -s -p <new-priority>  -i pid <process-id>
```

new-priority is the new priority for the process, and *process-id* is the PID of the process you want to change.

The following example sets the priority level for process 8200 to -5:

```
priocntl -s -p -5 -i pid 8200
```

The following example is used to set the priority (nice value) for every process created by a given parent process:

```
priocntl -s -p -5 -I ppid 8200
```

As a result of this command, all processes forked from process 8200 have a priority of -5.

The priority value assigned to a process can be displayed using the ps command, which was described earlier in this chapter.

The functionality of the priocntl command goes much further than what is described in this section. Consult the online manual pages for more information about the priocntl command.

Fair Share Scheduler (FSS) and the Fixed Scheduler (FX)

The *Fair Share Scheduler (FSS)* in Solaris 10 can be used to control the allocation of resources. The *Fixed Scheduler (FX)* is a fixed priority scheduler that provides an ensured priority for processes. Neither of these are objectives on the CX-310-200 exam and they are not covered in this chapter.

Using the Solaris Batch-Processing Facility

A way to divide processes on a busy system is to schedule jobs so that they run at different times. A large job, for example, could be scheduled to run at 2:00 a.m., when the system would normally be idle. Solaris supports two methods of batch processing: the `crontab` and `at` commands. The `crontab` command schedules multiple system events at regular intervals, and the `at` command schedules a single system event.

Configuring `crontab`

Objective:

Explain how to schedule the automatic recurring execution of a command.

`cron` is a Unix utility named after Chronos ("time"), the ancient Greek god of time. It enables you to execute commands automatically according to a schedule you define. The `cron` daemon schedules system events according to commands found in each `crontab` file. A `crontab` file consists of commands, one per line, that will be executed at regular intervals. The beginning of each line contains five date and time fields that tell the `cron` daemon when to execute the command. The sixth field is the full pathname of the program you want to run. These fields, described in Table 5.14, are separated by spaces.

TABLE 5.14 The `crontab` File

Field	Description	Values
1	Minute	`0` to `59`. A `*` in this field means every minute.
2	Hour	`0` to `23`. A `*` in this field means every hour.
3	Day of month	`1` to `31`. A `*` in this field means every day of the month.
4	Month	`1` to `12`. A `*` in this field means every month.
5	Day of week	`0` to `6` (`0 = Sunday`). A `*` in this field means every day of the week.
6	Command	Enter the command to be run.

Follow these guidelines when making entries in the crontab file:

- Use a space to separate fields.
- Use a comma to separate multiple values in any of the date or time fields.
- Use a hyphen to designate a range of values in any of the date or time fields.
- Use an asterisk as a wildcard to include all possible values in any of the date or time fields. For example, an asterisk (*) can be used in the first five fields (time fields) to mean all legal values.
- Use a comment mark (#) at the beginning of a line to indicate a comment or a blank line.
- Each command within a crontab file must consist of one line, even if it is very long, because crontab does not recognize extra carriage returns.
- There can be no blank lines in the crontab file. Although this is not documented well, and some crontab files I've seen contain blank lines, the system will generate an email to root with a message that "there is an error in your crontab file."

The following sample crontab command entry displays a reminder in the user's console window at 5:00 p.m. on the 1st and 15th of every month:

```
0 17 1,15 * * echo Hand in Timesheet > /dev/console
```

crontab files are found in the /var/spool/cron/crontabs directory. Several crontab files besides root are provided during the SunOS software installation process; they are also located in this directory. Other crontab files are named after the user accounts for which they are created, such as bill, glenda, miguel, or nicole. They also are located in the /var/spool/cron/ crontabs directory. For example, a crontab file named root is supplied during software installation. Its contents include these command lines:

```
10 3 * * * /usr/sbin/logadm
15 3 * * 0 /usr/lib/fs/nfs/nfsfind
30 3 * * * [ -x /usr/lib/gss/gsscred_clean ] && /usr/lib/gss/gsscred_clean
#10 3 * * * /usr/lib/krb5/kprop_script ___slave_kdcs___
```

The first command line instructs the system to run /usr/sbin/logadmin at 3:10 a.m. every day of the week. The second command line orders the system to execute nfsfind on Sunday at 3:15 a.m. The third command line runs each night at 3:30 a.m. and executes the gsscred command. The fourth command is commented out. The cron daemon never exits and is started via the svc:/system/cron:default service. The /etc/cron.d/FIFO file is used as a lock file to prevent running more than one instance of cron.

Creating and Editing a crontab File

Creating an entry in the crontab file is as easy as editing a text file using your favorite editor. Use the steps described next to edit this file; otherwise, your changes are not recognized until the next time the cron daemon starts up. cron examines crontab configuration files only during its own process-initialization phase or when the crontab command is run. This reduces the overhead of checking for new or changed files at regularly scheduled intervals.

Step by Step 5.2 tells you how to create or edit a crontab file.

STEP BY STEP

5.2 Creating or Editing a crontab File

1. (Optional) To create or edit a crontab file belonging to root or another user, become superuser.
2. Create a new crontab file or edit an existing one by typing the following:

```
# crontab -e
```

NOTE

crontab Default Editor The crontab command chooses the system default editor, which is ed, unless you've set the VISUAL or EDITOR variable to vi (or another editor), as follows:

```
# EDITOR=vi;export EDITOR
```

3. Add command lines to the file, following the syntax described in Table 5.14. Because cron jobs do not inherit the users environment, such as PATH, you should specify the full pathname for commands.
4. Save the changes and exit the file. The crontab file is placed in /var/spool/cron/crontabs.
5. Verify the crontab file by typing the following:

```
# crontab -l
```

The system responds by listing the contents of the crontab file.

Controlling Access to crontab

TIP

Many of the questions that you encounter regarding cron are related to controlling access to cron using the files described in this section. Make sure that you have a clear understanding of how you can control a user's access to cron by adding and removing entries in these files.

You can control access to crontab by modifying two files in the /etc/cron.d directory: cron.deny and cron.allow. These files permit only specified users to perform crontab tasks such as creating, editing, displaying, and removing their own crontab files. The cron.deny and cron.allow files consist of a list of usernames, one per line. These access control files work together in the following manner:

- If cron.allow exists, only the users listed in this file can create, edit, display, and remove crontab files.

- If cron.allow doesn't exist, all users may submit crontab files, except for users listed in cron.deny.
- If neither cron.allow nor cron.deny exists, superuser privileges are required to run crontab.

Superuser privileges are required to edit or create cron.deny and cron.allow.

During the Solaris software installation process, a default /etc/cron.d/cron.deny file is provided. It contains the following entries:

- daemon
- bin
- nuucp
- listen
- nobody
- noaccess

None of the users listed in the cron.deny file can access crontab commands. The system administrator can edit this file to add other users who are denied access to the crontab command. No default cron.allow file is supplied. This means that, after the Solaris software installation, all users (except the ones listed in the default cron.deny file) can access crontab. If you create a cron.allow file, only those users can access crontab commands.

Scheduling a Single System Event (at)

Objective:

Explain how to schedule an automatic one-time execution of a command using the command line.

The at command is used to schedule jobs for execution at a later time. Unlike crontab, which schedules a job to happen at regular intervals, a job submitted with at executes once, at the designated time.

To submit an at job, type at followed by the time that you would like the program to execute. You'll see the at> prompt displayed and it's here that you enter the at commands. When you are finished entering the at command, press control-d to exit the at prompt and submit the job as shown in the following example:

```
# at 07:45am today
at> who > /tmp/log
at> <Press Control-d>
job 912687240.a at Thu Jun 6 07:14:00
```

When you submit an at job, it is assigned a job identification number, which becomes its filename along with the .a extension. The file is stored in the /var/spool/cron/atjobs directory. In much the same way as it schedules crontab jobs, the cron daemon controls the scheduling of at files.

The command syntax for at is shown here:

```
# at [-m -l -r] <time> <date>
```

The at command is described in Table 5.15.

TABLE 5.15 at Command Syntax

Option	Description
-m	Sends you mail after the job is completed.
-l	Reports all jobs for the user.
-r	Removes a specified job.
<time>	The hour when you want to schedule the job. Add am or pm if you do not specify the hours according to a 24-hour clock. midnight, noon, and now are acceptable keywords. Minutes are optional.
<date>	The first three or more letters of a month, a day of the week, or the keywords today or tomorrow.

You can set up a file to control access to the at command, permitting only specified users to create, remove, or display queue information about their at jobs. The file that controls access to at is /etc/cron.d/at.deny. It consists of a list of usernames, one per line. The users listed in this file cannot access at commands. The default at.deny file, created during the SunOS software installation, contains the following usernames:

- daemon
- bin
- smtp
- nuucp
- listen
- nobody
- noaccess

With superuser privileges, you can edit this file to add other usernames whose at access you want to restrict.

Checking Jobs in Queue (atq and at -l)

To check your jobs that are waiting in the at queue, use the atq command. This command displays status information about the at jobs you created. Use the atq command to verify that you have created an at job. The atq command confirms that at jobs have been submitted to the queue, as shown in the following example:

```
# atq
```

The system responds with this:

```
Rank   Execution Date Owner  Job             Queue   Job Name
1st    Jun  6, 08:00  root   912690000.a       a     stdin
2nd    Jun  6, 08:05  root   912690300.a       a     stdin
```

Another way to check an at job is to issue the at -l command. This command shows the status information on all jobs submitted by a user, as shown in this example:

```
# at -l
```

The system responds with this:

```
user = root    912690000.a    Thu Jun  6 08:00:00
user = root    912690300.a    Thu Jun  6 08:05:00
```

Removing and Verifying Removal of at Jobs

To remove the at job from the queue before it is executed, type this:

```
# at -r [job-id]
```

job-id is the identification number of the job you want to remove.

Verify that the at job has been removed by using the at -l (or atq) command to display the jobs remaining in the at queue. The job whose identification number you specified should not appear. In the following example, you'll remove an at job that was scheduled to execute at 8:00 a.m. on June 6. First, check the at queue to locate the job identification number:

```
# at -l
```

The system responds with this:

```
user = root    912690000.a    Thu Jun  6 08:00:00
user = root    912690300.a    Thu Jun  6 08:05:00
```

Next, remove the job from the at queue:

```
# at -r 912690000.a
```

Finally, verify that this job has been removed from the queue:

```
# at -l
```

The system responds with this:

```
# user = root    912690300.a    Thu Jun  6 08:05:00
```

Job Scheduler

The Solaris Management Console (SMC) includes a graphical tool to create and schedule jobs on your system. You can use the Job Scheduler Tool to

- View and modify job properties
- Delete a job
- Add a scheduled job
- Enable or disable job logging

To open the Job Scheduler, follow the steps described in the "SMC Process Tool" section to start up the SMC using the `smc` command.

1. In the Navigation pane of the SMC Welcome window, open the Job Scheduler by clicking on the This Computer icon, then click on the Services icon, and then click on the Scheduled Jobs icon as shown in Figure 5.10.

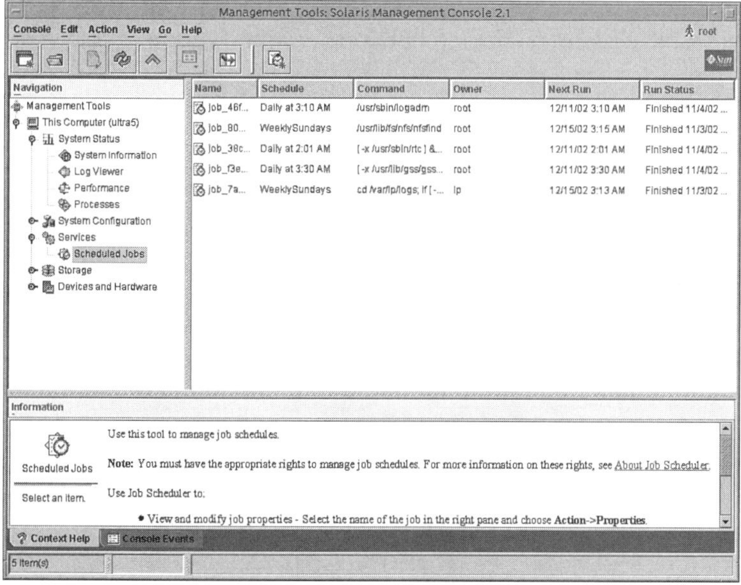

FIGURE 5.10 Opening the Job Scheduler.

2. You can add jobs to the `crontab` by selecting Action from the top toolbar as shown in Figure 5.11.

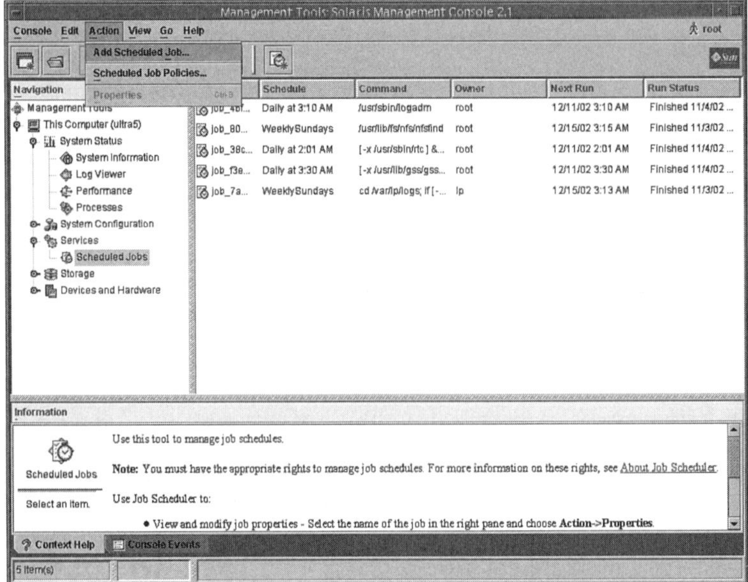

FIGURE 5.11 Adding a `cron` job.

3. Modify a `cron` job by double clicking on the job in the main window pane as shown in Figure 5.12.

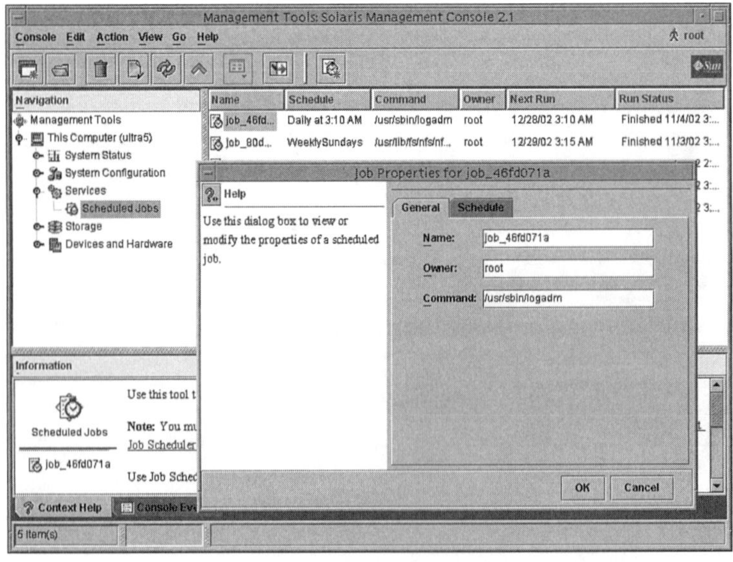

FIGURE 5.12 Modifiying a `cron` job.

Summary

This chapter described Solaris processes and the various Solaris utilities available to monitor them. Using commands such as `ps`, `prstat`, `pargs`, `sdtprocess`, and the SMC Process Tool, you can view all the attributes associated with a process. In addition, we described foreground and background jobs.

The concept of sending signals to a process was described. A signal is a message sent to a process to interrupt it and cause a response or action. You also learned how to send signals to processes to cause a response such as terminating a process.

Setting process priorities was described. We also described the concept of projects and tasks along with administrative commands used to administer them. The various commands, such as `nice` and `priocntl`, that are used to set and change process priorities were described. In addition, you learned how to use the `crontab` and `at` facilities. You can use these facilities to submit batch jobs and schedule processes to run when the system is less busy, to reduce the demand on resources such as the CPU and disks.

The system administrator needs to be aware of the processes that belong to each application. As users report problems, the system administrator can quickly locate the processes being used and look for irregularities. By keeping a close watch on system messages and processes, you'll become familiar with what is normal and what is abnormal. Don't wait for problems to happen—watch system messages and processes daily. Create shell scripts to watch processes for you and to look for irregularities in the system log files. By taking a proactive approach to system administration, you'll find problems before they affect the users.

In Chapter 6, "Managing the LP Print Service," we'll explore another topic that you'll need to become acquainted with—the LP Print Service, the facility responsible for printing within the Solaris environment.

Key Terms

- `at` command
- Process Manager GUI
- Child process
- `cron`
- `crontab`
- `crontab` file
- `mpstat`
- `ptree`
- `nice` command
- Parent process
- `pgrep` command
- `preap` command
- `priocntl` command
- Process
- Project (as it relates to process management)
- `prstat` command

- ps command
- Signals
- SMC Job Scheduler
- SMC Process Tool
- `time`
- Zombie process

Exercises

5.1 Displaying Process Information

In this exercise, you'll use the various utilities described in this chapter to display information about active processes.

Estimated time: 10 minutes

1. Log in as root into the Java Desktop Environment or CDE.
2. Open a new window and display the active processes using the `ps` command:

   ```
   # ps -ef
   ```

3. Open another new window and display the active processes using the `prstat` command:

   ```
   # prstat
   ```

   Notice how the `ps` command took a snapshot of the active processes, but the `prstat` command continues to update its display.
4. Type `q` to exit `prstat`.
5. Display the `dtlogin` process and all of its child processes. First obtain the PID of the `dtlogin` process with the `pgrep` command:

   ```
   # pgrep dtlogin
   ```

   Now use the `ptree` command with the PID of the `dtlogin` process to display the ancestry tree:

   ```
   # ptree <PID from dtlogin>
   ```

6. Now start the Process Manager.

   ```
   # sdtprocess &
   ```

   Notice how the window updates periodically.
7. In the sample field at the top of the window, change the sample period from 30 to 5 seconds.
8. Sort the processes by ID by clicking on the ID button in the header.

5.2 Using the Batch Process

In this exercise, you'll use `crontab` to configure a process to execute everyday at a specified time.

Estimated time: 10 minutes

1. Log in as root into a Java Desktop or CDE session.
2. Make sure your default shell editor is set to `vi` (EDITOR=vi;export EDITOR) before beginning this exercise.
3. Open a new window and edit the `crontab` entry.

   ```
   # crontab -e
   ```

4. Enter the following after the last line at the end of the file:

   ```
   0 11 * * * echo Hand in Timesheet > /dev/console
   ```

5. Save and close the file.

   Open a console window and at 11:00 a.m., you'll see the message `Hand in Timesheet` displayed.

Exam Questions

1. Which of the following commands finds all processes that have `dt` in the process argument string? Choose all that apply.

   ❍ **A.** `pgrep -l -f dt`

   ❍ **B.** `ps -ef dt`

   ❍ **C.** `ps -el dt`

   ❍ **D.** `ps -ef¦grep dt`

2. Which one of the following commands kills a process named `test`?

   ❍ **A.** `pkill test`

   ❍ **B.** `kill test`

   ❍ **C.** `ps -ef¦¦grep kill¦ kill -9`

   ❍ **D.** `kill -test`

3. Which commands display active system processes and update at a specified interval? Choose all that apply.

   ❍ **A.** `ps`

   ❍ **B.** `prstat`

   ❍ **C.** `sdtprocess`

   ❍ **D.** `ptree`

4. In output from the `ps` command, what does an `R` stand for in the `S` field?

   ❍ **A.** The process is on the run queue.

   ❍ **B.** The process is receiving input.

   ❍ **C.** It is a regular process.

   ❍ **D.** The process is sleeping, so it must be restarted.

5. In output from the `ps` command, which of the following does the `UID` field display?

   ❍ **A.** The parent process

   ❍ **B.** The process id

   ❍ **C.** The process owner

   ❍ **D.** The priority of the process

6. Which one of the following options to the `ps` command lists only processes for a particular user?

   ❍ **A.** `-P`

   ❍ **B.** `-f`

   ❍ **C.** `-l`

   ❍ **D.** `-u`

7. Which one of the following commands lists all processes running on the local system?

   ❍ **A.** `ps -e`

   ❍ **B.** `ps -a`

   ❍ **C.** `ps -f`

   ❍ **D.** `ps -t`

8. Which one of the following sends a terminate signal (signal 15) to a process with a PID of 2930?

❍ **A.** `kill 2930`

❍ **B.** `stop 2930`

❍ **C.** Ctrl+C

❍ **D.** `cancel 2930`

9. Which one of the following signals kills a process unconditionally?

❍ **A.** 9

❍ **B.** 0

❍ **C.** 15

❍ **D.** 1

10. Which of the following commands is used to change the priority on a process? Choose all that apply.

❍ **A.** `renice`

❍ **B.** `priocntl`

❍ **C.** `ps`

❍ **D.** `hup`

11. Which one of the following commands is issued to increase the priority of PID 8200?

❍ **A.** `renice -n -4 -p 8200`

❍ **B.** `nice -n -4 -p 8200`

❍ **C.** `nice -i 8200`

❍ **D.** `renice -I -p 8200`

12. Which utilities can be used to show the process ancestry tree? Choose all that apply.

❍ **A.** `ps`

❍ **B.** `ptree`

❍ **C.** `sdtprocess`

❍ **D.** `prstat`

13. Which of the following commands schedules a command to run once at a given time?

❍ **A.** `crontab`

❍ **B.** `priocntl`

❍ **C.** `at`

❍ **D.** `cron`

14. Which of the following commands show(s) the jobs queued up by the `at` command? Choose all that apply.

❍ **A.** `atq`

❍ **B.** `at -l`

❍ **C.** `ps`

❍ **D.** `crontab`

15. Which one of the following `crontab` entries instructs the system to run `logchecker` at 3:10 on Sunday and Thursday nights?

❍ **A.** `0 4 * * 10,3 /etc/cron.d/logchecker`

❍ **B.** `10 3 * * 0,4 /etc/cron.d/logchecker`

❍ **C.** `* 10 3 0,4 /etc/cron.d/logchecker`

❍ **D.** `10 3 * * 0-4 /etc/cron.d/logchecker`

16. Which one of the following logs keeps a record of all `cron` activity?

❍ **A.** `/var/cron/log`

❍ **B.** `/var/spool/cron/log`

❍ **C.** `/var/adm/cron`

❍ **D.** `/var/adm/messages`

17. A user wants to execute a command later today, after leaving work. Which one of the following commands will allow him to do this?

❍ **A.** `runat`

❍ **B.** `at`

❍ **C.** `submit`

❍ **D.** None of the above

18. You've added the user name bcalkins to the /etc/cron.d/cron.allow file. You've removed the name bcalkins from the /etc/cron.d/cron.deny file. Which statement is true regarding crontab?

❍ **A.** bcalkins cannot create crontab entries.

❍ **B.** bcalkins can create crontab entries.

❍ **C.** Only root can create crontab entries.

❍ **D.** No one can create crontab entries.

Answers to Exam Questions

1. **A, D.** Use the pgrep and ps commands to view processes running on your system. The commands pgrep -l -f dt and ps -ef¦grep dt find all the processes that have dt in the process argument string and display them.
2. **A.** The command pkill test kills a process named test.
3. **B, C.** The prstat and sdtprocess commands display active system processes and can be configured to update at a specified interval.
4. **A.** In output from the ps command, the R in the S field means that the process is on the run queue.
5. **C.** In output from the ps command, the UID field displays the process owner.
6. **D.** The -u option to the ps command lists only processes for a particular user.
7. **A.** The -e option to the ps command lists all processes currently running on the system. The other options only list processes for the local user.
8. **A.** The command kill 2930 sends a terminate signal (signal 15) to a process with a PID of 2930.
9. **A.** Signal 9 stops a process unconditionally.
10. **A, B.** The commands renice and priocntl are used to change the priority on a process.
11. **A.** The renice -n -4 -p 8200 command is issued to increase the priority of a process with a PID of 8200.
12. **B, C.** The utilities ptree and sdtprocess are used to show the process ancestry tree.
13. **C.** The at command schedules a command to run once at a given time.
14. **A, B.** The atq and at -l commands show the jobs queued up by the at command.
15. **B.** The crontab entry 10 3 * * 0,4 /etc/cron.d/logchecker instructs the system to run logchecker at 3:10 on Sunday and Thursday nights.

16. **A.** The log file named `/var/cron/log` keeps a record of all `cron` activity.
17. **B.** Use the `at` command to execute a command or script at a later time.
18. **B.** Users can manage jobs if their name appears in the `/etc/cron.d/cron.allow` file and does not appear in the `/etc/cron.d/cron.deny` file.

Suggested Reading and Resources

1. Calkins, Bill. *Inside Solaris 9*. New Riders Publishing. November 2002.

CHAPTER SIX

Managing the LP Print Service

Objectives

The following test objectives for Exam CX-310-200 are covered in this chapter:

Configure and administer Solaris 10 OS print services, including client and server configuration, starting and stopping the LP print service, specifying a destination printer, and using the LP print service.

- **You need to be able to describe how printers function in the Solaris operating environment. You need to be familiar with the tools used to manage printer queues and the various files and directories that support the print function.**
- **Be prepared to explain how to configure printer classes, set the default printer, change the default printer class, remove a printer's configuration, start the LP print service, and stop the LP print service using the appropriate commands.**
- **Understand how to manage printer queues, how to send jobs to a printer, and how to manage those jobs.**

Outline

Study Strategies

The following study strategies will help you prepare for the test:

- This chapter does not show many lengthy step-by-step procedures, but it does introduce several commands that you use to manage printers, and it provides examples on how to use these commands. You should practice the step-by-step procedures as well as the commands to make sure that you understand where and when to use them.
- You should pay close attention to the differences between the System V Release 4 (SVR4) and the Berkeley Software Distribution (BSD) print services. You need to understand the basic functions of the Solaris print service.
- You need to make sure you understand the difference between a print server and a print client. You must understand the differences between local and networked printers, and you should pay close attention to the various configuration files that are used to define a printer.

The Solaris OS Print Service (LP)

Printers are standard peripherals for many computer systems. One of the first devices added to almost any new system is a printer. The multi-user nature of the Solaris operating environment means that the Solaris printer software is more complex than that of a single-user operating system. This means that adding a printer to a Solaris system requires more than just plugging it in.

The basic function of the Solaris OS print service includes:

- Initialization: Before sending a print job to a printer, the Solaris OS initializes the printer to ensure that the printer is in a known state.
- Queuing: The Solaris OS schedules (queues) the print requests that are waiting for the printer to become available.
- Tracking: The Solaris OS tracks every print request and allows root and users to manage their print requests. The Solaris OS also logs any errors that may occur during the printing process.
- Fault Notification: If a problem occurs in the print server, the Solaris OS provides fault notification. Notification is sent via an error message on the console or an email to root.
- Filtering: Filtering is where the print service converts a print job to the appropriate type of file for the specific printer it is being sent to.

This chapter describes how to set up local printers, set up access to remote printers, and perform some printer administration tasks by using the Print Manager graphical user interface (GUI) or the command line. Print Manager should meet most of a system administrator's needs for setting up printing services, adding printers to servers, or adding access from print clients to remote printers on print servers.

Setting up a printer from the command line can be a complex task. This chapter examines the hardware issues involved in connecting a printer to a Solaris system and then moves on to examine the more complex part of the process—configuring the software.

The Solaris Print Service

Objective:

Describe the purpose, features, and functionality of printer fundamentals, including print management tools, printer configuration types, Solaris LP print service, LP print service directory structure, and the Solaris operating environment printing process.

The Solaris print service is a default cluster that is installed when the operating system is initially installed. The function of the Solaris print service is described later in this chapter. To verify that the package is installed, you should look for the following software packages by using the `pkginfo` command as described in Chapter 2, "Installing the Solaris 10 Operating Environment":

Package	Description
`SUNWlpmsg`	ToolTalk programs for passing printer alerts.
`SUNWfdl`	Solaris Desktop Font Downloader for Adobe PostScript printers.
`SUNWscplp`	Solaris Print-Source Compatibility package. This package contains print utilities for user-interface and source-build compatibility with SunOS 4.x. These utilities are located in the `/usr` directory.
`SUNWslpr`	root (`/`) file system portion of the Service Location Protocol (SLP) framework. Includes the SLP configuration file and start scripts for the SLP daemon.
`SUNWslpu`	`/usr` file system portion of the SLP framework.
`SUNWmp`	MP (make pretty) print filter.
`SUNWpcr`	Solaris print client configuration files and utilities for the print service (root).
`SUNWpcu`	Solaris print client configuration files and utilities for the print service (usr).
`SUNWppm`	Solaris Print Manager.
`SUNWpsr`	Configuration and startup files for the print service.
`SUNWpsu`	Solaris Print-LP Server configuration files and utilities for the print service (usr).

NOTE

SLP SLP is an Internet Engineering Task Force (IETF) protocol for discovering shared resources (such as printers, file servers, and networked cameras) in an enterprise network. The Solaris 10 operating environment contains a full implementation of SLP, including application programming interfaces (APIs) that enable developers to write SLP-enabled applications. SLP also provides system administrators with a framework for ease of network extensibility.

Setting up a Solaris printer involves setting up the spooler, the print daemon, and the hardware (that is, the printer and the printer port). The system administrator needs to verify that the computer has at least 2GB of disk space available for `/var/spool/lp`. Print files will be sent to this location to be prepared for printing. Other configuration files are created, but Solaris takes care of that part for you. When you are setting up a printer, Solaris makes the required changes in the system's `/etc/printers.conf` file and the `/etc/lp` directory.

LP Print Service Directories

The LP print service includes the following directory structure, files, and logs:

- **/usr/bin**—This dirctory contains thc LP print service user commands.
- **/usr/sbin**—This directory contains the LP print service administrative commands.
- **/usr/share/lib/terminfo**—This directory contains the `terminfo` database, which describes the capabilities of devices such as printers and terminals. The `terminfo` database is discussed later in this chapter.
- **/usr/lib/lp**—This directory contains the LP print service daemons, binary files used by the print service, PostScript filters, and default printer interface programs.
- **/usr/lib/lp/model**—This directory contains default printer interface programs (shell scripts) called `standard`, `standard foomatic`, `netstandard`, and `netstard foomatic`. The print service runs the `standard` interface script on local printers to do the following:
    - Initialize the printer port.
    - Initialize the printer.
    - Print a banner page.
    - Print the correct number of copies, as specified in the user's print request.
- The `netstandard` script is designed to support network printers. It collects the spooler and print database information and passes this information on to `/usr/lib/lp/bin/netpr`. `netpr` in turn opens the network connection and sends the data to the printer.
- When a print request is sent to a printer queue, the print service runs through the printer's standard script, which performs the following functions:
    - Initialize the printer port.
    - Initialize the actual printer, using the terminfo database to find the appropriate control sequences.
    - Print a banner page if configured to do so.
    - Print the specified number of copies.
- The `/usr/lib/lp/model` directory also contains the `standard_foomatic` and `netstandard_foomatic` scripts which are for printers which take advantage of the Raster Image Processor (RIP) and Postscript Printer Definition (PPD) features. RIP enables you to print to printers that do not have resident PostScript processing capabilities. In previous Solaris releases, you could only print to printers that understood PostScript natively, or you could only print plain ASCII text files. Through the use of additional transformation software, raster image processor (RIP), and PostScript Printer Definition (PPD) files, you can print to a wider range of printers. These scripts are located in the `/usr/lib/lp/model/ppd/system` directory.

- Printer interface file templates are located in the `/usr/lib/lp/model` directory. When a printer queue is created, this template file is copied to the `/etc/lp/interfaces` directory. The name of the interface file reflects the name of the printer. For example, a printer named `hpljet1` would have an interface file named `/etc/lp/interfaces/hpljet1`. Printer interface files are scripts that can be modified as needed to change the behavior of the printer, such as turning off the banner page and enabling two-sided printing.
- **`/usr/lib/lp/postscript`**—This directory contains all the PostScript filter programs that the Solaris LP print service provides. Print filters are used to convert the content of the print request to a format that is accepted by the destination printer.
- **`/etc/lp`**—This directory contains the LP service configuration files. These files are edited by using the print service configuration tools described later in this chapter.
- **`/etc/lp/fd`**—This directory contains a set of print filter descriptor files. The files describe the characteristics of the filter and point to the actual filter program.
- **`/etc/lp/interfaces`**—This directory contains each printer interface program file which is copied from the `/usr/lib/lp/model` directory as described earlier. Entries in this directory are specific for each printer installed on the system. Each printer interface file located in this directory reresents a shell script that sends the print job to the printer.
- **`/etc/lp/printers`**—This directory contains subdirectories for each local printer attached to the system. Each subdirectory contains configuration information and alert files for each printer.
- **`/var/spool/lp`**—All current print requests are stored here until they are printed.
- **`/var/lp/logs`**—This directory contains a history log of print requests.

The Print Spooler

Spool stands for simultaneous peripheral operations online. The spooler is also referred to as the *queue*. Users execute the print spooler `lp` program when they want to print something. The print spooler then takes what the user wants to print and places it in the predefined `/var/spool/lp` print spooling directory.

Spooling space is the amount of disk space used to store and process requests in the print queue. The size of the `/var` directory depends on the size of the disk and how the disk is partitioned. If `/var` is not created as a separate partition, the `/var` directory uses some root partition space, which is likely to be quite small. A large spool directory could consume several gigabytes of disk space. To get a feel for this, you should look at the size and partitioning of the disks available on systems that could be designated as print servers.

When connecting printers, you need to first carefully evaluate the users' printing needs and usage patterns. If users typically print only short ASCII files, without sophisticated graphics or formatting requirements, a print server with 200MB to 300MB of disk space allocated to `/var` is probably sufficient. However, if many users are printing lengthy PostScript files, they will probably fill up the spooling space quite frequently. When `/var` fills up and users cannot queue their jobs for printing, workflow is interrupted. The size of `/var` is set when the operating system is loaded and disks are partitioned.

CAUTION

Running Out of Space in `/var` Some print jobs consume large amounts of disk space. In fact, one of my clients had a report that consumed more than 800MB when it was spooled to the printer. When `/var` runs out of disk space, many system functions cannot continue, such as printing, message logging, and mail. Make sure you provide adequate space in `/var` when setting up your system.

The SVR4 `lp` program is equivalent to the BSD `lpr` print program. In SunOS the print spooler is located in `/usr/spool`.

NOTE

BSD Print Systems Throughout this chapter, I make reference to the BSD print system for system administrators who might be familiar with it. The BSD printing protocol is an industry standard. It is widely used and provides compatibility between different types of systems from various manufacturers.

For sites that have a mix of BSD and SVR4 Unix, Sun has provided compatibility for both print systems in Solaris.

The LP Print Daemons

The `/usr/lib/lp/local/lpsched` daemon, also called the print scheduler, is the Unix utility that is responsible for scheduling and printing in Solaris 10. The `lpsched` daemon is started by the service management facility command, `svcadm`. For example, to start the `lpsched` print service (bring it online), type

```
# svcadm enable application/print/server
```

To shut down the `lp` print service, type

```
# svcadm disable application/print/server
```

For compatibility, the `/usr/lib/lpsched` and `/usr/lib/lpshut` scripts are still available for starting and stopping the `lpsched` daemon, but these commands simply run the appropriate `svcadm enable` and `svcadm disable` commands.

Each print server has one `lpsched` daemon, which is started by the `svc:/application/print/server:default` service when the system is booted (provided a printer has been configured on this server). `lpsched` is also started automatically when a printer is added using the `lpadmin` command and disabled when the last printer has been removed.

The `lpsched` daemon starts or restarts the `lp` print service. Sometimes `lpsched` is referred to as the `lp` daemon. The `lp` daemon takes output from the spooling directory and sends it to the correct printer. It also tracks the status of printers and filters on the print server and is equivalent to the line printer daemon (`lpd`) in BSD Unix.

The service that handles the incoming print request from the network is `svc:/application/print/server:default`. You can check the status of this service using the `svcs` command described in Chapter 3, "Perform System Boot and Shutdown Procedures for SPARC, x64, and x86-Based Systems," as follows:

```
svcs svc:/application/print/server
```

You can enable or disable the service using the `svcadm` command described earlier in this section.

The Internet services daemon, `/usr/sbin/inetd`, is started at bootup by the SMF, and it listens for service requests that are currently enabled. When a request arrives, the `inetd` daemon executes the server program that is associated with the service. The `inetd` daemon is described in the *Solaris 10 System Administration Exam Prep Exam CX-310-202* book. Print servers listen for print requests with the `inetd` daemon. When receiving a request, `inetd` starts the protocol adaptor `in.lpd` daemon, which is managed by the `svc:/application/print/rfc1179:default` service. The protocol adaptor translates the print request, communicates it to the print spooler, and returns the results to the requester. This protocol adaptor starts on demand and exits when it has serviced the network request, eliminating idle system overhead for printing.

Many methods can be used to define a printer on a Solaris system. Table 6.1 describes the tools Solaris provides for adding printers.

TABLE 6.1 Solaris Tools for Adding Printers

Utility	Description
Solaris Print Client	An interface that was previously available only with the Solstice AdminSuite set of administration tools. It is now available as part of the standard Solaris distribution software and is used to set up print clients.
Print Manager	A GUI that is used to manage printers in a name service environment. Print Manager is somewhat limited for advanced tasks.
LP print service commands	The command-line utilities that are used to set up and manage printers. These commands provide complete functionality.

Setting Up the Printer Hardware

Connecting printers to a Unix system is no one's favorite activity because it can quickly become a time-consuming task. Many printers are on the market, each with a unique interface.

When connecting a printer locally to a Sun system, you have four options:

- Use an Ethernet connection.
- Use a parallel connection.
- Use a serial connection.
- Use a universal serial bus (USB) connection.

The type of connection depends on the connectivity options available on the printer. Most modern printers have either an Ethernet or USB connection. If Ethernet or USB connectivity is not an option, a parallel connection is the preferred method. If no parallel option exists, the final choice is a serial connection.

Ethernet Connections

Most modern printers provide an option to add an Ethernet interface. A printer with an Ethernet connection is referred to as a *network printer*. A network printer is a hardware device that provides printing services to print clients without being directly cabled to a print server. It is a print server with its own system name and IP address, and it is connected directly to the network. The Ethernet interface might be internal or external to the printer. Using an Ethernet interface to install a printer is recommended in particular because of its speed (1000Mbps).

Parallel Connections

Most printers, with a few rare exceptions, have parallel interfaces. A parallel interface has a speed advantage over a serial interface, especially if it uses a Centronics interface.

If your system has a parallel port, you simply connect the printer to the Sun system by using a Centronics parallel cable. Some Sun systems do not have parallel interfaces at all, so you might have to add a parallel interface by purchasing a parallel interface from Sun.

Serial Connections

Some printers support both parallel and serial connections. Sometimes a printer is connected via the serial interface because the Sun system does not have an available parallel interface. Connecting a device using a serial interface requires a thorough understanding of serial transmission. This method of connecting a printer is the most difficult because of the complexity in establishing the proper communications settings between the computer and the printer. It is also slower than other methods.

USB Connections

Most modern printers support USB connection, but some older Sun systems do not. If your Sun system has a USB port, this option provides a plug-n-play interface that is also hot-swappable, allowing devices to be plugged in and unplugged without the system being turned off. USB is intended to replace serial and parallel ports.

USB 1.0 has a maximum bandwidth of 12Mbps (which is equivalent to 1.5MBps) and up to 127 devices can be attached.

Setting Up a Network Printer

You use the vendor's software to configure the operating system of a network printer. After you have completed the vendor software installation, you don't need additional configuration. You must obtain this vendor software from the printer manufacturer and then install the printer on your system. Most network printers are easy to configure. The HP JetDirect print server is the most popular, but it is by no means the only print server available.

The first step in setting up the printer software is to connect the print server to the network and set its IP address and other network configuration settings. This process varies from one print server to another, so you need to follow the manufacturer's guidelines for information on how to do this. Next, you need to install the print server software and follow the manufacturer's guidelines for configuring the printer. The vendor's software configures everything; usually no additional software configuration is required.

CAUTION

Be Careful Using Print Manager to Add a Network Printer Unless a printer uses the `lpd` protocol, you should not use Print Manager to add, modify, or delete a network-based printer that is connected directly to a network with its own network interface card. You won't damage anything if you try this, but your printer will not be recognized by the system, even though the printer might appear in the printer tool window. You should always use the manufacturer-supplied software to manage the printer.

For printers that have parallel or serial connections, you must use the Solaris tools to configure the operating system to recognize the printer.

BSD Versus SVR4 Printing Software

BSD Unix and SVR4 Unix are similar and yet different when it comes to the software that drives the Unix printing process. The two print systems are similar in that both are based on the concept of spooling. Both SVR4 and BSD print services support the concept of an interface program, which acts as a filter through which all output sent to the printer is passed. The following are examples of the uses of interface programs:

- **Adding a banner page**—Most Unix systems automatically add a banner page to the front of a print job. The purpose of the banner page is to identify the owner of the printer output in a shared printer setting.
- **Adding or removing a line-feed character**—Unix uses just the line-feed character to separate lines. The first problem you might encounter when testing a printer is that the text might come out in a stair-step manner. This problem can be overcome by installing the vendor's print software or interface file.

The differences between BSD and SVR4 are in the configuration files and the spooling directories, which the Solaris operating environment configures automatically. Differences also exist in the way the `lpsched` daemon handles print jobs as compared to the way the `lpd` daemon handles them in BSD.

SVR4 Print Service

In SVR4, one `lpsched` daemon services all printers. The `lpsched` daemon is continually running, and it provides the power for the print service. Only one instance of `lpsched` should be running at any time.

The LP print service performs the following functions:

- Administers files and schedules local print requests
- Receives and schedules network requests
- Filters files (if necessary) so that they print properly
- Starts programs that interface with the printers
- Tracks the status of jobs
- Tracks forms mounted on the printer
- Delivers alerts to mount new forms or different print wheels
- Delivers alerts about printing problems

Most of the `lp` configuration files are located in the `/var/spool/lp` directory, except for the interface files, which are located in the `/etc/lp/interfaces` directory. A `SCHEDLOCK` file should exist in `/var/spool/lp` when `lpsched` is running; it is responsible for ensuring that there is only one instance of `lpsched`. You use the `lpadmin` command to add, configure, and delete printers from the system.

Information about printers can be found in the `/etc/printers.conf` file and in files located in the `/etc/lp` directory. Solaris Print Manager provides a graphical interface to many of the `lp` commands listed in Table 6.2.

TABLE 6.2 Solaris Printing Commands

Command	Description
`accept/reject`	Enables or disables any further requests for a printer or class entering the spooling area.
`cancel`	Lets the user stop the printing of information.
`enable/disable`	Enables or disables more output from the spooler to the printer.
`lp`	Places information to be printed into the spooler.
`lpadmin`	Allows the configuration of the print service.
`lpmove`	Moves print requests between destinations.
`lpsched`	A script that runs the `svcadm` command to start the print service.
`lpshut`	A script that runs the `svcadm` command to stop the print service.
`lpstat`	Displays the status of the print service.

Although Solaris uses the SVR4 print model, it still supports BSD-style printing to provide interoperability. The widely used BSD printing protocol provides compatibility between different types of Unix and non-Unix systems from various manufacturers.

Print Servers Versus Print Clients

A *print server* is a system that has a local printer connected to it and makes the printer available to other systems on the network. A *print client* is a remote system that can send print requests to a print server. A system becomes a print client when you install the print client software and enable access to remote printers on the system. Any networked Solaris system with a printer can be a print server, as long as the system has adequate resources to manage the printing load.

The print client issues print commands that allow it to initiate print requests. The `print` command locates a printer and printer configuration information.

When a print job is sent from the print client, the user issues either the SVR4-style `lp` command or the BSD-style `lpr` command. Any one of the styles shown in Table 6.3 can be used to submit a print request.

TABLE 6.3 Valid Print Styles

Style	Description
Atomic	The `print` command and option followed by the printer name or class. Here's an example: `lp -d neptune filename`
POSIX	The `print` command and option followed by the server printer. Here's an example: `lpr -P galaxy:neptune` *`filename`*
Context	Context-based style as follows: `lpr -d thisdept/service/printer/`*`printer-name filename`*

If the user doesn't specify a printer name or class in a valid style, the command follows the search order defined in the `/etc/nsswitch.conf` file. By default, the command checks the user's `PRINTER` or `LPDEST` environment variable for a default printer name. These variables can be set in the user's startup file to specify a default printer to use. If neither environment variable for the default printer is defined, the command checks the `.printers` file in the user's home directory for the default printer alias. If the command does not find a default printer alias in the `.printers` file, it then checks the print client's `/etc/printers.conf` file for configuration information. If the printer is not found in the `/etc/printers.conf` file, the command checks the name service (NIS or NIS+), if any.

TIP

The `lpadmin -d <printername>` command is used to define the system default printer from the command line. When this command is run, an entry for the default printer is made in the `/etc/printers.conf` file.

Configuring Software for a Solaris Printer

The print client software and the Print Manager application offer a graphical solution for setting up and managing printers in a networked environment. Print Manager provides a graphical interface to the `lp` commands listed in Table 6.2. The advantage of the Solaris Print Manager software is that it supports a name service (NIS or NIS+) that lets you centralize print administration for a network. If you're using a name service, Solaris Print Manager is the preferred method for managing printer configuration information. Using a name service for storing printer configuration information is desirable because it makes printer information available to all systems on the network, and that makes printing administration easier. The two tools are similar to one another and require the same type of information.

You can also use the `lpadmin` command at the command line to configure printers on individual systems. The next few sections describe how to set up a printer by using Print Manager and the command line.

Setting Up a Printer by Using Print Manager

Solaris Print Manager is a Java-based GUI that enables you to manage local and remote printer configuration. As with any Solaris GUI, your terminal must be able to display the X11 window environment in order to use this tool and you must be logged in as root.

You can follow the procedure in Step by Step 6.1 to set up a printer using the Printer Manager.

STEP BY STEP

6.1 Setting Up a Printer by Using Print Manager

1. Log in as root on the system to which you want to connect the printer. The system on which you install the printer becomes the printer server.
2. Connect your printer to the server and turn on power to the printer.
3. Start up Print Manager by typing the following:

   ```
   # /usr/sadm/admin/bin/printmgr &
   ```

   The windows shown in Figure 6.1 appear.
4. In the Select Naming Service window, select from the pull-down menu the name service you are using, as shown in Figure 6.2.
5. In the example in Figure 6.2, Files is selected from the pull-down menu because I am not using a name service at this time. After making your selection, click OK to continue. The Select Naming Service window closes.

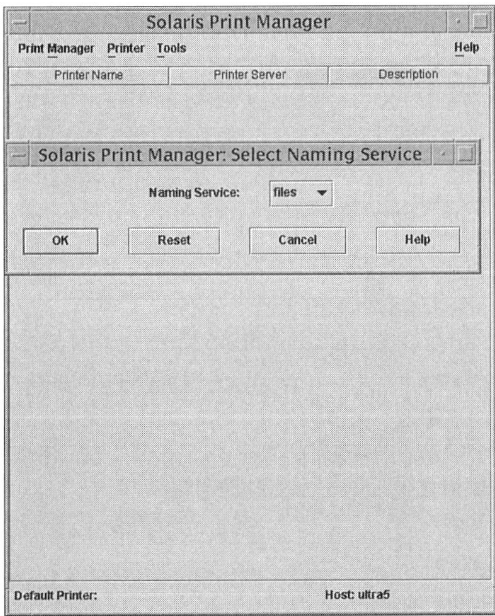

FIGURE 6.1 The Print Manager startup window.

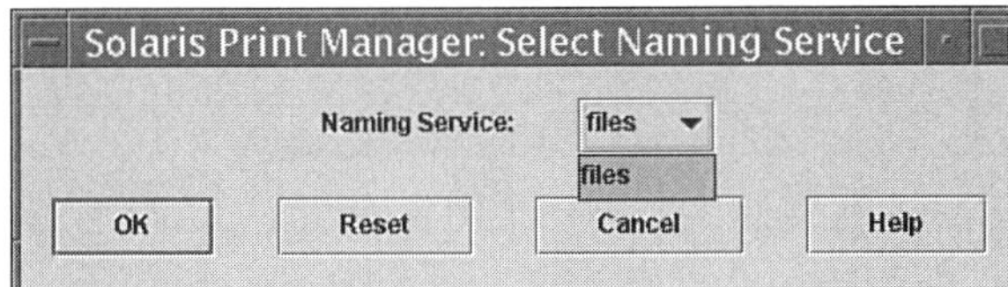

FIGURE 6.2 Selecting a name service.

6. From the main Solaris Print Manager window, click the Printer menu from the top toolbar and select New Attached Printer, as shown in Figure 6.3.

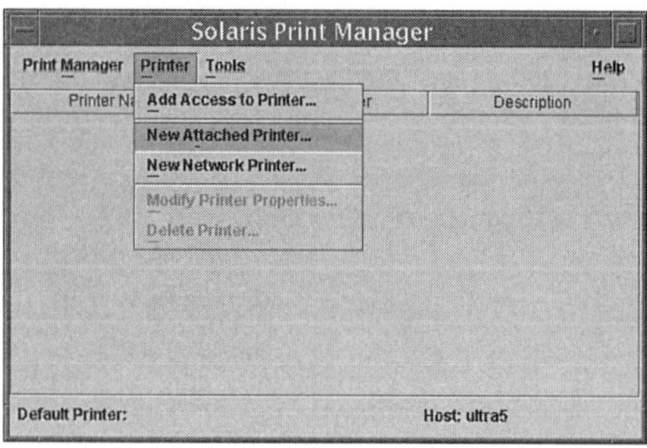

FIGURE 6.3 The Solaris Print Manager window.

The New Attached Printer window appears, as shown in Figure 6.4.

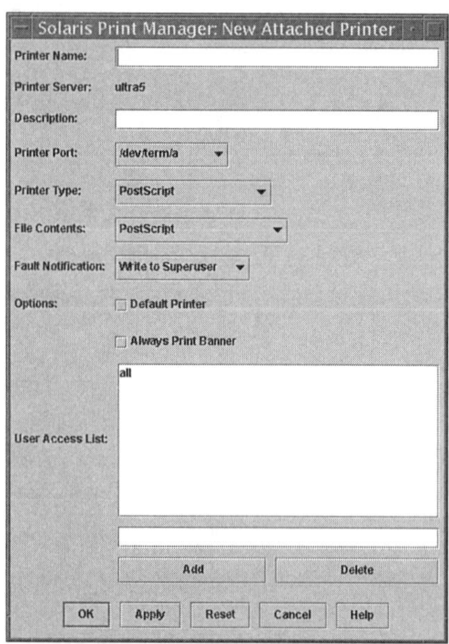

FIGURE 6.4 The New Attached Printer window.

7. Fill in the empty fields as follows:

   - **Printer Name**—Enter the name you want to give this printer.
   - **Description**—If you want to, enter a brief description of the printer.
   - **Printer Port**—Click the button and select the port to which the printer is connected:

     `/dev/term/a` is serial port A.

     `/dev/term/b` is serial port B.

     `/dev/bpp0` is the parallel port.

     `/dev/ecpp0` is the parallel port on Sun Ultra systems.

> **NOTE**
>
> **Parallel Port on PCI-Based Systems** On the PCI-based Sun systems (that is, AX machines and Ultra 30, 450, 5, 10, and 60), the parallel port is called `/dev/ecpp0` rather than `/dev/bpp0`, as on previous machines.

Select Other if you've connected an interface card with another device name.

- **Printer Type**—Click the button to select the printer type that matches your printer. The printer types here correspond to printers listed in the `/usr/share/lib/terminfo` directory. The printer type you select must correspond to an entry in the `terminfo` database. Unix works best with PostScript printers because page formatting of text and graphics from within the common desktop environment (CDE) is for a PostScript printer. If you want to set your printer type as a PostScript printer, your printer must be able to support PostScript. If you're using an HP LaserJet printer, you should choose `HPLaserJet` as the print type unless your LaserJet printer supports PostScript.
- **File Contents**—Click the button to select the format of the files that will be sent to the printer.
- **Fault Notification**—Click the button to select how to notify the superuser in case of a printer error.
- **Options**—Choose to print a banner or make this the default printer.

> **NOTE**
>
> **Default Printers** One printer can be identified as the default printer for the system. If a user does not specify a printer when printing, the job goes to the default printer.

- **User Access List**—If you want to, enter the names of the systems that are allowed to print to this printer. If nothing is entered, all clients are allowed access.

After you fill in all the fields, click the OK button. The window closes, and the new printer name appears in the Solaris Print Manager window, as shown in Figure 6.5.

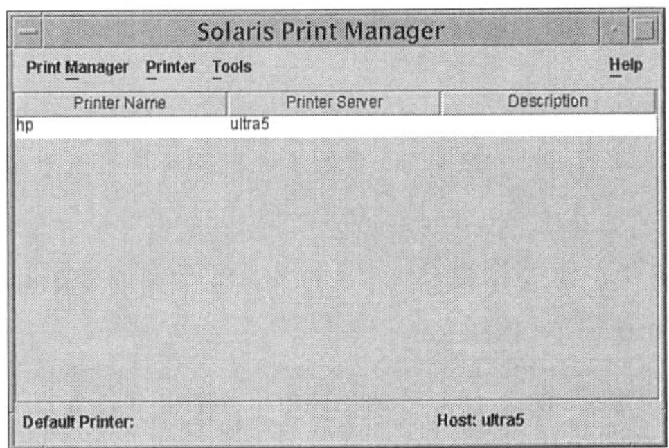

FIGURE 6.5 The new printer name in the Solaris Print Manager window.

Using a Printer Not Listed on the Printer Types Menu

Printer types listed in the Print Manager window correspond to printers listed in the `/usr/share/lib/terminfo` directory. If a printer type is not available for the type of printer you are adding, you might need to add an entry in the `/usr/share/lib/terminfo` database. Each printer is identified in the `terminfo` database by a short name; for example, an HP

LaserJet printer is listed under the `/usr/share/lib/terminfo/h` directory as `HPLaserJet`. The entries for PostScript printers are in `/usr/share/lib/terminfo/P`. The name found in the directory is the printer type you specify when setting up a printer.

If you cannot find a `terminfo` entry for your printer, you can try selecting a similar type of printer; however, you might have trouble keeping the printer set in the correct modes for each print request. If no `terminfo` entry exists for your type of printer and you want to keep the printer set in the correct modes, you can either customize the interface program used with the printer or add an entry to the `terminfo` database. You'll find the printer interface program located in the `/etc/lp/interfaces` directory. Editing an interface file or adding an entry to the `terminfo` database is beyond the scope of this book. A printer entry in the `terminfo` database contains and defines hundreds of items. Refer to the *Solaris System Administration Guide: Advanced Administration* at `http://docs.sun.com` for information on performing this task. Another good reference for this topic is John Strang and Tim O'Reilly's book *termcap & terminfo*, published by O'Reilly & Associates, Inc.

Setting Up a Printer by Using the `lpadmin` Command

If you are unable to use Print Manager, you can add a printer directly from the command line by using the `lpadmin` command. This method of setting up a printer provides the most flexibility, so if you're comfortable with using the command line, you should use it. The `lpadmin` command enables you to do the following:

- Define or remove printer devices and printer names.
- Specify printer interface programs and print options.
- Define printer types and file content types.
- Create and remove printer classes.
- Define, allow, and deny user lists.
- Specify fault recovery.
- Set or change the system default printer destination.

By using `lpadmin`, you can set all the print definitions, whereas Solaris Print Manager allows you to set only some of them when you install or modify a printer.

Before you use the `lpadmin` command to add a printer, you first need to gather the following information about the printer you are going to set up:

- Printer name
- Port device
- Printer type
- File content type

To set up a printer that is connected to the parallel port on a Sun Ultra system from the command line, you follow the procedure in Step by Step 6.2.

STEP BY STEP

6.2 Setting Up a Printer Using `lpadmin`

1. Use the `lpadmin` command to define the printer name and the port device that the printer will use:

```
# lpadmin -p ljet1 -v /dev/ecpp0
```

> **NOTE**
>
> **`lpadmin` Error Message** You might see an error such as this:
>
> ```
> UX:lpadmin: WARNING: "/dev/ecpp0" is accessible by others.
> TO FIX: If other users can access it you may get unwanted output. If this
> is not what you want change the owner to "lp" and change the mode to 0600.
> Processing continues.
> ```
>
> You can choose to modify permissions on this device file or leave them as is. If you modify permissions on `/dev/ecpp0`, when the print server and the print client are the same machine, the interface scripts run as the user that submitted the job. Therefore, if a user other than `lp` or root submits a job, the job will not have write access to `/dev/ecpp0`.

2. Set the printer type of the printer:

```
# lpadmin -p ljet1 -T PS
```

3. Specify the file content types to which the printer can print directly:

```
# lpadmin -p ljet1 -I postscript
```

4. Accept print requests for the printer:

```
# accept ljet1
```

The system responds with the following:

```
destination "ljet1" now accepting requests
```

5. Enable the printer:

```
# enable ljet1
```

The system responds with the following:

```
printer "ljet1" now enabled
```

6. Add a description for the printer:

```
# lpadmin -p ljet1 -D "Engineering PS Printer"
```

7. Verify that the printer is ready:

```
# lpstat -p ljet1
```

The system responds with the following:

```
printer ljet1 is idle. enabled since Jun 12 11:17 2008. available.
```

You now know how to set up a printer using the command line. Next you'll learn how to manage printers by using the `lpadmin` command.

Administering Printers

Objective:

Explain how to configure printer classes, set the default printer, change the default printer class, remove a printer's configuration, start the LP print service, and stop the LP print service using the appropriate commands.

- ▶ Given a scenario, identify the appropriate commands to specify a destination printer, accept and reject print jobs, enable and disable printers, and move print jobs.

Managing the print system involves monitoring the `lp` system and uncovering reasons it might not be working properly. Other routine tasks involve cancelling print jobs and enabling or disabling a printer while it's being serviced. The following sections provide instructions for the daily tasks you will perform to manage printers and the print scheduler.

Note that the commands described in the following sections require superuser access.

Deleting Printers and Managing Printer Access

You can use Print Manager to delete a printer from the system. To do so, in the Print Manager main window, highlight the printer that you want to delete and, from the top toolbar, select Printer. From the pull-down menu, select Delete Printer, as shown in Figure 6.6. The printer queue is deleted from the system.

To delete a printer from the command line, you issue the following command on the system where the printer is connected:

```
lpadmin -x <printer-name>
```

The printer is deleted from the system.

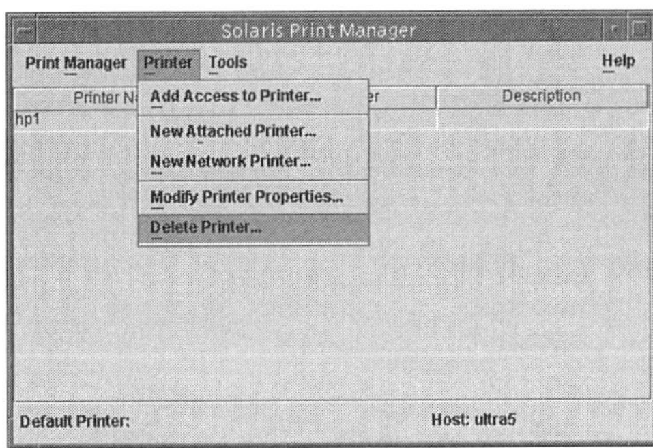

FIGURE 6.6 Deleting a printer.

Perhaps you do not want to remove the printer from the print server, but you want to keep a particular system from printing to the print server. In this case, you issue the following command on the print client from which you want to delete the printer:

```
# lpsystem -r <print-server>
```

The print server is deleted from the print client's `/etc/lp/Systems` file.

To stop accepting print requests on a particular printer—perhaps because a printer will be going offline for repairs—you type the following command on the system where the printer is physically connected:

```
# reject <printer-name>
```

This command prevents any new requests from entering the printer's queue while you are in the process of removing the printer. Use the `accept` command, described later in this section, to allow the queue to start accepting requests.

To allow a printer to keep taking requests but to stop the printer from printing the requests, you issue the following command on the system where the printer is physically connected:

```
# disable <printer-name>
```

Printing will be halted on this system until you issue the following command:

```
# enable <printer-name>
```

NOTE

Using `enable` in the bash Shell If you are using the `bash` shell, be aware that `enable` is a built-in shell command that conflicts with the LP system's `enable` command. When using `bash`, you must give the full path to `enable`, `/usr/bin/enable`.

When stopping or disabling a printer, you might need to move existing jobs that have been queued to that printer. To move print jobs from one printer to another, you use the `lpmove` command, as follows:

```
# lpmove <printer1> <printer2>
```

The arguments for the `lpmove` command are described in Table 6.4.

TABLE 6.4 `lpmove` Arguments

Argument	Description
<printer1>	The name of the printer from which all print requests will be moved
<printer2>	The name of the printer to which all print requests will be moved

If you move all the print requests to another printer, the `lpmove` command automatically stops accepting print requests for `printer1`. The following command is necessary if you want to begin accepting new print requests for the printer:

```
# accept printer1
```

In the following example, the `lpmove` command moves print requests from the printer `eps1` to the printer `eps2` (for example, when `eps1` is being taken down for maintenance). When the `eps1` printer is ready to start accepting print jobs again, you use the `accept` command to resume accepting print requests on `eps1`:

```
# lpmove eps1 eps2
# accept eps1
```

Creating Printer Classes

You can put several locally attached printers into a group called a *printer class*. This might be helpful if you have several printers sitting next to each other and it doesn't matter which printer your job goes to. After you have set up a printer class, users can specify the class (rather than individual printers) as the destination for a print request. The first printer in the class that is free to print is used. The result is faster turnaround because all printers are utilized. You create printer classes by issuing the `lpadmin` command with the `-c` option, as follows:

```
lpadmin -p <printer name> -c <class name>
```

No default printer classes are known to the print service; printer classes exist only if you define them. The following are three ways you can define printer classes:

- By printer type (for example, PostScript)
- By location (for example, 5th floor)
- By workgroup or department (for example, Accounting)

Alternatively, a class might contain several printers that are used in a particular order. The LP print service always checks for an available printer in the order in which printers were added to a class. Therefore, if you want a high-speed printer to be accessed first, you would add it to the class before you added a low-speed printer. As a result, the high-speed printer would handle as many print requests as possible. The low-speed printer would be used as a backup printer for when the high-speed printer was in use.

Printer class names must be unique and can contain a maximum of 14 alphanumeric characters and underscores. You are not obliged to define printer classes. You should add them only if you determine that using printer classes would benefit the users on the network.

Step by Step 6.3 describes how to define a printer class.

STEP BY STEP

6.3 Defining Printer Classes

1. Log in as superuser or issue the `lp` command on the print server.
2. Define a class of printers by using the `lpadmin` command:

```
# lpadmin -p <printer-name> -c <printer-class>
```

The arguments that are used with `lpadmin` to define printer classes are described in Table 6.5.

TABLE 6.5 `lpadmin` Arguments

Argument	Description
`-p <printer-name>`	This option allows you to specify the name of the printer you are adding to a class of printers.
`-c <printer-class>`	This option allows you to specify the printer class name.

The specified printer is added to the end of the class's list in the print server's `/etc/lp/classes/<printer-class>` file. If the printer class does not exist, it is created. You can verify what printers are in a printer class by using the `lpstat` command:

```
# lpstat -c <printer-class>
```

The following example adds the printer `luna` to the class `roughdrafts`:

```
# lpadmin -p luna -c roughdrafts
```

Checking Printer Status

You use the `lpstat` command to verify the status of a printer. You can use this command to determine which printers are available for use or to examine the characteristics of a particular printer. The `lpstat` command syntax is as follows:

```
lpstat [-a] [-d] [-p <printer-name> [-D] [-l]] [-t] [-u <logon_IDs>]
```

The `lpstat` command options are described in Table 6.6.

TABLE 6.6 `lpstat` Command Syntax and Options

Option	Description
`-a`	Reports whether printers are accepting requests. You can also specify a specific list of printers, as in `lpstat -a eps1 eps2 eps3`.
`-d`	Shows the system's default printer.
`-p <printer-name>`	Shows whether a printer is active or idle, when it was enabled or disabled, and whether it is accepting print requests. You can specify multiple printer names with this command. You use spaces or commas to separate printer names. If you use spaces, you need to enclose the list of printer names in quotes. If you don't specify the printer name, the status of all printers is displayed.
`-D`	Shows the description of the specified printer.
`-l`	Shows the characteristics of the specified printer.
`-t`	Shows status information about the LP print service, including the status of all printers—whether they are active and whether they are accepting print requests.
`-u <logon-IDs>`	Prints the status of output requests for users, in which `<logon-IDs>` can be one or all of the following: `<user>`—A user on the local system, as in `lpstat -u bcalkins`. `<host!user>`—A user on a system, as in `lpstat -u systema!bcalkins`. `<host!all>`—All users on a particular system, as in `lpstat -u systema!all`. `<all!user>`—A particular user on all systems, as in `lpstat -u all!bcalkins`. `all`—All users on all systems specified, as in `lpstat -u all`.

The following is an example of the `lpstat` command:

```
# lpstat -p hplaser
```

The system responds with this:

```
printer hplaser is idle. enabled since Jun 16 10:09 2008.
available.
```

The following example requests a description of the printers `hplaser1` and `hplaser2`:

```
# lpstat -p "hplaser1 hplaser2" -D
printer hplaser1 faulted. enabled since Jun 16 10:09 2008.
available.
unable to print: paper misfeed jam

Description: Printer by finance.
printer hplaser2 is idle. enabled since Jun 16 10:09 2008.
available.
Description: Printer in computer room.
```

The following example requests the characteristics of the printer `hplaser`:

```
# lpstat -p hplaser -l
printer hplaser disabled since Tue Jun 17 20:25:34 2008. available.
        new printer
        Form mounted:
        Content types: simple
        Printer types: unknown
        Description:
        Connection: direct
        Interface: /usr/lib/lp/model/standard
        PPD: none
        On fault: write to root once
        After fault: continue
        Users allowed:
                (all)
        Forms allowed:
                (none)
        Banner required
        Character sets:
                (none)
        Default pitch:
        Default page size:
        Default port settings:
```

Managing Printer Queues

The routine task of managing printers involves managing their queues. Occasionally, large jobs are submitted that are not needed and can be aborted. Other times you might want to put a high-priority job ahead of other jobs that are waiting to be printed. The following sections outline some of the routine tasks you might want to perform on the printer queues.

Viewing a Print Job

To remove someone else's print job from the print queue, you first need to become root. Then you need to determine the request ID of the print request to cancel, by using the `lpstat` command as follows:

```
# lpstat -u bcalkins
```

The system displays this:

```
eps1-1     bcalkins      1261     Mar 16 17:34
```

In this example, the user `bcalkins` has one request in the queue. The request ID is `eps1-1`.

Cancelling a Print Request

You can cancel a print request by using the `cancel` command, which has the following syntax:

```
cancel <request-ID> ¦ <printer-name>
```

The arguments for the `cancel` command are described in Table 6.7.

TABLE 6.7 `cancel` Arguments

Argument	Description
<request-ID>	The request ID of a print request to be cancelled. You can specify multiple request IDs. You use spaces or commas to separate request IDs. If you use spaces, you need to enclose the list of request IDs in quotes.
<printer-name>	Specifies the printer for which you want to cancel the currently printing print request. You can specify multiple printer names with this command. You can use spaces or commas to separate printer names.

The following example cancels the `eps1-3` and `eps1-4` print requests:

```
# cancel eps1-3 eps1-4
```

The system responds with this:

```
request "eps1-3" cancelled
request "eps1-4" cancelled
```

The following example cancels the print request that is currently printing on the printer `eps1`:

```
# cancel eps1
```

The system responds with this:

```
request "eps1-9" cancelled
```

Sending a Print Job at a Higher Priority

The `lp` command with the `-q` option assigns the print request a priority in the print queue. You specify the priority level as an integer from `0` to `39`. You use `0` to indicate the highest priority and `39` to indicate the lowest. If no priority is specified, the system administrator assigns the default priority for a print service.

The following example illustrates how to send a print job to the printer `eps1`, with the highest priority:

```
# lp -d eps1 -q 0 file1
```

If the printer exists on another server, send the print job to that server using the following command:

```
# /usr/bin/lp -d sysA:hpljet -q 0 myfile
```

In the above example, a file named "myfile" is sent to a printer named "hpljet" which is connected to a server named "sysA."

Limiting User Access to a Printer

You can allow or deny users access to a printer by using the `lpadmin` command and adding usernames to an access list. The access list can be a list of specific users who are denied access (deny access list) or a list of users who are allowed access (allow access list). By default, all users are allowed access to a printer. This is the syntax for modifying access lists using the `lpadmin` command:

```
lpadmin -p <printername> -u <lpadmin-argument>
```

The arguments for the `lpadmin` command that are used to control access to a printer are described in Table 6.8.

TABLE 6.8 `lpadmin` Arguments

Argument	Description
`-p <printer-name>`	This option allows you to specify the name of the printer to which the allow or deny user access list applies.
`-u allow:<user-list>`	This option allows you to specify the usernames to be added to the allow user access list. You can specify multiple usernames with this command. You use spaces or commas to separate names. If you use spaces, you need to enclose the list of names in quotes. Table 6.9 describes the valid values for `user-list`.
`-u deny:<user-list>`	This option allows you to specify the usernames to be added to the deny user access list. You can specify multiple usernames with this command. You use spaces or commas to separate names. If you use spaces, you need to enclose the list of names in quotes.

The specified users are added to the allow or deny user access list for the printer in one of the following files on the print server:

- `/etc/lp/printers/<printer-name>/users.allow`
- `/etc/lp/printers/<printer-name>/users.deny`

Table 6.9 provides the valid values for *user-list*.

TABLE 6.9 Values for Allow and Deny User Access Lists

Value for *user-list*	Description
user	A user on any system
all	All users on all systems
none	No user on any system
system!*user*	A user on the specified system only
!*user*	A user on the local system only
all!*user*	A user on any system
all!all	All users on all systems
system!all	All users on the specified system
!all	All users on the local system

NOTE

Specifying none in *user-list* If you specify none as the value for *user-list* in the allow user access list, the following files are not created for the print server:

```
/etc/lp/printers/<printer-name>/alert.sh
/etc/lp/printers/<printer-name>/alert.var
/etc/lp/printers/<printer-name>/users.allow
/etc/lp/printers/<printer-name>/users.deny
```

The following example gives only the users `bcalkins` and `bholzgen` access to the printer `eps1`:

```
# lpadmin -p eps1 -u allow:bcalkins,bholzgen
```

The following example denies the users `bcalkins` and `bholzgen` access to the printer `eps2`:

```
# lpadmin -p eps2 -u deny:"bcalkins bholzgen"
```

You can use the `lpstat` command to view access information about a particular printer. The following command displays access information for the printer named `eps1`:

```
# lpstat -p eps1 -l
```

The system responds with this:

```
printer eps1 is idle. enabled since Mon Jun 16 14:39:48 EST 2008.
available.

        Form mounted:
        Content types: postscript
        Printer types: PS
        Description: epson
        Connection: direct
        Interface: /usr/lib/lp/model/standard
        On fault: write to root once
        After fault: continue
        Users allowed:
        bcalkins
        bholzgen
        Forms allowed:
               (none)
        Banner not required
        Character sets:

        Default pitch:
        Default page size: 80 wide 66 long
        Default port settings:
```

Accepting or Rejecting Print Requests for a Printer

As root, you can stop accepting print requests for the printer by using the `reject` command. The command syntax is as follows:

```
reject [-r "reason"] <printer-name>
```

The arguments for the `reject` command are described in Table 6.10.

TABLE 6.10 `reject` Arguments

Argument	Description
`-r "reason"`	Tells the users why the printer is rejecting print requests. *reason* is stored and displayed whenever a user checks on the status of the printer by using `lpstat -p`.
`<printer-name>`	Specifies the name of the printer that will stop accepting print requests.

The following example stops the printer `eps1` from accepting print requests:

```
# reject -r "eps1 is down for repairs" eps1
```

The system responds with this:

```
destination "eps1" will no longer accept requests
```

Any queued requests will continue printing as long as the printer is enabled. The following example sets the printer `eps1` to accept print requests again:

```
# accept eps1
```

The system responds with this:

```
destination "eps1" now accepting requests
```

Cancelling a Print Request from a Specific User

You need to be the root or `lp` user if you want to cancel print requests of other users. You cancel a print request from a specific user with the `cancel` command. The syntax is as follows:

```
cancel -u <user-list> <printer-name>
```

The arguments for the `cancel` command are described in Table 6.11.

TABLE 6.11 `cancel` Arguments

Argument	Description
`-u <user-list>`	Cancels the print request for a specified user(s). *`user-list`* can be one or more usernames. You use spaces or commas to separate usernames. If you use spaces, you need to enclose the list of names in quotes.
`<printer-name>`	Specifies the printer(s) for which you want to cancel the specified user's print requests. You use spaces or commas to separate printer names. If you use spaces, you need to enclose the list of printer names in quotes. If you don't specify *`printer-name`*, the user's print requests will be cancelled on all printers.

The following example cancels all the print requests submitted by the user `bcalkins` on the printer `luna`:

```
# cancel -u bcalkins  luna
```

The system responds with this:

```
request "luna-23" cancelled
```

The following example cancels all the print requests submitted by the user `bcalkins` on all printers:

```
# cancel -u bcalkins
```

The system responds with this:

```
request "asteroid-3" cancelled
request "luna-8" cancelled
```

Changing the Priority of a Print Request

You can change the priority of a print request by using the following `lp` command:

```
lp -i <request-id> -H <change-priority> -q <priority-level>
```

The options for the lp command are described in Table 6.12.

TABLE 6.12 lp Options

Option	Description
-i *<request-id>*	Specifies the request ID(s) of a print request that you want to change. You use a space or a comma to separate request IDs. If you use spaces, you need to enclose the list of request IDs in quotation marks.
-H *<change-priority>*	Specifies one of the three ways to change the priority of a print request: hold—Places the print request on hold until you cancel it or instruct the LP print service to resume printing the request. resume—Places a print request that has been on hold in the queue. It will be printed according to its priority and placement in the queue. If you put a hold on a print job that is already printing, resume puts the print request at the head of the queue so that it becomes the next request printed. immediate—Places a print request at the head of the queue. If a request is already printing, you can put that request on hold to allow the next request to print immediately.
-q *<priority-level>*	Assigns the print request a priority in the print queue. You specify *priority-level* as an integer from 0 to 39. 0 indicates the highest priority, and 39 indicates the lowest priority.

In the following example, the command changes a print request with the request ID eps1-29 to priority level 1:

```
# lp -i eps1-29 -q 1
```

Restarting the Print Scheduler

The Solaris print scheduler, lpsched, schedules all print requests on print servers. If printouts are not coming out of the printer, you might need to restart the print scheduler. To restart the print scheduler, you use the svcadm restart svc:/application/print/server:default command. If a print request was printing when the print scheduler stopped running, that request would be printed in its entirety when you restart the print scheduler. You first stop the scheduler by typing the following:

```
# svcadm disable -t scv:/application/print/server:default
```

To restart the scheduler, you type the following:

```
# svcadm enable -t scv:/application/print/server:default
```

Setting a User's Default Printer

When you add a printer, you are given the option of selecting that printer as the default printer for that particular system. You might want to set the default printer at the user level so that, on a particular system, users can specify their own default printers. If a user doesn't provide a printer name when sending a print job, the print command searches for the default printer in the following order:

1. `LPDEST` variable
2. `PRINTER` variable
3. `$HOME/.printers`
4. System's default printer

These variables can be set in the user's `.profile` file. The `lp` command checks `LPDEST` and then `PRINTER`. If neither variable has been set, the print command searches for the variable named `_default` in the following file:

```
$HOME/.printers
```

An entry in this file that names `printer1` as the default printer looks like this:

```
default printer1
```

If the `$HOME/.printers` file does not exist, the `/etc/printers.conf` file is checked. An entry in this file would look like this:

```
_default¦lp:
        :use=system1:
        :bsdaddr=system1,printer1
```

If the `_default` variable is not set in the `/etc/printers.conf` file and you're running a name service, the name service database is checked. Refer to the *Solaris 10 System Administration Exam Prep: Exam CX-310-202* book for information on the name service database. If the destination printer name cannot be located in any of these files, the print request cannot be processed.

Modifying the Printer with Print Manager

You can use Solaris Print Manager to modify a printer after it has been added to the system. Modifications that can be made to a printer via Print Manager include the following:

- ▶ Giving the printer description
- ▶ Indicating the printer port
- ▶ Listing file contents
- ▶ Providing fault notification

- Selecting a default printer
- Printing a banner page
- Accepting and processing print requests
- Providing a user access list

To modify a printer via the Print Manager GUI, you select Printers from the top toolbar, and then you select Modify Printer Properties, as shown in Figure 6.7.

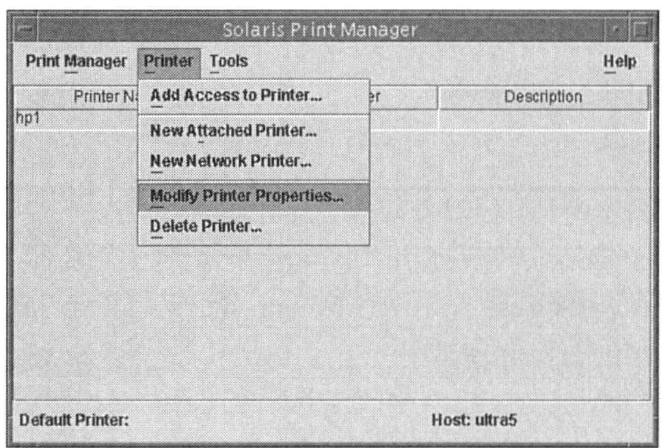

FIGURE 6.7 Modifying printers.

The Modify Printer Properties window appears, as shown in Figure 6.8.

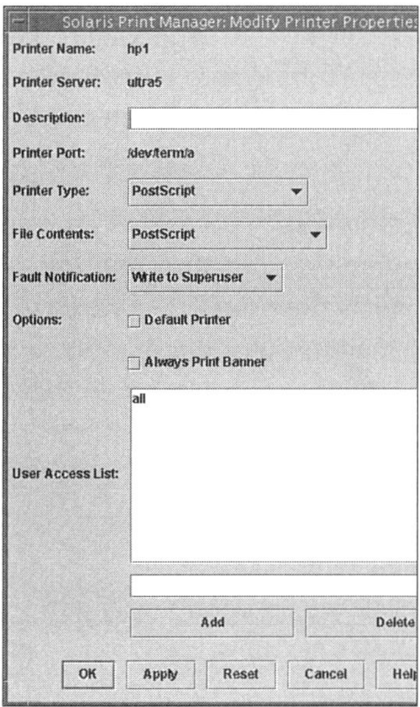

FIGURE 6.8 The Modify Printer Properties window.

You can modify the selected printer by selecting or filling in the appropriate fields in the Modify Printer Properties window.

Troubleshooting the Print Scheduler

The `lpsched` daemon keeps a log file of each print request that it processes and notes any errors that occur during the printing process. This log file is kept in the `/var/lp/logs/lpsched` file. By default, every Sunday at 3:13 a.m., the `lp cron` job renames the `/var/lp/logs/lpsched` file to a new `lpsched.n` file and starts a new log file. If errors occur or jobs disappear from the print queue, you can use the log files to determine what the `lpsched` daemon has done with a printing job.

Summary

As a system administrator, the majority of system problems I respond to are printer related. I could spend a great deal of time describing how to configure and troubleshoot the LP print service. I could explore a more in-depth discussion on configuring printer filters, creating `terminfo` databases, and troubleshooting printing problems, but that's beyond the scope of this book. To be prepared for the certification exam and basic system administration, you need to understand the basics of the LP print service, including the print spooler, print daemons, and printer configuration files. Also, you need to know where the printer related files and programs are stored in the Solaris 10 directory structure.

In addition to understanding the LP print service, you need to know how to use all the utilities and programs that are available to manage the LP print service. You need to know how to start and stop the print service and how to enable or disable it using all the methods described in this chapter.

You should also become familiar with third-party applications and how they prepare print jobs to be sent to the spooler. Many of the problems you may encounter are not with the Solaris print service but have to do with the way that the application formats the print job. This chapter introduces you to the Solaris print system and the `lpsched` daemon. For a more detailed discussion of the `lpsched` daemon, refer to *Solaris 10 System Administration Guide: Advanced Administration*, from Sun Microsystems.

Key Terms

- Default printer
- Local printer
- `lp`
- `lpd`
- `lpsched`
- Network printer
- Print client
- Print daemon
- Print queue
- Print Manager
- Print scheduler
- Print server
- Print service
- Printer class
- Spool
- `terminfo` database

Exercises

6.1 Configuring a Printer Using `lpadmin` at the Command Line

This exercise shows you how to add and remove a local LaserJet 5M printer on a print server. The commands in this example must be executed on the print server where the printer is connected. The following information is available for the installation:

Printer name: `hp1`

Port device: `/dev/ecpp0`

System type: Ultra5

Printer type: HP LaserJet5M

File content type: PostScript/PCL

Estimated time: 10 minutes

1. As root, use the `lpadmin` command to add the printer named `hp1` to the parallel port (`/dev/ecpp0`), set the printer type as `hplaser`, and specify the file content type as `any`:

   ```
   # lpadmin -p hp1 -v /dev/ecpp0 -T hplaser -I any
   ```

   Now, start accepting print requests for the printer and enable the printer:

   ```
   # enable hp1
   # accept hp1
   ```

2. Verify that the printer is set up and ready:

   ```
   # lpstat -p hp1 -l
   ```

3. Send a print job to the printer to test it:

   ```
   # lp -d hp1 /etc/hosts
   ```

4. Remove the printer:

   ```
   # lpadmin -x hp1
   ```

5. Verify that the printer has been removed:

   ```
   # lpstat -t
   ```

6.2 Configuring a Printer Using the Print Manager GUI

In this exercise, you add a LaserJet 5M printer to the print server using the Print Manager GUI.

Estimated time: 5 minutes

1. As root, start up Print Manager:

```
# /usr/sadm/admin/bin/printmgr &
```

2. From the `Printer` button at the top of Print Manager window, select `New Attached Printer`. Fill in the fields as follows:

   Printer name: `hp1`

   Description: `Hplaser 5M`

   Printer port: `/dev/eccp0`

   Printer type: `HP Printer`

   File contents: `Any`

   Fault notification: `Mail to Superuser`

   Click OK when you're finished, and then exit Print Manager.

3. Verify that the printer is set up and ready by typing the following:

```
# lpstat -p hp1 -l
```

6.3 Stopping and Starting the LP Print Service

In this exercise, you use the `svcadm` command to stop and start the LP print service.

Estimated time: 5 minutes

1. Halt the LP print service:

```
# svcadm disable application/print/server
```

   Any printers that are currently printing when the command is invoked are stopped.

2. Use the `svcadm enable` command to start the LP print service:

```
# svcadm enable application/print/server
```

   Printers that are restarted using this command reprint all jobs that were interrupted with the `svcadm disable` command.

6.4 Setting Up a Network-Based Printer

This exercise illustrates how to configure a printer named `hplaser` that is connected directly to the network via its own network interface card that has the IP address `192.168.1.10`. In this example, the printer is utilizing an HP JetDirect interface, and you use Hewlett-Packard's JetAdmin software to configure the printer.

Estimated time: 15 minutes

1. Obtain the JetAdmin software from Hewlett-Packard's website (`www.hp.com`) and install it using the `pkgadd` command, as described in Chapter 2, "Installing the Solaris 10 Operating Environment." Make sure you get the correct version of JetAdmin. As of this writing, the current version is named `SOLd621.PKG`. Put the downloaded file in your `/tmp` directory.

2. Install the JetAdmin package into the `/opt/hpnp` directory by using the `pkgadd` command:

   ```
   # pkgadd -d /tmp/SOLd621.PKG
   ```

   You should see the following output:

   ```
   The following packages are available:
     1  HPNP      JetAdmin for Unix
                  (sparc) D.06.21
   Select package(s) you wish to process\
    (or 'all' to process all packages).
   (default: all) [?,??,q]: 1
   ```

3. Type the following:

   ```
   1 <return>
   Processing package instance <HPNP> from </var/spool/pkg/SOLd621.PKG>
   JetAdmin for Unix
   (sparc) D.06.21
   (c)Copyright Hewlett-Packard Company 1991, 1992,\
    1993. All Rights Reserved.
   (c)Copyright 1983 Regents of the University of\
    California
   (c)Copyright 1988, 1989 by Carnegie Mellon\
    University
                RESTRICTED RIGHTS LEGEND
   Use, duplication, or disclosure by the U.S.\
    Government is subject to restrictions as set\
    forth in sub-paragraph (c)(1)(ii) of the Rights\
    in Technical Data and Computer Software clause\
    in DFARS 252.227-7013.
                       Hewlett-Packard Company
                       3000 Hanover Street
                       Palo Alto, CA 94304 U.S.A.
   Where should HPNP be installed?
   (<return> for /opt/hpnp) [?,q] <enter>
   ```

4. Keep all the default selections by pressing Enter `<return>` to install the JetAdmin package in the `/opt/hpnp` directory:

   ```
   HPNP will be installed in /opt/hpnp.
   Please configure the sub-packages you would like\
    to install.
   -----------------------------------------
   Done altering installation configuration
       1. [ N/A ]  JetPrint
   ```

```
    2. [ On  ]  JobMonitor
    3. [ On  ]  HPNPF
    4. [ On  ]  HPNPD
    5. [ On  ]  CONVERT
    ?.          Help
--------------------------------------------
Select a number to toggle an installation option.
When done select 0. Select ? for help information: 0
```

5. Enter `0 <return>`, and the JetAdmin package is installed. You should see the following messages appear onscreen as the package is installing:

```
Select a number to toggle an installation option.
When done select 0. Select ? for help information: 0
Using </> as the package base directory.
## Processing package information.
## Processing system information.
## Verifying disk space requirements.
## Checking for conflicts with packages already\
 installed.
The following files are already installed on the\
 system and are being used by another package:
  /etc <attribute change only>
  /etc/init.d <attribute change only>
  /etc/rc1.d <attribute change only>
  /etc/rc2.d <attribute change only>
  /usr <attribute change only>
  /usr/bin <attribute change only>
Do you want to install these conflicting files\
 [y,n,?,q] y
```

6. Enter `y <return>` to install the conflicting packages.

```
This package contains scripts which will be\
 executed with super-user permission during\
 the process of installing this package.
Do you want to continue with the installation\
 of <HPNP> [y,n,?] y
```

7. Enter `y <return>` to continue the installation. You should see a list of files being installed, followed by this message:

```
Installation of <HPNP> was successful.
```

8. Configure the HP LaserJet printer by using the JetAdmin utility that you just installed:

```
# /opt/hpnp/jetadmin
```

The following information is displayed:

```
************************************************
*                  MAIN MENU                   *
*  HP JetAdmin Utility for UNIX (Rev. D.06.21)  *
************************************************
   1) Configuration (super-user only):
     - configure printer, add printer to spooler
   2) Diagnostics:
     - diagnose printing problems
   3) Administration (super-user only):
     - manage HP printer, JetDirect
   4) Administration (super-user only):
     - manage JetAdmin
   5) Printer Status:
     - show printer status, location, and contact
                   ?) Help         q) Quit
Please enter a selection (q - quit):1
```

Enter 1 `<return>` to configure a new printer:

```
Printer Network Interface:
Create printer configuration in BOOTP/TFTP database
2) Remove printer configuration from BOOTP/TFTP
         Spooler:
Add printer to local spooler
Delete printer from local spooler
Modify existing spooler queue(s)
               ?) Help            q) Quit
Please enter a selection: 3
```

Enter 3 `<return>` to add your printer to the local spooler:

```
Enter the network printer name or IP address \
(q - quit): 192.168.1.10
```

Enter the IP address for your printer. In this example, I entered 192.168.1.10:

```
Following is a list of suggested parameter \
values for this queue. You can change any \
 settings by selecting the corresponding \
non-zero numbers. The values will be used to \
configure this queue when '0' is selected.
To abort the operation, press 'q'.
Configurable Parameters:           Current Settings
-----------------------            ----------------
   1) Lp destination (queue) name   [192_1]
   2) Status log                    [(No log)]
   3) Queue class                   [(not assigned)]
   4) JobMonitor                    [OFF]
   5) Default queue                 [NO]
```

```
   6) Additional printer configuration...
Select an item for change, or '0' to configure \
(q-quit):1
```

Enter 1 to change the name of the printer:

```
Currently used names:
hp1
Enter the lp destination name (default=192_1, q - quit): hplaser
```

Enter a name for the printer. In this example, I entered `hplaser`:

```
Following is a list of suggested parameter values \
for this queue. You can change any settings by \
selecting the corresponding non-zero numbers. \
The values will be used to configure this queue \
when '0' is selected.
To abort the operation, press 'q'.
Configurable Parameters:          Current Settings
-----------------------           ----------------
   1) Lp destination (queue) name   [hplaser]
   2) Status log                    [(No log)]
   3) Queue class                   [(not assigned)]
   4) JobMonitor                    [OFF]
   5) Default queue                 [NO]
   6) Additional printer configuration...
Select an item for change, or '0' to configure \
(q-quit):0
```

Enter `0` to configure the printer settings you've defined:

```
Ready to configure hplaser.
OK to continue? (y/n/q, default=y)y
```

Answer y to start the configuration process.

The system displays the following messages as the printer is being configured:

```
Finished adding "hplaser" to the spooler.
Press the return key to continue ...
```

Enter <`return`>, followed by q, and another q to exit the JetAdmin utility.

9. Verify that the printer is enabled and ready:

```
# lpstat -p hplaser -l
```

The system displays information about the printer.

Exam Questions

1. Which of the following commands does the Unix utility use for printing in SRV4 Unix?

   ❍ **A.** `lpr`

   ❍ **B.** `lp`

   ❍ **C.** `lpd`

   ❍ **D.** `spool`

2. Where is the spool directory located in Solaris?

   ❍ **A.** `/var/spool/lpd`

   ❍ **B.** `/var/spool/lp`

   ❍ **C.** `/usr/spool/lp`

   ❍ **D.** `/usr/spool/lpd`

3. Which of the following commands prevents queuing of print requests?

   ❍ **A.** `disable`

   ❍ **B.** `cancel`

   ❍ **C.** `reject`

   ❍ **D.** `lpshut`

4. Which of the following can be used to add a local printer to a print server? (Select the two best answers.)

   ❍ **A.** SMC

   ❍ **B.** Print Manager

   ❍ **C.** `lpadmin`

   ❍ **D.** `lp`

5. In Solaris 10, which of the following commands stops the print service?

   ❍ **A.** `lpsched`

   ❍ **B.** `lpshut`

   ❍ **C.** `cancel`

   ❍ **D.** `disable`

   ❍ **E.** `svcadm`

6. Which of the following commands submits the spooler information that is to be printed?

   ❍ **A.** `lpd`

   ❍ **B.** `print`

   ❍ **C.** `lpsched`

   ❍ **D.** `lp`

7. Which of the following statements is true of a print server? (Choose two.)

   ❍ **A.** It is a system that has a local printer connected to it.

   ❍ **B.** It is a remote system that can send print requests to another system for printing.

   ❍ **C.** It is a system that makes a printer available to other systems on the network.

   ❍ **D.** Printing can be initiated from it.

8. If the user doesn't specify a printer name, which of the following environment variables tells the print service where to print? (Choose two.)

   ❍ **A.** $HOME

   ❍ **B.** $LPDEST

   ❍ **C.** $PRINTER

   ❍ **D.** $DEFAULT_DEST

9. When adding a printer by using Print Manager, what is the Printer Server field used for?

   ❍ **A.** It defines the name of the system to which the printer is connected.

   ❍ **B.** It defines the system as a print server.

   ❍ **C.** It selects a system from which to download the print software.

   ❍ **D.** It defines a system that can spool to the local printers.

10. Which of the following is a serial port device?

   ❍ **A.** `/dev/bpp0`

   ❍ **B.** `/dev/term/ttya`

   ❍ **C.** `/dev/term/a`

   ❍ **D.** `/dev/fd`

11. Which of the following are valid printer ports? (Choose two.)

❍ **A.** `/dev/terma`

❍ **B.** `/dev/term/a`

❍ **C.** `/dev/ecpp0`

❍ **D.** `/dev/term/ttya`

12. Which of the following commands cancels all print requests for the user `bcalkins` on the printer `jetprint`?

❍ **A.** `lprm -bcalkins jetprint`

❍ **B.** `cancel -Pjetprint bcalkins`

❍ **C.** `cancel -u bcalkins jetprint`

❍ **D.** `lpremove -Pjetprint bcalkins`

13. Which of the following can be used to delete a printer? (Choose two.)

❍ **A.** `lpadmin -x`*<printer-name>*

❍ **B.** `lpshut` *<printer-name>*

❍ **C.** Print Manager

❍ **D.** `lpadmin -D` *<printer-name>*

14. Which of the following commands removes a job from the print queue?

❍ **A.** `lpmove`

❍ **B.** `cancel`

❍ **C.** `lpremove`

❍ **D.** `reject`

15. Which of the following daemons services all printers?

❍ **A.** `lpsched`

❍ **B.** `lpd`

❍ **C.** `lpr`

❍ **D.** `spoold`

16. Where is information on printers found? (Choose two.)

❍ **A.** `/etc/printers.conf`

❍ **B.** `/etc/lp`

❍ **C.** `/var/spool/lp`

❍ **D.** `/etc/print`

17. Which of the following is a system that has a local printer connected to it and makes the printer available to other systems on the network?

❍ **A.** Print server

❍ **B.** Print client

❍ **C.** Client

❍ **D.** Server

18. Which of the following commands adds the printer `luna` to the class `roughdrafts`?

❍ **A.** `lpadmin -p luna -c roughdrafts`

❍ **B.** `lpadmin -class roughdrafts -p luna`

❍ **C.** `lpadmin luna -c roughdrafts`

❍ **D.** `lpadmin -cp roughdrafts luna`

19. Which of the following commands displays the characteristics of the printer `hplaser`?

❍ **A.** `lpstat -p hplaser -l`

❍ **B.** `lpstat -p hplaser`

❍ **C.** `lpadmin -p hplaser -l`

❍ **D.** `lpstat -a -p hplaser -l`

20. Which of the following commands changes a print request with the request ID `eps1-29` to priority level 1?

❍ **A.** `lp -i eps1-29 -q 1`

❍ **B.** `lpadmin -i eps1 -q 0`

❍ **C.** `lp -i eps1-29 -q 39`

❍ **D.** `lpadmin -i eps1 -q 39`

Answers to Exam Questions

1. **B.** The Unix utility responsible for printing in SVR4 Unix is called `lp`. For more information, see the section "The Solaris Print Service."
2. **B.** For Solaris, the spool directory is located in `/var/spool/lp`. For more information, see the section "The Print Spooler."
3. **C.** The `reject` command disables any further requests for a printer or class that is entering the spooling area. For more information, see the section "SVR4 Print Service."
4. **B, C.** You can use Print Manager or `lpadmin` to add a local printer to a print server. For more information, see the section "Setting Up a Printer by Using the `lpadmin` Command."
5. **B, E.** The `lpshut` command is used to disable (stop) the print service; however, `svcadm disable` is preferred over `lpshut`. For more information, see the section "SVR4 Print Service."
6. **D.** The `lp` command places information to be printed into the spooler. For more information, see the section "The LP Print Daemons."
7. **A, C.** A print server is a system that has a local printer connected to it. A print server makes a printer available to other systems on the network. For more information, see the section "Print Servers Versus Print Clients."
8. **B, C.** If the user doesn't specify a printer name or class in a valid style, the print command checks the user's `PRINTER` or `LPDEST` environment variable for a default printer name. For more information, see the section "Setting a User's Default Printer."
9. **A.** When you use Print Manager to add a printer, the Printer Server field defines the name of the system (hostname) to which the printer is connected. For more information, see the section "Setting Up a Printer by Using Print Manager."
10. **C.** `/dev/term/a` is the serial port A device, the primary serial port on a Sun system. For more information, see the section "Setting Up a Printer by Using Print Manager."
11. **B, C.** Valid printer ports on a Solaris system include `/dev/term/a`, `/dev/term/b`, and `/dev/ecpp0`. For more information, see the section "Setting Up a Printer by Using Print Manager."
12. **C.** The following command cancels all print requests for the user `bcalkins` on the printer named `jetprint`:

    ```
    cancel -u bcalkins jetprint
    ```

    For more information, see the section "Cancelling a Print Request."
13. **A, C.** To delete a printer from the system, you can use either the `lpadmin -x` command or the Print Manager interface. For more information, see the section "Deleting Printers and Managing Printer Access."
14. **B.** You use the `cancel` command to remove a job from the print queue. For more information, see the section "Cancelling a Print Request."

15. **A.** The print scheduler, `lpsched`, handles print requests on print servers. For more information, see the section "Restarting the Print Scheduler."

16. **A, B.** When you set up a printer with Print Manager or `lpadmin`, Solaris makes the required changes in the system's `/etc/printers.conf` file and the `/etc/lp` directory. For more information, see the section "The Solaris Print Service."

17. **A.** The print server is a system that has a local printer connected to it and makes the printer available to other systems on the network. For more information, see the section "Print Servers Versus Print Clients."

18. **A.** To add a printer to a class, you use the following command syntax: `lpadmin -p <printer-name> -c <printer-class>`. For more information, see the section "Creating Printer Classes."

19. **A.** You use the `lpstat` command to display the characteristics of a particular printer: `lpstat -p <printer-name> -l`. For more information, see the section "Checking Printer Status."

20. **A.** You use the `lp` command to change the priority of a print job to priority level 1: `lp -i <job name> -q 1`. For more information, see the section "Changing the Priority of a Print Request."

Suggested Reading and Resources

For more information on this topic, refer to the *Managing Print Services* section of the *Solaris 10 Advanced System Administration Guide* by Sun Microsystems, part number 817-0403-10. This guide is available at `http://docs.sun.com`.

For more information on the reminfo database, refer to John Strang and Tim O'Reilly's book *termcap & terminfo*, published by O'Reilly & Associates, Inc.

A good book on the topic of Unix printing in general is *Network Printing*, by Matthew Gast and Todd Radermacher.

CHAPTER SEVEN

Performing System Backups and Restorations

Objectives

The following test objectives for Exam CX-310-200 are covered in this chapter:

Given a scenario, develop a strategy for scheduled backups, and back up an unmounted file system using the appropriate commands.

- Solaris 10 provides several utilities for copying data between disks, tapes, and other types of media. You need to understand the capabilities of each utility and determine which is best for a particular circumstance. This chapter describes all the utilities and commands used to back up and restore data on a Solaris system. When you're finished with this chapter, you should be able to develop a scheduled backup strategy and determine the number of tapes required, command protocols, and backup frequency/levels for any given scenario.

Back up a mounted file system by creating a UFS snapshot and performing a backup of the snapshot file.

- You need to understand how to create a read-only image of a mounted file system using the `fssnap` command. You also need to know how to back up the UFS snapshot to tape.

Restore data from a UFS snapshot and delete the UFS snapshot.

- You need to understand the methods of restoring an entire file system from a snapshot and removing a snapshot when it is no longer needed.

Perform Solaris 10 OS file system restores using the appropriate commands, including restoring a regular file system, the /usr file system, the / (root) file system, and performing interactive and incremental restores for SPARC, x64-, and x86-based systems.

- You need to understand all the steps required to restore a file or file system from tape for each of the various Solaris backup utilities and hardware platforms.

Outline

Study Strategies

The following study strategies will help you prepare for the test:

- As you study this chapter, make sure that you thoroughly understand the various backup tools available in Solaris. On the exam, you'll need to match the correct tool to the task it can perform or the correct description. The exam questions are primarily on `ufsdump` and `ufsrestore`. For the exam you need to develop various backup strategies using `ufsdump`. You also need to know how to restore the operating system from a backup using the `ufsrestore` command.
- You should practice the commands and all the options on a live Solaris 10 system (SPARC or x86). You should try to memorize the examples that are provided in this chapter. They illustrate the commands and options that are most likely to appear on the exam. It's best if you have a tape drive with which to practice, but if you don't have one, you can practice using the commands for moving files between two partitions on a disk. You need to pay special attention to the `ufsdump` and `ufsrestore` commands.
- You should familiarize yourself with the exercises in this chapter. You should memorize them, because the material they cover is on the exam.

Introduction

Backing up a system involves copying data from the system's hard disks onto removable media that can be safeguarded in a secure area. Backing up system data is one of the most crucial system administration functions and should be performed regularly. Backups are used to restore data if files become corrupted or if a system failure or another disaster destroys data. Having a fault-tolerant disk array is not enough. Disk mirroring and RAID 5 protect data in case of a hardware failure, but they do not protect against file corruption, natural disaster, or accidental deletion of a file. In other words, disk mirroring does not protect against flood damage or fire. In addition, if a program corrupts a particular file, the file will be just as corrupt on the mirrored copy as in the original. Therefore, you need to have in place some type of offline backup of your data. Backing up system data—the most important task you perform as a system administrator—must be done on a regular basis. Although even a comprehensive backup scheme can't guarantee that information will not be lost, you can use backups to make sure the loss will be minimal.

This chapter describes the methods available to perform backups, the types of backups, how to develop a solid backup strategy, and how to restore data if you encounter a loss. This chapter begins with a look at backup media and then an explanation of the `tar`, `dd`, `cpio`, and `pax` commands, which are used to copy data from disk to disk or from disk to tape. Then you'll learn about the `ufsdump` and `ufsrestore` utilities, the preferred methods of backing up and restoring data from a Solaris system to tape on a regular basis. This chapter also introduces a method of backing up live file systems, called `fssnap`. Finally, this chapter describes how to back up an entire Solaris operating environment using the Solaris Flash Archive.

Many third-party backup applications are available for Solaris but are not covered on the exam. Therefore, this chapter describes only the methods that are available in the standard Solaris 10 distribution.

Backup Media

Selecting backup media is as critical as selecting the program to perform the backup. Your backup media should be removable so that the information can be taken to another site for safe storage in case of fire, flood, or other natural disaster. In some cases, the backup medium is simply another system on the network that's located in a different building from the primary data. Most backup systems, however, use tape media. Magnetic tape still provides the lowest cost per gigabyte for storing data. Table 7.1 lists some typical tape devices that are used to store backed-up data.

Table 7.1 Common Tape Device Types

Media Type	Capacity
8mm cartridge tape	40GB to 70GB
4mm DAT cartridge tape (DDS-DDS4)	1GB to 40GB
DLT (Digital Linear Tape) 1/2-inch cartridge tape	20GB to 400GB
SDLT (Super Digital Linear Tape) cartridge tape	160GB to 320GB
SDLT II	300GB to 600GB
LTO (Linear Tape Open) cartridge tape	100GB to 200GB
LTO II	200GB to 400GB
LTO III	400GB to 800GB
LTO IV	800GB to 1.6TB

To achieve high capacity, one or more of these tape drives are often combined into cabinets called *tape libraries* or *tape silos*, which can store several terabytes of data, spread across tens or even hundreds of tapes. Robotic arms are used to locate, retrieve, and load tapes into a tape drive automatically to eliminate human intervention.

Tape Device Names

Chapter 1, "Managing File Systems," describes disk device names. Tape drives are also accessed through their logical device names. In fact, for each tape drive, you see 24 different logical device files assigned to each tape drive. These device files are located under the directory `/dev/rmt` and are composed of numbers and letters:

```
/dev/rmt/#cn
```

The following are the numbers and letters in the device files:

- `#`: This number refers to the tape drive's logical device number. The first tape drive found by the system is given the designation `0`, the second is `1`, the third is `2`, and so forth. These numbers do not correspond to SCSI ID numbers.
- `c`: The letter following the device number is the tape density. This can be `l` (low), `m` (medium), `h` (high), `c` (compressed), or `u` (ultra compressed).
- `n`: If an `n` is present after the tape density letter, it means "no rewind." Sometimes after a tape drive is finished, you do not want the tape to automatically rewind. If the `n` is not present in the device name, the tape automatically rewinds when the backup is complete. You must specify this option when backing up multiple file systems; otherwise, the tape will rewind after each file system has been backed up, overwriting each previous file system. The result would be that only the last file system has been stored to tape.

Table 7.2 describes 24 device files for a tape drive with a logical device number of `0`. Beside each device file listed is a description of what the letters mean. All these device files contain different attributes but refer to the same physical tape drive, `0`, and can be used at will.

Table 7.2 Tape Logical Device Files

Device Name	Description
`0`	SystemV (SysV)-style rewinding device with no compression. This is the standard tape device. When you use this device name, the tape rewinds when complete.
`0b`	Berkeley-style rewinding tape device with no compression.
`0bn`	Berkeley-style nonrewinding tape device with no compression.
`0c`	SysV-style rewinding tape device with compression.
`0cb`	Berkeley-style rewinding tape device with compression.
`0cbn`	Berkeley-style nonrewinding tape device with compression.
`0cn`	SysV-style nonrewinding tape device with compression.
`0h`	SysV-style rewinding tape device with high density.
`0hb`	Berkeley-style rewinding tape device with high density.
`0hbn`	Berkeley-style nonrewinding tape device with high density.
`0hn`	SysV-style nonrewinding tape device with high density.
`0l`	SysV-style rewinding tape device with low density.
`0lb`	Berkeley-style rewinding tape device with low density.
`0lbn`	Berkeley-style nonrewinding tape device with low density.
`0ln`	SysV-style nonrewinding tape device with low density.
`0m`	SysV-style rewinding tape device with medium density.
`0mb`	Berkeley-style rewinding tape device with medium density.
`0mbn`	Berkeley-style nonrewinding tape device with medium density.
`0mn`	SysV-style nonrewinding tape device with medium density.
`0n`	SysV-style nonrewinding tape device with no compression.
`0u`	SysV-style rewinding tape device with ultra compression.
`0ub`	Berkeley-style rewinding tape device with ultra compression.
`0ubn`	Berkeley-style nonrewinding tape device with ultra compression.
`0un`	SysV-style nonrewinding tape device with ultra .

NOTE

Compression Tape drives that support data compression contain internal hardware that performs the compression on-the-fly. You should check with your tape drive manufacturer to see if your tape drive supports compression.

Solaris Backup and Restoration Utilities

Objective:
Given a scenario, develop a strategy for scheduled backups, and back up an unmounted file system using the appropriate commands.

Solaris provides the utilities listed in Table 7.3. These backup utilities can be used to copy data from disk to removable media and to restore it.

Table 7.3 Backup Utilities

Utility	Description
`tar`	Creates tape or file-based archives. This format is commonly used for transferring collections of files between systems.
`dd`	Converts and copies a file or raw device.
`cpio`	Copies data from one location to another.
`pax`	Copies files and directory subtrees to a single tape or file. This utility provides better portability than `tar` and `cpio`, so it can be used to transport files to other types of UNIX systems.
`ufsdump`	Backs up all files in a file system.
`ufsrestore`	Restores some or all of the files archived with the `ufsdump` command.
`zip`	Packages and compresses archive files. This utility creates compressed archives that are portable across various platforms, including UNIX, VMS, and Windows.
Flash Archive	Combines the use of Jumpstart and backup utilities to provide an easy mechanism for restoring a system to its initial state or cloning systems.
`jar`	Leverages the portability and flexibility of Java to provide capabilities similar to those of `tar`, `cpio`, and `zip`.

The `tar` Utility

The primary use of the `tar` (which stands for *tape archiver*) command is to copy file systems or individual files between a hard disk and tape or from one file system to another. You can also use `tar` to create a `tar` archive on a floppy disk and to extract files from a `tar` archive on a floppy disk. The `tar` command is popular because it's available on most UNIX systems. If the data you are backing up requires more than one tape, you should use the `cpio`, `pax`, or `ufsdump` commands, which are described in the following sections. The `tar` command has the following syntax:

```
tar <options> <filename> <file-list>
```

You can replace *options* with the list of command options shown in Table 7.4.

Table 7.4 Command Options for `tar`

Option	Description
c	Creates a `tar` file.
t	Lists the names of the specified files each time they occur in the `tar` filename. If no file argument is given, the names of all files in the `tar` file are listed. When `t` is used with the v function modifier, additional information displays for the specified files. `t` stands for *table of contents*.
x	Extracts or restores files from a `tar` filename.
v	Outputs information to the screen as `tar` reads or writes the archive. v stands for *verbose*.
f	Uses the `tar` *<filename>* argument as the name of the `tar` archive. If `f` is omitted, `tar` uses the device indicated by the TAPE environment variable (if it is set). If the TAPE variable is not set, `tar` uses the default values defined in `/etc/default/tar`. If the name of the `tar` file is -, `tar` writes to the standard output or reads from the standard input.

For a more complete listing of command options, see the Solaris online man pages.

<filename> is used with the `f` option and can be any name you want. The filename can also be the name of a device, such as `/dev/rmt/0` or `/dev/rfd0`. *<file-list>* is a list of files you want to include in the archive.

`tar` Examples

The following examples illustrate the use of the `tar` command.

To create a tape archive of everything in the `/home/bcalkins` directory on tape device `/dev/rmt/0`, you type the following:

```
# tar cvf /dev/rmt/0 /home/bcalkins
```

NOTE

No hyphen Notice that the hyphen (-) is not used when specifying options to the `tar` command. This is a rare instance in which the options to a command do not require a hyphen.

To list the files in the archive, you type the following:

```
# tar tvf /dev/rmt/0
```

To restore the file `/home/bcalkins/.profile` from the archive, you type the following:

```
# tar xvf /dev/rmt/0 /home/bcalkins/.profile
```

You can use `tar` to create an archive file on disk instead of tape. The `tar` filename is `files.tar`:

```
# tar cvf files.tar /home/bcalkins
```

To extract files that were created using the preceding example, you type the following:

```
# tar xvf files.tar
```

NOTE

Modification time The modification time on any files restored by `tar` will be preserved and will reflect the time the file was last modified before the backup, *not* the time of the restore operation.

Notice the use of the full pathname when creating an archive with `tar`. Using the full pathname to create an archive ensures that the files will be restored to their original locations in the directory hierarchy. You cannot restore them elsewhere.

If you want to be able to restore files with a relative pathname in the preceding example, you can change to the `/home/bcalkins` directory and specify files to be archived as `* (asterisk)`. This puts the files into the archive, using a pathname that is relative to the current working directory rather than an absolute pathname (one beginning with a slash [`/`]). Files can then be restored into any directory. The use of relative pathnames is highly recommended so that you have the option of restoring an archive without overwriting files that exist but may be different from those in the archive.

The dd Utility

The main advantage of the `dd` command is that it quickly converts and copies files with different data formats, such as differences in block size, record length, or byte order.

The most common use of `dd` is to transfer a complete file system or partition image from a hard disk to a tape. You can also use it to copy files from one hard disk to another. When you're using it to copy data, the `dd` command makes an image copy (an exact byte-for-byte copy) of any medium, which can be either tape or disk. The syntax for the `dd` command is as follows:

```
dd if=<input-file> of=<output-file> <option=value>
```

The command arguments for `dd` are described in Table 7.5.

Table 7.5 dd Command Arguments

Argument	Description
`if`	Designates an input file. The input file can be a filename or a device name, such as `/dev/rmt/0`. If no input file is specified, input for `dd` is taken from the standard input.
`of`	Designates an output file. The output file can be a filename or a device name, such as `/dev/rmt/0`. If no output file is specified, output from `dd` is sent to the standard output.
<option=value>	Several other options can be used on the command line to specify buffer sizes, block sizes, and data conversions. See the Solaris online man page `dd` (1M) for a list of these options.

dd Examples

The next few examples illustrate the use of the `dd` command to copy data. The first example shows how the `dd` command is used to duplicate tapes:

```
# dd if=/dev/rmt/0 of=/dev/rmt/1
```

This procedure requires two tape drives—a source tape and a destination tape.

The next example uses `dd` to copy one entire hard disk to another hard disk:

```
# dd if=/dev/rdsk/c0t1d0s2 of=/dev/rdsk/c0t4d0s2 bs=128K
```

In this example, you need two disks, and both must have the same geometry. Disk geometry is discussed in Chapter 1.

CAUTION

Using `dd` to copy data between dissimilar disk drives Be careful when using `dd` to copy data between two different types of disk drives. We have used `dd` to move data from a 4GB disk to an 18GB disk, and the data transferred fine. We were able to access the data, and the option seemed to have completed correctly. Then we noticed that when we went into the `format` utility, the 18GB disk was labeled as a 4GB disk. This is because *everything* on the 4GB disk transferred to the 18GB disk—including the disk label! All our work was wasted. We had to reidentify the disk type, relabel, and repartition the disk to get it to recognize the disk as an 18GB disk.

In this example, the option `bs=128K` specifies a block size. A large block size, such as 128KB or 4096KB, can decrease the time to copy by buffering large amounts of data. Notice in the example that the raw device is specified. For this technique to work properly, you must use the raw (character) device to avoid the buffered (block) input/output (I/O) system.

You can use the dd command with tar to create an archive on a remote tape drive. In the next example, tar is used to create an archive on a remote system by piping the output to a tape drive called /dev/rmt/0 on a remote system named xena:

```
# tar cvf - <files> ¦ rsh xena dd of=/dev/rmt/0 obs=128
```

Another example would be to read tar data coming from another UNIX system such as older Silicon Graphics systems. The Silicon Graphics system swaps every pair of bytes, making a tar tape unreadable on a Solaris system. To read a tar tape from a Silicon Graphics system, you type the following:

```
# dd if=/dev/rmt/0 conv=swab ¦ tar xvf -
```

Note that the argument for the conv option is swab ("swap bytes") and not swap. In a similar way, a Solaris system can create a tar tape that a Silicon Graphics system can read:

```
# tar cvf - <files> ¦ dd of=/dev/rmt/0 conv=swab
```

The cpio Utility

The is used to copy data from one place to another. cpio stands for *copy input to output*. When copying files with cpio, you present a list of files to the system's standard input and write the file archive to the system's standard output. The principal advantage of cpio is its flexible syntax. The command acts as a filter program, taking input information from the standard input file and delivering its output to the standard output file. You can manipulate the input and output by using the shell to specify redirection and pipelines. The following are the advantages of cpio over other UNIX utilities:

- cpio can back up and restore individual files, not just whole file systems. (tar, pax, and ufsdump also have this capability.)
- Backups made by cpio are slightly smaller than those created with tar because the cpio header is smaller.
- cpio can span multiple tapes; tar is limited to a single tape.

cpio has more options and is therefore perceived as a more complex command than tar.

The cpio utility operates in one of three modes: copy out (cpio -o), copy in (cpio -i), or pass (cpio -p). You use copy-out mode when creating a backup tape and copy-in mode when restoring or listing files from a tape. The pass mode is generally used to copy files from one location to another on disk. You must always specify one of these three modes. The command syntax for the cpio command is as follows:

```
cpio <mode> <option>
```

mode is -i, -o, or -p, and *option* is one of the options described in Table 7.6.

Table 7.6 Command Options for `cpio`

Option	Description
`-c`	Writes header information in ASCII format for portability.
`-d`	Creates directories as needed.
`-B`	Specifies that the input has a blocking factor of 5,120-byte records instead of the default 512-byte records. You must use the same blocking factor when you retrieve or copy files from the tape to the hard disk as you did when you copied files from the hard disk to the tape. You must use the `-B` option whenever you copy files or file systems to or from a tape drive. Using a larger blocking factor increases the write speed. If you use too high a blocking factor, write errors will occur.
`-v`	Reports the names of the files as they are processed. `-v` stands for *verbose*.
`-u`	Copies unconditionally. Without this option, an older file does not replace a newer file that has the same name.
`-m`	Retains the previous file modification time. This option is ineffective on directories that are being copied.
`-P`	With output, causes existing access control lists (ACLs) to be written along with other attributes, except for extended attributes, to the standard output. With input, causes existing ACLs to be extracted along with other attributes from standard input. `-P` stands for *preserve ACLs*.

`cpio` Examples

The following example shows how to copy the directory `/work` and its subdirectories to a tape drive with the device name `/dev/rmt/0`:

```
# cd /work
# find . | cpio -ocB > /dev/rmt/0
```

In this example, the `find` command locates all of the files in the current working directory and pipes them to the `cpio` command. The `-o` option specifies copy-out mode, `-c` outputs the header information in ASCII format, and `-B` increases the blocking factor to 5,120 bytes to improve the speed.

The following example shows how to copy the files located on a tape back into the directory named `/work` on a hard disk:

```
# cd /work
# cpio -icvdB < /dev/rmt/0
```

The `-i` option specifies copy-in mode, `-d` creates directories as needed to restore the data to the original location, and `-v` displays all the output.

Backing Up Files with Copy-Out Mode

To use copy-out mode to make backups, you send a list of files to the `cpio` command via the standard input of `cpio`. You use the UNIX `find` command to generate the list of files to be backed up. You specify copy-out mode by using the `-o` option on the `cpio` command line. In the following example, a file named `list` contains a short list of files to be backed up to tape:

```
# cpio -ovB < list > /dev/rmt/1
```

Normally, as indicated in Table 7.6, `cpio` writes files to the standard output in 512-byte records. By specifying the `-B` option, you can increase the record size to 5,120 bytes to significantly speed up the transfer rate, as shown in the previous example. You can use UNIX commands to generate a list of files for `cpio` to back up in a number of other ways, as shown in the following examples.

You can back up files by entering filenames via the keyboard. You press Ctrl+D when you have finished typing filenames. For example, enter the following:

```
# cpio -oB > /dev/rmt/1
File1.txt
File2.txt
Ctrl+d
```

You can use the `ls` command to generate the list of files to be backed up by `cpio`. You type the following to back up all the files in the current directory but not the files in subdirectories:

```
# cd /home/bcalkins
# ls -d * ¦ cpio -oB >/dev/rmt/1
```

You need to be careful when using `ls` to generate the list of files to back up. In particular, you should be sure that the `ls` command specifies the full path to the files that should be backed up. You will be dissatisfied with the results if you try to use `ls -R` or any other `ls` command on a directory unless you specify the `-d` option to `ls`.

In general, the best command to use for generating a file list is `find`. You can use the `find` command to generate a list of files that the user `bcalkins` created and modified in the past five days. The following is the list of files to be backed up:

```
# find . -user bcalkins -mtime -5  -print ¦ cpio -oB > /dev/rmt/1
```

If the current tape fills up, the `cpio` program prompts you for another tape. You see a message such as the following:

```
If you want to go on, type device/file name when ready
```

You should then change the tape and enter the name of the backup device (for example, `/dev/rmt/1`).

Restoring Files with Copy-In Mode

You use the copy-in mode of cpio to restore files from tape to disk. The following examples describe methods used to restore files from a cpio archive.

The following example restores all files and directories from tape to disk:

```
# cd /users
# cpio -icvumB < /dev/rmt/1
```

The cpio options specified restore files unconditionally (-u) to the /users directory and retain previous file modification times (-m).

The following example selectively restores files that begin with database:

```
# cpio -icvdumB 'database*' < /dev/rmt/1
```

The -d option in this example creates directories as needed.

NOTE

Using wildcards with cpio You must use standard shell escapes to pass the wildcard argument (*) to cpio. For example, the wildcard argument can appear within single quotes.

To obtain a list of files that are on tape, you use the following code:

```
# cpio -ictB < /dev/rmt/1
```

The list of files on /dev/rmt/1 then appears onscreen.

Using Pass Mode

Pass mode is generally not used for backups. The destination must be a directory on a mounted file system, which means that pass mode cannot be used to transfer files to tape. However, you can use pass mode to copy files from one directory to another. The advantage of using cpio over cp is that original modification times and ownership are preserved. You specify pass mode by using the -p option with cpio.

The following example copies all files from /users to /bkup:

```
# cd /users
# mkdir /bkup
# find . ¦ cpio -pdumv /bkup
```

Files are listed onscreen as they are copied.

The pax Utility

The `pax` command has been included in Solaris since version 2.5. `pax` is a POSIX-conformant archive utility that can read and write `tar` and `cpio` archives. It is available on all UNIX systems that are POSIX compliant, such as IBM's AIX, Hewlett-Packard's HP-UX, and some Linux distributions.

`pax` can read, write, and list the members of an archive file and copy directory hierarchies. The `pax` utility supports a wide variety of archive formats, including `tar` and `cpio`.

If `pax` finds an archive that is damaged or corrupted while it is processing, `pax` attempts to recover from media defects. It searches the archive to locate and process the largest possible number of archive members.

The action to be taken depends on the presence of the `-r` and `-w` options, which together form the four modes of operation: list, read, write, and copy (as described in Table 7.7). The syntax for the `pax` command is as follows:

```
pax <mode> <options>
```

Table 7.7 Four Modes of Operation for pax

Option	Operation Mode	Description
`-r`	Read mode	When `-r` is specified but `-w` is not, `pax` extracts the filenames and directories found in the archive file. The archive file is read from disk or tape. If an extracted file is a directory, the file hierarchy is extracted as well. The extracted files are created relative to the current file hierarchy.
None	List mode	When neither `-r` nor `-w` is specified, `pax` displays the filenames or directories found in the archive file. The archive file is read from disk, tape, or the standard input. The list is written to the standard output.
`-w`	Write mode	When `-w` is specified but `-r` is not, `pax` writes the contents of the file to the standard output in an archive format specified by the `-x` option. If no files are specified, a list of files to copy (one per line) is read from the standard input. A directory includes all the files in the file hierarchy whose root is at the file.
`-rw`	Copy mode	When both `-r` and `-w` are specified, `pax` copies the specified files to the destination directory.

In addition to selecting a mode of operation, you can select one or more options to `pax` from Table 7.8.

Table 7.8 Command Options for pax

Option	Description
`-r`	Reads an archive file from the standard input and extracts the specified files. If any intermediate directories are needed to extract an archive member, these directories are created.
`-w`	Writes files to the standard output in the specified archive format. When no file operands are specified, the standard input is read for a list of pathnames—one per line, without leading or trailing blanks.
`-a`	Appends files to the end of an archive that was previously written.
`-b`	Specifies the block size, which must be a multiple of 512 bytes with a maximum of 32,256 bytes. A block size can end with `k` or `b` to specify multiplication by 1,024 bytes (1KB) or 512 bytes, respectively. `-b` stands for *block size*.
`-c`	Matches all file or archive members except those specified by the `pattern` and `file` operands.
`-f` *<archive>*	Specifies *<archive>* as the pathname of the input or output archive. A single archive can span multiple files and different archive devices. When required, `pax` prompts for the pathname of the file or device in the next volume in the archive.
`-I`	Interactively renames files or archive members. For each archive member that matches a pattern operand or file that matches a file operand, a prompt is written to the terminal.
`-n`	Selects the first archive member that matches each pattern operand. No more than one archive member is matched for each pattern.
`-p` *<string>*	Specifies one or more file-characteristic options (privileges). *string* is a string that specifies file characteristics to be retained or discarded when the file is extracted. The string consists of the specification characters `a`, `e`, `m`, `o`, `p`, and `v`. Multiple characteristics can be concatenated within the same string, and multiple `p` options can be specified. The meanings of the specification characters are as follows: `a`: Does not preserve file access times. `e`: Preserves everything: user ID, group ID, file mode bits, file access times, and file modification times. `m`: Does not preserve file modification times. `o`: Preserves the user ID and group ID. `p`: Preserves the file mode bits. `v`: Specifies verbose mode.
`-x` *<format>*	Specifies the output archive format, with the default format being `ustar`. `pax` currently supports `cpio`, `tar`, `bcpio`, `ustar`, `sv4crc`, and `sv4cpio`.

For additional options to the `pax` command, see the Solaris man pages.

When you use `pax`, you can specify the `file` operand along with the options from Table 7.7. The `file` operand specifies a destination directory or file pathname. If you specify a directory operand that does not exist, that the user cannot write to, or that is not of type `directory`, `pax` exits with a nonzero exit status.

The `file` operand specifies the pathname of a file to be copied or archived. When the `file` operand does not select at least one archive member, `pax` writes the `file` operand pathnames in a diagnostic message to standard error and then exits with a nonzero exit status.

Another operand is the `pattern` operand, which is used to select one or more pathnames of archive members. Archive members are selected by using the filename pattern-matching notation described by `fnmatch`. The following are examples of `pattern` operands:

`pattern` Operand	Description
`?`	Matches any character
`*`	Matches multiple characters
`[`	Introduces a `pattern` bracket expression

When a `pattern` operand is not supplied, all members of the archive are selected. When a `pattern` operand matches a directory, the entire file hierarchy rooted at that directory is selected. When a `pattern` operand does not select at least one archive member, `pax` writes the `pattern` operand pathnames in a diagnostic message to standard error, and then exits with a nonzero exit status.

pax Examples

The following examples illustrate the use of the `pax` command.

To copy files to tape, you issue the following `pax` command, using `-w` to copy the current directory contents to tape and `-f` to specify the tape device:

```
# pax -w -f /dev/rmt/0
```

To list a verbose table of contents for an archive stored on tape device `/dev/rmt/0`, you issue the following command:

```
# pax -v -f /dev/rmt/0
```

The tape device in these two examples could have been a filename to specify an archive on disk.

You use the following command to interactively select the files to copy from the current directory to the destination directory:

```
# pax -rw -i . <dest-dir>
```

Because `pax` understands `tar` and `cpio` formats, it is a very helpful tool when a `tar` or `cpio` archive contains absolute pathnames and the files should not be restored to their original locations. The key is the `-s` option, which allows files to be programmatically renamed. The following example uses the `-s` option to extract files from a `tar` archive, stripping the leading slash from any absolute pathname:

```
# pax -r -s ',^/,,' -f file.tar
```

As you become more familiar with the `pax` utility, you might begin to use it in place of `tar` and `cpio` for the following reasons:

- It is portable to other UNIX systems.
- It can recover damaged archives.
- It can span multiple volumes.

The `ufsdump` Utility

Objective:
Given a scenario, develop a strategy for scheduled backups, and back up an unmounted file system using the appropriate commands.

Whereas the other Solaris utilities discussed in this chapter can be used to copy files from disk to tape, `ufsdump` is designed specifically for backups and is the recommended utility for backing up entire Solaris file systems. The `ufsdump` command copies files, directories, or entire file systems from a hard disk to tape or from disk to disk. The only drawback of using `ufsdump` is that the file systems must be inactive (that is, unmounted or read-only) before you can conduct a full backup. If the file system is still active, nothing in the memory buffers is copied to tape, and you could end up with a corrupt backup.

You should back up any file systems that are critical to users, including file systems that change frequently. Table 7.9 suggests the file systems to back up and the suggested frequency.

Table 7.9 File Systems to Back Up

File System	Frequency
root (`/`)	If you frequently add and remove clients and hardware on the network or you have to change important files in root (`/`), this file system should be backed up. You should do a full backup of the root file system between once a week and once a month. If `/var` is in the root file system and your site keeps user mail in the `/var/mail` directory on a mail server, you might want to back up root daily.
`/usr`	The contents of this file system are fairly static and need to be backed up only between once a week and once a month—and after new software or patches are installed.
`/export/home`	The `/export/home` file system usually contains the home directories and subdirectories of all users on the system; its files are volatile and should be backed up daily.

The `ufsdump` command has many built-in features that the other archive utilities don't have, including the following:

- The `ufsdump` command can be used to back up individual file systems to local or remote tape devices or disk drives. The device to which the files are being backed up can be on any system in the network. This command works quickly because it is aware of the structure of the UNIX file system and it works directly through the raw device file.
- `ufsdump` has built-in options to create incremental backups that back up only the files that have been changed since a previous backup. This saves tape space and time.
- `ufsdump` can back up groups of systems over the network from a single system. You can run `ufsdump` on each remote system through a remote shell or remote login, and you can direct the output to the system on which the drive is located.
- With `ufsdump`, the system administrator can restrict user access to backup tables.
- The `ufsdump` command has a built-in option to verify data on tape against the source file system.

Backing up a file system with `ufsdump` is referred to as *dumping* a file system. When a file system is dumped, a level between 0 and 9 is specified. A level 0 dump is a full backup and contains everything on the file system. Levels 1 through 9 are incremental backups and contain only files that have changed since previous dumps at lower levels.

A recommended backup schedule involves a three-level dump strategy: a level 0 dump at the start of the month (manually), automated weekly level 5 dumps, and automated daily level 9 dumps. The automated dumps are performed at 4:30 a.m., for example—a time when most systems typically are idle. Automated daily dumps are performed Sunday through Friday mornings. Automated weekly dumps are performed on Saturday mornings. Backups are automated by creating a shell script and using `cron` to execute the script on a regular basis.

Table 7.10 shows the dump level performed on each day of a typical month. Note that the level 0 dump at the start of the month is performed manually because the entire system must be idle before you can back up the root file system. One way to ensure that the system is not being used is to put the system in single-user mode. The level 9 and 5 dumps are automated with `cron`, but also must be conducted when the file systems are not being used. See Chapter 5, "Managing System Processes," for more information on `cron`.

Table 7.10 File System Dump Schedule

Floating	Sun	Mon	Tues	Wed	Thurs	Fri	Sat
First of month	0						
Week 1	9	9	9	9	9	9	5
Week 2	9	9	9	9	9	9	5
Week 3	9	9	9	9	9	9	5
Week 4	9	9	9	9	9	9	5

The backup schedule shown in Table 7.10 accomplishes the following:

- Each weekday tape accumulates all files changed since the end of the previous week or the initial level 0 backup for the first week. All files that have changed since the lower-level backup at the end of the previous week are saved each day.
- Each Saturday tape contains all files changed since the last level 0 backup.

This dump schedule requires at least four sets of seven tapes—one set for each week and one tape for the level 0 dump. Each set will be rotated each month. The level 0 tapes should not be overwritten and should be saved for at least a year, depending on your company's and jurisdiction's data-retention policy.

Even with the backup schedule outlined in Table 7.10, data can still be lost. For example, if a hard disk fails at 3 p.m., all modifications since the preceding 4:30 a.m. backup are lost. Also, files that were deleted midweek will not appear on the level 5 tapes. Or a user may accidentally delete a file and not realize it for several weeks, but when the user wants to use the file, it is not there. If he asks you to restore the file from backup, the only tape it appears on is the level 0 backup, and it could be too far out of date to be useful. By not overwriting the daily level 9 tapes frequently, you can minimize this problem.

The syntax for the `ufsdump` command is as follows:

```
/usr/sbin/ufsdump <options> <arguments> <files-to-dump>
```

The options for the `ufsdump` command are described in Table 7.11.

Table 7.11 `ufsdump` Command Options

Option	Description
<options>	A single string of one-letter option names.
<arguments>	The argument that goes with each option. The option letters and the arguments that go with them must be entered in the same order.
<files-to-dump>	The files to back up. This argument must always come last. It specifies the source or contents of the backup. It usually identifies a file system, but it can also identify individual files or directories. For a file system, you specify the name of the file system or the raw device file for the disk slice where the file system is located.

Table 7.12 describes the options and arguments for the `ufsdump` command.

Table 7.12 Options for the `ufsdump` Command

Option	Description
0 to 9	Specifies the backup level. Level 0 is for a full backup of the entire file system. Levels 1 through 9 are for incremental backups of files that have changed since the last lower-level backup.
a *<archive-file>*	Instructs `ufsdump` to create an archive file. Stores a backup table of the tape contents in a specified file on the disk. The file can be understood only by `ufsrestore`, which uses the table to determine whether a file to be restored is present in a backup file and, if so, on which volume of the medium it resides.
b *<factor>*	Specifies the blocking factor: the number of 512-byte blocks to write to tape per operation.
c	Instructs `ufsdump` to back up to cartridge tape. When end-of-media detection applies, this option sets the block size to 126.
d *<bpi>*	Specifies the tape density. You should use this option only when `ufsdump` cannot detect the end of the medium.
D	Backs up to floppy disk.
f *<dump-file>*	Specifies the destination of the backup. *<dump-file>* can be one of the following: ▶A local tape drive or disk drive ▶A remote tape drive or disk drive ▶Standard output You use this argument when the destination is not the default local tape drive `/dev/rmt/0`. If you use the f option, you must specify a value for *dump-file*.
l	Specifies autoload. You use this option if you have an autoloading (stackloader) tape drive. When the end of a tape is reached, this option takes the drive offline and waits up to two minutes for the tape drive to be ready again. If the drive is ready within two minutes, it continues. If the drive is not ready after two minutes, autoload prompts the operator to load another tape.
n	Specifies notify. When intervention is needed, this option sends a message to all terminals of all users in the `sys` group.
o	Specifies offline. When `ufsdump` is finished with a tape or disk, it takes the drive offline, rewinds it (if it's a tape), and removes the medium, if possible. (For example, it ejects a disk or removes an autoloaded tape.)
s *<size>*	Specifies the length of tape, in feet, or the size of the disk, in the number of 1,024-byte blocks. You need to use this option only when `ufsdump` cannot detect the end of the medium.

Table 7.12 Options for the `ufsdump` Command

Option	Description
S	Estimates the size of the backup. This option determines the amount of space needed to perform the backup (without actually doing it) and outputs a single number that indicates the estimated size of the backup, in bytes.
t *<tracks>*	Specifies the number of tracks for 1/4-inch cartridge tape. You need to use this option only when `ufsdump` cannot detect the end of the medium.
u	Updates the dump record. For a completed backup of a file system, this option adds an entry to the file `/etc/dumpdates`. The entry indicates the device name for the file system's disk slice, the backup level (0 to 9), and the date. No record is written when you do not use the u option or when you back up individual files or directories. If a record already exists for a backup at the same level, it is replaced.
v	Verifies the contents of the medium against the source file system after each tape or disk is written. If any discrepancies appear, this option prompts the operator to mount a new medium and then repeats the process. You use this option on an unmounted or snapshot file system only; any activity in the file system causes it to report discrepancies.
w	Lists the file systems appearing in `/etc/dumpdates` that have not been backed up within a day. When you use this option, all other options are ignored.
W	Shows all file systems that appear in `/etc/dumpdates` and highlights file systems that have not been backed up within a day. When you use this option, all other options are ignored.

The `ufsdump` command uses these options by default:

```
ufsdump 9uf /dev/rmt/0 <files-to-back-up>
```

`ufsdump` Examples

The following examples illustrate the use of the `ufsdump` command.

The following is an example of a full backup of the `/users` file system:

```
# ufsdump 0ucf /dev/rmt/0 /users
  DUMP: Writing 63 Kilobyte records
  DUMP: Date of this level 0 dump: Mon Jun 16 10:43:25 2008
  DUMP: Date of last level 0 dump: the epoch
  DUMP: Dumping /dev/rdsk/c0t1d0s0 (pyramid1:/users) to /dev/rmt/0.
  DUMP: Mapping (Pass I) [regular files]
  DUMP: Mapping (Pass II) [directories]
  DUMP: Estimated 10168 blocks (4.96MB).
  DUMP: Dumping (Pass III) [directories]
  DUMP: Dumping (Pass IV) [regular files]
  DUMP: Tape rewinding
  DUMP: 10078 blocks (4.92MB) on 1 volume at 107 KB/sec
  DUMP: DUMP IS DONE
```

NOTE

No hyphen As noted earlier with the `tar` command, the `ufsdump` command does not require a hyphen before the options.

If you want to see how much space a backup will require, you issue the following command:

```
# ufsdump S <filesystem>
```

The estimated number of bytes needed on tape to perform the level 0 backup is displayed.

In the following example, the local `/export/home` file system on a Solaris 10 system is backed up to a tape device on a remote Solaris 10 system called `sparc1`:

```
# ufsdump 0ucf sparc1:/dev/rmt/0 /export/home
DUMP: Date of this level 0 dump: Mon Jun 16 10:43:25 2008
DUMP: Date of last level 0 dump: the epoch
DUMP: Dumping /dev/rdsk/c0t3d0s7 (/export/home) to /dev/rmt/0 \
 on host sparc1
DUMP: mapping (Pass I) [regular files]
DUMP: mapping (Pass II) [directories]
DUMP: estimated 19574 blocks (9.56MB)
DUMP: Writing 63 Kilobyte records
DUMP: dumping (Pass III) [directories]
DUMP: dumping (Pass IV) [regular files]
DUMP: level 0 dump on Mon Jun 16 10:43:25 2008
DUMP: Tape rewinding
DUMP: 19574 blocks (9.56MB) on 1 volume
DUMP: DUMP IS DONE
```

NOTE

The `/.rhosts` file The `/.rhosts` file must be correctly configured on the system, with the tape device attached to enable remote systems to successfully perform a backup to them. For more information on the `/.rhosts` file, see Chapter 4, "User and Security Administration."

In this example, the `-u` option is used with the `ufsdump` command. This causes `ufsdump` to make an entry into the `/etc/dumpdates` file, which records the file system that was backed up, the level of the last backup, and the day, date, and time of the backup. Here's an example of looking into the `/etc/dumpdates` file:

```
# more /etc/dumpdates
```

The system responds with the following:

```
/dev/rdsk/c0t0d0s7          0 Mon Jun 16 10:47:46 2008
/dev/rdsk/c0t0d0s6          0 Mon Jun 16 10:48:04 2008
```

When incremental backups are made using `ufsdump`, the `ufsdump` command consults the `/etc/dumpdates` file to find the date of the most recent backup at the next lower level. `ufsdump` then copies all files modified or added since the date of that lower-level backup. You can also determine whether backups are being done by viewing the contents of the `/etc/dumpdates` file. If a backup fails, it is not recorded in `/etc/dumpdates`.

Another useful example is using `ufsdump` to copy the contents of one file system to another. In the section "The `dd` Utility," you learned how to copy data from one disk to another, but only when the disk geometry is exactly the same for each disk. In other words, `dd` works when you want to copy a 73GB disk to another 73GB disk. But if you want to replace an older 4GB disk with a new 73GB disk, you should not use `dd` to copy the data; a better option is to use `ufsdump`. Moving data from disk to tape and then back to disk again can be time consuming. Here's a way to move data directly to that file system by using `ufsdump` without going to tape:

```
ufsdump 0f - /export/home | (cd /data; ufsrestore  -rf - )
```

In this example, all data in the `/export/home` file system is copied to the `/data` file system. Instead of specifying a tape device, this example specifies a `-` (hyphen). The hyphen dumps the data to standard output and restores the data from standard input rather than from a file or device. This creates and extracts the dump file in memory, speeding up the entire process.

The `ufsrestore` Utility

Objective:
Given a scenario, develop a strategy for scheduled backups, and back up an unmounted file system using the appropriate commands.

TIP

Restoring file systems You need to understand each step described in Step by Step 7.2 and Step by Step 7.3, along with the order in which each step is performed. Be sure that you understand what the `restoresymtable` file is used for.

You'll be given various scenarios that require you to restore data. Make certain that you understand the correct order in which to restore incremental backups. These topics are likely to be on the exam.

The `ufsrestore` command copies files from backups created using the `ufsdump` command. As root, you can use `ufsrestore` to reload an entire file system from a level 0 dump and any incremental dumps that follow it, or to restore one or more single files from any dump tape. `ufsrestore` restores files with their original owner, last modification time, and mode (permissions).

The syntax for the `ufsrestore` command is as follows:

```
ufsrestore  <options>  <arguments> <filename(s)>
```

The options for the `ufsrestore` command are described in Table 7.13.

Table 7.13 `ufsrestore` Command Options

Option	Description
`<options>`	Gives you the choice of one and only one of these options: `i`, `r`, `R`, `t`, or `x`.
`<arguments>`	Follows the `<options>` string with the arguments that match the options.
`<filename(s)>`	Specifies files to be restored as arguments to the `x` or `t` options and must always come last.

Table 7.14 describes some of the most common options and arguments for the `ufsrestore` command.

Table 7.14 Command Options for the `ufsrestore` Command

Option	Description
`h`	Turns off directory expansion. Only the directory file you specify is extracted or listed.
`i`	Runs `ufsrestore` in interactive mode. In this mode, you can use a limited set of shell commands to browse the contents of the medium and select individual files or directories to restore. Table 7.15 lists the available commands.
`r`	Restores the entire contents of the medium into the current working directory, which should be the top level of the file system. Information used to restore incremental dumps on top of the full dump is also included. To completely restore a file system, you use this option to restore the full (level 0) dump and then each incremental dump. This is intended for a new file system that was just created with the `newfs` command. `r` stands for *recursive*.
`R`	Resumes the restoration. Prompts for the volume from which to resume restoring, and restarts from a checkpoint. You rerun the `ufsrestore` command with this option after a full restore (`r` option) is interrupted.
`x <filename(s)>`	Selectively restores the files you specify, using the `<filename(s)>` argument. `<filename(s)>` can be a list of files and directories. All files under a specified directory are restored unless you also use the `h` option, which turns off directory expansion. If you omit `<filename(s)>` or enter `.` for the root directory, all files on all volumes of the medium (or from standard input) are restored. Existing files are overwritten, and warnings are displayed. `x` stands for *extract*.

Table 7.14 Command Options for the ufsrestore Command

Option	Description
t *<filename(s)>*	Checks the files specified in the *<filename(s)>* argument against the medium. For each file, the full filename and the inode number (if the file is found) are listed. If the filename is not found, ufsrestore indicates that the file is not on the volume, meaning any volume in a multivolume dump. If you do not enter the *<filename(s)>* argument, all files on all volumes of the medium are listed, without distinction as to the volume on which the files are located. When you use the h option, only the directory files specified in *<filename(s)>* not their contents—are checked and listed. The table of contents is read from the first volume of the medium or (if you use the a option) from the specified archive file. This option is mutually exclusive with the x and r options.
b *<factor>*	Specifies the number of 512-byte blocks to read from tape per operation. By default, ufsrestore tries to figure out the block size used in writing the tape. b stands for *blocking factor.*
m	Restores specified files into the current directory on the disk, regardless of where they are located in the backup hierarchy, and renames them with their inode numbers. For example, if the current working directory is /files, a file in the backup named ./database/test with inode number 156 is restored as /files/156. This option is useful when you are extracting only a few files.
s*<n>*	Skips to the nth backup file on the medium. This option is useful when you put more than one backup on a single tape.
v	Displays the name and inode number of each file as it is restored. v stands for *verbose.*

For a full listing of options for the ufsrestore command, see the Solaris man pages.

Table 7.15 lists the commands that can be used with ufsrestore when you're using interactive mode (that is, ufsrestore -i).

Table 7.15 Commands for Interactive Restoration

Command	Description
ls *<directory-name>*	Lists the contents of either the current directory or the specified directory. Directories are suffixed with a slash (/). Entries in the current list to be restored (extracted) are marked by an asterisk (*) prefix. If the v option is in effect, inode numbers are also listed.
cd *<directory-name>*	Changes to the specified directory in the backup hierarchy.
add *<filename>*	Adds the current directory or the specified file or directory to the list of files to extract (restore). If you do not use the h option, all files in a specified directory and its subdirectories are added to the list. Note that it's possible that not all the files you want to restore to a directory will be on a single backup tape or disk. You might need to restore from multiple backups at different levels to get all the files.

Table 7.15 Commands for Interactive Restoration

Command	Description
`delete <filename>`	Deletes the current directory or the specified file or directory from the list of files to extract (restore). If you do not use the `h` option, all files in the specified directory and its subdirectories are deleted from the list. Note that the files and directories are deleted only from the extract list you are building. They are not deleted from the medium.
`extract`	Extracts the files in the list and restores them to the current working directory on the disk. You should specify `1` when asked for a volume number. If you are doing a multitape or multidisk restoration and are restoring a small number of files, you should start with the last tape or disk.
`help`	Displays a list of the commands you can use in interactive mode.
pwd	Displays the pathname of the current working directory in the backup hierarchy.
`q`	Quits interactive mode without restoring additional files.
`verbose`	Turns the `verbose` option on or off. You can also enter verbose mode by entering `v` on the command line outside interactive mode. When `verbose` is on, the interactive `ls` command lists `inode` numbers, and the `ufsrestore` command displays information about each file as it is extracted.

`ufsrestore` Examples

The following examples illustrate how to restore data from a tape by using `ufsrestore`.

You can use the `ufsrestore` command to display the contents of a tape:

```
# ufsrestore tf /dev/rmt/0
     2      .
  4249      ./users
 12400      ./users/bill
 12401      ./users/bill/.login
 12402      ./users/bill/.cshrc
 12458      ./users/bill/admin
 12459      ./users/bill/junk
```

You can use `ufsrestore` to restore a file from a backup that was created using `ufsdump`:

```
# ufsrestore f /dev/rmt/0 <filename>
```

You may also use the interactive method of restoring a file from a `ufsdump` tape or file. For example, Step by Step 7.1 describes how to restore the `/etc/inet/hosts` file from the second `ufsdump` file on a tape.

STEP BY STEP

7.1 Interactively Restore a File from a ufsdump

1. Change to the /var/tmp directory. This is a temporary location where the file will be restored. This will prevent you from overwriting the current /etc/inet/hosts file.

2. Load the tape into the tape drive, and position the tape to the second ufsdump file on the tape as follows:

```
# mt -f /dev/rmt/0n fsf 1
```

   For information on the mt command, see the section "Tape Drive Control" later in this chapter.

3. Access the ufsdump file on tape using the i option. This puts ufsrestore in interactive mode and allows you to search for the file on the tape:

```
# ufsrestore ivf /dev/rmt/0
```

   Your prompt changes to the following:

```
ufsrestore>
```

4. While in interactive mode of ufsrestore, change to the /etc/inet directory:

```
ufsrestore> cd /etc/inet
```

5. Mark the hosts file for extraction using the add command:

```
ufsrestore> add hosts
```

   When you issue the ls command, an asterisk appears next to the hosts file:

```
ufsrestore > ls
./etc/inet:
   1386  ./                          21014  mipagent.conf-sample
     45  ../                         21015  mipagent.conf.fa-sample
   1498  datemsk.ndpd                21016  mipagent.conf.ha-sample
  90583  *hosts                        90584  netmasks
```

6. Extract the file from the tape to the /var/tmp directory:

```
ufsdump> extract
```

   The following message may appear:

```
Extract requested files
You have not read any volumes yet. Unless you know which volume your file(s)
are on you should start with the last volume and work towards the first.
Specify next volume #: 1
```

   Enter 1.

You see a message that the file is being extracted:

```
extract file ./etc/inet/hosts
Add links
Set directory mode, owner, and times.
set owner/mode for '.'? [yn]  y
Answer Y
```

7. Exit the interactive `ufsrestore` session by typing the following:

   ```
   ufsrestore> quit
   ```

8. Move the file from the `/var/tmp` directory to the `/etc/inet` directory as follows:

   ```
   # mv /var/tmp/etc/inet/hosts /etc/inet/hosts
   ```

You can restore entire directories from a remote drive located on the system called `sparc1` by adding `sparc1:` to the front of the tape device name, as illustrated in the following example:

```
# ufsrestore rf sparc1:/dev/rmt/0 filename
```

Occasionally, a file system becomes so damaged that you must completely restore it from a backup. If you have faithfully backed up file systems, you can restore them to the state of the last backup. The first step in recovering a file system is to delete everything in the damaged file system and re-create the file system by using the `newfs` command. To recover a damaged file system, follow the procedure described in Step by Step 7.2.

STEP BY STEP

7.2 Recovering and Restoring a Damaged File System on a SPARC System

1. Unmount the corrupted file system /*<filesystem>*:

   ```
   # umount  /<filesystem>
   ```

2. After you unmount the file system, issue the `newfs` command to create a new file system:

   ```
   # newfs /dev/rdsk/<disk-partition-name>
   ```

   <disk-partition-name> is the name of the raw disk partition that contains the corrupted file system. Make sure you are using the correct device name; otherwise, you might destroy another file system.

3. Although optional, it's a good idea to perform an `fsck` after creating a file system just to make sure that everything is clean before you start putting data into a file system. This is especially true on a file system that was corrupted.

4. Mount the file system to be restored, and change to that directory:

   ```
   # mount /dev/dsk/<c?t?d?s?> <directory>
   # cd /<directory>
   ```

5. Load the tape and issue the following command:

```
# ufsrestore rf /dev/rmt/0
```

The entire contents of the tape are restored to the file system. All permissions, ownerships, and dates remain as they were when the last incremental tape was created.

The next two steps are optional.

6. Remove the `restoresymtable` file created by the `ufsrestore` command. This is a temporary file that is created whenever you restore an entire file system from tape. The `restoresymtable` file is used only by `ufsrestore` for "checkpointing" when information is passed between incremental restorations. The `restoresymtable` file is not required after the file system has been successfully restored.

7. Unmount the file system and run `fsck` again to check the repaired file system.

Recovering the Root (/) or /usr File System

Objective:
Perform Solaris 10 OS file system restores using the appropriate commands, including restoring a regular file system, the /usr file system, the / (root) file system, and performing interactive and incremental restores for SPARC, x64-, and x86- based systems.

Sometimes a careless administrator with root access accidentally deletes part or all of the root or `/usr` file system. Other times the file system can become unusable because of a faulty disk drive or a corrupted file system. You can follow the procedure described in Step by Step 7.3 if you ever need to recover the root or `/usr` file system on a SPARC-based system.

STEP BY STEP

7.3 Recovering the Root or /usr File System on a SPARC System

1. Replace and partition the disk if it has failed.

2. Because the system cannot be booted from the boot disk, boot from the DVD or CD-ROM, and re-create the failed file system by issuing the `newfs` command:

```
# newfs /dev/rdsk/<disk-partition-name>
```

<disk-partition-name> is the name of the raw disk partition that contains the corrupted file system.

3. Check the new file system by using `fsck`:

```
# fsck /dev/rdsk/<disk-partiton-name>
```

4. Mount the new file system on a temporary mount point:

```
# mount /dev/dsk/<disk-partition-name> /mnt
```

5. Change to the `/mnt` directory:

```
# cd /mnt
```

6. Write-protect the tapes so that you don't accidentally overwrite them.

7. Load the tape and issue the following command:

```
# ufsrestore rf /dev/rmt/0
```

The entire contents of the tape are restored to the file system. All permissions, ownerships, and dates remain as they were when the last incremental tape was created.

8. Verify that the file system is restored:

```
# ls
```

9. Remove the `restoresymtable` file that is created and used by `ufsrestore` to checkpoint the restoration:

```
# rm restoresymtable
```

10. Change to the root (`/`) directory:

```
# cd /
```

11. Unmount the newly created file system:

```
# umount /mnt
```

12. Check the new file system with `fsck`:

```
# fsck /dev/rdsk/<disk-partition-name>
```

The restored file system is checked for consistency.

13. If you are recovering the root (`/`) file system, create the boot blocks on the root partition by using the `installboot` command:

```
# installboot  /usr/platform/'uname-I'/lib/fs/ufs/bootblk\
 /dev/rdsk/<disk-partition-name>
```

The `installboot` command installs the boot blocks onto the boot disk. Without the boot blocks, the disk cannot boot.

14. Insert a new tape into the tape drive and back up the new file system:

```
# ufsdump 0uf /dev/rmt/0n /dev/rdsk/<device-name>
```

A level 0 backup is performed. You should immediately make a backup of a newly created file system because `ufsrestore` repositions the files and changes the `inode` allocation.

15. Reboot the system with a reconfiguration reboot:

    ```
    # shutdown -y -g0 -i0
    ok boot -r
    ```

    The system is rebooted.

The following example is an actual session that restores the root (/) file system from tape device /dev/rmt/0 to Small Computer System Interface (SCSI) disk target 0, slice 0, on controller 0:

```
# mount /dev/dsk/c0t0d0s0 /mnt
# cd /mnt
# devfsadm -c tape
# ufsrestore rf /dev/rmt/0
```

NOTE

devfsadm The devfsadm command with the -c tape option creates the /dev entries for the tape drive only. It creates links in /dev/rmt to the actual tape device special files. The devfsadm command is covered in Chapter 1.

Files are restored from tape. When this is complete, you are returned to a shell prompt. You can then remove the restoresymtable file, unmount the file system, and use fsck on the device:

```
# rm restoresymtable
# cd /
# umount /mnt
# fsck /dev/rdsk/c0t0d0s0
```

The system displays the fsck passes as the file system is checked. The next step is to install the bootblock on the boot disk, which is described in Chapter 3, "Perform System Boot and Shutdown Procedures for SPARC, x64-, and x86-Based Systems":

```
# installboot
 /usr/platform/`uname -i`/lib/fs/ufs/bootblk /dev/rdsk/c0t0d0s0
# ufsdump 0uf /dev/rmt/0 /dev/rdsk/c0t0d0s0
# shutdown -y -g0 -i0
```

The system is halted. At the ok prompt, you perform a reconfiguration reboot:

```
ok boot -r
```

Performing a reconfiguration reboot ensures that all devices connected to the system have been configured properly in the kernel and in the /dev and /devices directories.

Follow the procedure described in Step by Step 7.4, if you ever need to recover the root (/) file system on an x86/x64-based system. It's similar to Step by Step 7.3, except that you also need to install the GRUB `stage1` and `stage2` programs onto the active Solaris partition.

STEP BY STEP

7.4 Recovering the Root (/) File System on an x86/x64-Based System

1. Replace and partition the disk if it has failed.

   Because the system cannot be booted from the boot disk, boot from the DVD or CD-ROM.

2. The system begins its boot process from the Solaris miniroot on DVD (or CD-ROM). The following list of boot choices is displayed:

   ```
   1. Solaris Interactive (default)
   2. Custom JumpStart
   3. Solaris Interactive Text (Desktop Session)
   4. Solaris Interactive Text (Console Session)
   5. Apply driver updates
   6. Single user shell
   Enter the number of your choice:
   ```

3. Select boot choice 6, the single user shell. If an instance of Solaris is found on the disk, the system asks if you want to mount it on `/a`. Answer `n` to avoid mounting an existing root file system.

4. Re-create the failed file system by issuing the `newfs` command:

   ```
   # newfs /dev/rdsk/<disk-partition-name>
   ```

   <disk-partition-name> is the name of the raw disk partition that contains the corrupted root file system.

5. Check the new file system by using `fsck`:

   ```
   # fsck /dev/rdsk/<disk-partiton-name>
   ```

6. Mount the new file system on a temporary mount point:

   ```
   # mount /dev/dsk/<disk-partition-name> /mnt
   ```

7. Change to the `/mnt` directory:

   ```
   # cd /mnt
   ```

8. Write-protect the tapes so that you don't accidentally overwrite them.

9. Load the tape and issue the following command:

   ```
   # ufsrestore rf /dev/rmt/0
   ```

The entire contents of the tape are restored to the file system. All permissions, ownerships, and dates remain as they were when the last incremental tape was created.

10. Verify that the file system is restored:

```
# ls
```

11. Remove the `restoresymtable` file that is created and used by `ufsrestore` to checkpoint the restoration:

```
# rm restoresymtable
```

12. Install the GRUB `stage1` and `stage2` programs on the Solaris partition. The `installgrub` command installs the GRUB `stage1` program in sector 0 and the GRUB `stage2` program beginning at sector 50. These sectors are within the reserved first cylinder of the partition. Depending on the nature of the damage, they may not require reinstallation.

    To install the `stage1` and `stage2` programs found in the `miniroot` from the Solaris DVD (or CD-ROM), use the following command:

```
# /sbin/installgrub  /boot/grub/stage1 /boot/grub/stage2 /dev/rdsk/<disk-partition-name>
```

13. Change to the root (`/`) directory:

```
# cd /
```

14. Unmount the newly created file system:

```
# umount /mnt
```

15. Check the new file system with `fsck`:

```
# fsck /dev/rdsk/<disk-partition-name>
```

    The restored file system is checked for consistency.

16. Perform a full backup of the file system:

```
ufsdump 0uf /dev/rmt/0 dev/rdsk/<disk-partition-name>
```

17. Reboot the system, but first eject the DVD (or CD-ROM) to prevent the system from booting to it again:

```
# init 6
```

Additional Notes About Restoring Files

When you restore files in a directory other than the root directory of the file system, `ufsrestore` re-creates the file hierarchy in the current directory. For example, if you restore to `/home` files that were backed up from `/users/bcalkins/files`, the files are restored in the directory `/home/users/bcalkins/files`.

When you restore individual files and directories, it's a good idea to restore them to a temporary directory such as /var/tmp. After you verify that you've retrieved the correct files, you can move them to their proper locations. You can restore individual files and directories to their original locations; however, if you do so, you should be sure that you do not overwrite newer files with older versions from the backup tape.

You should not forget to make regular backups of your operating system. Losing all the customization you do—such as adding user accounts, setting up printers, and installing application software—would be disastrous. Whenever you make modifications that affect the root (/), /usr, /opt, or other operating system directories, you should bring down the system into single-user mode and perform a level 0 dump.

Tape Drive Control

The mt command is used to communicate with the tape drive from the command line. Use the mt command to send instructions to the tape drive. The command syntax is as follows:

```
mt -f tape-device=name command count
```

The -f option is followed by the tape device name. If the -f option is not used, /dev/rmt/0 is used by default.

After specifying the *tape-device-name*, provide an mt command for the tape drive. The mt command is sent to the tape drive; it instructs the tape drive to perform an action. Table 7.16 lists a few of the common mt commands and their respective actions.

Table 7.16 mt Commands

Command	Description
mt status	Prints status information about the tape unit.
mt rewind	Rewinds the tape.
mt offline	Rewinds the tape and, if appropriate, takes the drive unit offline by unloading the tape.
mt fsf *count*	Forward spaces the tape over the requested number of sequential file marks.
mt eom	Spaces to the end of recorded media on the tape. This is useful for appending files onto previously written tapes.
mt erase	Erases the entire tape.
mt rewoffl	Rewinds the tape and, if appropriate, takes the drive unit offline by unloading the tape (the same as rewind)

For additional information and mt commands, refer to the mt man pages.

The UFS Snapshot Utility

Objective:
Back up a mounted file system by creating a UFS snapshot and performing a backup of the snapshot file.

You can use the `fssnap` command to create a read-only snapshot of a file system while the file system is mounted. A *snapshot* is a point-in-time image of a file system that provides a stable and unchanging device interface for backups. This snapshot uses the *backing-store file*. A few important points about the backing-store:

- The destination path of the backing store files must have enough free space to hold the file system data. The size of the backing store files vary with the amount of activity on the file system.
- The backing store file location must be different from the file system that is being captured in a snapshot.
- The backing-store files can reside on any type of file system, including another UFS file system or an NFS file system.
- Multiple backing-store files are created when you create a snapshot of a UFS file system that is larger than 512GB.

NOTE

File system snapshot It is *not* possible to perform a snapshot of a file system if the file system is in use by system accounting and if the file system is used as a backing store by real-time applications.

Unlike `ufsdump`, `fssnap` enables you to keep the file system mounted and the system in multiuser mode during backups. The snapshot is stored to disk, and then you can use Solaris backup commands such as `ufsdump`, `tar`, and `cpio` to back up the UFS snapshot. The result is a more reliable backup than you get with `ufsdump` alone.

When you use the `fssnap` command to create a file system snapshot, you should observe how much disk space the backing-store file consumes. The backing-store file itself uses no space initially, and then it grows quickly. As activity increases on the original file system, the backing-store file grows. This is because the size of the backing-store is activity related and is not related to the size of the original file system. It holds the original version of blocks that changed while the `fssnap` was active. If the file system has heavy use, the backing-store file increases in size quickly. On a heavily used file system, you need to make sure the backing-store file has enough space to grow.

NOTE

Disk space for the backing-store file If the backing-store file runs out of disk space, the snapshot might delete itself, causing the backup to abort. If you are experiencing problems with the backup, you should examine the `/var/adm/messages` file for possible snapshot errors.

Step by Step 7.5 describes how to create snapshots.

STEP BY STEP

7.5 Creating Snapshots

1. Determine which file system you want to create the snapshot of. For this example, assume that you want to create a snapshot of `/export/home`.
2. Determine where you will store the backing-store file (that is, the snapshot). That file system should be large enough to hold an expanding backing-store file. In this example, you will use `/var/tmp` as a location to store the backing-store file.
3. Create the snapshot:

   ```
   # fssnap -F ufs -o backing-store=/var/tmp /export/home
   ```

   `backing-store` can be abbreviated as `bs` (for example, `bs=/var/tmp`).

   The system responds with the name of the virtual device that is created:

   ```
   /dev/fssnap/0
   ```

4. Now you can back up the file system to tape (`/dev/rmt/0`) by specifying the virtual device (`/dev/fssnap/0`):

   ```
   # ufsdump 0ucf /dev/rmt/0 /dev/fssnap/0
   ```

   The virtual device `/dev/fssnap/0` is described later in this section.

Here's what happens after you create the snapshot using the `fssnap` command. A file, the backing-store file, is created in the `/var/tmp` file system. It's a normal file that can be listed just like any other file, by using the `ls` command:

```
# ls -l /var/tmp
```

The following backing-store file is listed:

```
-rw-------    1 root     other    196665344 Mar 27 15:05 snapshot0
```

`snapshot0` is the name of the backing-store file. The backing-store file is a bitmapped file that contains copies of presnapshot data that has been modified since the snapshot was taken. When you take the snapshot, the `snapshot0` file is created. As the original file system changes, the snapshot's backing-store file is updated, and the backing-store file grows.

To display a summary of all the snapshots that have been created on a system, along with their corresponding virtual devices, issue the following command:

```
# /usr/sbin/fssnap -i
```

The system displays each virtual device, followed by the corresponding file system:

```
1 /export/home
2 /data
3 /oracle
```

For more detailed information about snapshots, use the `/usr/lib/fs/ufs/fssnap -i` command. Notice the path to this command and how it differs from the previous `fssnap` command:

```
# /usr/lib/fs/ufs/fssnap -i /export/home
```

This `fssnap` command displays detailed information for a specific UFS snapshot:

```
# /usr/lib/fs/ufs/fssnap -i /export/home
Snapshot number               : 0
Block Device                  : /dev/fssnap/0
Raw Device                    : /dev/rfssnap/0
Mount point                   : /export/home
Device state                  : idle
Backing store path            : /var/tmp/snapshot0
Backing store size            : 0 KB
Maximum backing store size    : 512000 KB
Snapshot create time          : Wed Jun 18 08:58:33 2008
Copy-on-write granularity     : 32 KB
```

NOTE

Limiting the size of the backing-store file You can limit the size of the backing-store file by using the `maxsize` option:

```
# fssnap -F ufs -o maxsize=600m,backing-store=/var/tmp /export/home
```

In this example, the size of the backing-store file is limited to 600MB; however, the backing-store file is a sparse file. A sparse file uses less disk space than the file system it represents.

In addition, after you execute the `fssnap` command, two read-only virtual device files are created:

- `/dev/fssnap/0`: Block virtual device
- `/dev/rfssnap/0`: Raw virtual device

The virtual devices look and act like standard read-only devices, and you can use any of the existing Solaris commands with them. For example, you can mount the block virtual device by using the `mount` command:

```
# mount -F ufs -o ro /dev/fssnap/0 /mnt
```

NOTE

Mounting the snapshot Because the virtual devices are read-only, you need to mount the snapshot as read-only by using the `-o ro` option to the `mount` command.

You can go into the mount point and view the contents of the snapshot with the following:

```
# ls -l /mnt
```

The contents of the snapshot are displayed:

```
total 3810
drwxr-xr-x   2 wcalkins staff        512 Mar 12 14:14 bcalkins
-rw———-      1 root     other    1933312 Mar 27 10:15 dump
drwx———      2 root     root        8192 Feb 26 15:33 lost+found
```

In this case, there wasn't much in the file system when the snapshot was created.

Now you can list the contents of the "real" file system named `/export/home`; remember that this is the live file system from which the snapshot was taken:

```
# ls -l /export/home
total 3810
drwxr-xr-x   2 wcalkins staff        512 Mar 12 14:14 bcalkins
-rw———-      1 root     other    1933312 Mar 27 15:05 dump
-rw-r—r—     1 root     other         12 Mar 27 15:05 file1
drwx———      2 root     root        8192 Feb 26 15:33 lost+found
```

Notice in this example that things are changing. There is a new file named `file1`, and the dump file has a new time. The snapshot image, however, remains the way it was. None of the dates have changed, and none of the new files show up. When you back up the snapshot, you get a backup of the file system the way it was when you made the snapshot. Here's how you back up the snapshot by using the `ufsdump` command:

```
# ufsdump 0ucf /dev/rmt/0 /dev/rfssnap/0
```

Notice that you're backing up the virtual device named `/dev/fssnap/0`. The backup that was created from the virtual device is a backup of the original file system; it represents the state of the file system when the snapshot was taken. If you ever need to restore a file system from the backup, restore the data using `ufsrestore`, as if you had taken the backup directly from the original file system. For this recovery procedure, refer to the section "The `ufsrestore` Facility" earlier in this chapter.

You can use the `ufsdump` command to create incremental backups of UFS snapshots. Use the `N` option with the `ufsdump` command to create an incremental backup of the UFS snapshot that writes the name of the device being backed up, rather than the name of the snapshot device, to the `/etc/dumpdates` file. Step by Step 7.6 demonstrates how to use the `ufsdump` command to create an incremental backup.

STEP BY STEP

7.6 Create an Incremental Backup of a UFS Snapshot

1. We'll assume that a snapshot was created earlier, backed up using a level 0 dump, and then removed. To create an incremental backup, I'll create a new snapshot of the same file system that was already backed up earlier. I'll assume that the name of the raw virtual device is `/dev/rfssnap/0`.

2. Create an incremental backup of the snapshot:

```
# ufsdump 1ufN /dev/rmt/0 /dev/rdsk/c1t0d0s0 /dev/rfssnap/0
```

The backup contains all the files that were added or changed since the last level 0 dump.

Use a UFS snapshot of an existing file system to create, or clone, a new file system. For example, suppose that you have created a snapshot of the `/data` file system and the corresponding virtual device is named `/dev/rfssnap/0`. To create a new file system named `/data_new`, which will be an exact copy of the snapshot, issue the following commands:

```
# mkdir /data_new
# ufsdump 0ucf - /dev/rfssnap/0 | (cd /data_new; ufsrestore rf - )
```

To remove the snapshot, you issue the following command:

```
# fssnap -d  /export/home
```

`/export/home` was the name of the file system you created the snapshot of. The system responds with the following:

```
Deleted snapshot 0
```

When you create a UFS snapshot, you can specify that the backing-store file be unlinked, which means the backing-store file is removed after the snapshot is deleted. Here's how you do this:

```
# fssnap -F ufs -o unlink,backing-store=/var/tmp /export/home
```

When you use the `unlink` option, you cannot see the backing-store file. This might make administration more difficult because the file is not visible in the file system.

Earlier you did not specify the `-o unlink` option, so you have to delete the backing-store manually after you run the `fssnap -d` command:

```
# rm /var/tmp/snapshot0
```

The backing-store file occupies disk space until the snapshot is deleted, whether you use the `-o unlink` option to remove the backing-store file or you remove it manually.

Here are a few other facts about snapshots:

- The size of the backing-store file depends on how much data has changed since the snapshot was taken.
- A snapshot does not persist across system reboots.
- Snapshots are meant to be used on UFSs only.

For more information on options that can be used with the `fssnap` command to list and manage snapshots, refer to the man pages for `fssnap` and `fssnap_ufs`.

zip and unzip

`zip` is a compression and file-packaging utility that is now available on Solaris. `zip` is used on UNIX, Microsoft Windows, Macintosh, and many other operating systems to compress files and then put those files into an archive file. The `zip` program is useful for combining a set of files for distribution or for saving disk space by temporarily compressing unused files or directories. You are likely to see Solaris patches distributed in `zip` format. The section "Installing a Patch" in Chapter 2, "Installing the Solaris 10 Operating Environment," provides information on patches.

You use the `unzip` command to extract the compressed files from an archive. Other than for installing patches, the `zip` and `unzip` commands are not covered on the exam. For more information, consult the online man pages.

Solaris Flash Archive

EXAM ALERT

chapter because it is a method of backing up your system. For a more in-depth explanation of the Flash archive, refer to the *Solaris 10 System Administration Exam Prep: Exam CX-310-202* book.

You can back up your Solaris operating environment (not the data) by creating a Flash archive. Previously in this chapter, you learned how to back up your operating system by using `ufsdump` and specifying a level 0 dump of the root (`/`), `/usr`, and other operating system-related file systems. The Flash archive feature can be used as a backup or to replicate an installation on a number of systems, called *clone systems*. (Chapter 2 describes the Flash archive. Installing a Flash archive is described in the *Solaris 10 System Administration Exam Prep: Exam CX-310-202* book.)

After the system has been set up and configured (but before it goes into production) is a good time to create the archive. While you're in single-user mode, you use the `flarcreate` command to create the Solaris Flash archive. The following is the syntax for this command:

```
flarcreate -n <name> <options> <path>/<filename>
```

The arguments for the command are described in Table 7.17.

Table 7.17 Arguments to the `flarcreate` Command

Argument	Description
`<name>`	Specifies the name that you give the archive.
`<path>`	Specifies the path to the directory in which you want to save the archive file. If you do not specify a path for saving the archive, `flarcreate` saves the archive file in the current directory.
`<filename>`	Specifies the name of the archive file.

Many options are available for the `flarcreate` command, and they are described in the *Solaris 10 System Administration Exam Prep: Exam CX-310-202* book. The following example shows the use of the `-n` and `-t` options, used to create an archive of the entire operating environment on the local tape drive:

```
# flarcreate -n osarchive -t /dev/rmt/0
```

The `-n` option allows you to identify the archive with a unique name. It is not the name with which the archive will be stored, however. The `-t` option specifies that the archive will be stored to tape.

If the archive creation is successful, the `flarcreate` command returns the exit code `0`. If the archive creation fails, the `flarcreate` command returns a nonzero exit code.

You can use the `flar` command to administer archives. The `flar` command includes subcommands for extracting information, splitting archives, and combining archives.

You can use the `flar` command with the `-i` option to get information about archives you have already created:

```
# flar -i /data/vararchive
```

The system responds with the following:

```
files_archived_method=cpio
creation_date=20080327221216
creation_master=ultra5
content_name=vararchive
files_compressed_method=none
files_archived_size=34472960
content_architectures=sun4u
```

The `jar` Utility

The Java archive (JAR) file format enables you to bundle multiple files into a single archive file, much the same way you can bundle files by using the `tar` utility. Typically, a JAR file contains the class files and auxiliary resources associated with Java applets and applications.

The benefits of using the JAR file format include the following:

- **Security:** You can digitally sign the contents of a JAR file. Users who recognize your signature can then optionally grant your files security privileges that they wouldn't otherwise have.
- **Decreased download time:** If your applet is bundled in a JAR file, the applet's class files and associated resources can be downloaded to a browser in a single Hypertext Transfer Protocol (HTTP) transaction, without the need for opening a new connection for each file.
- **Compression:** The JAR format enables you to compress files for efficient storage.
- **Packaging for extensions:** The extensions framework provides a means by which you can add functionality to the Java core platform, and the JAR file format defines the packaging for extensions. Java 3D and JavaMail are examples of extensions developed by Sun. By using the JAR file format, you can turn your software into extensions as well.
- **Package sealing:** Packages stored in JAR files can optionally be sealed so that they can enforce version consistency. To seal a package within a JAR file means that all classes defined in that package must be found in the same JAR file.
- **Package versioning:** A JAR file can hold data about the files it contains, such as vendor and version information.
- **Portability:** The mechanism for handling JAR files is a standard part of the Java platform's core application programming interface (API).

The `jar` command is similar to the `tar` command in that it packages several files into a single file, but it also compresses the resulting file. It is a Java application that combines multiple files into a single JAR file. It is also a general-purpose archiving and compression tool that is based on Zip and the ZLIB compression format. The `jar` command was originally created so that Java programmers could download multiple files with one request rather than having to issue a download request for each separate file. `jar` is standard with the Solaris 10 operating system, and it is also available on any system that has a Java Virtual Machine (JVM) installed.

This is the syntax for the `jar` command:

```
jar <options> <jar-file> <input-file(s)>
```

Table 7.18 describes the options and arguments used with the `jar` command.

Table 7.18 `jar` **Command Options**

Option	Description
`c`	Indicates that you want to create a JAR file.*
`f`	Indicates that you want the output to go to a file rather than to the system's standard output.*
`i`	Generates index information for the JAR file(s).
`t`	Lists the table of contents for the archive.
`v`	Produces verbose output on standard output while the JAR file is being built. The verbose output tells you the name of each file as it is added to the JAR file.
`x`	Extracts files from an archive.
`0`	Indicates that you don't want the JAR file to be compressed.
`<jar-file>`	Specifies the name that you want the resulting JAR file to have. You can use any filename for a JAR file. By convention, JAR filenames are given a `.jar` extension, although that is not required.
`<input-file(s)>`	Specifies a space-separated list of one or more files that you want to be placed in your JAR file. The *`<input-file(s)>`* argument can contain the wildcard asterisk (`*`) symbol. If *`input-files`* is a directory, the contents of the directory are added to the JAR recursively.

*The `c` and `f` options can appear in either order, but there must not be any space between them.

You use the following to create a JAR file:

```
# jar cf <jar-file> <input-file(s)>
```

You use the following to view the contents of a JAR file:

```
# jar tf <jar-file>
```

You use the following to extract the contents of a JAR file:

```
# jar xf <jar-file>
```

You use the following to extract specific files from a JAR file:

```
# jar xf <jar-file> <archived-file(s)>
```

Here's an example of how to use `jar` to compress files located within two different directories. JAR files are packaged with the Zip file format, so you can use them for Zip-like tasks, such as lossless data compression, archiving, decompression, and archive unpacking. To package the audio and images directories into a single JAR file named `files.jar` in your default home directory, you would run the following command from inside the `/export/home/bcalkins` directory:

```
# jar cvf ~/files.jar files.class audio images
```

The `audio` and `images` arguments represent directories, so the JAR tool recursively places them and their contents in the JAR file. The generated JAR file `files.jar` is placed in the user's home directory. Because the command used the `v` option for verbose output, you see something similar to this output when you run the command:

```
adding: files.class (in=3825) (out=2222) (deflated 41%)
adding: audio/ (in=0) (out=0) (stored 0%)
adding: audio/beep.au (in=4032) (out=3572) (deflated 11%)
adding: audio/ding.au (in=2566) (out=2055) (deflated 19%)
adding: audio/return.au (in=6558) (out=4401) (deflated 32%)
adding: audio/yahoo1.au (in=7834) (out=6985) (deflated 10%)
adding: audio/yahoo2.au (in=7463) (out=4607) (deflated 38%)
adding: images/ (in=0) (out=0) (stored 0%)
adding: images/cross.gif (in=157) (out=160) (deflated -1%)
adding: images/not.gif (in=158) (out=161) (deflated -1%)
```

You can see from this output that the JAR file `files.jar` is compressed. The JAR tool compresses files by default. You can turn off the compression feature by using the `0` option; in that case, the command looks like this:

```
# jar cvf0 files.jar files.class audio images
```

Summary

This chapter has described the standard copy and backup utilities available in Solaris. It also describes the various types of backup media available. It discussed `tar`, `dd`, `cpio`, and `pax`, and it described how to use these utilities to copy and restore files, directories, and entire file systems.

This chapter also described how to use `ufsdump` and `ufsrestore` to perform regular backups on a system. It described a recommended backup schedule that you can implement to safeguard any system from deliberate or accidental loss of data. This chapter described how to recover data from backup media. It described the procedures to restore single files and entire file systems on both SPARC and x86/x64-based systems. The chapter also described how to use `fssnap` and Solaris Flash archive as further methods to back up live data.

Finally, this chapter described methods used to package and compress files (such as `zip` and `jar`).

As you're finding out with Solaris, there are often many ways to perform a task. You need to choose the method that best suits your environment. Although all the utilities described in this chapter do a good job of backing up your data, if your company has several servers and large storage pools, you might want to investigate some of the more robust backup packages available from third parties, such as Veritas and Legato. Sun also has a backup product, StorEdge Enterprise Backup, which is an optional package that can be purchased directly from Sun and added into your Solaris operating environment. Most of these add-on packages provide a comprehensive suite of utilities for conducting and managing backups in complex computing environments. In most cases, they allow single-point backups—not only for Solaris, but for other operating systems as well.

Key Terms

- Block size
- File system dump
- Full backup
- Incremental backup
- Tape archive
- Interactive restore
- File system restore
- Flash archive
- Java archive
- `zip`
- `dd`
- `tar`
- `cpio`
- `mt`
- `ufsdump`
- `ufsrestore`
- Snapshot

Exercises

These exercises utilize a tape drive connected as /dev/rmt/0. If your system does not have a tape drive attached to it, you should substitute the device /dev/rmt/0n for a filename such as /tmp/foo.

7.1 Using tar

In this exercise, you use the tar command to copy files from disk to tape.

Estimated time: 15 minutes (depending on the size of /export/home)

1. Log in as root, and insert a tape into the tape drive. The tape will be erased, so you should use a blank tape and make sure that the tape is not write-protected.
2. Create a tape archive of everything in the /export/home directory on tape device /dev/rmt/0:

```
# tar cvf /dev/rmt/0 /export/home
```

3. List the contents of the archive:

```
# tar tvf /dev/rmt/0
```

4. Add another tape archive to the same tape. This is referred to as a *stacked tape*. To do this, you first need to advance the tape past the first archive by using the mt command:

```
# mt  -f /dev/rmt/0n fsf 1
```

   The mt utility sends commands to a magnetic tape drive. It can be used to rewind, retension, and fast-forward a tape as well as many other operations. In the example, the fsf option moves the tape forward by one record.

   Notice the use of the "no rewind" device (that is, 0n rather than 0).

5. Add the next archive of the /var/adm directory:

```
# tar cvf /dev/rmt/0n /var/adm
```

6. Rewind the tape:

```
# mt -f /dev/rmt/0 rew
```

7. List the first archive on the tape:

```
# tar tvf /dev/rmt/0n
```

8. List the contents of the second tape archive on the stacked tape:

```
# tar tvf /dev/rmt/0
```

   Note that it's important to make a notation on the tape label that this is a stacked tape and also to record the order of each archive on the tape.

7.2 Using cpio and pax

This exercise demonstrates how to copy user files that have been modified in the past 30 days to a tape drive with the device name /dev/rmt/0. You should specify a larger-than-default blocking factor to increase the transfer speed.

Estimated time: 15 minutes (depending on the size of /export/home)

1. Log in as root and insert a tape in the tape drive. The tape will be erased, so you should use a blank tape and make sure the tape is not write-protected.

   ```
   # cd /export/home
   ```

2. Locate all files by using the find command and transfer them to tape by using cpio:

   ```
   # find . -mtime -30 -print ¦ cpio -oB > /dev/rmt/0
   ```

3. List all the files that were backed up in step 2:

   ```
   # cpio -ict < /dev/rmt/0
   ```

4. Use the pax utility to list the contents of the tape that was created by using cpio:

   ```
   # pax -v -f /dev/rmt/0
   ```

7.3 Using ufsdump and ufsrestore

In this exercise, you use the ufsdump command to back up an entire file system. You then use the ufsrestore command to restore a file.

This exercise destroys data This exercise removes and overwrites files in the /var file system. Therefore, you should not do this exercise on a production system.

NOTE

Estimated time: 20 minutes

1. Log in as root and insert a tape in the tape drive. The tape will be erased, so you should use a blank tape and make sure the tape is not write-protected.

2. Back up the entire /var file system to tape:

```
# ufsdump 0ucf /dev/rmt/0 /var
```

3. Remove the /var/adm/messages file:

   ```
   # rm /var/adm/messages
   ```

4. Restore the /var/adm/messages file by using ufsrestore:

```
# cd /var
# ufsrestore -ivf /dev/rmt/0
```

5. At the ufsrestore> prompt, verify that the messages file is on the tape:

```
ls adm/messages
```

6. Mark the file for extraction, and then extract the file:

```
add adm/messages
extract
```

When the system asks you to specify the next volume, type 1.

When the system says, set owner/mode for '.'?[yn], enter y.

Enter q to exit the ufsrestore utility.

7. Verify that the file has been restored to its proper location by using the ls -l command.

Exam Questions

1. What does the following command sequence do?

```
#cd /home/myjunk
#tar cvf /dev/rmt/0 .
```

❍ **A.** It takes all the files in /home/myjunk, packages them into a single tar archive on /dev/rmt/0, and prints a commentary on the process.

❍ **B.** It extracts the contents of the tape at /dev/rmt/0 to /home/myjunk.

❍ **C.** It tars all the files in /dev/rmt/0 to /home/myjunk, creates a table of contents, and ignores checksum errors.

❍ **D.** It tars all the files in the current directory into two separate archives—one for the contents of myjunk and one for the rest of /home.

2. Say you have the following backup schedule:

- First Monday of the month—level 0 (tape 1)
- All other Mondays—level 1 (tape 2)
- Wednesdays—level 2 (tape 3)
- Fridays—level 4 (tape 4)

Which tapes would be needed to fully restore the system if it goes down the second Saturday of the month?

- ❍ **A.** All four of them
- ❍ **B.** Tapes 2 through 4
- ❍ **C.** Tapes 1, 2, and 4
- ❍ **D.** Tapes 1, 3, and 4

3. Which of the following commands can be used in conjunction with the `cpio` command to perform incremental archives?

- ❍ **A.** `sort`
- ❍ **B.** `find`
- ❍ **C.** `grep`
- ❍ **D.** `diff`

4. Which of the following utilities has a built-in function to perform incremental backups?

- ❍ **A.** `tar`
- ❍ **B.** `cpio`
- ❍ **C.** `ufsdump`
- ❍ **D.** `dd`

5. Which of the following commands lists the contents of a `tar` file without actually extracting the file?

- ❍ **A.** `tar -cvf`
- ❍ **B.** `tar -xvf`
- ❍ **C.** `tar -tvf`
- ❍ **D.** `tar -txf`

6. Which of the following statements about `dd` is false?

- ❍ **A.** It quickly converts and copies files with different data formats.
- ❍ **B.** It is a good backup tool.
- ❍ **C.** It is used to transfer a complete file system or partition from a hard disk to a tape.
- ❍ **D.** It is used to copy all data from one disk to another.

7. Which of the following statements about the `cpio` command are true? (Choose three.)

 - ❍ **A.** It is used to copy data from one place to another.
 - ❍ **B.** It is not a good tool for backups.
 - ❍ **C.** It can back up and restore individual files, not just entire file systems.
 - ❍ **D.** Backups made by `cpio` are smaller than those created with `tar`.

8. Which statement about the `pax` utility is false?

 - ❍ **A.** It supports a wide variety of archive formats, including `tar` and `cpio`.
 - ❍ **B.** It is a POSIX-conformant archive utility.
 - ❍ **C.** It does not have a built-in function to perform incremental backups.
 - ❍ **D.** It is old and is not a recommended backup utility.

9. You need to perform a backup of the root file system without bringing the system to single-user mode or unmounting the root file system. Which is the best method of backing up an active, mounted file system?

 - ❍ **A.** `fssnap`, and then use `ufsdump` on the snapshot
 - ❍ **B.** `fnssnap`, and then use `ufsdump` on the snapshot
 - ❍ **C.** `flarcreate`, and then use `ufsdump` on the snapshot
 - ❍ **D.** `ufsdump` alone can be used to back up an active file system.
 - ❍ **E.** `fssnapshot`, and then use `ufsdump` on the snapshot

10. On an active file system, which command successfully backs up the root file system to the `/dev/rmt/0` tape device?

 - ❍ **A.** `ufsdump -S0uf /dev/rmt/0  /`
 - ❍ **B.** ``ufsdump 0uf /dev/rmt/0 `fssnap -o bs=/opt,raw` ``
 - ❍ **C.** ``ufsdump 0uf /dev/rmt/0 `fssnap -o bs=/export,raw /` ``
 - ❍ **D.** ``ufsdump 0uf /dev/rmt/0  `snapfs -o bs=/var/tmp,raw /` ``

11. Which statement about the `restoresymtable` file is true?

- ❍ **A.** The `restoresymtable` file manages the restoration of symbolic links to ensure that unnecessary copies of data are not restored.
- ❍ **B.** The `restoresymtable` file is used to coordinate the restoration of incremental dumps on top of a full dump. It can be deleted after the last incremental restoration.
- ❍ **C.** The `restoresymtable` file contains detailed information about the restored files. It's simply a log file that can be removed after the restoration of a full backup.
- ❍ **D.** The `restoresymtable` file is used for future full dumps of a file system that has been restored by using `ufsrestore`. It needs to be saved for when `ufsrestore` may be used to restore files to this file system later.
- ❍ **E.** You must not delete this binary file; it is needed by `ufsrestore` and `ufsdump`. You should put a backup copy of this file in another location.

Answers to Exam Questions

1. **A.** The first command changes your working directory, and the second creates the `tar` file. The commands shown in the example take all the files in the `/home/myjunk` directory, package them into a single `tar` archive on `/dev/rmt/0`, and print a commentary of the process. For more information, see the section "The `tar` Utility."
2. **A.** To restore the data from backups, you first load the level 0 tape created the first Monday of the month, followed by the level 2 tape, followed by the level 3 tape, and finally the level 4 tape. For more information, see the section "The `ufsdump` Utility."
3. **B.** You use the `find` command with `cpio` to perform incremental archives. For more information, see the section "The `cpio` Utility."
4. **C.** `ufsdump` has built-in options for creating incremental backups that back up only those files that were changed since a previous backup. This saves tape space and time. For more information, see the section "The `ufsdump` Utility."
5. **C.** The `-t` option with the `tar` command lists the contents of a `tar` file. For more information, see the section "The `tar` Utility."
6. **B.** The main advantage of the `dd` command is that it can quickly convert and copy files with different data formats, such as differences in block size or record length. The most common use of this command is to transfer a complete file system or partition from your hard disk to a tape. You can also use it to copy files from one hard disk to another. `dd` does not make a good backup tool. For more information, see the section "The `dd` Utility."
7. **A, C, D.** `cpio` is used to copy data and back up and restore files and file systems in a more compressed format than `tar`. For more information, see the section "The `cpio` Utility."

8. **D.** `pax` is a backup utility that has recently been added to Solaris. It works well as a backup utility. For more information, see the section "The `pax` Utility."

9. **A.** Unlike `ufsdump`, `fssnap` enables you to keep the file system mounted and the system in multi-user mode during backups. The snapshot is stored to disk, and then you can use Solaris backup commands such as `ufsdump`, `tar`, and `cpio` to back up the UFS snapshot. The result is a more reliable backup. For more information, see the section "The UFS Snapshot Utility."

10. **C.** The following example backs up the root (`/`) file system without requiring you to unmount the file system:

```
# ufsdump 0uf /dev/rmt/0 `fssnap  -o bs=/export,raw  /`
```

Because `ufsdump` requires the path to a raw device, the `raw` option is used. The command `fssnap  -o bs=/export,raw  /` is enclosed in backticks so that the file system snapshot is created in the `/export` file system and then backed up by `ufsdump`. After you use `ufsdump`, you need to ensure that you remove the snapshot to free up space on the backing store by using `fssnap -d` and by removing the temporary file created in `/export`. For more information, see the section "The UFS Snapshot Utility."

11. **B.** The `restoresymtable` file is created by the `ufsrestore` command when restoring an entire file system. This is a temporary file that is created whenever you restore an entire file system from tape. The `restoresymtable` file is used only by `ufsrestore` for "checkpointing," which involves information passed between incremental restorations. For example, if you perform an incremental restoration of data from backup tapes, the system uses information from the `restoresymtable` file to restore incremental backups on top of the latest full backup. The `restoresymtable` file is not required after the file system has been successfully restored, and it can be deleted by using the `rm` command. It is not removed automatically. For more information, see the section "The `ufsrestore` Utility."

Suggested Readings and Resources

Inside Solaris 9, by Bill Calkins (New Riders, 2002).

Unix Backup and Recovery, by W. Curtis Preston (O'Reilly, 1999).

System Administration Guide: Devices and File Systems, part number 817-5093-16, by Sun Microsystems. Available at http://www.docs.sun.com.

PART II

Final Review

Fast Facts

The Fast Facts listed in this chapter are designed as a refresher of key points, topics, and knowledge that are required to be successful on the Sun Certified System Administrator for the Solaris 10 Operating Environment—Part I exam (CX-310-200). By using these summaries of key points, you will refresh your understanding of key topics and ensure that you have a solid understanding of the objectives and the information required for you to succeed in each major area of the exam.

This chapter is designed as a quick study aid that you can use just prior to taking the exam. You should be able to review the Fast Facts for this exam in less than an hour. It cannot serve as a substitute for knowing the material supplied in these chapters. However, its key points should refresh your memory on critical topics. In addition to the information located in this chapter, remember to review the Glossary terms because they are intentionally not covered here.

Managing File Systems

A file system is a structure of files and directories used to organize and store files on disks and other storage media. All disk-based computer systems have a file system. In Unix, file systems have two basic components: files and directories. A *file* is the actual information as it is stored on the disk, and a *directory* is a listing of the filenames. In addition to keeping track of filenames, the file system must also keep track of files' access dates, permissions, and ownership.

A *hard disk* consists of several separate disk platters mounted on a common spindle. Data stored on each platter surface is written and read by disk heads. The circular path a disk head traces over a spinning disk platter is called a *track*.

Each track is made up of a number of sectors laid end to end. A *sector* consists of a header, a trailer, and 512 bytes of data. The header and trailer contain error-checking information to help ensure the accuracy of the data. Taken together, the set of tracks traced across all of the individual disk platter surfaces for a single position of the heads is called a *cylinder*.

Devices and Drivers

In Solaris, each disk device is described in three ways, using three distinct naming conventions:

- **Physical device name**—Represents the full device pathname in the device information hierarchy.
- **Instance name**—Represents the kernel's abbreviated name for every possible device on the system.
- **Logical device name**—Used by system administrators with most system commands to refer to devices.

The system commands used to provide information about physical devices are described in Table 1.

Table 1 Device Information Commands

Command	Description
`prtconf`	Displays system configuration information, including the total amount of memory and the device configuration, as described by the system's hierarchy. This useful tool verifies whether a device has been seen by the system.
`sysdef`	Displays device configuration information, including system hardware, pseudo devices, loadable modules, and selected kernel parameters.
`dmesg`	Displays system diagnostic messages as well as a list of devices attached to the system since the most recent restart.

You can add new devices to a system without requiring a reboot if your system supports hot-plug devices. It's all handled by the `devfsadmd` daemon that transparently builds the necessary configuration entries. Older commands such as `drvconfig`, `disks`, `tapes`, `ports`, and `devlinks` have been replaced by the `devfsadm` utility. The `devfsadm` command should now be used in place of all these commands; however, `devfsadmd`, the `devfsadm` daemon, automatically detects device configuration changes, so there should be no need to run this command interactively.

During the process of building the `/devices` directory, the `devfsadmd` daemon assigns each device a major device number by using the name-to-number mappings held in the `/etc/name_to_major` file. This file is maintained by the system. The major device number indicates the general device class, such as `disk`, `tape`, or `serial line`. The minor device number indicates the specific member within that class.

The `/dev/dsk` directory refers to the block or buffered device file, and the `/dev/rdsk` directory refers to the character or raw device file. The "r" in `rdsk` stands for "raw."

Instance Names

The instance name represents the kernel's abbreviated name for every possible device on the system. For example, on a SPARC system, `dad0` represents the instance name of the IDE disk drive, and `eri0` is the instance name for the network interface. Instance names are mapped to a physical device name in the `/etc/path_to_inst` file.

File Systems

Following are the four types of disk-based file systems used by Solaris 10:

- **UFS**—The Unix file system, which is based on the BSD Fast file system (the traditional Unix file system). The UFS is the default disk-based file system used in Solaris.
- **HSFS**—The High Sierra and ISO 9660 file system. The HSFS is used on CD-ROMs and is a read-only file system.
- **PCFS**—The PC file system, which allows read/write access to data and programs on DOS-formatted disks.
- **UDF (Universal Disk Format) file system**—UDF is the industry-standard format for storing information on the optical media technology called DVD (Digital Versatile Disc).

Virtual file systems, previously called pseudo file systems, are virtual or memory-based file systems that create duplicate paths to other disk-based file systems or provide access to special kernel information and facilities. Most virtual file systems do not use file system disk space, although a few exceptions exist. The following is a list of some of the more common types of virtual file systems:

- **Cachefs**—The cache file system.
- **TMPFS**—The temporary file system uses local memory for file system reads and writes.
- `/var/run`—`/var/run` is the repository for temporary system files that are not needed across systems.
- **MNTFS**—The MNTFS type maintains information about currently mounted file systems.
- **DEVFS**—DEVFS is used to manage the namespace of all devices on the system. This file system is used for the `/devices` directory.

Disks are divided into regions called disk slices or disk partitions using the `format` utility or the Solaris Management Console. Make sure you understand all of the Format menu options and what tasks they perform. The following displays the main menu options in the `format` utility:

```
disk - select a disk
    type - select (define) a disk type
    partition - select (define) a partition table
    current - describe the current disk
    format - format and analyze the disk
    repair - repair a defective sector
    label - write label to the disk
    analyze - surface analysis
    defect - defect list management
    backup - search for backup labels
    verify - read and display labels
    save - save new disk/partition definitions
    inquiry - show vendor, product and revision
    volname - set 8-character volume name
    !<cmd> - execute <cmd>, then return
    quit   -  Quit the format utility
```

Here are the menu options available in the partition section of the format utility:

```
PARTITION MENU:
  0 - change '0' partition
  1 - change '1' partition
  2 - change '2' partition
  3 - change '3' partition
  4 - change '4' partition
  5 - change '5' partition
  6 - change '6' partition
  7 - change '7' partition
  select - select a predefined table
  modify - modify a predefined partition table
  name - name the current table
  print - display the current table
  label - write partition map and label to the disk
  !<cmd> - execute <cmd>, then return
  quit   -  Quit the format utility
```

When you create a UFS, the disk slice is divided into cylinder groups. Disk configuration information is stored in the disk label. If you know the disk and slice number, you can display information for a disk by using the print volume table of contents (`prtvtoc`) command.

The slice is then divided into blocks to control and organize the structure of the files within the cylinder group. A UFS has the following four types of blocks. Each performs a specific function in the file system:

- **Bootblock**—Stores information used when booting the system
- **Superblock**—Stores much of the information about the file system
- **Inode**—Stores all information about a file except its name
- **Storage or data block**—Stores data for each file

File systems can be mounted from the command line by using the `mount` command. The commands in Table 2 are used from the command line to mount and unmount file systems.

Table 2 File System Commands

Command	Description
`mount`	Mounts specified file systems and remote resources
`mountall`	Mounts all file systems specified in a file system table (`vfstab`)
`umount`	Unmounts specified file systems and remote resources
`umountall`	Unmounts all file systems specified in a file system table (vfstab)

Common options used when mounting file systems are listed in Table 3.

Table 3 UFS Mount Options

Option	Description
`-rw|ro`	Specifies read/write or read-only. The default is read/write.
`-nosuid`	Disallows `setuid` execution and prevents devices on the file system from being opened. The default is to enable `setuid` execution and to allow devices to be opened.
`-f`	Fakes an entry in `/etc/mnttab` but doesn't really mount any file systems.
`-n`	Mounts the file system without making an entry in `/etc/mnttab`.
`-largefiles`	Specifies that a file system might contain one or more files larger than 2GB. It is not required that a file system mounted with this option contain files larger than 2GB, but this option allows such files within the file system. `largefiles` is the default.
`-nolargefiles`	Provides total compatibility with previous file system behavior, enforcing the 2GB maximum file size limit.
`-logging/nologging`	Enables/disables UFS logging on a file system; `logging` is the default in Solaris 10.

Use the `df` command and its options to see the capacity of each file system mounted on a system, the amount of space available, and the percentage of space already in use. Use the `du` (directory usage) command to report the number of free disk blocks and files.

Creating a UFS

`mkfs` constructs a file system on the character (or raw) device found in the `/dev/rdsk` directory. Again, it is highly recommended that you do not run the `mkfs` command directly, but instead use the friendlier `newfs` command, which automatically determines all the necessary parameters required by `mkfs` to construct the file system.

The `/etc/vfstab` (virtual file system table) file contains a list of file systems to be automatically mounted when the system is booted to the multi-user state. Each column of information follows this format:

- **`device to mount`**—The buffered (block) device that corresponds to the file system being mounted.
- **`device to fsck`**—The raw (character) special device that corresponds to the file system being mounted. This determines the raw interface used by `fsck`. Use a dash (`-`) when there is no applicable device, such as for `swap`, `/proc`, `tmp`, or a network-based file system.
- **`mount point`**—The default mount point directory.
- **`FS type`**—The type of file system.
- **`fsck pass`**—The pass number used by `fsck` to decide whether to check a file system. When the field contains a dash (`-`), the file system is not checked. When the field contains a value of `1` or greater, the file system is checked sequentially. File systems are checked sequentially in the order that they appear in the `/etc/vfstab` file. The value of the pass number has no effect on the sequence of file system checking.
- **`mount at boot`**—Specifies whether the file system should be automatically mounted when the system is booted. The RC scripts located in the `/etc` directory specify which file system gets mounted at each run level.
- **mount options**—A list of comma-separated options (with no spaces) used when mounting the file system. Use a dash (`-`) to show no options.

Use the `fsck` command to repair file systems. `fsck` is a multipass file system check program that performs successive passes over each file system, checking blocks and sizes, pathnames, connectivity, reference counts, and the map of free blocks (possibly rebuilding it). `fsck` also performs file system cleanup.

Volume Management

Volume management, with the vold daemon, is the mechanism that automatically mounts CD-ROMs and file systems when removable media containing recognizable file systems are inserted into the devices. The vold daemon is the workhorse behind volume manager. It is automatically started by SMF. The vold.conf file contains the volume manager configuration information that vold uses.

Several other commands help you administer the volume manager on your system. They are described in Table 4.

Table 4 Volume Manager Commands

Command	Description
rmmount	Removable media mounter. Used by vold to automatically mount a /cdrom, /floppy, Jaz, or Zip drive if one of these media types is installed.
volcancel	Cancels a user's request to access a particular CD-ROM or floppy file system. This command, issued by the system administrator, is useful if the removable medium containing the file system is not currently in the drive.
volcheck	Checks the drive for installed media. By default, it checks the drive pointed to by /dev/diskette.
volmissing	Specified in vold.conf and notifies the user if an attempt is made to access a removable media type that is no longer in the drive.
vold	The volume manager daemon, controlled by /etc/vold.conf.
volrmmount	Simulates an insertion so that rmmount will mount the media, or simulates an ejection so that rmmount will unmount the media.

Installing the Solaris 10 Operating Environment

The computer must meet the following requirements before you can install Solaris 10 using the interactive installation method.

Note that the requirements for a SPARC system are different than the x86/x64 platform:

- A SPARC system must have a minimum of 256MB of physical memory for a CLI installation and 512 Mbytes for a graphical based installation. Sun recommends 512 Mbytes and a minimum of 256 Mbytes.

  An x86/x64 based system must have a minimum of 384 Mbytes of physical memory for a CLI installation and 512 Mbytes for a graphical based installation. 512 Mbytes is recommended.

- A SPARC system must have a 200MHz or faster processor, while an x86/x64 based system must have a 120MHz or faster processor.
- The media is distributed on CD-ROM and DVD only, so a bootable CD-ROM or DVD-ROM drive is required either locally or on the network. You can use all of the Solaris installation methods to install the system from a networked CD-ROM or DVD-ROM.
- A minimum of 5GB of disk space is required for both SPARC and x86 platforms. See the next section for disk space requirements for the specific Solaris software you plan to install. Also, remember to add disk space to support your environment's swap space requirements.
- When upgrading the operating system, you must have an empty 512MB slice on the disk. The swap slice is preferred, but you can use any slice that will not be used in the upgrade such as root (/), `/usr`, `/var`, and `/opt`.
- The system must be a SPARC-based or supported x86/x64-based system.

Be familiar with the following software terms:

- **Software Package**—A collection of files and directories in a defined format.
- **Software Group**—Software packages are grouped into software groups, which are logical collections of software packages. Sometimes these groups are referred to as *clusters*.

For SPARC systems, software clusters are grouped into seven configuration groups to make the software installation process easier. These seven configuration groups are minimal core metacluster (SUNWmreq),reduced networking support (SUNWCrnet), core system support (SUNWcreq), end-user support (SUNWcuser), developer system support (SUNWcprog), entire distribution (SUNWCall), and entire distribution plus OEM system support (SUNWCXall). Make sure you know the package name for each Solaris software group.

You can use one of seven methods to install the Solaris software: interactive using a GUI, interactive using the command line, JumpStart, custom JumpStart, Flash Archive, WAN Boot, or Solaris Upgrade.

You have two upgrade options available. One upgrade option is available in the interactive installation if you are currently running Solaris 2.6, 7, 8, or 9 and you want to upgrade to Solaris 10. The other upgrade option is the Solaris Live upgrade, which enables an upgrade to be installed while the operating system is running and can significantly reduce the downtime associated with an upgrade. As described in Chapter 2, "Installing the Solaris 10 Operating Environment," both upgrade options preserve most customizations you made in the previous version of Solaris.

To view the names of cluster configurations on your system, look at the `/var/sadm/system/admin/.clustertoc` file using the following command:

```
grep METACLUSTER /var/sadm/system/admin/.clustertoc
```

To determine which cluster configuration has been installed on your system, type:

```
# cat /var/sadm/system/admin/CLUSTER
```

During the installation, Solaris allocates disk space into separate file systems. By default, the interactive installation program (`install-solaris`) sets up the root (`/`) and swap partitions. It's typical to add additional file systems. The following is a typical partitioning scheme for a system with a single disk drive:

- **root (`/`)**—Solaris normally creates the (/) root partition for itself. The installation program determines how much space you need. Most of the files in these two partitions are static. If the root (`/`) file system fills up, the system will not operate properly.
- **swap**—This area on the disk doesn't have files in it. In Unix you're allowed to have more programs running than will fit into the physical memory. The pieces that aren't currently needed in memory are transferred into swap to free up physical memory for other active processes.
- **`/export/home`**—On a single-disk system, everything not in root (`/`), `/usr`, or swap should go into a separate partition. `/export/home` is where you would put user home directories and user-created files.
- **`/var` (optional)**—Solaris uses this area for system log files, print spoolers, and email.
- **`/opt` (optional)**—By default, the Solaris installation program loads optional software packages here. Also, third-party applications are usually loaded into `/opt`.

Understand how to install the software on both SPARC and x86/x64-based systems.

Tools for Managing Software

Solaris provides tools for adding and removing software from a system. Those tools are described in Table 5.

Table 5 Tools for Managing Software

Command	Description
Managing Software from the Command Line	
`pkgadd`	Adds software packages to the system.
`pkgrm`	Removes software packages from the system.
`pkgchk`	Checks the accuracy of a software package installation.
`pkginfo`	Displays software package information.
`pkgask`	Stores answers in a response file so that they can be supplied automatically during an installation.
`pkgparam`	Displays package parameter values.
Managing Software from the Graphical User Interface	
Solaris Product Registry	Manages all of your Solaris software.
Web Start installer	Invokes a Web Start install wizard.

Software Patches

Another system administration task is managing system software patches. A *patch* is a fix to a reported software problem. Sun will ship several software patches to customers so that problems can be resolved before the next release of software. The existing software is derived from a specified package format that conforms to the ABI.

Patches are identified by unique alphanumeric strings. The patch base code comes first, then a hyphen, and then a number that represents the patch revision number. For example, patch `110453-01` is a Solaris patch to correct a known problem.

You might want to know more about patches that have previously been installed. Table 6 shows commands that provide useful information about patches already installed on a system.

Table 6 Helpful Commands for Patch Administration

Command	Function
`showrev -p`	Shows all patches applied to a system.
`pkgparam` *`<pkgid>`* `PATCHLIST`	Shows all patches applied to the package identified by *`<pkgid>`*.
`pkgparam` *`<pkgid>`* `PATCH INFO` *`<patch-number>`*	Shows the installation date and name of the host from which the patch was applied. *`<pkgid>`* is the name of the package (for example, `SUNWadmap`), and *`<patch-number>`* is the specific patch number.
`patchadd -R` *`<client_root_path>`* `-p`	Shows all patches applied to a client, from the server's console.

`patchadd -p`	Shows all patches applied to a system.
`patchrm <patchname>`	Removes a specified patch. `<patchname>` is the name of the patch to be removed.
`smpatch`	A tool for managing patches.
`Patch Tool`	Solaris Management Console Tool for managing patches.

System Startup and Shutdown

On a SPARC system, during system startup, or bootup, the boot process goes through the following phases:

1. **Boot PROM phase**—After you turn on power to the system, the PROM displays system identification information and runs self-test diagnostics to verify the system's hardware and memory. It then loads the primary boot program, called `bootblk`.

2. **Boot program phase**—The `bootblk` program finds and executes the secondary boot program (called `ufsboot`) from the UFS and loads it into memory. After the `ufsboot` program is loaded, it loads the two-part kernel.

3. **Kernel initialization phase**—The kernel initializes itself and begins loading modules, using `ufsboot` to read the files. When the kernel has loaded enough modules to mount the root file system, it unmaps the `ufsboot` program and continues, using its own resources.

4. **`init` phase**—The kernel starts the Unix operating system, mounts the necessary file systems, and runs `/sbin/init` to bring the system to the `initdefault` state specified in `/etc/inittab`.

   The kernel creates a user process and starts the `/sbin/init` process, which starts other processes by reading the `/etc/inittab` file.

   The `/sbin/init` process starts the run control (rc) scripts, which execute a series of other scripts. These scripts (`/sbin/rc*`) check and mount file systems, start various processes, and perform system maintenance tasks.

5. **`svc.startd` phase**—The `svc.startd` daemon starts the system services and boots the system to the appropriate milestone.

Understand, that on an x86/x64-based system, phase 1 and 2 are substantially different than the SPARC system. The main difference is that after powering on the system and after the initialization phase is complete, the BIOS loads the Grand Unified Boot Loader (GRUB) and the GRUB main menu is displayed which provides the following features:

- A boot menu where kernel and boot options can be configured.
- Can be used to boot a multitude of operating systems making it possible for the Solaris OS to coexist with other operating systems on the same disk.

OpenBoot Environment (SPARC Systems Only)

The hardware-level user interface that you see before the operating system starts is called the OpenBoot PROM (OBP). The primary tasks of the OpenBoot firmware are as follows:

- Test and initialize the system hardware.
- Determine the hardware configuration.
- Start the operating system from either a mass storage device or a network.
- Provide interactive debugging facilities for testing hardware and software.
- Allow modification and management of system startup configuration, such as NVRAM parameters.

Specifically, the following tasks are necessary to initialize the operating system kernel:

1. OpenBoot displays system identification information and then runs self-test diagnostics to verify the system's hardware and memory. These checks are known as a POST.
2. OpenBoot loads the primary startup program, `bootblk`, from the default startup device.
3. The `bootblk` program finds and executes the secondary startup program, `ufsboot`, and loads it into memory. The `ufsboot` program loads the operating system kernel.

A *device tree* is a series of node names separated by slashes (`/`). The top of the device tree is the root device node. Following the root device node, and separated by a leading slash (`/`), is a bus nexus node. Connected to a bus nexus node is a leaf node, which is typically a controller for the attached device. Each device pathname has this form:

```
driver-name@unit-address:device-arguments
```

Nodes are attached to a host computer through a hierarchy of interconnected buses on the device tree. OpenBoot deals directly with the hardware devices in the system. Each device has a unique name that represents both the type of device and the location of that device in the device tree. The OpenBoot firmware builds a device tree for all devices from information gathered at the POST. Sun uses the device tree to organize devices that are attached to the system.

Device pathnames tend to get very long; therefore, the OpenBoot environment utilizes a method that allows you to assign shorter names to the long device pathnames. These shortened names are called *device aliases* and they are assigned using the `devalias` command. Table 7 describes the `devalias` command, which is used to examine, create, and change OpenBoot aliases.

Table 7 devalias Commands

Command	Description
`devalias`	Displays all current device aliases.
`devalias_`*<alias>* `alias.`	Displays the device pathname corresponding to
`devalias_`*<alias> <device-path>*	Defines an `alias` representing `device-path`.

When the kernel is loading, it reads the `/etc/system` file where system configuration information is stored. This file modifies the kernel's parameters and treatment of loadable modules. It specifically controls the following:

- The search path for default modules to be loaded at boot time as well as the modules not to be loaded at boot time
- The modules to be forcibly loaded at boot time rather than at first access
- The root type and device
- The new values to override the default kernel parameter values

Various parameters are used to control the OpenBoot environment. Any user can view the OpenBoot configuration variables from a Unix prompt by typing the following:

```
# /usr/sbin/eeprom
```

OpenBoot can be used to gather and display information about your system with the commands described in Table 8.

Table 8 OpenBoot Commands

Command	Description
`banner`	Displays the power-on banner
`show disks`	Displays only the disk devices currently connected to the system.
`.enet-addr`	Displays the current Ethernet address
`.idprom`	Displays ID PROM contents, formatted
`.traps`	Displays a list of SPARC trap types
`.version`	Displays the version and date of the startup PROM
`.speed`	Displays CPU and bus speeds
`show-devs`	Displays all installed and probed devices

In addition, various hardware diagnostics can be run in OpenBoot to troubleshoot hardware and network problems.

The operating system is booted from the OpenBoot prompt using the `boot` command. You can supply several options to the OpenBoot `boot` command at the `ok` prompt. Table 9 describes each of these.

TABLE 9 `boot` Command Options

Option	Description
`-a`	An interactive boot
`-r`	A reconfiguration boot
`-s`	A single-user boot
`-v`	A verbose-mode boot
-m verbose	Displays more detailed messages during the boot process..
-m milestone	Allows the operator to enter which milestone to enter upon bootup

The following list describes the steps for booting interactively:

1. At the `ok` prompt, type **`boot -a`** and press Enter. The boot program prompts you interactively.
2. Press Enter to use the default kernel (`/kernel/unix`) as prompted, or type the name of the kernel to use for booting and press Enter.
3. Press Enter to use the default modules directory path as prompted, or type the path for the modules directory and press Enter.
4. Press Enter to use the default `/etc/system` file as prompted, or type the name of the system file and press Enter.

5. Press Enter to use the default root file system type as prompted (UFS for local disk booting, or NFS for diskless clients).
6. Press Enter to use the default physical name of the root device as prompted, or type the device name.

The Kernel

After the `boot` command initiates the kernel, the kernel begins several phases of the startup process. The first task is for OpenBoot to load the two-part kernel. The secondary startup program, `ufsboot`, which is described in the preceding section, loads the operating system kernel. The core of the kernel is two pieces of static code called `genunix` and `unix`. `genunix` is the platform-independent generic kernel file, and `unix` is the platform-specific kernel file. When the system boots, `ufsboot` combines these two files into memory to form the running kernel.

The kernel initializes itself and begins loading modules, using `ufsboot` to read the files. After the kernel has loaded enough modules to mount the root file system, it unmaps the `ufsboot` program and continues, using its own resources. The kernel creates a user process and starts the `/sbin/init` process.

During the init phase of the boot process, the `init` daemon (`/sbin/init`) reads the `/etc/default/init` file to set any environment variables. By default, only the `TIMEZONE` variable is set. Then, `init` reads the `/etc/inittab` file and executes any process entries that have `sysinit` in the action field, so that any special initializations can take place before users login.

After reading the `/etc/inittab` file, `init` starts the `svc.startd` daemon, which is responsible for starting and stopping other system services such as mounting file systems and configuring network devices. In addition, `svc.startd` will execute legacy run control (rc) scripts, which are described later in this section.

The kernel is dynamically configured in Solaris 10. The kernel consists of a small static core and many dynamically loadable kernel modules. Many kernel modules are loaded automatically at boot time, but for efficiency, others—such as device drivers—are loaded from the disk as needed by the kernel.

When the kernel is loading, it reads the `/etc/system` file where system configuration information is stored. This file modifies the kernel's parameters and treatment of loadable modules.

After control of the system is passed to the kernel, the system begins initialization and starts the `svc.startd` daemon. In Solaris 10, the `svc.startd` daemon replaces the init process as the master process starter and restarter. Where in previous version of Solaris, `init` would start all processes and bring the system to the appropriate "run level" or "init state," now SMF, or more specifically, the `svc.startd` daemon, assumes the role of starting system services.

The service instance is the fundamental unit of administration in the SMF framework and each SMF service has the potential to have multiple versions of it configured. An instance is a specific configuration of a service and multiple instances of the same version can run in the Solaris operating environment.

The services started by `svc.startd` are referred to as milestones. The milestone concept replaces the traditional run levels that were used in previous versions of Solaris. A milestone is a special type of service which represents a group of services. A milestone is made up of several SMF services. For example, the services which constituted run levels S, 2, and 3 in previous versions of Solaris are now represented by milestone services named.

`milestone/single-user` (equivalent to run level S)

`milestone/multi-user` (equivalent to run level 2)

`milestone/multi-user-server` (equivalent to run level 3)

Other milestones that are available in the Solaris 10 OE are

`milestone/name-services`

`milestone/devices`

`milestone/network`

`milestone/sysconfig`

An SMF manifest is an XML (Extensible Markup Language) file that contains a complete set of properties associated with a service or a service instance. The properties are stored in files and subdirectories located in `/var/svc/manifest`.

SMF provides a set of command-line utilities used to administer and configure SMF that are described in Chapter 3, "Perform System Boot and Shutdown Procedures for SPARC, x64, and x86-Based Systems."

A run level is a system state (run state), represented by a number or letter, that identifies the services and resources that are currently available to users. The `who -r` command can still be used to identify a systems run state as follows:

```
# who -r
```

The system responds with the following, indicating that run-level 3 is the current run state:

```
.       run-level 3  Aug  4 09:38     3      1  1
```

Since the introduction of SMF in Solaris 10, we now refer to these run states as milestones and Chapter 3 describes how the legacy run states coincide with the Solaris 10 milestones.

Commands to Shut Down the System

When preparing to shut down a system, you need to determine which of the following commands is appropriate for the system and the task at hand:

`/usr/sbin/shutdown`

`/sbin/init`

`/usr/sbin/halt`

`/usr/sbin/reboot`

`/usr/sbin/poweroff`

Stop+A or L1+A (to be used as a last resort)

User and Security Administration

Use the Solaris Management Console (SMC) GUI or the command line to create and manage user accounts.

Table 10 describes field entries you'll need to know when setting up a new user account using SMC.

Table 10 Add User Fields

Item	Description
User Name	Enter a unique login name that will be entered at the Solaris login prompt.
User ID	Enter the unique user ID (UID). SMC automatically assigns the next available UID; however, in a networked environment, make sure this number is not duplicated by another user on another system.
Primary Group	Enter the primary group name or GID (group ID) number for the group to which the user will belong.
Full Name/Description	These two fields are comment fields and are optional. Enter any comments such as the full username or phone number.
Password	Click this button to specify the password status. Selectable options are as follows: **User Must Set Password at First Login**—This is the default. The account does not have a password assigned. The user is prompted for a password on first login, unless `passreq=no` is set in `/etc/default/login`. **User Must Use This Password at First Login**—The account will have a password that you set in advance.
Path	This will be the location of the user's home directory and where his or her personal files will be stored.

Another way to manage user accounts is from the command line. Although using the command line is more complex than using the SMC GUI, the command line provides a little more flexibility. Solaris supplies the user administration commands described in Table 11 for setting up and managing user accounts.

Table 11 Account Administration Commands

Command	Description
`useradd`	Adds a new user account
`userdel`	Deletes a user account
`usermod`	Modifies a user account
`groupadd`	Adds a new group
`groupmod`	Modifies a group (for example, changes the group ID or name)
`groupdel`	Deletes a group
`smuser`	The command line equivalent of the SMC GUI tool that manages one or more user entries in the local `/etc` files, NIS, or NIS+ name service
`smgroup`	The command line equivalent of the SMC GUI tool that manages one or more group definitions in the group database for the local `/etc` files, NIS, or NIS+ name service

Shells and Initialization Files

The Solaris 10 operating environment offers five commonly used shells:

- **The Bourne shell (`/sbin/sh`)**—The default shell. It is a command programming language that executes commands read from a terminal or a file.
- **The C shell (`/bin/csh`)**—A command interpreter with a C-like syntax. The C-shell provides a number of convenient features for interactive use that are not available with the Bourne shell, including filename completion, command aliasing, and history substitution.
- **The TENEX C shell (`/bin/tcsh`)**—An enhanced version of the C shell with complete backward compatibility. The enhancements are mostly related to interactive use, including the ability to use arrow keys for command history retrieval and command-line editing.
- **The Korn shell (`/bin/ksh`)**—A command programming language that executes commands read from a terminal or a file.
- **The Bourne Again shell (`/bin/bash`)**—Bash is a sh-compatible command language interpreter that executes commands read from the standard input or from a file. Bash also incorporates useful features from the Korn and C shells (`ksh` and `csh`).

The login shell is the command interpreter that runs when you log in. The Solaris 10 operating environment offers the three most commonly used shells, as described in Table 12.

Table 12 Basic Features of the Bourne, C, and Korn Shells

Feature	sh	csh	tcsh	ksh	bash
Syntax compatible with `sh`	Yes	No	No	Yes	Yes
Job control	Yes	Yes	Yes	Yes	Yes
History list	No	Yes	Yes	Yes	Yes
Command-line editing	No	Yes	Yes	Yes	Yes
Aliases	No	Yes	Yes	Yes	Yes
Protect files from overwriting	No	Yes	Yes	Yes	Yes
Ignore Ctrl+D (`ignoreeof`)	No	Yes	Yes	Yes	Yes
Enhanced cd	No	Yes	Yes	Yes	Yes
Initialization file separate	No	Yes	Yes	Yes	Yes
Logout file	No	Yes	Yes	No	Yes
Functions	Yes	No	No	Yes	Yes
Arrow keys for command edits	No	No	Yes	No	Yes

The logout file functionality can be implemented with the use of a trap statement in `/etc/profile`:

```
trap 'test -f $HOME/.shlogout && . $HOME/.shlogout' EXIT
```

A shell initialization file is a shell script that runs automatically each time the user logs in. The initialization file will set up the work environment and customize the shell environment for the user.

C shell initialization files run in a particular sequence after the user logs in to the system. For the C shell and `tcsh`, initialization files are run in the following sequence:

1. Commands in `/etc/.login` are executed.
2. Commands from the `$HOME/.cshrc` file (located in your home directory) are executed. In addition, each time you start a new shell or open a new window in CDE, commands from the `$HOME/.cshrc` are run. In `tcsh`, if `$HOME/.tcshrc` exists, it is used instead of `$HOME/.cshrc`.
3. The shell executes commands from the `$HOME/.login` file (located in your home directory). Typically, the `$HOME/.login` file contains commands to specify the terminal type and environment.

4. Finally, when startup processing is complete, the C shell begins reading commands from the default input device, the terminal.
5. When the shell terminates, it performs commands from the `$HOME/.logout` file (if it exists in your home directory).

Bourne shell initialization files run in a particular sequence after the user logs in to the system. For the Bourne shell, initialization files are run in the following sequence:

1. Commands in `/etc/profile` are executed.
2. Commands from the `$HOME/.profile` file (located in your home directory) are executed. Typically, the `$HOME/.profile` file contains commands to specify the terminal type and environment.
3. Finally, when startup processing is complete, the Bourne shell begins reading commands from the default input device, the terminal.

Korn shell initialization files run in a particular sequence after the user logs in to the system. For the Korn shell, initialization files are run in the following sequence:

1. Commands in `/etc/profile` are executed.
2. Commands from the `$HOME/.profile` file (located in your home directory) are executed. Typically, the `$HOME/.profile` file contains commands to specify the terminal type and environment.
3. If the environment variable `$ENV` is set to the name of a file and that file is present, commands located in this file are executed. In addition, this initialization file gets read (and the commands get executed) every time a new Korn shell is started after login.
4. Finally, when startup processing is complete, the Korn shell begins reading commands from the default input device, the terminal.

Bash initialization files run in a particular sequence after the user logs in to the system. For the Bash shell, initialization files are run in the following sequence:

1. Commands in `/etc/profile` are executed.
2. Commands in `$HOME/.bash_profile` are executed. This file serves the same purpose as `$HOME/.profile` in the Bourne and Korn shells.
3. Commands in `$HOME/.bashrc` are executed, but only if this is not a login shell.
4. When startup processing is complete, `bash` begins reading commands from the default input device, the terminal.

5. As a login session exits, `$HOME/.bash_logout` is processed (if it exists in your home directory).

The Solaris 10 system software provides default user initialization files for each shell in the `/etc/skel` directory on each system. These files are listed in Table 13.

Table 13 Default Initialization Files

Name	Description
`local.cshrc`	The default `.cshrc` file for the C shell
`local.login`	The default `.login` file for the C shell
`local.profile`	The default `.profile` file for the Bourne and Korn shells

System Security

Protecting your system against unauthorized access or modification begins with controlling access to your system. Several files that control default system access are stored in the `/etc/default` directory. Table 14 summarizes the files in the `/etc/default directory`.

Table 14 Files in the `/etc/default` Directory

Filename	Description
`/etc/default/passwd`	Controls default policy on password aging.
`/etc/default/login`	Controls system login policies, including root access. The default is to limit root access to the console.
`/etc/default/su`	Specifies where attempts to `su` to root are logged and where these log files are located. The file also specifies whether attempts to `su` to root are displayed on a named device (such as a system console).

Controlling access to systems also involves using passwords and appropriate file permissions. Enforce the following guidelines on passwords:

- Passwords should contain a combination of six to eight letters, numbers, or special characters. Don't use fewer than six characters.
- Mix upper- and lowercase characters.
- Use a password with nonalphabetic characters, such as numerals or punctuation.
- Do not use words from a dictionary or easy-to-guess words.

Most of the user account information is stored in the `/etc/passwd` file; however, password encryption and password aging details are stored in the `/etc/shadow` file. Group information is stored in the `/etc/group` file.

Protecting Data

System security also involves protecting your data using standard Unix file permissions. File access permissions are shown by the `ls -la` command. The first column returned describes the type of file and its access permissions for the user, group, and others using letters. The `r`, `w`, and `x` are described in Table 15.

Table 15 File Access Permissions

Symbol	Permission	Means That Designated Users...
r	Read	Can open and read the contents of a file.
w	Write	Can write to the file (modify its contents), add to it, or delete it.
x	Execute	Can execute the file (if it is a program or shell script).
-	Denied	Cannot read, write to, or execute the file.

When listing the permissions on a directory, all columns of information are the same as for a file, with one exception. The `r`, `w`, and `x` found in the first column are treated slightly differently than for a file. These are described in Table 16.

Table 16 Directory Access Permissions

Symbol	Permission	Means That Designated Users...
r	Read	Can list files in the directory.
w	Write	Can add or remove files or links in the directory.
x	Execute	Can open or execute files in the directory. Also can make the directory and the directories beneath it current.
-	Denied	Do not have read, write, or execute privileges.

Use the commands listed in Table 17 to modify file access permissions and ownership, but remember that only the owner of the file or root can assign or modify these values.

Table 17 File Access Commands

Command	Description
chmod	Changes access permissions on a file. You can use either symbolic mode (letters and symbols) or absolute mode (octal numbers) to change permissions on a file.
chown	Changes the ownership of a file.
chgrp	Changes the group ownership of a file.

When a user creates a file or directory, the user mask controls the default file permissions assigned to the file or directory and is set using the `umask` command.

Access Control Lists (ACLs)

ACLs (pronounced *ackls*) can provide greater control over file permissions when the traditional Unix file protection in the Solaris operating system is not enough. An ACL provides better file security by enabling you to define file permissions for the owner, owner's group, others, specific users and groups, and default permissions for each of these categories. The following are commands used to set and modify ACL entries:

- **`setfacl`**—Set, modify, or delete ACL entries on a file

  Options to the `setfacl` command are:

  - **`-f`**—Set a file's ACL with the entries located in a file.
  - **`-m`**—Adds one or more new ACL entries and/or modifies one or more existing ACL entries on a file. If an entry already exists for a specified uid or gid, the specified permissions replace the current permissions. If an entry does not exist, an entry is created. When using the `-m` option to modify a default ACL, you must specify a complete default ACL (user, group, other, mask, and any additional entries) the first time.
  - **`-r`**—Recalculates the permissions for the ACL mask entry.
  - **`-s`**—Sets a file's ACL.

- **`getfacl`**—Display or copy the ACL entry on a file

  Options to the `getfacl` command are:

  - **`-a`**—Displays the filename, the file owner, the group owner, and the ACL of the file.
  - **`-d`**—Displays the filename, the file owner, the file group owner and trhe default ACL of the file, if it exists.

The mask entry indicates the maximum permissions allowed for users (other than the owner) and for groups. The mask is a quick way to change permissions on all the users and groups. The mask permission will override any specific user or group permissions.

Monitoring Users

As the system administrator, you'll need to monitor system resources and watch for unusual activity. Having a method to monitor the system is useful when you suspect a breach in security. The following commands are used to monitor users and system activity:

`logins` A command to monitor a particular user's activities.

`loginlog` A file that contains one entry for each failed login attempt.

`who` Shows who is logged into the system. `who` lists the login account name, terminal device, login date and time, and where the user logged in.

`whodo` Displays each user logged in and the active processes owned by that user. The output shows the date, time, and machine name. For each user logged in, the system displays the device name, UID, and login time, followed by a list of active processes associated with the UID.

`last` Displays the sessions of the specified users and terminals in chronological order. For each user, `last` displays the time when the session began, the duration of the session, and the terminal where the session took place

Network Security

It is critical to turn off all unneeded network services because many of the services run by `inetd`, such as `rexd`, pose serious security threats. `rexd` is the daemon responsible for remote program execution. On a system connected to the rest of the world via the Internet or other public network, this could create a potential entry point for a hacker. TFTP should absolutely be disabled if you don't have diskless clients using it. Most sites will also disable `Finger` so that external users can't figure out the usernames of your internal users. Everything else depends on the needs of your site.

Solaris 10's File Transfer Protocol (FTP) is a common tool for transferring files across the network. Although most sites leave FTP enabled, you need to limit who can use it. Solaris 10 contains a file named `/etc/ftpd/ftpusers` that is used to restrict access via FTP. The `/etc/ftpd/ftpusers` file contains a list of login names that are prohibited from running an FTP login on the system.

The `/etc/hosts.equiv` file contains a list of trusted hosts for a remote system and can present a potential security risk. When an entry for a host is made in `/etc/hosts.equiv`, that host is trusted and so is any user at that machine. If the username is also mentioned, the host is trusted only if the specified user is attempting access. A single line of + in the /etc/hosts.equiv file indicates that every known host, and every user on those hosts, is trusted—this should never be used.

The $HOME/.rhosts file is the user equivalent of the /etc/hosts.equiv file, except any user can create an $HOME/.rhosts file granting access to whomever the user chooses—without the system administrator's knowledge. The system administrator should disallow the use of .rhosts files—or even better, disable all R services.

It is recommended that you use the secure shell (ssh) when establishing communication between two hosts over insecure networks such as the Internet. The secure shell is much safer than previous methods used to access remote systems such as rlogin, rsh, and rcp. The secure shell daemon (sshd) listens for connections and handles the encrypted authentication exchange between two hosts. When authentication is complete, the user can execute commands and copy files remotely and securely.

Secure by Default can be enabled/disabled at the time of installation or later using the netservices open/closed commands. When Secure by Default is enabled, all unnecessary network services, except ssh, are disabled.

Restricting Root Access

Root access needs to be safeguarded against unauthorized use. You should assume that any intruder is looking for root access. You can protect the superuser account on a system by restricting access to a specific device through the /etc/default/login file. In the /etc/default/login file, you can control where root is able to log in by assigning one of the following values to the variable named CONSOLE:

CONSOLE=/dev/console	Root is only allowed to login from the console device.
CONSOLE=	With no value defined, root cannot log in from anywhere, not even from the console.

Users can still log in using a non-root login and issue the su command to switch from being a user to being root, but this activity is logged in the file /var/adm/sulog. The sulog file lists all uses of the su command—not only those used to switch from being a user to being superuser.

Managing Processes

A process is distinct from a job or command, which can be composed of many processes working together to perform a specific task. Each process has a process ID associated with it and is referred to as a pid. You can monitor processes that are currently executing by using one of the commands listed in Table 18.

Table 18 Commands to Display Processes

Command	Description
`ps`	Executed from the command line to display information about active processes.
`pgrep`	Executed from the command line to find processes by a specific name or attribute.
`prstat`	Executed from the command line to display information about active processes on the system.
`psrinfo`	Displays one line for each configured processor, displaying whether it is online, noninterruptible, offline, or powered off, as well as when that status last changed.
`pargs`	Used from the command line to examine the arguments and environment variables of a process (or number of processes). `pargs` can also be used to examine core files.
`sdtprocess`	A GUI used to display and control processes on a system. This utility requires a terminal capable of displaying graphics.
SMC	The Solaris Management Console Processes Tool to view, suspend, resume, and delete processes.

A process has certain attributes that directly affect execution. These are listed in Table 19.

Table 19 Process Attributes

Attribute	Description
`PID`	The process identification (a unique number that defines the process within the kernel).
`PPID`	The parent `PID` (the creator of the process).
`UID`	The user ID number of the user who owns the process.
`EUID`	The effective user ID of the process.
`GID`	The group ID of the user who owns the process.
`EGID`	The effective group ID that owns the process.
`Priority`	The priority at which the process runs.

Using the `kill` Command

The `kill` command sends a terminate signal (signal 15) to the process, and the process is terminated. Signal 15, which is the default when no options are used with the `kill` command, is a gentle kill that allows a process to perform cleanup work before terminating. Signal 9, on the other hand, is called a sure, unconditional kill because it cannot be caught or ignored by a process. If the process is still around after a `kill -9`, it is either hung up in the Unix kernel, waiting for an event such as disk I/O to complete, or you are not the owner of the process.

Another way to kill a process is to use the `pkill` command. A signal name or number may be specified as the first command-line option to `pkill`. For example, to kill the process named `psef`, issue the following command:

```
# pkill -9 psef
```

Using the Solaris Batch-Processing Facility

A way to divide processes on a busy system is to schedule jobs so that they run at different times. A large job, for example, could be scheduled to run at 2 a.m., when the system would normally be idle. Solaris supports three methods of batch processing: the `crontab` command, `at` command, and SMC Job Scheduler tool. The `crontab` command schedules multiple system events at regular intervals, and the `at` command schedules a single system event for execution at a later time. Unlike `crontab`, which schedules a job to happen at regular intervals, a job submitted with `at` executes once, at the designated time.

The `cron` daemon handles the automatic scheduling of `crontab` commands. Its function is to check the `/var/spool/cron/crontab` directory every 15 minutes for the presence of `crontab` files. It checks for new `crontab` files or changes to existing ones, reads the execution times listed within the files, and submits the commands for execution at the proper times.

Table 20 describes the fields in the `crontab` file for scheduling jobs to run on a regular basis.

Table 20 The `crontab` File

Field	Description	Values
1	Minute	0–59. An * in this field means every minute.
2	Hour	0–23. An * in this field means every hour.
3	Day of month	1–31. An * in this field means every day of the month.
4	Month	1–12. An * in this field means every month.
5	Day of week	0–6 (0 = Sunday). An * in this field means every day of the week.
6	Command	Enter the command to be run.

Control who can access the `crontab` file by configuring `/etc/cron.d/cron.deny` and `/etc/cron.d/cron.allow`. These access control files work together in the following manner:

- If `cron.allow` exists, only the users listed in this file can create, edit, display, and remove `crontab` files.
- If `cron.allow` doesn't exist, all users may submit `crontab` files, except for users listed in `cron.deny`.
- If neither `cron.allow` nor `cron.deny` exists, superuser privileges are required to run `crontab`.

The Solaris Management Console (SMC) includes a graphical tool to create and schedule `cron` jobs on your system. You can use the Job Scheduler Tool to

- View and modify job properties.
- Delete a job.
- Add a scheduled job.
- Enable or disable job logging.

The Job Scheduler tool is really just a GUI for managing `crontab` entries.

Managing the LP Print Service

Many methods can be used to define a printer on a Solaris system. The following tools are available in Solaris 10 to set up and administer printers:

- **Solaris Print Manager**—A GUI that provides the ability to configure and manage printers.
- **LP print service commands**—The various LP commands available from the command line to configure and manage printers.

Although the GUI is an easy tool to use, the LP commands used from the command line offer more functionality. Table 21 lists the `lp` commands, which are the command-line means for controlling printers and print queues.

Table 21 Solaris `lp` Commands

Command	Description
`accept/reject`	Enables or disables any further requests for a printer or class entering the spooling area.
`cancel`	Lets the user stop the printing of information.
`enable/disable`	Enables or disables any more output from the spooler to the printer.
`lp`	The user's print command. Places information to be printed into the spooler.
`lpadmin`	Allows the configuration of the print service.
`lpmove`	Moves print requests between destinations.
`lpsched`	Starts the print service.
`lpshut`	Stops the print service.
`lpstat`	Displays the status of the print service.

There are three types of printer configurations that you need to understand:

- **Local printer**—A printer physically connected to a system and accessed from that local system.
- **Network printer**—A printer physically attached to the network with its own hostname and IP address. A network printer provides print services to clients, but is not directly connected to a print server.
- **Remote printer**—A printer that users access over the network. This printer is either physically attached to a remote system or is physically attached to the network.

A *print server* is a system that has a local printer connected to it and makes the printer available to other systems on the network. A *print client* is a remote system that can send print requests to a print server. A system becomes a print client when you install the print client software and enable access to remote printers on the system. Any networked Solaris system with a printer can be a print server, as long as the system has adequate resources to manage the printing load.

The basic functions of the Solaris OS print service include:

- **Initialization**—The initialization function ensures that the printer is in a known state.
- **Queuing**—The queuing function schedules the print requests that are waiting to be sent to the printer.
- **Tracking**—Tracks the status of every print request and logs any errors that have occurred during the printing process.
- **Fault Notification**—Provides fault notification if a problem occurs in the print service. It will print an error message on the console or send an email to root.
- **Filtering**—Converts print jobs to the appropriate type of file for the destination printer.

When setting up printer services, you'll perform some or all of the following tasks:

1. **Set up the printer**: Physically connect the printer to the system or the network.
2. **Set up the print server**: Setup the system that will manage and provide access to the printer.
3. **Set up the print clients**: Configure remote systems (clients) to access a printer on the print server.
4. **Verify printer access**: Check that the print server recognizes all print clients and that each client recognizes the print server.

The LP Print Daemons

The `/usr/lib/lpsched`, also referred to as the scheduler daemon, is the Unix utility that is responsible for scheduling and printing in Solaris 10. Sometimes it is referred to as the `lp` daemon. The `lpsched` print daemon takes output from the spooling directory and sends it to the correct printer. `lpsched` also tracks the status of printers and filters on the print server. The `lpsched` daemon is started by the `svc:/application/print/server:default` service when the system is booted.

The `/usr/sbin/inetd` daemon is started at bootup by the service management facility, and it listens for service requests on all the ports associated with each of the services that are currently enabled. The service that handles incoming print requests from the network is `svc:/application/print/server:default`. When `inetd` receives a print request, `in.lpd` is started to service the connection. The `in.lpd` daemon exits after the request has been serviced.

The Solaris LP print service performs the following functions:

- **Initialization**—Initializes a printer prior to sending it a print request to ensure that the printer is in a known state.
- **Queuing**—Schedules the print requests that are waiting to be sent to the printer.
- **Tracking**—Tracks the status of every print request. It enables the system administrator to manage all of the requests and allows users to view or cancel their own requests. It also logs errors that may have occurred during the printing process.
- **Fault notification**—This function prints the error message on the console or sends the message via email to the user.
- **Filtering**—Converts the print jobs to the appropriate type of file for the destination printer.

Most of the `lp` configuration files are located in the `/var/spool/lp` directory, except for the interface files, which are located in the `/etc/lp/interfaces` directory. A `SCHEDLOCK` file should be in `/var/spool/lp`; it is responsible for ensuring that only one instance of `lpsched` runs. You use the `lpadmin` command to add, configure, and delete printers from the system.

You can put several locally attached printers into a group called a *printer class*. When you have set up a printer class, users can then specify the class (rather than individual printers) as the destination for a print request. The first printer in the class that is free to print is used. You create printer classes with the `lpadmin` command as follows:

```
# lpadmin -p <printer-name> -c <printer-class>
```

Set the system default printer by typing:

```
# lpadmin -d <printername>
```

Performing System Backups and Restorations

Solaris provides the utilities listed in Table 22. They can be used to backup data from disk to removable media and restore it.

Table 22 Backup Utilities

Utility	Description
`tar`	Archives data to another directory, system, or medium.
`dd`	Copies data quickly.
`cpio`	Copies data from one location to another.
`pax`	Copies files and directory subtrees to a single tape. This command provides better portability than `tar` or `cpio`, so it can be used to transport files to other types of Unix systems.
`ufsdump`	Backs up all files in a file system.
`ufsrestore`	Restores some or all of the files archived with the `ufsdump` command.
`zip`	This utility creates compressed archives that are portable across various platforms, including Unix, VMS, and Windows.
Web Start flash	Combines the use of JumpStart and backup utilities to provide an easy mechanism for restoring a system to its initial state or cloning systems.
`jar`	Uses Java to provide capabilities similar to those of `tar`, `cpio`, and `zip`.

You can use the `fssnap` command to create a read-only snapshot of a file system while the file system is mounted. A *snapshot* is a point-in-time image of a file system that provides a stable and unchanging device interface for backups. Unlike `ufsdump`, a UFS snapshot enables you to keep the file system mounted and the system in multiuser mode during backups. The snapshot is stored on disk, so you can use Solaris backup commands like `ufsdump`, `tar`, and `cpio` to backup the UFS snapshot.

Create the snapshot using the `fssnap` command as follows:

```
# fssnap -F ufs -o bs=/var/tmp /export/home
```

Another way to backup your Solaris operating environment (not the data) is to create a Flash archive, but that topic is covered on the 310-202 exam, so don't worry about it on the first exam.

Practice Exam

This exam consists of 31 questions reflecting the material covered in the chapters. The questions are representative of the types of questions you should expect to see on the Solaris exam; however, they are not intended to match exactly what is on the exam.

Some of the questions require that you choose the best possible answer. Often, you are asked to choose the best course of action to take in a given situation. The questions require that you read them carefully and thoroughly before you attempt to answer them. It is strongly recommended that you treat this practice exam as if you were taking the actual exam. Time yourself, read carefully, and answer all the questions to the best of your ability.

You can find the answers to all the questions in the "Answers to the Practice Exam" element that follows the exam. Check your answers against those provided, and then read the explanations. You may also want to return to the chapters to review the material associated with any incorrect answers.

Practice Exam Questions

1. The kernel consists of which of the following?

- ❍ **A.** The shell and environment variables
- ❍ **B.** A small static core and many dynamically loadable modules
- ❍ **C.** Boot PROM and the operating system
- ❍ **D.** System milestones

2. What are the characteristics of changing to the single-user run level? (Choose three.)

- ❍ **A.** It's equivalent to run level S.
- ❍ **B.** Shutdown state
- ❍ **C.** All users are logged out.
- ❍ **D.** File systems remain mounted.

3. Which daemon is responsible for maintaining system services?

   ❍ **A.** `init`

   ❍ **B.** `inetd`

   ❍ **C.** `startd`

   ❍ **D.** `svc.startd`

4. Which of the following is a service identifier used to identify a specific service within the Service Management Facility? (Choose two.)

   ❍ **A.** Milestone

   ❍ **B.** `lrc:/etc/rc3.d/S90samba`

   ❍ **C.** `svc:/system/filesystem/local:default`

   ❍ **D.** `/var/svc/manifest/milestone/multi-user.xml`

5. Which service state indicates that a service is not configured to start up and run?

   ❍ **A.** Uninitialized

   ❍ **B.** Offline

   ❍ **C.** Disabled

   ❍ **D.** Degraded

6. The bootstrap procedure consists of which of the following basic phases? (Choose three.)

   ❍ **A.** Load the kernel.

   ❍ **B.** Automatically boot the system if the `auto-boot?` parameter is set to `true`.

   ❍ **C.** Hardware powerup.

   ❍ **D.** Execute a power-on self-test (POST).

7. What is the best command to use to find your hardware platform and current operating system release?

   ❍ **A.** `init -q`

   ❍ **B.** `sysdef`

   ❍ **C.** `uname -a`

   ❍ **D.** `arch`

8. What information do you need during the installation process? (Choose three.)

❍ A. IP address

❍ B. Product code

❍ C. Time zone

❍ D. Root password

9. What does the `pkgchk` command do? (Choose two.)

❍ A. It displays information about software packages installed on the system.

❍ B. It stores answers in a response file so that they can be supplied automatically during an installation.

❍ C. It determines the accuracy of a software package installation.

❍ D. It determines whether a file's contents or attributes have changed since it was installed with the package.

10. In the Solaris Management Console, what field corresponds to the maximum number of days an account can go without being accessed before it is automatically locked?

❍ A. User Must Keep for:

❍ B. Max Inactive

❍ C. User Must Change Within:

❍ D. Expires if Not Used for:

11. Respectively, what are the user initialization files for the Bourne, Korn, and C shells?

❍ A. `.bshrc`, `.kshrc`, `.cshrc`

❍ B. `.exrc`, `.profile`, `.login`

❍ C. `.profile`, `.profile`, `.login`

❍ D. `.profile` works for all shells.

12. Which of the following file systems can reside on a local physical disk? (Choose two.)

❍ A. HSFS

❍ B. TMPFS

❍ C. UFS

❍ D. NFS

13. Which file system block contains information about the file system?

- ❍ **A.** Boot block
- ❍ **B.** Superblock
- ❍ **C.** Inode
- ❍ **D.** Data block

14. To view the capacity of all file systems mounted on a system, which command should you use?

- ❍ **A.** `du -a`
- ❍ **B.** `ls`
- ❍ **C.** `df`
- ❍ **D.** `mountall`

15. Which command is a friendlier way to create a file system?

- ❍ **A.** `mkfs`
- ❍ **B.** `newfs`
- ❍ **C.** `fsck`
- ❍ **D.** `mknod`

16. Which of the following commands cannot be used to copy file systems?

- ❍ **A.** `dd`
- ❍ **B.** `ufsdump`
- ❍ **C.** `fsck`
- ❍ **D.** `volcopy`

17. Which command might you use to see which process is preventing a file system from being unmounted?

- ❍ **A.** `ps`
- ❍ **B.** `mountall`
- ❍ **C.** `fsck`
- ❍ **D.** `fuser`

18. Which of the following are easily guessed passwords? (Choose two.)

❍ **A.** Britney

❍ **B.** TnK0Tb!

❍ **C.** Dietcoke

❍ **D.** ZunSp0ts

19. What would a default umask of 023 set as default permissions on new files?

❍ **A.** Owner no rights; Group write only; World write and execute only

❍ **B.** Owner read, write, execute; Group read only; World execute only

❍ **C.** Owner read, write; Group read only; World read only

❍ **D.** Owner no rights; Group read and execute only; World read only

20. The second field of the `/etc/group` file is used to store the group password. What is the effect of a group password?

❍ **A.** Access to each group is granted only to users in a group.

❍ **B.** Users who are not members of the group can access it if they know the password.

❍ **C.** Users who are primary members of the group are required to use the group password to gain access to the group.

❍ **D.** Users who are secondary members of the group are required to use the group password to gain access to the group.

21. What would you use the `prstat` command to do? (Choose two.)

❍ **A.** Get information on all the processes for a particular user.

❍ **B.** Determine disk usage.

❍ **C.** Determine which processes are consuming the most CPU cycles.

❍ **D.** Change system run levels.

22. Which of the following signals kills a process unconditionally?

❍ **A.** `SIGHUP`

❍ **B.** `SIGKILL`

❍ **C.** `SIGTERM`

❍ **D.** `SIGQUIT`

23. What does the `at` command do?

❍ **A.** It stands for "all terminate" and kills all nonroot processes.

❍ **B.** It runs a batch job once at a specific time in the future.

❍ **C.** It sets a repeating batch job to run at a specific time of day.

❍ **D.** It displays the time of last login for a user.

24. If a nonroot user does not want to use the system default printer, how can that user select another printer to be the default? (Choose two.)

❍ **A.** `lpadmin`

❍ **B.** Specify the printer in the $HOME/.printers file.

❍ **C.** `lpstat -d` *<printername>*

❍ **D.** Set the LPDEST variable.

❍ **E.** `/usr/sadm/admin/bin.printmgr`

25. Which command can tell you if a print queue is down?

❍ **A.** `lpadmin`

❍ **B.** `lpstat`

❍ **C.** Admintool

❍ **D.** `Print Manager`

26. What does the command `tar xvf /tmp/backup.tar` do? (Choose two.)

❍ **A.** It extracts the absolute paths of the archives in `/tmp/backup.tar`, creating new directories and overwriting files if necessary.

❍ **B.** It prints a verbose listing of the files and directories in `/tmp/backup.tar`.

❍ **C.** It compresses `/tmp/backup.tar`.

❍ **D.** It archives the current directory and its contents to `/tmp/backup.tar`.

27. Which of the following statements about the `dd` command is false?

❍ **A.** It quickly converts and copies files with different data formats.

❍ **B.** It can be used to copy an entire file system or partition to tape.

❍ **C.** It can compress files quickly and efficiently.

❍ **D.** It can be used to read standard input from another program to write to tape.

28. To what do the directories in `/proc` correspond?

❍ **A.** File systems

❍ **B.** Physical and virtual devices attached to the system

❍ **C.** Active process IDs

❍ **D.** Active UIDs

29. In Solaris, each disk device is described by which naming conventions? (Choose three.)

❍ **A.** Instance name

❍ **B.** Physical device name

❍ **C.** Virtual name

❍ **D.** Logical device name

30. Which statement about Solaris Management Console is false?

❍ **A.** It provides single-console, single-login administration of multiple Solaris systems.

❍ **B.** It provides an easy-to-navigate GUI console.

❍ **C.** It has a command-line interface in addition to the GUI controls.

❍ **D.** It uses Role-Based Access Control.

31. What can the SMC Toolbox Editor allow you to do? (Choose three.)

❍ **A.** Suspend, resume, monitor, and control processes.

❍ **B.** Install software packages.

❍ **C.** Schedule, start, and manage jobs.

❍ **D.** View and manage mounts, shares, and usage information.

Answers to the Practice Exam

Answers at a Glance to the Practice Exam

1. B
2. A, C, D
3. D
4. B, C
5. C
6. B, C, D
7. C
8. A, C, D
9. C, D
10. D
11. C
12. A, C
13. B
14. C
15. B
16. C
17. D
18. A, C
19. C
20. B
21. A, C

22. B

23. B

24. B, D

25. B

26. A, B

27. C

28. C

29. A, B, D

30. C

31. A, C, D

Answers with Explanations

1. **B.** The kernel consists of a small static core and many dynamically loadable kernel modules. Many kernel modules are loaded automatically at boot time, but for efficiency, others—such as device drivers—are loaded from the disk as needed by the kernel. The shell and environmental variables are user-specific and are loaded when each user logs in. The boot PROM is firmware and is considered part of the hardware. Answer A is incorrect because the kernel does not contain shell and shell environment variables. Answer C is incorrect because, although the kernel is part of the operating system, it does not contain the boot PROM code. Answer D is incorrect because the system milestones are part of the operating system, not the kernel. For more information, see Chapter 3, "Performing System Boot and Shutdown Procedures for SPARC, x64-, and x86-Based Systems."

2. **A, C, D.** The single-user milestone, also called run level S, is the single-user (system administrator) state. Only root is allowed to log in at the console, and any users logged in are logged out when entering this run level. All file systems previously mounted remain mounted and accessible. All services except the most basic operating system services are shut down in an orderly manner. Answer B is incorrect because the single-user run level is not considered a shutdown state. The shutdown state would be run level 0. For more information, see Chapter 3.

3. **D.** The `svc.startd` daemon is responsible for maintaining the system services and ensures that the system boots to the correct milestone. Answers A and B do not maintain system services. Answer C is not a Solaris daemon. For more information, see Chapter 3.

4. **B, C.** `lrc:/etc/rc3.d/S90samba` is the FRMI for a legacy service. `svc:/system/filesystem/local:default` is an example of a service identifier within the SMF. A milestone is a special type of service made up of a defined set of other services, but it does not define a specific service. `/var/svc/manifest/milestone/multi-user.xml` describes the dependencies for a milestone. For more information, see Chapter 3.

5. **C.** Disabled indicates that the service is not configured to start up and is not running. Uninitialized is the state of a service before the configuration has been read. Offline indicates that the service is not yet running but is configured to run. Degraded indicates that the service is enabled but is running at a limited capacity. For more information, see Chapter 3.

6. **B, C, D.** On SPARC-based Solaris systems, the bootstrap procedure consists of some basic phases. First, the system hardware is powered on, and the system firmware (PROM) executes a power-on self-test (POST). After the tests have completed successfully, the firmware attempts to autoboot if the appropriate OpenBoot configuration variable (`auto-boot?`) has been set to `true`. Otherwise, it enters interactive OpenBoot command mode. The bootstrap procedure does not include loading the kernel. For more information, see Chapter 3.

7. **C.** The `uname` command with the `-a` flag set displays basic information currently available from the system, including hardware platform and current operating system release. The `sysdef` command outputs the current system definition, such as hardware devices, loadable modules, and kernel parameters. The `init` command is used to start processes from information in the `inittab` file. The `arch` command displays the system's application architecture. For more information, see Chapter 2, "Installing the Solaris 10 Operating Environment."

8. **A, C, D.** The Solaris Installation program prompts you for the following: hostname, IP address, subnet mask, whether to install IPv6, name service, whether to use the Kerberos network authentication system, time zone, root password, and language. For more information, see Chapter 2.

9. **C, D.** The `pkgchk` command checks the accuracy of a software package installation. It also can be used to determine whether the contents or attributes of a file have changed since it was installed with the package. You use the `pkginfo` command to display software package information, and you use `pkgask` to store answers for an interactive installation. For more information, see Chapter 2.

10. **D.** "Expires if Not Used for:" is the correct option. Select how many days can elapse before the user's password expires if the user does not log in to this account. The "User Must Keep for:" field specifies the minimum number of days a user must wait before changing a password or reusing a previous password. The "User Must Change Within:" field allows you to set the maximum number of days that can elapse before a user must change his password. "Max Inactive" is an invalid field and does not appear in the SMC. For more information, see Chapter 4, "User and Security Administration."

11. **C.** Bourne and Korn shells initialize with a `.profile`, whereas the C shell uses `.login` and `.cshrc`. For more information, see Chapter 4.

12. **A, C.** The High Sierra file system (HSFS) is a read-only file system used on CD-ROMs. The UNIX file system (UFS) is the default disk-based file system used by Solaris. TMPFS resides in memory. Data in this type of file system is destroyed upon reboot. NFS is the Network File System, which is remotely mounted over the network. For more information, see Chapter 1, "Managing File Systems."

13. **B.** The superblock stores much of the information about the file system. The boot block stores information used to boot the system and does not store information about file systems. An inode stores all the information about a file except its name. A storage or data block stores the actual data for each file. For more information, see Chapter 1.

14. **C.** The `df` command and its options can be used to see the capacity of each file system mounted on a system, the amount of space available, and the percentage of space already in use. The `ls` command is used to list information about files and directories. The `du` command summarizes disk usage but does not provide file system capacity information. The `mountall` command is used to mount all file systems listed in the `/etc/vfstab` file. For more information, see Chapter 1.

15. **B.** The `newfs` command automatically determines all the necessary parameters to pass to `mkfs` to construct new file systems. `newfs` was added in Solaris as a friendly front end to the `mkfs` command to make the creation of new file systems easier. The `fsck` command is used to check and repair file systems. The `mknod` command is used to create special device files. For more information, see Chapter 1.

16. **C.** The `fsck` command checks and repairs file systems. Any of the others could be used to copy one file system to another. `dd` is used to convert and copy files reading input, one block at a time. `ufsdump` is used to perform file system dumps that can be used to copy file systems from one disk slice to another. `volcopy` is used to make an image copy of a file system. For more information, see Chapter 1.

17. **D.** The `fuser` command can be used to display which processes are using a particular file system. The following example uses the `fuser` command to find out why `/cdrom` is busy:

    ```
    fuser -c -u /cdrom
    ```

    The `fsck` command is used to check and repair file systems. The `mountall` command is used to mount all file systems listed in the `/etc/vfstab` file. The `ps` command is used to list system processes and report their status, but it does not identify which file system a process may be accessing. For more information, see Chapter 1.

18. **A, C.** Although it is debatable what a “good” password might be, a proper name (Britney) is easy for a password guesser to guess. A password should contain a combination of letters, numbers, and symbols (such as space, comma, period, and so on). Varying case and mixing words can also help expand the number of possibilities that must be covered by a password-guessing program before the password is discovered. For more information, see Chapter 4.

19. **C.** A umask of 023 makes a mask, automatically unsetting those permission bits from otherwise-full permissions. Because each digit represents an octal number corresponding, respectively, to Owner, Group, and World, the permissions displayed by the `ls` command would be `rw-r--r--`. The first 3 permission bits are `rw-` (read-write) for Owner, followed by `r--` (read-only) for Group, and finally `r--` (read-only) for World. For more information, see Chapter 4.

20. **B.** When using the `newgrp` command to switch your effective group ID, a password is demanded if the group has a password (the second field of the `/etc/group` file) and the user is not listed in `/etc/group` as being a member of that group. For more information, see Chapter 4.

21. **A, C.** The `prstat` command is used from the command line to monitor system processes. Like the `ps` command, it provides information on active processes. The difference is that you can specify whether you want information on specific processes, UIDs, CPU IDs, or processor sets. By default, `prstat` displays information about all processes sorted by CPU usage. `prstat` does not

display disk usage; you use the `df` command to display that information. `prstat` is not used to change system run levels; you use the `init` command for that. For more information, see Chapter 5, "Managing System Processes."

22. **B.** The `SIGKILL` signal can be sent to a process with `kill -9` or `kill -SIGKILL`. Signal 9 is called a sure, unconditional kill because a process cannot catch or ignore it. If the process is still around after a `kill -9`, either it is hung up in the UNIX kernel, waiting for an event such as disk I/O to complete, or you are not the owner of the process. `SIGHUP` is not used to kill a process. `SIGTERM` can be used to terminate a process, but not to kill it unconditionally. `SIGQUIT` sends a signal to the process to dump the core. For more information, see Chapter 5.

23. **B.** The `at` command is used to schedule jobs for execution at a later time. Unlike `crontab`, which schedules a job to happen at regular intervals, a job submitted with `at` executes once, at the designated time. For more information, see Chapter 5.

24. **B, D.** The Print Manager allows the system administrator to set the default printer. If the user doesn't specify a printer name or class in a valid style, the command checks the `printers` entry in the `/etc/nsswitch.conf` file for the search order. By default, the `/etc/nsswitch.conf` file instructs the command to search the user's `PRINTER` or `LPDEST` environment variable for a default printer name. The user can set these variables. If neither environment variable for the default printer is defined, the command checks the `.printers` file in the user's home directory for the default printer alias; again, the user can set up this file. If the command does not find a default printer alias in the `.printers` file, it checks the print client's `/etc/printers.conf` file for configuration information. If the printer is not found in the `/etc/printers.conf` file, the command checks the name service (NIS or NIS+), if any. You must be root or a member of group 14 to use the Print Manager or the `lpadmin` command to set a system default printer. For more information, see Chapter 6, "Managing the LP Print Service."

25. **B.** The `lpstat -p` <*`printer`*> command tells you whether a printer is active or idle, when it was enabled or disabled, and whether it is accepting print requests. The `lpadmin` command is used to configure the LP print service, such as adding printers. Print Manager can be used to create and remove printers, but it does not display information about printers. Admintool is not supported in Solaris 10. For more information, see Chapter 6.

26. **A, B.** This command uses the flags `x` (extract archive), `v` (verbose—lists all files and directories extracted), and `f` (archive is in the file following this argument). If `backup.tar` has files that specify absolute paths (for example, `/etc/shadow`), the files are extracted to disk using the absolute paths. New directories are created and files are overwritten, so be very sure that you trust the creator of a tar file before you extract it as root. Answer C is incorrect because the `tar` command does not compress data. Answer D is incorrect because the `x` option extracts files; the `c` option archives files. For more information, see Chapter 7, "Performing System Backups and Restorations."

27. **C.** The `dd` command quickly converts and copies files with different data formats, such as differences in block size or record length. `dd` can be used to copy an entire file system or partition to tape, and it can take input from other programs through standard input. It cannot, however, compress files as it copies, because it is a byte-by-byte image copy. For more information, see Chapter 7.

28. **C.** Each entry in the /proc directory is a decimal number corresponding to a process ID. Each directory in /proc has files that contain more-detailed information about that process. The /proc file system does not contain information about other file systems, devices, or active UIDs. For more information, see Chapter 5.

29. **A, B, D.** In Solaris, each disk device is described in three ways, using three distinct naming conventions:

    Physical device name: Represents the full device pathname in the device information hierarchy.

    Instance name: Represents the kernel's abbreviated name for every possible device on the system.

    Logical device name: Used by system administrators with most file system commands to refer to devices.

    For more information, see Chapter 1.

30. **C.** Although you can find command-line equivalents to SMC tools such as `smuser` and `smgroup`, no command-line interface exists for the Solaris Management Console. Answers A, B, and D are all true and represent functionality found in the SMC. For more information, see Chapter 4.

31. **A, C, D.** The SMC Toolbox Editor manages processes, users, file system mounts and shares, disks, and serial ports. It also schedules jobs and has a log viewer. You can also use SMC to install patches, but not to install software. For more information, see Chapter 4.

PART III
Appendixes

APPENDIX

What's on the CD-ROM

The CD features an innovative practice test engine by ExamGear, giving you one of the best tools for assessing your readiness for the exam. The CD also includes a PDF of the entire text of the book, accessible from the CD interface.

ExamGear, Exam Prep Edition

ExamGear, Exam Prep Edition is an exam environment developed for Que Certification. In addition to providing a means of evaluating your knowledge of the Exam Prep material, ExamGear, Exam Prep Edition features several innovations that help you improve your mastery of the subject matter.

For example, the practice exams enable you to check your scores by their correspondence to Sun Solaris exam objectives for the Solaris 10 System Administrator exam. In another mode, ExamGear, Exam Prep Edition enables you to obtain immediate feedback on your responses in the form of explanations for both correct and incorrect answers.

ExamGear, Exam Prep Edition is written to this book's Exam Prep content. It is designed to help you assess how well you understand the Exam Prep material that is related to the Sun exam objectives for the Solaris 10 System Administrator exam. ExamGear also presents the common question formats that you will see on the actual exam, including questions that use round option buttons (where you can choose only a single answer from all the options displayed) or square checkboxes (where you can choose one or more answers from all the options displayed, and the number of options you must choose is often provided). Thus, this tool serves as an excellent method for assessing your knowledge of the Exam Prep content and gives you the experience of taking an electronic exam.

For additional questions online that use the same test engine, visit http://www.UnixEd.com.

Glossary

A

access control list (ACL) Used in Solaris to provide greater control over file access permissions when traditional UNIX file protection is not enough. An ACL provides better file security by enabling you to define file permissions for the file owner, file group, other specific users and groups, and default permissions for each of those categories.

ARP (Address Resolution Protocol) The Internet protocol that dynamically maps Internet addresses to physical (hardware) addresses on LANs. ARP is limited to networks that support hardware broadcast.

array controller A storage array.

AutoClient A client system type that caches (locally stores copies of data as it is referenced) all its needed system software from a server. The AutoClient system has a local disk, but the root (`/`) and `/usr` file systems are accessed across the network from a server and are loaded in a local disk cache. Files in the `/` and `/usr` file systems are copied to the cache disk as they are referenced. If a Solstice AutoClient client accesses an application that is not already in its disk cache, that application is downloaded. If the application already resides in the client's disk cache, the application is accessed locally. AutoClient replaced the dataless client in Solaris 2.6.

AutoFS maps AutoFS files are called *maps*. These maps are as follows:

- **Master map** is read by the `automount` command during bootup. This map lists the other maps used to establish the AutoFS.
- **Direct map** lists the mount points as absolute pathnames. This map explicitly indicates the client's mount point.
- **Indirect map** lists the mount points as relative pathnames. This map uses a relative path to establish the mount point on the client.
- **Special** provides access to entries in `/etc/hosts` or the Federated Naming Services (FNS).

Automated Security Enhancement Tool Examines the startup files to ensure that the path variable is set up correctly and does not contain a dot (`.`) entry for the current directory.

B

bandwidth A measure of the capacity of a communication channel, which is usually specified in megabytes per second (MBps).

block A unit of data that can be transferred by a device, usually 512 bytes long.

block device A device file that calls for I/O operations based on a defined block size. The block size varies by device, but for a UFS, the default block size is 8KB.

block size Specifies the size of a section of data that is written to disk or tape at one time. Typical block sizes are 512 bytes and 1024 bytes.

boot The process of loading and executing the operating system. Sometimes called *bootstrapping*.

bootblock The boot program (`bootblk`) that is stored in a predictable area (sectors 1 to 15) on the system hard drive, CD-ROM, or other bootable device. The bootblock is responsible for loading the secondary boot program (`ufsboot`) into memory, which is located in the UFS on the boot device. Only the root (`/`) file system has an active bootblock, but each file system has space allocated for one.

boot server A server system that provides client systems on the same network subnet with the programs and information they need to start. A boot server is required to install over the network if the install server is on a different subnet than the systems on which Solaris software is to be installed.

bootstrapping The process a computer follows to load and execute the bootable operating system. The name comes from the phrase "pulling yourself up by your bootstraps." The instructions for the bootstrap procedure are stored in the boot PROM.

bundled software package A Solaris software package is the standard way to deliver bundled and unbundled software. Packages are administered using the package administration commands. They generally are identified by the SUNW*xxx* naming convention when supplied by Sun Microsystems. SUNW is Sun Microsystems' ticker symbol on the stock exchange.

bus A path for transferring data.

byte A group of adjacent binary digits (bits) that the computer treats as a unit. The most common-sized byte contains eight binary digits.

C

CDE Process Manager A GUI tool for viewing and managing system processes.

character device file A device file that calls for I/O operations based on the disk's smallest addressable unit, or sector. Each sector is 512 bytes in size. A character device is also called a *raw device*.

check script Used to validate the rules file that is required by the custom JumpStart installation software to match a system to a profile.

chunk A quantity of information that is handled as a unit by the host and array.

child process New processes created by a parent process.

class file A text file that defines how to install the Solaris software on a system.

client A system that relies on a server and uses the server's remote services.

client/server Describes the relationship between a server and its clients. *See* client and server.

cluster A group of patches (patch cluster) or a group of software packages (software cluster).

concatenated stripe A metadevice composed of both concatenated and striped components.

concatenation Combining two or more files to create one larger file. If partitions are concatenated, the component blocks are addressed on the components sequentially. This means that data is written to the first available stripe until it is full and then moves to the next available stripe.

configuration group On SPARC systems, software groups are placed in five configuration groups to make the software installation process easier. During the installation process, you are asked to install one of the five configuration groups. These five configuration groups are core system support, end-user support, developer system support, entire distribution, and entire distribution plus OEM system support.

configuration server A server that contains the JumpStart configuration files, used to install networked systems.

controller A device within the array that manages commands and data transfers from the host, delegates jobs to its processors, and maps the data locations in the array.

core file A point-in-time copy (snapshot) of the RAM allocated to a process. The copy is written to a more permanent medium, such as a hard disk. A core file is useful in analyzing why a particular program crashed. A core file is also a disk copy of the address space of a process at a certain point in time. This information identifies items such as the task name, task owner, priority, and instruction queue in execution at the time the core file was created.

crash dump A disk copy of the computer's physical memory at the time of a fatal system error.

`crontab` file Consists of commands, one per line, that are executed at regular intervals by the `cron` daemon.

Custom JumpStart Provides a way to install groups of similar systems automatically and identically.

cylinder A stack of concentric tracks.

cylinder group Each file system is divided into cylinder groups, with a minimum default size of 16 cylinders per group.

cylinder group block A table in each cylinder group that describes the cylinder group.

D

data block Units of disk space that are used to store data. Regular files, directories, and symbolic links use data blocks.

de-encapsulation When a header is removed from each segment received on the way up the layers.

default printer The printer designated to accept print jobs when a destination printer is not specified.

default shell The shell that is specified for each user account in the `/etc/passwd` file. When the user logs in, he is automatically placed in his default shell. If no shell is specified for the user, the `/sbin/sh` shell is his default shell.

device alias Device pathnames can be long and complex to enter. The concept of device aliases, like UNIX aliases, allows a short name to be substituted for a long name. An alias represents an entire device pathname, not a component of it.

device autoconfiguration Offers many advantages over the manual configuration method used in earlier versions of UNIX. With that method, device drivers were manually added to the kernel, the kernel was recompiled, and the system had to be restarted. *See also* reconfiguration boot.

device driver A low-level program that allows the kernel to communicate with a specific piece of hardware.

device hierarchy During a reconfiguration restart, this is created in the `/devices` directory to represent the devices connected to the system.

device tree Each device has a unique name representing both the type of device and the location of that device in the system addressing structure called the device tree. The OpenBoot firmware builds a device tree for all devices from information gathered at the power-on self-test (POST).

DHCP (Dynamic Host Configuration Protocol) An application-layer protocol that enables individual computers, or clients, on a TCP/IP network to extract an IP address and other network configuration information from a designated and centrally maintained DHCP server or servers. This facility reduces the overhead of maintaining and administering a large IP network.

direct map A type of automount map that lists the mount points as absolute pathnames. This type of map explicitly indicates the mount point on the client.

disk array A subsystem that contains multiple disk drives, designed to provide performance, high availability, serviceability, or other benefits.

disk-based file system Any file system created on a local disk. Disk-based file systems include UFS, HSFS, PCFS, and UDFs.

disk block The smallest addressable unit on a disk platter. One sector holds 512 bytes of data. Sectors are also called *disk blocks*.

disk label A special area of every disk that is set aside for storing information about the disk's controller, geometry, and slices.

diskless client A client that has no local disk or file systems. The diskless client boots from the server; remotely mounts its root (`/`), `/usr`, and `/export/home` file systems from a server; allocates swap space on the server; and obtains all its data from the server. Any files created are stored on the server.

disk partition *See* disk slice.

disk quota Enables system administrators to control the size of UFSs by limiting the amount of disk space and the number of I-nodes (which roughly corresponds to the number of files) that individual users can acquire.

disk set A grouping of two hosts and disk drives in which all the drives are accessible by each host in the set.

disk slice Groupings of cylinders that are commonly used to organize data by function.

DNS The name service provided by the Internet for Transmission Control Protocol/Internet Protocol (TCP/IP) networks. It was developed so that workstations on the network can be identified by common names instead of Internet addresses.

DNS resolver DNS clients use the dynamic library routines, collectively called the resolver, to locate a remote host. The resolver queries the DNS database on a name server, which eventually returns the hostname or IP address of the machine requested by the resolver.

domain A part of the Internet naming hierarchy. A domain represents a group of systems on a local network that share administrative files.

dynamic failover (as it relates to NFS) When high availability for read-only NFS resources is needed, dynamic failover provides an alternative NFS mount point if the primary mount point fails.

E–F

encapsulation When a header is added to each segment received on the way down the layers.

Ethernet A standard that defines the physical components a machine uses to access the network and the speed at which the network runs.

FDDI A standard for data transmission on fiber-optic lines in a LAN that can extend up to 200 km (124 miles).

file access permission Used in Solaris to provide control over file access.

filename The object most often used to access and manipulate files. A file must have a name that is associated with an I-node. *See also* I-node.

file system A structure used to organize and store files on disk.

file system dump A backup of a file system using the `ufsdump` command.

file system minfree space The portion of a file system that is reserved and held back from users. It is accessible only by root.

file system type Describes the type of file system, such as UFS, PROCFS, or TMPFS. Many file system administration commands require you to specify the file system type (`fstype`).

finish script Used in a JumpStart installation, this is a user-defined Bourne shell script, specified within the rules file, that performs tasks after the Solaris software is installed on the system, but before the system reboots. You can use finish scripts only with custom JumpStart installations.

flash archive Provides a method to store a snapshot of the Solaris operating environment, complete with all installed patches and applications.

flash installation A complete snapshot of a Solaris operating environment, including patches and applications.

fragment Also called fragmentation. The method used by the UFS to allocate disk space efficiently.

free block Blocks not currently being used as I-nodes, indirect address blocks, or storage blocks are marked as free in the cylinder group map.

free hog slice A temporary, automatically designated slice that expands and shrinks to accommodate the slice resizing operations.

full backup A backup that contains everything on the file system.

full device name A series of node names separated by slashes (/). The root of the tree is the machine node, which is not named explicitly but is indicated by a leading slash. Each device pathname has this form: driver-name@unit-address:device-arguments.

G–H

GB A gigabyte, or 1,024 megabytes (or 1,073,741,824 bytes).

group Used to control user access to files and directories. Users who need to share files are placed in the same group. A group can be a collection of users who are referred to by a common name. In NIS+, a group is a collection of users who are collectively given specified access rights to NIS+

objects. NIS+ group information is stored in the NIS+ group table. In UNIX, groups determine a user's access to files. The two types of groups are default user groups and standard user groups.

group ID (GID) The primary group number for the group to which the user will belong. This is the group that the operating system assigns to files created by the user. GIDs typically can range from 0 to 60,002, but they can go as high as 2,147,483,647.

hard link A file that has many names that all share the same I-node number.

hard mount A file system mounted using the `mount -o hard` option. The `hard` option indicates that the retry request is continued until the server responds. The default for the `mount` command is `hard`.

hardware port An electrically wired outlet on a piece of equipment into which a plug or cable connects.

hierarchical namespace Namespace information that is similar in structure to the UNIX directory tree. *See also* namespace.

home directory The portion of a file system allocated to a user for storing private files.

host A node on the network.

hostname Every system on the network usually has a unique hostname. Hostnames let users refer to any computer on the network by using a short, easily remembered name rather than the host's network IP address. Hostnames should be short, easy to spell, and lowercase, and they should have no more than 64 characters. The `hostname` command determines a system's host.

hot-pluggable A device that can be connected or disconnected while the system is running.

hot spare A slice reserved to substitute automatically for a failed slice in a submirror or RAID5 metadevice. A hot spare must be a physical slice, not a metadevice.

hot spare pool A collection of slices (hot spares) reserved for automatic substitution in case of slice failure in either a submirror or RAID5 metadevice. Hot spares are used to increase data availability.

hot-swappable A device that allows for the connection and disconnection of peripherals or other components without rebooting the operating system.

HSFS High Sierra File System.

hub The central device through which all hosts in a twisted-pair Ethernet installation are connected. A hub shares bandwidth between all systems that are connected to it. *See also* switch.

I

incremental backup Backs up only files that have been changed since a previous backup, saving tape space and time.

indirect map A type of automount map that lists mount points as relative pathnames. This map uses a relative path to establish the mount point on the client.

initial installation A Solaris 9 installation method. You perform an initial installation either on a system that does not have an existing Solaris operating system already installed on it or when you want to wipe out the existing operating system and reinstall it.

init state When a system begins initialization, it enters one of eight run states, also called init states. Because run state 4 currently is unused, only seven usable run states exist.

I-node The objects that the Solaris operating environment uses to record information about a file. I-nodes contain information about a file, its owner, its permissions, and its size. I-nodes are numbered, and each file system contains its own list of I-nodes.

installation media The Solaris 9 operating system software is distributed on CD-ROM and DVD and is called the Installation Media Kit.

install server A server that provides an image of the Solaris operating environment, which the JumpStart client uses as its source of data to install.

instance name Represents the kernel's abbreviation name for every possible device on the system.

interactive boot (`boot -a`) Stops and asks for input during the boot process. The system provides a dialog box in which it displays the default boot values and gives you the option of changing them. You might want to boot interactively to make a temporary change to the system file or kernel. Booting interactively lets you test your changes and recover easily if you have problems.

interactive installation The Solaris interactive installation program, `suninstall`, guides you step by step through installing the Solaris software.

interlace The number of blocks on a component of a striped or RAID metadevice that can be simultaneously accessed with the same number of blocks from another component. The interlace value dictates how much data Solaris Volume Manager places on a component of a striped or RAID metadevice before moving on to the next component.

IP address Each machine on a TCP/IP network has a unique 32-bit Internet address (or IP address) that identifies the machine to its peers on the network. An IP address in IPv4 consists of four numbers that are separated by periods (192.168.0.1, for example). Most often, each part of the IP address is a number between 0 and 225. However, the first number must be less than 224, and the last number cannot be 0.

IPv6 Version 6 of Internet Protocol (IP) that is designed to be an evolutionary step up from the current version, IPv4 (version 4).

ISO/OSI model The International Organization for Standardization (ISO)/Open Systems Interconnection (OSI) model is an ISO standard for worldwide communications that defines a framework for implementing protocols in seven layers. Control is passed from one layer to the next, starting at the application layer in one station, proceeding to the bottom layer, over the channel to the next station, and back up the hierarchy.

J–K

JavaStation Also called a *zero-administration client*, this client has no local file system, and its `/home` is accessed from a server across the network. The JavaStation runs only applications that are 100% pure Java.

journaling The recording of UNIX file system (UFS) updates in a log before the updates are applied to the UFS. This allows for increased data recovery in the event of a catastrophic system failure. Also called *logging*.

JumpStart client Also called an *Install client*, the JumpStart client uses the JumpStart automatic installation to install the Solaris operating environment across the network. JumpStart clients require support from a JumpStart server to find an image of the Solaris operating environment to install.

JumpStart server Provides all the directives for the JumpStart installation, including an image of the Solaris operating environment to install.

KB A kilobyte, or 1,024 bytes.

Kerberos A security system developed at MIT that authenticates users. It does not provide authorization to services or databases; it establishes identity at logon, which is used throughout the session. Kerberos (also spelled Cerberus) was a fierce, three-headed mastiff that guarded the gates of Hades in Greek mythology.

kernel The part of the operating system that remains running at all times until the system is shut down. It is the core and the most important part of the operating system.

L

LAN (local-area network) Multiple systems at a single geographic site connected for the purpose of sharing and exchanging data and software.

LAN/WAN Local-area network/wide-area network. *See* LAN and WAN.

large file A regular file whose size is greater than or equal to 2GB.

large-file-aware A utility is large-file-aware if it can process large files in the same manner that it does small files. A large-file-aware utility can handle large files as input and can generate large files as output. The `newfs`, `mkfs`, `mount`, `umount`, `tunefs`, `labelit`, and `quota` utilities are all large-file-aware for UFSs.

large-file-safe A utility is large-file-safe if it causes no data loss or corruption when it encounters a large file. A utility that is large-file-safe cannot properly process a large file, so it returns an appropriate error. Some examples of utilities that are not large-file-aware but that are large-file-safe are the `vi` editor and the `mailx` and `lp` commands.

LDAP (Lightweight Directory Access Protocol) The latest name-lookup service (directory service) to be added to Solaris.

live upgrade Provides a method of upgrading while your Solaris system is still running. The original system configuration remains fully functional and unaffected by the upgrade. The upgrade creates a duplicate boot environment that is activated when the system is rebooted. If a failure occurs, you can revert to the original boot environment, thereby eliminating the downtime associated with the normal test-and-evaluation process.

locale A geographic or political region or community that shares the same language, customs, or cultural conventions. For example, English for the United States is `en_US`, and English for the United Kingdom is `en_UK`.

local printer A printer that is physically connected to a system and is accessed from that system.

logical device name Symbolic links pointing to the physical device name stored in the `/devices` directory. A logical device's name is used to refer to a device when you are entering commands on the command line. All logical device names are stored in the `/dev` directory.

logging *See* journaling.

logical volume Allows file systems to span multiple disks and provide for improved I/O and reliability compared to the standard Solaris file system.

LPD (Line Printer Daemon) A TCP/IP printer protocol that provides print spooling and network printing. Originally developed for Berkeley UNIX (BSD UNIX), LPD has become the de facto cross-platform printing protocol.

`lpsched` *See* print scheduler.

M

MAC address The unique serial number burned into an Ethernet adapter that differentiates that network card from all others.

major device number Indicates the general device class, such as disk, tape, or serial line.

makefile Used to create the appropriate NIS maps.

master map A type of automount map that lists the other maps used to establish the AutoFS. The `automount` command reads this map at boot time.

master NIS server The center of the NIS network that is designated as the master server containing the set of maps that get updated.

MB A megabyte, or 1,024 kilobytes.

metadevice A Solaris Volume Manager (SVM) term used to describe a group of physical slices accessed as a single logical device. Metadevices are used like slices. The metadevice maps logical block addresses to the correct location on one of the physical devices. The type of mapping depends on the configuration of the particular metadevice. Also called a *pseudo device* or *virtual device* in standard UNIX terms.

metadisk A special driver that coordinates I/O to and from physical devices and volumes, allowing applications to treat a volume like a physical device.

metadriver A pseudo device driver that maps metadevice operations affiliated with commands to the metadevice components.

metastate database A database, stored on disk, that records configuration and the state of all metadevices and error conditions. This information is important to the correct operation of Solaris Volume Manager (SVM), and it is replicated. *See also* state database replica.

minor device number Indicates the specific member within a general device class (such as disk, tape, or serial line). All devices managed by a given device driver contain a unique minor number.

mirror Replicates all writes to a single logical device (the mirror) and then to multiple devices (the submirrors) while distributing read operations. This provides redundancy of data in the event of a disk or hardware failure.

mounted file system table (`mnttab`) A file system that provides read-only access to the table of mounted file systems for the current host.

multiuser mode A Solaris run state in which the system supports multiuser operations.

N

name service A network service that provides a means of identifying and locating resources such as hostnames and IP addresses available to a network. The default name service product available in the Solaris operating environment is Network Information Service Plus (NIS+).

name service switch Directs requests to the correct name service in use on the system or network.

namespace Stores name service information that users, workstations, and applications must have to communicate across the network. A namespace can also refer to the set of all names in a naming system:

- **NIS+ namespace** is a collection of hierarchical network information used by the NIS+ software.
- **NIS namespace** is a collection of nonhierarchical network information used by the NIS software.
- **DNS namespace** is a collection of networked workstations that use the DNS software.

network address The address, consisting of up to 20 octets, used to locate an Open Systems Interconnection (OSI) transport entity. The address is formatted into an initial domain part that is standardized for each of several addressing domains, and a domain-specific part that is the responsibility of the addressing authority for that domain.

network-based file system A file system accessed over the network. Typically, it resides on one system (the server) and is accessed by other systems (clients) across the network.

network class Network addresses are divided into three classes: A, B, and C. This addressing scheme is called *classful IPv4 addressing*.

network interface Also called a *network adapter* or *NIC* (network interface card). A printed circuit board that plugs into both the clients and servers in a network. It controls the exchange of data between them at the data link level, also called the *access method* (OSI layers 1 and 2).

network mask A number used by software to separate the local subnet address from the rest of a given Internet protocol address.

network port A software network port is an identified doorway (address) for communicating between a program and another communications system or program, often passing through a hardware port. The network port usually is numbered. A standard network implementation such as TCP, UDP, or IP attaches a port number to data it sends. The receiving implementation guards and listens at the attached port number (doorway) to figure out which program to send data to on its system. A port may send/receive data either in one direction at a time (simplex) or simultaneously in both directions (duplex). These software network ports may also connect internal programs on a single computer system. In TCP and UDP, the combination of a port and a network address (IP number) is called a *socket*.

network printer A printer that is physically attached to the network and that has its own hostname and IP address. A network printer provides printing services to print clients without being directly cabled to a print server.

network protocol The part of the network that you configure but cannot see. It's the software portion of the network that controls data transmission between systems across the network.

network service Describes services offered by servers to network clients, such as FTP, Telnet, and HTTP.

NFS (Network File System) A service that lets computers of different architectures, running different operating systems (OSs), share file systems across a network.

NFS client A system that mounts a remote file system from an NFS server.

NFS daemon A process that supports NFS activities. These daemons can support both NFS client and NFS server activity, NFS server activity alone, or logging of the NFS server activity.

NFS logging Provides a record of all NFS activity on network file systems that have been shared with the logging option enabled.

NFS server Shares resources to be used by NFS clients.

NIS (Network Information Service) A distributed service containing key information about the systems and the users on the network. The NIS database is stored on the master server and all the replica or slave servers.

NIS client The hosts in the NIS domain, including the master and slave servers.

NIS map Multicolumn tables used to store NIS information.

NIS+ Similar to NIS, but with more features. NIS+ is not an extension of NIS, but a new software program designed to replace NIS.

NIS+ authorization The process of granting NIS+ principals access rights to an NIS+ object.

NIS+ object A directory, table, or group within a namespace.

NIS+ security level Lets NIS+ administrators specify different read, modify, create, and destroy rights to NIS+ objects for each class.

node A host or router.

`nscd` A daemon that speeds up queries of the most common data to retrieve naming service information from specified databases.

NVRAM (nonvolatile random-access memory) Where the system identification information is stored, such as the hostid, Ethernet address, and time-of-day (TOD) clock. The NVRAM chip has user-definable system parameters and writeable areas for user-controlled diagnostics, macros, and device aliases.

O–Q

OBP (OpenBoot PROM) The hardware-level user interface that you see before the operating system starts. The OBP consists of two 8KB chips on the system board: the startup PROM itself, which contains extensive firmware allowing access to user-written startup drivers and extended diagnostics, and an NVRAM (nonvolatile random-access memory) chip.

OpenBoot The primary task of the OpenBoot firmware is to boot the operating system from either a mass storage device or the network. *See also* OBP.

packet The basic unit of information to be transferred over the network.

parallel Simultaneous. Usually applied to a RAID-3 environment in which a block of data is transferred by dividing it into smaller blocks, accessing all drives at once and simultaneously transferring the data.

parent process The main, or primary, program or first process loaded into memory. A parent process forks a child process, which, in turn, can fork other processes.

parity A method used by RAID5 configurations to provide data redundancy. Typically, a RAID5 configuration stores data blocks and parity blocks. In the case of a missing data block, the missing data can be regenerated using the other data blocks and the parity block.

partition table Identifies a disk's slices, the slice boundaries (in cylinders), and the total size of the slices.

password aging A system parameter set by the system administrator in the `/etc/default/password` file that requires users to change their passwords after a certain number of days.

password encryption The reversible transformation of a user's password from the original format (the plain text) to a difficult-to-interpret format (the cipher text). This is done to protect the password's confidentiality. Encryption uses an algorithm. The encrypted password consists of 13 characters chosen from a 64-character alphabet.

patchlist file Specifies a file containing a list of patches to install.

PCFS (Personal Computer File System) Allows read and write access to data and programs on DOS-formatted disks that are written for DOS-based PCs.

physical device name Represents the full device pathname in the device information hierarchy. Physical device names uniquely identify the physical location of the hardware devices on the system and are maintained in the `/devices` directory. The physical device name contains the hardware information, represented as a series of node names separated by slashes (/) that indicate the path to the device.

platform group A general term used to group Sun systems based on their hardware architecture. To determine the platform group that your Sun system belongs to, use the `uname -m` command. The system responds with the platform group and platform name for your system.

port *See* hardware port and network port.

POST (power-on self-test) When a system is turned on, the monitor runs a POST that checks such things as the hardware and memory on the system. If no errors are found, the automatic boot process begins.

power-management software Provided in the Solaris environment to automatically save the state of a system and turn off the system after it has been idle for 30 minutes. On newer systems that comply with the EPA's Energy Star guidelines, the power management software is installed by default. You are then prompted after rebooting to enable or disable the power-management software.

primary group Each user is assigned to a primary group when he or she logs in. This is the group that the operating system assigns to files created by the user.

print client A remote system that sends print requests to a print server.

print daemon A system process that supports printing activities.

printer class Several locally attached printers that are put into a group. A printer class is helpful if you have several printers sitting next to each other and it doesn't matter which printer your job goes to.

Print Manager A graphical user interface used to manage printers in a name service environment.

print scheduler The LP print service has a scheduler daemon called `lpsched`. This print scheduler daemon updates the LP system files with information about printer setup and configuration. This daemon schedules all the local print requests on a print server. It also tracks the status of printers and filters on the print server.

print server A system that has a local printer connected to it, makes the printer available to other systems on the network, and provides spooling for the client's print requests.

process A program in operation.

PROCFS (Process File System) A file system that resides in memory and contains a list of active processes.

profile A JumpStart configuration file that defines how the Solaris software is installed on the JumpStart client if a system matches the rule. Every rule in the rules file specifies a profile that defines how a system is to be installed when the rule is matched. You usually create a different profile for every rule. However, the same profile can be used in more than one rule. *See also* rights profile and rules profile.

PROM (Programmable Read-Only Memory) A permanent memory chip that is programmed, or filled, by the customer rather than by the chip manufacturer. It differs from a ROM, which is programmed at the time of manufacture. PROMs have been mostly superseded by EPROMs, which can be reprogrammed.

R

RAID (Redundant Array of Independent Disks) A disk subsystem that is used to increase performance and/or provide fault tolerance. RAID is a classification of different ways to back up and store data on multiple disk drives. RAID has seven levels:

- **Level 0**: Nonredundant disk array (striping)
- **Level 1**: Mirrored disk array
- **Level 2**: Memory-style Error Code Correction (ECC)
- **Level 3**: Bit-interleaved parity
- **Level 4**: Block-interleaved parity
- **Level 5**: Block-interleaved distributed parity
- **Level 6**: P + Q redundancy

SVM implements RAID levels 0, 1, and 5.

RARP (Reverse ARP) A method by which a client is assigned an IP address based on a lookup of its Ethernet address.

reconfiguration boot A method of booting a system so that it recognizes newly added peripheral devices and creates an entry in the `/etc/path_to_inst` file and the `/dev` and `/devices` directories.

reconfiguration startup *See* reconfiguration boot.

redundancy Duplication for the purpose of achieving fault tolerance. This refers to duplicating or adding components, data, and functions within the array.

replica One or more additional copies of the state database.

restricted shell Restricted versions of the Korn shell (rksh) and the Bourne shell (rsh) to limit the operations allowed for a particular user account. Restricted shells are especially useful for ensuring that time-sharing users, or users' guests on a system, have restricted permissions during login sessions.

rights profile Also called a *right* or *profile*. A collection of overrides used in Role-Based Access Control (RBAC) that can be assigned to a role or user. A rights profile can consist of authorizations; commands with set UIDs or GIDs, which are called security attributes; and other rights profiles.

router A machine that forwards Ethernet packets from one network to another.

RPC (Remote Procedure Call) A protocol that one program can use to request services from another system on the network.

rules file A text file that contains a rule for each group of systems (or a single system) that you want to install automatically using JumpStart. Each rule distinguishes a group of systems, based on one or more system attributes. The rules file links each group to a profile, which is a text file that defines how the Solaris 9 software is to be installed on each system in the group. *See also* profile.

`rules.ok` file A system-generated version of the rules file. The `rules.ok` file is required by the custom JumpStart installation software to match a system to a profile. You must use the check script to create the `rules.ok` file.

run control script Each `init` state has a corresponding series of run control (rc) scripts, located in the `/sbin` directory, to control each `init` state.

run state When a system begins initialization, it enters one of eight run states, also called `init` states. Because run state 4 currently is unused, only seven usable run states exist. A run state is also called a *run level*.

S

SCSI (Small Computer Systems Interface) An interface standard for peripheral devices and computers to communicate with each other.

secondary group Specifies additional groups, other than the primary group, that a user can belong to. Each user can belong to a maximum of 15 secondary groups.

secondary swap An additional swap added to a system's primary swap.

sector *See* disk block.

Secure Shell (SSH) Both a computer program and an associated network protocol designed for logging in to and executing commands on a networked computer. Secure Shell was designed to replace the earlier rlogin, Telnet, and rsh protocols, which are considered unsecure. SSH provides secure encrypted communications between two untrusted hosts over an unsecure network. Users of SSH can also use it for tunneling, forwarding arbitrary TCP ports and X11 connections over the resultant secure channel, and transferring files using the associated scp or sftp programs. An SSH server, by default, listens on the standard TCP port 22.

server A system that provides resources, services, or file systems, such as home directories or mailboxes, to other systems on the network.

shared resource A shared file system on an NFS server.

shell variable A structure that holds data and that is uniquely named by the user within the shell. It holds the data assigned to it until a new value is assigned or the program is finished.

single-user mode A Solaris run state in which the system does not support multiuser operations. This run state is used to perform system administration tasks.

slave NIS server A secondary NIS server that contains all the maps in case the primary server fails.

SMC (Solaris Management Console) A graphical user interface designed to ease several routine system administration tasks. SMC has a menu-like interface that is much easier to use than the ASCII interface supplied at the command prompt.

soft mount A file system mounted using the `mount -o soft` option. The `soft` option indicates that the retry request does not continue after the server becomes unresponsive. The default for the `mount` command is `hard`.

soft partition A new feature of SVM that breaks the traditional eight-slices-per-disk barrier by allowing disks, or logical volumes, to be subdivided into many more partitions.

software group A logical grouping of the Solaris software (clusters and packages). During a Solaris installation, you can install one of the following software groups: Core, End-user Solaris Software, Developer Solaris Software, Entire Solaris Software, or Entire Solaris Software Group Plus OEM Support.

software package The standard way to deliver bundled and unbundled Solaris software. Packages are administered by using the package administration commands. They generally are identified by the SUNW*xxx* naming convention when supplied by Sun Microsystems. SUNW is Sun Microsystems' ticker symbol on the stock exchange.

software patch A fix to a reported software problem. Sun ships software patches to customers so that problems can be resolved before the next release of the software.

software spool directory For convenience, you can copy frequently installed packages to a spool directory. This way, you don't need to use the CD each time you install the package.

Solaris Volume Manager object A graphical representation of the state database, metadevice or part of a metadevice, or hot spare pool.

spool Stands for simultaneous peripheral operations online. For printing, spooling is when an application generates the printer output and sends it to the print spooler. The spooler feeds the print images to the printer, one at a time, at slower printing speeds. The printing is then done in the background while the user interacts with other applications in the foreground. For software installation, spooling is the process of copying software packages from a CD-ROM to a directory on the local disk.

standalone system A client that uses remote services, such as installation software, from a server and that doesn't rely on a server to function.

state database replica A copy of the metadevice state database. Keeping copies of the metadevice state database protects from the loss of state and configuration information critical to metadevice operations.

sticky bit A permission bit that protects the files in a directory. If the directory has the sticky bit set, a file can be deleted only by its owner, by the owner of the directory, or by root.

storage block Occupies space allocated to the file system. *See also* data block.

stripe Accessing several disks at the same time in parallel to gain performance.

stripe width The amount of data written across a striped or RAID volume. In Solaris Volume Manager, this is the interlace size multiplied by the number of disks in the stripe.

striping Spreading, or interleaving, logical contiguous blocks of data across multiple independent disk spindles. Striping allows multiple disk controllers to simultaneously access data, improving performance.

submirror A metadevice that is part of a mirror. *See also* mirror.

superblock Stores much of the information about the file system. The superblock resides in the 16 disk sectors (sectors 16 to 31) that follow the bootblock. The superblock is a table of information that describes the file system. When a file system is created, each cylinder group replicates the superblock beginning at sector 32. The replication protects the critical data in the superblock from catastrophic loss.

SVM (Solaris Volume Manager) Uses virtual disks to manage physical disks and their associated data.

swap Space used as a virtual memory storage area when the system does not have enough physical memory to handle current processes. *See also* swap space.

swap file Physical memory is supplemented by this specially configured file on the physical disk. *See also* swap space.

swap space Swap space and necessary file system overhead are included in the disk space recommendations for each software group. A minimum of 512MB is required for swap space, but more space might be needed. By default, Solaris Web Start allocates 512MB for swap space. A swap partition or swap file is used to provide swap space.

switch The central device through which all hosts in a twisted-pair Ethernet installation are connected. Each port on the switch can give full bandwidth to a single server or client station. *See also* hub.

symbolic link A pointer to files anywhere on the network. The file or directory could exist in another file system, on another disk, or on another system on the network. Symbolic links contain only one type of data: the pathname of the file to which they point. The size of a symbolic link always matches the number of characters in the pathname it contains.

T

TCP/IP (Transmission Control Protocol/Internet Protocol) The protocol suite originally developed for the Internet. It is also called the *Internet protocol suite*. Solaris networks run on TCP/IP by default.

Terminfo database Describes the capabilities of devices such as printers and terminals.

throughput A measure of sequential I/O performance in MBps.

TMPFS (Temporary File System) A file system that uses local memory for file system reads and writes and that typically is much faster than a UFS.

track A series of sectors positioned end-to-end in a circular path. The number of sectors per track varies with the radius of a track on the platter. The outer tracks are larger and can hold more sectors than the inner tracks.

trusted host A host from which a user can log in without being required to enter a password.

U

UDF (Universal Disk Format) A file system used to store information on the optical media technology called DVD (Digital Versatile Disc or Digital Video Disc).

UFS (UNIX File System) The default disk-based file system for the Solaris operating environment.

ufsboot The secondary boot program. It locates and loads the two-part kernel. The kernel consists of a two-piece static core called `genunix` and `unix`.

UFS logging The process of storing file system operations to a log before the transactions are applied to the file system.

unbundled software package A Solaris software package is the standard way to deliver bundled and unbundled software. Packages are administered by using the package administration commands. They generally are identified by the SUNW*xxx* naming convention when supplied by Sun Microsystems. SUNW is Sun Microsystems' ticker symbol on the stock exchange.

upgrade Performed on a system that is already running Solaris 2.6, Solaris 7, Solaris 8, or a previous release of Solaris 9. An upgrade saves as many modifications as possible from the previous version of Solaris that is currently running on your system. *See also* live upgrade.

user ID (UID) A unique number assigned to each user account. All UIDs must be consistent across the network. The UID typically is a number between 100 and 60,002, but it can go as high as 2,147,483,647.

user initialization file A shell script that runs automatically each time the user logs in. The initialization file sets up the work environment and customizes the shell environment for the user. The primary job of the shell initialization file is to define the user's shell environment, such as the search path, environment variables, and windowing environment.

user mask Controls the default file permissions assigned to the file or directory.

V–Z

virtual file system (VFS) An architecture that provides a standard interface for different file system types. The VFS architecture lets the kernel handle basic operations, such as reading, writing, and listing files, and makes it easier to add new file systems.

virtual volume Grouping disk partitions across several disks to appear as a single volume to the operating system.

volume A group of physical slices that are accessed as a single logical device by concatenation, striping, mirroring, setting up RAID5 volumes, or logging physical devices. After they are created, volumes are used like slices. The volume maps logical block addresses to the correct location on one of the physical devices. The type of mapping depends on the configuration of the particular volume. Also called a *pseudo device* or *virtual device* in standard UNIX terms.

volume manager Simplifies the use of disks and CDs by automatically mounting them using the `vold` daemon.

volume name An eight-character name assigned to a disk drive.

WAN (wide-area network) A network that connects multiple local-area networks (LANs) or systems at different geographic sites via phone, fiber-optic, or satellite links.

warm plug The ability to replace a failed disk drive without powering down the storage array and without rebooting the host computer system. This is an important aspect of high availability. *See also* hot-pluggable.

Web Start An installation program located on the Solaris Installation CD-ROM that can be run with a graphical user interface (GUI) or command-line interface (CLI). Using Solaris Web Start and Sun's Web browser, you select either a default installation or a customize option to install only the software you want, including the Solaris software group, Solstice utilities, and additional software. You can also use Web Start to upgrade your operating system.

Web Start Flash An installation feature that lets you create a single reference installation (Web Start Flash archive) of the Solaris operating environment on a machine, which is called the master machine. After installing the operating system on the master machine, you can add or delete software and modify system configuration information as necessary. You then create a Web Start archive from this master machine. You can use this archive to replicate that installation on a number of systems, which are called clone machines.

XOR Exclusive OR. A binary mathematical operation performed on data to produce parity information. In RAID level 5, parity is generated from user data and is used to regenerate any user data that is lost due to a drive failure.

ZFS A highly scalable file system that uses pooled storage, protects against data corruption, and simplifies administration.

Index

A

B

C

D

E

F

G

L

O - P

Q - R

S

T

U

V

W - X

Y - Z

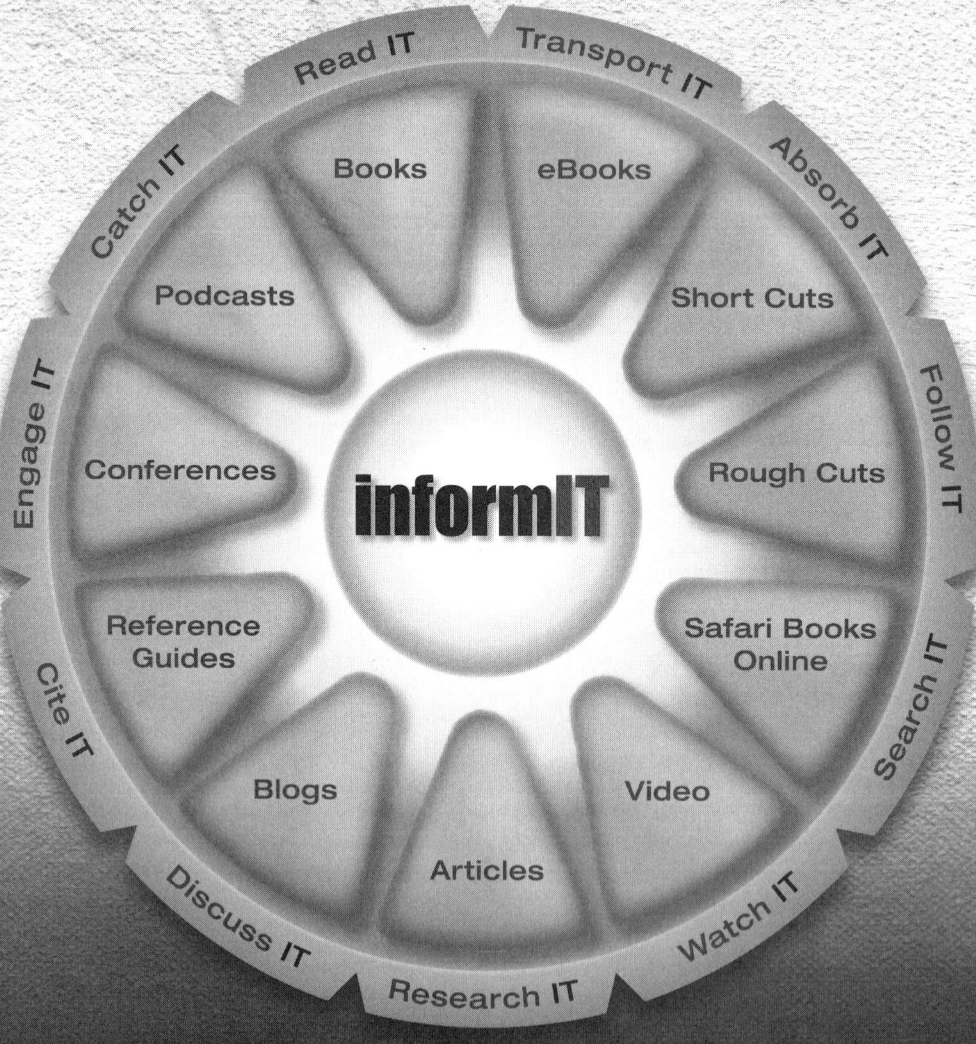